A Special Issue of
Visual Cognition

Visual search and attention

Guest Editors

Hermann J. Müller

and

Joseph Krummenacher

Ludwig-Maximilian-University Munich, Germany

Routledge
Taylor & Francis Group

LONDON AND NEW YORK

First published 2006 by Psychology Press

2 Park Square, Milton Park, Abingdon, Oxfordshire OX14 4RN
52 Vanderbilt Avenue, New York, NY 10017

Routledge is an imprint of the Taylor & Francis Group, an informa business

First issued in paperback 2018

British Library Cataloguing in Publication Data
A catalogue record for this book is available from the British Library

Cover design by Design Deluxe
Typeset in Ireland by Datapage International, Dublin

ISBN 13: 978-1-84169-806-9 (hbk)
ISBN 13: 978-1-138-87766-5 (pbk)

ISSN 1350-6285

Contents*

(*continued overleaf*)

---

* This book is also a special issue of the journal *Visual Cognition*, and forms issues 4, 5, 6, 7 & 8
of Volume 14 (2006). The page numbers are taken from the journal and so begin with p. 389.

VISUAL COGNITION, 2006, 14 (4/5/6/7/8), 389–410

Ψ **Psychology Press**
Taylor & Francis Group

Visual search and selective attention

Hermann J. Müller and Joseph Krummenacher

Ludwig-Maximilian-University Munich, Germany

Visual search is a key paradigm in attention research that has proved to be a test bed for competing theories of selective attention. The starting point for most current theories of visual search has been Treisman's "feature integration theory" of visual attention (e.g., Treisman & Gelade, 1980). A number of key issues that have been raised in attempts to test this theory are still pertinent questions of research today: (1) The role and (mode of) function of bottom-up and top-down mechanisms in controlling or "guiding" visual search; (2) in particular, the role and function of implicit and explicit memory mechanisms; (3) the implementation of these mechanisms in the brain; and (4) the simulation of visual search processes in computational or, respectively, neurocomputational (network) models. This paper provides a review of the experimental work and the—often conflicting—theoretical positions on these thematic issues, and goes on to introduce a set of papers by distinguished experts in fields designed to provide solutions to these issues.

A key paradigm in attention research, that has proved to be a test bed for competing theories of selective attention, is visual search. In the standard paradigm, the observer is presented with a display that can contain a target stimulus amongst a variable number of distractor stimuli. The total number of stimuli is referred to as the display size. The target is either present or absent, and the observers' task is to make a target-present vs. target-absent decision as rapidly and accurately as possible. (Alternatively, the search display may be presented for a limited exposure duration, and the dependent variable is the accuracy of target detection.) The time taken for these decisions (the reaction time, RT) can be graphed as a function of the display size (search RT functions). An important characteristic of such functions is its slope, that is, the search rate, measured in terms of time per display item. Based on the search RT functions obtained in a variety of search experiments, a distinction has been proposed between two modes of visual

Please address all correspondence to Hermann J. Müller, Department of Psychology, Allgemeine und Experimentelle Psychologie, Ludwig-Maximilian-University Munich, Leopoldstrasse 13, 80802 München, Germany. E-mail: mueller@psy.uni-muenchen.de

© 2006 Psychology Press Ltd
http://www.psypress.com/viscog   DOI: 10.1080/13506280500527676

search (e.g., Treisman & Gelade, 1980): Parallel and serial. If the search function increases only little with increasing display size (search rates < 10 ms/item), it is assumed that all items in the display are searched simultaneously, that is, in "parallel" ("efficiently"). In contrast, if the search functions exhibit a linear increase (search rates > 10 ms/item), it is assumed that the individual items are searched successively, that is, the search operates "serially" ("inefficiently").

This does not explain, of course, why some searches can operate efficiently, in parallel, while others operate inefficiently, (strictly) serially, and why, in some tasks, the search efficiency is found to lie in between these extremes. In order to explain this variability, a number of theories of visual search have been proposed, which, in essence, are general theories of selective visual attention. The starting point for most current theories of visual search has been Anne Treisman's "feature integration theory" of visual attention (e.g., Treisman & Gelade, 1980; see below). This theory led to a boom in studies on visual search; for example, between 1980 and 2000, the number of published studies rose by a factor of 10. A number of key issues that have been raised in attempts to test this theory are still pertinent questions of research today: (1) The role and (mode of) function of bottom-up and top-down mechanisms in controlling or "guiding" visual search; (2) in particular, the role and function of implicit and explicit memory mechanisms; (3) the implementation of these mechanisms in the brain; and (4) the simulation of visual search processes in computational or, respectively, neurocomputational (network) models.

The present *Visual Cognition* Special Issue presents a set of papers concerned with these four issues. The papers are based on the presentations given by some 35 leading visual-search experts worldwide, from a variety of disciplines—including experimental and neuropsychology, electro- and neurophysiology, functional imaging, and computational modelling—at the "Visual Search and Selective Attention" symposium held at Holzhausen am Ammersee, near Munich, Germany, June 6–10, 2003 ("Munich Visual Search Symposium", for short[1]). The aim of this meeting was to foster a dialogue amongst these experts, in order to contribute to identifying theoretically important joint issues and discuss ways of how these issues can be resolved by using convergent, integrated methodologies.

---

[1] Supported by the DFG (German National Research Council) and the US Office of Naval Research.

THE SPECIAL ISSUE

This Special Issue opens with Anne Treisman's (2006 this issue) invited "Special Lecture", which provides an up-to-date overview of her research, over 25 years, and her current theoretical stance on visual search. In particular, Treisman considers "how the deployment of attention determines what we see". She assumes that attention can be focused narrowly on a single object, spread over several objects or distributed over the scene as a whole—with consequences for what we see. Based on an extensive review of her ground-breaking original work and her recent work, she argues that focused attention is used in feature binding. In contrast, distributed attention (automatically) provides a statistical description of sets of similar objects and gives the gist of the scene, which may be inferred from sets of features registered in parallel.

The four subsequent sections of this Special Issue present papers that focus on the same four themes discussed at the Munich Visual Search Symposium (see above): I Preattentive processing and the control of visual search; II the role of memory in the guidance of visual search; III brain mechanisms of visual search; and IV neurocomputational modelling of visual search. What follows is a brief introduction to these thematic issues, along with a summary of the, often controversial, standpoints of the various experts on these issues.

I. Preattentive processing and the control of visual search

Since the beginnings of Cognitive Psychology, theories of perception have drawn a distinction between preattentive and attentional processes (e.g., Neisser, 1967). On these theories, the earliest stages of the visual system comprise preattentive processes that are applied uniformly to all input signals. Attentional processes, by contrast, involve more complex computations that can only be applied to a selected part of the preattentive output. The investigation of the nature of preattentive processing aims at determining the functional role of the preattentive operations, that is: What is the visual system able to achieve without, or prior to, the allocation of focal attention?

Registration of basic features. Two main functions of preattentive processes in vision have been distinguished. The first is to extract basic attributes, or "features", of the input signals. Since preattentive processes code signals across the whole visual field and provide the input information for object recognition and other, higher cognitive processes, they are limited to operations that can be implemented in parallel and executed rapidly.

Experiments on visual search have revealed a set of visual features that are registered preattentively (in parallel and rapidly), including luminance, colour, orientation, motion direction, and velocity, as well as some simple aspects of form (see Wolfe, 1998). These basic features generally correspond with stimulus properties by which single cells in early visual areas can be activated.

According to some theories (e.g., Treisman & Gelade, 1980; Wolfe, Cave, & Franzel, 1989), the output of preattentive processing consists of a set of spatiotopically organized feature maps that represent the location of each basic (luminance, colour, orientation, etc.) feature within the visual field. There is also evidence that preattentive processing can extract more complex configurations such as three-dimensional form (Enns & Rensink, 1990) and topological properties (Chen & Zhou, 1997). In addition, individual preattentively registered items can be organized in groups if they share features (Baylis & Driver, 1992; Harms & Bundesen, 1983; Kim & Cave, 1999) or form connected wholes (Egly, Driver, & Rafal, 1994; Kramer & Watson, 1996). Based on evidence that preattentive processes can also complete occluded contours, He and Nakayama (1992) proposed that the output of the preattentive processes comprises not only of a set of feature maps, but also a representation of (object) surfaces.

Guidance of attention.   Besides rendering an "elementary" representation of the visual field, the second main function of preattentive processes is the guiding of focal-attentional processes to the most important or "promising" information within this representation. The development of models of visual processing reveals an interesting tradeoff between these two functions: If the output of preattentive processing is assumed to only represent basic visual features, so that the essential operations of object recognition are left to attentional processes, focal attention must be directed rapidly to the (potentially) most "meaningful" parts of the field, so that the objects located there can be identified with minimal delay.

Preattentive processes must guarantee effective allocation of focal attention under two very different conditions. First, they must mediate the directing of attention to objects whose defining features are not predictable. This data-driven or bottom-up allocation of attention is achieved by detecting simple features (or, respectively, their locations) that differ from the surrounding features in a "salient" manner (e.g., Nothdurft, 1991). The parallel computation of feature contrast, or salience, signals can be a very effective means for localizing features that ought to be processed attentionally; however, at the same time it can delay the identification of a target object when there is also a distractor in the field that is characterized by a salient feature (Theeuwes, 1991, 1992). Numerous investigations had been concerned with the question under which conditions focal attention is "attracted" by a salient feature (or object) and whether the mechanisms that direct focal attention to salient features (or objects) are always and invariably operating or whether they can be modulated by the task set (e.g., Bacon & Egeth, 1997; Yantis, 1993).

Under other conditions, the appearance of a particular object, or a particular type of object, can be predicted. In such situations, preattentive processes must be able in advance to set the processing (top-down) for the corresponding object and initiate the allocation of focal attention upon its appearance. This can be achieved by linking the allocation of attention to a feature value defining the target object, such as blue or vertical (Folk & Remington, 1998), or to a defining feature dimension, such as colour or orientation (Müller, Reimann & Krummenacher, 2003). Although the top-down allocation of attention is based, as a rule, on the (conscious) intention to search for a certain type of target, it can also be initiated by implicit processes. If the preceding search targets exhibit a certain feature (even a response-irrelevant feature), or are defined within a certain dimension, attention is automatically guided more effectively to the next target if this is also characterized by the same feature or feature dimension (Krummenacher, Müller, & Heller, 2001; Maljkovic & Nakayama, 1994, 2000; Müller, Heller, & Ziegler, 1995).

An important question for theories of preattentive vision concerns the interaction between top-down controlled allocation of attention to expected targets and bottom-up driven allocation to unexpected targets. What is required is an appropriate balance between these to modes of guidance, in order to guarantee that the limited processing resources at higher stages of vision are devoted to the most informative part of the visual input. While there is a broad consensus that preattentive processes can guide visual search (i.e., the serial allocation of focal attention), there are a number of open questions concerning the interaction between top-down and bottom-up processing in the control of search, the top-down modifiability of pre-attentive processes, the interplay of feature- and dimension-based set (processes), etc. Further open questions concern the complexity of the preattentively computed "features". All these issues are addressed by the papers collected in the first section of this Special Issue, "Preattentive processing and the control of visual search".

The first set of three papers (Folk & Remington; Theeuwes, Reimann & Mortier; Müller & Krummenacher) is concerned with the issue whether and to what extent preattentive processing is top-down modulable.

More specifically, C. L. Folk and R. Remington (2006 this issue) ask to which degree the preattentive detection of "singletons" elicits an involuntary shift of spatial attention (i.e., "attentional capture") that is immune from top-down modulation. According to their "contingent-capture" perspective, preattentive processing can produce attentional capture, but such capture is contingent on whether the eliciting stimulus carries a feature property consistent with the current attentional set. This account has been challenged recently by proponents of the "pure- (i.e., bottom-up driven-) capture" perspective, who have argued that the evidence for contingencies in attentional capture actually reflects the rapid disengagement and recovery from capture. Folk and Remington present new experimental evidence to counter this challenge.

One of the strongest proponents of the pure-capture view is Theeuwes. J. Theeuwes. B. Reimann, and K. Mortier (2006 this issue) reinvestigated the effect of top-down knowledge of the target-defining dimension on visual search for singleton feature ("pop-out") targets. They report that, when the task required simple detection, advance cueing of the dimension of the upcoming singleton resulted in cueing costs and benefits; however, when the response requirements were changed ("compound" task, in which the target-defining attributes are independent of those determining the response), advance cueing failed to have a significant effect. On this basis, Theeuwes et al. reassert their position that top-down knowledge cannot guide search for feature singletons (which is, however, influenced by bottom-up priming effects when the target-defining dimension is repeated across trials). Theeuwes et al. conclude that effects often attributed to early top-down guidance may in fact represent effects that occur later, after attentional selection, in processing.

H. J. Müller and J. Krummenacher (2006 this issue) respond to this challenge by asking whether the locus of the "dimension-based attention" effects originally described by Müller and his colleagues (including their top-down modifiability by advance cues) are preattentive or postselective in nature. Müller and his colleagues have explained these effects in terms of a "dimension-weighting" account, according to which these effects arise at a preattentive, perceptual stage of saliency coding. In contrast, Cohen (e.g., Cohen & Magen, 1999) and Theeuwes have recently argued that these effects are postselective, response-related in nature. In their paper, Müller and Krummenacher critically evaluate these challenges and put forward counterarguments, based partly on new data, in support of the view that dimensional weighting operates at a preattentive stage of processing (without denying the possibility of weighting processes also operating post selection).

A further set of four papers (Nothdurft; Smilek, Enns, Eastwood, & Merikle; Leber & Egeth; Fanini, Nobre, & Chelazzi) is concerned with the influence of "attentional set" for the control of search behaviour.

H.-C. Nothdurft (2006 this issue) provides a closer consideration of the role of salience for the selection of predefined targets in visual search. His experiments show that salience can make targets "stand out" and thus control the selection of items that need to be inspected when a predefined target is to be searched for. Interestingly, salience detection and target identification followed different time courses. Even typical "pop-out" targets were located faster than identified. Based on these and other findings, Nothdurft argues in favour of an interactive and complementary function of salience and top-down attentional guidance in visual search (where "attention settings may change salience settings").

While top-down controlled processes may guide selective processes towards stimuli displaying target-defining properties, their mere involvement may also impede search, as reported by D. Smilek, J. T. Enns, J. D. Eastwood, and P. M. Merikle (2006 this issue). They examined whether visual search could be made more efficient by having observers give up active control over the guidance of attention (and instead allow the target to passively "pop" into their minds) or, alternatively, by making them perform a memory task concurrently with the search. Interestingly, passive instructions and a concurrent task led to more efficient performance on a hard (but not an easy) search task. Smilek et al. reason that the improved search efficiency results from a reduced reliance on slow executive control processes and a greater reliance on rapid automatic processes for directing visual attention.

The importance of executive control or (top-down) "attentional set" for search performance is further illustrated by A. B. Leber and H. E. Egeth (2006 this issue). They show that, besides the instruction and the stimulus environment, past experience (acquired over an extended period of practice) can be a critical factor for determining the set that observers bring to bear on performing a search task. In a training phase, observers could use one of two possible attentional sets (but not both) to find colour-defined targets in a rapid serial visual presentation stream of letters. In the subsequent test phase, where either set could be used, observers persisted in using their pre-established sets.

In a related vein, A. Fanini, A. C. Nobre, and L. Chelazzi (2006 this issue) used a negative priming paradigm to examine whether feature-based (top-down) attentional set can lead to selective processing of the task-relevant (e.g., colour) attribute of a single object and/or suppression of its irrelevant features (e.g., direction of motion or orientation). The results indicate that individual features of a single object can indeed undergo different processing fates as a result of attention: One may be made available to response selection stages (facilitation), while others are actively blocked (inhibition).

Two further papers (Pomerantz; Cave & Batty) are concerned with visual "primitives" that may form the more or less complex representations on which visual search processes actually operate—"colour as a Gestalt" and, respectively, stimuli that evoke strong threat-related emotions.

J. R. Pomerantz (2006 this issue) argues that colour perception meets the customary criteria for Gestalts at least as well as shape perception does, in that colour emerges from nonadditive combination of wavelengths in the perceptual system and results in novel, emergent features. Thus, colour should be thought of not as a basic stimulus feature, but rather as a complex conjunction of wavelengths that are integrated in perceptual processing. As a Gestalt, however, colour serves as a psychological primitive and so, as with Gestalts in form perception. may lead to "pop out" in visual search.

Recently, there have been claims (e.g., Fox et al., 2000; Öhman. Lundqvist & Esteves, 2001) that social stimuli, such as those evoking strong emotions or threat, may also be perceptual primitives that are processed preattentively (e.g., detected more rapidly than neutral stimuli) and, thus, especially effective at capturing attention. In their contribution, K. R. Cave and M. J. Batty (2006 this issue) take issue with these claims. A critical evaluation of the relevant studies leads them to argue that there is no evidence that the threatening nature of stimuli is detected preattentively. There is evidence, however, that observers can learn to associate particular features, combinations of features, or configurations of lines with threat. and use them to *guide* search to threat-related targets.

II. The role of memory in the guidance of visual search

Inhibition of return and visual marking.   A set of issues closely related to "preattentive processing" concerns the role of memory in the guidance of visual search, especially in hard search tasks that involve serial attentional processing (e.g., in terms of successive eye movements to potentially informative parts of the field). Concerning the role of memory, there are diametrically opposed positions. There is indirect experimental evidence that memory processes which prevent already searched parts of the field from being reinspected, play no role in solving such search problems. In particular, it appears that visual search can operate efficiently even when the target and the distractors unpredictably change their positions in the search display presented on a trial. This has given rise to the proposal that serial search proceeds in a "memoryless" fashion (cf. Horowitz & Wolfe, 1998). On the other hand, there is evidence that "inhibition of return" (IOR) of attention (Posner & Cohen. 1984) is also effective in the guidance of visual search, by inhibitorily marking already scanned locations and, thereby, conferring an advantage to not-yet-scanned locations for the allocation of attention (Klein, 1988; Müller & von Mühlenen. 2000; Takeda & Yagi, 2000).

Related questions concern whether and to what extent memory processes in the guidance of search are related to mechanisms of eye movement control and how large the capacity of these mechanisms is. For example, Gilchrist and Harvey (2000) observed that, in a task that required search for a target letter amongst a large number of distractor letters, refixations were rare within the first two to three saccades following inspection of an item, but afterwards occurred relatively frequently. This argues in favour of a short-lived (oculomotor) memory of a low capacity for already fixated locations. In contrast, Peterson, Kramer, Wang, Irwin, and McCarley (2001) found that, when observers searched for a "T" amongst "L"s, refixations occurred less frequently (even after long intervals during which up to 11 distractors were scanned) than would have been expected on the basis of a memoryless model of visual search. This argues in favour of a longer lasting memory of relatively large capacity.

Another, controversial form of search guidance has been proposed by Watson and Humphreys (1997), namely, the parallel "visual marking" of distractors in the search field: If, in conjunction search (e.g., for a red "X" amongst blue "X"s and red "O"s), a subset of the distractors (red "O"s) are presented prior to the presentation of the whole display (which includes the target), a search process that is normally inefficient is turned into an efficient search. Watson and Humphreys explained this in terms of the inhibitory marking (of the locations) of the prepresented distractors, as a result of which search for a conjunction target amongst all distractors is reduced to search for a simple feature target amongst the additional, later presented distractors (search for a red "X" amongst blue "X"s). However, whether Watson and Humphreys' findings are indeed based on the—memory-dependent—parallel suppression of distractor positions or, alternatively, the attentional prioritization of the display items that onset later (accompanied by abrupt luminance change) (Donk & Theeuwes, 2001), is controversial. (See also Jiang, Chun, & Marks, 2002, who argued that the findings of Watson and Humphreys reflect a special memory for stimulus asynchronies.)

Scene-based memory.   The idea, advocated by Watson and Humphreys (1997), of an inhibitory visual marking implies a (more or less implicit) memory of the search "scene". That a memory for the search scene exists is also documented by other studies of visual search for pop-out targets (Kumada & Humphreys, 2002; Maljkovic & Nakayama, 1996). These studies have shown that detection of a salient target on a given trial that appears at the same position as a target on previous trials is expedited relative to the detection of a target at a previous nontarget (or empty) position; in contrast, detection is delayed if a target appears at the position of a previously salient, but to-be-ignored distractor, relative to detection of a target at a nondistractor position. Such positive and negative effects on the detection of a target on the current trial could be traced back across five to eight previous trials (Maljkovic & Nakayama, 1996). The long persistence of these effects suggests that they are based on (most likely implicit) memory mechanisms of search guidance. That such mechanisms can also represent the arrangement of items in complex search scenes, is suggested by Chun and Jiang (1998). They found that the search (e.g., for an orthogonally rotated "T" amongst orthogonally rotated "L"s) on a trial was expedited if a certain, complex arrangement of display items (targets und distractors) was repeated, with some five repetitions of the arrangement (one repetition each per block of 24 trials) being sufficient to generate the learning effect.

With regard to scene-based memory, another controversial issue is: How much content-based information is retained from the (oculomotor) scanning of a natural scene in an enduring (implicit or explicit) representation? One position states that visual (object) representations disintegrate as soon as focal attention is withdrawn from an object, so that the scene-based representation is rather "poor" (e.g., Rensink, 2000a; Rensink, O'Regan, & Clark, 1997). An alternative position is that visual representations do not necessarily disintegrate after the withdrawal of attention; rather, representations from already attended regions can be accumulated within scene-based memory (e.g., Hollingworth, & Henderson, 2002; Hollingworth, Williams, & Henderson, 2001).

In summary, there is evidence that a set of implicit (i.e., preattentive), as well as explicit, memory mechanisms are involved in the guidance of visual search. Open questions are: How many mechanisms can be distinguished? What is their decay time? How large is their capacity? and so on. These questions are considered, from different perspectives, in this second section of papers in this Special Issue.

The first set of four papers (Klein & Dukewich; Horowitz; McCarley, Kramer, Boot, Peterson, Wang, & Irwin; and Gilchrist & Harvey) are concerned with the issue of memory-based control of covert and overt (i.e., oculomotor) attentional scanning in visual search.

R. Klein and K. Dukewich (2006 this issue) ask: "Does the inspector have a memory?" They start with elaborating the distinction between serial and parallel search and argue that serial search would be more efficient, in principle, if there were a mechanism, such as IOR, for reducing reinspections of already scanned items. They then provide a critical review and meta-analysis of studies that have explored whether visual search is "amnesic". They conclude that it rarely is; on the other hand, there is ample evidence for the operation of IOR in visual search. Finally, they suggest three approaches for future research (experimental, neuropsychological, and correlational) designed to provide convergent evidence of the role of IOR for increasing search efficiency.

The following paper, by T. S. Horowitz (2006 this issue), asks: "How much memory does visual search have?" The goal of this paper is less to find a definitive answer to this question than to redefine and clarify the terms of the debate. In particular, Horowitz proposes a formal framework, based on the "variable memory model" (Arani, Karwan, & Drury, 1984), which has three parameters—(1) encoding, (2) recall, and (3) target identification probability—and permits cumulative RT distribution functions to be generated. On this basis, the model can provide a common metric for comparing answers to the above question across different experimental paradigms, in terms that are easy to relate to the "memory" literature.

The next two papers are concerned with the control oculomotor scanning in visual search. Based on RT evidence in a novel, multiple-target visual search task, Horowitz and Wolfe (2001) suggested that the control of attention during visual search is not guided by memory for which of the items or locations in a display have already been inspected. In their contribution, J. S. McCarley, A. F. Kramer, W. R. Boot, M. S. Peterson, R. F. Wang, and D. E. Irwin (2006 this issue) present analyses of eye movement data from a similar experiment, which suggest that RT effects in the multiple-target search task are primarily due to changes in eye movements, and that effects which appeared to reveal memory-free search were produced by changes in oculomotor scanning behaviour.

Another form of oculomotor memory revealed by the systematicity of scan paths in visual search is examined by I. D. Gilchrist and M. Harvey (2006 this issue). They report that, with regular grid-like displays, observers generated more horizontal than vertical saccades. Disruption of the grid structure modulated, but did not eliminate, this systematic scanning component. Gilchrist and Harvey take their findings to be consistent with the scan paths being partly determined by a "cognitive" strategy in visual search.

The next set of two papers (Olivers, Humphreys, & Braithwaite; Donk) are concerned with the benefit deriving from a preview of one set of search items (prior to presentation of a second set containing the target). C. N. L. Olivers, G. W. Humphreys, and J. J. Braithwaite (2006 this issue) review a series of experiments that provide evidence for the idea that, when new visual objects are prioritized in the preview paradigm, old objects are inhibited by a top-down controlled suppression mechanism (visual marking): They show that new object prioritization depends on task settings and available attentional resources (top-down control aspect) and that selection of new items is impaired when these items share features with the old items (negative carryover effects within as well as between trials; inhibitory aspect). They then reconsider the various accounts of the preview benefit (visual marking and alternative accounts) and conclude that these are not mutually exclusive and that the data are best explained by a combination of mechanisms.

This theme is taken up by M. Donk (2006 this issue), who argues that the results of recent studies cannot easily be explained by the original (Watson & Humphreys, 1997) visual-marking account. She goes on to consider three alternatives: Feature-based inhibition (the preview benefit is mediated by inhibition applied at the level of feature maps), temporal segregation (the benefit results from selective attention to one set of elements that can be perceptually segregated, on the basis of temporal-asynchrony signals, from another set), and onset capture (the benefit is mediated by onset signals associated with the appearance of the new elements). She maintains that prioritization of new over old elements is primarily caused by onset capture; however, in line with Olivers et al. (2006 this issue), she admits that other mechanisms may play an additional role to optimize selection of the relevant subset of elements.

The final set of three papers (by Wolfe, Reinecke, & Brawn; Hollingworth; Woodman & Chun) are concerned with visual memory for (natural) scenes, short-term and long-term memory effects on search.

J. M. Wolfe, A. Reinecke, and P. Brawn (2006 this issue) investigated the role of bottlenecks in selective attention and access to visual short-term memory in observers' failure to identify clearly visible changes in otherwise stable visual displays. They found that observers failed to register a colour or orientation change in an object even if they were cued to the location of the object prior to the change occurring. This held true even with natural images. Furthermore, observers were unable to report changes that happened after attention had been directed to an object and before attention returned to that object. Wolfe et al. take these demonstrated failures to notice or identify changes to reflect "bottlenecks" in two pathways from visual input to visual experience: A "selective" pathway, which is responsible for object recognition and other operations that are limited to one item or a small group of items at any one time: and a "nonselective" pathway, which supports visual experience throughout the visual field but is capable of only a limited analysis of the input (visual short-term memory).

A. Hollingworth (2006 this issue) provides a review of recent work on the role of visual memory in scene perception and visual search. While some accounts (e.g., Rensink, 2000b: Wolfe, 1999) assume that coherent object representations in visual memory are fleeting, disintegrating upon the withdrawal of attention from an object, Hollingworth considers evidence that visual memory supports the accumulation of information from scores of individual objects in scenes, utilizing both visual short-term and long-term memory. Furthermore, he reviews evidence that memory for the spatial layout of a scene and for specific object positions can efficiently guide search within natural scenes.

The role of working (short-term) memory and long-term memory in visual search is further considered by G. F. Woodman and M. M. Chun (2006 this issue). Based on a review of recent studies, they argue that, while the working memory system is widely assumed to play a central role in the deployment of attention in visual search, this role is more complex than assumed by many current models. In particular, while (object) working memory representations of targets might be essential in guiding attention only when the identity of the target changes frequently across trials, spatial working memory is always required in (serial) visual search. Furthermore, both explicit and implicit long-term memory representations have clear influences on visual search performance, with memory traces of attended targets and target contexts facilitating the viewing of similar scenes in future encounters. These long-term learning effects (of statistical regularities) deserve more prominent treatment in theoretical models.

III. Brain mechanisms of visual search

Over the past 25 years, behavioural research has produced a considerable amount of knowledge about the functional mechanisms of visual search. However, detailed insights into the brain mechanisms underlying search became available only during the past 5–10 years—based on approaches that combined behavioural experimental paradigms with methods for measuring neuronal functions at a variety of levels: From single cell recording through the activation of component systems to the analysis of whole system networks. These approaches made it possible for the first time to investigate the interplay of different brain areas in the dynamic control of visual search.

The cognitive neuropsychology of visual search examines patients with selective brain lesions who show specific performance deficits in visual search, ranging from difficulties with simple feature discrimination to impaired (working) memory for objects at already scanned locations. If these deficits can be related to specific brain lesions, important indications may be gained as to the role of the affected areas in visual search (e.g., Humphreys & Riddoch, 2001; Robertson & Eglin, 1993).

Electrophysiological approaches examine the EEG/MEG as well as event-related potentials (ERPs) in visual search tasks, above all to reveal the time course of the processes involved in visual search (e.g., Luck, Fan, & Hillyard, 1993; Luck & Hillyard, 1995). Specific ERP components become manifest at different points in time, and these components may be associated, in terms of time, with processes of preattentive and attentional processing. Depending on how accurately the neural generators of these components can be localized, these approaches can also provide indications as to the neuronal sites where the corresponding processes are occurring (in addition to the time at which they occur).

Neurophysiological single-cell recording studies can provide precise information as to both the neuronal loci and the time course of processing in visual search (e.g., Chelazzi, Duncan, Miller, & Desimone, 1993; Motter, 1994a, 1994b; Treue & Maunsell, 1996), but they cannot reveal the interplay among different areas involved in (controlling) the search.

However, this information can be gained by functional-imaging approaches, such as PET and fMRI. Since these methods may be employed both for the imaging of patterns of activity across the whole brain and the detailed measurement of activation in specific cortical areas, they can provide information about the interplay among brain areas during the performance of visual search tasks as well as the areas that are specifically modulated by attention (e.g., Pollmann, Weidner, Müller, & von Cramon, 2000; Rees, Frith, & Lavie, 1997; Weidner, Pollmann, Müller, & von Cramon, 2002).

Recently, a further method: Transcranial magnetic stimulation (TMS) has been used to more precisely examine the role of certain brain areas in visual search (e.g., Walsh, Ellison, Asbridge, & Cowey, 1999). Whereas imaging research is "correlative" in nature, TMS can be applied to "causally" intervene in the processing—in that the targeted application of a time-locked magnetic impulse can simulate a temporary brain "lesion". If the affected areas play no causal role, then such temporary lesions should have little direct influence on specific components of visual search.

The seven papers collected in this section of this Special Issue provide examples of how these new approaches are used to reveal the brain mechanisms of visual search and attentional selection.

In a programmatic paper charting the field, G. W. Humphreys, J. Hodsoll, C. N. L. Olivers, and E. Young Yoon (2006 this issue) argue that an integrative, cognitive-neuroscience approach can contribute not only information about the neural localization of processes underlying visual search, but also information about the functional nature of these processes. They go on to illustrate the value of combining evidence from behavioural studies of normal observers and studies using neuroscientific methods with regard to two issues: First, whether search for form–colour conjunctions is constrained by processes involved in binding across the two dimensions— work with patients with parietal lesions suggests that the answer is positive; and second, whether the "preview benefits" (see Donk, 2006 this issue; Olivers, Humphreys, & Braithwaite, 2006 this issue) are simply due to onset capture—convergent evidence from electrophysiological, brain-imaging, and neuropsychological work indicates that the answer is negative.

Also using a neuropsychological approach, L. C. Robertson and J. L. Brooks (2006 this issue) investigated whether feature processing, as well as feature binding (see also Humphreys, Hodsall, & Olivers, 2006 this issue), is affected in patients with spatial-attentional impairments. They show that the mechanisms underlying "pop out" continue to function in the impaired visual field, albeit at a slowed rate.

The following two studies (Lavie & de Fockert; Pollmann, Weidner, Müller, & von Cramon), used event-related fMRI to examine top-down modulation of attentional capture and dimension-specific saliency coding processes, respectively. N. Lavie and J. de Fockert (2006 this issue) report that the presence (vs. absence) of an irrelevant colour singleton distractor in a visual search task was not only associated with activity in superior parietal cortex, in line with attentional capture, but was also associated with frontal cortex activity. Moreover, behavioural interference by the singleton was negatively correlated with frontal activity, suggesting that frontal cortex is involved in control of singleton interference (see also Folk & Remington, 2006 this issue).

S. Pollmann, R. Weidner, H. J. Müller, and D. Y. von Cramon (2006 this issue) review the evidence of a frontoposterior network of brain areas associated with changes, across trials, in the target-defining dimension in singleton feature, and conjunction, search (see also Müller & Krummenacher, 2006 this issue). They argue that anterior prefrontal components, reflecting transient bottom-up activation, are likely to be involved in the detection of change and the initiation and control of cross-dimensional attention ("weight") shifts. However, they provide new evidence that the attentional weighting of the target-defining dimension itself is realized in terms of a modulation of the visual input areas processing the relevant dimension (e.g., area V4 for colour and V5/MT for motion).

How attention modulates neural processing in one feature dimension, namely motion, is considered by S. Treue and J. C. Martinez-Trujillo (2006 this issue). Concentrating on single-cell recordings from area MT in the extrastriate cortex of macaque monkeys trained to perform visual tasks, they review evidence that, in MT, "bottom-up" filtering processes are tightly integrated with "top-down" attentional mechanisms that together create an integrated saliency map. This topographic representation emphasizes the behavioural relevance of the sensory input, permitting neuronal processing resources to be concentrated on a small subset of the incoming information.

Authors such as Treue and Martinez Trujillo and Pollmann et al. ascribe saliency coding to areas in extrastriate cortex. This position is challenged by Li Zhaoping and R. Snowden, (2006 this issue) who propose that V1 creates a bottom-up saliency map, where saliency of any location increases with the firing rate of the most active V1 output cell responding to it, regardless of the feature selectivity of the cell. Thus, for example, a red vertical bar may have its saliency signalled by a cell tuned to red colour, or one tuned to vertical orientation, whichever cell is the most active. This predicts interference between colour and orientation features in texture segmentation tasks where bottom-up processes are important. Consistent with this prediction, Zhaoping and Snowden report that segmentation of textures of oriented bars became more difficult as the colours of the bars were randomly drawn from larger sets of colour features.

Until recently, right posterior parietal cortex has been ascribed a preeminent role in visual search. This view is disputed by J. O'Shea, N. G. Muggleton, A. Cowey, and V. Walsh (2006 this issue), who provide a reassessment of the roles of parietal cortex and the human frontal eye fields (FEFs). They review recent physiological and brain-imaging evidence, and the results of a programme of TMS studies designed to directly compare the contributions of the parietal cortex and the FEFs in search. This leads them to argue that the FEFs are important for some aspects of search previously solely attributed to the parietal cortex. In particular, besides conjunction search tasks, the right FEF is activated in singleton feature search tasks that do not require eye movements; application of TMS to the right FEF slows RTs on target-present trials (in contrast to parietal cortex where both target-present and target-absent trials are affected); and search-related activation in the FEF starts as early as 40–80 ms post stimulus onset.

IV. Neurocomputational modelling of visual search

To provide explanations of the large data base that has been accumulated over 25 years of research on visual search, a variety of models have been developed. One class of model is rooted in Anne Treisman's "Feature Integration Theory" (FIT; Treisman & Gelade, 1980), which assumed a two-stage processing architecture: At the first, preattentive stage, a (limited) set of basic features are registered in parallel across the visual field; in the second, attentional stage, items are processed serially, one after the other. Accordingly, feature search operates in parallel (e.g., the time required to find a red target amongst green distractors would be independent of the display size because the target is defined by a unique basic feature—"red"); in contrast, conjunction search operates serially (e.g., the search for a "T" amongst "L"s in different orientations would increase with each additional "L", because the "L"s would have to be scanned one after the other before either the "T" is found or the search is terminated).

However, the strict dichotomy between parallel and serial searches postulated by FIT was cast into doubt by findings that performance in various search tasks could not be neatly assigned to one or the other category. In particular, search can be relatively efficient in tasks in which certain types of feature information can be exploited, even if the target is not defined by a single unique feature. For example, in search for a red "O" amongst black "O"s and red "N"s, observers are able to restrict search to a subset of display items; that is, search time is only dependent on the number of "O"s—the red "N"s can be effectively excluded from the search (Egeth, Virzi, & Garbart, 1984). In addition, it is also possible to exploit multiple features—so that, for example, search for a red vertical targets amongst red horizontal and green vertical distractors can be performed very efficiently, even though the target is not defined by a single feature (Wolfe, 1992). Findings along these lines led to the development of the "Guided Search" model (GS; Wolfe, 1994; Wolfe et al., 1989). GS maintains the two-stage architecture, but assumes that the serial allocation of attention can be guided by information from preattentive stages of processing. Cave's (1999) "FeatureGate" model implements similar ideas in a neural network.

Other models of search have avoided the notion of serial selection of specific items within a two-stage architecture—by, instead, postulating a single, parallel processing system. Information is accumulated from all items simultaneously (e.g., Eriksen & Spencer, 1969; Kinchla, 1974), and stimulus properties determine how fast an item can be classified or identified. Parallel models must be able to account for the increase in RT, or, respectively, the decrease in response accuracy, with increasing display size (without recourse to a serial processing stage along the lines of FIT and GS). Many parallel models assume that the "parallel processor" has a limited capacity (e.g., Bundesen, 1990); other models assume an essentially unlimited capacity. Although, according to these models, all items can be processed simultaneously, the result remains a signal that is embedded in a background of noise. With increasing display size, the number of sources of noise (i.e., uncertainty) increases and performance declines (Palmer, Verghese, & Pavel, 2000).

Indeed, visual search may be modelled as a signal detection problem. If the target signal is strong enough, the noise produced by the distractors will have little influence on performance. However, if the target signal is weak, more information will have to be accumulated in order to discriminate it from the background noise (Eckstein, Thomas, Palmer, & Shimozaki, 2000). Signal detection models have proved to be of particular relevance for (real-life) search tasks in which the targets are not clearly demarcated in the image (e.g., search for tumours in radiological images; Swensson & Judy, 1981).

Recently, there has been a blurring of the distinction between the model classes. For example, Bundesen (1998a, 1998b) proposed the parallel processing of item groups (instead of parallel processing of all items)—a proposal that combines aspects of serial and of parallel search models (see also Carrasco, Ponte, Rechea, & Sampedro, 1998; Grossberg, Mingolla, & Ross, 1994; Humphreys & Müller, 1993; Treisman, 1982). Moore and Wolfe (2001) proposed that, while items are selected serially, one at a time (like in FIT or GS), several items can be processed simultaneously. A "pipeline" or "car wash" facility serve as relevant metaphors: Only one car can enter the facility at a time, but several cars may be simultaneously inside it. Such a processing system displays aspects of both serial and (capacity-limited) parallel processing (Harris, Shaw, & Bates, 1979).

Besides these formal computational models of visual search, neurocomputational models have been developed increasingly over the past 15 years, to simulate processes of visual search (described by functional theories) within neuronal network systems (e.g., Cave, 1999; Deco & Zihl, 2000; Heinke, Humphreys, & di Virgilio, 2002; Humphreys & Müller, 1993; Itti & Koch, 2001). In as far as these models incorporate neuroscientifically founded assumptions with regard to the functional architecture of the search processes (and thus display a certain degree of "realism"), they bridge the gap between behavioural experimental and computational research on the one hand and neuroscientific research on the other.

This final section "Neurocomputational modelling of visual search" brings together three papers (Itti; Heinke, Humphreys, & Tweed; Deco & Zihl) that represent three major approaches to the modelling of visual search and illustrate the power of these approaches in accounting for visual-selection phenomena.

L. Itti (2006 this issue) provides an extension of his saliency-based (simulation) model of attentional allocation by investigating whether an increased realism in the simulations would improve the prediction of where human observers direct their gaze while watching video clips. Simulation realism was achieved by augmenting a basic version of the model with a gaze-contingent foveation filter, or by embedding the video frames within a larger background and shifting them to eye position. Model-predicted salience was determined for locations gazed at by the observers, compared to random locations. The results suggest that emulating the details of visual stimulus processing improves the fit between the model prediction and the gaze behaviour of human observers.

D. Heinke, G. W. Humphreys, and C. L. Tweed (2006 this issue) present an extended version of their "Selective Attention for Identification Model" (SAIM) incorporating a feature extraction mechanism. Heinke et al. show that the revised SAIM can simulate both efficient and inefficient human search as well as search asymmetries, while maintaining translation-invariant object identification. Heinke et al. then turn to the simulation of top-down modulatory effects on search performance reported in recent studies, and they present an experimental test of a novel model prediction. The simulations demonstrate the importance of top-down target expectancies for selection time and accuracy. Also, consistent with the model prediction, a priming experiment with human observers revealed overall RT and search rate effects for valid-prime relative to neutral- and invalid-prime conditions.

A powerful, "neurodynamic model" of the function of attention and memory in visual processing has been developed by G. Deco and his colleagues, based on Desimone and Duncan's (1995) "biased competition hypothesis". G. Deco and J. Zihl (2006 this issue) describe the scope of this model, which integrates, within a unifying framework, the explanation of several existing types of experimental data obtained at different levels of investigation. At the microscopic level, single-cell recordings are simulated; at the mesoscopic level of cortical areas, results of fMRI studies are reproduced; and at the macroscopic level, the behavioural performance in psychophysical experiments, such as visual-search tasks, is described by the model. In particular, the model addresses how bottom-up and top-down (attentional) processes interact in visual processing, with attentional top-down bias guiding the dynamics to focus attention at a given location or on a set of features. Importantly, the modelling suggests that some seemingly serial processes reflect the operation of interacting parallel distributed systems.

REFERENCES

Arani, T., Karwan, M. H., & Drury, C. G. (1984). A variable-memory model of visual search. *Human Factors, 26*, 631–639.

Bacon, W. F., & Egeth, H. E. (1997). Goal-directed guidance of attention: Evidence from conjunctive visual search. *Journal of Experimental Psychology: Human Perception and Performance, 23*, 948–961.

Baylis, G. C., & Driver, J. (1992). Visual parsing and response competition: The effect of grouping factors. *Perception and Psychophysics, 51*, 45–162.

Bundesen, C. (1990). A theory of visual attention. *Psychological Review, 97*, 523–547.

Bundesen, C. (1998a). A computational theory of visual attention. *Philosophical Transactions of the Royal Society London, Series B: Biological Sciences, 353*, 1271–1281.

Bundesen, C. (1998b). Visual selective attention: Outlines of a choice model, a race model, and a computational theory. *Visual Cognition, 5*, 287–309.

Carrasco, M., Ponte, D., Rechea, C., & Sampedro, M. J. (1998). "Transient structures": The effects of practice and distractor grouping on a within-dimension conjunction search. *Perception and Psychophysics, 60*, 1243–1258.

Cave, K. (1999). The FeatureGate model of visual selection. *Psychological Research, 62*, 182–194.

Chelazzi, L., Duncan, J., Miller, E., & Desimone, R. (1993). A neural basis for visual search in inferior temporal cortex. *Nature, 363*, 345–347.

Chen, L., & Zhou, W. (1997). Holes in illusory conjunctions. *Perception and Psychophysics, 4*, 507–511.

Chun, M. M., & Jiang, Y. (1998). Contextual cueing: Implicit learning and memory of visual context guides spatial attention. *Cognitive Psychology, 36*, 28–71.

Cohen, A., & Magen, H. (1999). Intra- and cross-dimensional visual search for single feature targets. *Perception and Psychophysics, 61*, 291–307.

Deco, G., & Zihl, J. (2000). Neurodynamical mechanism of binding and selective attention for visual search. *Neurocomputing, 32–33*, 693–699.

Desimone, R., & Duncan, J. (1995). Neural mechanisms of selective visual attention. *Annual Review of Neuroscience, 18*, 193–222.

Donk, M., & Theeuwes, J. (2001). Visual marking beside the mark: Prioritizing selection by abrupt onsets. *Perception and Psychophysics, 63*, 891–900.

Eckstein, M. P., Thomas, J. P., Palmer, J., & Shimozaki, S. S. (2000). A signal detection model predicts the effects of set size on visual search accuracy for feature, conjunction, triple conjunction, and disjunction displays. *Perception and Psychophysics, 62*, 425–451.

Egeth, H. E., Virzi, R. A., & Garbart, H. (1984). Searching for conjunctively defined targets. *Journal of Experimental Psychology: Human Perception and Performance, 10*, 32–39.

Egly, R., Driver, J., & Rafal, R. D. (1994). Shifting visual attention between objects and locations: Evidence from normal and parietal lesion subjects. *Journal of Experimental Psychology: General, 123*, 161–177.

Enns, J. T., & Rensink, R. A. (1990). Influence of scene-based properties in visual search. *Science, 247*, 721–723.

Eriksen, C. W., & Spencer, T. (1969). Rate of information processing in visual perception: Some results and methodological considerations. *Journal of Experimental Psychology, 79*, 1–16.

Folk, C. L., & Remington, R. (1998). Selectivity in distraction by irrelevant featural singletons: Evidence for two forms of attentional capture. *Journal of Experimental Psychology: Human Perception and Performance, 24*, 847–858.

Fox, E., Lester, V., Russo, R., Bowles, R. J., Pichler, A., & Dutton, K. (2000). Facial expressions of emotion: Are angry faces detected more efficiently? *Cognition and Emotion, 14*, 61–92.

Gilchrist, I. D., & Harvey, M. (2000). Refixation frequency and memory mechanisms in visual search. *Current Biology, 10*, 1209–1212.

Grossberg, S., Mingolla, E., & Ross, W. D. (1994). A neural theory of attentive visual search: Interactions of boundary, surface, spatial and object representations. *Psychological Review, 101*, 470–489.

Harms, L., & Bundesen, C. (1983). Color segregation and selective attention in a nonsearch task. *Perception and Psychophysics, 33*, 11–19.

Harris, J. R., Shaw, M. L., & Bates, M. (1979). Visual search in multicharacter arrays with and without gaps. *Perception and Psychophysics, 26*, 69–84.

He, Z. J., & Nakayama, K. (1992). Surface versus features in visual search. *Nature, 359*, 231–233.

Heinke, D., Humphreys, G. W., & di Virgilio, G. (2002). Modelling visual search experiments: The selective attention for identification model (SAIM). *Neurocomputing, 44–46*, 817–822.

Hollingworth, A., & Henderson, J. M. (2002). Accurate visual memory for previously attended objects in natural scenes. *Journal of Experimental Psychology: Human Perception and Performance, 28*, 113–136.

Hollingworth, A., Williams, C. C., & Henderson, J. M. (2001). To see and remember: Visually specific information is retained in memory from previously attended objects in natural scenes. *Psychonomic Bulletin and Review, 8*, 761–768.

Horowitz, T. S., & Wolfe, J. M. (1998). Visual search has no memory. *Nature, 394*, 575–577.

Horowitz, T. S., & Wolfe, J. M. (2001). Search for multiple targets: Remember the targets, forget the search. *Perception and Psychophysics, 63*, 272–285.

Humphreys, G. W., & Müller, H. J. (1993). SEarch via Recursive Rejection (SERR): A connectionist model of visual search. *Cognitive Psychology, 25*, 43–110.

Humphreys, G. W., & Riddoch, M. J. (2001). Detection by action: Evidence for affordances in search in neglect. *Nature Neuroscience, 4*, 84–88.

Itti, L., & Koch, C. (2001). Computational modelling of visual attention. *Nature Neuroscience Reviews, 2*, 194–203.

Jiang, Y., Chun, M. M., & Marks, L. E. (2002). Visual marking: Selective attention to asynchronous temporal groups. *Journal of Experimental Psychology: Human Perception and Performance, 28*, 717–730.

Kim, M.-S., & Cave, K. R. (1999). Grouping effects on spatial attention in visual search. *Journal of General Psychology, 126*, 326–352.

Kinchla, R. A. (1974). Detecting targets in multi-element arrays: A confusability model. *Perception and Psychophysics, 15*, 149–158.

Klein, R. (1988). Inhibitory tagging system facilitates visual search. *Nature, 334*, 430–431.

Kramer, A. F., & Watson, S. E. (1996). Object-based visual selection and the principle of uniform connectedness. In A. F. Kramer, M. G. H. Coles, & G. Logan (Eds.), *Converging operations in the study of visual selective attention* (pp. 395–414). Washington, DC: American Psychological Association.

Krummenacher, J., Müller, H. J., & Heller, D. (2001). Visual search for dimensionally redundant pop-out targets: Evidence for parallel-coactive processing of dimensions. *Perception and Psychophysics, 63*, 901–917.

Kumada, T., & Humphreys, G. W. (2002). Cross-dimensional interference and cross-trial inhibition. *Perception and Psychophysics*, *64*, 493–503.

Luck, S. J., Fan, S., & Hillyard, S. A. (1993). Attention-related modulation of sensory-evoked brain activity in a visual search task. *Journal of Cognitive Neuroscience*, *5*, 188–195.

Luck, S. J., & Hillyard, S. A. (1995). The role of attention in feature detection and conjunction discrimination: An electrophysiological analysis. *International Journal of Neuroscience*, *80*, 281–297.

Maljkovic, V., & Nakayama, K. (1994). Priming of pop-out: I. Role of features. *Memory and Cognition*, *22*, 657–672.

Maljkovic, V., & Nakayama, K. (1996). Priming of pop-out: II. The role of position. *Perception and Psychophysics*, *58*, 977–991.

Maljkovic, V., & Nakayama, K. (2000). Priming of popout: III. A short-term implicit memory system beneficial for rapid target selection. *Visual Cognition*, *7*, 571–595.

Moore, C. M., & Wolfe, J. M. (2001). Getting beyond the serial/parallel debate in visual search: A hybrid approach. In K. Shapiro (Ed.), *The limits of attention: Temporal constraints on human information processing* (pp. 178–198). Oxford, UK: Oxford University Press.

Motter, B. C. (1994a). Neural correlates of attentive selection for color and luminance in extrastriate area V4. *Journal of Neuroscience*, *14*, 2178–2189.

Motter, B. C. (1994b). Neural correlates of feature selective memory and pop-out in extrastriate area V4. *Journal of Neuroscience*, *14*, 2190–2199.

Müller, H. J., Heller, D., & Ziegler, J. (1995). Visual search for singleton feature targets within and across feature dimensions. *Perception and Psychophysics*, *57*, 1–17.

Müller, H. J., Reimann, B., & Krummenacher, J. (2003). Visual search for singleton feature targets across dimensions: Stimulus- and expectancy-driven effects in dimensional weighting. *Journal of Experimental Psychology: Human Perception and Performance*, *29*, 1021–1035.

Müller, H. J., & von Mühlenen, A. (2000). Probing distractor inhibition in visual search: Inhibition of return. *Journal of Experimental Psychology: Human Perception and Performance*, *26*, 1591–1605.

Neisser, U. (1967). *Cognitive psychology*. New York: Appleton-Century-Crofts.

Nothdurft, H. C. (1991). Texture segmentation and pop-out from orientation contrast. *Vision Research*, *31*, 1073–1078.

Öhman, A., Lundqvist, D., & Esteves, F. (2001). The face in the crowd revisited: A threat advantage with schematic stimuli. *Journal of Personality and Social Psychology*, *80*, 381–396.

Palmer, J., Verghese, P., & Pavel, M. (2000). The psychophysics of visual search. *Vision Research*, *40*, 1227–1268.

Peterson, M. S., Kramer, A. F., Wang, R. F., Irwin, D. E., & McCarley, J. S. (2001). Visual search has memory. *Psychological Science*, *12*, 287–292.

Pollmann, S., Weidner, R., Müller, H. J., & von Cramon, D.Y. (2000). A fronto-posterior network involved in visual dimension changes. *Journal of Cognitive Neuroscience*, *12*, 480–494.

Posner, M. I., & Cohen, Y. (1984). Components of visual orienting. In H. Bouma & D. G. Bouwhuis (Eds.), *Attention and performance X: Control of language processes* (pp. 531–556). Hove, UK: Lawrence Erlbaum Associates Ltd.

Rees, G., Frith, C. D., & Lavie, N. (1997). Modulating irrelevant motion perception by varying attentional load in an unrelated task. *Science*, *278*, 1616–1619.

Rensink, R. A. (2000a). The dynamic representation of scenes. *Visual Cognition*, *7*, 17–42.

Rensink, R. A. (2000b). Seeing, sensing, and scrutinizing. *Vision Research*, *40*, 1469–1487.

Rensink, E. A., O'Regan, J. K., & Clark, J. J. (1997). To see or not to see: The need for attention to perceive changes in scenes. *Psychological Science*, *8*, 368–373.

Robertson, L. C., & Eglin, M. (1993). Attentional search in unilateral visual neglect. In I. H. Robertson & J. C. Marshall (Eds.), *Unilateral neglect: Clinical and experimental findings* (pp. 169–191). Hove, UK: Lawrence Erlbaum Associates Ltd.

Swensson, R. G., & Judy, P. F. (1981). Detection of noisy visual targets: Models for the effects of spatial uncertainty and signal-to-noise ratio. *Perception and Psychophysics, 29*, 521–534.

Takeda, Y., & Yagi, A. (2000). Inhibitory tagging in visual search can be found if search stimuli remain visible. *Perception and Psychophysics, 62*, 927–934.

Theeuwes, J. (1991). Cross-dimensional perceptual selectivity. *Perception and Psychophysics, 50*, 184–193.

Theeuwes, J. (1992). Perceptual selectivity for color and form. *Perception and Psychophysics, 51*, 599–606.

Treisman, A. (1982). Perceptual grouping and attention in visual search for features and for objects. *Journal of Experimental Psychology: Human Perception and Performance, 8*, 194–214.

Treisman, A., & Gelade, G. (1980). A feature-integration theory of attention. *Cognitive Psychology, 12*, 97–136.

Treue, S., & Maunsell, J. H. R. (1996). Attentional modulation of visual motion processing in cortical areas MT and MST. *Nature, 382*, 539–541.

Walsh, V., Ellison, A., Asbridge, E., & Cowey, A. (1999). The role of the parietal cortex in visual attention: Hemispheric asymmetries and the effects of learning: A magnetic stimulation study. *Neuropsychologia, 37*, 245–251.

Watson, D. G., & Humphreys, G. W. (1997). Visual marking: Prioritizing selection for new objects by top-down attentional inhibition of old objects. *Psychological Review, 104*, 90–122.

Weidner, R., Pollmann, S., Müller, H. J., & von Cramon, D. Y. (2002). Top-down controlled visual dimension weighting: An event-related fMRI study. *Cerebral Cortex, 12*, 318–328.

Wolfe, J. M. (1992). "Effortless" texture segmentation and "parallel" visual search are not the same thing. *Vision Research, 32*, 757–763.

Wolfe, J. M. (1994). Guided Search 2.0: A revised model of visual search. *Psychonomic Bulletin and Review, 1*, 202–238.

Wolfe, J. M. (1998). What can 1,000,000 trials tell us about visual search? *Psychological Science, 9*, 33–39.

Wolfe, J. M. (1999). Inattentional amnesia. In V. Coltheart (Ed.), *Fleeting memories* (pp. 71–94). Cambridge, MA: MIT Press.

Wolfe, J. M., Cave, K. R., & Franzel, S. L. (1989). Guided Search: An alternative to the feature integration model for visual search. *Journal of Experimental Psychology: Human Perception and Performance, 15*, 419–433.

Yantis, S. (1993). Stimulus-driven attentional capture. *Current Directions in Psychological Science, 2*, 156–161.

VISUAL COGNITION, 2006, 14 (4/5/6/7/8), 411–443

Ψ Psychology Press
Taylor & Francis Group

How the deployment of attention determines what we see

Anne Treisman

Princeton University, NJ, USA

Attention is a tool to adapt what we see to our current needs. It can be focused narrowly on a single object or spread over several or distributed over the scene as a whole. In addition to increasing or decreasing the number of attended objects, these different deployments may have different effects on what we see. This article describes some research both on focused attention and its use in binding features, and on distributed attention and the kinds of information we gain and lose with the attention window opened wide. One kind of processing that we suggest occurs automatically with distributed attention results in a statistical description of sets of similar objects. Another gives the gist of the scene, which may be inferred from sets of features registered in parallel. Flexible use of these different modes of attention allows us to reconcile sharp capacity limits with a richer understanding of the visual scene.

Perception comprises a range of different ways of informing ourselves about the environment for a variety of different purposes including understanding, recognition and prediction, aesthetic appreciation, and the control of action. One important tool adapting the visual system to different perceptual tasks is the set of control systems that we call attention. Attention can be allocated to different aspects of the environment and in different ways, ranging from the focused analysis of local conjunctions of features to the global registration of scene properties. I will describe some research exploring the effects of these different ways of allocating attention to displays with multiple stimuli.

GENERAL FRAMEWORK

I will start by illustrating the framework I use to help me think about the results. Figure 1 shows a first rapid pass through the visual system before

Please address all correspondence to Anne Treisman, Psychology Department, Princeton University, Princeton, NJ 08544-1010, USA. Email: treisman@princeton.edu

http://www.psypress.com/viscog
DOI: 10.1080/13506280500195250

**First feedforward pass
(or later passes with attention focused elsewhere)**

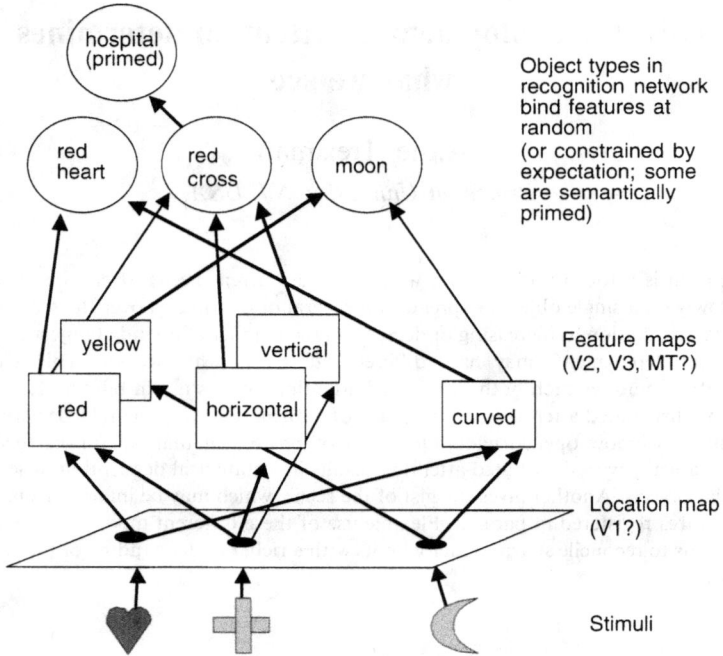

Figure 1. Sketch of model before attention acts (preattentive processing) or when attention is focused elsewhere (inattention).

attention is brought to bear, or when attention is focused elsewhere. Visual stimuli are initially registered as implicit conjunctions of features by local units in V1 that respond to many of their properties. At this level they function as filled locations in a detailed map of discontinuities, although of course the information about their properties is implicitly present to be extracted by further processing. Contingent adaptation effects (McCollough, 1965) are probably determined at this early level, since they are retinotopically determined, and independent of attention (Houck & Hoffman, 1986).

Specialized units then respond selectively to different "features", and form feature maps in various extrastriate areas. A "red" unit, for example, would pick up from any V1 detectors that respond to red stimuli in their receptive fields, regardless of the other properties to which they are tuned. The feature maps retain implicit information about the spatial origins through their links back to V1 but they do not otherwise make the locations explicitly available.

At a higher level in the ventral pathway, nodes in a recognition network representing object types for familiar entities are activated to different degrees, depending on how many of their features are present but regardless of how these are conjoined.[1] The recognition network is a long-term store of knowledge used to identify objects but not to represent the current scene. In this preattentive or inattentive phase, features activate any object types with which they are individually consistent, and may inhibit those with which they conflict, activating particular recognition nodes to differing degrees depending on the level of feature support. Top-down expectations may also prime predicted objects. Because the feature access is nonselective, illusory conjunctions will be activated as well as correct conjunctions. Figure 1 shows the nodes for a red cross, and, through associative priming, for hospital, being activated by what is actually a yellow cross and a red heart. The initial access to identities on the first pass is very fast, taking only 150 ms or so (Thorpe, Fize, & Marlot, 1996), although not all are later confirmed and consciously seen. So far the information is mostly unconscious and not explicitly available, although it may trigger responses based on the semantic categories activated (see below).

Our hypothesis (Treisman & Gelade, 1980) was that incorrect conjunctions are weeded out by focused attention. Figure 2 shows the attention window narrowly focused onto one object location and suppressing any features outside the currently selected area. One way this might be implemented is through a reentry process, controlled by parietal areas, acting back on the map of locations, perhaps in V1, to serially select the contents of different locations (Treisman, 1996). An "object file", addressed by its location at a particular time, is formed to represent the attended object (Kahneman, Treisman, & Gibbs, 1992). Within it, the selected features are bound and then compared to the set of currently active representations in the recognition network to retrieve the identity of the object—in this example the moon. Conscious perception depends on these object files.[2]

---

[1] Note, however, that some physical conjunctions may create emergent features, which could also play a part in activating only recognition units with which they are compatible (see, for example, Treisman & Paterson, 1984).

[2] While conscious perception in the theory depends on object files, the converse may not be the case. Binding can sometimes occur without the bound objects becoming consciously accessible. For example, in the negative priming paradigm with only two objects present, accurate binding can happen without attention. The attended object is consciously and correctly bound, and the remaining features belonging to the unattended object are bound by default, with the resulting object tokens surviving sometimes for several days or weeks (Treisman & DeSchepper, 1996). However, the unattended shape may fail to be consciously registered.

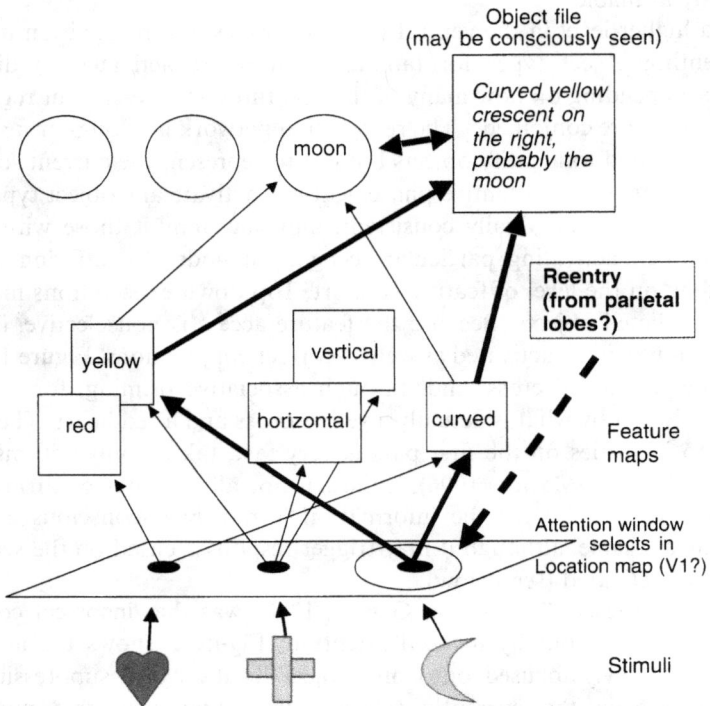

Figure 2. Sketch of model with attention focused on one object. The features in the selected location are collected in an object file where they are bound. Nonselected features are excluded from the object file but may still prime object nodes in recognition network.

The window of attention set by the parietal scan can take on different apertures, to encompass anything from a finely localized object to a global view of the surrounding scene. The resulting object file may represent the scene as a whole (e.g., an ocean beach), a pair of objects within the scene (e.g., a woman walking her dog), or even a single part of one object (e.g., the handle of a cup). In combination, these samples at differing scales build up a representation both of a background setting and of some objects within it.

This account provides a dual representation of object identities, one implicit and unconscious and the other explicit and conscious: On the one hand, there is a continuum of activation in the recognition network of object types, modulated both by expectations, and by the amount of feature support allowed through at any time by the window of attention. In addition, the attended features are assembled to form a few explicit object tokens or "object files" that encode information from particular objects in their particular current instantiation, specifying the spatial relations and conjunctions of features, and mediating conscious experience. The number of object files that can be set up and maintained in working memory is very limited—only two to four bound objects (Luck & Vogel, 1997). However, the semantic knowledge primed in the recognition network may be much richer (see discussion below).

EVIDENCE FOR FEATURE INTEGRATION THEORY

The evidence that led to Feature Integration Theory (FIT) includes the following findings:

1. Search for a conjunction target requires focused attention, whereas targets coded by separate features can be found through parallel search. This early claim was supported by several experiments (Treisman & Gelade, 1980), but its generality was soon challenged. When the features of the conjunction are defined by separate dimensions and are highly discriminable, a strategy for guiding the search can bypass the need to bind every distractor (Treisman, 1988; Treisman & Sato, 1990; Wolfe, Cave, & Franzel 1989). Because the strategy also depends on spatial selection (controlled from the relevant feature maps), this strategy fails for conjunctions of parts within objects, for example a rotated T among rotated Ls, where both parts are present in every item and only their arrangement changes. It also cannot be used when the target is unknown and defined as the odd one out in a background of known conjunctions (Treisman & Sato, 1990).
2. Participants make binding errors if attention is diverted or overloaded. When we flashed displays of three coloured letters and asked observers to attend primarily to two flanking digits, they reported many illusory conjunctions such as a red E or a green T when the stimuli were actually a red O, a blue T, and a green E (Treisman & Schmidt, 1982).
3. A spatial cue in advance of the display helps the identification of a conjunction target much more than the identification of a feature target (Treisman, 1988)
4. Boundaries or shapes defined only by conjunctions are difficult to see, whereas feature-defined boundaries give easy segregation and shape recognition (Treisman & Gelade, 1980; Wolfe & Bennett, 1997). It seems that we cannot "hold onto" more than one conjunction at a time.
5. Priming can be object specific. For example, a letter primes report of a matching letter when it reappears in the same frame, even after the frame has moved to a new location (Kahneman et al., 1992). This

suggests that temporary episodic object tokens are set up to represent objects in their current specific instantiations, and to bind their features across space and time.

6. Search for conjunctions activates the same parietal areas as shifting attention spatially (Corbetta, Shulman, Miezin, & Petersen, 1995).

7. Patients with bilateral parietal lesions lose their ability to localize objects spatially. Since this rules out spatial attention, FIT predicts that they should experience problems with binding and with individuating objects. This prediction is confirmed (Humphreys, Cinel, Wolfe, Olson, & Klempen, 2000; Robertson, Treisman, Friedman-Hill, & Grabow-ecky, 1997). The patient we studied saw illusory conjunctions even with long displays of only two objects. He was unable to find conjunction targets in visual search tasks but had no problem searching for targets defined by a single feature. If the deficit reflects a perceptual space that has collapsed down to a single functional location, it could also explain the simultanagnosia. Our account of these deficits is depicted in Figure 3. The model gives a way of integrating the two symptoms described by

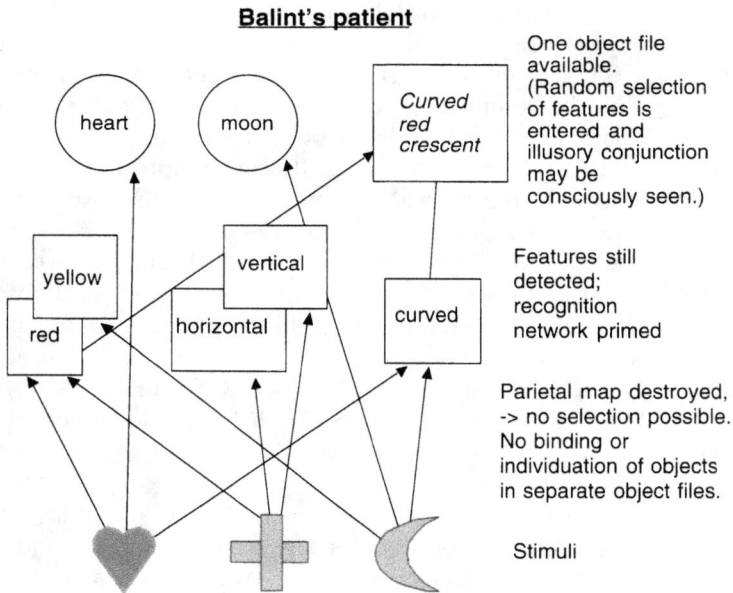

Figure 3. Sketch of model for Balint's patient with bilateral parietal damage. The location map has been destroyed, preventing feature binding and the individuation of different simultaneously presented objects through spatial attention. As a result, binding errors are frequent and only one object file is available at any given time.

Balint (1909)—localization failures and simultanagnosia—while adding the third prediction, that these patients should have major problems with binding.

BINDING, PERCEPTUAL ORGANIZATION, AND VISUAL SEARCH

The first new experiment that I will describe, done in collaboration with my students, Evans and Hu, explored the effect of perceptual organization on search for conjunction targets, specifically, what determines the units that are entered into object files. A debate over whether attention selects locations or objects has been going on for years. Debates that last that long usually get the answer "both". It is certainly the case that one can attend to a particular currently empty location and that this causes a faster response to whatever appears in that location. But it is also true that object characteristics can mould attention to fit them, and that responses are triggered faster to two parts of the same object than to equidistant parts of two different objects (Egly, Driver, & Rafal, 1994).

But what defines an object before it has been selected and attended? In Feature Integration Theory, preattentive grouping must take place either in the separate feature maps, where it will be defined by separate colours, orientations, directions of movement, and so on, but not by conjunctions of those features, or in the map of filled locations where properties such as connectedness, proximity, and colinearity could play a role in defining the candidate objects for focused attention. Grouping can also be influenced by top-down control, in a recursive interaction.

Balint's patients may also provide some useful empirical evidence on what counts as a perceptual unit. Their simultanagnosia allows them to perceive only a single object, so an object may be whatever they can see at any given time. The circularity can be broken by seeing how well their responses predict attentional performance in normal participants. Humphreys and Riddoch (1993) showed a Balint's patient an array of dots in either one or two colours. He was unable to tell whether the array contained two colours or not, since he saw only one dot of the many presented. However, when heterogeneous pairs of dots were joined with connecting lines he was suddenly able to do the task. The lines made each pair into a unitary object so that two dots of different colours were now consciously accessible instead of one. However, when the lines connected matching pairs he failed. Robertson and I tried replicating this experiment with our Balint's patient. Unfortunately he did not show the effect. However, he did make an intriguing remark that is also relevant to our question. He said "You know I can only see 1 or 2 of the whole bunch of them". Now where was that "bunch" that he knew about but allegedly could not see? Our guess is that he occasionally opened a larger object file, letting in a patch of dots as a single object. I will return to that observation later in the paper.

Inspired by Humphrey's patient, Evans, Hu, and I explored a prediction about perceptual units and binding in normal participants. The target in our visual search task was a conjunction of shape and colour—a blue circle among green circles and blue triangles. We used displays with lines that either connected the elements or left them unconnected. The lines connected either mixed or matching pairs (see Figure 4). The Balint's data suggest that connecting lines make perceptual units out of the pairs. If so, the linking might help when the pairs match, since there would be fewer items to search. But it should hinder when they are mixed because each object would contain both target features—circle and blue. Attention would have to narrow down to the separate shapes within the pairs, breaking the natural units. Search should be slower, and the risk of illusory conjunctions should increase.

The four conditions, mixed linked, mixed separate, matching linked, and matching separate, were randomly mixed within blocks. There were three display sizes: For each condition: 4 pairs in a 4×3 matrix; 9 pairs in a 5×5 matrix; and 16 pairs in a 7×7 matrix. The 3×4 and 5×5 matrixes were randomly located in the 7×7 matrix, which was centred on the screen, so the densities and the average distances of elements from the initial fixation point were approximately matched. A target was present on half the trials. The displays remained visible until participants responded. There were 12 participants, all students at Princeton University.

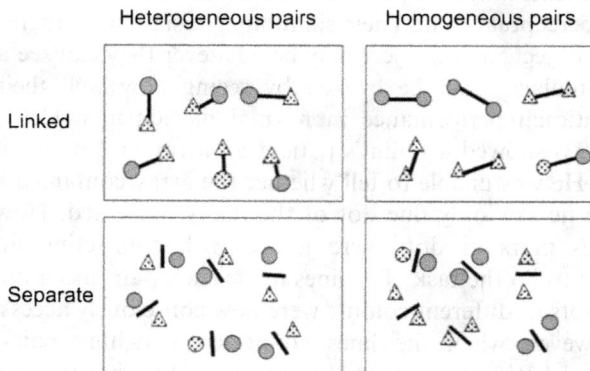

Figure 4. Stimuli used in visual search and grouping experiment (Evans, Hu, & Treisman, unpublished). The target was a blue circle (shown as speckled) among blue triangles and green circles (shown as grey).

Participants missed far more targets in some conditions than in others, implying that they sometimes stopped the search without completing it, making it difficult to compare search times across conditions. To correct for the different numbers of missed targets, we reasoned as follows: If participants missed targets with probability p in displays of n items, they presumably searched only $(1 - p)$ of the n items. We calculated the search rates replacing the objective display sizes with these estimates of the number of items searched. Since the functions appeared to increase linearly with the number of items and the slope ratios of target absent to target present were close to 2 to 1 (averaging 2.1), we assumed that they reflected serial self-terminating search. To get a concise summary of performance in the four conditions, we took the mean of the slopes for target absent and twice the slopes for target present (since only half the items would be checked in a self-terminating search). These are shown in Table 1.

The mixed linked condition, as predicted, gave by far the worst performance—search times per item nearly double those for the matching linked, and much worse than those for the mixed separate. The object files that preattentive processes deliver up for attentive checking in this condition are poorly adapted to the task of finding the blue circle target, because each pair creates a potential illusory conjunction. It has to be broken up perceptually before being rejected.

COMPONENTS OF BINDING

Once the candidate objects for attention are specified, how do we actually bind their features? The second experiment, done with Seiffert and Weber, is an attempt to analyse the binding process and to see what brain mechanisms are involved. We distinguish three different components to the binding task in visual search: Shift, suppress, and bind.

TABLE 1
Search functions for the four conditions shown in Figure 4

	Mixed pairs			Matching pairs		
	Slope estimate	Intercept	Mean % missed targets	Slope estimate	Intercept	Mean % missed targets
Linked	187	359	21	108	470	12
Separate	130	452	8	98	480	5

Slopes are means of 2 (target present) and (target absent), calculated after correcting the display sizes for the proportion of targets missed on target present trials at each display size.

1. We must *shift* the attention window in space to select one object after another.
2. We must exclude or *suppress* features of other objects, to prevent illusory conjunctions.
3. Finally we must *bind* the selected features together.

We used a difficult conjunction search task, initially tested by Wolfe and Bennett (1997), to try to separate the contribution of each of these components. The target was a plus with a blue vertical and a green horizontal bar. It appeared among either conjunction distractors—pluses with a green vertical and blue horizontal bar, or feature distractors with a unique feature not shared by the target (see Figure 5). In one experiment, the feature distractors differed from the target either in colour or in orientation. They were a plus tilted 20 degrees left or right, or a plus with a purple bar. In another experiment, they differed from the target either in colour or in shape. They were a plus with a purple bar or a T with blue vertical and green horizontal bars. When the distractors have a purple bar or tilt, or when they differ from the target in a simple feature of shape, there should be no need to bind. They can be rejected on the basis of the unique nontarget feature. But when the target and distractors have the same colours and bars, the only way to determine whether they match the target is to bind the colour, orientation, or T feature to the bars for each distractor in turn.

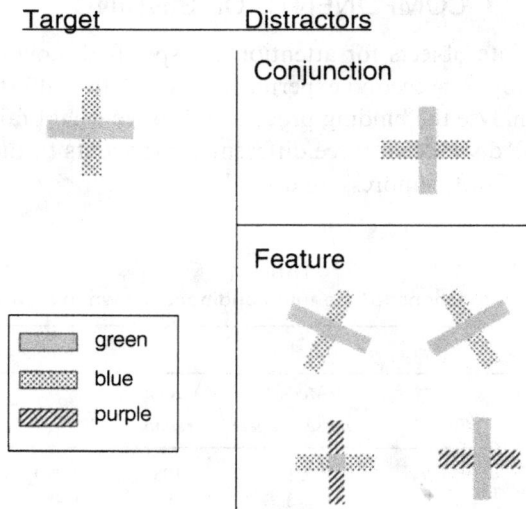

Figure 5. Stimuli used by Seiffert, Weber, and Treisman (unpublished) to test separate components of the binding process.

We presented strings of sequential displays, consisting of two components: Eight items in successive cued locations that could contain the target with 50% probability (we call this the target sequence), and a fixed set of five additional distractor items in other randomly selected uncued locations (we call this the surround; see Figure 6 for an example). At the end of each string of eight displays, participants were asked whether a target (a plus with a blue vertical and green horizontal bar) was present anywhere in the sequence. It could only appear in one of the cued locations. We isolated the *binding* component by comparing detection rates when the target sequence consisted of conjunction distractors and when it consisted of feature distractors. We tested the *spatial shifting* component by presenting the items in the target sequence in different randomly selected locations, each one precued by a black dot, and comparing this shifting sequence with a sequence that appeared in a single cued location. We tested the *distractor suppression* component by varying the nature of the items in the surround. The five additional distractors could be conjunction distractors or feature distractors. The conjunction distractors should need active suppression to prevent their features from forming illusory conjunctions with those in the cued location.

Figure 7 shows the error rates (false alarms plus omissions) in each condition. There was a large effect of shifting attention around in the display: Significant, $F(1, 8) = 61.28, p < .001$. There was also a large effect of conjunction versus feature distractors in the sequence of cued locations, $F(1, 8) = 37.86, p < .001$. This is the component that reflects the need to bind the

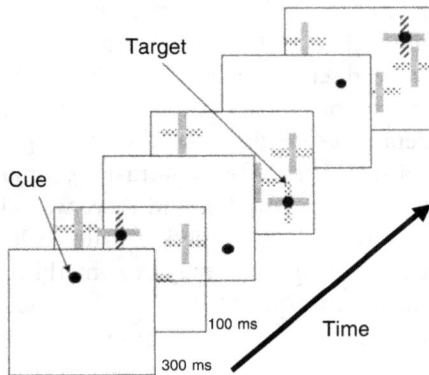

Figure 6. Example of trial in components of binding experiment. Each trial comprised a sequence of 8 cued items, interleaved with a spatial cue (a black dot) preceding each display. If present (50% trials), the target always appeared at a cued location. The distractors differed from the target in either a feature (colour or tilt), or the conjunction of features. Distractors were added in the surround to test suppression of nontarget items. The figure shows the first three displays in a trial in which the shift-attention and suppress-surround components are needed, but not the binding component for the cued sequence, since the cued items differ from the target in a simple feature (colour).

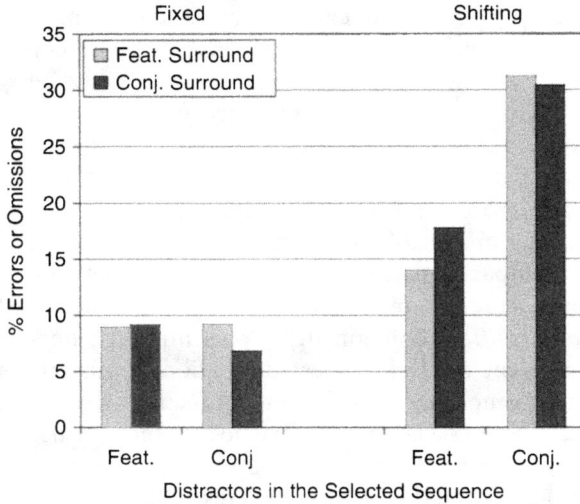

Figure 7. Percentage errors and omissions made in the different conditions of experiment testing components of binding. Trials requiring shifts of attention are slower than those with fixed attention. When attention must be reset for each item. trials with conjunction distractors in the cued sequence are slower than those with feature distractors. suggesting that binding increases the difficulty. However. there is no overall effect of conjunction distractors relative to feature distractors in the surround.

colours and bars. There was also an interaction between the effects of shifting and binding. $F(1, 8) = 42.8$, $p < .001$. When the relevant location was fixed, there was little effect of the cued distractors. They interfere mostly when attention must be reset for each item. Finally there was no overall effect of having conjunction versus feature distractors in the surround. Looking in more detail at the data for the shifting sequence only, we found that there was a significant effect contrasting conjunction with *colour* distractors in the surround (Figure 8a). and there was also an effect in the second experiment contrasting conjunction with colour or with shape distractors (see Figure 8b). Thus there may be something special that makes orientation feature distractors in the surround harder to suppress than colour or shape feature distractors and as hard as conjunction distractors. Finally in both experiments. when there were conjunction distractors in the cued sequence there was no additional decrement from replacing feature distractors in the surround with conjunction distractors. A possible reason could be the greater heterogeneity in the display with two different distractor types (feature and conjunction) compared to one (all conjunction distractors). We are currently testing with two kinds of feature distractors (e.g., colour distractors in the cued locations and orientation distractors in the

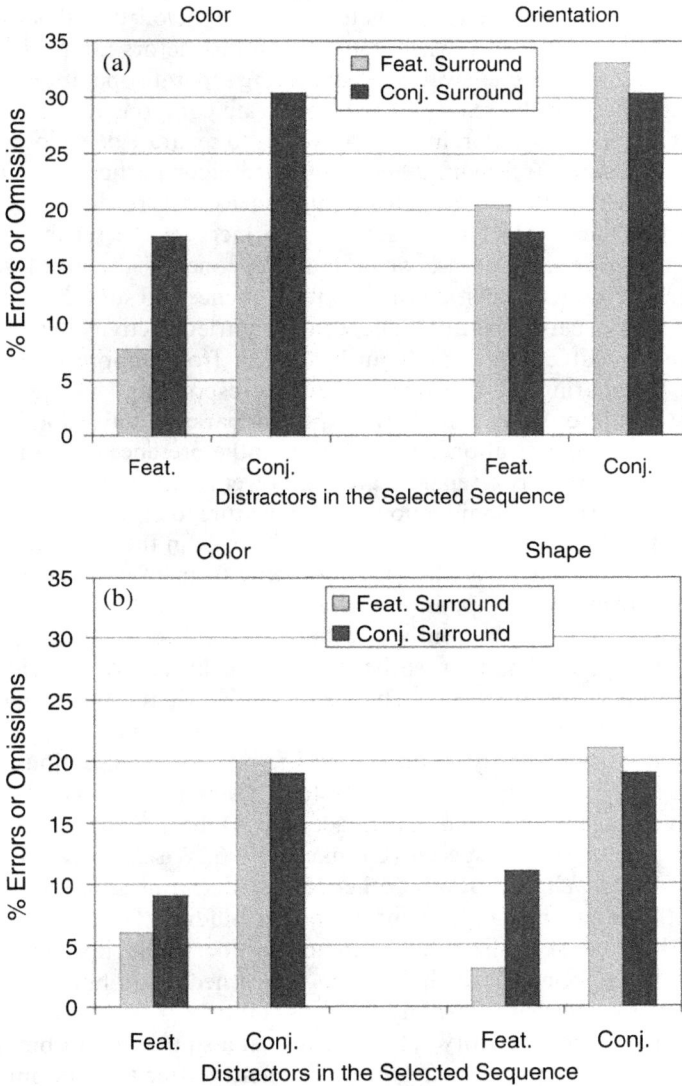

Figure 8. (a) Separating trials with colour feature and trials with orientation feature distractors shows that tilt distractors are as difficult as conjunction distractors to suppress, but colour feature distractors are easier. (b) Separate analysis of shape and colour distractors (in shifting attention trials only) shows that both feature types are easier than conjunction distractors to suppress. However, neither of the experiments shows increased difficulty when conjunction distractors in the surround are added to conjunction distractors in the cued sequence. This may be because display heterogeneity is greater with feature distractors in the surround and conjunction distractors in the sequence. Two different distractor types must be excluded rather than a single type.

surround), and we find that, with heterogeneity controlled in this way, there is clearly more interference when conjunction distractors are present.

Brain imaging offers a new tool for dissecting separate operations. We were interested in testing the reality of these separate components of binding by relating them to different brain areas as well as to separate behavioural effects (Seiffert, Weber, & Treisman, 2003). We tested eight participants doing the first experiment with colour and orientation as feature distractors in the Princeton Siemens fMRI brain scanner. To increase the sensitivity in the shifting attention conditions, we tested only one of the fixed sequence conditions (conjunction distractors in both sequence and surround). Previous studies (e.g., Corbetta et al., 1995) have shown parietal activity in conjunction search, but most did not distinguish shifting from suppression or from binding. Comparing the activation in the corresponding shifting and fixed sequence conditions, we found the expected parietal activation, and also plenty of occipital activation, probably due to the presence of motion. More interesting, we found two separate areas that were activated selectively in the *binding* comparison—conjunction versus feature distractors in the cued sequence. One was a medial frontal area, close to or in the anterior cingulate. This tends to be activated when there is some form of conflict present. In binding, there may be competition between relevant and irrelevant features to be integrated into the currently selected object. The other area showing activity selective to binding was the left anterior insula. We also found this area in another conjunction search experiment, so we think it may be a real effect. But its function is more mysterious. The anterior insula appears to be activated in a wide variety of rather specific but diverse situations, ranging from disgust (Critchley, Wiens, Rotshtein, Öhman, & Dolan, 2004), to imitation of facial expressions (Carr, Iacoboni, Dubeau, Mazziotta, & Lenzi, 2003), to articulation in speech (Dronkers, 1996; Wise, Greene, Buchel, & Scott, 1999), as well as to several other equally disparate situations. It seems unlikely that what they all have in common is binding! Of course there may well be different specialized subareas *within* the insula involved in these different tasks, one of which may be concerned with binding. Further research will be needed to explore that possibility.

There is no complete story yet on the neural instantiation of binding. My speculation is that it reflects a process of reentry after the first initial pass through the sensory hierarchy, returning to the early visual areas where fine localization and detailed features can be retrieved. The idea of reentry (first proposed in the context of memory by Damasio, 1989) is very much in the air these days. For example it is used in the Reverse Hierarchy Theory proposed by Hochstein and Ahissar (2002) and in the model of visual masking by object substitution proposed by Di Lollo, Enns, and Rensink (2000). I suggested that it may also play a role in binding, as follows (Treisman, 1996). The first response to visual stimulation may activate feature detectors in early striate and extrastriate areas that connect automatically to the temporal lobe object nodes with which they are compatible, and perhaps inhibit those with which they conflict. To check whether the conjunctions are real, the features must be retraced to the early visual areas V1 or V2 where localization is more precise. Parietal areas may then control a serial reentry scan through these areas to retrieve the features present in each. The binding itself might involve the area we found in the anterior insula combining the selected features to form an integrated object representation.

DISTRIBUTED ATTENTION

The second part of this paper explores the effects of deploying attention more globally over several objects at once or over the display as a whole. The hypothesis is that this provides different information from that available in the focused binding mode. Figure 9 shows the attention window encompassing

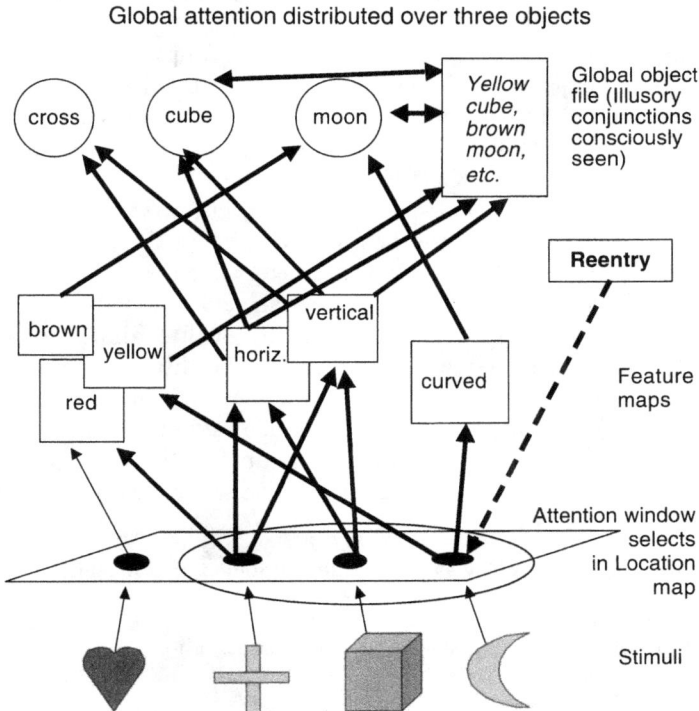

Figure 9. Sketch of model with attention spread over three items rather than focused on one. The hypothesis is that this produces binding failures within the attention window.

three objects instead of one, making all their features available to potential object files. A separate choice can then be made of whether to open separate object files for the individual elements, running the risk that a random selection of features may result in illusory conjunctions. The yellow cube in the figure is an illusory conjunction of two attended features that actually belong to different objects. Because it is in an object file, it could become consciously available. Alternatively one could choose to open a single object file for the attended group as a whole, making a different set of properties available, including the global shape, global boundaries, and global relations between elements. The "whole bunch of dots" reported by our Balint's patient may reflect processing of a global patch as a unitary object.

What useful information might this global deployment provide? Table 2 summarizes the following suggestions.

1. First, it could be an efficient way of revealing the presence of a target feature anywhere in the display. If we are looking for something "red" and red appears in the global object file, we can detect its presence, and then rapidly home in on it in the location map with more narrowly focused attention.
2. It might define global boundaries between groups of objects where the groups differ in some feature that is shared by elements within each group and differs for elements between groups. Groups defined only by conjunctions of features do not create boundaries that are perceptually available (Treisman & Gelade, 1980).
3. It should give the global shape of the objects, at some expense to the local objects that compose them (Navon, 1977).
4. It should provide some general parameters like the global illumination of the elements, allowing us to detect an odd object that is lit from a different direction or oriented differently in three dimensional space, even though the unique object seems to be distinguished only by a conjunction of shape and contrast (Enns & Rensink, 1990).
5. With more complex natural scenes, global attention may also give us the gist of the scene—for example a mountain landscape, or a kitchen, perhaps through priming from disjunctive sets of features (see below).

TABLE 2

Information potentially available with distributed or global attention

1. Target with unique feature (popout effect in search)
2. Global boundaries defined by features (not conjunctions)
3. Global shape
4. Global illumination and 3D orientation
5. Gist of the scene (e.g. mountain landscape, or kitchen)
6. Statistical properties

6. Finally, our current hypothesis is that it may offer some simple statistical properties of sets of similar objects.

STATISTICAL PROCESSING WITH DISTRIBUTED ATTENTION

The world is full of sets that vary on a range of different dimensions, for example the cars in a parking lot, or the apples on a tree. It would be wasteful and probably beyond our attentional capacity to specify each element in the representation we form. Instead we may generate a statistical description, including the frequencies of different element types, the mean, the range and the variance of sizes, colours, orientations that they encompass, facilitating rapid decisions based, for example, on the quality of the fruit, the density of the traffic, or the rockiness of the terrain (see Figure 10).

One important proviso is that this statistical information should be restricted to features, since it comes from pooled feature maps rather than from individuated objects. I recently tested this prediction by asking participants to judge the frequencies either of features or of conjunctions. I presented brief displays of coloured shapes—the letters, O, X, and T in red, green, and blue—and asked people to estimate proportions, for example

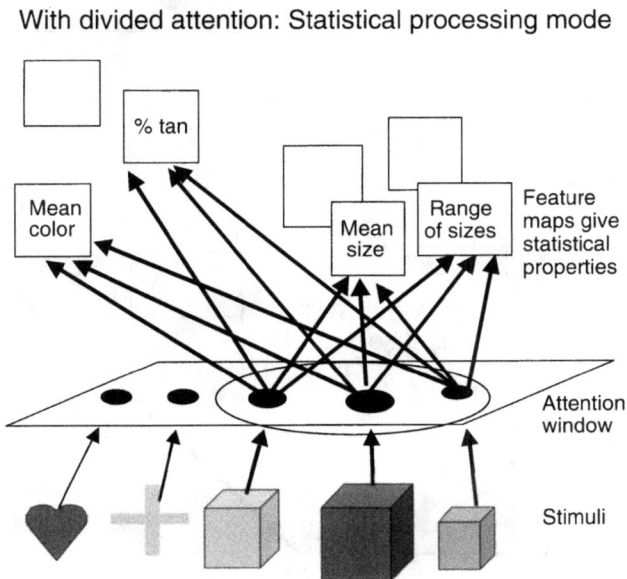

Figure 10. Statistical properties may be automatically computed at the feature level when attention is distributed over sets of similar items.

what proportion were green, or were Ts, or were green Ts. I postcued which feature or conjunction was relevant (Figure 11). On each trial, participants saw the display for 500 ms, then 500 ms blank screen, and then a single colour patch or a single white letter or a single coloured letter as a probe. The task was to say what proportion of the display that particular feature or conjunction represented. Participants were good at judging the proportions of the separate features that were present, but very poor at judging the proportions of conjunctions. For example, they gave similar estimates for the proportion of blue Xs in the two displays of Figure 12a and 12b. The two displays contain exactly the same proportions of the different features—half blue letters, half Xs, a quarter each red letters, green letters, Ts, and Os, but the features are differently bound in the two conditions. The first display actually has 33% blue Xs and the second has none. Yet the mean estimates hardly differed: They were 15% and 11%. Global attention gives us good estimates of feature proportions, but it does not yield proportions for bound objects.

Also exploring this framework of statistical perception, my student Chong and I have done some research on judgements of mean size with heterogeneous arrays of circles. Our starting point was a paper by Ariely (2001) in which he showed that the mean size of a set of circles is recognized better than any individual size in the set, and that extraction of the mean is

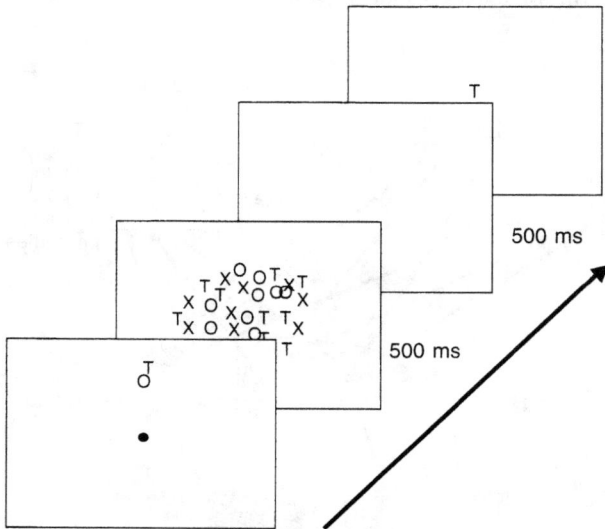

Figure 11. Experiment testing participants' ability to estimate the proportions of different features or of different conjunctions. The set of relevant targets to be reported (e.g., red items, Ts, or red Ts) was specified immediately after the display was presented.

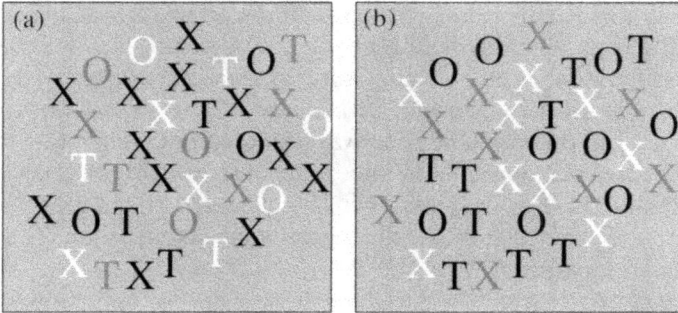

Figure 12. Examples of two displays with equal numbers of each feature type but different numbers of various conjunctions. Black represents blue letters. The display in (a) has 36% blue Xs and the display in (b) has none. The mean estimates were 15% and 11%, respectively.

not impaired by increasing the number of items in the display. We found this result quite surprising and it piqued our curiosity. First we compared the threshold for judging mean sizes with the threshold for judging the size of an individual circle presented alone, to see just how good the statistical judgement is (Chong & Treisman, 2003). With a single item, we can focus attention and give it our full resources, so we might expect to get much more accurate discriminations. We used forced choice judgements of which side of a display had the larger size, or the larger mean size, and we added a third condition in which people judged the sizes of circles in two homogeneous sets (Figure 13). We found very little difference between the three conditions.

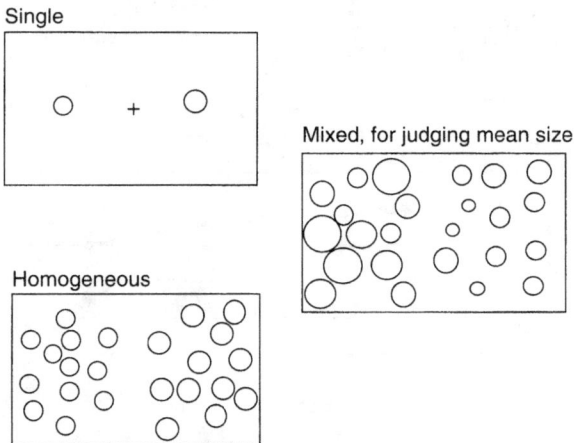

Figure 13. Examples of stimuli for size judgements. Participants decided which side had the larger size or the larger mean size.

Computing the mean size in heterogeneous arrays was about as accurate as judging the presented size of single circles or of homogeneous arrays. Next we tried varying the exposure duration. If the mean is computed by serially adding each individual size and dividing by N, we would expect a clear deterioration as the available time was reduced. But we found very little. Moreover, the decrement was no larger for the mean than for the homogeneous displays (Figure 14). The measure is the size threshold, expressed as a percentage of the difference in diameter required to give 75% correct discrimination.

Do the displays have to be simultaneously available, or can we hold onto one in memory? We compared simultaneous with successive presentations of the two displays (Figure 15), and used two delays in the successive condition (100 ms and 2 s) to see whether performance depended on perceptual availability or whether the first display could be briefly retained in visual memory. Again there was surprisingly little difference between any of these conditions (Figure 16). The mean judgement showed a small decrement with the 2 s ISI but so did the single circles. Either we compute the mean and hold that in memory, or we store the display as such and make the comparison when the second display appears.

Were participants really computing the mean? Or might they be, for example, looking just at the largest size. To find out, we tested them on displays with 12 items to the left and 12 to the right of the centre (see Figure 17). The task was to say which side of the display had the

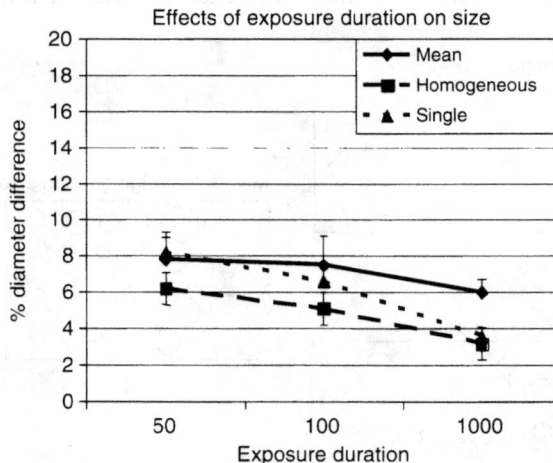

Figure 14. Effects of exposure duration on mean thresholds for size judgement with single circles, homogeneous sets, or mixed sets. The measure is the percentage diameter difference giving 75% accuracy in the forced choice judgement.

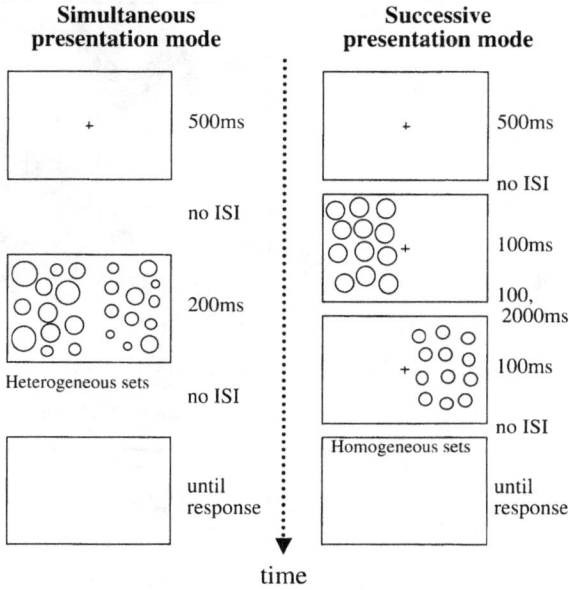

Figure 15. Procedure for comparing simultaneous presentation with successive presentation of two displays.

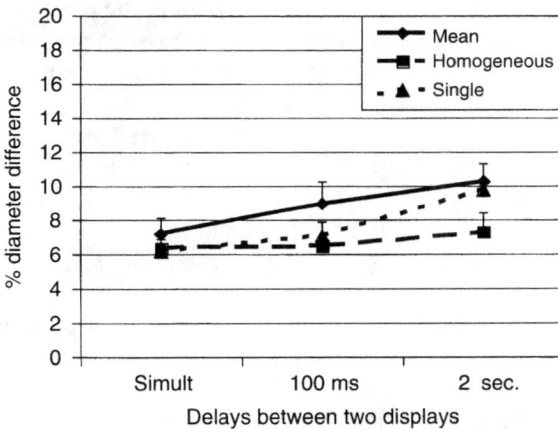

Figure 16. Effects of delay between the two sets of stimuli on thresholds for judging size or mean size.

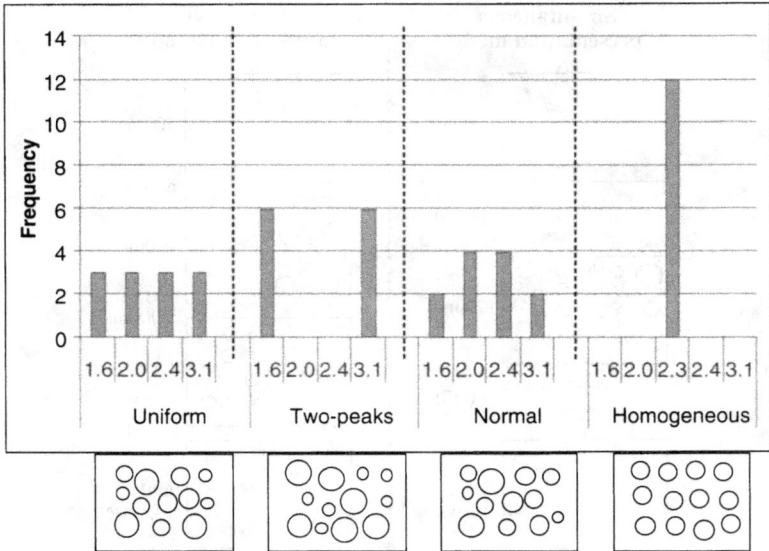

Figure 17. Different distributions tested in mean size judgements. Comparisons were made both within and across distributions. The numbers indicate the mean diameter size in degrees of visual angle.

larger mean size. The two sets could either be drawn from the same distribution (one of the following: Uniform—four equiprobable sizes; two peaks—two equiprobable sizes, the largest and smallest of the four previous sizes; normal—an approximation to a normal distribution; and homogeneous—an homogeneous display of circles all at the mean size of the other displays), or they could be generated from any possible pair of these different distributions. Again people were surprisingly good at making these statistical judgements (Figure 18). They were only slightly worse comparing across two different distributions than comparing two samples from the same distributions. See, for example, the threshold for normal versus normal and for normal versus homogeneous—they are about the same, although the sizes are identical in the normal versus normal and have no overlap in the normal versus homogeneous. This suggests that participants really were computing the mean.

Our hypothesis is that statistical processing occurs automatically when attention is globally distributed over a set of similar items. To test this we tried a couple of dual task paradigms, both using the same displays of 12 circles of four different sizes (Chong & Treisman, 2004). We combined tests of statistical judgements of the mean size with one of two visual search tasks, one that seems to require focused attention to each item in turn and one that

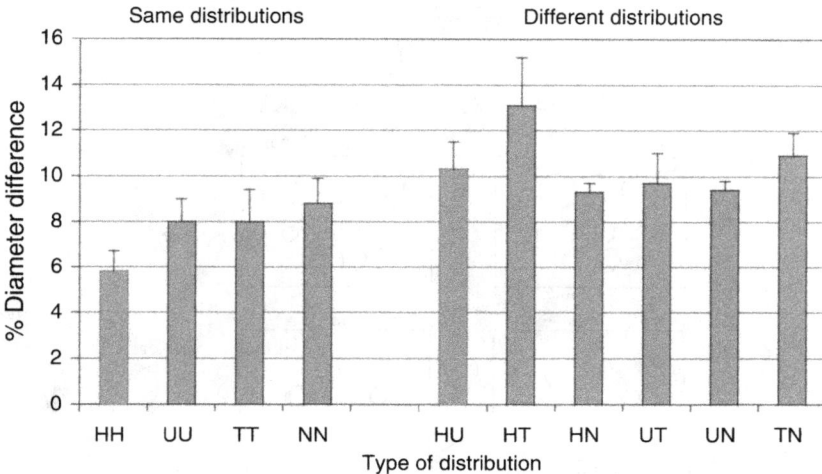

Figure 18.   Mean thresholds within and across distributions. H = Homogeneous, U = Uniform, T = Two peaks, N = Normal.

gives popout or parallel processing and that, according to our hypothesis, is done with global attention to the display as a whole. The focused attention task was search for a closed circle among circles with gaps, and the parallel processing version was search for a circle with a gap among closed circles (Figure 19). Participants saw the display and did the search task as quickly as they could. As soon as they pressed a key to signal target present or absent, two probe circles appeared and participants made a forced choice judgement of which matched either the mean size or the size of an individual circle sampled at random from the display. The location of the relevant circle was postcued by a small location marker presented at the same time as the two probe circles. We obtained the predicted interaction: Significant, $F(1, 11) = 9.6$, $p < .05$. Performance was better on the mean judgement (threshold 22%) when the concurrent task was the popout task using global attention, compared to when the concurrent task required serial search (threshold 25%), even though the display duration (determined by the search reaction time) was considerably longer with the focused attention task. On the other hand participants were better on the individual item size judgement when the concurrent task required focused attention (threshold 24%) compared to when the target popped out (threshold 28%).

Does the extra task impair the statistical processing at all, or is the mean size computed automatically? We compared performance in the dual task with attention globally deployed and performance when the statistical task was the only one required. There was no decrement with the global attention version of the dual task, relative to single task thresholds. It seems that when

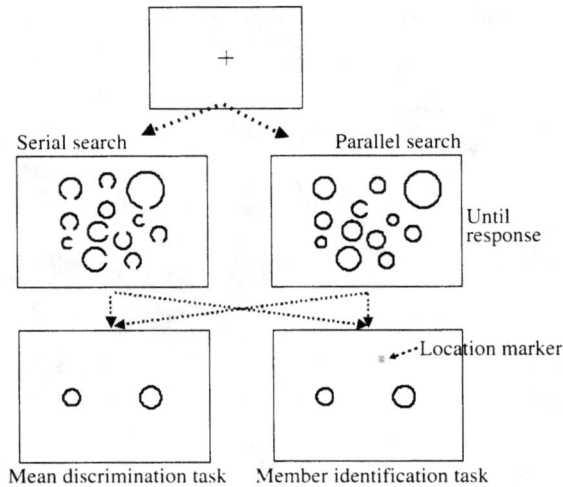

Figure 19. Design of experiment testing the effect of a concurrent task requiring either focused attention (search for a closed circle among circles with gaps) or distributed attention (search for a circle with a gap among closed circles) on two size judgement tasks—judgement of the mean size and judgement of the size of an individual postcued circle.

attention is spread over the display as a whole, the mean size is automatically extracted with no demand for additional resources.

We tested the automaticity idea in a different way as well, by seeing whether the extraction of the mean size is automatic in the sense of producing implicit priming. We presented an array of 12 circles of just two sizes, large and small, followed by a speeded same–different matching task on two new circles (Figure 20). One or both the target circles would match either the mean of the previous set, or one of the two presented sizes, or some other size, either within the range of presented sizes or outside the range. If observers automatically form a representation of the mean size when they see a heterogeneous display, we might expect priming for subsequent perception of an individual circle at the mean size, and that is what we found (Figure 21). The latency to respond same or different was shorter for circles primed by the mean size than for any other size, including the ones that were physically presented.

Finally Chong and I tested the psychological reality of the mean size by seeing whether it would generate false positive responses in a visual search task. Would people see illusory targets when the real target matched the mean size of the search display? We controlled for discriminability by matching the difference between the target and the nearest distractor size. The stimuli were selected from six possible sizes, two distractor sizes that were always present (fixed), a third optional distractor size that was either

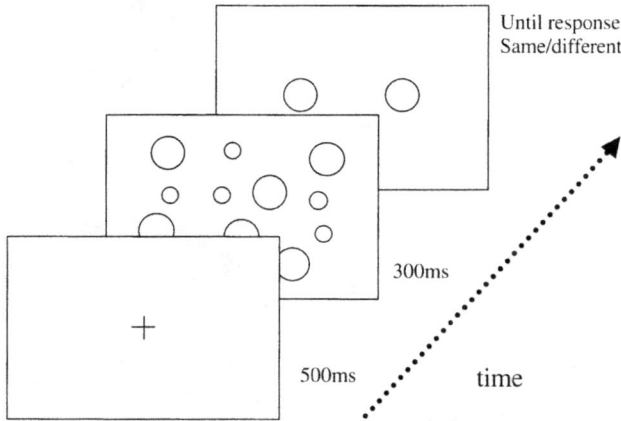

Figure 20. Design of experiment testing whether perception of the mean size of the preceding display is favoured in a subsequent same–different judgement task.

the largest or the smallest size (extreme), and another size that was either the target size or another distractor size (critical). The choice of which extreme distractor size was included determined which of the critical sizes matched the mean size of the display (see Figure 22). The displays contained 12 circles, including 3 each of the two fixed distractor sizes, 3 of one extreme size, and 3 of one of the critical sizes. By adding either the large or the small extreme distractor size, we could shift the mean size of the display to one or

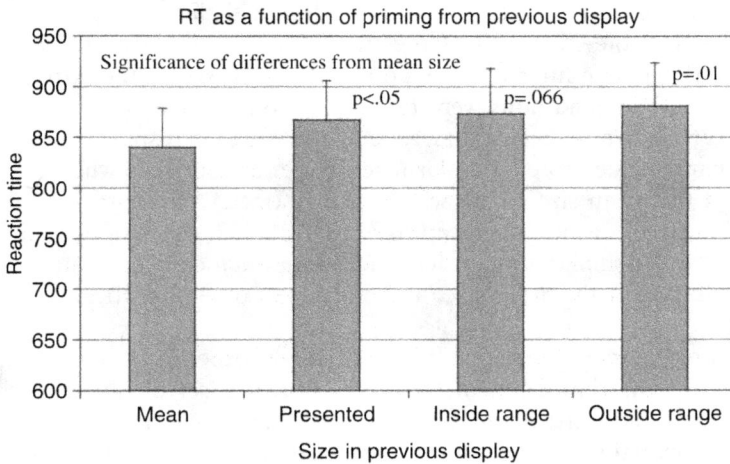

Figure 21. Mean response times as a function of which size from the preceding display was primed in the same–different judgement. The mean gives the shortest latencies, even compared to the sizes that were actually present in the display.

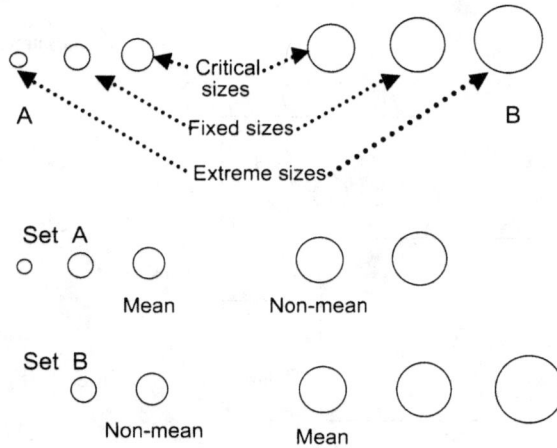

Figure 22.   Schematic representation of stimuli to test the effect of target size in relation to the mean of the display in a visual search task. The fixed distractor sizes appeared in all displays and one of the two extreme distractor sizes was added. Depending on which was added, one or other of the critical sizes became the mean size and the other the control size. One of these was designated the target size and could be either present or absent. When it was absent the other critical size was present as a fourth distractor size. Each display had three instances of each of the four relevant sizes. The target size was cued in advance of each display.

other of the two possible critical sizes (see Figure 22). There were four conditions: Target present with targets at the mean size, target present with targets at the other critical size, target absent with additional distractors at the mean size, and target absent with additional distractors at the other critical size. Note that each of the two critical sizes played all four roles across different conditions. All that differed was the size of the extreme set of distractors. The conditions were randomly mixed across trials and participants were shown the relevant target circle before each display. As predicted, participants made more false alarms on target absent trials when the target matched the mean size of the search display (mean 34% compared to 28% when the target was not the mean size, $t(13) = 2.437$, $p < .05$, suggesting that seeing a set of similar stimuli does indeed automatically generate a mental representation of the mean size (and perhaps of other statistical parameters as well).

So what conclusions emerge from these experiments on statistical processing? Discrimination of the mean size of a set of objects seems to occur very rapidly and about as accurately as discrimination of the size of a single individual object. It seems to be automatic, provided that attention is globally deployed. Even when the display contains just two sizes, a representation is formed of the mean size, which primes subsequent perception more strongly than do either of the sizes that were actually presented. We plan to look at other dimensions and other statistical measures, but we think we have some evidence for a separate mode of processing visual information using distributed or global attention, which contrasts with the focused mode used in binding and individuating separate objects.

PERCEPTION OF MEANING AND GIST

Returning again to the general framework: Is this enough to get us seeing the everyday world? I am not sure. There are some puzzling results in the literature. So far I have discussed results obtained with simple displays, designed to tease apart particular mechanisms underlying performance. However, the world we deal with is normally rich, complex, full of meaning and emotional associations. I will contrast some research findings that deal with this richer world and ask what implications they have for a more complete understanding. One recent paradigm studying change blindness fits well, suggesting that we deal with the complexity quite simply by ignoring it. Rensink, Simons, and others showed that, if simple low level cues to change (like apparent motion and visual transients) are removed or masked, we are very slow to detect quite salient changes in natural scenes (O'Regan, Rensink, & Clark, 1999; Rensink, 1998, 2000; Simons, 1996; Simons & Levin, 1998). If we happen to attend to the changing object, we are likely to become aware of the change, but otherwise it may take us several seconds to find it. O'Regan et al. (1999) suggest that we briefly summarize the scene and rely on the world itself to store the information in case we need to refer to any part of it in detail. Note, however, that the change detection task requires us not only to form representations of all the objects in the scene, but also to store and compare them across successive frames. It does not rule out more complex perception, which is instantly lost or erased by the next display (Wolfe, 1998).

The other contrasting line of research probes immediate perception rather than memory and suggests a much larger capacity and the possibility of attention-free semantic processing. It goes back to Potter's demonstrations in the 1970s (Potter, 1975), in which she showed strings of natural scenes at high speed, successively in the same location, and asked people to find semantic targets, for example, a clown, or an aeroplane, or a donkey. She found that they could do this pretty well at presentation rates of up to 10 pictures/second, although memory for the nontarget pictures was very poor. More recently, Li, VanRullen, Koch, and Perona (2002) have looked at the attention demands of this task and found a surprising result. They occupied attention at a foveal location by asking people to decide whether five small letters—Ts and/or Ls in random orientations—were all the same or contained one odd letter. This is a very demanding task and leaves people badly impaired in discriminating a single target letter in the periphery. However, when Li et al. briefly flashed a picture of a natural scene in the periphery, and asked people to determine whether it contained an animal or not, performance was just as good when attention was focused on the foveal T/L task as when the scene classification task was the only one required.

So we have an apparently paradoxical pair of findings. You cannot even see a salient object like an aeroplane engine coming and going in the change blindness picture, but you can detect the presence of an unknown animal in a 50 ms exposure while focused on a completely different set of stimuli. Can we reconcile those findings? How would they fit the framework I proposed? The animal detection task clearly is not using the binding mode with focused attention, since that is devoted to the foveal letter task. But my suggestion was that even without attention, on the first rapid pass through the visual system, we can detect disjunctive sets of features. In searching for a target category, participants may be set to sense, in parallel, a highly overlearned vocabulary of features that characterize a particular semantic category. For example animals might be signalled by the presence of a compact curvilinear figure against the background, a set of legs, a head, an eye, wings, or fur. If present, these animal features would prime the general, semantic category and could perhaps distinguish a slide with an animal from one without (cf. Levin, Takarae, Miner, & Keil, 2001). Evans and I (Evans & Treisman, 2005) have shown that detecting an animal in RSVP strings of natural scenes is much harder when the scenes also contain humans than when they do not (58% vs. 76% hits), presumably because shared features required observers to raise their criteria. On the other hand, detecting a vehicle is not affected by whether or not humans are present in the distractor slides. Vehicles and people share no obvious features. Participants were also quite bad at locating the target animal (to the left, centre, or right of the scene), suggesting a failure to bind the features to their locations. Of the 67% correct detections, only 53% were also correctly located, (where chance was 33%). The target animal was correctly identified on only 46% of the hit trials (e.g., as a bear, a butterfly, or a goldfish), although observers had at least some information about the superordinate category (e.g., mammal, insect, or fish), and were correct on the superordinate category on 81% of trials. The categories should be available from one or more distinctive features (wings, fur, etc.).

One objection that might be raised is that these animal features are *physically* more complex than the colours, shapes, and orientations used in my earlier research. They do not sound like features in the usual sense of the term. Firstly, however, I do not claim in the theory to have defined a priori any specific set of features. They cannot be specified independently of the contrast set from which they are to be discriminated in any given setting.

The set of feature detectors used in any task is an empirical question, to be tested with a set of converging operations such as those shown in Table 3. This is a boot-strapping account, but if the tests do converge, we have learned something. Secondly, the animal features may not be more complex for the visual system than the "simple" colours, line orientations, directions of motion, and so on tested in the usual psychophysical experiments. We have evolved to detect the natural components of real-world objects and their natural textures and colours. Gross, Rocha-Miranda, and Bender (1972) showed that single units in area IT respond to monkey hands or faces, and Tanaka (1993) found many units in IT that respond to what look like elementary components of natural objects.

Animals are a natural category with which we have evolved, so it might make sense to have fur and eye detectors. However, another possible objection arises when we consider that Li et al. (2002) got similar results using the category of vehicles. Admittedly, it is harder to tell an evolutionary story about the features of constructed objects like cars and aeroplanes. I would not expect wheel and engine detectors to be part of our innate repertoire. However, there is a great deal of plasticity in the brain, and feature detectors may be created to carry out any discrimination that proves useful. Evolution would provide the plasticity at the feature level to enable whatever elements prove consistently useful to be detected automatically. Freedman, Riesenhuber, Poggio, and Miller (2001, 2002) recorded from single units in prefrontal cortex of monkeys, discriminating members of the cat family from various breeds of dogs, together with many intermediate morphs. When the reward contingencies were changed from distinguishing cats and dogs to distinguishing creatures that varied on the orthogonal dimension—dog/catness versus cat/dogness—the same units learned to respond selectively to one of the new categories.

Given the possibility of flexible feature sets, we may be able to account for visual category detection within the framework I am using, as shown in Figure 23. Once the category is primed, if the target animal or vehicle is still present and attention can home in on it, we can form an object file to make it consciously accessible. If not, we may be able to tell simply from its features

TABLE 3

Diagnostics for separable perceptual features (see Treisman, 1986)

Mediate parallel search
Support perceptual grouping and segregation
Can migrate independently in illusory conjunctions
Can be separately attended
Neural evidence-separate populations of single units
Show selective adaptation and selective masking

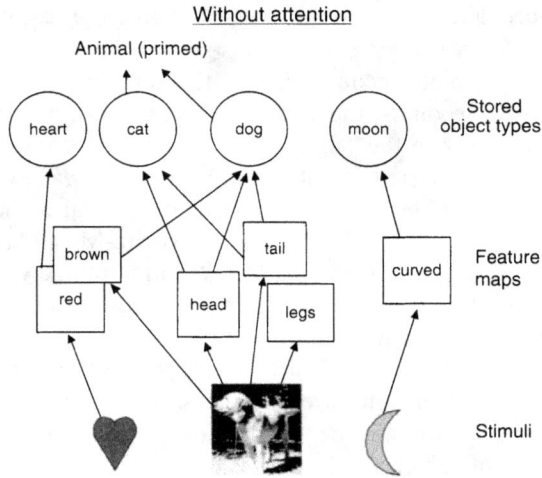

Figure 23. Sketch of model to account for detection of high-level perceptual categories. The suggestion is that sets of learned features may be detected in parallel and prime their category without being bound through focused attention.

which animal it is likely to be—cats seldom have wings and beaks. But we might make mistakes.

Why would this framework not also predict easy change detection? There are a number of differences that could make change detection harder than category detection: First, change detection depends on comparing successive displays, thus involving both visual memory and the need to match a current display to a stored one; secondly participants are not cued in advance with the relevant category (or the relevant sets of features) to look for. Primed detection of a prespecified category could potentially be mediated by unbound features, whereas the change detection task imposes a much heavier load involving both binding, nonselective memory, and a nonselective comparison process.

This paper has specified three ways of deploying attention and three types of information that they may provide: (1) Focused attention, offering conscious access to individuated objects with bound features in their current locations, viewpoints, and configurations; (2) at the other end of what is actually a continuum, global or distributed attention, offering global and statistical properties of groups of objects or the general layout of a scene; (3) rapid preattention, or more prolonged inattention, offering parallel and automatic access to sets of unbound features that can also prime semantic categories in a recognition network. Perhaps in combination, these parallel feature detectors, flexibly evolved through learning, together with the attention-controlled construction of a small set of explicit object files, and the statistical descriptions of sets of similar elements, may approach the outlines of an explanation for our amazing ability to see and interact with the world around us, even with the limited resources set by visual attention.

REFERENCES

Ariely, D. (2001). Seeing sets: Representation by statistical properties. *Psychological Science*, *12*, 157–162.

Balint, R. (1909). Seelenlahmung des "Schauens", optische Ataxie, raumliche Storung der Aufmerksamkeit. *Monatschrift fur Psychiatrie nd Neurologie*, *25*, 5–81.

Carr, L., Iacoboni, M., Dubeau, M. J., Mazziotta, J., & Lenzi, G. (2003). Neural mechanisms of empathy in humans: A relay from neural systems for imitation to limbic areas. *Proceedings of the National Academy of Sciences*, *100*, 5497–5502.

Chong, S., & Treisman, A. (2003). Representation of statistical properties. *Vision Research*, *43*, 393–404.

Chong, S.-C., & Treisman, A. (2004). Attentional spread in the statistical processing of visual displays. *Perception and Psychophysics*, *66*, 1282–1294.

Corbetta, M., Shulman, G. L., Miezin, F. M., & Petersen, S. E. (1995). Superior parietal cortex activation during spatial attention shifts and visual feature conjunction. *Science*, *270*, 802–805.

Critchley, H., Wiens, S., Rotshtein, P., Öhman, A., & Dolan, R. (2004). Neural systems supporting interoceptive awareness. *Nature Neuroscience*, *7*(2), 189–195.

Damasio, A. R. (1989). Time-locked multiregional retroactivation: A systems-level proposal for the neural substrates of recall and recognition. *Cognition*, *33*, 25–62.

Di Lollo, V., Enns, J. T., & Rensink, R. (2000). Competition for consciousness among visual events: The psychophysics of reentrant visual process. *Journal of Experimental Psychology: General*, *129*, 481–507.

Dronkers, N. F. (1996). A new brain region for coordinating speech articulation. *Nature*, *384*, 159–161.

Egly, R., Driver, J., & Rafal, R. (1994). Shifting visual attention between objects and locations: Evidence from normal and parietal lesion subjects. *Journal of Experimental Psychology: General*, *123*(2), 161–177.

Enns, J. T., & Rensink, R. A. (1990). Influence of scene-based properties on visual search. *Science*, *247*, 721–723.

Evans, K., & Treisman, A. (2005). Perception of objects in natural scenes: Is it really attention-free? *Journal of Experimental Psychology: Human Perception and Performance*, *31*, 1476–1492.

Freedman, D. J., Riesenhuber, M., Poggio, T., & Miller, E. K. (2001). Categorical representation of visual stimuli in the primate prefrontal cortex. *Science*, *291*, 312–316.

Freedman, D., Riesenhuber, M., Poggio, T., & Miller, E. (2002). Visual categorization and the primate prefrontal cortex: Neurophysiology and behavior. *Journal of Neurophysiology*, *88*(2), 929–941.

Gross, C., Rocha-Miranda, C. E., & Bender, D. B. (1972). Visual properties of neurons in inferotemporal cortex of the macaque. *Journal of Neurophysiology*, *35*, 96–111.

Hochstein, S., & Ahissar, M. (2002). View from the top: Hierarchies and reverse hierarchies in the visual system. *Neuron*, *36*, 791–804.

Houck, M. R., & Hoffman, J. E. (1986). Conjunction of color and form without attention: Evidence from an orientation-contingent color aftereffect. *Journal of Experimental Psychology: Human Perception and Performance, 12,* 186–199.

Humphreys, G. W., Cinel, C., Wolfe, J. M., Olson, A., & Klempen, N. (2000). Fractionating the binding process: Neuropsychological evidence distinguishing binding of form from binding of surface features. *Vision Research, 40*(10–12), 1569–1596.

Humphreys, G. W., & Riddoch, M. J. (1993). Interactions between object and space systems revealed through neuropsychology. In D. E. Meyer & S. Kornblum (Eds.), *Attention and performance XIV: Synergies in experimental psychology, artificial intelligence, and cognitive neuroscience* (pp. 183–218). Cambridge, MA: MIT Press.

Kahneman, D., Treisman, A., & Gibbs, B. (1992). The reviewing of object files: Object-specific integration of information. *Cognitive Psychology, 24,* 175–219.

Levin, D. T., Takarae, Y., Miner, A. G., & Keil, F. (2001). Efficient visual search by category: Specifying the features that mark the difference between artifacts and animals in preattentive vision. *Perception and Psychophysics, 63,* 676–697.

Li, F., VanRullen, R., Koch, C., & Perona, P. (2002). Rapid natural scene categorization in the near absence of attention. Proceedings of the National Academy of Sciences, *USA, 99*(14), 9596–9601.

Luck, S. J., & Vogel, E. K. (1997). The capacity of visual working memory for features and conjunctions. *Nature, 390,* 279–281.

McCollough, C. (1965). Color adaptation of edge-detectors in the human visual system. *Science, 149,* 1115–1116.

Navon, D. (1977). Forest before trees: The precedence of global features in visual perception. *Cognitive Psychology, 9,* 353–383.

O'Regan, J. K., Rensink, R. A., & Clark, J. J. (1999). Change-blindness as a result of "mudsplashes". *Nature, 398,* 34.

Potter, M. (1975). Short-term conceptual memory for pictures. *Science, 187,* 965–966.

Rensink, R. A. (1998). *Mindsight: Visual sensing without seeing* [Abstract]. *Investigative Ophthalmology and Visual Science, 39,* 631.

Rensink, R. A. (2000). Visual search for change: A probe into the nature of attentional processing. *Visual Cognition, 7,* 345–376.

Robertson, L., Treisman, A., Friedman-Hill, S., & Grabowecky, M. (1997). The interaction of spatial and object pathways: Evidence from Balint's syndrome. *Journal of Cognitive Neuroscience, 9,* 254–276.

Seiffert, A. E., Weber, M., & Treisman, A. (2003, November). *Isolating feature binding in visual search.* Paper presented at the meeting of the Society for Neuroscience, New Orleans.

Simons, D., & Levin, D. (1998). Change blindness. *Trends in Cognitive Science, 1,* 261–267.

Simons, D. J. (1996). In sight, out of mind. *Psychological Science, 7,* 301–305.

Tanaka, K. (1993). Neuronal mechanisms of object recognition. *Science, 262,* 685–688.

Thorpe, S., Fize, D., & Marlot, C. (1996). Speed of processing in the human visual system. *Nature, 381,* 520–522.

Treisman, A. (1986). Properties, parts and objects. In K. Boff, L. Kaufman, & J. Thomas (Eds.), *Handbook of perception and human performance* (Vol. 2, Ch. 35, pp. 1–70). New York: Wiley.

Treisman, A. (1988). Features and objects: The Fourteenth Bartlett Memorial Lecture. *Quarterly Journal of Experimental Psychology, 40A,* 201–237.

Treisman, A. (1996). The binding problem. *Current Opinion in Neurobiology, 6,* 171–178.

Treisman, A., & DeSchepper, B. (1996). Object tokens, attention, and visual memory. In T. Inui & J. McClelland (Eds.), *Attention and Performance: XVI. Information integration in perception and communication* (pp. 15–46). Cambridge, MA: MIT Press.

Treisman, A., & Gelade, G. (1980). A feature integration theory of attention. *Cognitive Psychology, 12,* 97–136.

Treisman, A., & Paterson, R. (1984). Emergent features, attention and object perception. *Journal of Experimental Psychology: Human Perception and Performance, 10,* 12–21.

Treisman, A., & Sato, S. (1990). Conjunction search revisited. *Journal of Experimental Psychology: Human Perception and Performance, 16,* 459–478.

Treisman, A., & Schmidt, H. (1982). Illusory conjunctions in the perception of objects. *Cognitive Psychology, 14,* 107–141.

Wise, R., Greene, J., Buchel, C., & Scott, S. (1999). Brain regions involved in articulation. *The Lancet, 353,* 1057–1061.

Wolfe, J. M. (1998). Inattentional amnesia. In V. Coltheart (Ed.), *Fleeting memories* (pp. 71–94). Cambridge, MA: MIT Press.

Wolfe, J. M., & Bennett, S. C. (1997). Preattentive object files: Shapeless bundles of basic features. *Vision Research, 37,* 25–44.

Wolfe, J. M., Cave, K. R., & Franzel, S. L. (1989). Guided search: An alternative to the feature integration model for visual search. *Journal of Experimental Psychology: Human Perception and Performance, 15,* 419–433.

Section I.

Preattentive processing and the control of visual search

VISUAL COGNITION, 2006, 14 (4/5/6/7/8), 445–465

Ψ Psychology Press
Taylor & Francis Group

Top-down modulation of preattentive processing: Testing the recovery account of contingent capture

Charles L. Folk and Roger Remington

Ames Research Center, Villanova University NASA, Villanova, PA, USA

One highly controversial issue with respect to preattentive processing concerns the degree to which the preattentive detection of "singletons" elicits an involuntary shift of spatial attention (i.e., attentional capture) that is immune from top-down modulation. According to the "pure-capture" perspective, preattentive processing drives the allocation of spatial attention in a purely bottom-up manner, in order of relative salience. According to the "contingent-capture" perspective, preattentive processing can produce attentional capture, but such capture is contingent on whether the eliciting stimulus carries a feature property consistent with the current attentional set. Pure-capture proponents have recently argued that the evidence for contingencies in attentional capture actually reflects the rapid disengagement and recovery from capture. Two spatial cueing experiments tested the rapid recovery by measuring (1) compatibility effects associated with irrelevant distractors and (2) inhibition of return to irrelevant distractors. These two measures provide converging evidence against the rapid recovery account.

Over the last three decades, a general consensus has emerged concerning the role of preattentive processing in visual search tasks that require the allocation of focused attention. According to what one might refer to as the "standard model", preattentive processing is a preliminary stage of analysis that provides a quick representation of the visual field in terms of "simple" or "basic" visual features such as colour, orientation, shape, brightness, etc. (Treisman & Gelade, 1980; Treisman & Souther, 1995; Wolfe, 1994). These simple features are assumed to be encoded into retinotopically organized "feature maps" by independent processing modules operating simultaneously, in a spatially parallel fashion, and with unlimited capacity. In addition to encoding the features themselves, preattentive representations are assumed to provide a bottom-up component that, through interaction

---

Please address all correspondence to Charles L. Folk, Department of Psychology, Villanova University, Villanova, PA 19085, USA. E-mail: charles.folk@villanova.edu

The authors thank Jan Theeuwes for comments on an earlier version of this paper.

DOI: 10.1080/13506280500193545

with top-down goal-driven processing, guides the serial allocation of attentional resources (Cave & Wolfe, 1990; Wolfe, 1994).

There is far less agreement, however, concerning the nature of preattentive processing in visual search tasks that do not require focused attention. These tasks have been referred to as "feature" or "singleton" search, because the target is typically defined by a single feature that differs from an otherwise homogeneous set of distractors (e.g., a red circle among green circles). Although it is generally agreed that the preattentive detection of such singletons can result in a compulsory shift of attentional resources to the location of the singleton (i.e., attentional "capture"), there is a heated debate concerning the degree to which this process is encapsulated, or cognitively penetrable. At one end of the theoretical spectrum is the "pure capture" perspective, according to which preattentive processing results in the purely bottom-up or stimulus-driven allocation of attention that is completely impervious to top-down attention set or behavioural goals. From this perspective, a singleton will capture attention regardless of whether or not an observer is actually looking for that particular singleton (Theeuwes, 1992, 1996). At the other end of the spectrum is the "contingent capture" perspective, according to which the compulsory allocation of attention can be modulated by top-down attentional set. Adherents of this view argue that attentional capture is contingent on the match between the properties of the eliciting stimulus and the top-down "set" of the observer (Folk & Annett, 1994; Folk & Remington, 1998; Folk, Remington, & Johnston, 1992; Folk, Remington, & Wright, 1994). Thus, a red singleton will capture attention if an observer is looking for the colour red, but not if they are looking for the colour green.

Part of the difficulty in resolving this debate has been the fact that the two theoretical perspectives emerged from two fundamentally different experimental paradigms. The pure-capture perspective is based primarily on data from the "additional singleton" paradigm, in which capture is inferred from costs in performance associated with the presence of an irrelevant singleton distractor. For example, Theeuwes (1992) had subjects search for a singleton target defined as a green diamond among a variable number of green circles. Response time to discriminate the orientation of a line segment inside the target diamond was measured. On half of the trials, one of the circles appeared in red, creating an additional singleton in a dimension that was irrelevant to the target task. The presence of an irrelevant colour singleton produced a significant cost in response time, suggesting that the singleton had "captured" attention even when it was not part of the attentional "set" of the observer. Moreover, Theeuwes established that this irrelevant singleton effect was dependent on the relative salience of the target and distractor. When the target was defined by a colour singleton, a less-salient form singleton had no effect on performance. Theeuwes has also shown that irrelevant singletons consisting of a new, abruptly onset object produce significant costs in searching for targets defined by a colour singleton (Theeuwes, 1994). These results are consistent with a model in which preattentive processing directs the allocation of attention to locations or objects in order of relative salience, and that this process is immune from top-down modulation (see also Nothdurft, 2006 this issue, for additional discussion of salience-based models of allocation of attention).

The contingent-capture perspective, on the other hand, is based primarily on data collected in the modified spatial cueing paradigm (Folk & Remington, 1998, 1999; Folk et al., 1992, 1994; Gibson & Kelsey, 1998). In this paradigm, singleton target displays are preceded by a "cueing" display that contains a singleton distractor at one of the four locations. Across trials, the location of the distractor is completely uncorrelated with the location of the target, providing no incentive to voluntarily allocate attention to the distractor location. Thus, any location congruence or "cueing" effects can be attributed to the involuntary capture of attention by the distractor. The influence of top-down set is tested by manipulating the relationship between the features that define the target and distractor singletons. For example, Folk et al. (1992) presented subjects with target displays consisting of either a single, abruptly onset character (onset target) appearing in one of the boxes, or one red character in one box and three white characters in each of the other boxes (colour target). The onset target condition was assumed to encourage a top-down attentional set for onset, and the colour target condition a top-down set for colour. Target displays were preceded by a distractor display consisting of the abrupt onset of four small circles surrounding one box (onset distractor) or a set of red circles surrounding one box and three sets of white circles surrounding the other three boxes (colour distractor). Folk et al. found location congruence effects consistent with attentional capture only when targets and distractors were both defined by onsets or were both defined by colour. No location congruence effects were observed when onset (colour) distractors were paired with colour (onset) targets. Folk and Remington (1998) reported a similar pattern when the distractors and targets were both colour singletons, but the relationship between the particular colour of the distractor and target was systematically varied. Specifically, red distractors produced evidence of capture when paired with red targets, but not when paired with green targets. Likewise, green distractors produced capture when paired with green targets, but not when paired with red targets. These results are consistent with a model in capture by preattentively detected singletons is contingent on whether the singleton is defined by a feature that is consistent with top-down attentional set.

Each of the perspectives outlined above is, at the same time, entirely consistent with the data from the paradigm of choice, and entirely

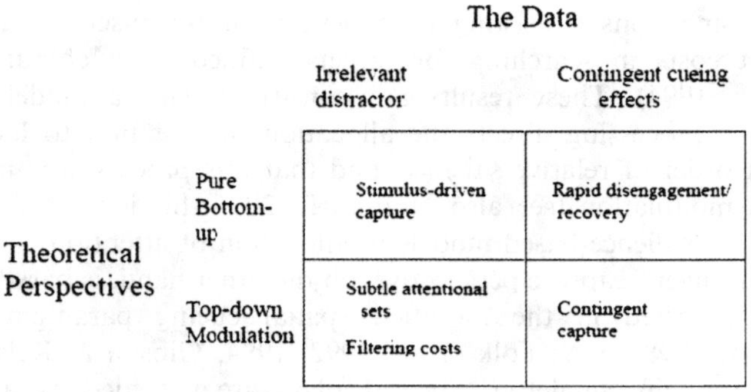

The Data

		Irrelevant distractor	Contingent cueing effects
Theoretical Perspectives	Pure Bottom-up	Stimulus-driven capture	Rapid disengagement/ recovery
	Top-down Modulation	Subtle attentional sets Filtering costs	Contingent capture

Figure 1.   The attentional capture debate.

inconsistent with the data from the other paradigm. The viability of the pure-capture perspective is dependent on the ability to explain contingent cueing effects in the spatial cueing paradigm, and the viability of the contingent-capture perspective requires an account of irrelevant singleton effects. Figure 1 provides a summary of the debate. The cells on the main diagonal represent the theoretical perspectives and the data on which they are based. The remaining two cells represent data that is inconsistent with each perspective, and yet must be accounted for. The entries in these two cells summarize the accounts each perspective has offered to reconcile the discrepant data.

Consider first contingent capture accounts of irrelevant singleton effects (lower left cell of Figure 1). At least two explanations have been offered to explain why, if top-down set modulates capture, irrelevant singletons nonetheless produce costs in performance. The first explanation is that the additional singleton task may actually induce a subtle attentional set for the irrelevant singleton. This idea is based on the notion of "search mode", as introduced by Bacon and Egeth (1994). Specifically, it has been argued that when a target is a singleton in a given dimension (e.g., a diamond among circles), subjects tend to adopt "singleton search mode" in which the system is set to respond to singletons in general, rather than a singleton defined by a specific feature. According to this view, capture by an irrelevant singleton reflects the fact that the system is set to respond to singletons, and is therefore consistent with the contingent capture perspective. In support of this claim, Bacon and Egeth showed that when subjects are forced to look for a target defined by a specific feature (i.e., when they adopt "feature search mode"), the effect of irrelevant singletons is eliminated (but see Theeuwes, 2004).

The second account of irrelevant singleton effects proposes that irrelevant singletons do not capture spatial attention, but instead produce a form of nonspatial interference first referred to by Kahneman, Treisman, and Burkell (1983) as "filtering costs". According to this account, the presence of an irrelevant singleton results in a display in which two objects "pop out"—the target and the distractor. Displays containing no distractor, on the other hand, result in just one object popping out—the target. Thus, the cost associated with the presence of an irrelevant distractor in Theeuwes' experiments may reflect a delay in attentional deployment as the system determines to which of the two objects attention should be allocated. Consistent with this proposed dissociation between filtering costs and spatial attention shifts, Folk and Remington (1998) found that even when distractors in a spatial cueing task produce no evidence of capture (i.e., when the distractor does not carry the defining feature of the target), they nonetheless yield a cost in performance relative to conditions where no distractor is presented.

Theeuwes (1996) argued against the "filtering cost" interpretation of irrelevant singleton effects by manipulating the compatibility of the characters appearing at the distractor and target locations. He reasoned that any effect of the identity of the character at the distractor location on responses to the target would indicate that attention had been allocated to the distractor location. As predicted, significant distractor compatibility effects were obtained. Lavie (1995), however, has shown that under conditions of low perceptual load, the identities of a small number of objects can be processed in parallel. Thus, assuming that a display in which two salient objects pop out can be considered a "low-load", it is possible that the compatibility effects associated with Theeuwes' distractors may reflect parallel processing of the distractor and target rather than the selective allocation of spatial attention to the distractor.

Now consider pure-capture accounts of conditional cueing effects in the upper right-hand cell of Figure 1. The primary explanation here is that attention really is captured in all conditions, but that when the distractor does not match the target property, attention can be "disengaged" quickly, such that the system has "recovered" by the time the target display appears. Two lines of support have been offered for this account. First, Theeuwes, Atchley, and Kramer (2000) used the additional singleton paradigm, but varied the timing of the distractor singleton's onset relative to target onset. They found significant costs associated with the presence of the irrelevant distractor singleton at SOAs of 50 and 100 ms, but no cost at 150 ms, suggesting that attention had been captured early on, but recovered within 150 ms. Similar results have recently been reported by Lamy and Egeth (2003), but only under conditions that encourage singleton search mode. The second line of support comes from a study by Theeuwes and Godijn (2002) that used Inhibition of Return (IOR) to index involuntary shifts of spatial attention. IOR is a phenomenon found at long SOAs in spatial cueing studies in which response times to targets appearing at the cued location are significantly longer than response times to targets appearing at noncued locations. This inhibitory effect is assumed to reflect the involuntary allocation of attention to a cued location (Posner & Cohen, 1984), and serves to bias the system against reallocating attention to a previously attended location (see Taylor & Klein, 1998, for a review of IOR mechanisms). Theeuwes and Godijn (2002) found that irrelevant colour-singleton distractors produced IOR even when subjects were searching for a target defined by luminance offset. Assuming IOR does indeed result from the reflexive allocation of attention, these data would appear to provide evidence that irrelevant singletons capture attention even when they do not match the defining features of the target.

Although both of these studies are consistent with a recovery account of contingent capture, the data from each are subject to alternative interpretations. Given the importance of this work to the theoretical debate outlined above, the purpose of the present study was to critically evaluate the evidence from each study, and then provide a critical test of alternative accounts.

In the Theeuwes et al. (2000) study, subjects were presented with displays similar to those used by Theeuwes (1992) in which targets were defined by a diamond among circles, and subjects made timed responses to the orientation of a character (a forward or backward "C") in the diamond. Target displays were revealed by removing line segments from premasks. At various stimulus onset asynchronies (SOAs) prior to the presentation of the target display, one of the premasks changed colour, creating an irrelevant additional singleton distractor. Relative to no-distractor trials, the additional singleton produced a significant cost at short SOAs (i.e., 50 and 100 ms), but had no effect on performance at SOAs greater than 100 ms. These results are consistent with the notion that attentional capture occurs early on, but the system is able to recover within 150 ms.

As additional evidence that attention was allocated to the distractor singleton, Theeuwes et al. (2000) varied the response compatibility between a grey character appearing at the distractor location and the target character. They reasoned that if attention is captured by the irrelevant colour singleton, then the identity of the attended grey character should be processed, producing a compatibility effect in response times to the target. Moreover, they argued that "if attention is not captured by the coloured singleton, then there should be no congruency effect on RT" (p. 113). In line with the recovery account, significant compatibility effects were obtained at SOAs of 50, 100, but not at the 200 ms SOA.

Although these results seem to provide strong evidence of capture by irrelevant singletons followed by rapid disengagement and recovery, they are subject to the same alternative account as the original additional singleton studies. Specifically, as the distractor and target move closer to simultaneity (i.e., as the SOA shortens), the potential for nonspatial filtering costs also increases as the system has to determine to which object (target or distractor) attention should be allocated. Moreover, the compatibility effects associated with the distractor could reflect parallel processing of the identity of distractor and target characters. Finally, there is no evidence that the costs associated with the presence of the distractor are spatial in nature, because there was no explicit manipulation of spatial relationship between target and distractor. In short, the data from Theeuwes et al. are inconclusive with respect to the recovery account of contingent cueing effects.

In an attempt to provide a more conclusive test of the recovery account, the first experiment replicated the design of Folk and Remington (1998) in which colour-singleton targets were preceded by colour-singleton distractors that either matched the target colour or did not match the target colour. Recall that Folk and Remington found that only matching distractors produced location congruence effects consistent with attentional capture. Of critical interest for the present experiment, however, were the "mismatch" conditions where the distractor produced no location congruence effects. According to the recovery account, attention is captured even in these conditions, but the system recovers within the 150 ms distractor–target SOA. One straightforward way of addressing this possibility would be to reduce the SOA, as in Theeuwes et al. (2000). However, as argued above, reducing the SOA introduces the possibility of filtering costs on trials where the distractor is in a different location than the target. (Note that on same-location trials, filtering costs would not be predicted because the distractor and target merge into a single object appearing at one location.) Thus, what is needed is an index of attention allocation that does not require a reduction in distractor–target SOA. To this end, Experiment 1 introduced a compatibility manipulation much like that employed by Theeuwes and colleagues (Theeuwes, 1996; Theeuwes et al., 2000) as well as Folk and Remington (1999).

EXPERIMENT 1

In the first experiment, subjects searched for a red or green singleton target, which was preceded by a red or green irrelevant distractor that appeared at the target location on 25% of the trials and at a nontarget location on 75% of the trials (i.e., distractor location and target location were uncorrelated). Unlike the additional singleton paradigm, the explicit manipulation of the spatial relationship between distractor and target, combined with the relatively long distractor–target SOA, ensures that any effects of the distractor are tied to spatial attention rather than nonspatial filtering costs. The critical manipulation, however, was the appearance of a grey, response compatible/incompatible character *simultaneous* with the distractor, and at the distractor location. This distractor character was then followed by a pattern mask, which was then followed by the target display. The logic of this manipulation was identical that of Theeuwes et al. (2000). If attention is captured even on those trials where the colour of the distractor does not match the colour of the target. but then recovers before the target display appears 150 ms later, then presenting a distractor character *simultaneous* with the appearance of the distractor should ensure that it is attended. Thus, assuming the allocation of attention results in the processing of the character's identity, compatibility effects should be evident even in the absence of any location congruence effects. If, on the other hand, attention is never oriented to the location of the distractor (as predicted by the contingent capture perspective), then on colour mismatch trials no compatibility effect should obtain.

Method

Subjects.　　Thirty-two undergraduates from Villanova University participated in partial fulfilment of a course requirement. Subjects ranged in age from 18 to 20 years, and all were tested for normal or corrected-to-normal binocular near visual acuity (20/30 or better) and normal colour vision using a Titmus II vision tester.

Apparatus.　　Stimuli were generated and responses collected by a Zenith 386 microcomputer equipped with a Sigma Design, colour 400 (680 × 400) graphics board. Stimuli were displayed on a Princeton Graphics Systems Ultrasync monitor. The monitor was placed in an enclosed viewing box at a distance of 50 cm.

Stimuli.　　Each trial consisted of four basic displays: Fixation display, distractor display, mask display, and target display (see Figure 2). The fixation display consisted of a central fixation square (0.34° × 0.34° visual angle) flanked by four peripheral boxes (1.15° × 1.15°) at the 12, 3, 6, and 9 o'clock positions on an imaginary circle with a diameter of 8.2°. All boxes were light grey (IBM colour designation no. 7) against the black background of the CRT screen. Distractor displays consisted of the fixation display with the addition of sets of four small circles (0.23 in diameter) in a diamond configuration, surrounding each of the four peripheral boxes. Three of the sets of circles were white (IBM colour no. 15), and one set of circles was either red (IBM colour no. 12) or green (IBM colour no. 10). In addition, an "X" or " =" (the distractor character), subtending approximately 0.57° in height and width, appeared inside the box surrounded by the coloured circles. The mask display was identical to the distractor display for a given

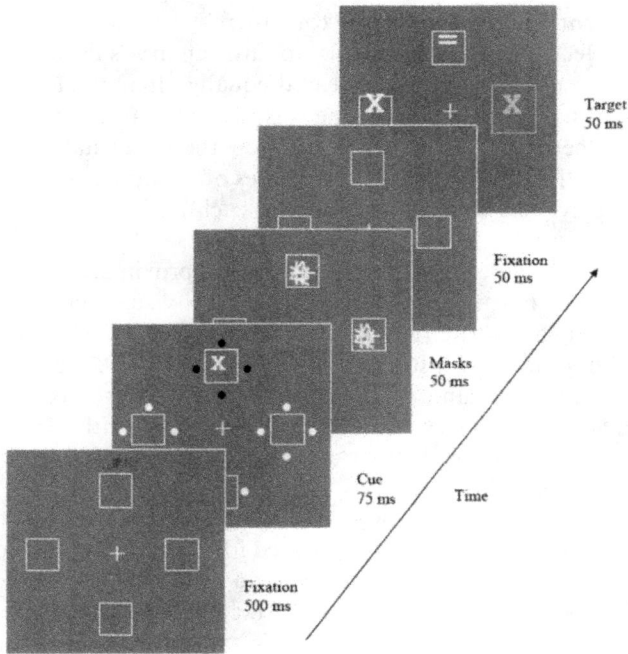

Figure 2. Displays and trial sequence on a typical trial in Experiment 1. The dark grey distractor represents the colour red, and the light grey target represents the colour green. This would be an example of a trial on which the distractor and target were defined by different colours, and the distractor character was incompatible.

trial, except that the distractor character was removed, and a pattern mask appeared in each of the four peripheral boxes. The mask consisted of short, vertical, horizontal, and diagonal line segments pseudorandomly distributed in an imaginary square subtending $0.6° \times 0.6°$ visual angle. The target display consisted of the fixation display with the addition of an "X" or " =" ($0.57°$ in height and width) in each of the peripheral boxes. Three of the characters were white and one was either red or green.

Design. Half of the subjects were randomly assigned to look for a red target, and half were assigned to look for a green target. Distractor colour (red vs. green) was varied within subjects but was blocked in units of four blocks of 64 trials, with order of units balanced across subjects. Within a given block, the four possible target locations were factorially crossed with the four possible distractor locations, yielding 16 trials (25%) on which the distractor and target appeared at the same location and 48 trials (75%) on which they appeared at different locations. Uncorrelating distractor and target position in this way ensures that there is no incentive to voluntarily allocation attention to the distractor, thereby allowing any location congruence effects to be attributable to involuntary shifts of attention. Each of the two possible targets appeared equally often at each of the four locations. On half of the trials the distractor character matched the subsequent target (compatible distractor); on the other half they did not match (incompatible distractor). The identities of the nontarget characters in the target display were chosen randomly on each trial.

   Procedure.   The experimental session lasted approximately 1 hour, beginning with tests for normal or corrected-to-normal visual acuity and colour vision, followed by written and oral descriptions of the stimuli and procedures. Subjects were instructed to respond as quickly and accurately as possible, and to maintain fixation on the central fixation square throughout each. Subjects were also fully informed with respect to the uninformative nature of the distractors, and were encouraged to "ignore the distractor if possible".

   The trial sequence was as follows (see Figure 2). First, the central fixation square and four surrounding boxes appeared for 500 ms. The fixation square then blinked off for 100 ms then back on for a randomly varying foreperiod of either 100, 200, 300, or 400 ms. The distractor display then appeared for 75 ms, followed by the mask display for 50 ms. The fixation display then reappeared for 50 ms, followed by the target display for 50 ms, followed once again by the fixation display. The next trial sequence was initiated 1000 ms after a response was made. Phenomenally, the four display boxes and the fixation cross appeared to remain on the CRT screen for the duration of each trial, as well as the intertrial interval. The SOA between cue and target was 175 ms, making contamination of response times by eye movements unlikely.

   Responses consisted of a press of the "." or "0" key on the numeric keypad of the keyboard for "X" and " = " targets, respectively (the keys were appropriately labelled). The "X" response was assigned to the right index finger and the " = " response to the left index finger. Response time was measured from the onset of the target display. If a response was not initiated within 1500 ms, an error was scored and the next trial sequence initiated. Incorrect responses elicited a 500 ms, 1000 Hz computer tone, and were followed by a "buffer" trial with parameters drawn randomly from the set for that block. Response times for error and buffer trials were not included in the data analysis.

Results

Mean response times as a function of distractor type (i.e., same or different colour as target), distractor compatibility (compatible vs. incompatible), and distractor location (same or different as target), collapsed across target colour are shown in Figure 3. Corresponding error rates are presented in parentheses at each data point. A mixed analysis of variance (ANOVA) with target colour as the single between-subjects variable, and distractor type, distractor compatibility, and distractor location as the three within-subjects variables, was used. The main effect of target colour did not approach significance, nor did it interact with any of the other variables. Significant main effects were found for distractor compatibility, $F(1, 30) = 10.25$, $MSE = 1065$, $p < .01$, and distractor location, $F(1, 30) = 67.9$, $MSE = 515$, $p < .001$. More importantly, two theoretically critical interactions were reliable. First, distractor location interacted with distractor type, $F(1, 30) = 15.18$, $MSE = 724$, $p < .001$, confirming what is obvious in Figure 3; the congruence of distractor and target location had a significantly larger effect on trials where the distractor colour matched the target colour than on trials where the distractor and target were different colours. This pattern replicates the basic contingent capture effect. Simple effects analyses confirmed a significant 36 ms location effect for same colour distractors, $F(1, 31) = 69.64$, $MSE = 306$, $p < .001$. Surprisingly, the 11 ms location effect for different colour distractors was also reliable, $F(1, 31) = 10.25$, $MSE = 296$, $p < .05$. Second, distractor compatibility also interacted with distractor type, $F(1, 30) = 18.84$, $MSE = 697$, $p < .001$. Again, as is obvious in the figure, distractor compatibility only affected trials on which the distractor colour matched the target colour. Simple effects confirmed that the 28 ms

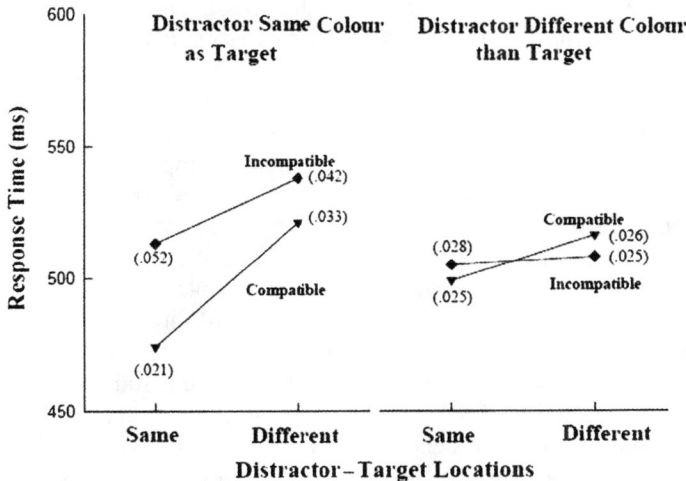

Figure 3.   Average mean response times and error rates as a function of distractor type, distractor location, and compatibility in Experiment 2.

compatibility effect for same-colour distractors was reliable, $F(1, 31) = 25.97$, $MSE = 462$, $p < .001$, but the -1 ms compatibility effect for different-colour distractors was not, $F(1, 31) = 0.06$, $MSE = 414$, $p > .05$. Finally, distractor compatibility also interacted with distractor location, $F(1, 30) = 20.27$, $MSE = 264$, $p < .001$, with compatible distractors producing a larger location effect than incompatible distractors. No other main effects or interactions were significant.

A similar analysis was conducted on mean error rates. The main effect of distractor compatibility was significant, $F(1, 30) = 4.39$, $MSE = 0.00146$, $p < .05$, with incompatible distractors producing significantly more errors (3.7%) than compatible distractors (2.7%). In addition, the interaction between distractor compatibility and distractor location was significant, $F(1, 30) = 4.64$, $MSE = 0.0006$, $p < .05$, with larger location effects on compatible trials than on incompatible trials. Finally, distractor location interacted with target colour, $F(1, 30) = 6.81$, $MSE = 0.0005$, $p < .05$, with larger location effects for subjects searching green targets than for subjects searching for red targets. Generally, the analysis of error rates reveals the same pattern as response times, suggesting that subjects did not trade speed for accuracy.

Discussion

The results of the present experiment replicate those of Folk and Remington (1998), in that distractor location effects depended critically on whether the colour of the distractor matched that of the target. This pattern is consistent with the notion that capture by featural singletons is contingent on a top-down set for the defining feature. However, it is also consistent with a pure-capture account if one assumes that attention disengages more rapidly from mismatching distractors such that recovery is complete before the target display appears. We turn then to the distractor compatibility manipulation to distinguish between these two possibilities. If attention is allocated to the distractor location, then given that the distractor character appears simultaneously with the singleton distractor, compatibility effects should obtain, even if attention subsequently disengages from the distractor location. Two aspects of the obtained compatibility results are critical. First, highly significant compatibility effects were evident when the distractor colour matched the target colour. This establishes that when attention is allocated to the distractor location, the distractor character is in fact processed and can influence response time to the target. Second, and most important, there was no evidence of a compatibility effect when the distractor was a different colour than the target. This result, combined with the presence of the compatibility effect in the same-colour condition, suggests that attention was not allocated to the distractor location in the different-colour conditions. In other words, the results are not consistent with a rapid disengagement/recovery account of contingent capture effects.

Although the data are clearly inconsistent with a recovery account, there are two alternative interpretations that need to be considered. First, one might argue that, in the different-colour conditions, attention is allocated to the distractor, but disengages so rapidly that the identity of the distractor character is not processed. However, Theeuwes et al. (2000) found that irrelevant singletons produced costs in performance of up to 100 ms, suggesting that disengagement takes at least that long. Assuming the same time course in the present experiment, the distractor character would have been attended for the full 75 ms presentation of the distractor display. Thus, it is unlikely that the system did not have enough time to process the identity of the distractor character.

The second alternative account is that because the distractor character is white (i.e., not the target colour) the system is able to "filter out" or even inhibit the character such that its identity is not processed. However, the same white distractor character appeared in the same-colour distractor conditions. Thus, if the distractor character can be filtered out or inhibited because it is white, one would expect no compatibility effects here either. The highly significant compatibility effects in the same-colour condition there-fore argue against a colour-filtering/inhibition account. Moreover, Theeuwes et al. (2000), using the additional singleton paradigm, also found distractor compatibility effects associated with white distractor characters, suggesting that filtering of attended objects on the basis of colour is not possible.

There is one unexpected aspect of the present results that needs to be addressed. Although the overall distractor location effect was dramatically reduced when the distractor was a different colour than the target, it was nonetheless reliable. Thus, one might argue that this result suggests that attention was indeed captured in the different-colour distractor condition. This possibility is unlikely for several reasons. First, the magnitude of the location effect (11 ms) is much smaller than in any previous spatial cueing studies of attentional capture. Second, inspection of Figure 1 suggests that the location effect is driven primarily by trials on which the distractor character was compatible with the target. We suspect that the small location effect may actually reflect a form of perceptual (as opposed to response) priming of the target character by compatible distractors. Specifically, it is possible that parts of the distractor character may actually "survive" the presentation of the mask, and then combine with a compatible target character to enhance its perceptual quality. Note that a similar pattern is evident in the same-colour distractor condition, in that compatible trials produced larger distractor location effects than incompatible trials.

We now turn to the second line of evidence for the recovery account of contingent capture—the finding that irrelevant singleton distractors produce IOR. Theeuwes and Godijn (2002) presented subjects with displays consisting of eight equally spaced grey circles, each containing a small grey square (see Figure 4a). The subjects' task was to detect the offset of one of the small squares. On each trial, one of the circles (the singleton distractor) turned red 1300 ms prior to the offset of the target. The location of the distractor was uncorrelated with the subsequent location of the target. Theeuwes and Godijn found that target detection times were significantly longer when the target appeared at the distractor location than when it appeared at a nondistractor location. They concluded that the presence of IOR confirms that attention was reflexively allocated to the distractor, even though the distractor was not part of the observer's attentional set for offsets. Thus the results are consistent with the pure-capture perspective, and suggest that the lack of location congruence effects at earlier SOAs reflects rapid disengagement/recovery.

The stimuli used by Theeuwes and Godijn (2002), however, are somewhat unusual in that the target task involved the detection of an offset, whereas most of the work on contingent capture has used onset targets. It is possible that the use of the offset target task may have induced an attentional set that would encompass the characteristics of the distractor. Specifically, as is evident in Figure 4a, the offset of one of eight squares actually produces a "singleton" consisting of an empty circle among filled circles. Moreover, this singleton is revealed dynamically, in the sense that only one of the elements

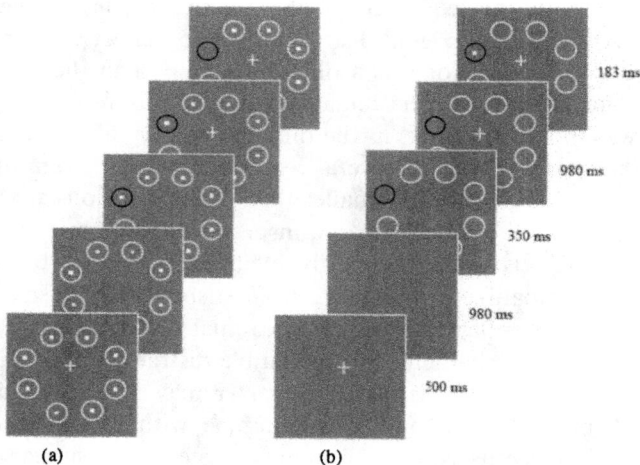

Figure 4.   (a) Displays and trial sequence used by Theeuwes and Godijn (2002). (b) Displays and trial sequence used in Experiment 2b.

changes across time. Now consider the distractor. It also consists of a dynamic singleton, in that it is revealed through a change in colour at one location across time. Thus, if subjects are set for dynamic singletons in general, it is not surprising that the colour singleton produced evidence of attentional capture (i.e., IOR). In fact, when Theeuwes and Godijn reduced the distractor–target SOA to 133 ms (Exp. 2), targets appearing at the distractor location were responded to significantly faster than targets at nondistractor locations. This suggests that not only were subjects captured by the distractor, they were also unable to "disengage" from the distractor, which is precisely what one would expect if the distractor were consistent with subjects' attentional set. Thus, the results of Theeuwes and Godijn do not provide unambiguous evidence for IOR to distractors that do not match the defining properties of the target. A strong test of the recovery account requires measuring IOR to irrelevant colour singletons under conditions where no evidence of capture is found at the typical 150 ms SOA, such as when a static colour singleton is paired with an onset target (Folk & Remington, 1999; Folk et al., 1992, 1994). Experiment 2 was conducted with this goal in mind.

EXPERIMENT 2

Experiment 2 consisted of two subexperiments. Experiment 2a was an attempt to first replicate the results of Theeuwes and Godijn (2002) in which a dynamic colour singleton produced IOR when paired with an offset target. Experiment 2b provided the critical test of the recovery account by measuring IOR under conditions known to elicit no evidence of capture at early SOAs. Specifically, a "static" colour singleton was paired with a target consisting of the onset of a single small square (see Figure 4b). Note that we refer to the colour singleton as "static" because, although all circles appeared abruptly in time, it was the difference in colour across space that defined the location of the distractor. If attention is captured by irrelevant singleton distractors regardless of attentional set (but recovers quickly when the distractor does not match the target), then evidence of IOR should obtain in both versions of Experiment 2. If, however, irrelevant singletons only capture attention when they are consistent with the top-down attentional set for the target, then IOR should obtain in Experiment 2a (assuming subjects are indeed set for dynamic singletons), but not in Experiment 2b.

Method

Subjects. Thirty-six undergraduates from Villanova University participated in partial fulfilment of a course requirement. Half the subjects participated in Experiment 2a, and half in Experiment 2b. One subject was replaced in Experiment 2b because of error rates approaching 50%. Subjects ranged in age from 18 to 20 years, and all reported normal or corrected-to-normal visual acuity and normal colour vision.

Apparatus.   The apparatus was the same as that used in Experiment 1.

Stimuli.   For both experiments, displays consisted of eight circles (1.15° in diameter) equally spaced on the circumference of an imaginary circle (8.2° in diameter) centred on a fixation cross (0.34° × 0.34°). For the distractor displays, seven of the circles were light grey (IBM colour designation no. 7) and one circle was red (IBM colour no. 12). In Experiment 2a each circle also contained a small, light grey, central square (0.25° × 0.25°), with the exception that the square in one of the circles was removed on the target display. In Experiment 2b, the target display included one circle in which a light grey square was added.

Design.   An experimental session consisted of four blocks of 76 trials. Each block consisted of 64 target trials and 12 "catch" trials. On catch trials in Experiment 2a no square was removed from the target display; on catch trials in Experiment 2b no target square appeared. Subjects were instructed not to respond to catch trials. Within a block, both the target and distractor appeared equally often in each of the eight circles. However, distractor and target locations were uncorrelated, such that the target appeared at the distractor location on one-eighth of the trials.

Procedure.   The experimental session lasted approximately 1 hour. Subjects were instructed to respond as quickly and accurately as possible, and to maintain fixation on the central fixation cross throughout each trial. Subjects were also fully informed with respect to the uninformative nature of the distractors, and were encouraged to "ignore the distractor if possible".

The trial sequence for Experiment 2a was identical to that used by Theeuwes and Godijn (2002), and is shown in Figure 4a. First, the fixation cross and eight circles appeared for 500 ms followed by the removal of the fixation cross for 980 ms. One of the eight circles then turned red and after 350 ms the fixation cross reappeared. After another 980 ms one of the grey squares was removed for 183 ms, after which the entire display was extinguished. The sequence for the Experiment 2b was the same as that for 2a, with the following exceptions. First, no circles appeared until the onset of the distractor display, at which point all eight (empty) circles appeared simultaneously and remained on the screen until the end of the trial. Second, the target display consisted of the onset of a single grey square in one of the eight circles.

Subjects responded to target trials by pressing the "0" key on the numeric keypad of the keyboard with the forefinger of the their dominant hand as soon as the target event occurred. On catch trials subjects were instructed to withhold any response. Response time was measured from the onset of the target display. Incorrect responses elicited a 500 ms, 1000 Hz computer tone, and were followed by a "buffer" trial with parameters drawn randomly from the set for that block. Response times for error and buffer trials were not included in the data analysis.

Results

For Experiment 2a, mean response times for targets appearing at the distractor vs. nondistractor locations were 364 and 308 ms, respectively. This difference was highly significant, $F(1, 17) = 46.91$, $MSE = 829$, $p < .01$. Error rates showed the same pattern: 11.7% for targets appearing at the distractor location versus 1.5% at nondistractor locations. For Experiment 2b, mean response times for targets appearing at the distractor and nondistractor locations were 276 ms and 285 ms, respectively, which did not differ significantly, $F(1, 7) = 2.59$, $MSE = 105$, $p > .05$. The corresponding error rates were 1.6% and 1.1%, respectively. In addition to the separate analyses, a mixed ANOVA on response times, with Experiment 2a versus 2b as the between-subjects variable, yielded main effects of experiment, $F(1, 15) = 8.42$, $MSE = 7278$, $p < .05$, and distractor location, $F(1, 15) = 8.76$, $MSE = 491$, $p < .01$, as well as a significant interaction, $F(1, 15) = 16.35$, $MSE = 491$, $p < .01$.

Discussion

The results of this experiment are clear. The Theeuwes and Godijn (2002) results were replicated, showing that dynamic colour-singleton distractors produce IOR when subjects are searching for dynamic offset singletons. More importantly, static colour-singleton distractors produced no evidence of IOR when paired with onset targets. Assuming IOR is a measure of the reflexive allocation of attention, this latter result is consistent with the claim that attention was not captured by the colour singleton and inconsistent with the rapid recovery account. We acknowledge, however, that the lack of IOR (i.e., a null effect) does not necessarily rule out the possibility that attention was allocated to the colour singleton. Nonetheless, the fact that IOR was obtained in Experiment 2a suggests that the experimental procedures were sensitive enough to pick up the effect if present. Moreover, the present results are consistent with other studies that have explored the influence of top-down attentional set on IOR. For example, Gibson and

Amelio (2000) found that abrupt onset distractors produced IOR when paired with abrupt onset targets, but not when paired with colour targets, consistent with the contingent capture perspective.

Interestingly, Gibson and Amelio (2000) also found that colour-singleton distractors produced no evidence of IOR regardless of whether they were paired with onset targets or colour-singleton distractors. Pratt, Sekuler, and McAuliffe (2001) also found no evidence of IOR associated with colour singletons, regardless of whether subjects were looking for colour-singleton targets or onset targets. It is unclear at this point why the colour singletons in the present Experiment 2a, as well as in that of Theeuwes and Godijn (2002), produced IOR when these singletons in these previous studies did not. Note, however, that in both Gibson and Amelio and Pratt et al. the colour singletons were "static" in the sense defined above. Thus, it is possible that it is the dynamic nature of the singleton distractor that results in IOR when the target is also defined by a dynamic event.

GENERAL DISCUSSION

The degree to which preattentive processing yields purely stimulus-driven shifts of spatial attention remains a controversial issue. Resolution of the debate requires reconciling discrepant results from the additional singleton and spatial cueing paradigms. The present experiments were conducted to test one potential resolution to the empirical discrepancy; that contingent cueing effects reflect rapid disengagement and recovery from capture when the eliciting distractors that do not match the attentional set of the observer. Two converging measures of attentional allocation, compatibility effects and IOR, were employed to probe for capture by distractors that otherwise show no location effects. Neither measure provided any evidence of capture by such distractors.

In fact, the evidence shows a strong degree of convergence among the three measures of attention allocation (i.e., facilitatory location effects, compatibility effects, and IOR). Specifically, Experiment 1 shows that distractors that share the defining features of the target produce facilitatory location effects at early SOAs as well as significant compatibility effects. Moreover, assuming that dynamic colour-singleton distractors are consistent with a top-down set for dynamic offset singleton target, Theeuwes and Godijn (2002), as well as Experiment 2a of the present paper, show that such distractors produce both facilitatory location effects at short SOAs and IOR at long SOAs. Thus, the three measures provide converging evidence that attention is captured under these conditions. In contrast, when the distractors and targets do not share defining features, none of the three effects are evident. Experiment 1 shows that when the distractors are a different colour than the target, neither early location effects nor compatibility effects obtain. Folk et al. (1994), along with Experiment 2b of the present paper, show that when paired with onset targets, static colour-singleton distractors produce neither early location facilitation effects (Folk et al., 1994) nor IOR at long SOAs (Experiment 2b). Thus, the three measures provide converging evidence that attention is not captured or allocated to the distractor location under these conditions. In short, the data from these spatial cueing studies appear to be consistent with a true contingent capture perspective and inconsistent with the rapid recovery account of contingent cueing effect.

A recent study by Lamy and Egeth (2003) provides further evidence against a rapid recovery account of capture by irrelevant featural singletons. These authors manipulated both the SOA between the irrelevant distractor and the target as well as the spatial congruency of the distractor and target locations. When paired with targets defined by a shape singleton, irrelevant colour-singleton distractors produced significant spatial congruency effects at early (i.e., 50–100 ms) SOAs, which disappeared by 150 ms (Exp. 5), a result consistent with Theeuwes et al. (2000) and suggestive of early capture followed by rapid disengagement. However, when subjects were forced to adopt feature search mode for a particular shape, the only spatial congruency effects consisted of a small but reliable cost associated with targets that appeared at the *same* location as the distractor (Exp. 6). The authors conclude that under strict feature search mode, capture by irrelevant colour singletons is eliminated, and inhibition is applied to the distractor location. As further evidence for the influence of top-down search strategies, Lamy and Egeth report that spatial congruency effects were *not* eliminated for those subjects who had previously been forced to search for shape singletons targets (rather than targets defined by a specific shape). For these subjects, the singleton strategy apparently carried over to the feature search conditions, yielding capture by the irrelevant colour-singleton distractor.

In short, these results are consistent with the notion that capture by irrelevant featural singletons is contingent on top-down attentional control/search settings. It should be noted, however, that Lamy and Egeth (2003) also show that when the distractor was defined by an abrupt luminance transient (rather than a colour singleton), spatial congruency effects were obtained at early SOAs regardless of the attentional search strategy adopted by subjects. Based on this result, the authors argue that abrupt changes in luminance may indeed have some special status with regard to attentional prioritization. Even here, however, the authors acknowledge the possibility that because the presentation of the target search display was characterized by strong luminance transients at all locations, subjects may have adopted an attentional set for onsets as an informative "displaywide" characteristic (see Gibson & Kelsey, 1998).

Although the results of the present spatial cueing experiments are consistent with the contingent capture perspective, the data from the additional singleton paradigm remain controversial. For example, it remains unclear why Theeuwes et al. (2000) found that the presence of an irrelevant colour distractor produced no effect at SOAs of 150 ms (consistent with the spatial cueing work), but nonetheless produced significant costs and response compatibility effects at earlier SOAs (50 and 100 ms). As discussed above, it is possible that the effects at the very early SOAs reflect nonspatial filtering costs and parallel processing of the identities of the distractor and target. One way of testing this possibility might be to take advantage of Lavie's (1995) work showing that parallel processing is affected by processing load. If the costs and compatibility effects associated with irrelevant distractors reflect filtering costs and the parallel processing distractor identity, then increasing processing load should leave filtering costs in place, but eliminate compatibility effects. Clearly additional experiments are needed to explore the various interpretations of the costs associated with distractors in the additional singleton paradigm.

REFERENCES

Bacon. W. F., & Egeth, H. E. (1994). Overriding stimulus-driven attentional capture. *Perception and Psychophysics, 55,* 485–496.

Cave. K. R., & Wolfe, J. (1990). Modeling the role of parallel processing in visual search. *Cognitive Psychology, 22,* 225–271.

Folk. C. L., & Annett, S. (1994). Do locally defined feature discontinuities capture attention? *Perception and Psychophysics, 56,* 277–287.

Folk. C. L., & Remington, R. W. (1998). Selectivity in distraction by irrelevant featural singletons: Evidence for two forms of attentional capture. *Journal of Experimental Psychology: Human Perception and Performance, 24,* 847–858.

Folk. C. L., & Remington, R. W. (1999). Can new objects override attentional control settings? *Perception and Psychophysics, 61,* 727–739.

Folk. C. L., Remington, R. W., & Johnston, J. C. (1992). Involuntary covert orienting is contingent on attentional control settings. *Journal of Experimental Psychology: Human Perception and Performance, 18,* 1030–1044.

Folk, C. L., Remington, R. W., & Wright, J. H. (1994). The structure of attentional control: Contingent attentional capture by apparent motion. abrupt onset. and color. *Journal of Experimental Psychology: Human Perception and Performance, 20,* 317–329.

Gibson. B. S., & Amelio, E. (2000). Inhibition of return and attentional control settings. *Perception and Psychophysics, 62,* 496–504.

Gibson, B. S., & Kelsey. E. M. (1998). Stimulus-driven attentional capture is contingent on attentional set for displaywide visual features. *Journal of Experimental Psychology: Human Perception and Performance, 24,* 699–706.

Kahneman. D., Treisman. A., & Burkell. J. (1983). The cost of visual filtering. *Journal of Experimental Psychology: Human Perception and Performance, 9,* 510–522.

Lamy, D., & Egeth, H. E. (2003). Attentional capture in singleton-detection and feature-search modes. *Journal of Experimental Psychology: Human Perception and Performance*. *29*, 1003–1020.

Lavie, N. (1995). Perceptual load as a necessary condition for selective attention. *Journal of Experimental Psychology: Human Perception and Performance*, *21*, 451–468.

Nothdurft, H.-C. (2006). Salience and target selection in visual search. *Visual Cognition*. *14*, 514–542.

Posner, M. I., & Cohen, Y. (1984). Components of visual orienting. In H. Bouma & D. G. Bouwhuis (Eds.), *Attention and performance X: Control of language processes*. Hove, UK: Lawrence Erlbaum Associates Ltd.

Pratt, J., Sekuler, A. B., & McAuliffe, J. (2001). The role of attentional set on attentional cueing and inhibition of return. *Visual Cognition*, *8*, 33–46.

Taylor, T. L., & Klein, R. M. (1998). On the causes and effects of inhibition of return. *Psychonomic Bulletin and Review*, *5*, 625–643.

Theeuwes, J. (1992). Perceptual selectivity for color and form. *Perception and Psychophysics*. *51*, 599–606.

Theeuwes, J. (1994). Stimulus-driven capture and attentional set: Selective search for color and visual abrupt onsets. *Journal of Experimental Psychology: Human Perception and Performance*, *20*, 799–806.

Theeuwes, J. (1996). Perceptual selectivity for color and form: On the nature of the interference effect. In A. F. Kramer, M. Coles, & G. Logan (Eds.), *Converging operations in the study of visual selective attention* (pp. 297–314). Washington DC: American Psychological Association.

Theeuwes, J. (2004). Top-down search strategies cannot override attentional capture. *Psychonomic Bulletin and Review*, *11*, 65–70.

Theeuwes, J., Atchley, P., & Kramer, A. F. (2000). On the time course of top-down and bottom-up control of visual attention. In S. Monsell & J. Driver (Eds.), *Attention and performance XVIII: Control of cognitive performance* (pp. 105–124). Cambridge, MA: MIT Press.

Theeuwes, J., & Godijn, R. (2002). Irrelevant singletons capture attention: Evidence from inhibition of return. *Perception and Psychophysics*, *64*, 764–770.

Treisman, A., & Gelade, G. (1980). A feature integration theory of attention. *Cognitive Psychology*, *12*, 97–136.

Treisman, A., & Souther, J. (1985). Search asymmetry: A diagnostic for preattentive processing of separable features. *Journal of Experimental Psychology: General*, *114*, 285–310.

Wolfe, J. (1994). Guided Search 2.0: A revised model of visual search. *Psychonomic Bulletin and Review*, *1*, 202–238.

VISUAL COGNITION, 2006, 14 (4/5/6/7/8). 466–489

Ψ Psychology Press
Taylor & Francis Group

Visual search for featural singletons: No top-down modulation, only bottom-up priming

Jan Theeuwes

Vrije Universiteit, Amsterdam, Netherlands

Brit Reimann

Dresden University of Technology, Germany

Karen Mortier

Vrije Universiteit, Amsterdam, Netherlands

The present study investigated the effect of top-down knowledge on search for a feature singleton (a "pop-out target"). In a singleton detection task, advance cueing of the dimension of upcoming singleton resulted in cueing costs and benefits (Experiment 1). When the search for the singleton stayed the same but only the response requirements were changed. advance cueing failed to have an effect (Experiments 2 and 3). In singleton search only bottom-up priming plays a role (Experiments 4 and 5). We conclude that expectancy-based, top-down knowledge cannot guide the search for a featural singleton. Bottom-up priming that does facilitate search for a featural singleton cannot be influenced by top-down control. The study demonstrates that effects often attributed to early top-down guidance may represent effects that occur later in processing or represent bottom-up priming effects.

Every day we spend a lot of time searching for important things such as a traffic sign at a busy crossroad, or one of our kids in a busy shopping centre. When searching for an object we have to keep in mind what we are looking for. A target template describing the target (its colour, its shape. its location, etc.) is kept in memory to guide our search process. For example when searching for one of our lost kids in a shopping centre, we try to remember

---

Please address all correspondence to Jan Theeuwes, Dept. of Cognitive Psychology. Vrije Universiteit, van der Boechorststraat 1, 1081 BT Amsterdam. The Netherlands. E-mail: J.Theeuwes@ psy.vu.nl

We would like to thank Hermann Müller for valuable comments on an earlier draft of this paper.

http://www.psypress.com/viscog

DOI: 10.1080/13506280500195110

what the child was wearing that day so that colour may guide our search process.

It appears to be obvious that knowledge of what we are looking for helps our search process. Indeed almost all theories of visual search assume that preknowledge may generate top-down activation that can guide the search process. Top-down activation refers to the extent to which an item matches the current attentional set. For example, when instructed to search for a red target among green nontargets, the red element will receive high top-down activation. Visual search models assume that attentional serial search is guided by information that is available at the early preattentive level (Wolfe, 1994). Various studies have demonstrated that knowledge of the specific task demands may guide attention to only those locations that match the target-relevant feature. For example, Kaptein, Theeuwes, and van der Heijden (1995) showed that participants can restrict search for a colour-orientation conjunction target to a colour-defined subset. Thus, when searching for a red vertical line segment between red tilted and green vertical line segments, participants searched serially among the red items while they completely ignored the green line segments.

Even though it may be obvious that top-down knowledge can guide search in environments that require effortful serial search (e.g., when searching for a conjunction target), it is not clear whether top-down knowledge guides search when the target is unique in a basic feature dimension. When confronted with a display in which one element is unique in a basic feature dimension (such as a red element surrounded by green elements) the element pops out from the display. Without any effort one is able to detect such a *feature singleton*. The question is whether top-down knowledge can affect search for a singleton target (i.e., a "pop-out target").

When confronted with a display, it is first segmented into basic stimulus attributes in different dimension-specific "modules" (such as colour, orientation, etc.). For each stimulus location, each module computes a bottom-up saliency signals indicating the feature difference between one particular item relative to all other items represented within the same module. The more dissimilar an item is, the greater its saliency (see, e.g., Cave & Wolfe, 1990; Theeuwes, 1992, 1994; Wolfe, 1994). Maps of saliency signals are computed in parallel in all modules, and these signals are summed onto a master map of activations. The activity on the master map guides focal attention to the most active location. Focal attention gates the passage of information to higher stages of processing (visual object recognition and response systems). The question we address is whether top-down knowledge can affect the already high bottom-up activity generated by the singleton.

There is evidence that top-down knowledge speeds up search even when one is searching for a feature singleton. While knowing the actual feature value of the target (whether it is blue, red, or white between green nontargets) hardly speeded search. Treisman (1988) showed that knowing the dimension of the target (whether it would be a unique colour or a unique shape) speeded search with about 100 ms. Treisman (1988) suggested that there is no top-down selectivity within dimensions; yet, across dimensions knowing in what dimension the target will be presented speeds up search significantly. More recently, Müller and colleagues (e.g., Found & Müller, 1996; Müller, Heller, & Ziegler, 1995; Müller, Reimann, & Krummenacher, 2003) also provided evidence that knowing for which dimension one is looking speeds up search even when one is searching for a singleton target.

Müller et al. (1995) investigated search for singleton targets within and across stimulus dimensions. Typically, in these experiments, participants search for three possible targets, which all are defined within one dimension (e.g., orientation) or are defined across dimensions (e.g., orientation, colour, and size). In their Experiment 1, the detection of a common right-tilted target was 60 ms slower in the cross-dimension relative to both the intradimension condition and the control condition. In addition, Müller et al. reported dimension-specific intertrial effects: There was an RT advantage when the previous trial contained a target defined in the same dimension relative to a target defined in a different dimension (see also, Found & Müller, 1996).

To account for data like these, Müller and colleagues developed a "dimensionweighting" account of visual selection (Found & Müller, 1996; Müller et al., 1995). In cross-dimensional singleton feature search, observers have to detect the presence of an odd-one-out target object (a feature singleton). Because the target-defining dimension varies from trial to trial, the target is not known in advance. In these conditions, the target does not simply "pop out" from the background in a purely bottom-up fashion. Rather it is claimed that that target detection involves "an attentional mechanism that modifies the processing system by allocating selection weight to the various dimensions that potentially define the target" (Müller et al., 2003, p. 1021). According to the dimension-weighting account, there is a limit to the total attentional weight available to be allocated at any one time to the various dimensions of the target object. It is assumed that potential target-defining dimensions are assigned weight in accordance with their instructed importance and their variability across trials. The greater the weight allocated to a particular dimension, the faster can the presence of a target defined in that dimension be discerned. Dimensional weighting is similar to Guided Search (Wolfe, 1994) except that it focuses specific on dimension specific signals.

Recently, Wolfe, Butcher, Lee, and Hyle (2003) conducted experiments similar to those of Müller and colleagues and Treisman (1988). For example, in Wolfe et al. participants searched a whole block of trials for a red target between green nontargets (i.e., colour singleton) or for a vertical line between horizontal line segments (i.e., shape singleton). These blocked conditions were compared to mixed conditions consisting of blocks of trials in which the target could either be red, green, vertical, or horizontal. On the basis of these data Wolfe et al. concluded "top-down information makes a substantial contribution to RT even for the simplest of feature searches. Fully mixed RTs are about 80 ms slower than are blocked RTs" (p. 485). Wolfe et al. explain these experiments in the same vein as Müller and colleagues: In a blocked condition in which the target is always the same, as much weight as possible can be placed on one dimension (e.g., orientation), allowing for a strong signal to guide search. In a mixed condition, all features have some weight. When in the mixed condition the target happens to be an orientation singleton, there is a weaker signal to guide search, and noise from other dimensions (colour and size) may slow search. Note that both in Müller's and Wolfe's accounts top-down knowledge guides the search process, i.e., top-down knowledge influences the selection process of the featural singleton.

In general, studies demonstrating top-down effects on singleton search use the same straightforward approach. In Treisman (1988) participants either know or did not know in which dimension the target singleton would pop out. Not knowing the dimension of the target generated a large cost. Similarly, in Wolfe et al.'s (2003) experiments participants know which target they are looking for because they search a whole block for the same singleton (for example a red line). This performance is compared to mixed blocks in which the target singleton can either be the same red line or a singleton unique in another dimension (e.g. orientation, size, shape). In Müller's experiments participants typically search for three possible targets that all are defined within one dimension (e.g., orientation) or are defined in one of several possible dimensions (e.g., orientation, colour, and size). Typically, search time in conditions in which the target dimension (or feature) is known are faster than those in mixed blocks in which the target dimension (or target feature) is not known (cross-dimensional search costs).

Even though on the face of it this approach seems valid, it may appear to be impossible to determine whether the effects reflect knowledge, expectancy-based top-down effects, or merely passive bottom-up priming (cf. Maljokovic & Nakayama, 1994). As outlined by Müller et al. (2003) the design of experiments in which mixed versus blocked conditions are compared introduces intertrial effects that may have nothing to do with top-down effects. For example, showing faster RT when one type of singleton is presented throughout a whole block of trials relatively to a condition in which the type of singleton varies from trial to trial would not necessarily imply top-down modulation. In other words, participants may not be faster in a blocked condition because they actively prepare for the upcoming target singleton (as a top-down approach would assume) but are faster because the target singleton on the current trial is simply the same as the one on the previous trial. Indeed, Maljkovic and Nakayama's (1994) research demonstrated that it is impossible to counteract the priming of a previous trial. Intertrial facilitation could not be abolished or reduced even when participants knew exactly which target would be presented on the next trial. Participants could not actively set themselves for a target that was different from that of the previous trial (but see Hillstrom, 2000).

To rule out the possibility that the effects are due to passive bottom-up priming, instead of using a blockwise cueing procedure, Müller et al (2003) employed a trial-by-trial cueing procedure. Before each trial, a verbal cue (the word "colour" and "shape") indicated the likely target-defining dimension. It is assumed that the cue allows participants to actively set themselves for the likely upcoming stimulus dimension. In terms of the dimensional weighting account (Müller et al., 2003) or guided search (e.g., Wolfe et al., 2003) it is assumed that participants use the advance cue to allocate attentional weight to the likely target dimension. In the current experiments, we used the same trial-by-trial cueing procedure as Müller et al. In addition to examining the attentional set induced by the cue it allows an analysis of the intertrial effects to examine the bottom-up priming effects.

EXPERIMENT 1

To ensure that the task was a singleton task we used the same displays as used by Theeuwes (1992). For the current shape and colour singleton, Theeuwes (1992) demonstrated flat search functions indicating parallel (preattentive) search.

Experiment 1 consisted of a singleton search task in which participants had to respond to the presence or absence of a shape or colour singleton. On each trial participants were cued regarding the dimension of the singleton that was most likely to be presented (cue validity of 83%).

Method

Participants. Twelve participants ranging in age between 18 and 30 years participated as paid volunteers. All had self-reported normal or corrected-to-normal vision and reported having no colour vision defects.

Apparatus. A Dell Pentium Optiplex GX-1 with a Dell SVGA colour monitor controlled the timing of the events, generated stimuli and recorded reaction times. The "/" key and the "z" key of the computer keyboard were used as response buttons.

Stimuli. The visual field consisted of nine green elements equally spaced around the fixation point on an imaginary circle (3.4° radius). The search displays were identical to Theeuwes' (1992) "display-size-nine" displays consisting of outline circles (1.4° in diameter) and possibly one diamond of 1.4° side length, each element containing a line segment (0.5°) that was tilted 22.5° to either side of the horizontal or vertical plane. These oriented lines (which were irrelevant in Experiment 1) were randomly distributed in the display. In the colour target-present condition one of the green circles was replaced by a red circle. In the shape target-present condition, one of the green circles was replaced by a green diamond shape. The target-singleton position was randomly chosen among the nine possible element positions. In the target-absent conditions all nine circles were green.

Initially, a centre fixation cross was presented for 900 ms. This was replaced by a verbal cue presented at the centre of the screen indicating with an 83% probability the dimension of the upcoming singleton. In other words, if a singleton was present then the cue indicated this with an 83% probability. For example, if the cue indicated "colour" and a target was present, in 83% of the trials a colour singleton was presented (valid cue condition) and in 17% of the trials a shape singleton (invalid cue condition) was presented. If the cue indicated "shape" and a target was present, in 83% of the trials a shape singleton was presented and in 17% of the trials a colour singleton. In the neutral condition the word "equal" was presented as a cue indicating that there was an equal probability of receiving a shape or a colour singleton appearing on the upcoming trial. After 700 ms the cue was replaced by the centre fixation point. After an ISI of 850 ms the display consisting of the nine elements along with the fixation point was presented. The search display remained on until a response was given (with a maximum of 2 s). Figure 1 gives an example of the displays.

Design and procedure. Each participant performed both the cue and neutral conditions which were varied between blocks. Half of the partici-pants started with the neutral condition, the other half with the cue condition. Each participant performed 360 cue trials and 180 neutral trials. In half of the trials were target-present trials. Half of the participants responded with the "z" key for target present and "/" key for target absent. This response assignment was reversed for the other half.

Participants were told to keep their eyes fixated at the fixation cross. Participants received 270 practice trials prior to the experimental trials. Participants were told to respond to the presence of a singleton regardless of type of singleton. They were informed that the cue would indicate with a high probability the dimension of the upcoming singleton target.

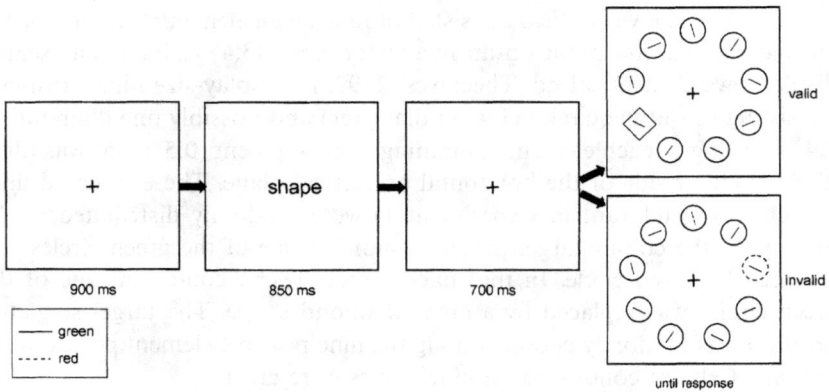

Figure 1. An example of a trial sequence. A verbal cue indicated with 83% validity the dimension ("shape" or "colour") of the upcoming colour or shape singleton target. Participants responded to the presence of a singleton regardless of the type of singleton.

Results

All RTs lasting longer than 750 ms were counted as errors, which led to a loss of well under 1% of the trials.

Figure 2 presents the mean RTs for target-present trials. The individual mean RTs for target-present trials were submitted to an analysis of variance (ANOVA) with cue validity (valid, invalid, or neutral) and singleton type (colour singleton or shape singleton) as factors. There were main effects of

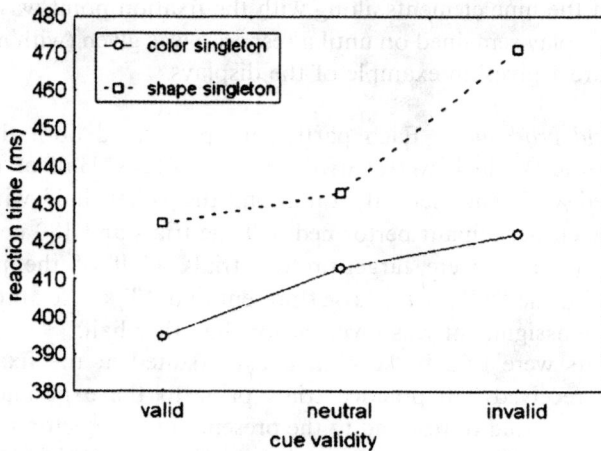

Figure 2. Experiment 1: Mean reaction time as a function of cue validity in a feature detection task when searching for a colour singleton and when searching for a shape singleton.

cue validity, $F(2, 22) = 11.3$, $p < .001$, and of singleton type, $F(1, 11) = 39.2$, $p < .0001$. The interaction was also reliable, $F(2, 22) = 7.4$, $p < .01$. Additional planned comparisons showed that the response times in the valid cue condition were significantly faster than those in the neutral cue condition (411 ms vs. 423 ms; $p = .005$). In addition, the neutral cue condition generated faster RTs than the invalid cue condition (423 ms vs. 447 ms; $p = .019$). As is clear from Figure 2, identical to Theeuwes (1992), colour singleton generated faster response times than shape singletons.

Present responses were not faster than absent responses (418 vs. 425 ms; $F < 1$) providing additional evidence that the current task was a singleton detection task (see Theeuwes, Kramer, & Atchley, 1999).

To determine whether there were any intertrial facilitation effects (cf. Found & Müller, 1996; Maljkovic & Nakayama, 1994), we determined for target-present trials the mean RTs to a target on trial N dependent on the dimensional definition of target on trial $N-1$ (dimension not switch versus dimension switched). An ANOVA showed a main effect of switch (dimension not switch vs. dimension switch: 410 ms vs. 444 ms), $F(1, 11) = 11.4$, $p = .006$. It is important to note that the factor switch did not interact with singleton type or with cue validity, $F(2, 22) = 1.27$, $p = .30$, indicating that the above reported validity effects are not modulated by any passive, bottom-up, priming (cf. Maljkovic & Nakayama, 1994) and do not depend on the singleton type one has to respond to.

An ANOVA on the error rates for target-present trials showed a main effect of validity, $F(2, 22) = 4.0$, $p < .05$. Since error rates mimicked the validity effect on RT (valid 2.4%, neutral 3.6%, and invalid 7.5% errors), differences in response latencies cannot be attributed to a speed–accuracy tradeoff.

Discussion

The present findings show dimension-specific cueing effects and basically represent a replication of the experiments conducted by Müller et al. (2003). Relative to the neutral condition there were reliable benefits for valid cue and reliable costs for invalid cue conditions. The results indicate that advance knowledge regarding the dimension of the upcoming singleton affects the speed of responding. The present results are in line with theories that assume that top-down knowledge can improve visual search for a singleton target. For example, in line with the dimension-weighting account of Müller et al. (1995, 2003; Found & Müller, 1996) or the guided search account of Wolfe et al. (2003), the present results seem to indicate that target selection is modulated by intentional, knowledge-based processes. Because processing is tuned to a specific dimension (i.e., the cued dimension), it is assumed that visual search for the relevant feature dimension is speeded.

The observation of an intertrial facilitation effect that does not interact with any top-down cueing conditions is in line with Maljokovic and Nakayama (1994), who argued that intertrial facilitation is a passive bottom-up priming effect, which cannot be modulated by top-down processing. Priming is a process that is assumed to be cognitively inaccessible (see also Kristjansson, Wang, & Nakayama, 2002).

EXPERIMENT 2

Experiment 2 was identical to Experiment 1 except that participants responded to the orientation of the line segment located in the target singleton. In such a "compound" search task (cf. Duncan, 1985), there is a clear separation between perceptual and response selection factors (see also Theeuwes, 1991, 1992). Employing this task makes it possible to determine whether the cueing effect reported in Experiment 1 represents cueing effects operating at perceptual or response selection levels. Participants searched for exactly the same singletons as in Experiment 1 yet they responded to the line segment inside the singleton. Identical to Experiment 1 the dimension of the upcoming target singleton was cued with a validity of 83%.

Method

Participant. Fourteen participants ranging in age between 18 and 30 years participated as paid volunteers.

Stimuli. The stimuli and trial sequence were identical to those in Experiment 1 except that the line segment inside the target singleton was either vertical or horizontal, the orientation determining the appropriate response keys (left for vertical and right for horizontal).

Design and procedure. Cue validity was again 83%. Participants performed 360 trials (200 valid, 40 invalid, and 120 neutral). Cue and neutral conditions were again varied between blocks of trials. Participants received a block of 180 practice trials. Again, they were informed that the cue would indicate with a high probability the dimension of the upcoming singleton in which the target line segment was located. It was made explicitly clear that they should use the cue as much as possible to reduce reaction time. Note that unlike in Experiment 1 there were no target-absent trials.

Results

All RTs lasting longer than 1200 ms were counted as errors, which led to a loss of less than 1% of the trials.

Figure 3 presents the mean RTs. The individual mean RTs were submitted to the same analysis of variance with cue validity (valid, invalid, or neutral) and singleton type (colour singleton or shape singleton) as factors. There was only a main effect of singleton type, $F(1, 13) = 35.0$, $p < .0001$. Identical to Experiment 1, colour singletons generated faster responses than shape singletons. There was no effect of cue validity, $F(1, 13) = 0.06$. The mean RT in the valid cue condition was 585 ms, in the neutral cue condition it was 585 ms and in the invalid cue condition it was 589 ms. Cue validity did not interact with singleton type, $F(2, 26) = 0.65$. As in Experiment 1 we did find a reliably intertrial effect, $F(1, 13) = 4.74$, $p < .05$. Participants responded faster (mean of 582 ms) when the target did not switch dimensions than when it did switch (mean of 592 ms).

Error rates (about 8.3%) were slightly higher than in Experiment 1. More errors were made in the shape singleton condition (9.4%) than in the colour singleton condition (7.2%), $F(1, 13) = 6.9$, $p < .05$, effects that mimic the effects on RT.

Discussion

The current experiment clearly indicates that the same cue that was able to generate cue benefits and costs in Experiment 1 failed to produce cueing

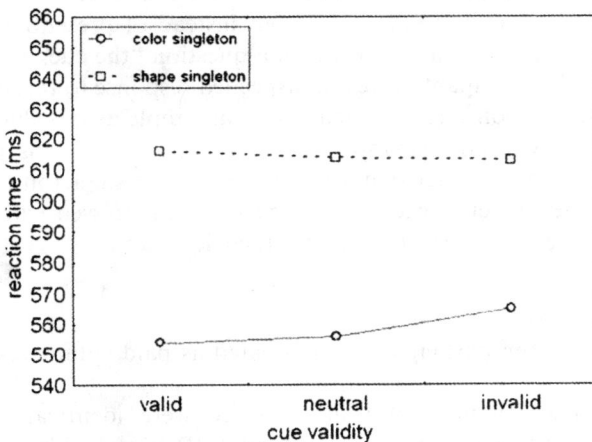

Figure 3. Experiment 2: Mean reaction time as a function of cue validity in a compound search task when searching for a colour singleton and when searching for a shape singleton.

effects in Experiment 2. Unlike Experiment 1 in which participants responded to the presence or absence of the singleton, in Experiment 2 participants searched for the singleton but responded to the line segment located in it.

Experiment 2 was identical to Experiment 1 (i.e., same type of cues, same targets, same cue validity) except that now participants responded to the line segment located inside the singleton. Just by changing the response requirement the reliable cueing effect of Experiment 1 was not present anymore. If the cue would affect (preattentive) search processes for the odd-one-out singleton as many theories of visual search assume (cf. Muller et al., 2003; Wolfe et al., 2003) then one would expect a validity effect in Experiment 2 as well. The results clearly show no sign of cue validity whatsoever. The differential cueing effects between Experiment 1 and 2 demonstrates that effects that typically have been attributed to early top-down visual modulation (e.g., Found & Müller, 1996; Müller et al., 1995; Wolfe et al., 2003) represent effects that occur much later in processing.

EXPERIMENT 3

One may argue that the verbal cue in Experiment 2 did not have a cueing effect because participants did not actively process the cue. Since it may have been difficult to establish a top-down set for a cued dimension and at the same time hold the response mapping for the orientation task, participants may simply have ignored the cue altogether. To determine whether participants actually processed the cue, in Experiment 3 we interleaved some "validation" trials with the search trials. In these validation trials, the cue was presented as in a search trial but instead of presenting the search display, the participant was probed with a question "the cue, was it SHAPE or COLOUR?" Participants gave a nonspeeded response to this question. To ensure that the response requirements were as simple as possible, instead of using an arbitrary response mapping involving line orientations, participants had to respond to the letter that appeared inside the singleton target. If the letter inside the singleton was an "R" participants pressed with their right hand; if it was an "L" the pressed with their left hand.

Method

Participant.   Ten participants participated as paid volunteers.

Stimuli.   The stimuli and trial sequence were identical to those in Experiment 2 except that there were capital "R"s and "L"s placed inside each of the elements (see Theeuwes, 1995, in which exactly the same task was used). The letter that appeared inside the singleton (which was either colour or shape) determined the appropriate response keys (left for "L" and right for "R"). In case of a validation trial, instead of presenting the search display a question was displayed in the middle of the screen saying "SHAPE or COLOUR?" Participants made a nonspeeded response, typing the "S" key when the verbal cue said SHAPE and a "C" when the verbal cue said COLOUR. If they made an error, they received feedback stating "please process the cue".

Design and procedure.   For search trials cue validity was 80% (160 valid cues and 40 invalid cues). Forty validation trials were randomly interleaved.

Results

The first trial following a validation trial was considered a warm-up trial and was therefore excluded from the analysis. Figure 4 presents the mean RTs. There was only a main effect of singleton type, $F(1, 9) = 35.3$, $p < .0001$. As in Experiments 1 and 2, colour singletons generated faster responses than shape singletons. Even though numerically there appears to the be some effect in the right direction (valid cue condition: 586 ms vs. invalid cue condition: 598 ms), statistically cue validity, $F(1, 9) = 1.7$, was not reliable. Cue validity did not interact with singleton type, $F(1, 9) = 0.0004$. Intertrial analyses were not performed since there were not enough trials in the invalid cue condition.

Of the 400 validation trials participants were wrong on only 3 trials (<1%), suggesting that they processed the verbal cue correctly. Error rates

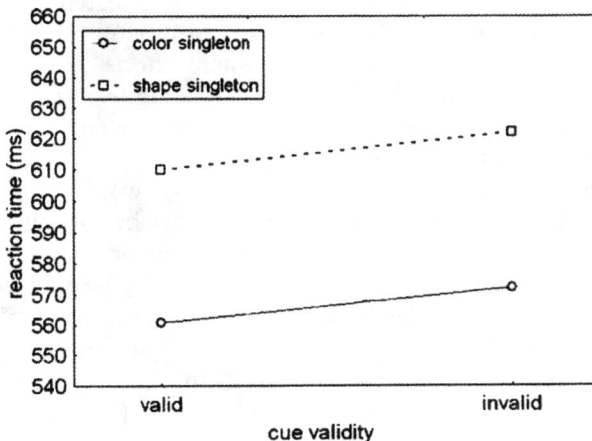

Figure 4.   Experiment 3: Mean reaction time as a function of cue validity in a compound search task when searching for a colour singleton and when searching for a shape singleton.

in the search task were very low (about 2.8%) and were therefore not further analysed.

Discussion

Experiment 3 clearly demonstrates that participants processed the cue. Participants correctly identified the cue in 99.2% of the trials. Also, the task, which required participants only to press right when a "R" was presented and press left when an "L" was presented, was slightly easier. Even though participants did not respond faster they made significantly less errors in Experiment 3 than in Experiment 2 (2.8% vs. 8.3%). Even though the response requirements were fairly simple and there was evidence that participants processed the cue (i.e., they did not simply ignore the cue), the results basically replicate those of Experiment 2: Dimension cueing does not affect search for a feature singleton. The finding that cueing had no effect suggests that the cue cannot speed up or slow down the actual search for the odd-one-out singleton.

EXPERIMENT 4

Given the results of Experiments 1–3, one may ask the question whether there can be any top-down guidance of visual search when searching for a featural singleton (i.e., pop-out target). In other words, is it possible to design an experiment that results in reliable cueing effects that operate on the actual search processes. As noted above there have been demonstrations that cueing may speed up the response when participants search for the presence or absence of a feature singleton (e.g., Müller et al., 1995, 2003). Experiments 1–3 suggest, however, that these effects that typically have been attributed to early top-down visual modulation (e.g., Found & Müller, 1996; Müller et al., 1995, 2003; Wolfe et al. 2003) may represent effects that occur later in processing.

The question arises which conditions, if any, would allow top-down guidance for singleton search. One argument may be that the verbal cues used in Experiments 1–3 may be less optimal to obtain early modulation of visual search processes. Even though verbal cues may be effective when the design of the experiments is such that it allows response bias (as for example in Müller et al., 2003), they may be less effective when response bias is taken out as an explanatory mechanism (as in Experiments 2 and 3).

In Experiments 4 and 5, instead of a verbal cue, we used the actual singleton as a cue presented at the centre of the screen. The cue (e.g., a red circle or a green diamond) was identical to the target singleton that was most likely to be presented on the upcoming trial (80% validity). As in

Experiments 2 and 3, participants searched a target singleton and responded to the orientation of the line segment therein. If we find any cueing effects, these conditions ensure that possible cueing effects represent facilitation at the perceptual selection level and not at the response selection level.

Method

Participants.   Twelve participants participated as paid volunteers.

Stimuli.   The stimuli and trial sequence were identical to those in Experiment 2 except that, instead of using a verbal cue, a symbolic (direct) cue was used. The symbolic cue, which was presented in the centre of the display, was identical to the shape singleton (i.e., the green diamond) or the colour singleton (i.e., the red circle) participants had to search for in the search display. The cue was presented just as in Experiment 1 for 850 ms followed by a 700 ms ISI before the search display was presented.

Design and procedure.   The cue indicated with a probability of 80% the target singleton for the upcoming trial. If the cue was a green diamond, there was an 80% probability that the target singleton was a green diamond and a 20% probability that the target singleton was a red circle. If the cue was a red circle, there was an 80% probability that the target singleton was a red circle and a 20% probability that the target singleton was a green diamond. Each participant performed 240 experimental trials consisting of 200 validly and 40 invalidly cued trials. Participants performed 240 practice trials. Participants were told to respond to the presence of a singleton regardless of type of singleton. They were informed that the cue would indicate with a high probability the dimension of the upcoming singleton target.

Results

All RTs lasting longer than 1200 ms were counted as errors, which led to a loss of less than 1% of the trials. There were main effect of cue validity, $F(1, 11) = 6.3$, $p < .05$, and of singleton type, $F(1, 11) = 27.0$, $p < .001$. The interaction was not reliable ($F < 1$). In line with previous experiments, responses to the colour singletons were faster (586 ms) than responses to shape singletons (617 ms). The results indicate that cueing was effective. In case of a valid cue participants were faster than when the cue is invalid (593 ms vs. 610 ms).

There was a reliable Intertrial × Cue validity interaction, $F(1, 11) = 6.5$, $p < .05$. The validity manipulation had a much larger effect (582 ms for valid vs. 612 ms for invalid) when the target dimension did not switch than when it switched from one dimension to another (603 ms for valid vs. 610 ms for invalid).

Error rates were low (6.3%) and were not systematically related to any of the variables manipulated.

Discussion

The present results suggest that there is top-down guidance of visual search for featural singletons. Even when it is ensured that cueing can only operate on the search process itself (and not on the response selection process) a clear cueing effect was found.

One may argue that the absence of a cueing effect in Experiments 2 and 3 may have been due to the fact that a verbal cue may not be effective in generating a top-down set that can guide search for the featural singleton. Even though on the face of it these results suggest that top-down knowledge can help attentional selection of a featural singleton, it remains a question whether this cueing effect is genuinely top-down. Indeed, the SOA between cue and target display was 1.5 s. which seems enough to cognitively prepare for the upcoming target singleton. Also. participants had every reason to prepare themselves for the upcoming singleton because most of the time the cue was correct (80% of the trials).

Even though this seems to be a reasonable interpretation, it is also possible that this cueing benefit is a bottom-up priming effect that is independent of any top-down set. This is in line with Maljkovic and Nakayama (1994), who showed that intertrial facilitation in visual search is most likely a passive bottom-up priming effect that cannot be influenced by any top-down processing.

In line with such a bottom-up priming account is the interaction between cue validity and intertrial target switches. The analysis suggests that the validity effect was due to fast response times when both the cue and the previous trial contained the same singleton. Only in this condition RT was fast (mean RT of 582 ms) while in all other conditions RTs were relatively slow and had about the same value (612 ms for no switch invalid, 603 ms for switch valid, and 610 ms for switch invalid). In all these latter conditions there was always a singleton as a cue or as a target in the previous trial that did not match the target singleton of the current trial. If bottom-up priming extends to several previous instances of the stimulus (see, e.g., Hillstrom, 2000) then these results can be expected. The fact that there are basically no cue validity effects when the previous trial contained a singleton that was different from the current trial suggests that actively preparing for the upcoming trial on the basis of the cue cannot counteract the bottom-up priming effect from the previous trial.

EXPERIMENT 5

Experiment 5 was designed to determine whether the cueing effect obtained in Experiment 4 is a top-down attentional set effect or a bottom-up priming effect. The cue indicated the upcoming target singleton with a low probability of only 16.6%. For example, when a colour singleton was presented as a cue, in 16.6% a colour target singleton would be presented and in 83.4% a shape singleton would be presented. If with this low validity, a valid cue still would result in faster response times, one would have strong evidence for bottom-up priming.

Method

Participants.   Twelve new participants participated as paid volunteers.

Stimuli.   The experiment was exactly the same as Experiment 1 except that now there were 40 validly cued trials and 200 invalidly cued trials implying that the cue was only valid on 16.6% of the trials. Participants were informed about these probabilities. Again there were 240 practice and 240 experimental trials.

Results

RTs lasting longer than 1200 ms were counted as errors, which led to a loss of less than 1% of the trials. There were main effects of cue validity, $F(1, 11) = 5.5$, $p < .05$, and of singleton type, $F(1, 11) = 16.9$, $p < .001$. The interaction was not reliable ($F < 1$). Again, RTs to the colour singletons were faster (555 ms) than responses to shape singletons (586 ms). Even though the cue did not have predictive value regarding the upcoming target singleton, cueing was effective. Where the cue happened to be valid (which was only in 16.6% of the trials), RTs were faster (565 ms) than when the cue was invalid (577 ms).

Again there was a reliable Intertrial × Cue validity interaction, $F(1, 11) = 7.8$, $p < .05$. The validity manipulation had a larger effect when the target dimension was switched (561 ms for valid vs. 584 ms for invalid) than when it was not switched (569 ms for valid vs. 570 ms for invalid. Error rates were low (5.2%) and not systematically related to any of the variables manipulated.

Discussion

The results of Experiment 5 are quite striking. Even though the cue had no predictive value, there was a reliable cueing effect for the valid versus invalid cue condition. In fact, an additional analysis with "Experiment 4 vs. 5" as a between-subject factor confirmed the notion that the cueing effect was not altered by the predictive value of the cue: The factor "experiment" was not reliable ($F < 1$) and did not interact with any of the other variables (all $Fs < 1$). Figure 5 gives the cueing effects for Experiments 4 and 5.

The current findings indicate that the cueing effect in Experiment 4 is not due to a top-down attentional set. Indeed the current data indicate that there is no top-down control to actively prepare for the upcoming dimension. If observers had been able to set themselves in a top-down fashion to search for the appropriate target singleton then one would expect to find a reverse cueing effect. For example, seeing a diamond as a cue predicts with 83% validity that a colour target singleton (a red circle) would be presented. Also, seeing a red circle as a cue predicts with 83% validity that a shape singleton (a green diamond) would be presented. If observers had been able to exert top-down control then invalidly cued trials should have been faster than validly cued trial. We found the opposite. providing evidence for bottom-up priming effects in visual search.

The intertrial analysis also suggests that bottom-up priming plays a major role. In this experiment the slowest RT is found when both the cue preceding

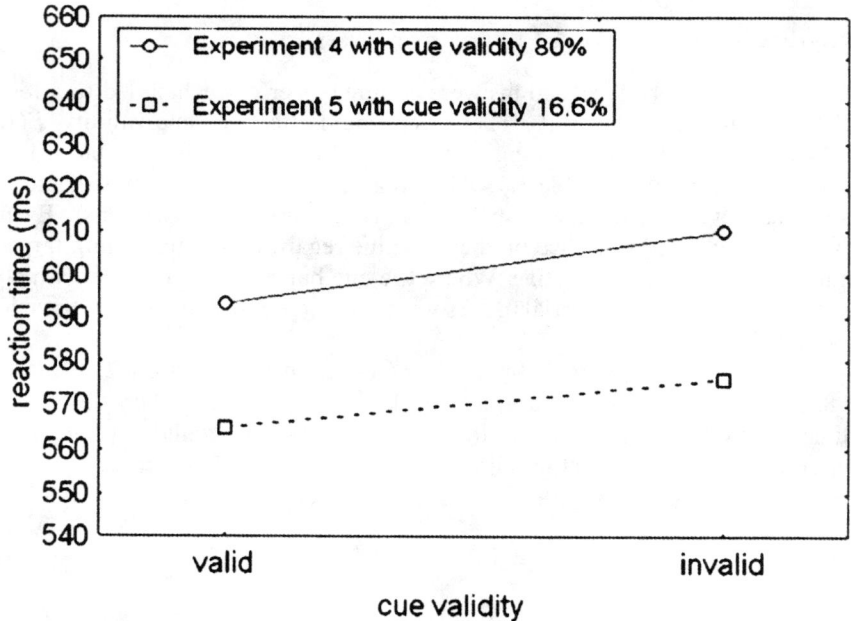

Figure 5.   The cueing effect for Experiment 4 in which the cue had a validity of 80% and Experiment 5 in which the cue had a validity of 16.6%.

the trial and the target singleton of the previous trial are the same and both are different from the target singleton of the current tri al (mean RT of 584 ms). In all other conditions either the cue or the target in the previous trial matched that of the target in the current trials. These RTs are all relatively fast (569ms for no switch valid; 570 ms for no switch invalid; 561 ms for switch valid). It seems that in this experiment participants became very slow when both the cue and the previous trial did not match the singleton of the current trial regardless of the actual validity.

GENERAL DISCUSSION

The current results are important in our thinking regarding top-down control in visual search for featural singletons. It is intuitively plausible to assume that observers can set themselves to search for a particular feature in a top-down knowledge-based way. Indeed most theories of visual search assume that top-down knowledge guides the actual search process for the featural singleton (e.g., Müller et al., 2003; Wolfe et al., 2003). The current study shows, however, that:

1. Expectancy-based, top-down knowledge induced by a verbal cue that is assumed to guide the search process (e.g., Müller et al., 1995, 2003) may represent effects that occur after visual selection has taken place (i.e., postselective).
2. Cueing that does affect the actual search for the featural singleton is not due to expectancy-based, top-down settings but is due to bottom-up priming.
3. Deliberate top-down control cannot counteract the bottom-up priming effects of the cue and of previous trials.

Experiment 1, which uses a verbal cue to induce expectancy-based top-down settings, basically replicates the main findings of Müller et al. (2003). Like Müller et al. we show that knowledge of the upcoming target dimension affects the speed of responding. When the verbal cue induced the correct expectations regarding the upcoming stimulus dimension participants were fast; if expectations were incorrect participants were slow. The typical explanation for these findings is that top-down modulation can guide search for a singleton target (e.g., Müller et al., 1995, 2003; Treisman, 1988; Wolfe, 1994; Wolfe et al., 2003). For example, according to the dimensional weighting account of Müller et al. (2003; see also Wolfe et al., 2003), knowing the dimension in advance allows attentional weight to be assigned to the relevant (known, precued) dimension. According to Müller et al., assigning weights according to the known likelihood of a target appearing in a particular dimension permits a rapid search. Experiment 2 was identical to Experiment 1 (i.e., same type of cues, same targets, same cue validity) except that now participants responded to the line segment located inside the singleton. Just by changing the response requirement the reliable cueing effect of Experiment 1 was not present anymore in Experiment 2. If the cue would guide search processes for the odd-one-out singleton, as many theories of visual search assume, then one would expect a validity effect in Experiment 2 as well. The results clearly show no sign of cue validity whatsoever. Experiment 3 demonstrated that participants did not simply ignore the cue: Participants processed the cue and knew exactly which cue was presented; yet they were not able to use this knowledge to speed up the search process. Experiment 1 shows that a verbal cue can have an effect on the speed of responding when searching for a singleton; Experiments 2 and 3 show that when one ensures that this advance cueing cannot affect response selection processes but only the actual search processes, cueing effects are no longer present. Our Experiments 1–3 suggest that effects that have been attributed to early top-down visual guidance (e.g., Müller et al., 2003; Wolfe et al., 2003) may represent effects that occur much later in processing.

Experiments 4 and 5 show that it is possible to obtain cueing effects that operate on the actual search process. As in Experiments 2 and 3, a compound search task was used in which the target one is searching for is different from what one has to respond to. Instead of using verbal cues, Experiment 4 demonstrated that a symbolic cue showing the actual singleton that would be the most likely target on the upcoming trial resulted in a cueing effect. On the basis of this finding one could conclude that participants used the cue to actively prepare for the most likely target singleton. Indeed the cue indicated with an 80% probability the upcoming target singleton. However, Experiment 5 shows that predictability of the cue did not alter the size of the cueing effect, suggesting that the cueing effect is not due to actively preparing for the most likely target singleton but may represent bottom-up priming. Indeed, if participants are able to actively set themselves for the most likely target singleton one would have expected a reversed cueing effect. Seeing one particular cue (e.g., a red circle) should have allowed participants to actively prepare for the shape dimension (the shape singleton) because in 83% of the trials a colour cue was followed by a shape singleton. The results suggest that participants did not and pre-sumably could not set themselves for the most likely target singleton. The cueing effect was not reversed but basically identical to the cueing effect of Experiment 4 in which the cue was predictive of the upcoming target singleton. The fact that the size of the cueing effect is not modulated by its validity suggests that top-down processing cannot counteract bottom-up priming.

Our claim that in feature search only bottom-up priming occurs, which cannot be counteracted by top-down, expectation-based modulation, is in line with the findings of Maljkovic and Nakayama (1994), who investigated intertrial effects in feature search. Even when a target on a given trial was 100% predictable (e.g., target definition changed in an AABBAAB-BAA ... manner), knowledge-based expectations could not modulate feature-specific intertrial effects. Maljkovic and Nakayama conclude that their intertrial effects reflect passive priming that are not top-down penetrable. This conclusion is completely in line with our study that used cues to induce top-down expectancies: In feature search there is no top-down modulation, only bottom-up priming. Maljkovic and Nakayama referred to this findings as "priming of pop-out". Kristjansson et al. (2002) found priming effects in conjunctive visual search. They show, similar to our Experiment 5, a counterintuitive result: Knowing what the target is on a given trial does not facilitate conjunction search. More importantly, they argue that, in addition to priming, there are no benefits for top-down guidance. They conclude, "the role of priming in visual search is underestimated in current theories of visual search and that differences in search times often attributed to top-down guidance may instead reflect the benefits of priming" (p. 37).

The effects reported in our Experiments 4 and 5 (and those reported by Kristjansson et al., 2002; Maljkovic & Nakayama, 1994) should be considered as the result of priming and not of some form of top-down processing. Wolfe et al. (2003) referred to the intertrial effects revealed in their study as being top-down in nature. Even though it is generally agreed that priming is basically a bottom-up process (e.g., Posner, 1978), Wolfe et al. (2003) called these effects top-down because "it relies on what the observer has learned about the prior trial and does not rely solely on the state of the stimulus" (p. 483). Even though the intertrial effects reported by Wolfe et al. are due to bottom-up priming in the sense of Maljokovic and Nakayama (1994, 1996; Kristjansson et al., 2002) given their definition that priming is top-down, it is not surprising that Wolfe et al. called his intertrial effects the results of *top-down guidance* in terms of Guided Search. Calling these effects top-down because they rely on what an observer has learned may be problematic. The word "learning" may be misleading because the change of state that priming induces has nothing to do with conscious effort or explicit knowledge. In fact priming effects may represent the most important example of effects that are impervious to prior knowledge and/or top-down processing. In line with others (Kristjansson et al., 2002; Maljkovic & Nakayama, 1994), we consider the intertrial effects the results of passive bottom-up priming that is not top-down penetrable.

In line with the notion that priming is impervious to prior knowledge or top-down processing our Experiments 4 and 5 show that top-down processing has no effect on priming. Our Experiment 5 shows that even when the cue was highly unpredictive (i.e., it indicated with 83% that the other singleton would be presented) it still caused priming effects. If there had been any top-down processing (i.e., preparing for the upcoming singleton) that could have counteracted the bottom-up priming one should have at least expected some attenuation of the priming effect. The results show that there is basically no difference in priming dependent on whether the cue was predictive (Experiment 4) or not (Experiment 5). In line with Kristjansson et al. (2002) we conclude that indeed "there are no benefits for top-down guidance over and above the effect of priming" (p. 49).

If one adheres the position that there should be top-down guidance in singleton search, one may argue that in experiments in which cueing effects are found participants actively processed and used the cue to set up top-down expectations, and in experiments in which there are no cueing effects participants just ignored the cue and did not bother to actively set-up top-down expectations. In other words, according this line of reasoning top-down effects on visual search are assumed even when cueing has no effect. If no effects of the cue are found it is assumed that observers did not bother to use it. This may especially be true for singleton search because this type of search is easy and of low effort. There are, however, arguments that do not seem to fit this interpretation. First, the claim that participants do not bother to set up top-down expectations when the task is very easy is not consistent with studies investigating location cueing. For example, in Remington and Pierce (1984) participants had to detect the onset of a luminance dot presented on the left or right of fixation. A symbolic cue (an arrow) pointed with 80% validity to the location where the dot was most likely to appear. In this extremely simple task (i.e., detecting a luminance onset) the symbolic cue had a clear validity effect: Valid cues gave faster detection times than invalid cues. It is clear that the detection of a luminance onset is very easy and can be done without setting up top-down expectations. Yet in this study participants used the symbolic location cue to improve their performance. Therefore it seems fair to conclude that the simplicity of the task should not prevent participants from setting up top-down expectations. Second, one may argue the opposite, that is, the task used in the present study is not too simple but to complex too show validity effects. For example, cueing in singleton search only may work in simple search and not in compound search because it take much longer to respond in a compound search task than in a simple search task. Indeed, in our Experiment 1 the mean RT was 422 ms and in Experiment 2 it was 586 ms. It is claimed that early cueing effects are obscured by the longer response times associated with the more difficult response requirements of the compound search task. This argument seems to suggest that the more difficult a task the harder it is to obtain cueing effects. Experiments 4 and 5, which also consisted of compound search, provide evidence that cue validity effects can be found even when the response times are high. Indeed, the mean RT in Experiment 4 was 600 ms and a clear validity effect was obtained. Third, the notion that participants simply do not process the cue is invalidated by Experiment 3, which shows that participants knew which cue was presented. Even though this experiment cannot prove that participants actively tried to set up an expectation for the upcoming singleton, the experiment proves that participants processed the cue and knew what the cue entailed.

Our notion that typical cueing effects as reported by Müller et al. (1995, 2003) represent effects that operate on response selection processes is in line with the claims of Cohen and colleagues (Cohen & Feintuch, 2002; Cohen & Magen, 1999; Cohen & Shoup, 1997). Cohen assumes separate response selection mechanism for different visual dimensions. A cross-dimensional task involves multiple response selection mechanisms, whereas an intradimensional task involves just one such mechanism. Similar to our claims, Cohen and Magen (1999) argue that the search processes in simple and compound search are exactly the same (i.e., search for a singleton). In line with Cohen is our argument that the cueing procedure in Experiment 1 did not cue the search process; instead it allowed to activate (feature-specific) response selection processes. Our claim and that of Cohen is that attention is necessary to make an overt response (see also Duncan, 1985). In order to be able to respond to a singleton, attention has to be directed to the location of the singleton. In this sense our view (and that of Cohen) implies that overt responses are postselective, i.e., overt responses can only be made after attention has been focused on the location of the target. Müller et al. (2003) suggest that some responses can be made directly on the detection of activity in the master map. It is assumed that one can respond to the target singleton (i.e., something unique is present) without waiting for complete knowledge to become available through focal attention. Cueing is assumed to affect the preattentive perceptual stage and a response can be given directly on the overall saliency signal.

The current findings suggest that early spatially parallel visual processes cannot be modulated by intentional, top-down processes. The results are consistent with Theeuwes (1991, 1992, 1994), who argued that there is no top-down control at the early preattentive level. Theeuwes concluded this on the basis of studies showing that a top-down attentional set cannot prevent attentional capture by an irrelevant, salient singleton. If there would have been top-down control at the early preattentive level then it should have been possible to increase the top-down "weight" of the relevant dimension thereby eliminating the interference from the irrelevant dimension. The results show that this did not occur, not even after 2000 trials of practice (see Theeuwes, 1992, Exp. 2). The current results suggest that in simple singleton search ("pop-out tasks") the salient element pops out from the background and deliberate top-down operations seem to have no influence on these processes. It should be noted, however, that the present findings suggest that bottom-up priming may play a role at the early preattentive level of processing and it is to be expected that priming will modulate attentional capture.

In conclusion, the simplest search (i.e., search for a pop-out target) appears to be driven in a bottom-up way. There is no evidence for expectancy-based top-down guidance of the search process. Only bottom-up priming affects feature singleton search. Priming occurs independently of top-down processing and its effect cannot even be counteracted by active top-down processing. Therefore, when looking at a cue with a red colour, cells in our brain representing "red" get active causing a selective and automatic enhancement of processing of objects with the colour red. Even though we may know that we do not want to look for red (e.g., our kid was wearing a green sweater that day) by looking at red we cannot avoid red objects receivimg attentional priority.

REFERENCES

Cave, K. R., & Wolfe, J. M. (1990). Modeling the role of parallel processing in visual search. *Cognitive Psychology*, *22*, 225–271.

Cohen, A., & Feintuch, U. (2002). The dimensional-action system: A distinct visual system. In W. Prinz & B. Hommel (Eds.), *Attention and performance: XIX. Common mechanisms in perception and action* (pp. 587–608). Oxford, UK: Oxford University Press.

Cohen, A., & Magen, H. (1999). Intra- and cross-dimensional visual search for single-feature targets. *Perception and Psychophysics*, *61*, 291–307.

Cohen, A., & Shoup, R. (1997). Perceptual dimensional constraints in response selection processes. *Cognitive Psychology*, *32*(2), 128–181.

Duncan, J. (1985). Visual search and visual attention. In M. I. Posner & O. S. M. Marin (Eds.), *Attention and performance: XI. Attention and neuropsychology* (pp. 85–106). Hillsdale, NJ: Lawrence Erlbaum Associates, Inc.

Found, A., & Müller, H. J. (1996). Searching for unknown feature targets on more than one dimension: Investigating a "dimension-weighting" account. *Perception and Psychophysics*, *58*, 88–101.

Hillstrom, A. (2000). Repetition effects in visual search. *Perception and Psychophysics*, *62*, 800–817.

Kaptein, N. A., Theeuwes, J., & van der Heijden, A. H. C. (1995). Search for a conjunctively defined target can be selectively limited to a colour-defined subset of elements. *Journal of Experimental Psychology: Human Perception and Performance*, *21*, 1053–1069.

Kristjansson, A., Wang, D., & Nakayama, K (2002). The role of priming in conjunctive visual search. *Cognition*, *85*, 37–52.

Maljkovic, V., & Nakayama, K. (1994). The priming of Pop-Out I: Role of features. *Memory and Cognition*, *22*, 657–672.

Maljkovic, V., & Nakayama, K. (1996). The priming of Pop-Out II: Role of position. *Perception and Psychophysics*, *58*, 977–991.

Müller, H. J., Heller, D., & Ziegler, J. (1995). Visual search for singleton feature targets within and across feature dimensions. *Perception and Psychophysics*, *57*, 1–17.

Müller, H. J., Reimann, B., & Krummenacher, J. (2003). Visual search for singleton feature targets across dimensions: Stimulus- and expectancy-driven effects in dimensional weighting. *Journal of Experimental Psychology: Human Perception and Performance*, *29*(5), 1021–1035.

Posner, M. I. (1978). *Chronometric explorations of mind*. Hillsdale, NJ: Lawrence Erlbaum Associates, Inc.

Remington, R., & Pierce, L. (1984). Moving attention: Evidence for time-invariant shifts of visual attention. *Perception and Psychophysics*, *35*, 393–399.

Theeuwes, J. (1991). Cross-dimensional perceptual selectivity. *Perception and Psychophysics*, *50*, 184–193.

Theeuwes, J. (1992). Perceptual selectivity for colour and form. *Perception and Psychophysics*, *51*, 599–606.

Theeuwes, J. (1994). Bottom-up capture and attentional set: Selective search for colour and visual abrupt onsets. *Journal of Experimental Psychology: Human Perception and Performance*, *20*, 799–806.

Theeuwes, J., Kramer, A. F., & Atchley, P. (1999). Attentional effects on preattentive vision: Spatial precues affect the detection of simple features. *Journal of Experimental Psychology: Human Perception and Performance*, *25*, 341–347.

Treisman, A. (1988). Features and objects: The fourteenth Bartlett memorial lecture. *Quarterly Journal of Experimental Psychology*, *40A*, 201–237.

Wolfe, J. M. (1994). Guided Search 2.0: A revised model of visual search. *Psychonomic Bulletin and Review*, *1*, 202–238.

Wolfe, J. M., Butcher, S. J., Lee, C., & Hyle, M. (2003). Changing your mind: On the contributions of top-down and bottom-up guidance in visual search for feature singletons. *Journal of Experimental Psychology: Human Perception and Performance*, *29*, 483–502.

VISUAL COGNITION, 2006, 14 (4/5/6/7/8), 490–513

Ψ Psychology Press
Taylor & Francis Group

Locus of dimension weighting:
Preattentive or postselective?

Hermann J. Müller and Joseph Krummenacher

Department Psychologie, Allgemeine und experimentelle Psychologie,
Ludwig-Maximilians-Universität München, Germany

In visual search for singleton feature targets, detection RTs are faster when the target-defining dimension is constant across trials rather than variable; in the latter case, RTs are faster when the target dimension on a trial is the same, rather than different, relative to preceding trial (with little effect of a feature change within a repeated dimension); and RTs are expedited when the target dimension is validly indicated by a symbolic precue on a given trial (e.g., Found & Müller, 1996; Müller, Heller, & Ziegler, 1995; Müller, Reimann, & Krummenacher, 2003). Müller and his colleagues have explained these effects in terms of a "dimension-weighting" account, according to which these effects arise at a preattentive, perceptual stage of saliency coding. In contrast, Cohen (e.g., Cohen & Magen, 1999) and Theeuwes (e.g., Theeuwes et al., 2006 this issue) have recently argued that these effects are postselective, response-related in nature. The present paper examines these challenges and puts forward counterarguments in support of the view that dimensional weighting operates at a preattentive stage of processing.

DIMENSION-BASED VISUAL SELECTION

Dimension-based theories of visual selective attention propose that selection is limited by the nature of the required discriminations between different stimulus attributes, more precisely, between dimensions of attributes. However, early dimension-based accounts, such as the "analyser theory" (Allport, 1971, 1980; Treisman, 1969), were not well supported empirically (see Duncan, 1984, for a critical review). Recently, an alternative, "dimension-weighting" account of visual selection has been developed (Found & Müller, 1996; Müller, Heller, & Ziegler, 1995), based mainly on studies of cross-dimensional singleton feature search. In this task, observers have to discern the presence of an odd-one-out object, a single-feature target, within a background field of homogeneous nontarget objects under conditions in

Please address all correspondence to Hermann J. Müller, Department of Psychology, Allgemeine und experimentelle Psychologie, Ludwig-Maximilians-Universität München, Leopoldstr. 13, D-80802 Munich, Germany. E-mail: Mueller@psy.uni-muenchen.de

DOI: 10.1080/13506280500194154

which the target-defining dimension varies from trial to trial and, thus, is not known in advance. Search performance under such conditions indicates that the target does not simply "pop out" of the field on the basis of some early, preattentive, detection mechanism operating in a purely bottom-up fashion. Rather, target detection involves an attentional mechanism that modifies the processing system by allocating "selection weight" to the various dimensions that potentially define the target (i.e., dimensions in which the target might differ from nontarget objects). According to the dimension-weighting account, there is a limit to the total attentional weight available to be allocated at any one time to the various dimensions of the target object, with potential target-defining dimensions being assigned weight in accordance with their instructed importance and their variability across trials. The greater the weight allocated to a particular dimension, the faster can the presence of a target defined in that dimension be discerned.

VISUAL SEARCH FOR ODD-ONE-OUT FEATURE TARGETS

It is well established that targets that differ from distractors in certain single salient attributes, or features, can be rapidly discerned irrespective of the number of items in the display (the display size). Visual features that support set size-independent search are generally assumed to be registered in parallel across the visual field. Such features are regarded as primitive image descriptors organized along a set of feature dimensions (e.g., colour and orientation). A number of feature dimensions have been shown to support parallel search, including: orientation, size, colour, stereo depth, and motion (see Wolfe, 1998, for a review).

One influential account of how salient feature differences in the field may be detected is Guided Search (GS; Cave & Wolfe, 1990; Wolfe, 1994, 1998). GS assumes that the visual field is initially represented, in parallel, as a set of basic stimulus attributes in different dimension-specific "modules" (such as colour, orientation, etc.). Each module computes saliency signals for all stimulus locations, indicating the feature contrast between one particular item, relative to the various other items represented within the same module: The more dissimilar an item is compared to the others, the greater its saliency. Maps of saliency signals are computed in parallel in all modules, and then these signals are summed onto a master map of activations. The activity on the master map guides focal attention, the most active location being sampled with priority. Focal attention gates the passage of information to higher stages of processing (visual object recognition and response systems). Thus, any odd-one-out feature target will generate a strong contrast signal within its own dimension. Even given some variability due to noise, the target's saliency signal on the master map should always be larger than those of distractor items, and attention should always be deployed first to its location.

However, recent investigations of singleton feature search under conditions in which the dimension defining the target is uncertain on a trial have produced results that are inconsistent with the assumption that saliency signals from relevant dimensions are integrated by the master map units in an equally weighted fashion.

Cross-dimension search cost

Müller et al. (1995) investigated search for singleton feature targets within and across stimulus dimensions. In their Experiment 1, search for three possible targets all defined *within* the orientation dimension (left-tilted, horizontal, and right-tilted small grey bars) was compared with search for three possible targets defined *across* three different— orientation, colour, and size—dimensions (a *right-tilted* grey small bar, a vertical *black* small bar, or a grey vertical *large* bar). The distractors in both uncertainty conditions, within- (intra-) and cross-dimension, were the same: Small grey vertical bars. There was also a no-uncertainty control condition in which the target was always known to be a small grey *right-tilted* bar among small grey vertical bars. Although search was parallel in all conditions, detection of the common right-tilted target was 60 ms slower in the cross-dimension condition relative to both the intradimension and the control condition—a considerable RT cost in view of the fast base RTs (see also Treisman, 1988, who found a 100 ms cost for cross-dimension search relative to intradimension search). That there was a RT cost only in the cross-dimension condition, but not the intradimension condition, suggests that, to detect the presence of a target, observers had to "determine" in which dimension a feature difference was present: orientation, colour, or size.

Dimension-specific intertrial transition effect

One related finding of Müller et al. (1995) was that, in cross-dimension search, there was an RT advantage for a target on a given trial if the previous trial contained a target defined in the same dimension, relative to a target defined in a different dimension—suggesting a *dimension*-specific intertrial (transition) effect. Found and Müller (1996, Exp. 1) demonstrated that the intertrial effect is indeed *dimension*-specific, rather than *feature*-specific, in nature. On positive trials, displays contained one of four possible targets: Either a left- or a *right-tilted* white bar (orientation target) or a *red* or a *blue* vertical bar (colour target). The results showed clear intertrial facilitation of 30–40 ms when consecutive trials contained targets defined in the same dimension, relative to targets defined in different dimensions. This was the case irrespective of whether a target (on trial N) was preceded by a featurally identical target (on trial $N-1$) or by a dimensionally identical, but featurally nonidentical target. For example, there was a RT advantage for a red target preceded by either a red or a blue target, relative to a preceding orientation target; but there was little (extra) advantage for a red target preceded by a red target, relative to a preceding blue target. This is consistent with the intertrial effect being dimension-specific in nature.[1]

Dimensional weighting

Müller and his colleagues (Found & Müller, 1996; Müller et al., 1995) took the cross-dimension cost and dimension-specific intertrial effects to argue for a dimension-weighting account of visual search for feature targets. Similar to visual search theories such as GS, this account assumes that attention operates on a master map of integrated (summed) saliency signals derived separately in dimension-specific input modules. However, unlike (earlier versions of) GS, intradimensional saliency processing is attentionally "weighted" prior to signal integration by the master map units. The greater the weight assigned to the target dimension, the faster the rate at which evidence for a feature difference within this dimension accumulates at the master map level. In the intradimension conditions described above, the target dimension was always constant and so weighted consistently, permitting rapid search. However, in the cross-dimension condition, the search involved a time-consuming "weight-switching" process to determine the target's dimension and render it salient at the master map level. The weight setting established in this process persists into the next trial, producing a dimension-specific RT advantage for a target defined within the same dimension as the preceding target. The crucial assumption is that there is a limit to the total attentional weight available to be allocated at any one time to the various dimensions of the target object. Potential target-defining dimensions may be assigned weight in accordance with their instructed importance (intentionally, top-down) and/or their variability across trials (automatically, bottom-up).

---

[1] Found and Müller (1996) obtained evidence of some feature-specific intertrial facilitation only for the colour-defined targets (there was a RT advantage for, say, a red target preceded by a red target, relative to a preceding blue target), but not orientation-defined targets, consistent with work on colour and orientation grouping (Nothdurft, 1993; Wolfe, Chun, & Friedman-Hill, 1995).

TOP-DOWN WEIGHTING OF DIMENSIONS

One important, and controversial, question concerns whether (and to what extent) the weighting of dimensions can be top-down modulated by knowledge- and expectation-based processes, or whether it is a stimulus-driven process that is cognitively impenetrable. There is behavioural evidence that, in simple singleton feature search tasks of the type described above ("pop-out" tasks), the target-defining attributes are determined and weighted relatively automatically, without involving deliberate (top-down) control operations. For example, Maljkovic and Nakayama (1994) reported that their observers were unable to overcome the priming of an upcoming target by the target on the previous trial(s) even when changes in target definition across trials were made entirely predictable. In (most of) Maljkovic and Nakayama's experiments, observers had to produce a form-based discrimination response to an odd-one-out colour target; the target could be, variably across trials, red amongst green distractors or green amongst red distractors. Thus, the task involved, first, detection of the differently coloured target and, second, a form-based response to that target (indicating on which side, left or right, a corner section was "cut off"). Maljkovic and Nakayama found that the form-based response was significantly expedited on a given trial when the target on preceding trials, in particular, the immediately preceding trial, was defined by the same colour. That is, there was feature-specific intertrial facilitation for colour-defined targets, consistent with Found and Müller (1995; see also footnote 1). Maljkovic and Nakayama reported further (see their Experiment 3a) that the effect could not be abolished, or reduced, by making the intertrial transition perfectly predictable, which should have permitted participants to actively set themselves for a same-coloured or a differently-coloured target relative to the target on the preceding trial. Maljkovic and Nakayama therefore characterized their intertrial facilitation effect as a passive-priming effect, reflecting the operation of a cognitively inaccessible "short-term implicit memory for the attention-focusing feature". [However, while Maljkovic and Nakayama (1994) failed to find evidence for top-down modulation of their feature repetition/change effects, Hillstrom (2000) did report evidence for top-down modulation in a variety of tasks adapted from Maljkovic and Nakayama: in particular, in her Experiment 1, Hillstrom found that "Responses were 115 msec faster, on average, to trials in the alternating sequences [of target color; i.e., AABBAABB...-sequences] than to trials in the random sequences ..., a result which reflects expectancy" (p. 803).]

On the other hand, Müller, Reimann, and Krummenacher (2003) have provided evidence that observers can modulate the dimensional weight setting in a top-down fashion. They used a trial-by-trial symbolic cueing procedure to make observers set themselves for the indicated target dimension or feature, respectively. In their Experiments 1 and 2, precueing of the likely target-defining dimension on a given trial (by the cue words "colour" or "orientation") produced RT benefits for valid-cue trials, on which the target was defined in the cued dimension, and costs for invalid-cue trials, on which the target was defined in an uncued dimension, relative to a neutral-cue condition (with the cue word "neutral"). Furthermore, the dimension-specific intertrial effects were reduced for both valid and invalid trials relative to neutral trials. However, residual intertrial effects on valid trials remained evident even when the cue indicated the target dimension with 100% validity (Experiment 2). Experiment 3 showed that, even when a specific target feature (e.g., red) was precued to be likely, while another feature in the same dimension (i.e., colour, e.g., blue) was unlikely, the cueing effects were dimension specific in nature; that is, there were benefits of the cueing even for unlikely features within the same dimension as the cued features (while there were costs only for features in a different dimension). This was the case even when a (noncued) feature within the dimension of the cued feature was extremely rare (Experiment 4).[2]

This pattern of results is consistent with the idea that observers can use the advance cue to allocate attentional weight to the likely target dimension. However, the fact that there remained a residual intertrial transition effect even with 100% valid precues suggests that top-down control processes cannot completely overcome automatic priming processes (which last for several seconds). Taken together, Müller et al. (2003) took these results to

---

[2] Consistent with this, Meeter and Theeuwes (2006) have recently reported that precueing the dimension or, respectively, feature of an upcoming target obligatorily sets the system to (all) odd-one-out stimuli defined within the precued dimension, rather than the precise feature defining the target (at the exclusion of features defining distractors). Meeter and Theeuwes presented an odd-one-out "distractor" (in a display matrix of homogeneous nontarget elements) that could be defined within either the same precued dimension as the singleton target or within a noncued dimension (same-dimension distractor, e.g., "colour"-cue, colour-defined distractor; different-dimension distractor, e.g., "colour"-cue, orientation-defined distractor). The featural identity of the distractor was fixed (e.g., the colour-defined distractor was always red), providing observers with an incentive to ignore/suppress the distractor feature—so as to be able to respond as fast as possible to the presence of a target, avoiding the standard distractor interference effect demonstrated by Theeuwes (1992). Besides a general RT cueing benefit relative to a neutral-cue condition, Meeter and Theeuwes found that a same-dimension distractor produced greater interference than a different-dimension distractor, whether the cue specified the dimension of the upcoming target or the precise target feature. For target-present trials, the distractor effects were assessed against a redundant-target condition (in which the singleton target was defined in both the colour and the orientation dimension). Yet, the results showed a pattern of distractor interference effects only relative to the cued dimension of the target. Meeter and Theeuwes took this pattern to suggest that observers can set can themselves, in top-down manner, only to the precued dimension generally, but not to specific features within this dimension.

suggest that dimension switching can operate relatively automatically, in a largely stimulus-driven manner, once the basic operating parameters are set (e.g., between which dimensions weight shifting must be carried out). However, dimension shifting may also be top-down controlled when there is an advantage, or a need, to do so.

LOCUS OF DIMENSION WEIGHTING: PREATTENTIVE OR POSTSELECTIVE?

Although the notion of dimension weighting as such is "agnostic" with respect to the locus of dimension-weighting effects, Müller and his colleagues (e.g., Found & Müller, 1996; Krummenacher, Müller, & Heller, 2001, 2002a; Müller et al., 1995) interpreted these effects as arising at a *preattentive perceptual* stage of processing: The overall-saliency map. Above-threshold activity of an overall-saliency map unit summons an attentional orienting response and may trigger a direct (manual) detection response. Furthermore, it is assumed that what is integrated at this stage are dimension-specific saliency signals which carry no information as to the precise feature(s) or dimension(s) by which a singleton feature (pop-out) target differs from the distractors. Only responses based on *explicit* target identity (i.e., feature or dimension) information require focal attention.

This interpretation has recently been challenged by Cohen and Magen (1999; Cohen & Feintuch, 2002; Cohen & Shoup, 1997, 2000; Feintuch & Cohen, 2002; see also Kumada, 1999, 2001) and Theeuwes (Mortier, Theeuwes, & Starreveld, 2005; Theeuwes, Reimann, & Mortier, 2006 this issue; see also Theeuwes, 1992, 1996; Theeuwes, Atchley, & Kramer, 2000; Theeuwes & Godijn, 2001), who argued that these effects reflect response stage processes. Although related, these challenges are subtly different and will be addressed in turn.

Cohen's challenge

The "dimensional action system" account proposed by Cohen and his colleagues (see Cohen & Feintuch, 2002, for a review) envisages dimensional modules, each consisting of a set of spatiotopically organized feature maps, which have separate response selection devices. The dimensional response units, which represent *feature*-based decisions, are mutually inhibitory, so that one response must win the competition to be transferred to the central response execution stage. With multiple stimuli in the display, such as in the "flanker" paradigm used by Cohen and Shoup (1997), multiple (incompatible) response units may be activated in parallel by the central target and the flanking stimuli, respectively. To resolve the ensuing competition, spatial attention must be focused on the task-critical, central, stimulus for its associated response to win the competition. That is, the mechanism by which a dimensional response decision unit is "assigned" to a specific stimulus is *location*-based attention.

This account makes a strong prediction, namely: With targets redundantly defined in multiple dimensions (e.g., a single *red* and *right-tilted* target amongst green vertical distractors), coactivation of the central response execution stage by separate dimensional response decision units (in the example, colour and orientation) is possible only within the focus of attention (Feintuch & Cohen, 2002). This prediction was recently examined by Krummenacher et al. (2002a, Exp. 3), who presented observers with a single dimensionally redundant target either within a spatially precued ($p = .8$) or an uncued ($p = .2$) region of the search display. While there was a significant cueing effect (i.e., expedited detection of targets within the cued region), detection responses were found to be "coactivated" by dimensionally redundant targets in *uncued* as well as *cued* display regions; that is, detection RTs to redundant targets were found to violate Miller's (1982) "race model inequality" (RMI) irrespective of whether a target appeared inside or outside the attended region. This pattern of results suggests that the integration of dimensionally redundant target signals occurs *independently of* and *prior to* the allocation of spatial attention, providing a challenge to response-based accounts that assume a critical role of spatial attention for the integration of response unit activity in separate dimensions.

An alternative, response-based account, which does not assume a critical role for spatial attention (e.g., Mordkoff & Yantis, 1993), might conceive of the dimensional response devices as units that pool activity across target-relevant feature maps (e.g., Treisman, 1988). That is, an activated dimensional response unit would indicate the presence of an odd-one-out stimulus in the corresponding dimension, but not carry information as to its location. (If it were carrying location information, the response-based account would become indistinguishable from the account of Müller and his colleagues, whose dimension-specific saliency map units might be regarded as location-specific "response selection devices".) Consequently, equivalent redundancy gains should arise with single targets redundantly defined in two dimensions (e.g., a single *red and right-tilted* target amongst green vertical distractors) and dual targets each defined in a different dimension (e.g., one *red* vertical target and one green *right-tilted* target amongst green vertical distractors), and the gains with dual targets should be independent of their spatial separation. In both cases, and for all separations, the dimensional response units would be activated to the same extent, so that the redundant-target effects should exhibit no difference. At variance with this prediction, Krummenacher et al. (2002a, Exp. 2) found that the redundant-target gains decreased as a function of the target signals' separations. That is: The integration of the target signals in separate dimensions is *location-specific*, which challenges the alternative response-based account.

Note that Krummenacher et al. (2001) had provided evidence that the integration of dimensionally redundant target signals is subject to intertrial effects. An analysis of doublets of repeated targets (with the first target being dimensionally different to the preceding target) revealed (1) expedited RTs to the second redundant target, R R, relative to the first redundant target, R R, and (2) more robust violations of the race model inequality for the second redundant target, R R (compared to the second colour, C C, and the second orientation target, O O), relative to the first redundant target, R R (compared to the first colour, C C, and the first orientation target, O O). This pattern of results argues that the integration stage is modulated by dimension-specific intertrial effects. In terms of the dimension weighting account, the first redundant target adjusts (i.e., equalizes) the weights so as to optimize the integration of the target signals from the two dimensions.

The implication for the present findings (in particular, the dimension-based modulation of the intertrial effects by symbolic dimension and feature cueing) is as follows. Given that the coactivation effects arise at a preattentive stage and are subject to intertrial effects, the intertrial effects themselves must operate at a preattentive level. Consequently, the modulation of the intertrial effects demonstrated in the present study may be interpreted as a top-down modulation of a preattentive processing stage.

Theeuwes' challenge

A somewhat different, but related, challenge to the present findings was provided by Theeuwes (personal communication, 30 October, 2001; Mortier et al., 2005; Theeuwes et al., 2006 this issue). Although he accepts the existence of the cueing effects revealed in the study of Müller et al. (2003), he does not agree that "that these data show any top-down modulation on the speed with which the target is *detected*". Instead, he argues, "that knowing for what you are searching (by means of a cue) will facilitate the speed with which one can give a response *after the target has been detected*", that is, "after the target was selected" (personal communication). In the words of Theeuwes (1992, p. 605): "knowing the task-relevant stimulus feature might speed up the identification of an item that has already been selected"; "in other words, after entering the second [attentional] stage of processing, less sensory evidence is required to decide whether an item is a target or a distractor" (e.g., Broadbent's, 1970, 1982, "response set").

These statements are based on Theeuwes' (1992) strong claim that the parallel stage of overall-saliency computation is top-down impenetrable. This claim rests on his finding that, in a search task for a shape-defined singleton in which observers had to respond to the orientation of a line within the target shape (i.e., the task was a "compound" task in terms of Duncan, 1985, in that target detection was based on a separate attribute to the response), a task-irrelevant colour-defined singleton distractor caused interference (i.e., tended to capture attention)—even after extended practice (some 2000 trials). Importantly, the colour singleton was more salient than the shape singleton, and interference was found only when the distractor salience was greater than the target salience (i.e., there was no interference when the target was colour-defined and the distractor shape-defined). With respect to the dimension weighting account, Theeuwes (personal communication) asks: Why, in the above task, was not all selection weight allocated to target shape, in order to effectively filter out the colour distractor? Concerning this question, Müller et al. (1995) argued that the weight is never set to zero for a given dimension; to do so would be maladaptive, as a singleton signal in a—for the current task—"irrelevant" dimension would then go completely undetected, even though it might provide an important warning ("interrupt") signal for another, survival-relevant task to be performed with priority. If this assumption is correct, then, given that the colour distractor was more salient than the shape target, its saliency signal would have become available faster (at least on some fraction of the trials) within the colour dimension and, as a consequence, at the overall saliency stage. Consequently, the colour distractor may have attracted attention before the colour target, producing interference. [Consistent with this, Theeuwes, Kramer, Hahn, Irwin, and Zelinsky (1999) found that, in an eye movement task in which observers had to make a speeded saccade to the target, only a *fraction* (some 30–40%) of *first* saccades were misdirected to the distractor (these saccades were fast and followed by a short latency prior to a corrective saccade to the target), indicative of attention capture by the distractor.]

To decide between the preattentive and postselective accounts of dimension-based effects (cross-dimension cost, dimension-specific intertrial effect, top-down modification of these effects) in singleton feature search, Mortier et al. (2005) examined whether similar effects would also be found in a "nonsearch" task, in which there was only one element in the display.

For example, in their Experiment 1, they compared a standard singleton feature search task, in which observers had to discern the presence of a target in a array of distractors/nontargets (presence/absence decision), with a nonsearch task, in which there was only a single stimulus and observers had to indicate whether this stimulus was a target or a nontarget (identity decision). Both tasks were performed under within- and cross-dimension conditions. In the within-conditions, possible targets were a *red*, a yellow, or a green circle; nontargets were grey circles (a single grey circle in the nonsearch task). In the cross-conditions, possible targets were a *red* circle (colour target), a grey triangle (shape target), or a large grey circle (size target), and nontargets were grey circles. Stimuli (targets and distractor stimuli in the search task, the single stimulus in the nonsearch task) were presented at positions on an imaginary circle around a central fixation cross. The only significant effect was a main effect of condition: RTs to the common, red target were slower for cross- relative to within-conditions, not only for the search task, but also for the nonsearch task. This cross-dimension cost in the nonsearch task was confirmed in Experiment 2, in which the single stimulus was always presented in the display centre (to remove any uncertainty concerning the critical stimulus location).[3]

Two further experiments revealed dimension-based intertrial and cueing effects in a nonsearch task with a single central stimulus, in agreement with those reported by Müller et al. (2003) for standard singleton search tasks. For example, in Experiment 3, the cues to the likely target dimension ($p = .8$) were the words "colour" or "shape", respectively, and the targets could be either a red or a green circle (colour targets) or either a grey triangle or a grey square (shape targets); the nontarget was a grey circle. There was a significant cueing effect, for both colour and shape targets. In addition, for valid-cue trials, there was an intertrial effect: Expedited RTs when the target on trial n was defined within the same, as compared to a different, dimension as the target on trial $n-1$. Mortier et al. (2005, p. 544) concluded from these findings that "effects that typically have been attributed to early top-down modulation of visual search processes may

---

[3] In this context, it is worth noting that Müller and O'Grady (2000) have already shown that performance in a nonsearch task, even with only a single stimulus object in the display, is dependent on dimensional processing limitations. In the study of Müller and O'Grady, stimulus displays were presented briefly (for less than 50 ms) and then masked, and the emphasis was on response accuracy, rather than RT. Yet, essentially the same cross-dimension cost was obtained, even when there was only one object in the display. In the latter case, the task required observers to judge one-and-the-same object in terms of dual colour (saturation *and* hue) or dual form (line size *and* texture)—that is, *within*-dimension—judgements or in terms of one colour (saturation *or* hue) and one form (line size *or* texture)—that is, *cross*-dimension—judgements (e.g., hue *and* texture). Judgement accuracy was reduced for cross-dimension, relative to within-dimension, judgements (essentially the same cross-dimension cost was obtained when judgements were to be directed to two separate objects, though in this case there was an additional object-based effect). Judgements/responses were made by observers mouse-clicking one of several visually displayed response alternatives (click panels, presented 1033 ms after display termination): The panel that matched the perceived (to-be-reported) stimulus properties (i.e., observers had to select the appropriate panel, move the mouse cursor there, and click it—without any time pressure). Response-selection processes (i.e., processes that select a response appropriate to the information derived from the brief displays) were unlikely to be a performance-limiting factor in this situation. Rather, the finding of cross-dimensional cost effects in this condition argues that these effects arise at a perceptual "locus" of stimulus processing.

represent effects that occur later in processing possibly related to response selection processes".

However, this conclusion is based on only a "partial" understanding of the dimension-weighting account, which assumes that, when the task requires processing of (or discrimination within) a particular dimension, the mechanisms that process this dimension are "attentionally weighted" and these weights persist across trials.

In visual search, the task requires target detection and, possibly, localization to analyse the target further. Thus, in singleton search tasks, the priming would influence mechanisms that support target detection and localization, that is, mechanisms that compute target–distractor contrast. In "nonsearch" tasks of the kind used by Mortier et al. (2005), the demand on these mechanisms may be minimal, though they would still be involved to some extent. Even if it is known exactly where the critical stimulus is going to appear (so that spatial attention can be directed in advance to its location), its appearance in the display still needs to be discerned before the stimulus can be analysed further. With single items, it is stimulus–background contrast (rather than target–distractor contrast) that is important for discerning stimulus presence. A "saliency" signal would be computed even in this case (at least, this would be assumed by most models of saliency signal computation; e.g., Itti, personal communication, 4 February, 2004; Itti, & Koch, 2001), and the computation would be subject to the same (dimension-specific) influences that also operate in (search) tasks requiring target–distractor discrimination.

However, while in a search task, it would be sufficient to respond on the basis of the presence of an above-threshold saliency signal, this would not suffice in the nonsearch task—in which the stimulus would need to be analysed further to be compared against memorized target or, respectively, nontarget descriptions. That is, the task requires identity analysis, which, on the dimension-weighting account, requires focal attention. In the cross-dimension task, the comparison required involves checking of potential target dimensions. Now assume that, in order to determine that the stimulus presented matches a target description or deviates from the nontarget description, the relevant dimension needs to be weighted (processed) attentionally and that this weight setting is carried over onto the next trial (so that there is a bias towards commencing processing of the next stimulus with the same dimensional "bias"). This would expedite both target detection and any subsequent identity analysis. Accordingly, the patterns of effects demonstrated by Mortier et al. (2005) are perfectly consistent with the dimension-weighting account.

The above account, in terms of dimension weighting, predicts that, when target identity needs to be analysed in addition to simple detection of its presence, the cross-dimension and intertrial effects are increased. Müller,

Krummenacher, and Heller (2004) have recently obtained evidence to this effect. They compared two cross-dimension search tasks in which observers had to encode either the target feature or target dimension (for possible later report) to a task in which simple detection of a target was sufficient to produce a search task response (independent groups of observers). In the "encode" conditions, the RTs were some 50 ms slower than in the "nonencode" condition (500 ms vs. 450 ms; significant), while the dimension-specific intertrial effects were increased (51 ms vs. 35 ms; significant). This is consistent with the idea that the "depth" of analysis of the target dimension that is required by the task determines the amount of weight allocated to this dimension (i.e., deeper processing requires greater weight).

In summary, it remains an open issue whether the patterns of effects described by Müller et al. (2004) and replicated by Mortier et al. (2005) with a nonsearch task arise at a perceptual or a response-related processing stage. The mere fact that similar effects arise under both search and nonsearch conditions is not conclusive with respect to this issue.

In another empirical attempt to decide between preattentive and postselective accounts of dimension-based effects, Theeuwes et al. (2006 this issue) compared top-down (cueing) effects in a standard singleton feature search and a "compound" task. In both tasks, the target was uniquely defined in either the colour or the shape dimension. In the standard search task (Experiment 1), observers gave a RT response to the detection of a singleton target. In contrast, in the compound task (Experiment 2), observers gave a two-alternative forced-choice response to the orientation of a line presented within the boundary contour of the singleton target; in other words, the response-relevant information was different from the information on which target detection was based (i.e., the "response set" shared no "features" with the "selective" set underlying target detection). Top-down effects on singleton detection were examined by presenting observers with a symbolic precue indicating the likely dimension, "colour" or "shape", in which the odd-one-out target was defined (83% of the cues were valid). This precue condition was compared to a neutral condition in which targets were equally likely to be defined by an odd-one-out colour or shape.

Theeuwes et al. (2006 this issue) found significant overall cueing effects (i.e., benefits for validly cued targets and costs for invalid targets, relative to the neutral condition) only for the simple-detection task, but not the compound task. Furthermore, there were significant intertrial effects (i.e., expedited RTs to target n when it was defined in the same, rather than a different, dimension to the preceding target $n-1$ in both tasks); these intertrial effects were, however, less marked with the compound task than with the simple simple-detection task (consistent with Krummenacher, Müller, & Heller, 2002b) and they were not significantly influenced by cue validity (i.e., they were not reduced for valid- as compared to neutral-cue trials, at variance with Müller et al., 2003).

Theeuwes et al. (2006 this issue) concluded that, in the simple-detection task, the cueing effects arise at a postselective, response-related stage of processing. Their argument is as follows: Given that the targets were detected by the same (preattentive) mechanisms, then why should there be a cueing effect only in the simple-detection task, but not the compound task? Since the two tasks differ only in terms of the information on which the response is based, the manifestation of a cueing effect in only the simple-detection task suggests that the effect arises at a response-related stage of processing, that is, the response decision (rather than target detection) is expedited when the target is defined within the precued (likely) dimension. In contrast, Theeuwes et al. took the finding of significant intertrial effects in both tasks to suggest that these effects arise at the preattentive (detection) stage, which (as the intertrial effects were not modulated by the precueing) is not top-down penetrable.

However, while this pattern of findings is theoretically interesting, there are at least two questions that remain unanswered. These questions will be addressed in turn below.

The first question concerns the lack of an overall cueing effect in the compound task (note, though, that there was a tendency towards an effect). This lack of an effect might simply be due to this task being more complex than the simple-detection task. Because of this, observers may not have attempted to (consistently) set themselves to the cued dimension (given that the target would "pop out" eventually by itself, use of the cue was not necessary to perform the task). To examine this possibility, we repeated the compound task of Theeuwes et al. (2006 this issue), but provided observers with an extra incentive to use the cue (see Appendix for details). The target was a singleton element amongst eight green-outline distractor circles, defined either by colour (the only *red* circle) or by shape (the only green *diamond*). All stimuli contained an oriented white bar inside, tilted randomly to either the left or the right (see Figure 1). Observers had to indicate the tilt direction of bar inside the target stimulus (left-tilted =left-hand response, right-tilted =right-hand response). In one condition, 10 observers were presented with a central symbolic dimension precue, the words "colour" or "shape", which indicated the likely target dimension on a given trial ($p =$ .80); the cue duration was 500 ms, and the cue–target SOA was 1000 ms. Observers were fully informed of the cue validity and instructed to make use of the cues. To ensure that observers actually attempted to so, they had to rate, at the end of each trial block, how well they had set themselves in response to the cue (rating scale, from 0 ="did not use cue" to 3 ="used cue consistently")—the mean rating was about 2.4 ($SD =0.5$, range $=2–3$). Performance in these (blocked) precue conditions was compared with that

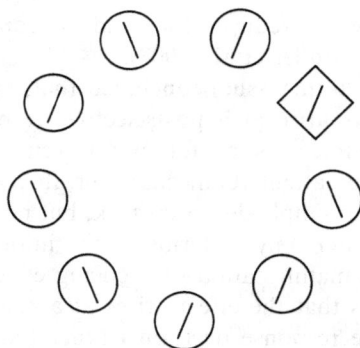

Figure 1.   Schematic depiction of the search display as used in the cueing experiments. The diamond shape (upper right) is the to-be-identified target: the shapes containing a right-tilted line indicate a right-button press.

under (blocked) neutral-cueing conditions in which the cue word was "neutral" (indicating that colour- and shape-defined targets were equally likely). In another condition, 10 different observers were presented with a direct precue in the display centre, either a red circle or a green diamond, indicating the likely target stimulus on a given trial; in neutral-trial blocks, the cue was a green circle (actually symbolizing a distractor: Same shape as colour cue, same colour as shape cue). In all other respects, the procedure was the same as in the symbolic-cueing condition. Mean cue compliance rating was 2.2 ($SD = 0.6$, range $= 1-3$).

Using the above "incentive" to pay attention to the cue (i.e., to be able to give a high rating of "compliance" with the task instruction), the results, presented in Figure 2, revealed cueing RT costs-plus-benefits (i.e., an RT difference between invalid- and valid-cue trials) of around 11 ms in the compound task. Although the cueing effect was numerically only about 11 ms, a mixed ANOVA with the factors cue condition (between-subject: Symbolic, direct) and cue validity (within-subject: Valid, invalid, neutral) revealed the main effect of cue validity, $F(2, 36) = 6.62$, $p < .004$; 558.1 (valid) vs. 568.7 (invalid) vs. 563.6 ms (neutral) to be significant. Planned t-tests conducted separately for the symbolic- and the direct-cue conditions revealed the costs-plus-benefits to be significant with both symbolic (9.3 ms), $t = -2.295$, $p < .0235$) and direct cues (11.9 ms), $t = -3.651$, $p < .0025$. Furthermore, there was no significant difference in the magnitude of the cueing effects between the two types of cue (i.e., the two-way interaction was nonsignificant), $F(2, 36) < 1$; main effect of cue condition, $F(1, 18) < 1$.

This pattern of results indicates that *significant* effects of symbolic dimension cueing can be obtained with compound tasks (see also Theeuwes et al., 2006 this issue, who reported nonsignificant costs-plus-benefits of

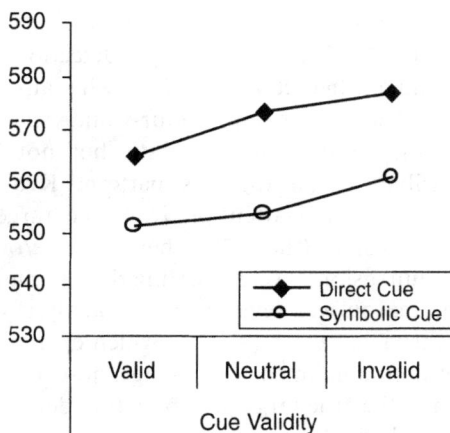

Figure 2. Results of the "compliance with the cue" rating conducted following the cueing experiment.

9 ms for the compound task when observers had to retain a memory of the cue), and that the cueing effects may be as large with symbolic precues as with direct precues (but see Theeuwes et al., 2006 this issue, who reported larger effects with direct cues). The significant effects of symbolic cueing in the compound task challenge the argument of Theeuwes et al. that top-down effects can arise only at a postselective, response-related stage of processing. At the very least, the finding of compound-task effects would leave it open where the effects arise: At a preattentive, perceptual or at a postselective, response-related stage of processing. [Further analyses revealed small, but significant intertrial effects, of 5 and 8 ms under symbolic and direct cueing conditions, respectively, but these effects were not significantly influenced by cue validity (valid- vs. neutral-cue trials: 5 vs. 7 ms). A mixed ANOVA with the between-subject factor cue condition (symbolic, direct) and the within-subject factors cue validity (valid, neutral), target feature (colour, form), and intertrial transition (same, different dimension) revealed the main effect of intertrial transition to be significant, $F(1, 18) = 33.101$, $p < .001$, while the Cue validity $\times$ Intertrial transition interaction was nonsignificant, $F(1, 18) < 1$. However, given the small size of the overall cueing effects (of some 11 ms), such a cue-dependent modulation may be difficult to demonstrate.]

A second question concerns why the intertrial effects (as well as the cueing effects) were greatly reduced in the compound task relative to the simple-detection task: 9 vs. 34 ms in the study of Theeuwes et al. (2006 this issue). [It is not clear how Theeuwes et al. explain this difference, given that they assume that both tasks involve the same preattentive (priming) mechanisms that give rise to the intertrial effects.] A reduction in the magnitude of the intertrial effects in compound relative to simple-detection tasks was reported previously by Krummenacher et al. (2002b), who also found that these effects were asymmetrical between colour- and shape-defined targets (significant effects for colour-defined targets, but not for shape-defined targets). As a possible reason for this pattern, Krummenacher et al. considered the need to switch attention from the target-defining to the response-relevant dimension (the latter being shape/orientation), which might influence the dimensional weight setting determining target detection.

Another possible reason was revealed in a reanalysis of the compound-task data of Krummenacher et al. (2002b), which examined the effects of a change in the target-defining dimension (change, no-change) contingent on a change in the response (i.e., the target attribute that determined the response hand) (change vs. no-change).

Interestingly, the results, illustrated in Figure 3A, revealed a significant interaction between these two factors, $F(1, 15) = 15.74$, $p < .001$, as follows: There was a dimension change cost (i.e., a disadvantage for a dimension change relative to a no-change) on trial n only when the target attribute that determined the response hand did not change from trial $n-1$ to trial n. However, this effect was abolished (or tended to be reversed) when the response attribute changed. This pattern was also evident in the dimension-cueing experiment reported above (see Figure 3B), $F(1, 9) = 20.541$, $p < .001$, and it was replicated by Pollmann, Weidner, Müller, Maertens, and von Cramon (2006a), who required observers to make alternative responses

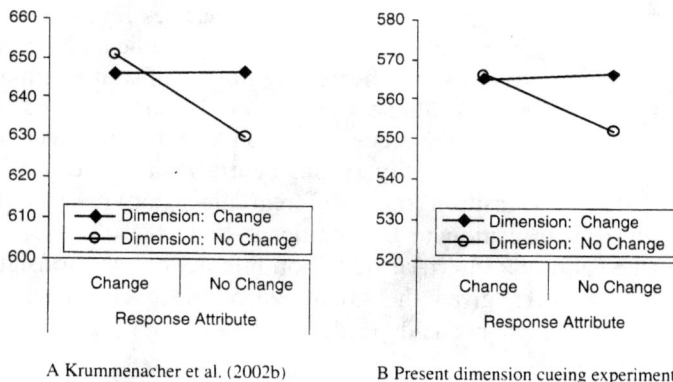

A Krummenacher et al. (2002b)   B Present dimension cueing experiment

Figure 3. Mean target-present RTs in trials N separately for four intertrial transition conditions relative to trials $N-1$. The response-hand condition is shown on the abscissa with response changes in panel A and no response change (i.e., the response is given with the same hand in both trials N and $N-1$) in panel B. Changes (and nonchanges, respectively) of the target-defining dimension are given in separate lines.

using the index and middle fingers of their right hand (see also Hillstrom, 2000; Hommel, 1998; Kingstone, 1992; Lockhead, Gruenewald, & King, 1978). This pattern suggests that, although, statistically, there is no correlation between the two types of change (target-defining dimension, response attribute), the processing system "assumes" there is one. If the target dimension (the task attribute that becomes available first) remains unchanged, then the system implicitly assumes that the attribute on which the response is based will stay the same, too; that is, the unchanged response will be facilitated, and there is a cost if the response attribute actually changes. In contrast, if the dimension changes, the system cancels any prior assumption as to the response to the response attribute to be expected, and starts processing from scratch. This is, perhaps, the most appropriate account of the pattern found by Pollmann et al. (2006a) and in the above dimension-cueing experiment (where there was no significant difference between response attribute change and no-change conditions when the dimension changed).

Whatever the explanation, the overall intertrial effects in compound tasks are reduced because of some (in terms of event statistics wholly unsupported) linkage between dimension and response changes. This linkage may exist because, for the system, it may be easier to change both task "parameters", dimension and response, than to change just one parameter (see Hillstrom, 2000, and Kingstone, 1992, for similar arguments). In any case, the interaction revealed in compound-task studies strongly suggests that the central assumption implicitly made by Theeuwes et al. (2006 this issue), namely, that the processes of dimensional selection (assumed to be preattentive, perceptual) and of response selection (assumed to be post-selective) are independent of each other, is not tenable. Given this, the use of a compound task will not permit perceptual and response-related processes to be disentangled in any simple and straightforward manner. [Similar arguments would apply to explaining why overall cueing effects are reduced in compound tasks, and why valid cueing does not reliably reduce the intertrial effects for valid- relative to neutral-cueing conditions.]

In summary, effects of symbolic dimension cueing may also be found with compound tasks (albeit of reduced magnitude relative to simple detection tasks), suggesting top-down modifiability of preattentive target selection mechanisms—at variance with Theeuwes et al. (2006 this issue). The fact that the cueing effects are reduced with compound tasks may be, at least in part, explained by implicit linkages the system makes between the information required for target and response selection, respectively. Thus, the compound-task findings do not rule out that dimensional weighting, including the top-down modulation of the weight setting, operates at an early, perceptual stage of processing, as assumed by the dimension-weighting account.

Evidence from functional imaging

Similar to the "early vs. late selection" debate, behavioural evidence alone may not be sufficient to answer the question of whether the dimensional weighting effects arise at early perceptual or later response-based stages of processing. In situations such as these, neuroscience data may be able to resolve the issue. Consistent with a perceptual interpretation, there is evidence from functional imaging studies that dimensional weighting modulates neuronal activity in extrastriate visual areas involved in the processing of features of the respective dimensions, and thus the early saliency signal computation in dimension-specific visual input modules. For example, Corbetta, Miezin, Dobmeier, Shulman, and Petersen (1991) compared two conditions. In the first, observers could allocate their "undivided" attention to a constant dimension, such as motion. In contrast, in the second, "divided attention" baseline, condition, observers could not predict the target dimension (form, colour, or motion) with certainty. Corbetta et al. found that, when observers could consistently allocate their attention to a single dimension, the neural activity in the task-relevant cortical processing area (e.g., V5 in the case of motion) was increased relative to the baseline condition. Pollmann, Weidner, Müller, and von Cramon (2006b this issue; see also Pollmann, Weidner, Müller, & von Cramon, 2000; Pollmann et al., 2006a; Weidner, Pollmann, Müller, & von Cramon, 2002) have recently confirmed this finding in an fMRI study of cross-dimension singleton search, in which the target was defined by either colour or motion (direction). An analysis of trial "epochs" with successive targets defined in the same dimension revealed tonically increased activation in posterior fusiform gyrus (which contains human area V4) for colour target epochs and, respectively, in lateral occipital cortex (which contains the hMT+ complex) for motion target epochs. This represents a dimension-specific "memory" that biases the system towards detecting signals in the respective dimension (i.e., signals in this dimension tend to reach threshold faster, either due to a baseline shift or a greater gain in activation). Traditionally (e.g., in Desimone & Duncan's, 1995, biased-competition model), such modulations of neuronal activity in extrastriate visual processing areas have been interpreted in terms of perceptual selection, rather than response selection (though decision and response related processes may, of course, also be affected). Consistent with this, Pollmann et al. (2005, 2006b this issue) observed these modulations even in compound tasks, where the response to be executed was independent of the colour or motion attributes of the target.

CONCLUSION

In summary, there are good grounds, based on both behavioural and neuroimaging studies, to argue that the dimensional effects reviewed in the present study arise largely at a preattentive stage of processing, even though contributions by a postselective stage are not ruled out (see also Krummenacher et al., 2002a).

One further point is important: Even if Cohen and Theeuwes were correct and the dimensional cueing effects originate entirely at a postselective stage of processing, it would still have to be explained why the effects are (predominantly) dimension-specific, rather than feature-specific, in nature. That is, why should the target-defining *dimension* be more important at the postselective stage than the target-defining *feature*? Arguably, one might expect the opposite, as "dimensions" are conceptual abstractions, whereas "features" are phenomenal givens. To accommodate these findings, the Theeuwes account would have to be extended to include (to-be-specified) postselective mechanisms that give rise to the dimension specificity of the cueing effects demonstrated in the present study. In contrast, the dimension-weighting account assumes that these effects arise from top-down modulation of a preattentive stage, dimension-specific saliency computation—that is, a stage that is incorporated in mainstream theories of visual search (such as GS).

REFERENCES

Allport, D. A. (1971). Parallel encoding within and between elementary stimulus dimensions. *Perception and Psychophysics, 10*, 104–108.

Allport, D. A. (1980). Attention and performance. In G. Claxton (Ed.), *Cognitive psychology: New directions* (pp. 112–153). London: Routledge & Kegan Paul.

Broadbent, D. E. (1970). Stimulus and response set: Two kinds of selective attention. In D. Mostofsky (Ed.), *Attention: Contemporary theories and analysis* (pp. 51–60). New York: Appleton Century Crofts.

Broadbent, D. E. (1982). Task combination and selective intake of information. *Acta Psychologica, 50*, 253–290.

Cave, K. R., & Wolfe, J. M. (1990). Modelling the role of parallel processing in visual search. *Cognitive Psychology, 22*, 225–271.

Cohen, A., & Feintuch, U. (2002). The dimensional-action system: A distinct visual system. In W. Prinz & B. Hommel (Eds.), *Attention and performance: XIX. Common mechanisms in perception and action* (pp. 587–608). Oxford, UK: Oxford University Press.

Cohen, A., & Magen, H. (1999). Intra- and cross-dimensional visual search for single feature targets. *Perception and Psychophysics, 61*, 291–307.

Cohen, A., & Shoup, R. (1997). Perceptual dimensional constraints on response selection processes. *Cognitive Psychology, 32*, 128–181.

Cohen, A., & Shoup, R. (2000). Response selection processes for conjunctive targets. *Journal of Experimental Psychology: Human Perception and Performance, 26*, 391–411.

Corbetta, M., Miezin, F. M., Dobmeyer, S., Shulman, G. L., & Petersen, S. E. (1991). Selective and divided attention during visual discriminations of shape, colour and speed: Functional anatomy by positron emission tomography. *Journal of Neuroscience, 11*, 2382–2402.

Desimone, R., & Duncan, J. (1995). Neural mechanisms of selective visual attention. *Annual Review of Neuroscience, 18*, 193–222.

Duncan, J. (1984). Selective attention and the organization of visual information. *Journal of Experimental Psychology: General, 113*, 501–517.

Duncan, J. (1985). Visual search and visual attention. In M. Posner & O. Marin (Eds.), *Attention and performance XI* (pp. 85–106). Hillsdale, NJ: Lawrence Erlbaum Associates, Inc.

Feintuch, U., & Cohen, A. (2002). Visual attention and co-activation of response decisions for features from different dimensions. *Psychological Science, 13*, 361–369.

Found, A. P., & Müller, H. J. (1996). Searching for feature targets on more than one dimension: Investigating a dimension weighting account. *Perception and Psychophysics, 58*, 88–101.

Hillstrom, A. P. (2000). Repetition effects in visual search. *Perception and Psychophysics, 62*, 800–817.

Hommel, B. (1998). Automatic stimulus–response translation in dual-task performance. *Journal of Experimental Psychology: Human Perception and Performance, 24*, 1368–1384.

Itti, L., & Koch, C. (2001). Computational modeling of visual attention. *Nature Neuroscience Reviews, 2*, 194–203.

Kingstone, A. (1992). Combining expectancies. *Quarterly Journal of Experimental Psychology, 44A*, 69–104.

Krummenacher, J., Müller, H. J., & Heller, D. (2001). Visual search for dimensionally redundant pop-out targets: Evidence for parallel-coactive processing of dimensions. *Perception and Psychophysics, 63*, 901–917.

Krummenacher, J., Müller, H. J., & Heller, D. (2002a). Visual search for dimensionally redundant pop-out targets: Parallel-coactive processing of dimensions is location-specific. *Journal of Experimental Psychology: Human Perception and Performance, 28*, 1302–1322.

Krummenacher, J., Müller, H. J., & Heller, D. (2002b). Visual search for dimensionally redundant pop-out targets: Redundancy gains in compound tasks. *Visual Cognition, 9*, 801–837.

Kumada, T. (1999). Limitations in attending to a feature value for overriding stimulus-driven interference. *Perception and Psychophysics, 61*, 61–79.

Kumada, T. (2001). Feature-based control of attention: Evidence for two forms of dimensional weighting. *Perception and Psychophysics, 63*, 698–708.

Lockhead, G. R., Gruenewald, P., & King, M. (1978). Holistic vs. attribute repetition effects in classifying stimuli. *Memory and Cognition, 6*, 438–445.

Maljkovic, V., & Nakayama, K. (1994). Priming of pop-out: I. Role of features. *Memory and Cognition, 22*, 657–672.

Meeter, M., & Theeuwes, J. (2006). Cueing the dimension of a distractor: Verbal cues of target identity also benefit same-dimension singleton distractors. *Psychonomic Bulletin and Review, 13*, 118–124.

Miller, J. (1982). Divided attention: Evidence for co-activation with redundant signals. *Cognitive Psychology, 14*, 247–279.

Mordkoff, J. T., & Yantis, S. (1993). Dividing attention between color and shape: Evidence of co-activation. *Perception and Psychophysics, 53*, 357–366.

Mortier, K., Theeuwes, J., & Starreveld, P. (2005). Response selection modulates visual search within and across dimensions. *Journal of Experimental Psychology: Human Perception and Performance, 31*, 542–557.

Müller, H. J., Heller, D., & Ziegler, J. (1995). Visual search for singleton feature targets within and across feature dimensions. *Perception and Psychophysics, 57*, 1–17.

Müller. H. J., Krummenacher, J., & Heller, D. (2004). Dimension-specific intertrial facilitation in visual search for pop-out targets: Evidence for a top-down modulable visual short-term memory effect. *Visual Cognition*, *11*, 577–602.

Müller. H. J., & O'Grady, R. B. (2000). Dimension-based visual attention modulates dual-judgment accuracy in Duncan's (1984) one- versus two-object report paradigm. *Journal of Experimental Psychology: Human Perception and Performance*, *26*, 1332–1351.

Müller, H. J., Reimann, B., & Krummenacher, J. (2003). Stimulus-driven and expectancy-driven effects in dimensional weighting. *Journal of Experimental Psychology: Human Perception and Performance*, *29*, 1021–1035.

Nothdurft, H. C. (1993). The role of features in preattentive vision: Comparison of orientation, motion and color cues. *Vision Research*, *33*, 1937–1993.

Pollmann, S., Weidner, R., Müller, H. J., & von Cramon, D. Y. (2000). A fronto-posterior network involved in visual dimension changes. *Journal of Cognitive Neuroscience*, *12*, 480–494.

Pollmann, S., Weidner, R., Müller, H. J., Maertens, M., & von Cramon, D. Y. (2006a). Selective and interactive neural correlates of visual dimension changes and response changes. *NeuroImage*, *30*, 254–265.

Pollmann, S., Weidner, R., Müller, H. J., & von Cramon, D. Y. (2006b). Neural correlates of visual dimension weighting. *Visual Cognition*, *14*, 877–897.

Theeuwes, J. (1992). Perceptual selectivity for color and form. *Perception and Psychophysics*, *51*, 599–606.

Theeuwes, J. (1996). Perceptual selectivity for color and form: On the nature of the interference effect. In A. F. Kramer & M. G. H. Coles (Eds.), *Converging operations in the study of visual selective attention* (pp. 297–314). Washington, DC: American Psychological Association.

Theeuwes, J., Atchley, P., & Kramer, A. F. (2000). On the time course of bottom-up and top-down control of visual attention. In S. Monsell & J. Driver (Eds.), *Attention and performance: XVIII. Control of cognitive performance* (pp. 357–376). Cambridge, MA: MIT Press.

Theeuwes, J., & Godijn, R. (2001). Attentional and oculomotor capture. In C. L. Folk & B. S. Gibson (Eds.), *Attraction, distraction, and action: Multiple perspectives on attentional capture* (pp. 121–150). Amsterdam: Elsevier Science/North Holland.

Theeuwes, J., Kramer, A. F., Hahn, S., Irwin, D. E., & Zelinsky, G. J. (1999). Influence of attentional capture on oculomotor control. *Journal of Experimental Psychology: Human Perception and Performance*, *25*, 1595–1608.

Theeuwes, J., Reimann, B., & Mortier, K. (2006). Visual search for featural singletons: No top-down modulation, only bottom-up priming. *Visual Cognition*, *14*, 466–489.

Treisman, A. (1969). Strategies and models of selective attention. *Psychological Review*, *76*, 282–299.

Treisman, A. (1988). Features and objects: The fourteenth Bartlett Memorial Lecture. *Quarterly Journal of Experimental Psychology*, *40A*, 201–236.

Weidner, R., Pollmann, S., Müller, H. J., & von Cramon, D. Y. (2002). Top-down controlled visual dimension weighting: An event-related fMRI study. *Cerebral Cortex*, *12*, 318–328.

Wolfe, J. M. (1994). Guided Search 2.0: A revised model of visual search. *Psychonomic Bulletin and Review*, *1*, 202–238.

Wolfe, J. M. (1998). Visual search. In H. Pashler (Ed.), *Attention* (pp. 13–74). Hove, UK: Psychology Press.

Wolfe, J. M., Chun, M. M., & Friedman-Hill, S. R. (1995). Making use of texton gradients: Visual search and perceptual grouping exploit the same parallel processes in different ways. In T. V. Papathomas & C. Chubb (Eds.), *Early vision and beyond* (pp. 189–197). Cambridge, MA: MIT Press.

APPENDIX

Participants

Twenty observers (14 female, 6 male), with ages ranging between 21 and 32 (average 25.4) years, participated in the experiment; 10 of the observer were randomly assigned to the symbolic-cue condition, the other 10 to the direct-cue condition. All observers reported normal vision (including colour vision). Observers were paid at a rate of €7.50 per hour.

Apparatus

Search displays were presented on a 17-inch Sony 17 Trinitron colour monitor controlled by IBM-compatible VGA graphics board. The chromatically coloured (red and green) display items were isoluminant at 3.7 cd/m^2, white elements (tilted lines and semantic cues) were somewhat brighter at 12 cd/m^2; all elements were presented on a black background (0.1 cd/m^2). Observers' viewing distance from the monitor was about 57 cm, with distance maintained by the use of a chinrest. Observers responded by pressing the left or right button of a mouse with the left or right index finger, respectively.

Stimuli

The display on each trial consisted of nine elements arranged with equal spacing around a virtual circle with a diameter of approximately 7° of visual angle. Display elements were either circles or diamonds subtending maximal angles of 1.4° and 1.7°, respectively. Each element contained a line 1.0° in length, which was tilted 22.5° to either the left or the right relative to the vertical. Distractors were always green circles, with the tilt (left or right) of the line inside chosen randomly. Target items were either red circles or green diamonds (displayed amongst the green circle distractors) randomly displayed at one of the nine possible locations. Cues were presented at the centre of the display. Direct cues consisted of the precise element that was likely to be the target in the upcoming search display (a red circle or a green diamond). Semantic cues, the German words "FORM" (form), "FARBE" (colour), or "NEUTRAL", were displayed in capital letters at the centre of the screen (subtending an angle of 2.8° horizontally and 0.7° vertically). Targets were presented on each trial, with 50% colour and 50% form target. Half of the lines displayed within the target were tilted to the left and half to the right, so as to ensure an equal frequency of left and right responses.

Procedure

Each of the two conditions (symbolic cue and direct cue) consisted of a total of 2400 trials, presented in two sessions on consecutive days. Each session consisted of 15 blocks of 80 trials. There were two types of block: "attention cue" blocks (10 per session), with the cues displayed indicating the likely target colour and form, respectively; and "neutral-cue" blocks (five per session), which were randomly interspersed amongst the attention cue blocks. At the beginning of each block, observers were informed about the specific cue condition to be performed, by the labels (displayed for 5 s) "attention cue" and "neutral cue", respectively.

Each trial started with the presentation, for 800 ms, of a central fixation dot (0.2° of visual angle) followed by the cue, displayed for 500 ms: The German word for "form", "colour", or "neutral" in the semantic-cue condition; the visual representation of the target—a red circle (colour cue), a green diamond (form cue), or a green circle (neutral cue)—in the direct-cue condition. The cue was then replaced by the fixation dot, and, after an interval of 500 ms, the search array was displayed until the observer responded.

VISUAL COGNITION, 2006, 14 (4/5/6/7/8), 514–542

Ψ **Psychology Press**
Taylor & Francis Group

Salience and target selection in visual search

Hans-Christoph Nothdurft

Visual Perception Laboratory Göttingen, Germany

Why is it easy to find strawberries and difficult to collect gooseberries or green tomatoes? Why don't we see the tree in the forest but do see the single tree in the garden? Various explanations have been given to account for these phenomena. The present paper is concentrating on salience, a property apparently important for search but not frequently discussed in this context. Salience lets targets stand out and thus controls the selection of items that need to be investigated when a certain target is to be searched for. This proposal was tested in two series of experiments. It was found that salience detection and target identification followed different time courses: even typical "pop-out" targets (bright or dark blobs, gaps) were faster located than identified. The importance of salience in visual search was further investigated by manipulating target salience without affecting stimulus properties that are assumed to be relevant for search. When the salience of individual items was increased, the effective set size was reduced and search performance improved. This suggests an interactive and complementary function of salience and attention which is further discussed.

Our life is full of search. We begin early in the morning, searching for the alarm-clock button, the toothbrush, and maybe our glasses, and continue to search throughout the day (parking lot, notes we made yesterday, a particular cheese we ought to buy) until late at night when we search for the right keys and perhaps even the keyhole in the door. This important role in everyone's life is reflected in the number of publications on visual search, which has strongly increased during the last 25 years and still is growing (Figure 1).

Part of the strong interest in visual search comes from the compelling observation that some targets are found immediately, whereas others require scrutiny and careful strategies to be found (Julesz, 1981; Treisman, 1985; cf. Figure 2). This difference has challenged researchers, and a number of models have been developed to explain these observations. Some of the early models proposed distinct mechanisms for fast and slow visual search, such

Please address all correspondence to Christoph Nothdurft, c/o MPI Biophysical Chemistry, 37070 Göttingen, Germany. E-mail: hnothdu@gwdg.de

I am very grateful to J. R. Pomerantz and an anonymous referee for helpful comments.

http://www.psypress.com/viscog   DOI: 10.1080/13506280500194162

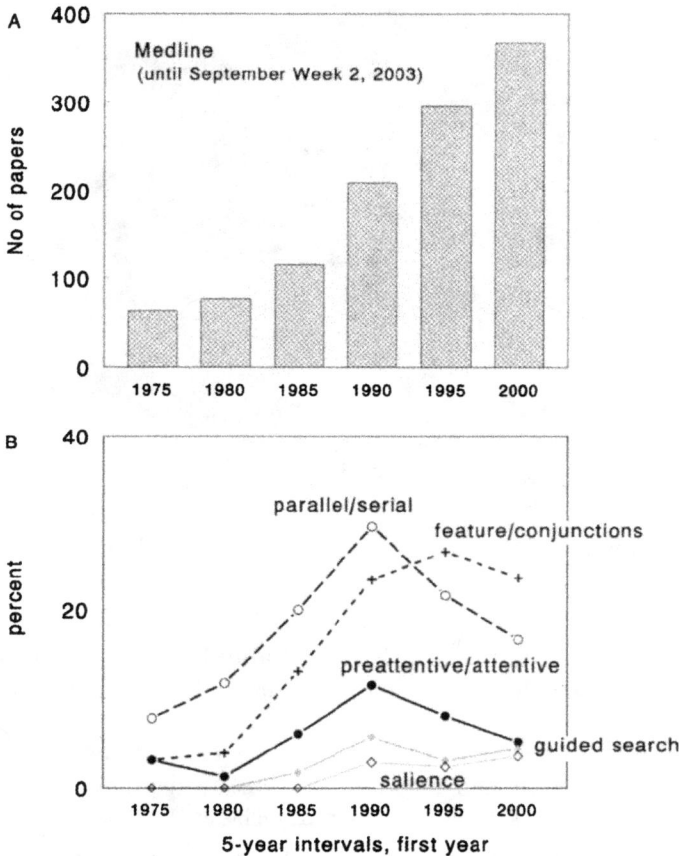

Figure 1.   Research on search. Graphs plot the number of publications in 5-year periods that cite the term "visual search" in title or abstract (A) and the percentage of these addressing the terminology of major models (B). Medline Database (1966 to September Week 2 2003); note that the last interval is shorter than 5 years. The number of publications on visual search has been growing since 1980 and some models had an enormous impact on this area of research. The present paper is on salience.

as parallel vs. serial processing, preattentive vs. attentive search, or feature vs. conjunction analysis (e.g., Treisman, 1985; Treisman & Gelade, 1980). However, although most of these "great dichotomies" have been very stimulating when originally brought up (cf. Figure 1B), it often turned out that the observed differences in search performance were not always, and not necessarily, associated with those distinctions. For example, the set-size effect obtained with some search tasks, that is, the increase of search time with the number of displayed items, may reflect serial search but would also be seen in a parallel search process with limited capacity (Townsend, 1971, 1976,

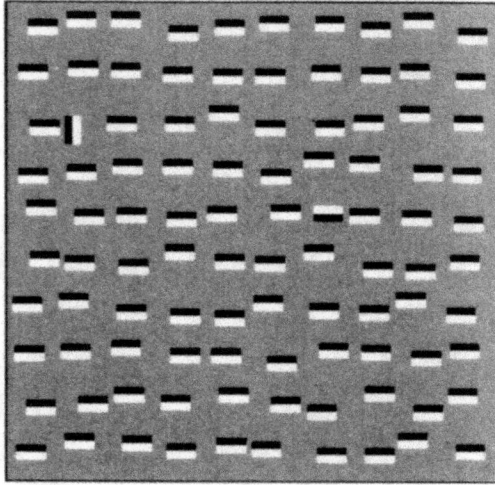

Figure 2. One of the key issues in visual search is the observation of fast and slow search performance. Two items differ from the rest: one is found immediately, the other requires time consuming search by scrutiny (from Nothdurft, 1994).

1990). Similarly, it was found that directed spatial attention is not only involved in "attentive" search but may also be required for so-called "preattentive" search (Bravo & Nakayama, 1992; Joseph, Chun, & Nakayama, 1997; Nothdurft, 1999; Theeuwes, Kramer, & Atchley, 1999)—leaving aside the fact that inattentive observers will miss a large number of targets in both attentive and preattentive search. Finally, the model of feature integration (Treisman & Gelade, 1980) would predict that triple conjunctions should be, at least, as difficult to find as paired ones, which is not the case. This discrepancy has led to the model of Guided Search (Wolfe, 1994; Wolfe, Cave, & Franzel, 1989; for an overview of experiments and models in visual search see, e.g., Wolfe, 1998).

In the present paper I would like to propose another view on visual search, which stresses the role of salience. So far, salience has not often been referred to in the context of visual search (cf. Figure 1B), although such a link would be obvious. The Merriam-Webster dictionary (1993) describes salience as "the quality or state of being salient", which is explained as "projecting beyond a ... surface, or level" and "standing out conspicuously". This description is reminiscent of "pop-out", a term frequently used in the visual search literature; also the term "conspicuity" was used in earlier papers (e.g., Engel, 1971, 1974; Jenkins & Cole, 1982). However, although salience may be nothing else than conspicuous pop-out, it seems preferable to use the term salience, for two reasons. First, pop-out has become popular in the context of features (it was said that certain features "pop out"), whereas salience is an attribute on its own, which depends on several properties including the context in which an object occurs. Second, salience is graded and can be quantified (we can compare two salient objects and notice that one is more salient than the other; cf. Nothdurft, 1993a), while such a gradation is usually not connected to feature-based pop-out.

The two targets in Figure 2 obviously differ in salience; one is salient and found immediately, the other is nonsalient and only found by chance (or scrutiny).[1] I will not discuss here, why the one target is salient and the other is not,[2] but would rather like to emphasize the role of salience in this example.

How could salience account for fast or slow visual search and for the presence or absence of set-size effects? It has been proposed that salience helps to select an item for visual analysis (cf. Koch & Ullman, 1985). Thus, if the target is the only salient item in a pattern, like in pop-out, it should be found immediately, independent of the number of other items available. There should be no set-size effect in such a search. If, on the other hand, there is no salient item, the target cannot be easily selected, and several items must be checked to find it—the more, the more items are present. Search time will increase with set size in that case. (The same should be true if a distractor, but not the target, were salient and item selection would thus not help to find the target.)

The role of salience in visual search is further illustrated in Figure 12A towards the end of this paper on page 537 (take a quick look—but please do not spend more than 1–2 seconds on looking at it for the first time).

What have you seen? Did you see the book? Did you see the grapefruit, the pistol, the cat? If you looked at the picture for a short moment, you may, or may not have seen the book. However, you likely have seen the strawberries and the grapefruit, but probably not the turkey. Somehow the strawberries are far more salient than the turkey and probably more salient than the book. In Figure 12B it is almost impossible to ignore the book, because it was deliberately made salient by adding a marker to it. If you did not spend much time on inspection of the pattern, you might have missed the turkey again.

If we assume that salience is an independent stimulus property and not based on only one feature of an object, we may expect two consequences that

---

[1] In this particular example, the difference in salience is very large and could indeed be described in the pop-out terminology: One target pops out; the other doesn't. However, graded differences in salience may be important in other examples.

[2] There are numerous explanations of why a certain target pops out or does not. In the feature-search model (e.g., Treisman, 1985), for example, the left-hand target is assumed to be immediately detected because one of its features (vertical) is preattentively processed. In a different view the target is salient because it differs in orientation from that of neighbouring bars (Nothdurft, 1992). The issue of the present paper, however, goes beyond such a distinction. It argues that salience itself, however it is produced, is a major key in fast visual search.

do not immediately follow from other, e.g., feature-based, explanations of fast visual search. First, the detection of salience itself may follow a different time course than the detection of other target properties, perhaps even of those that are believed to make the target pop out. Thus, we may perhaps detect a pop-out target before we could tell why it pops out. Second, since salience depends on several stimulus aspects including target context, it should be possible to manipulate salience, with strong effects on search speed, even when leaving the important and search-relevant properties unchanged. The paper presents evidence for both predictions.

GENERAL METHODS

All stimuli were generated on a colour monitor with a 100 Hz frame rate using standard DOS graphic routines. Stimulus onset and offset were linked to frame rate, thus allowing for presentation times at multiples of 10 ms. Viewing distance was 67 cm, corresponding to a visual angle of about 15 deg × 15 deg for the full monitor display. Items in the stimulus patterns (small squares, circles, oblique lines) were arranged in rasters (9 × 9 or 7 × 7), with or without jitter, which were centred on a green fixation point (0.1 deg × 0.1 deg; 55 cd/m^2) in the middle of the screen. All tests were performed under fixation, which was regularly controlled for by means of a video camera.

Subjects were students (20–34 years; 4 female, 1 male), who were paid for the time in experiment, and the author (54 years; male); all subjects had normal or corrected-to-normal visual acuity.

Each trial began with a 500–1000 ms presentation of the fixation point before the test pattern was presented, which was then replaced by a mask (not in the search tasks). Subjects entered their responses by pressing specific keys on a computer keyboard; reaction time (from stimulus onset) and/or performance (correct or not) were measured. Immediate feedback was only given in the search task (Experiments 3–5); in all other experiments, performance summaries were shown at the end of a run. Immediately after the subject's response a new trial was started with the (ongoing) presentation of the fixation point.

Tests were performed in sessions of up to 2 hours each. The various conditions in each experiment were blocked (see below), but related conditions were tested in an interleaved manner. In all experiments, subjects were given an initial period of training, during which they could familiarize with the task and improve performance.

Statistical significance was established using a two-factor, repeated measures ANOVA.

RESULTS

Different time courses for salience detection and target identification

When an array of bars is shown and one of the bars is later made salient, this bar is detected and located faster than it is identified (Nothdurft, 2002). The difference cannot be explained by a possibly slower identification process, since the bars were shown long before the salience cue. It rather may indicate a temporal sequence of selection and identification. Can similar differences be seen for targets that pop out? Are typical pop-out targets also faster located than identified? I addressed this question in two experiments measuring the time course of pop-out with typical features frequently studied in visual search, bright or dark blobs, and gaps.

Experiment 1: Detection and identification of luminance targets

Methods. Four subjects participated in the experiment. Targets were bright or dark single squares (0.4 deg × 0.4 deg; 12 or 60 cd/m²) on an intermediate background (35 cd/m²) (Figure 3). After presentation time (10–150 ms), test patterns were masked by a 9 × 9 raster (raster width 1.8 deg) of randomly brighter and darker squares (1 and 80 cd/m², respectively). Targets occurred (randomly) at one of 12 raster locations, six on either side of the fixation point, at an eccentricity of 3.6–5.7 deg (mean 4.7 deg). Subjects had to indicate, in different but interleaved tasks, on which half of the screen the target had occurred (detection task), and whether the target was bright or dark (identification task). Conditions were blocked for the task, with 20 repetitions per data point; up to 5 repetitions of each block were interleaved (giving up to 100 repetitions for each data point from every subject).

Results. All subjects could detect and locate the salient item from shorter presentations than were necessary to identify whether that item was bright or dark (Figure 4). This difference was consistently found, although performance and time courses varied between subjects. A two-factor, repeated measures ANOVA revealed a highly significant difference between the two tasks, $F(1, 3) = 32.9$, $p < .001$.

Experiment 2: Detection and identification of gap targets

Methods. Four subjects participated in the experiment. Targets were circles (1.0 deg diameter) with a gap of 50°, embedded in a 7 × 7 array (raster width 2.3 deg ±0.4 deg jitter) of circles of the same size without gaps (Figure 5A), at 11 cd/m² on 2.5 cd/m² background luminance. Targets could

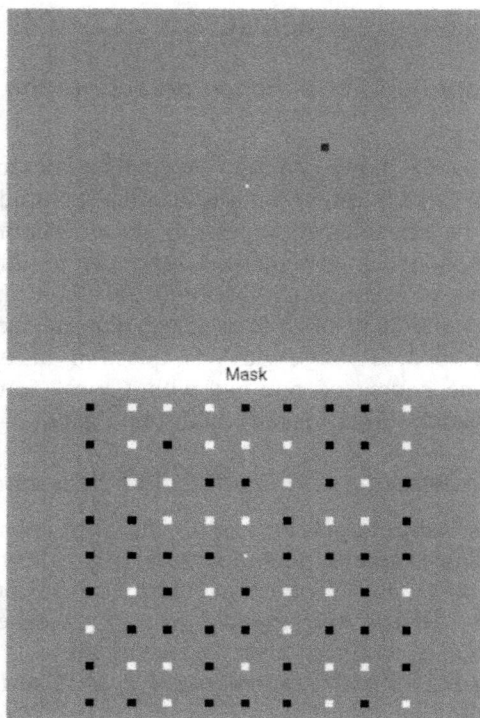

Mask

Figure 3. Experiment 1: Luminance pop-out. Subjects saw a bright or dark square (A) that was replaced by a masking pattern with randomly very bright or very dark squares (B). In different tasks subjects were asked to locate the target (detection task) and to distinguish its contrast polarity (identification task), while presentation time was varied.

occur at one of eight raster locations, four on each side, at an eccentricity of 2.3–4.6 deg (mean 3.3 deg). After presentation time (50–500 ms) all circles were masked by brighter circles (36 cd/m^2) with gaps, at the same locations (Figure 5B). While target gaps were located on either the left or the right side of the circle, mask gaps were randomly located at one of four locations (left, right, top, bottom); gaps in the target and target mask had different locations.

In separate but interleaved tests subjects had to indicate, on which half of the screen the target occurred (detection task) and whether the target had the gap on its right ("C") or left ("mirrored C") side (identification task). Target identification was also measured in a second test in which subjects had to indicate whether the target was a gap or a bright circle (discrimination task). In this test, targets were either gaps, as described before, or circles without a gap at increased luminance. In order to match luminance targets and gap

Luminance Pop-out

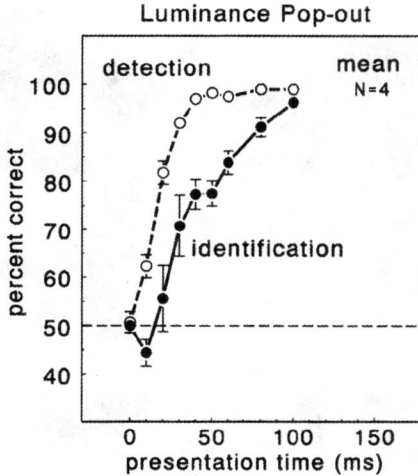

Figure 4.   Mean performance of four subjects in Experiment 1. Error bars (only plotted if larger than symbol size) in this and the following figures indicate SEM. Targets were faster detected and located than identified, indicating the importance of salience in luminance pop-out.

targets in salience, subjects first performed a salience matching task (Figure 5C), in which two targets, a circle with a gap and a bright circle, were shown simultaneously, one on each side of the screen (randomly assigned). The luminance setting of the brighter circle was varied (11–33 cd/m^2), and subjects were asked to indicate on which side of the screen the most salient item occurred (cf. Nothdurft, 1993a, 2000a). To let subjects evaluate and compare the two salient items, presentation time was set to 400 ms and patterns were not masked afterwards.

The various tests of Experiment 2 were carried out in the following sequence. Subjects first performed the salience matching task; test conditions (seven luminance settings of the bright circle) were intermixed, with 20 repetitions per block. The task was repeated three to five times to provide a reliable salience matching profile (cf. Figure 6), which was then fitted by a cumulate function to find the point of equal salience (50% preference for either target). This value was taken as the luminance setting of bright targets in the subsequent discrimination task. In the second step of Experiment 2, detection, identification, and discrimination tasks were tested in interleaved blocks, each containing all conditions of the particular task with 20 repetitions per data point. Since most subjects first had difficulties to detect the gap target from very short presentations, one or two experimental sessions were devoted to train subjects in all these tasks, until performance was settled. Thereafter, each test was repeated five times, in an interleaved fashion, thus giving 100 trials for every data point.

A stimulus

B mask

C salience match

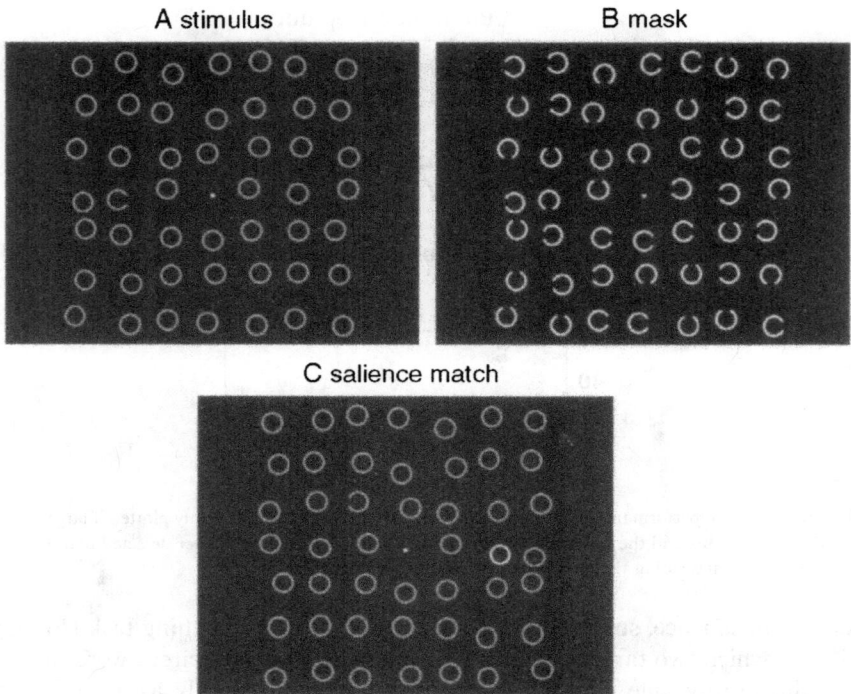

Figure 5. Experiment 2: Gap pop-out. (A) In an array of circles the one with a gap is quickly found. (B) Patterns were masked by an array of bright circles, all with gaps. In different tasks subjects had to detect (locate) or to identify the target, while presentation time was varied. (C) In a second test of Experiment 2, gap targets were distinguished from gap-free circle targets that popped out from luminance contrast. The pattern illustrates the salience matching task in which both targets were compared for salience.

Results. All subjects detected and located gap targets from shorter presentations than were necessary to identify the targets (Figure 7A); the difference was significant, $F(1, 3) = 6.18$, $p < .02$. The finding is similar to that of Experiment 1 (Figure 4), although the detection and identification of luminance targets in Experiment 1 was generally faster than that of gap targets in Experiment 2 (note the different time scales).

One could argue that the target identification task (for which gaps had to be located on the left or right side of an individual item) had required much finer spatial resolution than the target detection task (for which the gap had only to be coarsely located in either half of the screen). This difference in spatial resolution might have accounted for the curve shifts in Figure 7A. Therefore, another task was included in which gap targets had to be distinguished from luminance targets (Figure 5C). In order to perform the

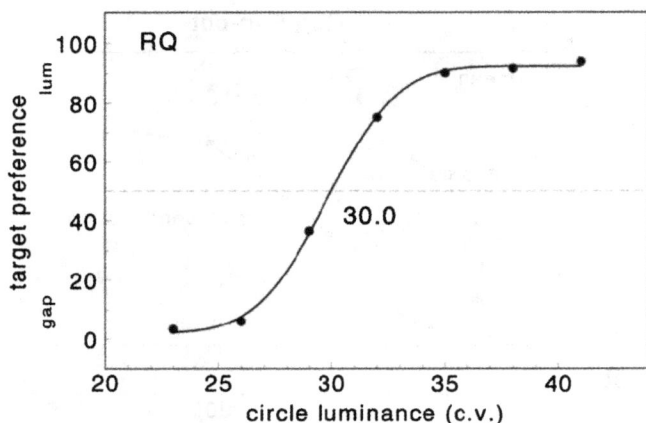

Figure 6. Typical rating profile in the salience matching task. Gap targets were presented together with luminance targets at various contrast (cf. Figure 6C), and subjects were asked to indicate which target was more salient. Luminance settings are indicated by their computer values (c.v.). In comparison with luminance targets that were not much brighter than the background circles (c.v. =23), subjects selected the gap target as more salient (ratings <50%), whereas bright circles (c.v. >32) were seen as more salient than the gaps (ratings >50%). For each subject, the data were fitted by cumulative functions and the luminance setting at equal salience (50% rating) was used in the discrimination task of Experiment 2.

discrimination properly, the two pop-out effects, gap and luminance, had first to be matched in salience (see Methods).

In the salience matching task, subjects compared two targets, one on each half of the screen, for their relative salience. One of the two targets was a circle with a gap; the other target was a bright ring, the luminance of which was varied. Figure 6 shows a typical matching profile obtained in this task. When the luminance target was only little brighter than the circles in the background, subjects choose the gap target as being more salient. When the luminance target was very bright, they choose this target as the more salient one. The measurements revealed a systematic transition between these two extremes, from which the point of isosalience (50%) was easily found. A luminance target at this contrast would have appeared as salient to the subject as the gap target.

The individual settings obtained from the salience matching task were used for the luminance targets in the discrimination task, which was tested in interleaved sequence with the other test series of Experiment 2. As Figure 7B shows, performance in the discrimination task was also deteriorated compared to the gap detection task; all subjects needed longer presentation times to distinguish the gap from the luminance target than to detect the salience effect produced by the gap, $F(1, 3) = 5.54$, $p < .025$.

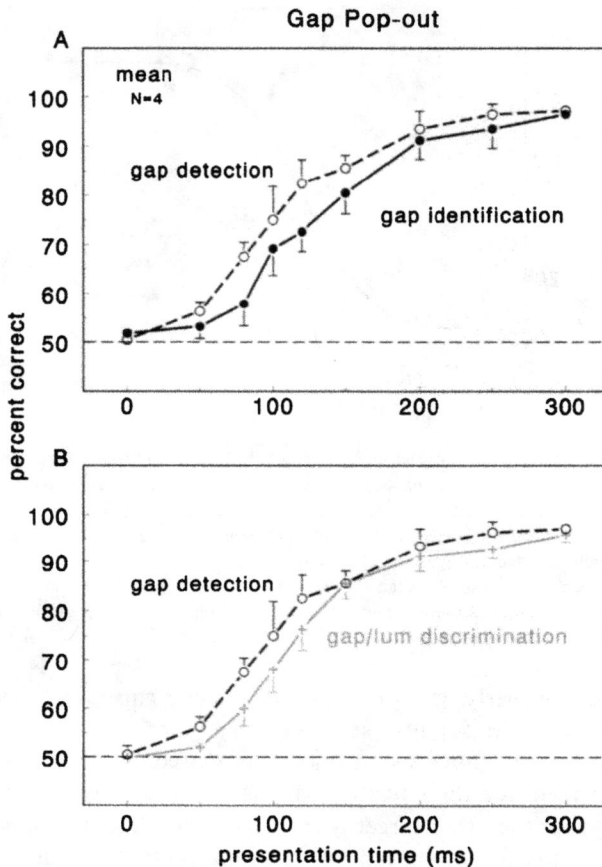

Figure 7. Mean performance of four subjects in Experiment 2: (A) detection and identification task, (B) detection and discrimination task. Subjects could faster detect the gap than they could either identify it or discriminate it from a luminance target of similar salience.

Discussion. Experiments 1 and 2 have shown that even in typical "feature search" salience detection and target identification can be distinguished; salient targets were faster located than identified, irrespective of how salient the target was and how quickly it was detected (cf. Figures 4 and 7). This finding is in agreement with the proposed model of salience-based selection and (subsequent) target identification.

Differences in the time course of salience detection and target identification have been reported earlier (Nothdurft, 2002; Sagi & Julesz, 1985; Scialfa & Joffe, 1995), but had then been attributed to shifts of focal attention. In the present study, typical pop-out targets were studied, which are assumed to be found preattentively. That even pop-out targets attract attention in visual search was shown in a number of studies (Joseph & Optican, 1996; Nothdurft, 1999). However, the demand on attention may be small, in particular when targets are easily discriminated from distractors (Braun & Julesz, 1998; Bravo & Nakayama, 1992). The present data suggest that it is not a certain feature (e.g., a bright or dark blob, a gap) that is (immediately) detected but that these features appear as salient when presented in the context of other items with different features. This salience is detected faster than the feature supposed to provide pop-out.

Note that the argument is not that gaps and luminance blobs would not pop out and that something else had made these targets salient. In fact, both features might well have provided the measured salience effects. Sufficient luminance contrast is a strong salience marker (Braun, 1994; Nagy & Sanchez, 1992; Nothdurft, 2000a, 2002; Turatto & Galfano, 2000), as are gaps (Mori, 1997; Treisman & Souther, 1985), although other stimulus properties that coincide with the occurrence of gaps might also account for their salience, e.g., differences in spatial frequency composition (Caelli & Moraglia, 1985). The point made here is that, even for features that pop out, salience is faster detected than are these features identified. This underlines the important role of salience in (fast) visual search.

One might argue against this interpretation by assuming that the different speed of performance in detection and identification tasks merely reflects the difficulty of the respective tasks rather than a functional difference. Thus, the differences might have disappeared if the identification task had been made easier. However, such an assumption would unlikely explain the present observations. Salience detection was measured in a (coarse) location task, and locating a target may, in fact, be more difficult than simply detecting its presence. Thus, the detection task might have already been suboptimal in this respect. The identification tasks, on the other hand, were straightforward in asking for bright vs. dark targets and bright circles vs. circles with gaps. It is difficult to imagine how such an identification task could be made easier. Only the location of gaps in the identification task of Experiment 2 might have been relatively difficult (as discussed above); for this reason the additional discrimination task was included.

In order to avoid that subjects discriminated targets in this task just by differences in salience, targets had to be matched in salience beforehand. The salience matching task was the first task subjects had performed on gaps, and it turned out that matches were most reliable when presentation time was not too short and patterns were not masked afterwards. As a consequence, however, the (variable) presentation time used in the discrimination task did not exactly correspond to the presentation time in the matching task. I did not notice any problems due to this fact, but it would, in principle, be possible that the salience of the two targets did not grow similarly fast with presentation time. We cannot be sure that a bright circle that is as salient as a gap when both targets are presented for 400 ms would also be as salient as the gap when both targets are presented for, say, 150 ms. But given that performance was to be measured over various presentation times, this seems to be an unavoidable problem. However, variations of presentation time in the matching task did not produce a systematic shift in one subject tested.

Salience affects the speed of visual search

The salience of an object depends not only on properties of that object but also on its context, that is on properties of other objects nearby. Thus, by varying the arrangement of items in a scene, or by replacing items in the neighbourhood, the salience of an object can be changed (Nothdurft, 1993a, 2000b). This has already been used to distinguish the role of salience vs. features in visual search (Nothdurft, 1992, 1993b). A target that was difficult to find because it was not more salient than other items in the pattern, was quickly found when its salience was increased. While salience manipulations in the search relevant dimension (orientation) might have improved target discrimination from nearby distractors, search time was also dramatically reduced when the target was made salient from feature contrast in another dimension (colour, luminance, motion, or disparity) that was irrelevant for the task, without changing the difficulties in the search-relevant dimension.

In the present paper, subjects were asked to perform a (difficult) conjunction search while certain items were made salient and thus could be selected for identification. There were three experiments (Experiments 3– 5), which differed in the combination of test conditions and in the way of how salience was produced.

Experiments 3 and 4: Conjunction search with and without markers

Methods. Targets were green bars tilted to the right, which were presented together with isoluminant red bars at the same orientation and orthogonal green bars (Figure 8). Subjects were asked to fixate a central spot on the screen and, when the pattern was switched on, to indicate correctly and as fast as possible whether or not the target was present. "Yes" and "no" responses were entered on different keys of the computer keyboard. Reaction time (RT), measured from stimulus onset, and the correctness of responses were analysed. Errors were indicated by a short beep after the response.

Bars were 0.8×0.2 deg in size, at 19 cd/m^2, and were arranged in a regular 9×9 raster with 1.8 deg raster width. In some trials, individual bars were

A

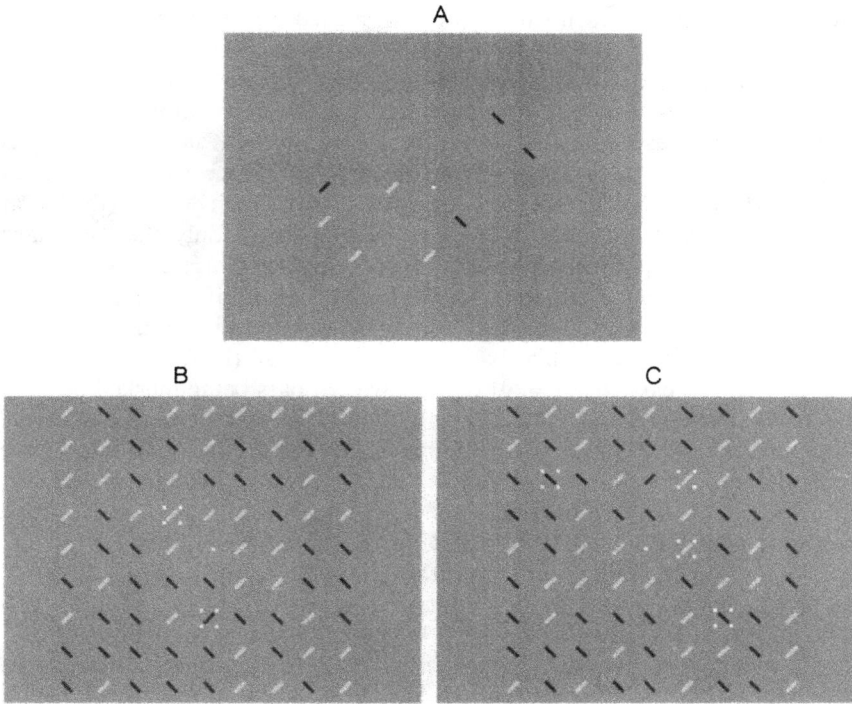

B   C

Figure 8.   Experiments 3 and 4: Conjunction search with and without salience markers. (A) Standard search; the number of items in the display (set size) is varied. (B, C) Examples of full pattern search with marked items. Subjects searched for a green bar (here, black) tilted to the right among similarly oriented, isoluminant red bars (white) and orthogonal green bars; background was dark. Salience markers were white four-dot cues presented for 20 ms at 100 ms delay. All search tests were done under fixation (white dot in the centre). The pictures illustrate various target-present conditions; standard search with variable set size (A), full set with the target (and other items) marked (B), full set with only nontargets marked (C).

marked by four dots (0.2 deg × 0.2 deg) that were symmetrically arranged around the bar at a radial distance of 0.6 deg (Figure 8B and C). The markers were white (84 cd/m^2) and were shown 100 ms after stimulus onset, for 20 ms. To minimize border effects and effects from decreasing visual acuity towards periphery, the occurrence of markers and targets was restricted to a central window including all locations in rows 3–7 and columns 2–8; targets were further excluded from the corner positions of this window. This resulted in a total of 34 possible marker and 30 possible target locations in the raster, at eccentricities of 1.8–5.7 deg (mean 3.6 deg). Subjects were not informed about this restriction.

Isoluminance of red and green stimuli was achieved from a separate test before the experiment, using heterochromatic flicker photometry. The individual settings of each subject were then used for his or her tests in the search task.

Each trial started with the presentation of the fixation point. After 1 s, the test pattern was switched on and remained visible until the subject responded. On response, the pattern was switched off, and after analysis and eventually feedback the next trial started. The number of items varied between the tasks. Most tests used full raster displays with 80 bars (the bar at the fixation point was always left out, cf. Figure 8); only the "standard search" task in Experiment 3 did also include smaller samples of up to eight bars. In Experiment 3, three different stimulus conditions were tested in separate blocks, which were repeated in an interleaved sequence. These conditions were (a) individual bars ($n = 1$, 2, 4, 6, 8), (b) full patterns ($n = 80$), and (c) full patterns ($n = 80$) with individual bars being marked ($n_m = 1$, 2, 4, 6, 8). The target was present in half of the trials and, when markers were shown (condition c), was one of the marked items. In the other half of the trials the target was absent and only nontargets were marked in condition c. In Experiment 4, all test conditions were intermixed; these were (a) full patterns, with individual bars including the target being marked ($n = 80$; $n_m = 1$, 2, 4, 6, 8), (b) full patterns with nothing being marked ($n = 80$; $n_m = 0$), and (c) full patterns with only nontargets being marked ($n = 80$; $n_m = 1$, 2, 4, 6, 8). Again, the target was present in half of the trials so that condition c now covered patterns with a target, in which only nontargets were marked (cf. Figure 8C).

Six subjects participated in Experiment 3, and five in Experiment 4. They all underwent an initial training period of up to one session (2 hours) and were reminded to search carefully and not respond too fast, when the number of errors was high. Only correct trials were used for analysis.

Results.

Standard search: Figure 9 shows the performance (mean RT) of six subjects in Experiment 3. When the pattern contained only few bars (Figure 9A), responses revealed the set-size effect to be expected for such a task, although it is not quite clear why hits and rejections with few items followed the same slope. Search took much longer and RTs for hits and rejections differed, when the target had to be detected in full size patterns ($n = 80$). When the slopes for $n = 1$, 2, 4, 6, 8 are extrapolated, RTs for hits in full size patterns would correspond to $(n + 1)/2 = 19.3$, which is below the theoretical value for $n = 80$, but close to that for the true number of possible target locations ($n = 30$).

Rejections in full-size patterns took relatively long; this may reflect the subjects' particular care not to miss a target that was not yet seen. In general, the search time in target-absent trials depends on many aspects that cannot be easily controlled (e.g., the subject's bias to avoid false rejections).

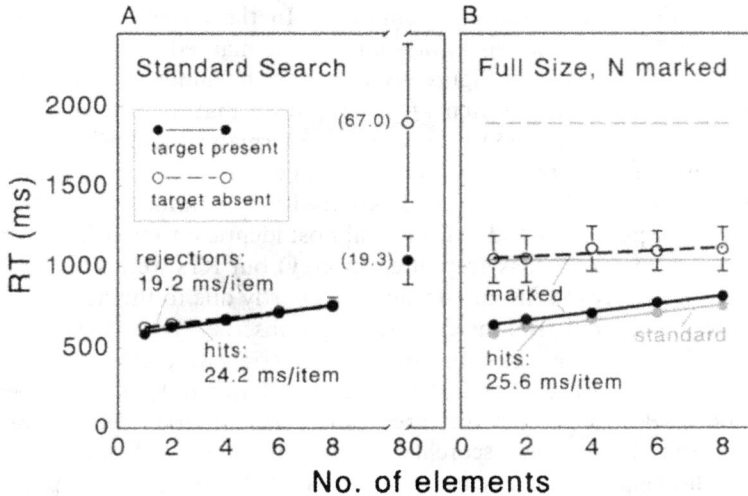

Figure 9.   Mean performance of six subjects in Experiment 3. (A) Standard search. Slopes for target-present ("hits") and target-absent trials ("rejections") indicate clear set-size effects as to be expected for conjunction search (error bars smaller than data symbols). The two separate data points represent standard search on full patterns (80 elements); the values in brackets indicate the corresponding number of elements when regression lines for hits and rejections are extrapolated. (B) Full pattern search with some items marked (abscissa). In contrast to the expected performance (horizontal grey lines, from data points in A) reaction times were shorter when the target was marked, and were modulated with the number of salient items ("marked"). The slope for search with salience selection is similar to the set-size effect in standard search (grey lines, replotted from A). In this and the following figures, target-present and target-absent cases are indicated by different symbols, as shown in the inset.

Therefore, analysis was based primarily (but not exclusively) on the performance with target-present trials.

The data confirm that search for a green bar among similarly oriented red and orthogonal green bars is not an easy task. The set-size effect was significant, $F(1, 4) = 7.15$, $p < .001$. Search time differed by 395 ms between the single bar ($n = 1$) and the full pattern ($n = 80$), thus revealing the typical characteristics of conjunction search. The question is: Can salience help to select the target in such a task and thus speed up search?

Cued selection: In order to study this, some items were marked and thus made salient. The markers in Experiment 3 and 4 were "cues" whose selection efficiency has been established in other studies (Enns & Di Lollo, 1997). These cues were briefly shown during stimulus presentation to increase the salience of certain items and thus select them for visual processing. To measure the effect of selection by salience, the number of marked items was varied in the same manner as the number of items in the standard test before, that is, one to eight bars (of the 80 bars on display) were marked in different stimulus presentations. In the target-present trials of Experiment 3, the target was always among the marked items (Figure 8B).

The results are shown in Figure 9B; note that the numbers on the abscissa now refer to the number of items marked. Given that there were always 80 bars, one should expect constant search performance with RTs similar to those in the standard test (grey, horizontal lines). However, RTs were much shorter, $F(1, 4) = 21.4$, $p < .001$, and varied with the number of salient items. In fact, the slope for marked items was almost identical to that for small sets in the standard search task (replotted in grey) but RTs were systematically delayed. This delay (54 ms, on average) was partly due to the delay at which the markers occurred (100 ms after stimulus onset).

Interestingly, search times for target-absent trials were also much shorter than in the standard test (dashed-line curves). This would not be predicted by salience selection. When the target was absent, markers could not help and subjects should have searched across all items. But apparently the markers did help to reduce search time. This was likely due to the particular test situation of Experiment 3. If items were marked, the target was either one of them (in target-present trials) or not at all present. Obviously, subjects had adapted to this coincidence and quickly rejected patterns with salient items if none of them was the target.

Experiment 4 was designed to test for this assumption. It was a replication of Experiment 3 except that (1) targets could be salient or nonsalient even when other items were marked, (2) all test conditions were intermixed, and (3) the standard test was removed (except for $n = 80$) for the brevity of experiment. The results are shown in Figure 10. Two target-present conditions are now distinguished. When the target was among the marked items (continuous black line), performance was comparable to that in Experiment 3. But Experiment 4 also included target-present patterns, in which only nontargets were marked. With these patterns, performance should not be improved compared to marker-free presentations, as targets were not selected by salience. This was indeed the case (grey line). The data seem to suggest that the wrong selections even delayed performance (cf. RT for "nothing marked"; light grey), as if salience had misled the search process; in the mean data, however, this difference is not significant, $F(1, 4) = 3.76$, $p < .06$. There also was a strong speed–accuracy tradeoff in both conditions (see next paragraph). Finally, as to be expected, all target-absent trials in Experiment 4 required similarly long RTs (dashed lines), as the markers *per se* did not indicate whether or not the target was present.

Error analysis: While the mean error rates in the different conditions were generally below 3.5% (false alarms <2.5%), there were two conditions (both target-present) in which the number of misses was noticeably increased. These conditions were full-size target search ($n = 80$) without salience markers (mean error rates were 14.9% in Experiment 3 and 11.5% in

mixed presentation

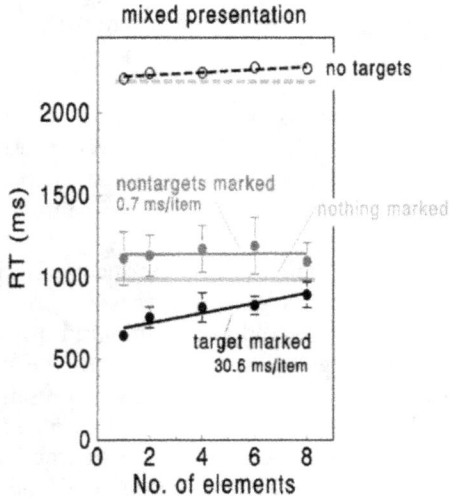

Figure 10. Mean performance in Experiment 4; five subjects. Test conditions were similar to those in Experiment 3 but also included target-present trials with markers on nontargets (cf. Figure 8C). Error bars are not plotted for rejections (target-absent trials) which produced large variations in reaction times. Light grey lines give performance on full patterns in standard search without any markers.

Experiment 4) and full-size patterns with only nontargets marked (12.6%). The fact that subjects missed quite a few targets in these conditions indicates that they did not search long enough on some of these patterns, and thus have partly preferred fast responses over accurate ones (speed–accuracy tradeoff). Since all data analysis was restricted to correct trials, averaged RT in these two conditions might thus have been too small.

Altogether, salience markers strongly affected search performance; salient targets were faster detected than nonsalient targets. This is consistent with the model that targets are found fast if salience helps to select them for further processing. If several items are salient, the probability that the target is processed first is reduced, and hence search time should increase. If all items are nonsalient, none is selected and search has to cover virtually all items, thus being slow. Search may be even slower if only nontargets are made salient; in that case the wrong items are selected by salience and the number of items to be checked until the target is found would statistically increase.

Experiment 5: Selection by advanced onset

In order to test the generality of the salience model, another salience and selection mode was used in Experiment 5. Instead of external markers, items were presented slightly in advance. Reaction time was always measured from the onset of the target bar or, in target-absent trials, from the onset of background bars.

Methods.   The experimental setup was identical to that of Experiment 4 except that selected items were not marked but were presented 30 ms before the rest of the pattern. All bars then remained visible until the subject reacted. Four subjects participated in this experiment.

Results.   Onset-defined salience effects produced a similar pattern as cue-based salience effects (Figure 11). If the target was among the selected items (black lines), search time was reduced compared to patterns in which nothing was selected (light grey), and varied with the number of selected items. There was no obvious cost effect in target-present trials when only nontargets were marked (grey lines), $F(1, 3) < 0.3$, $p > .59$, suggesting that the salience effect from advanced onset was less distractive than the salience effect produced by the four-dot cues in Experiments 3 and 4. It was, however, strong enough to let items be selected for analysis and the target quickly be found, $F(1, 3) > 4.72$, $p < .05$. Similar to Experiment 4, salience had no effect on target-absent trials (dashed lines).

Mean error rates for target-present trials were 4.6% (target advanced), 7.3% (nontargets advanced), and 6.5% (all bars simultaneous); the error rates for target-absent trials were < 2.5%.

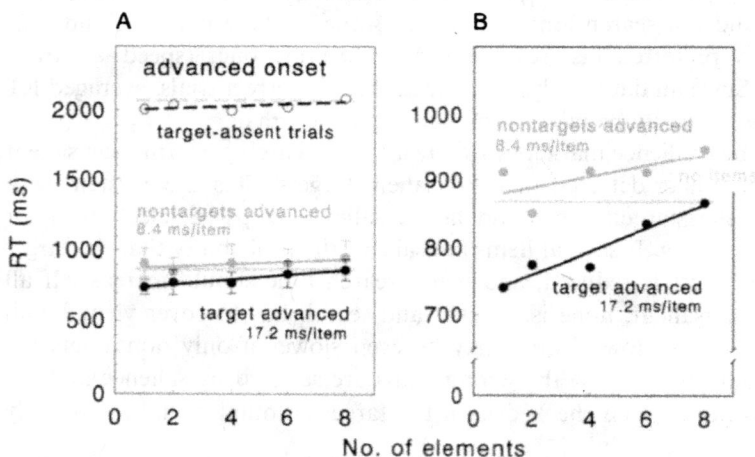

Figure 11.   Mean performance in Experiment 5 where salience effects were produced from 30 ms advanced onset of items; four subjects. (A) Data from both target and no-target trials; (B) enlarged presentation of target-present trials. Onset-based salience effects produced the same performance characteristics as marker-based salience effects (Figure 10). although search modulation was less pronounced. as was the salience from advanced onset itself. Performance in standard search is shown in light grey, for comparison.

Abrupt onset is considered being a strong salience effect that may capture attention (Jonides & Yantis, 1988; Remington, Johnston, & Yantis, 1992). However, with the relatively small luminance contrast of the bars, the salience of a 30 ms advanced onset was small and not even noticed by the observers, although such an asynchrony is reliably detected in a forced choice experiment under sufficient contrast (cf. Experiment 1; Figure 4). Nevertheless, the improvement in RT was in the order of 125 ms, if only the target was marked.

Discussion. Experiments 3–5 have shown that even in conjunction search the manipulation of salience may improve performance; salient targets were detected faster than nonsalient targets. Search time was still reduced, when several items were marked (in addition to the target). This is in close agreement with the proposed model that salience helps to select and locate possible targets, which then may have to be processed in detail to find out whether they display the feature that is being searched for. The fact that RT increased linearly with the number of salient items further supports this model. There were always 80 items on the display and no reason why search should be modulated unless salient elements were preferably checked. The slope of salience-based search in Experiment 3 was almost identical to that for small sets of bars in the standard search condition (Figure 9B), suggesting that indeed the salient items were selected and items in the background were ignored. Thus, search among salient bars in a large field was not different from search among individual bars as numerous as the salient bar sample.

The role of salience in conjunction search has been claimed before (Sobel & Cave, 2002; but see Bacon & Egeth, 1997), although then related to groups of items rather than to individual bars. Whether salience effects do automatically attract attention (e.g., Kim & Cave, 1999; Theeuwes, 1992, 1994a, 1999b; Theeuwes & Burger, 1998; but see Bacon & Egeth, 1994; Yantis & Egeth, 1999) or are controlled by an observer's general attention setting and strategy (Bacon & Egeth, 1994; Folk & Remington, 1999; Folk, Remington, & Johnston, 1992; Yantis & Jonides, 1990) has been a matter of dispute. In the present experiments, subjects made use of the salience markers in speeding up their responses and improving performance.

The gradual differences between Experiments 4 and 5 are best explained by the different strengths of the two salience effects. While the dot cues in Experiment 4 were strong salience markers, the advanced onset in Experiment 5 remained unnoticed by the observers. Consistent with this difference, both the advantage of salience markers for target selection and the possible cost effect for nontarget selection were more pronounced in Experiment 4 than in Experiment 5.

Salience markers as those used in Experiments 3 and 4 are reminiscent of cues that are used to attract attention to a certain location in the visual field. In particular for the four-dot cues used here, prominent masking effects have been reported (Di Lollo, Enns, & Rensink, 2000; Enns & Di Lollo, 1997, 2000). However, given the conditions under which such masking is predominant (long and ongoing presentation of the cue that remains visible after the target has already been switched off), masking effects should not have been pronounced in the present work (short cue presentation, long lasting presentation of the stimulus). In fact, all subjects had found the marked (i.e., cued) items faster than the noncued items.

A different question is whether the markers had indeed made items salient or had rather attracted attention to the cue location. We will come back to this issue in the General Discussion. Since salient targets may attract attention (Joseph & Optican, 1996; Nothdurft, 2002), it is not clear whether or not such a distinction would be meaningful and at all important. However, it must be stressed that in the present study several cues had been presented together and thus had marked several items simultaneously. Even in trials with eight markers, RTs for hits were still reduced compared to trials without salience markers (Figure 9B); thus all these markers must have had an effect. This would be different to the capture of a presumably unique focus of attention in cueing experiments (e.g., Posner, 1980).

The saliency effects studied in Experiment 5 are related to visual marking experiments (Watson & Humphreys, 1997; Watson, Humphreys, & Olivers, 2003), although the paradigms are very different. In visual marking, a subsample of nontarget items is shown relatively long (400 ms or more) before the full pattern; this subsample (which does not contain the target) is then found to be ignored from further search. In the present experiment a subsample of elements was shown only 30 ms before the rest of the pattern and search was found to be speeded up if the target was among this sample. Both paradigms merge on the conclusion that the onset of objects is a strong salience cue, which helps to select items (Donk & Theeuwes, 2001; cf. Gibson & Jiang, 2001).

GENERAL DISCUSSION

The introduction proposed that the distinction of fast and slow visual search could depend on target salience in the different tasks. If the target is the only salient item in a pattern, search time should not depend on the number of other items in the scene, and should not show a set-size effect. However, if the target is nonsalient and hence not easily selected for analysis, then search will remain nonguided by the stimulus, and eventually be time consuming. It was conjectured that we should expect two effects, if this model were correct.

First, for a target that is quickly found in visual search (e.g., a target that "pops out"), its salience should be detected fast, and perhaps faster than the properties that are believed to provide pop-out. Second, for targets that are generally not quickly found (like targets in a conjunction search task), an increase of target salience should speed up search. Both conjectures were experimentally confirmed, thus supporting the proposed model and providing evidence for the importance of saliency effects in visual search.

Saliency effects in visual search

The proposal that salience controls visual search, is not entirely new. In particular, the role of salience for attracting attention has been stated before. Itti and Koch (2000), for example, following an earlier proposal of Koch and Ullman (1985), considered salience-based search as the basis for overt and covert shifts of attention. Closely related to their "salience map" is the "activation map" of Guided Search 2.0 (Wolfe, 1994). The neural equivalent of such a salience map is not yet clear, however. While some authors had located it in lateral parietal cortex, area LIP (Kusunoki, Gottlieb, & Goldberg, 2000), one must also consider area V1 as one of its representations (Li, 2002). Thus, it may be that saliency effects are distributed in the brain and that a distinct saliency map does not exist, as was recently proposed (van Rullen, 2003).

Several earlier findings seem to confirm the important role of salience in visual search, although results were not always looked at this way. For instance, Sagi and Julesz (1985) have demonstrated that orientation pop-out targets could be quickly detected even when these were not yet all correctly identified; the proposed difference of "where" and "what" in vision already suggested that stimulus features themselves (like orientation) are not the only aspect relevant for search. However, salience was not yet generalized at that time but was linked to one of its many properties, namely orientation (contrast). As demonstrated later, several such properties contribute to the salience of an object, each alone being able to speed up search (Nothdurft, 1993b). Effects from different dimensions may even add, thus increasing the general salience of an object (Nothdurft, 2000a). Only that concept of the nonspecificity of individual saliency effects would lead to the concept of generalized salience; the present study shows that even cues and onset asynchrony add to this quality.

The fact that salience is graded, and can be measured, provides a fruitful perspective towards understanding the graded variations between very fast and very slow visual search; search performance is often less qualitatively distinct than would be suggested by a strict dichotomy. Variations in salience may also account for phenomena in visual search that are hitherto not yet fully understood. One such example is the asymmetry in search performance when the brightest or the dimmest of several bright items have to be found (Braun, 1994; Schiller & Lee, 1991). It was shown (Nothdurft, 2006) that targets in these conditions differ in salience, and that these differences (wherever they come from) lead to different performance in visual search. Of particular interest is the observation that salience and directed attention seemed to act in a complementary way. The less salient a target was, the more attention was required to detect it and the more strongly search performance was deteriorated when attention was simultaneously drawn to another task. We will come back to these complementary actions.

Top-down influences on bottom-up salience

Although salience in the present study was manipulated in visual input and thus was strictly bottom-up, it should be stressed that this is not necessarily the case. Salience can also be modulated by attention, for example when observers in the conjunction task would concentrate on (i.e., attend to) the green bars and try to ignore all red items (cf. Egeth, Virzi, & Garbart, 1984; Kaptein, Theeuwes, & van der Heijden, 1995). In that case, red bars might be suppressed leading to a selected perception of green bars, among which the now appearing orientation contrast would increase the salience of the target and make it pop out. There are several reports of top-down control on salience effects (Bacon & Egeth, 1997; Lamy & Tsal, 1999). For example, attention can amplify the salience of an attended colour by up to 30% (Sperling, Reeves, Blaser, Lu, & Weichselgartner, 2001).

This modulation does not even have to be intended or conscious. It was shown that learning can increase stimulus salience (Jagadeesh, Chelazzi, Mishkin, & Desimone, 2001); priming also may affect the salience of a target (Maljkovic & Nakayama, 1994; Olivers & Humphreys, 2003). Despite those examples of top-down modulation of saliency effects, the proposed model still holds. Provided that an observer is willing to search for a target and has adequately set attention, increased salience will enhance the neural representation of the object, improving the possibility of it being selected for processing and quickly found.

Figure 12 (opposite).   Salience effects in visual search. (A) If you look at this pattern the first time. please do restrict inspection time to 1–2 seconds. Have you seen the strawberries. the grapefruit. the pistol. the book? See the introduction for further instructions. (B) Salient items are seen immediately. Look there for just one second. Have you now seen the book? (C) Salience and attention modulate the neural representation in a similar way as does luminance contrast. If the contrast of one item is increased. corresponding to making it salient or attending to it. this item is quickly found.

Figure 12 (see caption opposite).

Encoding of salience

How is salience encoded in neural activity? One possible correlate of perceptual pop-out was found in the responses of neurons in area V1. Items that display feature contrast (e.g., local differences in orientation or motion) generate, on average, larger responses than items in homogeneous fields (Kastner, Nothdurft, & Pigarev, 1997; Knierim & van Essen, 1992; Nothdurft, Gallant, & Van Essen, 1999). Perceptually, such items are salient and pop out in many conditions (Nothdurft, 1993c). Thus, in area V1, salience seems to coincide with locally increased responses of the neural representation.

This is similar to the modulation of neural responses by focal attention. When attention is directed to a certain location in the visual field, the responses of neurons representing this location are increased (Kastner, Pinsk, de Weerd, Desimone, & Ungerleider, 1999; McAdams & Maunsell, 1999, 2000; Treue & Martínez-Trujillo, 1999; cf. Treue, 2001). Reynolds and Desimone (2003) have recently shown that this response modulation by attention is equivalent to a variation of stimulus contrast; by increasing the luminance contrast of a nonattended object, responses can be made similar to those of an attended object at lower contrast (see also Treue & Martinez-Trujillo, 2006 this issue). However, increasing the contrast of an object also increases its salience. Therefore, whatever we might do to increase the responses of an object's neural representation, whether we increase its salience or attend to it, it would make this object distinct from other objects and thus more easily found.

This is illustrated in Figure 12C. When we increase the luminance contrast of one item (here done by decreasing the luminance contrast of all other items), we modulate this object's salience—alternatively we could have left the object unchanged and attended to this location—and make that object found immediately. In this way, either by increasing its salience or by attending to it, the turkey that might have been missed in previous inspections is now quickly found.

Salience vs. attention—is it all the same in visual selection?

Given the similarity of effects on behaviour (the salient turkey should be found as fast as the attended turkey) and probably on neural representations, too, one would need to think about reliable distinctions. Obviously, we can attend to an object at one location and present a second, highly salient object at a different location, without having difficulties to name and distinguish the two perceptual phenomena. In that case, attention is top-down, salience is bottom-up, and we will likely agree on what one should call attention and what salience. However, salience may attract attention, so that, after a moment, the second object is attended, too—or is it still salient, or both? We may then deliberately attend to a third object, which was neither attended to nor salient before but now becomes salient in perception—or is it only attended, or both?

There seems to be an agreement that salience should be merely defined by the stimulus, and thus bottom-up, whereas attention would be mentally controlled, and thus top-down. However, this distinction would be difficult when the two processes interfere. The previously discussed example of a conjunction search in which we voluntarily attend to bars of one colour, and thus see the target pop out, has already illustrated that attention settings may change salience settings. Something that was not salient before may become salient from top-down modulation. Similarly, attention can be driven by bottom-up saliency effects. If we bring all these phenomena together, adding priming and perhaps even intention, it could indeed become difficult to decide whether an object is found from salience or from attention.

REFERENCES

Bacon, W. J., & Egeth, H. E. (1994). Overriding stimulus-driven attention capture. *Perception and Psychophysics*, *55*, 485–496.

Bacon, W. J., & Egeth, H. E. (1997). Goal-directed guidance of attention: Evidence from conjunctive visual search. *Journal of Experimental Psychology: Human Perception and Performance*, *23*, 948–961.

Braun, J. (1994). Visual search among items of different salience: Removal of visual attention mimics a lesion in extrastriate area V4. *Journal of Neuroscience*, *14*, 554–567.

Braun, J., & Julesz, B. (1998). Withdrawing attention at little or no cost: Detection and discrimination tasks. *Perception and Psychophysics*, *60*, 1–23.

Bravo, M. J., & Nakayama, K. (1992). The role of attention in different visual-search tasks. *Perception and Psychophysics*, *51*, 465–472.

Caelli, T., & Moraglia, G. (1985). On the detection of Gabor signals and discrimination of Gabor textures. *Vision Research*, *25*, 671–684.

Di Lollo, V., Enns, J. T., & Rensink, R. A. (2000). Competition for consciousness among visual events: The psychophysics of reentrant visual processes. *Journal of Experimental Psychology: General*, *129*, 481–507.

Donk, M., & Theeuwes, J. (2001). Visual marking beside the mark: Prioritizing selection by abrupt onsets. *Perception and Psychophysics*, *63*, 891–900.

Egeth, H. E., Virzi, R. A., & Garbart, H. (1984). Searching for conjunctively defined targets. *Journal of Experimental Psychology: Human Perception and Performance*, *10*, 32–39.

Engel, F. L. (1971). Visual conspicuity, directed attention and retinal locus. *Vision Research*, *11*, 563–576.

Engel, F. L. (1974). Visual conspicuity and selective background interference in eccentric vision. *Vision Research*, *14*, 459–471.

Enns, J. T., & Di Lollo, V. (1997). Object substitution: A new form of masking in unattended visual locations. *Psychological Science*, *8*, 135–139.

Enns, J. T., & Di Lollo, V. (2000). What's new in visual masking? *Trends in Cognitive Sciences*, *4*, 345–352.

Folk, C. L., & Remington, R. (1999). Can new objects override attentional control settings? *Perception and Psychophysics, 61,* 727–739.

Folk, C. L., Remington, R. W., & Johnston, J. C. (1992). Involuntary covert orienting is contingent on attentional control settings. *Journal of Experimental Psychology: Human Perception and Performance, 18,* 1030–1044.

Gibson, B. S., & Jiang, Y. (2001). Visual marking and the perception of salience in visual search. *Perception and Psychophysics, 63,* 59–73.

Itti, L., & Koch, C. (2000). A saliency-based search mechanism for overt and covert shifts of visual attention. *Vision Research, 40,* 1489–1506.

Jagadeesh, B., Chelazzi, L., Mishkin, M., & Desimone, R. (2001). Learning increases stimulus salience in anterior inferior temporal cortex of macaque. *Journal of Neurophysiology, 86,* 290–303.

Jenkins, S. E., & Cole, B. L. (1982). The effect of the density of background elements on the conspicuity of objects. *Vision Research, 22,* 1241–1252.

Jonides, J., & Yantis, S. (1988). Uniqueness of abrupt visual onset in capturing attention. *Perception and Psychophysics, 43,* 346–354.

Joseph, J. S., Chun, M. M., & Nakayama, K. (1997). Attentional requirements in a "preattentive" feature search task. *Nature, 387,* 805–807.

Joseph, J. S., & Optican, L. M. (1996). Involuntary attentional shifts due to orientation differences. *Perception and Psychophysics, 58,* 651–665.

Julesz, B. (1981). Textons, the elements of texture perception, and their interactions. *Nature, 290,* 91–97.

Kaptein, N. A., Theeuwes, J., & van der Heijden, A. H. C. (1995). Search for a conjunctively defined target can be selectively limited to a color-defined subset of elements. *Journal of Experimental Psychology: Human Perception and Performance, 21,* 1053–1069.

Kastner, S., Nothdurft, H. C., & Pigarev, I. N. (1997). Neuronal correlates of pop-out in cat striate cortex. *Vision Research, 37,* 371–376.

Kastner, S., Pinsk, M. A., de Weerd, P., Desimone, R., & Ungerleider, L. G. (1999). Increased activity in human visual cortex during directed attention in the absence of visual stimulation. *Neuron, 22,* 751–761.

Kim, M. S., & Cave, K. R. (1999). Top-down and bottom-up attentional control: On the nature of interference from a salient distractor. *Perception and Psychophysics, 61,* 1009–1023.

Knierim, J. J., & Van Essen, D. C. (1992). Neuronal responses to static texture patterns in area V1 of the alert macaque monkey. *Journal of Neurophysiology, 67,* 961–980.

Koch, C., & Ullman, S. (1985). Shifts in selective visual attention: Towards the underlying neural circuitry. *Human Neurobiology, 4,* 219–227.

Kusunoki, M., Gottlieb, J., & Goldberg, M. E. (2000). The lateral intraparietal area as a salience map: The representation of abrupt onset, stimulus motion, and task relevance. *Vision Research, 40,* 1459–1468.

Lamy, D., & Tsal, Y. (1999). A salient distractor does not disrupt conjunction search. *Psychonomic Bulletin and Review, 6,* 93–98.

Li, Z. (2002). A saliency map in primary visual cortex. *Trends in Cognitive Sciences, 6,* 9–16.

Maljkovic, V., & Nakayama, K. (1994). Priming of pop-out: I. Role of features. *Memory & Cognition, 22,* 657–672.

McAdams, C. J., & Maunsell, J. H. R. (1999). Effects of attention on orientation-tuning functions of single neurons in macaque cortical area V4. *Journal of Neuroscience, 19,* 421–441.

McAdams, C. J., & Maunsell, J. H. R. (2000). Attention to both space and feature modulates neuronal responses in macaque area V4. *Journal of Neurophysiology, 83,* 1751–1755.

Merriam-Webster (1993). *Webster's Third New International Dictionary of the English Language Unabridged: A Merriam-Webster.* Chicago: Encyclopaedia Britannica Inc.

Mori, S. (1997). Effect of absolute and relative gap sizes in visual search for closure. *Canadian Journal of Experimental Psychology*, *51*, 112–125.

Nagy, A. L., & Sanchez, R. R. (1992). Chromaticity and luminance as coding dimensions in visual search. *Human Factors*, *34*, 601–614.

Nothdurft, H. C. (1992). Feature analysis and the role of similarity in pre-attentive vision. *Perception and Psychophysics*, *52*, 355–375.

Nothdurft, H. C. (1993a). The conspicuousness of orientation and motion contrast. *Spatial Vision*, *7*, 341–363.

Nothdurft, H. C. (1993b). Saliency effects across dimensions in visual search. *Vision Research*, *33*, 839–844.

Nothdurft, H. C. (1993c). The role of features in preattentive vision: Comparison of orientation, motion, and color cues. *Vision Research*, *33*, 1937–1958.

Nothdurft, H.-C. (1994). Cortical properties of preattentive vision. In B. Albowitz, K. Albus, U. Kuhnt, H.-C. Nothdurft, & P. Wahle (Eds.), *Structural and functional organization of the neocortex* (pp. 375–384). Berlin: Springer.

Nothdurft, H. C. (1999). Focal attention in visual search. *Vision Research*, *39*, 2305–2310.

Nothdurft, H. C. (2000a). Salience from feature contrast: Additivity across dimensions. *Vision Research*, *40*, 1183–1201.

Nothdurft, H. C. (2000b). Salience from feature contrast: Variations with texture density. *Vision Research*, *40*, 3181–3200.

Nothdurft, H. C. (2002). Attention shifts to salient targets. *Vision Research*, *42*, 1287–1306.

Nothdurft, H.-C. (2006). Salience-controlled visual search: Are the brightest and the least bright targets found by different processes? *Visual Cognition*, *13*, 700–732.

Nothdurft, H. C., Gallant, J. L., & van Essen, D. C. (1999). Response modulation by texture surround in primate area V1: Correlates of "popout" under anesthesia. *Visual Neuroscience*, *16*, 15–34.

Olivers, C. N. L., & Humphreys, G. W. (2003). Attentional guidance by salient feature singletons depends on intertrial contingencies. *Journal of Experimental Psychology: Human Perception and Performance*, *29*, 650–657.

Posner, M. I. (1980). Orienting of attention. *Quarterly Journal of Experimental Psychology*, *32*, 3–25.

Remington, R. W., Johnston, J. C., & Yantis, S. (1992). Involuntary attentional capture by abrupt onsets. *Perception and Psychophysics*, *51*, 279–290.

Reynolds, J. H., & Desimone, R. (2003). Interacting roles of attention and visual salience in V4. *Neuron*, *37*, 853–863.

Sagi, D., & Julesz, B. (1985). "Where" and "what" in vision. *Science*, *228*, 1217–1219.

Schiller, P. H., & Lee, K. (1991). The role of the primate extrastriate area V4 in vision. *Science*, *251*, 1251–1253.

Scialfa, C. T., & Joffe, K. M. (1995). Preferential processing of target features in texture segmentation. *Perception and Psychophysics*, *57*, 1201–1208.

Sobel, K. V., & Cave, K. R. (2002). Roles of salience and strategy in conjunction search. *Journal of Experimental Psychology: Human Perception and Performance*, *28*, 1055–1070.

Sperling, G., Reeves, A., Blaser, E., Lu, Z. L., & Weichselgartner, E. (2001). Two computational models of attention. In J. Braun & C. Koch (Eds.), *Visual attention and cortical circuits* (pp. 177–214). Cambridge, MA: MIT Press.

Theeuwes, J. (1992). Perceptual selectivity for color and form. *Perception and Psychophysics*, *51*, 599–606.

Theeuwes, J. (1994a). Endogenous and exogenous control of visual selection. *Perception*, *23*, 429–440.

Theeuwes, J. (1994b). Stimulus-driven capture and attentional set: Selective search for color and visual abrupt onsets. *Journal of Experimental Psychology: Human Perception and Performance*, *20*, 799–806.

Theeuwes, J., & Burger, R. (1998). Attentional control during visual search: The effect of irrelevant singletons. *Journal of Experimental Psychology: Human Perception and Performance*, *24*, 1342–1353.

Theeuwes, J., Kramer, A. F., & Atchley, P. (1999). Attentional effects on preattentive vision: Spatial precues affect the detection of simple features. *Journal of Experimental Psychology: Human Perception and Performance*, *25*, 341–347.

Townsend, J. T. (1971). A note on the identifiability of parallel and serial processes. *Perception and Psychophysics*, *10*, 161–163.

Townsend, J. T. (1976). Serial and within-stage independent parallel model equivalence on the minimum completion time. *Journal of Mathematical Psychology*, *14*, 219–239.

Townsend, J. T. (1990). Serial and parallel processing: Sometimes they look like Tweedledum and Tweedledee but they can (and should) be distinguished. *Psychological Science*, *1*, 46–54.

Treisman, A. (1985). Preattentive processing in vision. *Computer Vision, Graphics and Image Processing*, *31*, 156–177.

Treisman, A. M., & Gelade, G. (1980). A feature-integration theory of attention. *Cognitive Psychology*, *12*, 97–136.

Treisman, A., & Souther, J. (1985). Search asymmetry: A diagnostic for preattentive processing of separable features. *Journal of Experimental Psychology: General*, *114*, 285–310.

Treue, S. (2001). Neural correlates of attention in primate visual cortex. *Trends in Neurosciences*, *24*, 295–300.

Treue, S., & Martinez-Trujillo, J. C. (1999). Reshaping neuronal representations of visual scenes through attention. *Cahiers de Psychologie Cognitive/Current Psychology of Cognition*, *18*, 951–972.

Treue, S., & Martinez-Trujillo, J. C. (2006). Visual search and single-cell electrophysiology of attention: Area MT, from sensation to perception. *Visual Cognition*, *14*, 898–910.

Turatto, M., & Galfano, G. (2000). Color, form and luminance capture attention in visual search. *Vision Research*, *40*, 1639–1643.

Van Rullen, R. (2003). Visual saliency and spike timing in the ventral visual pathway. *Journal of Physiology (Paris)*, *97*, 365–377.

Watson, D. G., & Humphreys, G. W. (1997). Visual marking: Prioritizing selection for new objects by top-down attentional inhibition of old objects. *Psychological Review*, *104*, 90–122.

Watson, D. G., Humphreys, G. W., & Olivers, C. N. L. (2003). Visual marking: Using time in visual selection. *Trends in Cognitive Sciences*, *7*, 180–186.

Wolfe, J. M. (1994). Guided Search 2.0: A revised model of visual search. *Psychonomic Bulletin and Review*, *1*, 202–238.

Wolfe, J. M. (1998). Visual search. In H. Pashler (Ed.), *Attention* (pp. 13–73). Hove, UK: Psychology Press.

Wolfe, J. M., Cave, K. R., & Franzel, S. L. (1989). Guided search: An alternative to the feature integration model for visual search. *Journal of Experimental Psychology: Human Perception and Performance*, *15*, 419–433.

Yantis, S., & Egeth, H. E. (1999). On the distinction between visual salience and stimulus-driven attentional capture. *Journal of Experimental Psychology: Human Perception and Performance*, *25*, 661–676.

Yantis, S., & Jonides, J. (1990). Abrupt visual onsets and selective attention: Voluntary versus automatic allocation. *Journal of Experimental Psychology: Human Perception and Performance*, *16*, 121–134.

VISUAL COGNITION, 2006, 14 (4/5/6/7/8), 543–564

Ψ Psychology Press
Taylor & Francis Group

Relax! Cognitive strategy influences visual search

Daniel Smilek and James T. Enns

University of British Columbia, Vancouver, BC, Canada

John D. Eastwood

York University, Toronto, Ontario, Canada

Philip M. Merikle

University of Waterloo, Waterloo, Ontario, Canada

Two experiments evaluated whether visual search can be made more efficient by having participants give up active control over the guidance of attention. In Experiment 1 participants were instructed to search while either *actively* directing their attention to the target or by *passively* allowing the target to just "pop" into their minds. Results showed that passive instructions led to more efficient search on a hard task but not on an easy task. In Experiment 2 participants completed the search task either by itself or concurrently with a memory task. This yielded the same pattern of results as Experiment 1; a hard search was completed more efficiently when performed concurrently with a memory task than when performed alone. These findings suggest (a) that the efficiency of some difficult searches can be improved by instructing participants to relax and adopt a passive cognitive strategy and (b) the improved efficiency results from a reduced reliance on slow executive control processes and a greater reliance on rapid automatic processes for directing visual attention.

Visual search has become a model task for exploring the nature of attentional processes, as attested to by the other articles in this special issue. In a typical study, participants look for a target item that is presented along with a number of distractor items. The total number of items in a

Please address all correspondence to J. T. Enns, Department of Psychology, University of British Columbia, 2136 West Mall, Vancouver, BC, Canada V6T 1Z4. E-mail:jenns@ psych.ubc.ca

This research was supported by the grants from the Natural Science and Engineering Research Council of Canada to D. Smilek, J. T. Enns, J. D. Eastwood, and P. M. Merikle. D. Smilek was also supported by postdoctoral fellowships from Killam Trusts, the Michael Smith Foundation for Health Research, and the Natural Sciences and Engineering Research Council of Canada. We thank Sherry Trithart for her assistance with data collection.

http://www.psypress.com/viscog
DOI: 10.1080/13506280500193487

display is varied so that it is possible to examine the time it takes to find a target, or the accuracy of the search, as a function of the set size. The resulting function is often linear and its slope is taken as an index of the difficulty, or inversely the efficiency, of search. Shallow slopes reflect easy or efficient search; steep search slopes reflect hard or inefficient searches. Following Wolfe (1998) we use the term *search efficiency* as a theory-neutral term for how search for a target is influenced by adding distractor items to a search display.

Most studies of visual search have varied either the *display characteristics* or the *knowledge* (i.e., expectations) that participants bring to the task. Often-studied display characteristics include target–distractor similarity (Duncan & Humphreys, 1989), item density (Cohen & Ivry, 1991), retinal eccentricity (Carrasco & Yeshurun, 1998), and whether a simple feature or a conjunction of features defines the target (Triesman & Sato, 1990). Variations in task knowledge and expectations have included prior visual versus conceptual information about the target (Wolfe, Butcher, Lee, & Hyle, 2003), prior experience with specific display configurations (Chun & Jiang, 1998), and whether the target must be detected, identified, or localized (Bravo & Nakayama, 1992; Liu, Healey, & Enns, 2003).

Results from these studies have led to numerous theories regarding how attention is guided during search. Most theories propose that search is optimally efficient when it is guided by an appropriate balance of *automatic* or involuntary processes that analyse the visual display and *controlled* or voluntary processes that place the proper weight on the output of these automatic processes. A representative theory of this kind is Guided Search Theory (Wolfe, 1994), which proposes that search depends both on the extent to which target–distractor differences correspond to the organization of early visual processes *and* the extent to which the participant has actively tuned his/her control processes to optimize search for a given set of displays. The dimensional weighting theory of Müller and his colleagues (Found & Müller, 1996; Müller, Reimann, & Krummenacher, 2003) also emphasizes the balanced contributions of automatic and controlled processes in efficient search.

One issue that has been surprisingly neglected in this context is the extent to which search efficiency is influenced by the general cognitive strategy brought by the participant to the task. By cognitive strategy, we are referring to processes that are under the observer's voluntary control, but the term is intended to apply to cognitive control settings that are distinct from any specific knowledge the participant may have about the search items, the stimulus displays, or the responses that will be made in the search task.

One reason to suspect that cognitive strategy plays an important role in search is that it influences performance in other tasks involving categorization, memory, and perception. For example, in studies of categorization where items in different categories have very similar nondefinitional surface features, individuals are often more accurate at categorizing items when they adopt a feature-based (analytic) strategy compared to when they adopt a holistic (nonanalytic) strategy (Jacoby & Brooks, 1984; Whittlesea, Brooks, & Westcott, 1994). Similarly, in studies of memory where items from a number of different sources must be memorized, later recognition of items from a given source is much higher when participants base their judgements on retrieval of the previous study context, than when they base them on the familiarity of the items (see Jacoby & Brooks, 1984).

Studies of perception show that the context can bias participants undertaking a search to adopt either a singleton mode or a feature mode (Bacon & Egeth, 1994) and that singleton distractors defined by a different feature than the target interfere less with performance when participants search in feature mode than when they search in singleton mode (but see Theeuwes, 2004). In Lange's (1888) classic studies of speeded responding, average reaction times were found to be much faster (about 100–120 ms) when participants were instructed adopt an "extreme muscular mode" and focus on generating a response than when they were instructed to adopt an "extreme sensory mode" and focus on the incoming stimulus. Even in studies of perception without awareness, the strength of the unconscious influence of a briefly presented stimulus is greater when the participant allows the stimulus to "pop" into their mind, as opposed to actively looking for the stimulus (Marcel, 1983; Snodgrass, Shevrin, & Kopka, 1993a, 1993b; van Selst & Merikle, 1993).

Another reason to believe that cognitive strategy may influence search comes from anecdotes provided by researchers who regularly use this task. For example, Jeremy Wolfe believes that some conjunction searches can be made more efficient by instructing participants to relax and to observe the display passively rather than to search with a great deal of cognitive effort. He refers colloquially to this strategy as "using the force" (Wolfe, personal communication, 2004). Similarly, in our laboratories we have often instructed visual search participants to "let the search items come to you rather than looking hard to find them". We arrived at these instructions because we noted that experienced participants reported doing this spontaneously, whereas naïve searchers were expending great mental effort but searching less efficiently. Although anecdotes such as these have received wide circulation among researchers, there is little formal evidence supporting the effectiveness of the claim that searching "passively" is more efficient. A primary purpose of the present study was therefore to simply document the influence of this cognitive strategy on visual search.

Preliminary evidence that cognitive strategy influences search comes from a recent study by Smilek, Dixon, and Merikle (2006a). Simple differences in the pretask instructions given to participants were reported to influence search for items that had recently been associated with meaningful verbal labels. In a first phase of the study, participants learned to associate verbal labels with simple shapes (e.g., vertical and right oblique were both called an "elephant" and left oblique was called a "pencil"). Counterbalancing the labels used by different groups of participants ensured that the visual similarity of the items was controlled. In one condition, target and distractor shapes were from the same category, so that participants had to search for an "elephant" among "elephants". In another condition, target and distractor shapes were from different categories, so that now a "pencil" had to be found among "elephants".

The critical manipulation in the study involved instructing one group of participants to search for the target by *actively* directing their attention to the target; the other group of participants was told to let the target "pop" *passively* into their mind. The results showed that the categorical relationship between target and distractors influenced search only when participants adopted a passive search strategy. Specifically, when target and distractors differed in category membership, search was much more efficient for participants following *passive* instructions than for those given *active* instructions. These results were interpreted to suggest that the conceptual categories of targets and distractors influences search only when participants adopt a *passive* strategy.

Although the Smilek et al. (2006a) study demonstrates that cognitive strategy can influence search, several important questions remain. First, it is not known whether cognitive strategies will influence search when no newly acquired meanings have been linked to the display items. It is possible that the search task of Smilek et al. required participants to base their search on a more conceptual and abstract representation of the items in the displays. Conceptual representations may simply be more susceptible to strategic influence than representations of spatial and geometric characteristics (Pylyshyn, 2003). On the other hand, it is possible that control processes are able to influence attentional guidance at the earliest stages and therefore influence search based on a simple visual discrimination.

Another question that remains unanswered is whether cognitive strategies interact with the overall difficulty of the search task. If instructions have an influence at the level of altering the decision criteria used by participants to select a response, with passive instructions simply leading to a more relaxed decision rule, then the instructions should have a similar influence on search tasks of all levels of difficulty. On the other hand, if instructions influence the cognitive control processes of participants, and more difficult searches bias participants to attempt to exert greater cognitive control over the task, then one would expect instructions to have a greater influence only on more difficult searches. This prediction is consistent with anecdotes that a passive search strategy is particularly effective for conjunction searches and that experienced searchers have learned that a passive strategy is most effective.

EXPERIMENT 1

The goals of Experiment 1 were twofold. First, we asked whether search efficiency is influenced by active and passive search instructions when the search task involves only geometric visual discriminations. Second, we evaluated whether the influence of instructions depends on the relative difficulty of the search.

Participants searched for a circle that had a gap either on the left side or on the right side, among circles that had a gap on both the left and right side. They were required to respond by indicating as quickly and accurately as possible whether the target gap was on the left or the right. Search difficulty was varied by testing participants in an *easy* discrimination (target gap was large) and a *hard* discrimination (target gap was small) in separate blocks of trials. *Active* and *passive* search instructions were given to two different groups of participants. Search efficiency was indexed by measuring search slopes for response time and accuracy over three different levels of set size: Two, four, and six display items.

Method

Participants.   Twenty-four undergraduate students reporting normal or corrected-to-normal vision participated in a 30-minute session for extra course credit at the University of British Columbia. Twelve participants were randomly assigned to each instructional group.

Stimuli.   Examples of the visual search displays are shown in Figure 1. Each display consisted of a target (circle with gap on left or right) and one, three, or five distractors (circle with a gap on the left and the right). Each

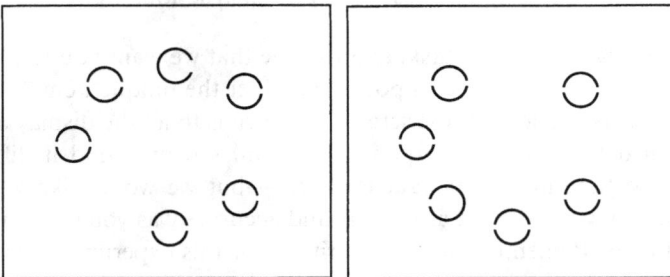

Figure 1.   Examples of easy (left) and hard (right) search displays used in Experiments 1 and 2.

item occupied one of eight possible locations, equally spaced on an imaginary circle centred on fixation. Item location was selected randomly. The size of the gap in the target circle was varied between blocks to vary the overall difficulty of the search: Easy (large gap) and hard (small gap). Examples of the easy and hard search displays are shown on the left and right sides of Figure 1, respectively.

Displays were presented on an Apple iMac computer running VScope experimental software (Enns & Rensink, 1992). The monitor resolution was 800×600 pixels and the refresh rate was 112 Hz. At this resolution, items in the search display measured 0.8 cm in diameter and subtended 0.8 degrees visual angle at a viewing distance of 57 cm. The gaps in the distractor items, the targets with the small gaps and the targets with the large gaps measured 0.1 cm (0.1°), 0.15 cm (0.15°), and 0.3 cm (0.3°), respectively. The imaginary circle on which the items were placed had a radius of 4.0 cm (4.0°).

Procedure. Each participant was tested in a single experimental session consisting of 8 practice trials and two blocks of 144 experimental trials. Order of search difficulty (easy, hard) was counterbalanced across participants. Within each block, the three set sizes (2, 4, and 6) and two targets (gap on left, gap on right) yielded six possible conditions, which were repeated 24 times, with each display configuration determined randomly.

Each trial began with a fixation cross at the centre of the screen for 500 ms. Following a blank interval of 400 ms, a search display was presented and remain on view until response or until 1800 ms had elapsed. Participants' index fingers rested on the "z" key (gap on left) and the "/" key (gap on right), which they depressed when they identified the target. Participants were instructed to respond as rapidly as possible without sacrificing accuracy for speed. Responses made after the end of the 1800 ms period in which the visual search display was presented were recorded as errors.

The two groups of participants differed only in the instructions given prior to the search task. The *passive* group instructions were:

The best strategy for this task, and the one that we want you to use in this study, is to be as receptive as possible and let the unique item "pop" into your mind as you look at the screen. The idea is to let the display and your intuition determine your response. Sometimes people find it difficult or strange to tune into their "gut feelings"—but we would like you to try your best. Try to respond as quickly and accurately as you can while using this strategy. Remember, it is very critical for this experiment that you let the unique item just "pop" into your mind.

The *active* group instructions were:

The best strategy for this task, and the one that we want you to use in this study, is to be as active as possible and to "search" for the item as you look at the screen. The idea is to deliberately direct your attention to determine your response. Sometimes people find it difficult or strange to "direct their attention"—but we would like you to try your best. Try to respond as quickly and accurately as you can while using this strategy. Remember, it is very critical for this experiment that you actively search for the unique item.

Results

Correct response time (RT).   Before examining the RT data of each participant, the outliers in each condition were removed using a recursive procedure (see van Selst & Jolicoeur, 1994). The data were then evaluated by a mixed analysis of variance (ANOVA) that assessed the between-group factors of instruction (active, passive) and order (hard search first, easy search first), and the within-participant factors of search difficulty (easy, hard) and set size (2, 4, and 6).

Figure 2 shows the mean correct RT. This pattern of results points to two main conclusions, which were corroborated by ANOVA. First, simply instructing participants to search actively or passively influences the efficiency of their search, with a passive strategy resulting in greater efficiency. Second, the passive strategy is effective only when the search is relatively difficult.

ANOVA showed that mean correct RT increased linearly with set size, $F(1, 20) = 246.74$, $MSE = 3744.9$, $p < .001$, as is the case in many studies of visual search. Also, the slopes of the search functions were steeper in the difficult search condition than in the easy search condition, $F(2, 40) = 39.96$, $MSE = 1241.0$, $p < .001$, indicating that variation of the target's gap size was effective in influencing search difficulty. Most importantly, the slopes of the search functions were shallower when participants adopted a passive strategy than when they adopted an active strategy, $F(2, 40) = 7.081$, $MSE = 2401.2$, $p < .003$, pointing to the role of cognitive strategy in search efficiency. However, whether strategy influenced the slopes also depended on the difficulty of search, $F(2, 40) = 11.617$, $MSE = 1241.0$, $p < .001$. Testing order had no influence on search strategy, $F < 1$, nor on its interaction with hard and easy search conditions, $F(2, 40) = 1.287$, $MSE = 1241.0$, $p = .287$.

To further examine how instructions interacted with search difficulty, we examined the data separately in the hard and easy search conditions. These analyses revealed that instructions had a substantial effect on the search slope when search was hard, $F(2, 40) = 12.477$, $MSE = 2503.3$, $p < .001$, but

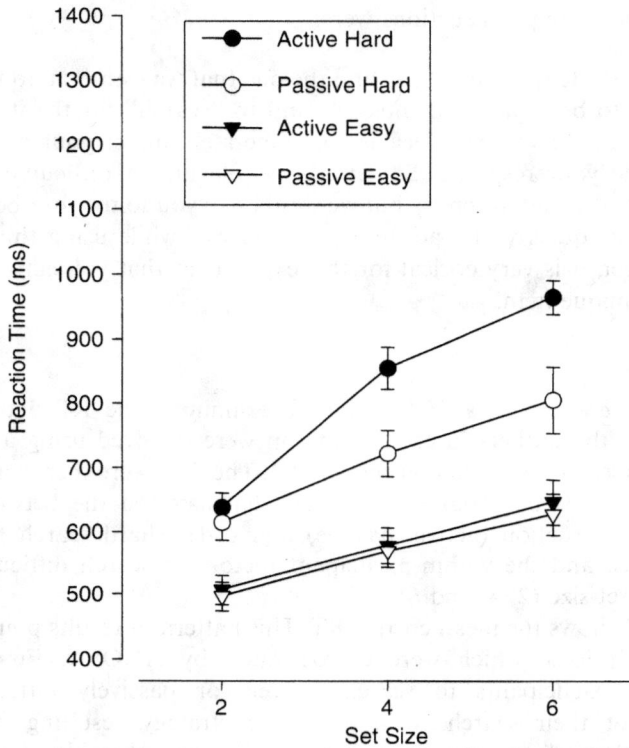

Figure 2. Mean correct response times for identifying the target in Experiment 1. The error bars represent one standard error of the mean.

not when search was easy, $F < 1$. In the hard search condition, the difference between active and passive search slopes was nominally greater when hard search was done after the easy search (slope difference of 45 ms/item) than when hard search was done before easy search (slope difference of 23 ms/item), but this interaction did not reach statistical significance, $F(2, 40) = 1.207$, $MSE = 2503.3$, $p = .310$.

Error data. The conclusions derived from the RT data are only valid if the error data indicate that participants are not trading response speed for accuracy. The error rates for each condition are shown in Table 1 and they indicate that speed–accuracy trading relations are not a concern for out interpretation. In particular, there was no evidence that the differences in the slopes of the RT functions associated with two instructional sets were the result of participants trading speed for accuracy.

TABLE 1
Mean percentages of errors in Experiment 1

	Set size		
	2	4	6
Active			
Hard	3.1	4.9	15.5
Easy	3.0	2.1	2.6
Passive			
Hard	9.7	10.7	20.8
Easy	5.2	6.9	9.0

These data were analysed in the same way as the RT data. ANOVA revealed that participants made more errors when search was hard than when search was easy, $F(1, 20) = 35.036$, $MSE = 0.00368$, $p < .001$, that errors increased linearly with set size, $F(1, 20) = 35.300$, $MSE = 0.00308$, $p < .001$, and this increase was greater in the hard search condition than in the easy search condition, $F(2, 40) = 15.000$, $MSE = 0.00243$, $p < .001$. Although there were more errors in the passive search condition than in the active search condition, $F(1, 20) = 8.472$, $MSE = 0.1166$, $p < .01$, there was no measurable influence of search strategy on the slopes of the error functions, $F < 1$, and this did not differ across hard and easy search conditions, $F < 1$.

Inefficiency scores. Speed–accuracy trading relationships can be subtle and difficult to detect when error rates are low (Pachella, 1974; Wickelgren, 1977). One sensitive way to assess whether they are playing a role in the data is to combine RT and errors in single measure of *search inefficiency*, by dividing mean correct RT for each participant in each condition by the mean proportion correct (Townsend & Ashby, 1983). This is a measure that corrects the RT measure by its appropriate level of accuracy in a very intuitive way: if accuracy is perfect in a condition, the inefficiency score will be identical to mean RT; as accuracy is decreased the inefficiency score will increase in proportion to the level of errors being made. The main assumption underlying the interpretation of these scores is that mean correct RT increases linearly as mean proportion accuracy decreases. This was supported in the present data by a correlation of $-.29$, $p < .001$.

The inefficiency scores for Experiment 1 are shown on the left side of Figure 5 (see later). Their pattern makes it clear that the benefit of the passive instructions was not the result of shifting participants' response criteria. Instead, using a passive strategy resulted in greater search efficiency in the hard search condition and had no measurable influence on the easy search. ANOVA conducted on the inefficiency scores showed the identical pattern of results as reported for the correct mean RT data.

EXPERIMENT 2

Having established that instructing participants to adopt an active or a passive strategy influences the efficiency of search, we sought to explore the reasons that passive search leads to more efficient search. One possibility is that these instructions influence the extent to which participants employ executive control mechanisms to direct their attention during search. Specifically, it is possible that active search instructions increase participants' propensity to employ cognitive control, whereas passive search instructions decrease their efforts to use such control. On this view, search is less efficient when following active instructions because exerting executive control over search is inefficient, relative to allowing search to proceed on the basis of the rapid and automatic mechanisms that are involved in passive search.

Tentative support for this hypothesis comes from a recent study of the effects of memory load on visual search performance (Woodman, Vogel, & Luck, 2001). In one of the experiments in this report, participants completed a relatively difficult search task either as a single or dual task. The dual-task condition was designed to interfere as much as possible with the short-term memory requirements that might be shared in both tasks. As such, participants were required to remember an array of four visual items that were very similar in appearance to the search items, prior to completing the search task. Upon completion of the search, they were required to indicate whether a test memory display was the same of different from the studied memory display.

The results showed that search was overall much slower in the dual-task condition than in the single task condition. However, the slope of the search function in the dual-task condition was slightly shallower than the slope in the single task condition (though the difference in search slopes did not reach statistical significance in that experiment). As such, the authors concluded that search efficiency is unaffected by memory load. However, we believe the data is suggestive for our claim that search may be accomplished *more* efficiently when participants are unable to exert strong executive control during the search. If so, then increasing the difficulty of the memory task might actually improve the efficiency of search task, in much the same way as following passive instructions, provided the memory task also requires executive control functions.

In Experiment 2 participants performed a concurrent memory task with visual search, in a test of this hypothesis. As in Experiment 1, participants completed the hard and easy search tasks in separate blocks of trials. However, instead of varying search instructions across participants, we varied executive processing demands by having some participants complete the search task as a single task, and others as part of a dual task, together with a demanding visual memory task.

The sequence of displays used in Experiment 2 consisted of a memory study display, a visual search display, and, finally, a memory test display. Examples of the memory study and test displays are shown in Figure 3. In the single task, participants were required to simply complete the search task and to ignore the two memory displays. In the dual task, participants were required to first memorize the study display, complete the search task, and then report whether the memory test display was same as or different to the memory study display. To ensure that the memory task was difficult and required considerable executive control, we followed Woodman et al. (2001) in designing memory study and test displays that were highly confusable with each other, as well as being confusable with the targets in the search display.

We expected that, as in Woodman et al. (2001), search should generally take longer when it is done as a dual task than when it is done as a single task. However, if passive instructions lead to more efficient search because they encourage participants to exert less executive control over search, then preventing participants from using executive control during search, by having them perform a concurrent memory task, should have a similar impact on search as did the passive instructions. Specifically, this would mean that search slopes in the dual task should be shallower than those for the single task when search is hard, but not when search is easy. On the other hand, if the influence of passive search observed in Experiment 1 is not a matter of decreasing the use of executive control mechanisms, then the slopes

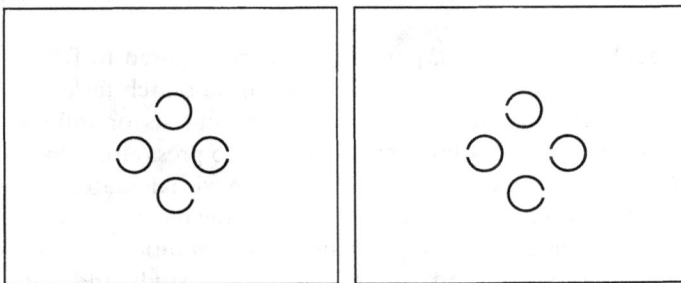

Figure 3. Examples of the memory study (left) and memory test (right) displays used in Experiment 2.

of the search functions should be equivalent across single and dual tasks for both easy and hard search.

Method

Participants. Twenty-four undergraduate students reporting normal or corrected-to-normal vision participated in a 45 minute session for extra course credit at the University of British Columbia. Twelve participated were randomly assigned to either the single- or the dual-task condition.

Stimuli. The search displays in Experiment 2 were identical to those in Experiment 1. In addition, Experiment 2 also included memory study and memory test displays. An example of a study display is shown in Figure 3. Each display consisted of four circles, each of which had a gap either on the left or on the right, with the constraint that not all of the circles had a gap on the same side. The circles were 2.0 cm (2.0 deg) above, below, to the left, and to the right of fixation. Figure 3 also shows an example of a memory test display. On half of the trials the memory test display on a given trial was identical to the study display; on the other half of the trials the orientation of one of the items in the test display differed from its counterpart in the study display.

Procedure. The main change in the procedure was that all participants were given neutral search instructions in Experiment 2. Participants were simply instructed to find the unique item in each display and, using their left hand, to press the "z" key if the gap was on the left or the "x" key if the gap was on the right. What did vary between observers was whether search was done as a single or a dual task. This meant that the sequence of displays used on each trial of Experiment 2 included a fixation cross presented for 500 ms, a blank interval for 400 ms, a memory study display for 1800 ms, a visual search display presented until response or until 2700 ms elapsed, a blank interval for 400 ms, and, finally, a memory test display presented for 2500 ms.

In the dual-task condition, participants were required to first memorize the items in the study display, complete the visual search task, and, finally, report whether the memory test display was same as or different to the memory study display by using their right hand to press either the "." key or the "/" key, respectively. The response to the visual search display was speeded as in Experiment 1, but the response to the memory test display was not. In contrast, participants in the single-task condition were required to complete the search task and ignore the memory study and test displays. They simply pressed the "/" key to advance to the search display each time the memory test display was presented.

Results and discussion

Response times.   As in Experiment 1, a recursive procedure was used to remove the outliers in each cell before the RTs for the correct responses were analysed. The data were then submitted to a mixed ANOVA that assessed the between-group factors of task (single, dual) and order (hard search first, easy search first) and the within-participant factors of search difficulty (easy vs. hard) and set size (2, 4, and 6).

The mean correct RT is shown in Figure 4. With the exception of the overall slowing in responses in the dual-task condition relative to the single task condition, the pattern of results is strikingly similar to that of Experiment 1. Like the passive search instructions in Experiment 1, performing search with a concurrent memory task led to more efficient search when search was hard, but no reliable influence when search was easy.

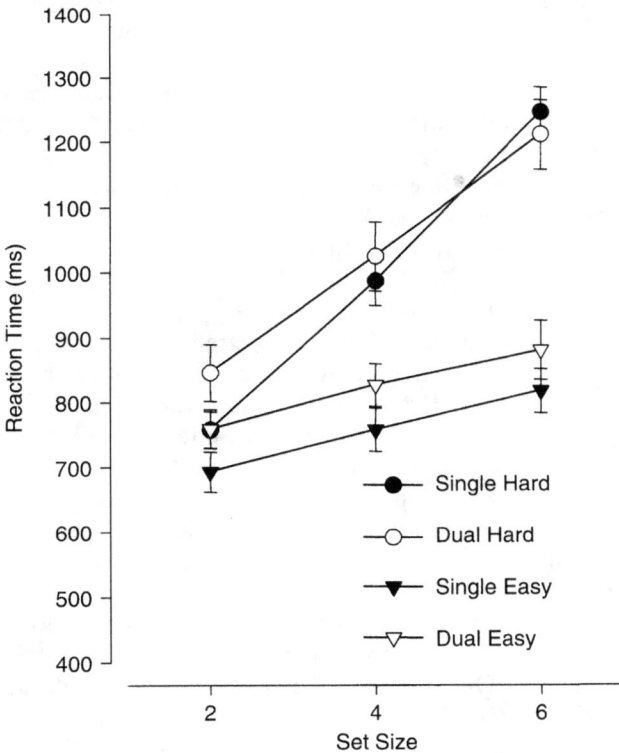

Figure 4.   Mean correct response times for identifying the target in Experiment 2. The error bars represent one standard error of the mean.

The findings suggest that preventing participants from using executive control during search, by having them do a concurrent memory task, has a similar impact as the passive instructions. Assuming that a concurrent memory task influences the same factors as do the passive search instructions, the findings imply that passive instructions increase search efficiency by encouraging participants to give up executive control during search and instead rely on more rapid automatic processes.

These conclusions were supported by the ANOVA. As in Experiment 1, RT increased linearly with set size, $F(1, 22) = 449.731$, $MSE = 4057.3$, $p < .001$, and the slopes of the search functions were much steeper in the difficult search condition than in the easy search condition, $F(2, 40) = 92.424$, $MSE = 3008.2$, $p < .001$. Although RT for the dual task was higher than for the single task, this main effect did not reach statistical significance, $F(1, 20) = 1.128$, $MSE = 76,453.9$, $p = .301$. Most importantly, however, the results revealed that search slopes were shallower in the dual-task condition than in the single-task condition, $F(2, 40) = 4.274$, $MSE = 2803.4$, $p = .021$, indicating that the presence of a concurrent memory task influenced the efficiency of search. Furthermore, the extent to which the dual task influenced the search slopes depended on the difficulty of search, $F(2, 44) = 3.604$, $MSE = 2955.0$, $p = .036$. Neither of these latter two findings depended on the order of the hard and easy search conditions, both $Fs < 2.605$, both $ps > .09$.

To evaluate how the influence of the dual task depended on the difficulty of search, the data for the hard and easy search conditions were further analysed separately. This revealed that the dual task had a substantial effect on slopes for hard search, $F(2, 40) = 6.351$, $MSE = 3557.1$, $p < .005$, but did not have any measurable influence for easy search, $F < 1$. Though the difference between single and dual task search slopes in the hard search condition was greater when hard search was done after the easy search (slope difference of 45 ms/item) than when hard search was done before easy search (slope difference of 15 ms/item), this effect of order did not reach statistical significance, $F(2, 40) = 2.661$, $MSE = 3557.1$, $p = .082$.

Overall, the RT search slopes in Experiment 2 are steeper than those in Experiment 1, as seen in a comparison of Figures 2 and 4. A similar comparison of the errors in Tables 1 and 2 reveals that these slopes were shallower in Experiment 2 than in Experiment 1. This pattern of findings suggests that participants responded with a different criterion in the two experiments. There are two possible reasons for such a criterion shift between experiments. One is that participants strategically adopted a stricter criterion in Experiment 2 because they had to complete an additional memory task. Another possible reason is that participants failed to respond more often before the visual search display timed-out in Experiment 1 than in Experiment 2. Indeed, the maximum exposure duration of the displays

TABLE 2
Mean percentages of errors in Experiment 2

	Set size		
	2	4	6
No load			
Hard	3.4	0.8	2.3
Easy	1.8	0.5	0.8
Load			
Hard	2.1	3.5	2.6
Easy	2.6	4.2	2.9

was made longer in Experiment 2 (2700 ms) than in Experiment 1 (1800 ms), to accommodate the increase in task difficulty in Experiment 2. Because responses that occurred after the display timed-out were recorded as errors this difference between the two experiments would be similar to participants adopting different criteria across experiments. To demonstrate that these two possibilities do not cause a problem for our interpretation of the RT data, and to facilitate comparison across experiments, we analysed both the errors and the inefficiency scores.

Error data and inefficiency scores. We first considered the possibility that the RT results might be due in part to the trading relationship between speed and accuracy. The error rates for each condition in Experiment 2 are shown in Table 2 and they indicate that speed–accuracy tradeoffs pose no problems for our interpretation of the RT data. Error rates were relatively low overall and there was no evidence that the differences in the slopes of the RT functions associated with the single and dual tasks were the result of participants trading speed for accuracy. These conclusions were corroborated by a mixed ANOVA similar to the one used to analyse the RT data. The analysis revealed no significant main effects or interactions, all Fs < 3.894, all ps $> .06$.

To bolster our conclusion that trading relations between speed and accuracy do not contaminate the RT data, we calculated the inefficiency scores, as shown on the right side of Figure 5. This shows that when RT and errors are combined, the pattern of data is the same as the pattern revealed by considering the RT data alone. Namely, the dual task led to increased search efficiency in the hard search condition but had no measurable influence in the easy search condition.

Having calculated the inefficiency scores for both Experiments 1 and 2, it is now possible to directly compare the results of the two experiments

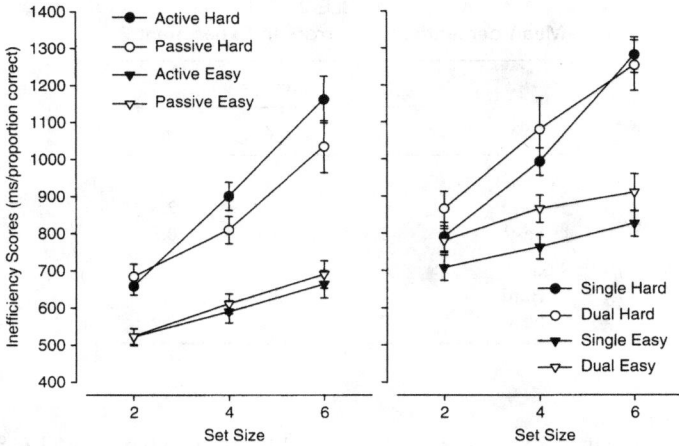

Figure 5. Mean search inefficiency scores (correct RT/proportion correct) for identifying the target in Experiment 1 (left) and Experiment 2 (right). The error bars represent one standard error of the mean.

because the inefficiency scores eliminate differences in response criterion between experiments. Note that the slopes of the inefficiency functions for Experiment 2 (right side of Figure 5) are very similar to those of Experiment 1 (left side of Figure 5). This further indicates that performing a concurrent memory task has the same impact on search efficiency as does instructing participants to search passively through the displays, once the different baseline rates of error in the two experiments have been factored in.

Memory data. The memory task was completed with an overall accuracy of 84.5%. The percentages of correct responses for the easy search condition were 80.4, 83.9, and 88.3, for set sizes 2, 4, and 6, respectively. The corresponding percentages for the hard search condition were 84.8, 82.8, and 87.0. The accuracy scores were evaluated using a mixed ANOVA, which assessed the between-group factor of order (hard search first, easy search first) and the within-participant factors of search difficulty (hard, easy) and set size (2, 4, and 6). The analysis revealed that memory performance increased with set size, $F(1, 11) = 22.616$, $MSE = 0.001322$, $p < .001$. No other main effects or interactions reached significance, all $Fs < 2.301$, all $ps > .126$.

A consideration of the visual search data together with the memory data suggests that our interpretation of the visual search slopes is not compromised by a tradeoff between tasks. If the shallower search slopes in the dual-task condition been accompanied by a decrease in memory performance as set size increased, it could be interpreted as a tradeoff between tasks. Such a pattern could be explained by positing that the shallower search slopes in the dual-task condition occurred because, as set size increased, resources were progressively shifted from the memory task to the search task. However, the pattern of data just described was not found in this experiment. Rather, memory performance increased with set size. Thus, any task tradeoff would actually lead to an underestimation of the influence of memory load on search efficiency and would further support our interpretation of the search findings.

GENERAL DISCUSSION

There is considerable anecdotal evidence that some visual search tasks can be made more efficient by instructing participants to simply relax, that is, to take a passive cognitive approach to an otherwise difficult task. In Experiment 1 we tested this possibility formally by instructing participants to complete a search task either by *actively* directing their attention to the target or by *passively* allowing the target item to just "pop" into their minds. The results showed that passive search instructions led to greater efficiency when the search task was hard but these instructions had no observable influence when the search task was easy. Our tentative hypothesis was that the passive instructional set induced participants to rely less on their control processes and to rely more on the unconscious processes that are able to distinguish the target from the distractors.

This hypothesis was put to the test in Experiment 2 where the amount of executive control available during the search task was reduced by having participants complete the search task while concurrently holding similar visual items in short-term memory. The results were strikingly similar to those in Experiment 2. As with passive search instructions, completing search concurrently with a memory task led to more efficient search when search was hard but had no observable influence on search efficiency when search was easy.

Taken together, these results support the following conclusions. First, visual search can be made more efficient by instructing participants to adopt a passive cognitive strategy, consistent with previous anecdotal evidence. This increase in efficiency is not simply the result of a tradeoff between speed and accuracy; both response times and errors agree that search is more efficient with passive instructions. Second, passive instructions influence searches that are relatively hard but do not influence searches that are relatively easy. This is consistent with passive instructions having their influence primarily on tasks on which participants are likely to try to exert strong cognitive control. It also shows in another way that passive instructions do not simply alter the decision criteria used by participants, since that effect should be evident in both hard and easy searches. Third, the similarity in the search results for passive instructions (Experiment 1) and for a difficult concurrent memory task (Experiment 2) is consistent with the improved efficiency deriving from a reduced reliance on slow executive control processes and a forced reliance on more rapid automatic processes for directing attention during search.

The present findings extend the work showing that active and passive cognitive strategies influence search for items associated with conceptual categories (Smilek et al., 2006a). A potential criticism of this work, considered in isolation, was that conceptual or abstract representations might be more susceptible to strategic influences than basic visual discriminations. The present findings show that this is clearly not the case. Cognitive strategy is able to influence attentional guidance at early stages of perception, where only acuity-based visual discriminations are required.

We must also emphasize that our conclusions regarding the influence of a concurrent memory task on search efficiency differ considerably from the conclusion reached by Woodman et al. (2001). These authors concluded that a concurrent memory task has no influence on the efficiency of visual search. Their conclusion was based on the fact that they failed to find a statistically significant *increase* in the slopes of the search functions under dual task conditions. However, in their Experiment 2, when the memory task was particularly difficult, the search slope in the dual-task condition was actually shallower than the slope in the single-task condition, although not significantly so. In our study, this trend was statistically significant when the search task was made sufficiently difficult. This finding therefore leads us to conclude that performing a concurrent memory task can in fact influence search efficiency; but it does so by *improving* the efficiency of difficult searches.

The present findings are consistent with a recent report by Olivers and Nieuwenhuis (2005), who showed that the temporal dynamics of attention is influenced by inducing a "distributed state of mind" in participants. In their study, participants were required to report two successively presented visual targets. As is typically the case in such studies, participants were much poorer at reporting the second target when the two targets are presented in close succession than when the targets were widely separated in time, a finding known as the attentional blink. The important new finding, however, was that this dual-task deficit was completely eliminated when participants were presented with rhythmic music simultaneously with the visual stream of items. The authors argued that under normal circumstances, participants focus on the first of the two targets and that this effortful focusing of attention leads to the exclusion of the second target, thus yielding the AB deficit. In contrast, when rhythmic music is played, participants are placed into a "distributed sate of mind" allowing both the first and second target to be processed, which eliminates the typical AB deficit. We find these results relevant because, in our view, music might have a similar influence as our passive search instructions in that they both lead participants to relinquish executive control and to rely more heavily on automatic, and perhaps implicit, processes. As such, it would be interesting to see whether our active and passive instructions also influence the size of the AB deficit and whether playing music during search improves search efficiency.

Do passive instructions always benefit performance?

Although adopting a passive cognitive strategy improved search in the present study, it is conceivable that a passive strategy may be detrimental in other situations. Indeed, in other domains, such as conceptual categorization, it is well known that a nonanalytic approach can either help or hurt performance relative to an analytic approach (see Whittlesea et al., 1994). The same is likely true of active and passive cognitive strategies on perception. Specifically, we predict that any task that requires participants to analyse a display into its component parts would be done more effectively using an active rather than a passive cognitive strategy.

One situation in which adopting a passive cognitive strategy seems to hurt perception is when participants judge the clarity of coarse quantized images (e.g., a face of Abraham Lincoln). Typically, when participants view such images they rate the clarity of a quantized image overlaid with a screen as higher than the same image viewed without a screen, a finding that we refer to as the *illusion of clarity* (Smilek, Rempel, & Enns, 2006b). The illusion of clarity occurs because participants actively segregate the screen from the quantized image and, in the process, they attribute the high frequency edges created by quantization to the screen rather than to the face. The end result is a clearer view of the face. In this task, our findings indicate that adopting a passive cognitive strategy decreases the perceived clarity of images, relative to when an active strategy is adopted. This demonstrates that there is at least one case in which a passive strategy impairs a perceptual process. We believe there will be others, even in search, provided that the search task requires an active segmentation or individuation of component features of the display.

Implications of the present findings

A prediction that follows from this interpretation is that passive search instructions should magnify the extent to which attention is oriented on the basis of information processed only implicitly, or without awareness. This follows from our conclusion that passive instructions encourage participants to rely less on conscious control processes. This prediction was recently tested in a study of contextual cueing (Lleras & von Mühlenen, 2004). Contextual cueing refers to the guidance of attention by implicit memory of previously encountered search displays (Chun & Jiang, 1998). In an initial attempt to obtain contextual cueing, Lleras and von Mühlenen failed to replicate the findings of Chun and Jiang; participants searched as efficiently on new search displays as on those they had previously encountered. Based on the present findings, Lleras and von Mühlenen hypothesized that a passive cognitive strategy may be critical to obtaining guidance by implicit memory. In a subsequent experiment, they therefore instructed participants to search either actively or passively through displays, using the same instructional sets used in the present study. The results showed a robust contextual cueing effect for individuals instructed to search passively, but no contextual cueing effect for individuals who were instructed to search actively. This is consistent with the hypothesis that passive instructions induce less reliance on conscious control processes.

Another prediction that emerges from our interpretation is that individuals with deficits in executive control functions should be able to search more efficiently under some conditions than individuals with unimpaired executive control functioning. This prediction is supported by findings showing that children with autism, who are known to have deficits in executive control, perform difficult visual search tasks more efficiently than normally developing children (O'Riordan, Plaisted, Driver, & Baron-Cohen, 2001). However, not all individuals with reduced executive control capacities show generally enhanced search efficiency. For instance, the elderly (Trick & Enns, 1998), young children (Plude, Enns, & Brodeur, 1994), and individuals with frontal damage (Kumada & Humphreys, 2002) all tend to show substantial reductions in visual search efficiency when compared to young healthy adults. One reason why these individuals may show reduced search efficiency is that they are actually trying to exert control over their search, and in their case, their control is poor or inappropriately matched to the task. If so, the search efficiency of these individuals might actually increase if they relaxed and gave up trying to exert conscious control, relying instead on their implicit processes. On the other hand, these individuals may also have other deficits, such as a reduced functional field of view that contributes to the reduction of their search efficiency for other reasons. Clearly more research is needed to understand fully how instructional sets can alter the guidance of visual attention. The findings to date on this issue suggest that this may well be a fruitful avenue of study.

REFERENCES

Bacon, W. F., & Egeth, H. E. (1994). Overriding stimulus-driven attentional capture. *Perception and Psychophysics*, *55*, 485–496.

Bravo, M., & Nakayama, K. (1992). The role of attention in different visual search tasks. *Perception and Psychophysics*, *51*, 465–472.

Carrasco, M., & Yeshurun, Y. (1998). The contribution of covert attention to the set-size and eccentricity effects in visual search. *Journal of Experimental Psychology: Human Perception and Performance*, *24*, 673–692.

Chun, M. M., & Jiang, Y. (1998). Contextual cueing: Implicit learning and memory of visual context guides spatial attention. *Cognitive Psychology*, *36*, 28–71.

Cohen, A., & Ivry, R. B. (1991). Density effects in conjunction search: Evidence for coarse location mechanism of feature integration. *Journal of Experimental Psychology: Human Perception and Performance*, *17*, 891–901.

Duncan, J., & Humphreys, G. W. (1989). Visual search and stimulus similarity. *Psychological Review*, *96*, 433–458.

Enns, J. T., & Rensink, R. (1992). *VScope™ software and manual (version 1.0): Vision testing software for the Macintosh*. Vancouver, Canada: Micropsych Software.

Found, A., & Müller, H. J. (1996). Searching for unknown feature targets on more than one dimension: Investigating a "dimension-weighting" account. *Perception and Psychophysics*, *58*, 88–101.

Jacoby, L. L., & Brooks, L. R. (1984). Nonanalytic cognition: Memory, perception, and concept learning. *Psychology of Learning and Motivation*, *18*, 1–46.

Kumada, T., & Humphreys, G. W. (2002). Early selection induced by perceptual load in a patient with frontal lobe damage: External vs. internal modulation of processing control. *Cognitive Neuropsychology*, *19*, 49–65.

Lange, L. (1888). Neue Experimente uber den Vorgang der einfachen Reaktion auf Sinneseindrucke. *Philosophische Studien*, *4*, 479–510.

Liu, G., Healey, C. G., & Enns, J. T. (2003). Target detection and localization in visual search: A dual systems perspective. *Perception and Psychophysics*, *65*, 678–694.

Lleras, A., & von Mühlenen, A. (2004). Spatial context and top-down strategies in visual search. *Spatial Vision*, *17*, 465–482.

Marcel, A. J. (1983). Conscious and unconscious perception: Experiments on visual masking and word recognition. *Cognitive Psychology*, *15*, 197–237.

Müller, H. J., Reimann, B., & Krummenacher, J. (2003). Visual search for singleton feature targets across dimensions: Stimulus- and expectancy-driven effects in dimensional weighting. *Journal of Experimental Psychology: Human Perception and Performance*, *29*, 1021–1035.

Olivers, C. N., & Nieuwenhuis, S. (2005). The beneficial effects of concurrent task-irrelevant mental activity on temporal attention. *Psychological Science*, *16*, 265–269.

O'Riordan, M. A., Plaisted, K. C., Driver, J., & Baron-Cohen, S. (2001). Superior visual search in autism. *Journal of Experimental Psychology: Human Perception and Performance*, *27*, 719–730.

Pachella, R. G. (1974). The interpretation of reaction time in information-processing research. In B. H. Kantowitz (Ed.), *Human information processing: Tutorials in performance and cognition* (pp. 41–82). Hillsdale, NJ: Lawrence Erlbaum Associates, Inc.

Plude, D., Enns, J. T., & Brodeur, D. A. (1994). The development of selective attention: A lifespan overview. *Acta Psychologica*, *86*, 227–272.

Pylyshyn, Z. W. (2003). *Seeing and visualizing: It's not what you think*. Cambridge, MA: MIT Press/Bradford Books.

Smilek, D., Dixon, M. J., & Merikle. P. M. (2006a). Revisiting the category effect: The influence of meaning and search strategy on the efficiency of visual search. *Brain Research*, *1080*, 73–90.

Smilek, D., Rempel, M. I., & Enns. J. T. (2006b). The illusion of clarity: Image segmentation and edge attribution without filling-in. *Visual Cognition*, *14*, 1–36.

Snodgrass, M., Shevrin, H.. & Kopka. M. (1993a). The mediation of intentional judgements by unconscious perceptions: The influences of task strategy, task preference. word meaning, and motivation. *Consciousness and Cognition*, *2*, 169–193.

Snodgrass, M., Shevrin, H.. & Kopka. M. (1993b). Absolute inhibition is incompatible with conscious perception. *Consciousness and Cognition*, *2*, 204–209.

Theeuwes, J. (2004). Top-down search strategies cannot override attentional capture. *Psychonomic Bulletin and Review*, *11*(1), 65–70.

Townsend, J. T., & Ashby, F. G. (1983). *Stochastic modeling of elementary psychological processes*. New York: Cambridge University Press.

Treisman. A., & Sato, S. (1990). Conjunction search revisited. *Journal of Experimental Perception and Performance*, *16*, 459–478.

Trick. L., & Enns, J. T. (1998). Lifespan changes in attention: The visual search task. *Cognitive Development*, *13*, 369–386.

Van Selst. M., & Jolicoeur, P. (1994). A solution to the effect of sample size on outlier elimination. *Quarterly Journal of Experimental Psychology*, *47A*, 631–650.

Van Selst. M.. & Merikle, P. M. (1993). Perception below the objective threshold? *Consciousness and Cognition*, *2*, 194–203.

Whittlesea. B. W. A., Brooks, L. R., & Westcott. C. (1994). After the learning is over: Factors controlling the selective application of general and particular knowledge. *Journal of Experimental Psychology: Learning, Memory, and Cognition*, *20*, 259–274.

Wickelgren. W. A. (1977). Speed–accuracy tradeoff and information processing dynamics. *Acta Psychologica*, *41*, 67–85.

Wolfe. J. M. (1994). Guided Search 2.0: A revised model of visual search. *Psychonomic Bulletin and Review*, *1*, 202–238.

Wolfe. J. M. (1998). What can 1,000,000 trials tell us about visual search? *Psychological Science*, *9*(1), 33–39.

Wolfe. J. M.. Butcher. S. J., Lee. C.. & Hyle. M. (2003). Changing your mind: On the contributions of top-down and bottom-up guidance in visual search for feature singletons. *Journal of Experimental Psychology: Human Perception and Performance*, *29*, 483–502.

Woodman. G. F., Vogel, E. K., & Luck. S. J. (2001). Visual search remains efficient when visual working memory is full. *Psychological Science*, *12*, 219–224.

VISUAL COGNITION, 2006, 14 (4/5/6/7/8), 565–583

Ψ Psychology Press
Taylor & Francis Group

Attention on autopilot: Past experience and attentional set

Andrew B. Leber and Howard E. Egeth

Department of Psychological and Brain Sciences, Johns Hopkins University, Baltimore, MD, USA

What factors determine the implementation of attentional set? It is often assumed that set is determined only by experimenter instructions and characteristics of the immediate stimulus environment, yet it is likely that other factors play a role. The present experiments were designed to evaluate the latter possibility; specifically, the role of past experience was probed. In a 320-trial training phase, observers could use one of two possible attentional sets (but not both) to find colour-defined targets in a rapid serial visual presentation (RSVP) stream of letters. In the subsequent 320-trial test phase, where either set could be used, observers persisted in using their pre-established sets through the remainder of the experiment, affirming a clear role of past experience in the implementation of attentional set. A second experiment revealed that sufficient experience with a given set was necessary to facilitate persistence with it. These results are consistent with models of executive control (e.g., Norman & Shallice, 1986), in which "top-down" behaviours are influenced by learned associations between tasks and the environment.

Attentional set—a preparatory state of the information processing system that prioritizes stimuli for selection based on simple visual features—is a powerful tool that allows observers to solve efficiently the various visual search challenges they may be faced with at any particular moment. Much is known about the types of sets, or strategies, at the observers' disposal (e.g., colour, orientation, or motion; see Wolfe & Horowitz, 2004, for a recent review), but less is known about how these sets are chosen. What are the determining factors?

An intuitive—albeit simplistic—answer holds that observers always choose the attentional set that they think will optimize performance. One

Please address all correspondence to Andrew Leber, Department of Psychology, Yale University, PO Box 208205, New Haven, CT 06520-8205, USA. E-mail: andrew.leber@yale.edu

This research was supported in part by a grant from the FAA (2001-G-020). We thank Chip Folk, Roger Remington, Steve Yantis, and an anonymous reviewer for thoughtful comments and suggestions on previous versions of this paper. Additionally, we thank James Drakakis, Sarah James, and Lindsay Vodoklys for assistance with data collection.

DOI: 10.1080/13506280500193438

prediction that can be drawn from this "maximal efficiency" account is that observers should attempt to establish sets that prevent unnecessary processing of known-to-be irrelevant stimuli. For example, in a search for a vertical bar among horizontal bars, observers could engage in an attentional set for "vertical", so as to avoid interference by a salient item possessing no informative value regarding the target's location (e.g., a singleton bar that is red when the remaining bars are all grey). Indeed, many reports in the literature have documented successful avoidance of distraction from feature singletons that were not predictive of the target location (e.g., Bacon & Egeth, 1994; Folk, Remington, & Johnston, 1992; Jonides & Yantis, 1988; Theeuwes, 1990; Yantis & Egeth, 1999). However, several other reports have shown that known-to-be-irrelevant singletons sometimes do interfere with search (e.g., Bacon & Egeth, 1994; Theeuwes, 1991, 1992; Todd & Kramer, 1994; Turatto & Galfano, 2001). In some cases, patterns of seemingly inconsistent results have been obtained in essentially the same paradigm. For example, Folk et al. (1992) initially found that irrelevant green singletons interfered with search for red singletons in one experiment, but later work using similar stimulus conditions showed that observers effectively ignored the green singletons (Folk & Remington, 1998).

Why would observers sometimes adopt clearly nonoptimal sets that permit distraction by irrelevant items, if they are capable of more efficient behaviour? One possibility, suggested by Bacon and Egeth (1994), is that even when participants are capable of using attentional sets to avoid distraction, it is not necessarily their top priority to do so.

Following a speculation by Pashler (1988), Bacon and Egeth (1994) proposed two distinct attentional sets: *Singleton detection mode* and *feature search mode*. They described the former as a diffuse set that grants priority to the most salient information (e.g., feature singletons) in the visual field. Singleton detection mode does not discriminate between salience on the target's defining dimension and salience on other dimensions; thus, irrelevant singletons can capture attention when singleton detection mode is used. In contrast, Bacon and Egeth described feature search mode as a narrow attentional set that is limited to the target's defining feature; therefore, interference from salient information not matching the attentional set should be minimal. Bacon and Egeth speculated that singleton detection mode may be less effort-intensive to employ than feature search mode, so it may be appealing to tolerate a small decrement in search performance as a tradeoff with effort expended. Feature search mode, however, should be used when singleton detection mode would result in performance below some putative criterion of effectiveness.

To support their theoretical framework, Bacon and Egeth (1994) adapted a paradigm from Theeuwes (1991, 1992) that, in some experiments, yielded significant interference from irrelevant colour singletons while participants searched for shape singletons. Bacon and Egeth's implementation contained conditions where the shape targets were not singletons, which rendered singleton detection mode ineffective. Trials of these conditions were mixed within blocks with trials like those of Theeuwes where the targets were singletons, under the assumption that observers would maintain a feature search mode for the shape target across all trial types. Bacon and Egeth found that the colour-singleton distractors did not interfere in any of these conditions, including trials like those of Theeuwes where the target was a singleton, suggesting that feature search mode was used. These results supported the notion that participants were capable of adopting feature search mode in experiments such as those of Theeuwes, but they exhibited a preference for singleton detection mode in those experiments because such a strategy, although susceptible to more distraction than feature search mode, was still sufficient to locate the shape targets. Accordingly, Bacon and Egeth's results suggest that sets are not solely established to maximize performance. Rather, other factors may play a role.

Unfortunately, few subsequent research efforts have sought to reveal what factors are involved in determining attentional set (but see the section on intertrial contingencies in the General Discussion). In fact, it is often still assumed by researchers that the set of the observer should be based only on factors such as experimenter instructions or characteristics of the stimulus displays. These assumptions, however, are surely insufficient to predict the visual search strategies employed by observers, as evidenced by the contradictory findings in the attention capture literature. In this paper, we entertain the notion that additional forces are at work in determining the attentional set of observers.

Perhaps first acknowledging that attentional set is mediated by top-down control mechanisms can facilitate insight into how sets are determined. Research into executive control processes has long shown that human behaviour is not always optimal or straightforward.

Consider the classic "water jug" experiments carried out by Luchins and Luchins (Luchins, 1942; Luchins & Luchins, 1950; described in Woodworth & Schlosberg, 1960). Observers were asked to solve a mathematical word problem that involved measuring an exact quantity of water by using three separate jars of varying size. The first five trials could be solved by the same somewhat complicated algorithm. On the sixth, critical, trial that algorithm would still work; however, a considerably easier solution was also available. Luchins observed that observers not only continued to use the now inefficient routine on this critical trial, but they persisted with it for several more trials. As a result, it was concluded that "Einstellung", or "mental set", is not constantly evaluated to ensure that the most efficient strategies are carried out.

This notion that humans do not constantly evaluate their performance is central to modern models of executive control. One influential model, the "Attention to Action" model of Norman and Shallice (1986), assumes that behavioural routines, or "schemas", are carried out automatically, triggered by environmental cues (or the output of other schemas). For example, the repeated association between entering a dark room and reaching to the wall for the light switch eventually leads to a high activation level for the "turn on the lights" schema as one enters a darkened room. Evidence for such automatic influences on behaviour comes from many sources, but introspection is often the most compelling; most people can easily recall at least one anecdote where absent-mindedness led them to perform an action sequence against their goals (e.g., setting out to go to the grocery store on a Saturday and inadvertently driving all the way to work; for studies of such "action lapses" or "capture errors", see Norman, 1981; Reason, 1979, 1984). While automatic processes may be most evident when they lead to unintended actions, Norman and Shallice theorized that these processes are always at work. In effect, the influence of automatic processes could be pervasive, biasing actions toward a particular behaviour in each learned environment. Only when the output of a schema fails to reach behavioural goals within an acceptable range—which can happen, for example, when a new goal arises in a familiar environment—does an executive monitoring process (what Norman & Shallice call the "supervisory attentional system") take over to inhibit some schemas while preferentially activating others.

Do the properties of executive control, such as persistence with a pre-established strategy (as Luchins & Luchins observed), govern the implementation of attentional set? Or, alternatively, is attentional set always determined solely by current task demands and stimulus characteristics? In the present experiments, we studied the role of past experience. Observers participated in a training phase of visual search trials designed to encourage the use of a particular strategic behaviour (i.e., attentional set); one group of observers was required to use singleton detection mode while another group was required to use feature search mode. After training, all observers were treated in the same manner; a test phase of trials that could be adequately searched with either attentional set (singleton detection or feature search mode) was presented. Would performance in the test phase be influenced by the conditions of the training phase?

EXPERIMENT 1

In carrying out this study, some methodological concerns were addressed. First, the paradigm would need to contain conditions where more than one set was available to the observer. Second, it would need to incorporate a robust tool that could characterize the set used by the observer. The paradigm of Folk, Leber, and Egeth (2002) was deemed adequate to satisfy both of these requirements.

Folk et al. (2002) asked participants to monitor a rapid serial visual presentation (RSVP) of 15 letters at fixation for a single colour-defined target. These streams appeared at a rate of approximately 10 letters per second. In their first experiment, the target colour was consistent across trials (e.g., red), and nontargets were always grey. To find the target letter, either singleton detection mode or feature search mode could be used (the target was always unique with respect to the homogeneously coloured nontargets, making singleton mode a viable strategy, and its consistent colour made feature search mode for the specific target colour a viable set). Because two suitable sets were available on these trials, they can be referred to as *option* trials. Folk et al. were able to determine which set was used, by measuring the interference created by briefly presented peripheral distractors, which contained four pound-signs (i.e., "#"; see Figure 1). Three types of distractor displays were used (in addition to a no-distractor condition). In

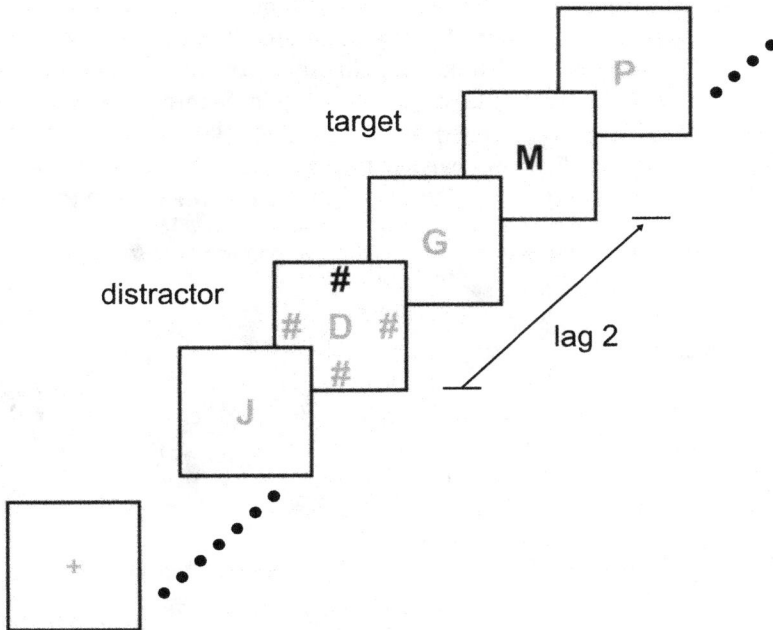

Figure 1. Representation of trial events in Experiment 1 of Folk et al. (2002). In this example, a distractor display containing a colour singleton appears at a "lag" of two items (approximately 200 ms) prior to the target. Black characters were coloured red or green (see text for details). Figure reprinted with permission of the Psychonomic Society.

the "all-grey" distractor display. all four "#"'s were coloured grey. In the "same-coloured singleton" display. three "#"'s were grey, and the remaining "#" was the same colour as the target (red or green). The "different-coloured singleton" display contained a singleton colour item that did not match the target colour (green or red, depending on the target colour). Folk et al. reasoned that if a singleton distractor could not be excluded by the attentional set, it would interfere with search performance (in comparison to the no-distractor and neutral all-grey distractor displays). They found that both same- and different-coloured singleton distractors interfered, and the cost was greatest at a distractor–target "lag" of two, that is, when the distractors were presented simultaneously with the letter appearing two frames (i.e.. approximately 200 ms) prior to the target (see Figure 2, left panel). The fact that interference was created by both same- and different-coloured singletons suggested that singleton detection mode was used.

In a second experiment, Folk et al. (2002. Exp. 2) made the nontargets in the stream heterogeneous in colour. This manipulation rendered singleton detection mode ineffective (the target did not stand out as a singleton), so it was predicted that feature search mode would be adopted. The results confirmed this prediction; interference from same-coloured distractors was not observed in comparison to the all-grey condition (although both all-grey and different-coloured singletons were slightly worse than the no-distractor condition). while target-coloured distractors significantly impaired perfor-mance (see Figure 2, right panel). Similar to what Bacon and Egeth (1994) showed with static displays, participants in temporal search tasks (i.e., RSVP) tended to operate in singleton detection mode when given the option.

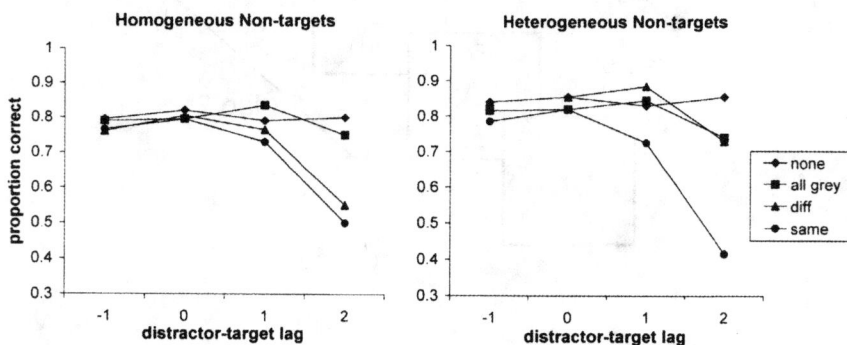

Figure 2. Data from the first (left) and second (right) experiments of Folk et al. (2002). Mean proportion correct is plotted as a function of distractor–target lag. by distractor condition. "None" refers to trials where no distractors were presented. All peripheral "#" items were grey on "all-grey trials", one of the four items was a nontarget-coloured singleton on "diff" trials. and one of the four items was a target-coloured singleton on "same" trials; see text for additional details. Reprinted with permission of the Psychonomic Society.

However, when singleton detection mode was rendered ineffective, they exhibited the ability to use feature search mode.

The paradigm of Folk et al. (2002) was used in the present experiments to determine if past experience could influence an observer's attentional set. In these experiments a "test phase" of option trials (e.g., like those used in Experiment 1 of Folk et al., 2002) was preceded by a "training phase" containing one of two trial types: One group of observers was influenced to use feature search mode for roughly 30 minutes while another group of observers was influenced to use singleton detection mode. To encourage feature search mode in the former group, observers were exposed to a block of practice trials in which they searched for a target of a known colour among heterogeneous nontargets (similar to Folk et al., 2002, Exp. 2). To encourage singleton detection mode in the latter group, observers were required in practice trials to search for targets of randomly varying colour embedded among grey nontargets (feature search mode would be ineffective, since target colour was unpredictable). Additionally, the distractor–target lag was held constant at two on all trials; since the present aim was to determine which sets were used, the lag known to yield the largest interference was chosen.

The analysis focused primarily on the test phase trials (i.e., the option trials), which were identical for both groups of observers. If past experience influences current attentional set, then participants should maintain the set used in the training phase throughout the option trials in the experimental trials. Alternatively, if attentional set is based solely on the current task demands and stimulus environment, then both groups of participants should ultimately converge upon the same set in the experimental trials, regardless of the set used during practice trials. Note that this latter alternative is agnostic as to what set should be converged upon; the key question was whether convergence would occur at all.

Method

Participants

Forty-eight Johns Hopkins undergraduates with self-reported normal or corrected-to-normal visual acuity and normal colour vision participated in a session lasting approximately 50 minutes.

Materials

Stimuli were generated with a personal computer and displayed on a 19 inch VGA monitor. Participants stabilized their heads with a chinrest placed at a viewing distance of 55 cm. Letters from the English alphabet (excluding

I, O, W, and Z), used for RSVP streams, were $1.0°$ tall $\times 1.0°$ wide with a stroke of $0.3°$; each letter, depending on variables described below, was grey, blue, purple, green, or red. When present, "#" distractors ($1.0°$ tall, $1.0°$ wide, stroke $=0.3°$) were centred $5.2°$ above, below, to the right, and to the left of fixation; they were grey, red, or green. All stimuli were presented on a black background.

Design

The experiment consisted of a *training phase* and *test phase* for all observers. For the training phase, half of the observers were assigned to the "feature group"; the remaining observers were assigned to the "singleton group". During the test phase, all observers—irrespective of training assignment—were treated similarly. Within each group, *colour assignment*, a variable that was used to determine the observer's target colour, was counterbalanced between observers: half of the observers were assigned "red" and the remaining observers were assigned "green".

For both groups (singleton and feature), and within each phase, three independent variables were manipulated within observers to determine the stimulus characteristics on each trial: *Distractor type* (four levels), *singleton location* (four levels), and *temporal distractor position* (five levels). This yielded 80 unique conditions, which were each presented four times in each phase for a total of 320 trials per phase; presentation order was randomized within each phase. Variables are described as follows.

- *Distractor type*. On 25% of the trials, no distractors were presented. On the remaining trials, one of three displays was presented (each 25% of the trials), which are described as follows. The "all-grey" display contained four grey "#"s. The "same-coloured singleton" display contained three grey "#"s and one "#" that matched the colour assignment (red or green, depending on the observers' colour assignment); and the "different-coloured singleton" display contained three grey "#"s and one nontarget-coloured "#" (green or red, depending on the observers' colour assignment).
- *Singleton location*. Singleton distractors (i.e., the uniquely coloured peripheral distractors), when present, appeared equally often at each of the four peripheral distractor locations.
- *Temporal distractor position*. The distractor display was presented simultaneously with the letter occupying one of five serial positions (10–14, each used equally often) in the stream. The position of the target item in the stream depended on the distractor position, as it always appeared two positions later. On no-distractor trials, distractor position was "dummy coded" to keep target position balanced.

Training phase. Depending on group assignment, observers were exposed to one of two *stream types.* (1) Observers in the feature group searched for a target of consistent colour every trial (red or green, depending on colour assignment), which was embedded in a stream of heterogeneous nontargets (grey, blue, purple, and green); the colour of each nontarget stream letter in these trials was selected randomly with replacement. (2) Observers in the singleton group searched for a target that on a given trial could be any one of five colours selected randomly with replacement. One colour was determined by the observers' colour assignment (red or green); the remaining colours were purple, blue, yellow, and orange for all observers. The target colour on each trial was unannounced to observers; thus, it was unpredictable. The nontargets in the stream, for the singleton group in this phase, were all homogeneous in colour (grey) on every trial.

Note that for the singleton group, the colour assignment variable only determined the target colour on one-fifth of the trials. (It is in the nature of the singleton detection condition to present several unpredictable targets so that observers are forced to adopt a singleton detection mode.) However, the use of colour assignment to determine *one* of the possible target colours affords a comparison between two theoretically interesting distractor types. Consider an observer whose set of possible targets includes, say, red. On some trials this observer will be shown a peripheral distractor display that contains a red "#"; this is referred to as the "same singleton" condition because the coloured "#" is the same as one of the colours in the set of possible target colours. On some other trials this observer will see a peripheral distractor that is green; this is referred to as the "different singleton" condition. Note that for this observer green is never the target.

Test phase. All observers were presented with "option" trials in this phase. In these trials, a consistently coloured target was embedded in a stream of homogeneously coloured (grey) distractors. The target colour, determined by the colour assignment variable, was the same in the test phase as it was for the training phase; for example, an observer in the feature search group who had searched for red targets in the training phase would continue to search for red targets in the test phase.

Procedure

Participants were instructed to identify a target, defined by colour, that was embedded in a rapid stream of letters at the fixation location. During the training phase, observers in the singleton group were instructed to search for the uniquely coloured item in the RSVP stream, whereas observers in the feature group were instructed to search for the red (or green) item in the stream. In the test phase, all observers were informed that the target would be consistently coloured (i.e., red for some observers or green for other observers) for the remainder of the experiment. All observers were asked to report the target's identity by entering the correct letter into a computer keyboard after the completion of the RSVP stream. Also, they were informed about the peripheral distractors and told to ignore them. Accuracy was emphasized (speeded responses were not necessary, nor could they be advantageous, since responses were only accepted after the completion of the RSVP stream). The experiment consisted of 24 practice trials, followed by 320 training phase trials, which were in turn followed by 320 test phase trials. After the practice trials, breaks were given every 40 trials (including one between the two phases).

Trials were initiated by a spacebar press, which prompted a blank-screen presentation for 1000 ms. A white fixation cross was then presented for 500 ms, followed by a 200 ms interstimulus interval. Next, the RSVP stream consisting of 20 letters began. Each letter was selected randomly without replacement from the 22-letter set and presented for 50 ms, followed by a 50 ms blank interval, yielding a rate of 100 ms/letter. At the completion of the RSVP stream, participants were prompted to report the target letter. A 250 ms feedback tone was presented for incorrect responses.

Results and discussion

To determine the use of set, the approach was to measure the interference caused by the singleton distractors by comparing them to the all-grey condition (which was deemed the most appropriate baseline following the results of Folk et al., 2002); thus the no-distractor condition was not analysed (however, it is included with the plotted means).

Training phase. Data from the training phase were analysed to determine if the experimental manipulation succeeded in inducing the observers in the two groups (feature and singleton) to adopt divergent sets.

For the feature group, mean accuracy scores in the four conditions (none, all-grey, same singleton, and different singleton) were 77%, 69%, 59%, and 72%, respectively. Two-tailed t-tests showed that performance on same singleton trials was worse than in the all-grey condition, $t(23) = 4.238$, $p < .001$; performance on different singleton trials was not different than on the all-grey trials, $t(23) = 1.440$, ns. Additionally, performance on the same singleton trials was worse than on the different singleton trials, $t(23) = 4.873$, $p < .001$. The selective interference by only the target-coloured distractor indicates that feature search mode was used on these trials.

For the singleton group, mean accuracy scores in the four distractor conditions (none, all-grey, same singleton, and different singleton) were 86%,

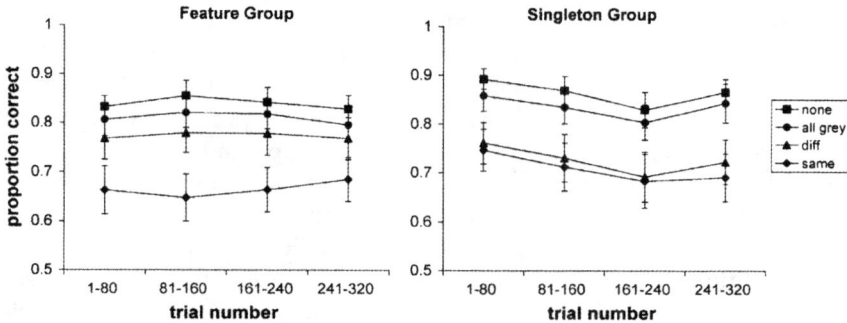

Figure 3. Performance on the test phase of Experiment 1. Left: Mean proportion correct for the feature group as a function of distractor type and trial number (placed into four bins of 80 trials). Right: Mean proportion correct for the singleton group.

83%, 68%, and 65%, respectively.[1] Performance on both "same" and "different" conditions was worse than in the all-grey condition: $t(23) = 4.917$, $p < .001$, and $t(23) = 5.038$, $p < .001$, respectively. Additionally, performance in the "same" and "different" singleton conditions did not differ significantly, $t(23) = 1.852$, ns. The observation that both singletons worsened performance suggests that singleton detection mode was used on these trials.

Test phase. Data from the test phase were plotted in bins of 80 trials to observe potential gradual changes in set over the 320 option trials (see Figure 3). The data were first analysed within each training group assignment to determine how attentional set was used (while collapsing across bin).

In the feature group, observers appeared to continue using feature search mode on the option trials; whereas the difference between performance on different singleton and all-grey trials was nonsignificant, $t(23) = 1.911$, performance was markedly worse on same singleton trials than on both all-grey trials, $t(23) = 5.249$, $p < .001$, and different singleton trials, $t(23) = 4.730$, $p < .001$. In contrast, observers in the singleton group appeared to continue using singleton detection mode on the option trials; performance was worse on both same and different singleton trials than the all-grey baseline, $t(23) = 4.227$, $p < .001$, and $t(23) = 4.185$, $p < .001$, respectively, and no difference was observed between same and different singleton trials, $t(23) = 0.907$, ns.

---

[1] The reader is reminded that "same" and "different" singleton conditions should be interpreted in the proper context, for the singleton group, during the training phase; the "different" singleton distractor never matched the colour of the target, but the "same" singleton distractor matched the actual target colour 20% of the time, as the target could be one of five colours.

Two more questions were probed within the test phase data. First, it was necessary to determine if the patterns of distractor interference in the test phase differed significantly between training phase groups. The second question concerned whether the patterns of interference changed throughout the course of the test phase. For both training groups, and within each bin of 80 trials, we computed distractor interference effects for both same and different distractor conditions. This was done by subtracting the accuracy scores for each of the respective distractor conditions from that of the all-grey condition. The resulting interference cost data were subjected to a three-factor mixed model ANOVA, which included *singleton condition* (two levels: same and different, *bin* (four levels), and *training group assignment* (two levels: feature and singleton). Speaking to the first question, it appears that the two groups used disparate sets during the test phase, as the interaction between training group assignment and singleton condition was significant, $F(1, 46) = 9.391$, $MSE = 0.200$, $p < .005$. Regarding the second question, observers did not significantly change their sets during the test phase, as no main effect of bin was observed. $F(3, 138) < 1$, nor did it enter into any interactions.

The results are clear. Set was not determined solely by the current task demands and stimulus environment. If such were the case, then both groups would have converged upon the same set. Rather, both groups persisted in using their respective training-phase sets for the 320 option trials of the test phase.

EXPERIMENT 2

Experiment 1 provided compelling evidence—in the form of an effect of past experience—that attentional set is not determined only by factors such as the immediate stimulus environment. On the heels of this result, however, comes a new question. *How* does past experience influence attentional set? We considered earlier that automatic control factors could be responsible (Norman & Shallice, 1986). However, one may question whether the results of Experiment 1 are truly indicative of automatic control over attentional set; rather than persisting because they failed to reevaluate their sets in the test phase, it is possible that observers simply decided consciously not to change their strategies. This would be plausible if, perhaps, the difference in the subjective desirability of feature search mode and singleton detection mode on the option trials was so negligible to observers that switching to the most preferred set would not have been worth the effort of reconfiguring attentional set (for evidence of costs for switching attentional set, see Hillstrom, 2000; Leber & Egeth, 2001).

Experiment 2 evaluates the role of automatic control in the persistence of attentional set. On the account that observers evaluated their current task demands and voluntarily chose not to reconfigure attentional set, one should expect that they would persist with a pre-established set regardless of their amount of experience with using it. The alternative, however, is that attentional set is influenced by automatic factors, which can be strengthened, with more experience with one set, to bias the automatic activation level of one set over another (e.g., as the model of Norman & Shallice, 1986, would predict). On this account, the duration of the training phase should influence how likely observers are to persist in the test phase.

In the present experiment, the duration of the training phase was reduced to 40 trials. Observers were expected to achieve their required sets by the end of the training phase (i.e., feature search mode or singleton detection mode, depending on group assignment); the question was whether they would persist with them in the test phase.

Method

Participants

Thirty-six Johns Hopkins undergraduates with self-reported normal or corrected-to-normal visual acuity and normal colour vision participated in a session lasting approximately 35 minutes.

Materials, design, and procedure

This experiment was identical to Experiment 1, except the training phase was dramatically reduced; instead of 24 practice trials followed by a 320 trial training phase, observers only received 40 total trials of training; these trials were each sampled randomly without replacement from the 80 unique conditions generated by crossing *distractor type* (four levels), *singleton location* (four levels), and *temporal distractor position*. After training, all subjects participated in the 320 trial test phase.

As in Experiment 1, half of the participants were assigned to the feature group, and the other half were assigned to the singleton group. Additionally, within each group, half were assigned the target colour red and the other half were assigned the target colour green.

Results and discussion

Training phase. An examination of the means (excluding the first 10 trials, during which familiarization with the task likely was taking place), confirms that the expected sets were used.

For the feature group, mean accuracy in the four distractor conditions (none, all-grey, same singleton, and different singleton) was 80%, 79%, 54%, and 77%, respectively; t-tests revealed that performance on same singleton trials was worse than in the all-grey condition, $t(17) = 4.035$, $p < .001$; performance on different singleton trials was not different than in the all-grey trials, $t(17) = 0.819$, ns. Additionally, performance on the same singleton trials was worse than on the different singleton trials, $t(17) = 2.724$, $p < .02$.

For the singleton group, mean accuracy in the four distractor conditions (none, all-grey, same singleton, and different singleton) was 86%, 78%, 51%, and 46%, respectively. On both "same" and "different" singleton conditions, performance was worse than in the all-grey condition: $t(17) = 3.719$, $p < .002$, and $t(17) = 5.050$, $p < .001$, respectively. Additionally, performance in the "same" and "different" singleton conditions did not differ significantly, $t(17) = 1.227$, ns.

Test phase.   Data from the test phase were analysed in the same fashion as Experiment 1; mean accuracy scores are plotted in Figure 4.

In the feature group, data are not easily categorized as indicative of either feature search mode or singleton detection mode. On the one hand, performance was worse in same and different singleton conditions than in the all-grey condition, $t(17) = 5.518$, $p < .001$, and $t(17) = 2.994$, $p < .01$, respectively. On the other hand, performance in the same singleton condition was worse than in the different singleton condition, $t(17) = 4.050$, $p < .001$.

Data were similar in the singleton group. Performance in the same and different singleton conditions was worse than in the all-grey condition, $t(17) = 4.962$, $p < .001$, and $t(17) = 4.262$, $p < .01$, respectively. Also, same

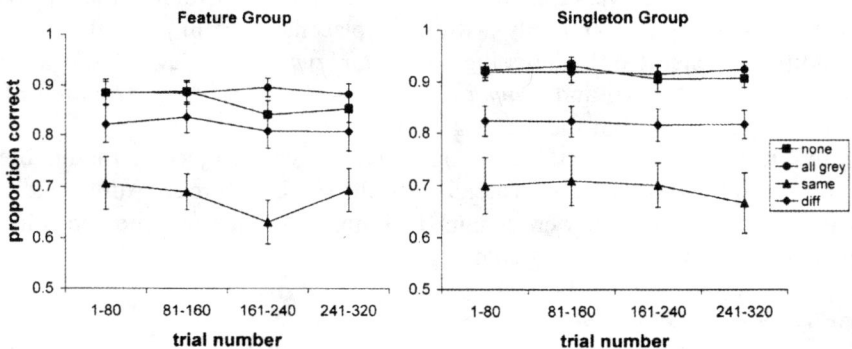

Figure 4. Performance on the test phase of Experiment 2. Left: Mean proportion correct for the feature group as a function of distractor type and trial number (placed into four bins of 80 trials). Right: Mean proportion correct for the singleton group.

singleton performance was worse for same singleton distractors than different singleton distractors, $t(17) = 4.026$, $p < .001$.

Performance did not vary as a function of bin, as this variable did not yield a significant main effect and did not enter into any significant interactions (all Fs < 1) in the *singleton condition* (2 levels) × *bin* (4 levels) × *training group* (2 levels) ANOVA. Additionally, the pattern of singleton costs did not significantly vary as a function of training group, as this interaction was not significant, $F(1, 34) < 1$.

Apparently, the separate treatment of the two groups of observers during the shortened training phase failed to significantly influence their performance in the test phase. Even though the patterns of distractor interference from the training phase showed that observers entered the test phase using divergent sets, the observers did not carry these divergent sets forward into the test phase. Thus, it appears that the likelihood of persistence is dependent on how much experience one has with a given set. This result is consistent with the notion that automatic processes, which are built upon past associations between the environment and relevant tasks, play a role in the implementation of attentional set.[2]

GENERAL DISCUSSION

We set out to explore the determining factors of attentional set. In particular, the role of past experience was probed, and the results revealed that sufficient past experience exerted a strong influence on attentional set; it caused observers to maintain divergent sets under identical stimulus conditions for up to 30 minutes (i.e., 320 trials), with no sign of subsiding. However, in line with influential models of executive control (e.g., Norman & Shallice, 1986), observers needed sufficient experience with a given set in order to persist with it; Experiment 2 revealed that after two groups of observers entered disparate sets in a training phase, they did not maintain them during the test phase.

Our work is not the first to assert a relationship between past experience and attentional set. For example, Müller and colleagues (e.g., Found & Müller, 1996; Müller, Heller, & Ziegler, 1995; see Müller & Krummenacher, 2006 this issue, for a review) have shown that visual search for feature singleton targets is faster when targets in the previous trial "pop out" on the same dimension as the target on the current trial, compared to when targets

---

[2] We acknowledge a limitation in drawing strong conclusions favouring our automaticity account from the results of Experiment 2 alone, as alternative explanations could account for our data. For example, an observer's subjective assessment of the costs of switching to a new set could increase as a function of experience with the old set.

in previous trials pop out on a different dimension. This phenomenon of dimensional "intertrial facilitation" may suggest that top-down attentional set is reconfigured to prioritize defining feature dimensions based on recent stimuli (see Krummenacher, Müller, & Heller, 2003; Olivers & Humphreys, 2003; Wolfe, Butcher, Lee, & Hyle, 2003). However, it has also been argued that these effects reflect benefits/costs at postselection decision or response stages of processing (e.g., Feintuch & Cohen, 2002; Kumada, 2001; Theeuwes, Reimann, & Mortier, 2006 this issue). Such "response priming" effects would be unrelated to attentional set. Researchers have not yet reached a consensus on the level at which dimensional effects occur and, in fact, the debate is still quite lively.

In addition to the dimensional effects are feature-specific intertrial modulations, which arise when targets on previous trials either share or do not share the specific feature value (e.g., red or vertical) with the current target ("priming of pop out"; Maljkovic & Nakayama, 1994, 2000). While these effects may be viewed as simply acting at a more specific level of the same hierarchy as the dimensional effects, they differ qualitatively in several ways. For example, when observers have to make a discrimination about a property that is orthogonal to the target's defining pop-out characteristic (e.g., if the object has a "chip" in the left or right side), the dimensional effects can be weak while feature priming effects remain intact (see Kumada, 2001; Theeuwes et al., 2006 this issue; but see Müller & Krummenacher, 2006 this issue; Pollmann, Weidner, Müller, & von Cramon, 2006 this issue). Thus, even if the dimensional effects are not related to attentional set, one might question whether feature-specific effects are related. However, one central finding that is at odds with such speculation is that feature-specific priming appears to be dissociable from top-down expectancies (Maljkovic & Nakayama, 1994, 2000). This characteristic of the phenomenon separates it from attentional set, where observers are capable of dramatically reconfiguring their preparedness from trial to trial, albeit with some costs (e.g., Leber & Egeth, 2001).[3]

All things considered, the present work is most distinct in *duration* from the intertrial effects, whose temporal range does not exceed more than a few trials. The central reason our effects persist for so long is that observers in this study (Experiment 1) are influenced to use a particular attentional set—a strategy determined by executive control functions—in the test phase; such strategies, although influenced by experience, are clearly not directly

---

[3] While we view priming as a phenomenon that is distinct from attentional set, we do not think that one has to reject the possibility that it operates in a top-down manner. Granted, priming may not be determined by expectancy, but it is not clear that this should be taken as a defining characteristic of a top-down process.

determined by the immediate stimulus, or even stimuli from the very recent past.

We find a link between these results and studies of "contextual cueing" (e.g., Chun, 2000; Chun & Jiang, 1998), where search performance benefits when associations between invariant display properties (e.g., spatial layouts of search items) and target properties (e.g., location or identity) are learned implicitly by observers.

In sum, the observations in the present experiments support the notion that observers do not continually evaluate their chosen sets based on current task demands and stimulus characteristics. If they had done so, they would have converged upon similar sets in Experiment 1. Rather, automatic control processes are likely at work. These results carry methodological and theoretical implications for research on attentional set, as they demonstrate that the set of an observer cannot be inferred by solely evaluating his/her real-time sensory input and task demands. Owing to their past experience, observers in this study used divergent sets under *identical* stimulus conditions with *identical* task requirements. While these results were observed in the context of a highly controlled laboratory experiment, they are consistent with the notion that any attentional set used by a participant at the beginning of an experiment can be influenced by a wide range of events—specific to that individual—occurring prior to the testing session. Efforts to further explore how past experience influences attentional set may succeed not only in reconciling inconsistent findings in the attention capture literature, but in facilitating a broader understanding of the properties of attentional control.

REFERENCES

Bacon, W. F., & Egeth, H. E. (1994). Overriding stimulus-driven attentional capture. *Perception and Psychophysics*, *55*, 485–496.

Chun, M. M. (2000). Contextual cueing of visual attention. *Trends in Cognitive Sciences*, *4*, 170–178.

Chun, M. M., & Jiang, Y. (1998). Contextual cueing: Implicit learning and memory of visual context guides spatial attention. *Cognitive Psychology*, *36*, 28–71.

Feintuch, U., & Cohen, A. (2002). Visual attention and coactivation of response decisions for features from different dimensions. *Psychological Science*, *13*(4), 361–369.

Folk, C. L., Leber, A. B., & Egeth, H. E. (2002). Made you blink! Contingent attentional capture produces a spatial blink. *Perception and Psychophysics*.

Folk, C. L., & Remington, R. W. (1998). Selectivity in distraction by irrelevant featural singletons: Evidence for two forms of attentional capture. *Journal of Experimental Psychology: Human Perception and Performance*, *24*, 847–858.

Folk, C. L., Remington, R. W., & Johnston, J. C. (1992). Involuntary covert orienting is contingent on attentional control settings. *Journal of Experimental Psychology: Human Perception and Performance*, *18*, 1030–1044.

Found, A., & Müller, H. J. (1996). Searching for unknown feature targets on more than one dimension: Investigating a "dimension weighting" account. *Perception and Psychophysics*, *58*, 88–101.

Hillstrom, A. P. (2000). Repetition effects in visual search. *Perception and Psychophysics*, *62*, 800–817.

Jonides, J., & Yantis, S. (1988). Uniqueness of abrupt visual onset in capturing attention. *Perception and Psychophysics*, *43*, 346–354.

Krummenacher, J., Müller, H. J., & Heller, D. (2003). Visual search for dimensionally redundant pop-out targets: Parallel-coactive processing of dimensions is location specific. *Journal of Experimental Psychology: Human Perception and Performance*, *28*(6), 1303–1322.

Kumada, T. (2001). Feature-based control of attention: Evidence for two forms of dimension weighting. *Perception & Psychophysics*, *63*, 698–708.

Leber, A. B., & Egeth, H. E. (2001, November). *Attentional control, task switching, and a new definition for the residual switch cost*. Poster presented at the annual Object Perception and Memory (OPAM) workshop, Orlando, FL.

Luchins, A. S. (1942). Mechanization in problem solving: The effect of Einstellung. *Psychological Monographs*, *54*, 248.

Luchins, A. S., & Luchins, E. H. (1950). New experimental attempts at preventing mechanization in problem solving. *Journal of General Psychology*, *42*, 279–297.

Maljkovic, V., & Nakayama, K. (1994). Priming of pop-out: I. Role of features. *Memory and Cognition*, *22*, 657–672.

Maljkovic, V., & Nakayama, K. (2000). Priming of pop-out: III. A short-term implicit memory system beneficial for rapid target selection. *Visual Cognition*, *7*(5), 571–595.

Müller, H. J., Heller, D., & Ziegler, J. (1995). Visual search for singleton feature targets within and across feature dimensions. *Perception and Psychophysics*, *57*, 1–17.

Müller, H. J., & Krummenacher, J. (2006). Locus of dimension weighting: Preattentive or postselective? *Visual Cognition*, *14*, 490–513.

Norman, D. A. (1981). Categorisation of action slips. *Psychological Review*, *88*(1), 1–15.

Norman, D. A., & Shallice, T. (1986). Attention to action: Willed and automatic control of behavior. In R. J. Davidson, G. E. Schwartz, & D. Shapiro (Eds.), *Advances in research: Vol. IV. Consciousness and self-regulation* (pp. 1–18). New York: Plenum Press.

Olivers, C. N. L., & Humphreys, G. W. (2003). Attentional guidance by salient feature singletons depends on intertrial contingencies. *Journal of Experimental Psychology: Human Perception and Performance*, *29*, 650–657.

Pashler, H. (1988). Cross-dimensional interaction and texture and texture segregation. *Perception and Psychophysics*, *43*, 307–318.

Pollmann, S., Weidner, R., Müller, H. J., & von Cramon, D.Y. (2006). Neural correlates of visual dimension weighting. *Visual Cognition*, *14*, 877–897.

Reason, J. T. (1979). Actions not as planned: The price of automatization. In G. Underwood & R. Stevens (Eds.), *Aspects of consciousness*. London: Academic Press.

Reason, J. T. (1984). Lapses of attention in everyday life. In W. Parasuraman & R. Davies (Eds.), *Varieties of attention*. Orlando, FL: Academic Press.

Theeuwes, J. (1990). Perceptual selectivity is task dependent: Evidence from selective search. *Acta Psychologia*, *74*, 81–99.

Theeuwes, J. (1991). Cross-dimensional perceptual selectivity. *Perception and Psychophysics*, *50*, 184–193.

Theeuwes, J. (1992). Perceptual selectivity for color and form. *Perception and Psychophysics*, *51*, 599–606.

Theeuwes, J., Reimann, B., & Mortier, K. (2006). Visual search for featural singletons: No top-down modulation, only bottom-up priming. *Visual Cognition*, *14*, 466–489.

Todd, S., & Kramer, A. F. (1994). Attentional misguidance in visual search. *Perception and Psychophysics*, *56*(2), 198–210.

Turatto, M., & Galfano, G. (2001). Attentional capture by color without any relevant attentional set. *Perception and Psychophysics*, *63*, 286–297.

Wolfe, J. M., Butcher, S. J., Lee, C., & Hyle, M. (2003). Changing your mind: On the contributions of top-down and bottom-up guidance in visual search for feature singletons. *Journal of Experimental Psychology: Human Perception and Performance*, *29*, 493–502.

Wolfe, J. M., & Horowitz, T. S. (2004). What attributes guide the deployment of visual attention and how do they do it? *Nature Reviews Neuroscience*, *5*, 1–7.

Woodworth, R. S., & Schlosberg, H. (1960). *Experimental psychology* (Rev. ed.). New York: Henry Holt.

Yantis, S., & Egeth, H. E. (1999). On the distinction between visual salience and stimulus-driven attentional capture. *Journal of Experimental Psychology: Human Perception and Performance*, *25*, 661–676.

VISUAL COGNITION, 2006, 14 (4/5/6/7/8), 584–618

Ψ Psychology Press
Taylor & Francis Group

Selecting and ignoring the component features of a visual object: A negative priming paradigm

Alessandra Fanini

Department of Neurological and Vision Sciences, Section of Physiology, University of Verona, Verona, Italy, and Department of Neurobiology, Harvard Medical School, MA, USA

Anna Christina Nobre

Department of Experimental Psychology, University of Oxford, Oxford, UK

Leonardo Chelazzi

Department of Neurological and Vision Sciences, Section of Physiology, University of Verona, Verona, Italy

Decades of investigation have led to tremendous progress in our understanding of the mechanisms that underlie selective attention to spatial locations and to individual objects. Much less work has been devoted so far to exploring the ability of humans to select the individual features of a multidimensional visual object. Here we report the results of two related experiments in which we used a negative priming procedure to assess whether and under which conditions attention mechanisms can lead to selective processing of the relevant feature of an object (e.g., colour) and/or suppression of the irrelevant features of the same object (e.g., direction of motion or orientation). Results showed that: (1) Individual features of a single object can indeed undergo different processing fates as a result of attention. While one is made available to response selection stages, others are actively blocked. (2) Feature-selective attention most likely operates through a combination of facilitatory and inhibitory mechanisms. (3) In particular, the engagement of inhibitory mechanisms appears to be critically dependent upon the

Please address all correspondence to Leonardo Chelazzi, Department of Neurological and Vision Sciences, Section of Physiology, University of Verona, Strada Le Grazie 8, I-37134 Verona, Italy. E-mail: leonardo.chelazzi@univr.it

This work was supported by grants to LC from the Italian Government (Ministero dell'Istruzione, Universita' e Ricerca scientifica, MIUR) and the Human Frontier Science Program (HFSP), and by a joint grant to LC and ACN from the McDonnell-Pew Program in Cognitive Neuroscience. AF was receiving a fellowship covered by the grant from the McDonnell-Pew Program in Cognitive Neuroscience. We wish to thank Giuseppe di Pellegrino and Gianfrancesco Gervasoni, who were involved in the early development of this work. Special thanks to Rebecca Saxe, who gave a critical contribution to performing Experiment 2.

http://www.psypress.com/viscog   DOI: 10.1080/13506280500195367

need to resolve response conflict interference between the constituent features of the object. These results are discussed in relation to several ongoing debates concerning the cognitive architecture of attention, including the processing stages at which attentional mechanisms intervene and the types of representation upon which they act.

In the last few decades a vast body of research has been devoted to discovering the representations upon which visual selective attention operates. Numerous findings have indicated the key role of location information to control the deployment of attention (Nissen, 1985; Posner, Snyder, & Davidson, 1980; Tsal & Lavie, 1988). This has been shown with a variety of approaches, including spatial cueing (Posner et al., 1980) and response-competition paradigms, such as the flanker task (Eriksen & Eriksen, 1974). As an alternative to space-based models of attention, some researchers have suggested that integrated objects are the natural targets of attentional selection (Blaser, Pylyshyn, & Holcombe, 2000; Duncan, 1984; Egly, Driver, & Rafal, 1994; Kahneman & Henik, 1977; Neisser, 1967; Treisman, Kahneman, & Burkell, 1983; Valdes-Sosa, Cobo, & Pinilla, 2000). According to this theoretical framework, the visual field is first preattentively segmented into separate figural units, or objects, on the basis of Gestalt principles of scene organization (e.g., continuity, similarity, etc.). At a second stage, focal attention is deployed to an individual object, aiding more detailed analysis and perceptual awareness. The focusing of attention onto a particular object results in the mandatory perception of all the features of that object, since object features have already been grouped together by the preattentive computations. Thus, different features of an object are processed in parallel, whereas different objects are selected one at the time. The evidence so far actually supports the existence of both space-based and object-based modes of attentional selection, and indicates that the two kinds of attentional selection can intervene even in the same task (Egly et al., 1994; Kramer & Jacobson, 1991). Perhaps, any comprehensive theory of visual attention should include the principles guiding the flexible intervention of either one mechanism over the other, or of both together, depending on task variables (Vecera & Farah, 1994).

Consistent with the general notion of a flexible implementation of attention, researchers have also demonstrated the existence of another putative form of attentional selection, namely the selective processing of individual features and feature dimensions (Cohen & Magen, 1999; Cohen & Shoup, 1997; Found & Müller, 1996; Garner, 1974; Kanwisher, Driver, & Machado, 1995; Kumada, 2001; Maruff, Danckert, Camplin, & Currie, 1999; Müller & O'Grady, 2000; Müller, Reimann, & Krummenacher, 2003;

Remington & Folk, 2001; Rossi & Paradiso, 1995). This form of selection is important whenever the cognitive system needs to emphasize processing of one property of an object (e.g., colour), while concurrently discarding information regarding other properties of the same object (e.g., shape). For instance, if we are trying to locate a ripe fruit among unripe ones on a tree, we will probably emphasize colour (and not shape) to distinguish ripe from unripe pomes by a rapid glance. Subsequently, however, when we are about to grasp the ripe fruit, we will probably emphasize its location and shape (but not colour) to guide the reaching movement and shape the hand correctly. Feature selective attention is also specifically tapped in classical neuropsychological tests, like the Wisconsin card-sorting task (Milner, 1963) and the Stroop task (Stroop, 1935).

By means of a flanker interference paradigm (Eriksen & Eriksen, 1974), Cohen and Shoup (1997) demonstrated how behavioural goals constrain selective processing of visual information in favour of the relevant feature of objects. Stimuli were bars varying either in colour or orientation. Some bars were associated to a response on the basis of their colour (red or green vertical bars); others were associated to a response on the basis of their orientation (blue bars tilted to the left or right). The subjects' task was to discriminate the feature dimension of the central target while ignoring the irrelevant flankers. The results showed that incongruent flankers (i.e., those associated with a different response from the target) interfered with the response to the central target when flankers and target belonged to the same dimension, but not when they belonged to different dimensions (see also Maruff et al., 1999, and Remington & Folk, 2001).

Kanwisher et al. (1995) used a repetition blindness paradigm (Kanwisher, 1987) and provided elegant evidence in favour of an attentional mechanism for single features. Subjects reported the colours or identities of two simultaneous letters briefly presented on each side of fixation. When the same dimension (e.g., colour) had to be reported for both stimuli, performance was affected by repetition along the relevant dimension, whereas repetition along the irrelevant (unreported) dimension had no effect. However, when different dimensions were to be reported for the two stimuli (e.g., colour for one stimulus and identity for the other), performance was affected by repetition on both dimensions.

Both studies show that behavioural performance is influenced by whichever feature dimension is relevant in a given trial, suggesting that subjects can selectively attend to one feature dimension, such that features belonging to a different and irrelevant dimension do not affect behaviour. It thus appears that the parallel encoding of the multiple perceptual dimensions of an object, as assumed by object-based models, is optional rather than obligatory, and can be modulated according to task demands. The aim of the present study is to provide further evidence for a feature-based attentional mechanism. In particular, we investigated whether the selection of the relevant feature of a multidimensional object is accompanied by the active suppression of the irrelevant feature of the same object. The studies cited above have provided incomplete answers to this issue. In the study of Cohen and Shoup (1997), and in that of Kanwisher et al. (1995), the irrelevant feature dimension did not affect behavioural performance, which suggests three possible explanations. One explanation is that the irrelevant feature dimension was effectively "filtered out" by an early-level attention mechanism. A second possibility is that the irrelevant feature dimension was actively suppressed and disconnected from the response selection stages by the intervention of a late-level attention mechanism. Finally, the third explanation goes as follows. In both studies, lack of processing of the irrelevant feature was indexed by the absence of an effect: Repetition cost in the study of Kanwisher et al., and flanker interference in the study of Cohen and Shoup. It might be suggested that both repetition blindness and flanker interference are only exerted by visual representations that are currently mapped onto the appropriate behavioural responses within procedural working memory. That is, repetition blindness and flanker interference might only occur for stimulus properties to which subjects are prepared to respond or that they are actively encoding. If this were the case, then it would be premature to conclude that absence of either effect is due to an attention mechanism allowing selection of a relevant feature and concurrent filtering or suppression of the irrelevant one. Thus, although still attentional in some sense, the effects reported by Cohen and Shoup and Kanwisher et al. would not entail any attentional mechanism directly acting on the irrelevant dimension of an object.

Let us consider the results from the study of Kanwisher et al. (1995) in more detail. Evidence in favour of selective processing of one perceptual dimension of the two simultaneously presented objects came principally from the results of Experiment 1 and from the "sustained-attention" conditions of Experiments 3 and 4. In all these cases, observers had to identify overtly (Experiment 1), or encode covertly (sustained-attention conditions of Experiments 3 and 4), the relevant property of one object and then identify the same property of the other object. Repetitions along the relevant dimension elicited repetition costs, whereas repetitions along the irrelevant dimension had no effect on performance. However, the presence of repetition blindness whenever the two stimuli were the same along the perceptual dimension that subjects had to identify (overtly or covertly) could be explained in terms of a refractoriness to activate the same visual category (type) twice in a rapid temporal sequence. As such, we submit that this finding does not demonstrate the ability of a putative attention mechanism to selectively process one of the constituent features of an object. More specifically, it does not demonstrate the ability of this mechanism to suppress perceptual representations of the irrelevant features of the same object.

Hardly anyone would argue, for instance, that when one utters the word "apple" in response to the view of a red apple, one applies an attention mechanism to suppress the perceptual representation of the red colour of the apple. Of course, this is a possibility, but one that would have to be demonstrated. In conclusion, the results from the above studies cannot decide unequivocally among the three alternative accounts.

Feature-based attentional mechanisms have also been shown to affect early stages of visual processing, in particular the perceptual salience of an attended feature relative to an unattended one. In the study by Rossi and Paradiso (1995), subjects discriminated either the spatial frequency or the orientation of Gabor patches presented at the centre of gaze. On a third of the trials, they also had to detect the presence of a near-threshold annular grating presented around the central patch, which also varied in either spatial frequency or orientation. It was found that the detection rate for the peripheral grating was specifically enhanced when the two stimuli were similar along the feature dimension of the central patch to be discriminated in the given task condition. While this finding nicely demonstrates facilitatory consequences of feature-selective processing, again we simply do not know whether the ignored feature dimension was inhibited or unaffected during the selective processing of the relevant one.

To demonstrate directly the existence of inhibitory mechanisms operating on the irrelevant feature dimension of a multidimensional visual object we have developed variants of the negative priming paradigm (Dalrymple-Alford & Budayr, 1966; Neill, 1977; Tipper, 1985; for extensive reviews see Neill & Valdes, 1996; Tipper, 2001). The general logic of the approach is as follows: If the internal representation of a distracting stimulus is actively inhibited in a given trial, then the processing of a target stimulus requiring the inhibited representation in the subsequent trial will be impaired. In a classic experiment (Tipper, 1985), subjects were required to identify one of two superimposed line drawings of familiar objects. Responses to a target drawing that had been the distracting drawing in the previous trial were slower and less accurate relative to a baseline condition—the negative priming (NP) effect. Nowadays it remains actively disputed whether negative priming reflects the intervention of an inhibitory selection mechanism—as originally believed (Tipper, 1985), or some other perceptual (Lowe, 1979; MacDonald & Joordens, 2000; Park & Kanwisher, 1994) or mnemonic (Fox & de Fockert, 1998; Milliken, Joordens, Merikle, & Seiffert, 1998; Neill & Valdes, 1992; Neill, Valdes, Terry, & Gorfein, 1992) process. On balance, however, there seems to be good ground to believe that inhibitory mechanisms play an important role in generating negative priming effects, perhaps in combination with other factors (Lavie & Fox, 2000; Tipper, 2001).

Inhibitory processes revealed by negative priming have been shown to act on both spatial locations (Milliken, Tipper, & Weaver, 1994; Tipper, Brehaut,

& Driver, 1990) and objects (Fox, 1998; Tipper, 1985; Tipper et al., 1990). Closest to our objective, the earliest demonstrations of NP were obtained with the Stroop paradigm, which taps a specific form of feature selective attention (Dalrymple-Alford & Budayr, 1966; Neill, 1977; see also Lowe, 1979, 1985). In the typical Stroop paradigm (Stroop, 1935), an observer is asked to name the ink colour in which a colour word is printed. The Stroop effect refers to the massive interference occurring when the colour word itself conflicts with the ink colour to be named. Dalrymple-Alford and Budayr (1966) found that the total time to name ink colours in a list of Stroop words was longer if each colour corresponded to the distractor word immediately preceding it in the list, relative to a control condition in which such immediate repetition did not occur (see also Neill, 1977; Lowe, 1979, 1985). Although the aforementioned studies have certainly provided suggestive evidence to the existence of inhibitory attention mechanisms for the component features of multidimensional visual objects, the general notions that can be derived from those studies are limited by a number of factors. First, even though Stroop words are a clear example of a stimulus consisting of two competing features, ink colour and word identity, these features are both mapped onto members of the same semantic category (colour names). Second, even if one were to ignore this property of Stroop words, demonstrations of NP with these stimuli would still only concern one special type of feature combination, namely that of colour and graphemic form, which makes it difficult to generalize findings with Stroop words to other kinds of low-level feature combinations. Third, previous studies with Stroop words have attested inhibitory mechanisms acting upon only one of the constituent stimulus features, word identity; they have not explored similar mechanisms acting on the other feature of the stimuli, colour of the ink. Finally, and perhaps most importantly, previous studies using Stroop stimuli did not explore the extent to which NP effects for individual object features depend critically on the need to resolve response conflict interference. The present study attempts to provide evidence of feature selective attention mechanisms in vision, in particular of inhibitory mechanisms aiding feature selection, while overcoming the above concerns about Stroop stimuli. Moreover, we systematically tested whether NP for elemental object features is only observed under conditions of response conflict interference.

EXPERIMENT 1

The aim of the first experiment was to develop a new paradigm to investigate the ability of human observers to attend to the component features of a single visual object. The paradigm comprised the sequential presentation of a prime and a probe stimulus, each requiring a key-press response. As to the prime stimuli, the paradigm was built around two critical properties. First, it was essential that observers could not rely on space-based or object-based attention mechanisms. For this reason, prime stimuli consisted of foveally presented bars, whose colour, orientation, and direction of motion were varied from trial to trial. Three types of prime stimuli were used, each defined by two dimensions: Prime stimuli defined by colour and orientation (coloured oriented bars), by colour and motion direction (coloured moving squares), and by motion direction and orientation (oriented grey moving bars). At the beginning of each trial, subjects were given an instruction cue indicating whether the colour, the orientation, or the motion direction of the stimulus had to be discriminated, with the other feature serving as distracting information. The second key property of our paradigm pertained to the response assignments of the two stimulus features in each type of prime. Given that it is perhaps unnatural to select one or the other feature of the same object (Duncan, 1984; Treisman, 1969), the boundary condition to engage feature selective attention might be a strong competition between the component object features for controlling behaviour. This is why in our task we have placed the two features of the prime stimulus in direct competition with one another. Specifically, in half of the trials, the response called for by the relevant feature was different from that called for by the irrelevant feature. We predicted that attention mechanisms would try to counteract this response–conflict interference by strongly inhibiting the processing of the irrelevant feature and/or by preventing its access to response selection stages.

To directly demonstrate the intervention of suppressive attentional mechanisms in this paradigm we analysed responses to probe stimuli, which followed prime stimuli on each trial and also required discrimination of colour, orientation, or motion direction. Contrary to prime stimuli, however, probe stimuli were unidimensional, i.e., they consisted of coloured stationary squares (colour probes), achromatic and stationary oriented bars (orientation probes), or moving grey squares (motion probes), thus they did not pose any response conflict and were not preceded by an instruction cue. The priming procedure allowed us to assess whether the previously ignored feature continued to suffer from a significant processing cost some time after selection had occurred. The specific hypothesis was that subjects would be significantly slower and less accurate to process a probe stimulus corresponding to the ignored feature in the preceding prime display—the hallmark of negative priming effects.[1]

---

[1] We chose to use one-dimensional, instead of two-dimensional probes, after pilot experiments had shown that reliable negative priming effects could be obtained with probes devoid of any element of response conflict interference.

Methods

Subjects. Fourteen subjects, mostly students at the University of Verona, took part in this experiment (aged between 20 and 27, 7 females). They were naive as to the purposes of the experiment and were paid for their participation. All reported normal or corrected-to-normal acuity and colour vision.

Apparatus. Presentation of stimulus displays and collection of behavioural responses were controlled by the software Micro Experimental Laboratory (MEL 2.0; Schneider, 1988) running on an IBM PC-compatible computer. Subjects were tested in a sound attenuated, dimly lit room, and viewed the display from about 57 cm.

Stimuli. Target features comprised: Red and green for the colour dimension, 45° tilted to the right and to the left from the vertical for the orientation dimension, upwards and downwards direction for the motion dimension. Prime and probe stimuli were randomly presented either at fixation, 1° of visual angle above or 1° below fixation, in order to avoid any spatial cue for discriminating motion direction. In this and in the following experiment, flicker photometry (Kaiser & Boynton, 1996) was applied to the individual subjects to match the subjective brightness of colours.

Prime stimuli were defined by two dimensions, and were of three different types: Colour-orientation primes were oblique coloured bars; colour-motion stimuli were moving coloured squares; orientation-motion stimuli were oblique grey moving bars (Figure 1). The width and length of the bars were 1° and 2.6° of visual angle, respectively. The side of the square measured 1.5°. The speed of moving stimuli was 2°/s. An instruction cue (the capital letter "C" for colour, "F" for orientation, and "M" for motion) presented before prime onset informed the subject as to which discrimination was required for the upcoming prime stimulus. Probe stimuli were defined by a single perceptual dimension. Colour probes were red or green stationary squares. Orientation probes were right-tilted or left-tilted grey stationary bars. Motion probes were upward-moving or downward-moving grey squares.

Design. Each trial consisted of the sequential presentation of an instruction cue, a prime, and a probe. The subject's task was to discriminate the relevant feature of the prime stimulus, as indicated by the instruction cue, while ignoring its distracting feature, and then to discriminate the only (response-associated) feature of the probe stimulus. Prime stimuli were classified into congruent and incongruent depending on the response assignment of their constituent features. In the congruent condition, the irrelevant feature was mapped onto the same response as the relevant one; in

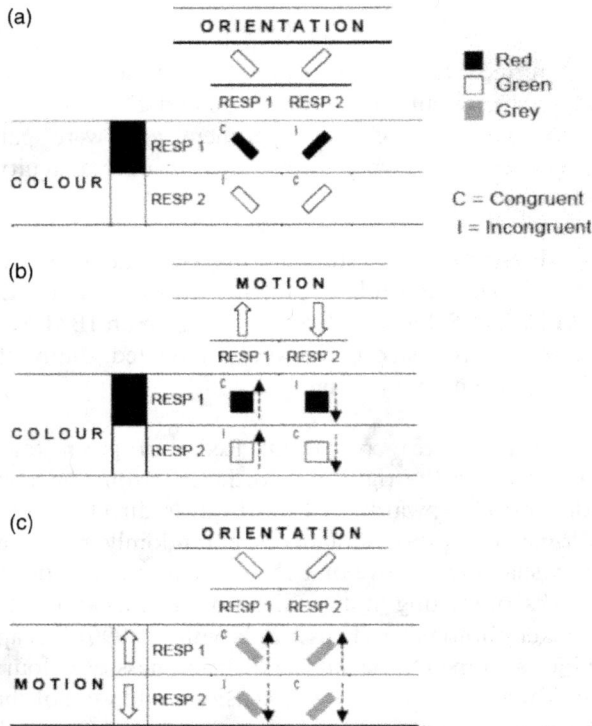

Figure 1. Experiment 1. Prime conditions and response assignments for each of the three types of prime stimuli: (a) Colour-orientation primes. (b) colour-motion primes, and (c) motion-orientation primes.

the incongruent condition, the irrelevant feature was mapped onto a different response from the relevant one. Note that in this context, relevant and irrelevant features are defined on a trial-by-trial basis, and they correspond to the to-be-attended and the to-be-ignored prime feature, respectively, depending on the preceding cue. One key-press response was assigned to the colour red, the left tilted orientation and the upward motion, and a second key-press response was assigned to the colour green, the right tilted orientation and the downward motion (Figure 1). For instance, a square moving upwards was congruent if its colour was red, and incongruent if its colour was green; similarly, a grey oblique bar moving upwards was congruent if it was tilted to the left, and incongruent if it was tilted to the right. Response assignments for probes were the same as those for prime stimuli, and no instruction cue was presented before probe onset.

Conditions for the prime stimuli resulted from any combination of task (colour, orientation, motion) and congruency (congruent, incongruent). We expected to find slower reaction times (RTs) and higher error rates in response to incongruent than congruent prime stimuli (interference effect).

The priming effects for the ignored feature in the prime display were assessed by analysing responses to the subsequent probe display. The relationship between the irrelevant feature in the prime display and the feature presented in the probe display produced two priming conditions. In the ignored feature (IF) condition, the irrelevant feature in the prime display was repeated as the response-associated (target) feature in the subsequent probe display. In the control (CTRL) condition the irrelevant feature (and perceptual dimension) in the prime display was different from the target feature (and perceptual dimension) in the subsequent probe display. The IF condition followed either a congruent or an incongruent prime stimulus, and so did the corresponding CTRL condition, thus eliminating any potential confound due to differential task difficulty in responding to congruent versus incongruent prime stimuli. The IF condition will be termed IFi in relation to incongruent primes and IFc in relation to congruent primes, and similarly the CTRL condition will be termed CTRLi and CTRLc in relation to incongruent and congruent primes, respectively.

Since we hypothesized the intervention of a feature-based inhibitory mechanism, aiding the selection of the relevant feature from the prime stimulus, especially under conditions of response conflict, our main interest was for the IF-condition probes following incongruent primes (IFi condition). As an example, Figure 2a illustrates the corresponding comparison conditions for a red colour probe. A negative priming effect for the ignored feature would be revealed by longer RTs and lower accuracy in the IFi condition relative to the CTRLi condition. To assess directly the crucial role of response conflict in triggering inhibitory mechanisms, we also compared performance across the IFc and CTRLc conditions for probes following congruent rather than incongruent primes. Comparison conditions in this case were identical to those illustrated in Figure 2a, except that the prime stimuli were congruent instead of incongruent (for the example shown, a red left-tilted bar in the IFc condition and a grey left-tilted bar moving upwards in the CTRLc condition).

Note that this design makes it possible to dissociate the contribution of stimulus-related and response-related components to the NP effect for the individual feature. In the IFi and CTRLi conditions (exemplified in Figure 2a) the features ignored in the preceding prime displays belong to different perceptual dimensions (colour and motion, respectively), but afford the same key-press response. By doing this, any inhibitory effect related to the key-press response itself is eliminated in the comparison. Also note that all comparison conditions testing negative priming effects were equated for the sequence of tasks and key-press responses required by the prime and probe stimuli in each trial.

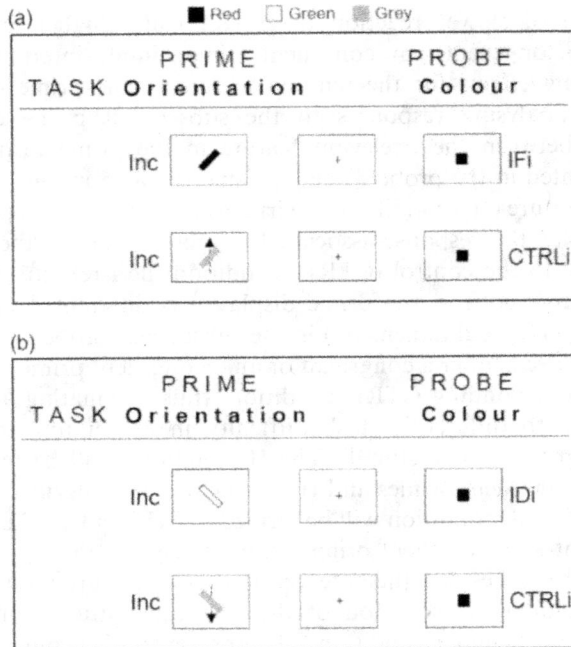

Figure 2. Experiment 1. Probe conditions (a) IFi and CTRLi, and (b) IDi and CTRLi. for an example red colour probe.

The task allowed us to test for another form of negative priming, which we will refer to as negative priming for the perceptual dimension. Impaired processing of a given probe target (e.g.. red) might occur not only when it matched the ignored feature (red) in the immediately preceding prime display, but also when the immediately preceding prime display contained the other, response-associated feature of the same ignored dimension (e.g., green). In other words, since the selection in the prime display was between two features belonging to different perceptual dimensions, we investigated whether the inhibitory mechanism applied to the irrelevant feature of the prime stimulus could spread to the other feature of the same perceptual dimension. Such an effect, if present, could be interpreted as reflecting active inhibition of the perceptual channel responsible for encoding the dimension of the irrelevant and potentially interfering feature of the prime stimulus, and/or its functional disconnection from response-selection stages. This would be an interesting finding, because to our knowledge it is not known whether negative priming can occur at the level of perceptual dimensions. Example comparison conditions to test for this effect are shown in Figure 2b for a red colour probe. In the ignored dimension (ID) condition, the feature ignored in the prime display was the other response-associated feature of the same perceptual dimension (green). In the control (CTRL) condition the ignored dimension in the prime display was different from the ignored dimension in the ID condition. Similar to what we saw earlier for the feature-specific effects, the ID condition followed either a congruent or an incongruent prime stimulus, and so did the corresponding CTRL condition. In the following, the ID condition will be termed IDi in relation to incongruent primes and IDc in relation to congruent primes, and similarly the CTRL condition will be termed CTRLi and CTRLc in relation to incongruent and congruent primes, respectively. As stated previously in the case of feature-specific effects, we hypothesized that inhibitory mechanisms might intervene only in the presence of response–conflict interference, i.e., following incongruent (IDi vs. CTRLi) but not following congruent (IDc vs. CTRLc) prime stimuli. As an example, Figure 2b illustrates for a red colour probe the comparison conditions IDi and CTRLi to assess negative priming for the perceptual dimension. To ascertain once more the putative role of response conflict in triggering inhibitory mechanisms, we also compared performance across the IDc and CTRLc conditions for probes following congruent instead of incongruent primes. Comparison conditions in this case were identical to those illustrated in Figure 2b, except that the prime stimuli were congruent rather than incongruent (for the example shown, a green right-tilted bar in the IDc condition and a grey right-tilted bar moving downwards in the CTRLc condition).

Finally, since trials in which discrimination of the same perceptual dimension was required for both the prime and the probe (same-task sequence trials) were not relevant to test our hypotheses, they comprised only one-eighth the number of the different-task sequence trials, and they will not be considered further.

Procedure.   The Italian word "PRONTO" (ready) appeared in the centre of the screen, and subjects initiated the trial by pressing the spacebar. After a 700 ms blank display, the instruction cue appeared in the centre of the screen for 400 ms and was then replaced by an achromatic fixation cross. After another 700 ms interval the prime display was presented for 177 ms and then replaced by a blank screen. The screen remained blank until a response was made or until 2000 ms had elapsed. The fixation cross then reappeared for 350 ms, followed by the probe display presented for 177 ms. This was again followed by a blank screen until a response was made or until 2000 ms had elapsed. An error tone was presented for 1000 ms following incorrect responses. Both speed and accuracy were emphasized.

Responses were produced by pressing either of two keys on the numeric keypad of the computer keyboard. Half the subjects were instructed to press the "1" key for the red colour, the left-tilted orientation, and the upwards motion, and the "2" key for the green colour, the right-tilted orientation, and the downwards motion; the remaining subjects had the reverse assignment. Subjects used the index and middle finger of their right hand to produce responses.

Each subject completed five experimental sessions, run on consecutive days. Each session consisted of five blocks of 108 trials. In each block there were 18 prime stimuli for the congruent and for the incongruent conditions, separately for each of the three tasks. As for the probe conditions, there were four trials for each of the priming conditions, separately for the three tasks, and separately following incongruent (IFi, CTRLi, IDi, CTRLi) and congruent (IFc, CTRLc, IDc, CTRLc) prime stimuli. This totaled 96 trials with a different-task sequence between prime and subsequent probe, with 12 additional trials using the same-task sequence. Over the entire experiment, each prime condition comprised 450 trials, and each probe condition in different-task sequences comprised 100 trials.

Before starting the first experimental session, subjects completed as many practice blocks (each of 108 trials) as they needed to achieve an accuracy level of at least 90%. On average, subjects reached this criterion after two blocks of practice (minimum 1 and maximum 6). Each experimental session lasted approximately 1 hour.

Results

Correct mean RTs and error percentages were analysed separately for prime and probe stimuli. In the analyses on probes, only RTs and errors that followed correct responses to immediately preceding prime stimuli were considered.

Prime stimuli. Preliminary analyses of the data showed a consistent pattern of interference depending on the dimension being ignored and not on the task being performed (note, however, that the mean RT for the three tasks was different: 552 ms for colour, 578 ms for orientation, and 621 ms for motion). Thus, data were averaged across tasks and submitted to an ANOVA with irrelevant dimension (colour, orientation, motion) and congruency (congruent, incongruent) as within-subjects factors. Results are summarized in Table 1.

In the analysis of RTs, the main effect of irrelevant dimension was significant but uninteresting, as it was a trivial consequence of averaging data from different pairs of tasks for the three irrelevant dimensions. This is not a problem, however, since we were specifically interested in the differences between congruent and incongruent conditions. The main effect of congruency was highly significant, $F(1, 13) = 54.93$, $p < .001$, revealing

TABLE 1
Mean RTs and error percentages (in parentheses)
to prime conditions of Experiment 1

| | Ignored dimension | | |
	Colour	Orientation	Motion
Cng	575 (0.6)	564 (0.3)	553 (0.5)
Inc	605 (2)	630 (6.2)	576 (3.3)

the presence of a robust interference effect. Moreover, the two effects interacted significantly with one another, $F(2, 26) = 13.46$, $p < .001$. Post hoc comparisons[2] showed that RTs to incongruent prime stimuli were significantly longer than RTs to congruent prime stimuli for each irrelevant dimension ($p < .001$ in all cases), but the effect was larger when the distracting dimension was orientation (66 ms) than when it was colour (30 ms), $t(13) = 3.98$, $p < .001$, or motion (22 ms), $t(13) = 3.93$, $p < .001$.

The pattern of results for error rates was similar to that found for RTs. The two main effects were significant, $F(2, 26) = 9.29$, $p = .001$ for the irrelevant dimension, and $F(1, 13) = 26.99$, $p < .001$ for congruency, as well as their interaction, $F(2, 26) = 15.08$, $p < .001$. More errors were produced in the incongruent (4%) than in the congruent (0.5%) condition. The difference in error rates between the incongruent and congruent conditions was larger for orientation (5.8%) than for colour (1.7%), $t(13) = 3.76$, $p < .001$, and motion (2.7%), $t(13) = 3.83$, $p < .01$.

Probe stimuli. The results for each probe condition, separately for each task and following incongruent and congruent prime stimuli, are summarized in Table 2.

To assess negative priming for the ignored feature of the prime, means of correct RTs and error percentages for probes following incongruent primes were submitted separately to a 3 (task: Colour, orientation, motion) $\times 2$ (priming: IFi, CTRLi) repeated-measures ANOVA. The task performed for the previous prime stimulus was not included as a factor in the ANOVA, since preliminary analyses did not show any significant difference due to this variable. The analysis of RTs revealed a significant main effect of task, $F(2, 26) = 12.44$, $p < .001$. RTs were slower for motion (684 ms) than for colour (616 ms), $t(13) = 3.38$, $p < .05$, and orientation (590 ms), $t(13) = 4.23$, $p < .01$, probes. The main effect of priming was also significant, $F(1, 13) = 25.08$, $p < .001$, revealing the presence of a negative priming effect for the

---

[2] We used pairwise t-test comparisons for post hoc analyses throughout, with the Bonferroni correction when required.

TABLE 2
Mean RTs and error percentages (in parentheses) to probe
conditions of Experiment 1

Prime	Probe	Colour	Orientation	Motion
	IFi	624 (2.8)	613 (1.9)	709 (5.9)
	CTRLi	609 (0.6)	566 (10.3)	660 (1.5)
Inc				
	IDi	644 (3.6)	607 (1.6)	701 (5.1)
	CTRLi	635 (2.6)	597 (0.3)	682 (2.4)
	IFc	596 (1)	585 (2.1)	651 (1.4)
	CTRLc	643 (1.9)	602 (2.9)	682 (2.4)
Cng				
	IDc	586 (0.4)	562 (0.6)	626 (0.4)
	CTRLc	614 (0.4)	568 (03)	644 (0.1)

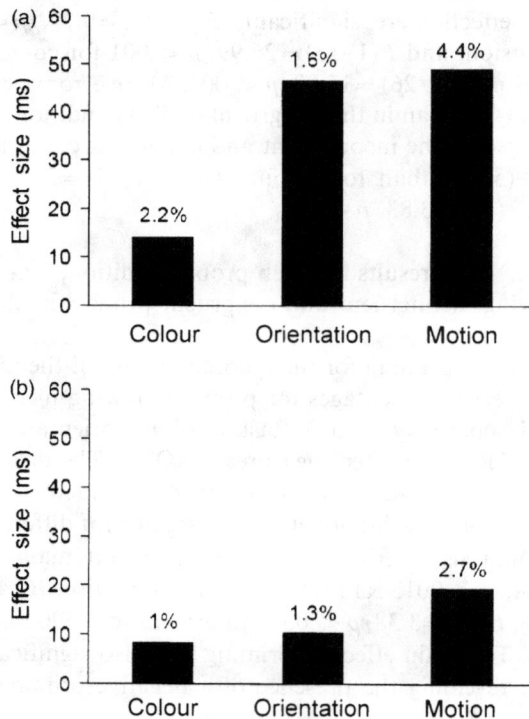

Figure 3. Experiment 1. Negative priming effect for (a) the feature (IFi-CTRLi) and (b) the dimension (IDi-CTRLi), with the corresponding error rate effect above each column.

individual feature. Figure 3a shows negative priming effects (IFi–CTRLi) for the ignored feature in the three tasks. As shown in the figure, the effect differed in size depending on the specific feature, consistent with the significant interaction between task and priming, $F(2, 26) = 10.01$, $p = .001$. RTs were longer in the IFi than in the CTRLi condition in all tasks, although the effect was not significant for the colour task (14 ms), $t(13) = 1.5$, $p > .1$. In the corresponding error-rate analysis, the main effect of task was significant, $F(2, 26) = 4.97$, $p < .05$, with more errors produced for discriminating motion (3.7%) than orientation (1%), $t(13) = 2.88$, $p < .05$, and colour (1.7%), although the latter was not a significant difference, $t(13) = 1.81$, $p > .1$. More importantly, subjects were less accurate in the IFi than in the CTRLi condition (3.5% vs. 0.8%), $F(1, 13) = 26.62$, $p < .001$. Finally, the interaction was significant, $F(2, 26) = 4.38$, $p < .05$. The error rate was significantly higher in the IFi than in the CTRLi condition in each task ($p < .01$ in all cases), although this difference was larger for discriminating motion (4.4%) than for colour (2.2%) and orientation (1.6%).

A similar analysis was performed on correct RTs and error rates obtained in the IDi and CTRLi conditions. Results are shown in Figure 3b. Although the effect was rather small, there was a consistent trend for the IDi condition to yield slower RTs than the CTRLi condition (651 ms vs. 638 ms), revealing the presence of negative priming for the perceptual dimension across tasks. At the ANOVA the main effect of priming was significant, $F(1, 13) = 5.95$, $p < .05$; the interaction between task and priming was not significant, $F(2, 26) = 1.01$, $p > .1$. The factor task was also significant, $F(2, 26) = 11.38$, $p < .001$, with slower RTs to discriminate motion (691 ms) than colour (640 ms), $t(13) = 2.6$, $p = .06$, and orientation (602 ms), $t(13) = 4.72$, $p = .001$. The analysis of error rates gave similar results. The factor task was significant, $F(2, 26) = 8.23$, $p < .01$, with more errors produced for discriminating motion (3.8%) than orientation (1%), $t(13) = 4$, $p < .01$, but not colour (3%), $t(13) = 1$, $p > .1$. Consistent with RT results, more errors were produced in the IDi (3.4%) than in the CTRLi (1.8%) condition, $F(1, 13) = 12.96$, $p < .01$. There was also a significant interaction between task and priming, $F(2, 26) = 3.58$, $p < .05$. The difference in error rate between the IDi and CTRLi condition was significant for all tasks ($p < .05$ in all cases). However, it was larger for motion (2.7%) than for colour (1%) and orientation (1.3%).

The probe results illustrated so far indicated the presence of negative priming for the irrelevant feature/dimension of an incongruent prime stimulus. Our hypothesis was that selective suppression of the to-be-ignored feature (and dimension) of the prime stimulus might be unnatural unless it is associated with a different and competing behavioural response relative to the relevant feature of the same stimulus. To test whether this was the boundary condition to observe negative priming, we investigated the priming effects following congruent prime stimuli (IFc vs. CTRLc and IDc vs. CTRLc).

In the RT analysis of priming effects for the individual feature the main effect of task was significant, $F(2, 26) = 7$, $p < .01$. RTs to discriminate motion (667 ms) were longer than RTs to discriminate colour (620 ms), although not significantly, $t(13) = 2.09$, $p > .1$, and orientation (594 ms), $t(13) = 3.67$, $p < .01$. The main effect of priming was also significant, $F(1, 13) = 15.65$, $p < .01$, as was the interaction, $F(2, 26) = 5.29$, $p < .05$. In contrast to what found following incongruent prime stimuli, RTs in the IFc condition were faster than in the CTRLc condition (611 ms vs. 642 ms), revealing positive, rather than negative, priming. This facilitatory effect was significant for all tasks ($p < .01$ in all cases), but it was smaller for the orientation (-18 ms) than for the colour (-47 ms) and motion (-30 ms) features. In the analysis of error rates, only the main effect of priming was significant, $F(1, 13) = 15.65$, $p < .01$, with fewer errors in the IFc than in the CTRLc condition (1.5% vs. 2.4%).

Similar results were obtained for the perceptual dimension. Again, task was significant, $F(2, 26) = 7.86$, $p < .01$, with slower RTs to motion (635 ms) than to colour (600 ms), $t(13) = 1.94$, $p > .1$, and orientation (565 ms), $t(13) = 3.67$, $p < .01$, features. More importantly, RTs in the IDc condition were faster than in the CTRLc condition (591 ms vs. 609 ms), $F(1, 13) = 25.23$, $p < .001$, but this effect was not significant in the orientation task (-5 ms), consistent with a significant interaction, $F(2, 26) = 3.83$, $p < .05$. The analysis on error rates was not performed, as too few errors were made (on average 0.5%; see Table 2).

After having demonstrated negative and positive priming effects, both for the individual feature and for the perceptual dimension, it was important to establish whether feature and dimension effects were of significantly different size. Two separate ANOVAs were performed to compare the magnitude of the feature and dimension effects, one using probe RTs following incongruent primes and one using probe RTs following congruent primes, with task and type of priming (for the feature and for the dimension, respectively) as main factors. The analysis on probe RTs following incongruent primes revealed that the negative priming effect for the individual feature was significantly greater than the negative priming effect for the perceptual dimension, $F(1, 13) = 27.21$, $p < .001$. The main effect of task was also significant, $F(2, 26) = 7.73$, $p < .01$, as well as the interaction, $F(2, 26) = 4.04$, $p < .05$. While feature and dimension effects reliably differed from one another for the orientation and motion tasks, this was not the case for the colour task, $t(13) = 0.58$, $p > .1$.[3] The corresponding analysis on probe RTs

---

[3] A comparison of the feature and dimension effects for colour probes in terms of error rates revealed a trend for more errors in the former condition, $t(13) = 2.10$, $p = .056$.

following congruent primes revealed that the effect for the individual feature was larger than that for the dimension, $F(1, 13) = 10.62$, $p < .01$. The main effect of task was also significant, $F(2, 26) = 6.49$, $p < .01$, while the interaction was not, $F(2, 26) = 0.26$, $p > .1$.

Discussion

The results of Experiment 1 are consistent with the general notion that attention can select the individual features of a multidimensional visual object (Cohen & Shoup, 1997; Garner, 1974; Kanwisher et al., 1995; Maruff et al., 1999; Remington & Folk, 2001; Rossi & Paradiso, 1995). More importantly, the use of a negative priming procedure allowed us to demonstrate that selective processing of the relevant feature of a prime stimulus was accompanied by active suppression of the irrelevant feature of the same stimulus (Tipper, Weaver, & Houghton., 1994). However, negative priming effects for the individual feature were only present when the response assignment for the irrelevant feature of the prime stimulus was incongruent with the response required by the relevant feature of the same stimulus. This suggests that mechanisms of active inhibition were only engaged under conditions of strong response conflict. Negative priming effects were replaced by positive priming effects following congruent primes, i.e., in the absence of such potential for response conflict.

Interestingly, RT measures of negative priming for the individual feature indicated a larger effect for orientation and motion probes than for colour probes, the latter yielding only a nonsignificant trend.[4] To note, however, that a reliable negative priming effect for the individual feature emerged for all three kinds of probes, including colour probes, in terms of error rates. One could try to relate this variability to the differential interference exerted by the three stimulus features, as measured by the difference in responding to congruent vs. incongruent primes. For example, one could reason that the greater the power of a given feature to intrude into discrimination of another feature (as attested by the size of the interference effect), the stronger might be the engagement of inhibitory mechanisms to try to mitigate the resulting interference, in turn resulting in larger negative priming effects (cf. Lavie & Fox, 2000). This reasoning is in line with the "reactive inhibition" view of negative priming phenomena (Tipper, 2001). Though appealing, this scenario does not seem to be supported by the results of the experiment. Although motion and orientation probes engendered similar amounts of

---

[4] We are fully confident that this is not due to noise in the present data, since previous and subsequent experiments in our laboratories have revealed only weak (and sometimes negligible) negative priming effects for colour features.

feature-specific negative priming, in turn much larger than that engendered by colour probes, the interference exerted on responses to prime stimuli by orientation information was much larger than that exerted by colour and motion information, in turn highly similar to one another. Thus, although interference and negative priming may be linked to one another to some degree (e.g., Kramer, Humphrey, Larish, Logan, & Strayer, 1994; Lavie & Fox, 2000; Paquet, 2001; Ruthruff & Miller, 1995; but see Allport, Tipper, & Chmiel, 1985; Driver & Tipper, 1989; Fox, 1994), the link is probably a rather complex one. For instance, the amount of interference exerted by a given stimulus feature may result from the interplay between at least three factors: (1) The salience and discriminability of the feature, together with the strength of its mapping to behavioural responses; (2) the efficiency with which the feature can be filtered out by early-level attentional mechanisms (whose action is not reflected in negative priming effects); and (3) the efficiency with which the feature can be suppressed by late-level attentional mechanisms (whose action results in negative priming; cf. Lavie & Fox, 2000; Paquet, 2001; Ruthruff & Miller, 1995).

In addition to the feature-specific effect, we obtained the unexpected finding of a reliable negative priming effect for the perceptual dimension to which the ignored feature of the prime stimulus belonged. This finding suggests that active inhibition was not only applied to the irrelevant and potentially interfering, specific feature of the prime stimulus, but also to the other response-associated feature of the same perceptual dimension, and perhaps to the perceptual channel as a whole. Again, the negative priming effect for the perceptual dimension was only obtained under conditions of response conflict, i.e., following incongruent primes.

As already noted, a necessary condition for (feature-specific and dimensional) negative priming to occur was a conflicting stimulus–response (S–R) mapping between relevant and irrelevant features of the prime stimulus, as we found negative priming effects following incongruent but not following congruent prime stimuli. These results indicate that inhibition (and facilitation) is likely triggered at a central locus where stimulus representations and responses are linked together, that is at the interface between perception and action (Neill, Lissner, & Beck, 1990; Tipper, MacQueen, & Brehaut, 1988). We will return to this issue in the General Discussion.

EXPERIMENT 2

Experiment 1 has demonstrated robust negative priming for the individual stimulus feature (as well as for the perceptual dimension), and we have interpreted these effects as reflecting active suppression of the ignored (and potentially conflicting) feature of the prime. However, an alternative interpretation could perhaps account for the feature-specific negative priming, and it is important to discard this possibility directly.[5] Previous studies have shown that in dichotomous-choice tasks, response repetition/ alternation effects are likely to be modulated by a strategy of comparing the current stimulus to the previous one (the probe and prime stimulus in our task). Thus, if there is a feature match between the two stimuli, subjects will be biased to repeat the same response; if there is a mismatch, they will be biased to switch response (e.g., Bertelson, 1963; Fletcher & Rabbitt, 1978; Terry, Valdes, & Neill, 1994). In our first experiment, feature-specific NP was always assessed on probe stimuli following an incongruent prime (i.e., the relevant and irrelevant attributes were associated to opposite responses). Hence, such trials always required a response alternation. Consequently, a feature match, as in the IFi condition, might slow such responses via the bias to repeat the same response, and this could have caused what appears to be a negative priming effect for the individual feature. This might also explain why the irrelevant feature appears to cause what seems to be a positive priming effect when the prime is congruent: Here, the probe requires a response repetition. This possible explanation of the feature-specific priming effects obtained in Experiment 1 would not hold if the different features were each mapped onto a separate finger/key, since a response repetition/ alternation strategy would not be very helpful in this case. Experiment 2 addressed this issue by having four response-associated stimulus features, each mapped onto a separate finger/key. Response-associated features were the red and green colours, and the upwards and downwards drift of a moving grid. A prime–probe procedure was used as before.

Methods

Subjects.   Eight new subjects, all students at the University of Oxford, took part in this experiment (aged 19 to 25, 3 females). They were naive as to the purposes of the experiment and were paid for their participation. All reported normal or corrected-to-normal acuity and colour vision.

Apparatus and stimuli.   Stimulus presentation and response collection were handled with the MEL software running on a PC computer (graphics resolution set at 640×480 pixels). Subjects were seated in a sound attenuated, dimly lit room, and viewed the display from a distance of about 100 cm.

Stimuli consisted of a grid made of three horizontal and three vertical stripes. Each stripe subtended approximately 1.5° of visual angle in length

---

[5] We thank Tram Neill for pointing out to us this alternative interpretation.

and 0.2° in width, and the distance between two adjacent stripes was also 0.2°. Stripes could be red, green, blue, or yellow (or grey), and could move upwards, downwards, leftwards, or rightwards (or be stationary). Only the red and green colours, and the upwards and downwards motions, were task-relevant (response-associated) features, the others being control features. The up/down motion was obtained by drifting the horizontal stripes within a fixed window, while keeping the vertical stripes stationary, and vice versa for the left/right motion. The speed of the horizontal and vertical stripes was 8.2°/s and 8°/s, respectively (since the motion was produced by shifting the stripes of the same number of pixels, the slight difference in speed was due to the rectangular shape of a single pixel). Once a moving stripe reached the border of the window and then disappeared, it was replaced with a new stripe appearing at the opposite border. As before, flicker photometry was used to ensure equal subjective brightness among the different colours. The background was approximately 0 cd/m².

Design.   Each trial comprised the sequential presentation of a prime and a probe stimulus, each requiring a response. The prime was a coloured moving grid (two-dimensional stimulus). The subject's task was to discriminate either the colour or the direction of motion of the stripes depending on an instruction cue (the letter "C" for colour and "M" for motion) presented before the prime stimulus onset. The relevant and irrelevant features were the selected and the ignored feature, respectively.

Different responses were assigned to each task-relevant feature: One response for red, another for green, a third response for upwards direction and a fourth response for downwards direction. Blue and yellow colours (and grey), and leftwards and rightwards motion (and stationary) were control features for the colour and motion dimension, respectively, and they had no response assignment. The prime stimulus was defined as incongruent when its irrelevant feature was associated to a different response from that associated to its relevant feature: it was defined as control when the irrelevant feature had no response assignment (see Figure 4a). Given that each feature was assigned to a different response there were no congruent primes in this experiment.

The probe stimulus was also a grid but defined by one feature only (one-dimensional stimulus). Colour probes were red or green stationary grids, and motion probes were grey upward or downward moving grids. The subject's task was always to discriminate the colour or the direction of motion of the probe stimulus. As the probe was always one-dimensional, no instruction was presented before its onset. All subjects produced responses by using four fingers/keys. The four fingers belonged to the same hand in half the sessions, while two fingers of each hand were used in the remaining half of the sessions.

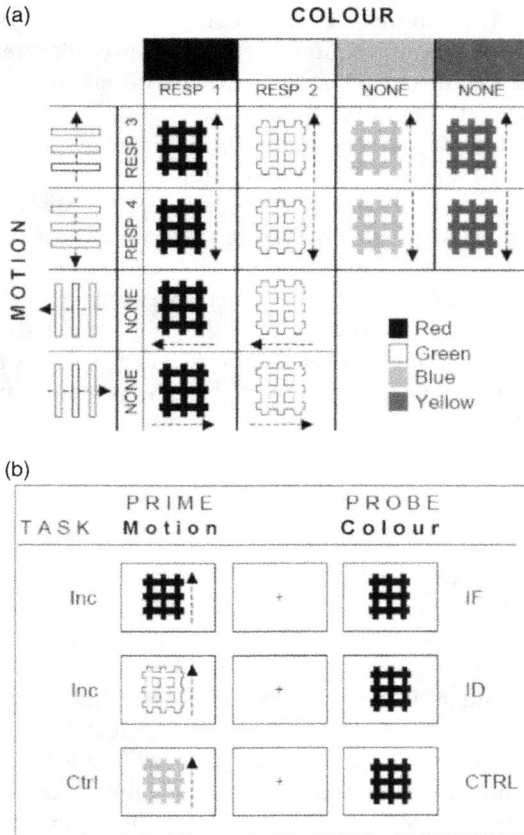

Figure 4. Experiment 2. (a) Prime conditions. (b) Probe conditions IF, ID, and CTRL.

For the prime stimuli a $2 \times 2 \times 2$ within-subjects design was used, and the factors were hands (one vs. two), task (colour vs. motion), and congruency (incongruent vs. control). As to the probe stimulus, the relationship between task in the prime and task in the probe defined the task-sequence factor (same vs. different). As in the previous experiment, to assess the NP effect for the individual feature, we presented the ignored feature in the prime as the (only) response-associated (target) feature in the subsequent probe. As a consequence, a change of task between prime and subsequent probe was a necessary condition to investigate the existence of negative priming effects, and for this reason only different-task sequences will be considered in the Results section below. The relationship between the irrelevant feature in the prime and the target feature of the probe produced the probe factors:

Ignored feature (IF), ignored dimension (ID), and control (CTRL). In the IF condition, the irrelevant feature in the prime was repeated as the target feature of the probe. In the ID and CTRL conditions the irrelevant feature in the prime was different from that presented in the probe, but both belonged to the same perceptual dimension (see Figure 4b). The two conditions differed in that the former followed an incongruent prime stimulus, whereas the latter followed a control prime stimulus. A pure NP effect for the feature is revealed by slower (and more error-prone) responses in the IF than in the ID condition. Instead, a dimension effect could in principle be measured as the difference between the ID and CTRL conditions, but this comparison would be contaminated by differential task difficulty in responding to an incongruent vs. control prime stimulus and thus will not be considered further. For the present purposes, we will only focus on the former effect. As a consequence, a $2 \times 2 \times 2$ design (one vs. two hands, colour vs. motion task, IF vs. ID condition) within-subjects design will be used to analyse the probe data.

Procedure. Each trial began with the word "READY" written in the centre of the screen and the subject had to press the spacebar to start the trial. After a 700 ms blank period, the instruction cue was presented in the centre of the screen for 500 ms. The cue was replaced by an achromatic fixation cross serving also as a marker for the location of the upcoming stimuli. After an interval varying randomly between 500 and 800 ms, the prime stimulus was presented and remained visible for 150 ms. After a response was made (or 1850 ms had elapsed) the fixation cross reappeared. After a variable interval of between 350 and 650 ms, the probe stimulus was shown for 150 ms and a second response had to be given. A fixed intertrial interval of 700 ms was allowed before the word "READY" was again presented. An error tone was delivered for 500 ms following incorrect responses.

In the one-hand condition responses were produced by pressing with the right hand one of four keys (the characters "v", "b", "n", and "m") on the computer keyboard. In the two-hands condition, each hand pressed one of two keys (the characters "z" and "x" for the left hand, and the characters "n" and "m" for the right hand). The order of response instructions was counterbalanced across subjects: Half the subjects run the first three sessions with one hand and the remaining three sessions with two hands; the other subjects had the reverse assignment. Response assignments were also counterbalanced across subjects such that each key/finger could map each of the four features.

Subjects were given a short practice session until they felt comfortable with the task requirements. They then performed six experimental sessions of 96 trials each. In each session the number of trials for the incongruent and control prime stimuli was 64 and 32, respectively (pooled across tasks). The corresponding number of trials for each of the probe conditions (IF, ID, and CTRL) was 16 (again pooled across tasks).[6]

Results

Prime stimuli. Prime errors (4.2% overall) and correct mean prime RTs were separately submitted to a $2 \times 2 \times 2$ within-subjects repeated-measures ANOVA. The main effect of congruency on RTs was significant, $F(1, 7) = 18.04$, $p < .01$, with longer RTs to incongruent (705 ms) than control (668 ms) stimuli. No other effect or interaction approached significance. The analysis of errors revealed that subjects made more errors in the incongruent than in the control trials (6% vs. 3%), $F(1, 7) = 14.77$, $p < .01$. There was also a significant interaction between hand condition and task, $F(1, 7) = 8.82$, $p < .05$: In the one-hand condition, subjects made more errors in the colour than in the motion task (4% vs. 3%); an opposite trend was present in the two-hand condition (4% vs. 5%). No other main effect or interaction approached significance.

Probe stimuli. We only analysed errors and correct mean RTs to probes following correct responses to preceding primes. Two ANOVAs were performed, one on correct mean RTs and one on error rates, with the factors hand condition (one vs. two), task (colour vs. motion), and probe condition (IF vs. ID). The analysis on RTs revealed a nonsignificant main effect of probe condition (737 and 708 ms, in the IF and ID condition, respectively), $F(1, 7) = 2.94$, $p > .1$, and a significant interaction between probe condition and task, $F(1, 7) = 5.11$, $p = .05$. Post hoc analyses showed a significant feature-specific NP effect for motion (59 ms), $t(7) = 2.40$, $p < .05$, but not for colour (-2 ms).[7] No other main effect or interaction approached significance. A similar analysis on error rates (4.9% overall) showed that only the main effect of probe condition approached significance, $F(1, 7) = 4.00$, $p = .08$, with more errors overall in the IF than ID condition (7.2% vs. 4.3%).

---

[6] There were several methodological differences between Experiments 1 and 2. To a large extent this is due to the fact that Experiment 2 had the additional objective of allowing us the scalp recording of event-related electrical potentials (ERPs) during task performance, and some features of the paradigm were chosen accordingly. Nonetheless, we believe that such methodological differences between the two experiments do not weaken our discussion of the behavioural results of Experiment 2 for the present purposes.

[7] A robust and highly significant negative priming effect for motion has been found in successive replications of this experiment.

Discussion

The results of Experiment 2 speak against the possibility that the feature-specific NP effects obtained in the previous experiment could be due to a response repetition/alternation strategy modulated by the degree of feature overlap between consecutive stimuli (primes and probes in our paradigm). In this experiment, unlike in the previous one, each response-associated feature was mapped onto a separate finger/key. Given this larger variety of possible responses, it is very unlikely that subjects generated a bias in favour of any particular finger/key to respond to a probe stimulus on the basis of which finger/key they had just used to respond to the previous prime stimulus. Although this factor has been shown to influence the speed of responding in other contexts (e.g., Bertelson, 1963; Fletcher & Rabbitt, 1978; Terry et al., 1994), it appears that the NP effects for the individual features, as shown in the present study, are not determined by mere biases to repeat or alternate responses across consecutive stimuli.

Results of Experiment 2, in addition to confirming feature-specific NP, also confirmed that this effect may be strongly asymmetric depending on the competing features. Although a large and reliable feature-specific NP effect was found for motion features, no such effect was observed for colour features (see footnote 4), replicating the results of Experiment 1. As discussed earlier, it is a challenging exercise to try and relate such asymmetrical NP effects to any asymmetry in the degree of interference exerted by colour vs. motion features.

GENERAL DISCUSSION

The overall pattern of results from the two experiments reported here provides strong support to the notion that attention can operate on the individual features and feature dimensions of a multidimensional visual object. Although similar conclusions were reached earlier by a number of authors (Boucart & Humphreys, 1994; Cohen & Shoup, 1997; Found & Müller, 1996; Garner, 1974; Kanwisher et al., 1995; Kumada, 2001; Maruff et al., 1999; Remington & Folk, 2001; Rossi & Paradiso, 1995), the present findings may be the first to demonstrate directly that selective processing of the relevant feature of an object can be accompanied by active suppression of the irrelevant feature of the same object, suggesting that feature selective attention operates through a combination of facilitatory and inhibitory mechanisms. Although the studies cited above were all able to demonstrate the privileged processing of object features that are relevant to current behaviour, they were neutral with respect to the processing fate of the ignored features of the same object. None of them assessed whether ignored object features were filtered out by early level-mechanisms, actively suppressed by late-level mechanisms, or simply unaffected during selective processing of task-relevant information. Perhaps the only exception is the work of Tipper et al. (1994), who employed a negative priming paradigm to test the idea that selective inhibition of task-irrelevant features of an object can be controlled and constrained by the behavioural goals at hand. While maintaining a constant stimulus set, the authors demonstrated that when the goal of the task was to indicate the location of a target, NP for the location of the ignored distractor was obtained, but not for its identity. Conversely, when the task was to identify the target, the location of the distractor did not produce NP. However, in the latter situation, NP for the identity of the distractor was not observed either, which would be predicted by the hypothesis. Overall, a complex pattern of results emerged from the experiments of this study, which makes it difficult to draw any firm conclusion regarding the underlying attentional mechanisms. In addition, in the paradigm of Tipper et al., different tasks required that individual stimulus features be mapped onto different types of behavioural response, which further limits the generality of the observation that active ignoring can be applied to individual object features. In our study we were able to reveal inhibitory attention mechanisms for the elemental features of a single multidimensional object when relevant and irrelevant features of the object were mapped onto the same response scheme.

Selective attention to the individual object features, as shown in the present study, should be clearly distinguished from other feature-based attention phenomena, like in Guided Search (e.g., Wolfe, Cave, & Franzel, 1989; see also Found & Müller, 1996; Treisman & Sato, 1990; Tsal & Lavie, 1988). In guided search, feature information is used for the top-down guidance of object-based (and space-based) attention towards objects of interest. In our task, space- and object-based attention mechanisms are simply excluded or overridden.

It may appear that the present demonstration of feature selective processing is at odds with the well-established notion of object-based attention (e.g., Blaser et al., 2000; Duncan, 1984; Egly et al., 1994; Kahneman, Treisman, & Burkell, 1983; Valdes-Sosa et al., 2000). Object-based models of attention posit that all features of an attended object are concurrently selected. However, in our view there is actually no contradiction between these two notions. Whereas object-based selection has been shown to constrain the degree to which attention can be divided between multiple sources of information (with minimal cost), the present data demonstrate that under conditions where selective processing is of the essence, attention can be directed to the component features of an object. The fact that under divided attention conditions it is easier to process two features of the same object than two features of different objects does not predict that, when required by the task, subjects cannot break down perceptual objects to achieve selective processing of their component features. In general, although object-based models capture the natural tendency of attentional processing to treat objects as perceptual wholes, the present data imply that selection of whole objects is optional, and perhaps highly natural, but not mandatory (Lamy & Egeth, 2002; Müller & O'Grady, 2000; Shomstein & Yantis, 2002). In general, the present data strongly argue in favour of a highly flexible implementation of attentional selection in vision, which can be directed to restricted spatial regions, to whole objects or just to a single object feature depending on task demands (Treisman, 1969). However, it is also noteworthy that feature selective processing was far from optimal in our paradigm, as attested by large interference effects, and this may reflect the natural tendency of attention mechanisms to select together the multiple features of a single object, at least at an initial stage of processing (Duncan, 1996).

An important issue raised by the present findings concerns the processing level at which feature selective attention intervenes, and consequently the representations upon which it acts. We have already emphasized that robust negative priming effects were only obtained in conditions of response conflict, i.e., following incongruent primes affording competing stimulus–response mappings. In contrast, positive priming effects were observed with probe stimuli following congruent primes. This clearly indicates that the inhibitory mechanisms revealed with our priming procedure were engaged at (or determined by) a processing stage where the irrelevant feature of the prime stimulus had been tacitly identified and its response mapping retrieved. In accordance with this interpretation, incongruent prime stimuli invariably engendered strong interference effects. In summary, suppression of the irrelevant feature of the prime stimulus must have occurred at a stage of incipient response activation (Coles, Gratton, Bashore, Eriksen, & Donchin, 1985). Having said this, one should not disregard the possibility that, although selective inhibition was triggered after the ignored prime feature had undergone a substantial degree of processing, nonetheless inhibition might have "spread back" onto earlier perceptual representations of the same feature, thus leading to perceptual effects as well. We are currently testing this possibility in our laboratories through behavioural and electrophysiological methods.

Somehow related to the same issue, the possibility should also be entertained that selection of the relevant feature of the prime, and concurrent suppression of the irrelevant feature of the same prime, was aided in part by an early-level filtering mechanism. In other words, it is conceivable that the late inhibitory mechanism, resulting in negative priming effects, was simply engaged to the extent that the irrelevant feature of the prime had escaped an early filtering or attenuation mechanism. At any rate, the hypothesis that an early-level attention mechanism aided task performance could not be tested in our paradigm, as it would require a way of comparing the speed and depth of perceptual processing of the relevant and irrelevant feature of the same object. Again, such a possibility will have to be tested in future experiments.

Whether or not early-level attention mechanisms were engaged at all to aid task performance in our paradigm, the negative priming effects we obtained were caused by a late attention mechanism sensitive to conflicting stimulus–response mappings. It has been reported that reducing the impact of a distractor on task performance, for instance by optimally cueing the task-relevant target (Kramer et al., 1994; Paquet, 2001; Ruthruff & Miller, 1995; but see Fox, 1994) or by increasing the perceptual load for the task-relevant stimulus set (Lavie & Fox, 2000), has the consequential effect of reducing negative priming as well. The explanation for these results is that effective cueing of the target or an increase in the perceptual load engage powerful early-level filtering mechanisms, thus blocking the irrelevant distractor from further processing. A blocked distractor does not lend itself to be further suppressed by a late attention mechanism. In our paradigm, instead, space-based and object-based filtering mechanisms were not available, and the perceptual load imposed by the prime stimulus was very low, presumably rendering the representation of the irrelevant feature readily available for processing. Suppression of the irrelevant feature by a late inhibitory mechanism thus became the primary option.

The foregoing discussion might create the false belief that interference and negative priming are always related to one another in a simple fashion. The greater the interference engendered by a distractor, the larger the resulting negative priming effect. Unfortunately such a straightforward relation has not been found (i.e., it may exist, but be masked by other parallel factors; e.g., Driver & Tipper, 1989; Fox, 1994). As discussed earlier with reference to the results of Experiment 1, this is probably because the overall pattern of interference and negative priming in a given paradigm results from the combination of many factors. Particularly relevant to our concern is the combination of early-level filtering mechanisms and late-level, reactive inhibitory mechanisms.

Interference by an incompatible distractor may thus be low either because an early filtering mechanism has prevented the distractor from being encoded, or because a late (reactive) inhibitory mechanism has prevented the distractor from gaining access to response selection stages of processing (Lavie & Fox, 2000; Paquet, 2001; Ruthruff & Miller, 1995; Tipper, 2001). Negative priming will be obtained in the latter but not in the former scenario.

Of particular interest was the unexpected finding in Experiment 1 of reliable negative priming effects for the perceptual dimension. We have used this term to refer to the impaired processing of a given probe target (e.g., red) when the immediately preceding prime display contained the other, response-associated feature of the same ignored dimension (e.g., green). Our tentative interpretation of the effect is in terms of a negative priming effect for the perceptual dimension to which the irrelevant feature of the prime stimulus belongs. When the irrelevant feature of the prime is actively inhibited, inhibition spreads to the other (response-associated) feature of the same dimension, or perhaps to the perceptual dimension in general, including feature values that are not mapped onto any response within the context of the current task. This might entail a sort of functional disconnection (gating) of the ignored perceptual channel from the response selection stages of processing (Cohen & Feintuch, 2002; Cohen & Shoup, 1997; see also Müller & O'Grady, 2000, for a compatible view).

However, alternative interpretations of this finding can be put forward in relation to the literature on the so-called task-switching costs. In particular, both the notion of backward inhibition (Mayr & Keele, 2000) and that of task set inertia (and its more recent development, the retrieval hypothesis; Allport & Wylie, 1999, 2000) could perhaps provide an account for what we have termed negative priming for the perceptual dimension. According to these notions, task alternation costs result from the involuntary persistence of stimulus–response mappings for the preceding trial(s) into the processing of the next (switch) trial—a form of proactive interference of task set. In this perspective, what we have termed negative priming for the perceptual dimension could be interpreted as a manifestation of proactive interference as well. When the subject faces an incongruent prime, the task associated to the relevant feature must be performed while the task associated to the irrelevant feature must be suppressed. Suppression of the irrelevant task is especially required because that task has been recently performed, its stimulus–response mappings have been recently practised, and it is thus active in the subject's procedural working memory (Allport & Wylie, 2000). The need to suppress the competing task is further increased when the irrelevant feature is a potent cue to retrieve the stimulus–response mappings of the task.

At present we do not know which is the most likely explanation for the phenomenon we have termed negative priming for the perceptual dimension, and it is actually not entirely clear whether our own account and those suggested by the work of Mayr and Keele (2000) and of Allport and Wylie (Allport & Wylie, 1999, 2000) are fundamentally different or simply represent different versions of a similar explanation. As a way to shed some light on these issues, in the future it will be important to assess the magnitude of negative priming for the perceptual dimension depending on whether the relevant and irrelevant features of the prime stimulus belong to well separable perceptual dimensions (and stimulus–response sets), such as colour and motion, or instead they belong to distinct stimulus–response sets arbitrarily defined within the boundaries of a common perceptual channel, such as speed and direction of motion. The outcome of this type of experiment should tell us whether our finding of a negative priming effect for the perceptual dimension is better conceptualized in terms of gating of perceptual channels by feature-based attention or of task-switching operations.

The cognitive psychology of visual selective attention has enjoyed an epoch of extraordinary advancement over the past few decades. However, compared to other forms of attentional processing, namely space- and object-based selection, feature-selective attention has been relatively neglected until recently, with the notable exception of a handful of studies (Cohen & Shoup, 1997; Found & Müller, 1996; Garner, 1974; Kanwisher et al., 1995; Maruff et al., 1999; Müller & O'Grady, 2000; Müller et al., 2003; Remington & Folk, 2001; Rossi & Paradiso, 1995; and the present work). This gap between feature-selective attention and other forms of attention has so far been even more profound with respect to cognitive neuroscience approaches. Thus, while the neural underpinnings of space-based and object-based attention have been charted out to a remarkable degree of detail with a variety of methods in humans and animals (for review see, e.g., Corbetta & Shulman, 2002; Desimone & Duncan, 1995; Kastner & Ungerleider, 2000; Luck & Hillyard, 2000; Nobre, 2001; Reynolds & Chelazzi, 2004), feature selective attention has been explored so far only by a small number of neuroscience studies (Anllo-Vento & Hillyard, 1996; Beauchamp, Cox, & DeYoe, 1997; Chawla, Rees, & Friston, 1999; Corbetta, Miezin, Dobmeyer, Shulman, & Petersen, 1990; Giesbrecht, Woldorff, Song, & Mangun, 2003; Huk & Heeger, 2000; Liu, Slotnick, Serences, & Yantis, 2003; Maunsell & Hochstein, 1991; McClurkin & Optican, 1996; Treue & Trujillo, 1999; Weidner, Pollmann, Müller, & von Cramon, 2002). A great deal remains to be understood of our ability to select the component features of a single multidimensional object by the convergent use of behavioural and cognitive neuroscience methods.

REFERENCES

Allport, D. A., Tipper, S. P., & Chmiel, N. R. J. (1985). Perceptual integration and postcategorical filtering. In M. I. Posner & O. S. M. Marin (Eds.), *Attention and performance: XI. Attention and neuropsychology* (pp. 107–132). Hillsdale, NJ: Lawrence Erlbaum Associates, Inc.

Allport, D. A., & Wylie, G. (1999). Task-switching: Positive and negative priming of task-set. In G. W. Humphreys, J. Duncan, & A. M. Treisman (Eds.), *Attention, space and action: Studies in cognitive neuroscience* (pp. 273–296). Oxford, UK: Oxford University Press.

Allport, D. A., & Wylie, G. (2000). Task-switching, stimulus–response bindings, and negative priming. In S. Monsell & J. S. Driver (Eds.), *Attention and performance: XVIII. Control of cognitive performance* (pp. 35–70). Cambridge, MA: MIT Press.

Anllo-Vento, L., & Hillyard, S. A. (1996). Selective attention to the color and direction of moving stimuli: Electrophysiological correlates of hierarchical feature selection. *Perception and Psychophysics, 58,* 191–206.

Beauchamp, M. S., Cox, R. W., & DeYoe, E. A. (1997). Graded effects of spatial and featural attention on human area MT and associated motion processing areas. *Journal of Neurophysiology, 78,* 516–520.

Bertelson, P. (1963). S–R relationships and reaction times to new versus repeated signals in a serial task. *Journal of Experimental Psychology, 65,* 478–484.

Blaser, E., Pylyshyn, Z. W., & Holcombe, A. O. (2000). Tracking an object through feature space. *Nature, 408,* 196–199.

Boucart, M., & Humphreys, G. W. (1994). Attention to orientation, size, luminance, and color: Attentional failure within the form domain. *Journal of Experimental Psychology: Human Perception and Performance, 20,* 61–80.

Chawla, D., Rees, G., & Friston, K. J. (1999). The physiological basis of attentional modulation in extrastriate visual areas. *Nature Neuroscience, 2,* 671–676.

Cohen, A., & Feintuch, U. (2002). The dimensional-action system: A distinct visual system. In W. Prinz & B. Hommel (Eds.), *Attention and performance: XIX. Common mechanisms in perception and action* (pp. 587–608). Oxford: Oxford University Press.

Cohen, A., & Magen, H. (1999). Intra- and cross-dimensional visual search for single-feature targets. *Perception and Psychophysics, 61,* 291–307.

Cohen, A., & Shoup, R. (1997). Perceptual dimensional constraints in response selection processes. *Cognitive Psychology, 32,* 128–181.

Coles, M. G. H., Gratton, G., Bashore, T. R., Eriksen, C. W., & Donchin, E. (1985). A psychophysiological investigation of the continuous flow model of human information processing. *Journal of Experimental Psychology: Human Perception and Performance, 11,* 529–553.

Corbetta, M., Miezin, F. M., Dobmeyer, S., Shulman, G. L., & Petersen, S. E. (1990). Attentional modulation of neural processing of shape, color, and velocity in humans. *Science, 248,* 1556–1559.

Corbetta, M., & Shulman, G. L. (2002). Control of goal-directed and stimulus-driven attention in the brain. *Nature Reviews Neuroscience, 3,* 201–215.

Dalrymple-Alford, E. C., & Budayr, B. (1966). Examination of some aspects of the Stroop color–word test. *Perceptual and Motor Skills, 23,* 1211–1214.

Desimone, R., & Duncan, J. (1995). Neural mechanisms of selective visual attention. *Annual Review of Neuroscience, 18,* 193–222.

Driver, J., & Tipper, S. P. (1989). On the nonselectivity of "selective" seeing: Contrasts between interference and priming in selective attention. *Journal of Experimental Psychology: Human Perception and Performance, 15,* 304–314.

Duncan, J. (1984). Selective attention and the organization of visual information. *Journal of Experimental Psychology: General, 113,* 501–517.

Duncan, J. (1996). Cooperating brain systems in selective perception and action. In T. Inui & J. L. McClelland (Eds.), *Attention and performance: XVI. Information integration in perception and communication* (pp. 549–578). Cambridge, MA: MIT Press.

Egly. R., Driver, J., & Rafal, R. D. (1994). Shifting visual attention between objects and locations: Evidence from normal and parietal lesion subjects. *Journal of Experimental Psychology: General*, *123*, 161–177.

Eriksen, B. A., & Eriksen, C. W. (1974). Effects of noise letters upon the identification of a target letter in a nonsearch task. *Perception and Psychophysics*, *16*, 143–149.

Fletcher, B., & Rabbitt, P. M. (1978). The changing pattern of perceptual analytic strategies and response selection with practice in a two-choice reaction time task. *Quarterly Journal of Experimental Psychology*, *30*, 417–427.

Found, A., & Müller, H. J. (1996). Searching for unknown feature targets on more than one dimension: Investigating a "dimension-weighting" account. *Perception and Psychophysics*. *58*, 88–101.

Fox, E. (1994). Interference and negative priming from ignored distractors: The role of selection difficulty. *Perception and Psychophysics*, *56*, 565–574.

Fox, E. (1998). Perceptual grouping and visual selective attention. *Perception and Psychophysics*, *60*, 1004–1021.

Fox, E., & de Fockert, J. W. (1998). Negative priming depends on prime–probe similarity: Evidence for episodic retrieval. *Psychonomic Bulletin and Review*, *5*, 107–113.

Garner, W. R. (1974). *The processing of information and structure*. Hillsdale. NJ: Lawrence Erlbaum Associates, Inc.

Giesbrecht, B., Woldorff, M. G., Song, A. W., & Mangun, G. R. (2003). Neural mechanisms of top-down control during spatial and feature attention. *Neuroimage*, *19*, 496–512.

Huk, A. C., & Heeger, D. J. (2000). Task-related modulation of visual cortex. *Journal of Neurophysiology*, *83*, 3525–3536.

Kahneman, D., & Henik, A. (1977). Effects of visual grouping on immediate recall and selective attention. In S. Dornič (Ed.), *Attention and performance VI* (pp. 307–331). Hillsdale, NJ: Lawrence Erlbaum Associates, Inc.

Kahneman, D., Treisman, A., & Burkell, J. (1983). The cost of visual filtering. *Journal of Experimental Psychology: Human Perception and Performance*, *9*, 510–522.

Kaiser, P. K., & Boynton, R. M. (1996). *Human color vision*. Washington, DC: Optical Society of America.

Kanwisher, N. (1987). Repetition blindness: Type recognition without token individuation. *Cognition*, *27*, 117–143.

Kanwisher, N., Driver, J., & Machado, L. (1995). Spatial repetition blindness is modulated by selective attention to color and shape. *Cognitive Psychology*, *29*, 303–337.

Kastner, S., & Ungerleider, L. G. (2000). Mechanisms of visual attention in the human cortex. *Annual Review of Neuroscience*, *23*, 315–341.

Kramer, A. F., Humphrey, D. G., Larish, J. F., Logan, G. D., & Strayer, D. L. (1994). Aging and inhibition: Beyond a unitary view of inhibitory processing in attention. *Psychological Aging*, *9*, 491–512.

Kramer, A. F., & Jacobson, A. (1991). Perceptual organization and focused attention: The role of objects and proximity in visual processing. *Perception and Psychophysics*, *50*, 267–284.

Kumada, T. (2001). Feature-based control of attention: Evidence for two forms of dimension weighting. *Perception and Psychophysics*, *63*, 698–708.

Lamy, D., & Egeth, H. (2002). Object-based selection: The role of attentional shifts. *Perception and Psychophysics*, *64*, 52–66.

Lavie, N., & Fox, E. (2000). The role of perceptual load in negative priming. *Journal of Experimental Psychology: Human Perception and Performance*, *26*, 1038–1052.

Liu, T., Slotnick, S., Serences, J., & Yantis, S. (2003). Cortical mechanisms of feature-based attentional control. *Cerebral Cortex*, *13*, 1334–1343.

Lowe, D. G. (1979). Strategies, context, and the mechanism of response inhibition. *Memory and Cognition*, *7*, 382–389.

Lowe, D. G. (1985). Further investigations of inhibitory mechanisms in attention. *Memory and Cognition*, *13*, 74–80.

Luck, S. J., & Hillyard, S. A. (2000). The operation of selective attention at multiple stages of processing: Evidence from human and monkey electrophysiology. In M. S. Gazzaniga (Ed.), *The new cognitive neurosciences* (pp. 687–700). Cambridge, MA: MIT Press.

MacDonald, P. A., & Joordens. S. (2000). Investigating a memory-based account of negative priming: Support for selection–feature mismatch. *Journal of Experimental Psychology: Human Perception and Performance*, *26*, 1478–1496.

Maruff, P., Danckert, J.. Camplin. G.. & Currie, J. (1999). Behavioral goals constrain the selection of visual information. *Psychological Science*, *10*, 522–525.

Maunsell. J. H. R., & Hochstein. S. (1991). Effects of behavioral state on the stimulus selectivity of neurons in area V4 of the macaque monkey. In B. Blum (Ed.), *Channels in the visual system: Neurophysiology, psychophysics, and models* (pp. 447–470). London: Freund.

Mayr. U., & Keele, S. W. (2000). Changing internal constraints on action: The role of backward inhibition. *Journal of Experimental Psychology: General*, *129*, 4–26.

McClurkin, J. W., & Optican, L. M. (1996). Primate striate and prestriate cortical neurons during discrimination: I. Simultaneous temporal encoding of information about color and pattern. *Journal of Neurophysiology*, *75*, 481–507.

Milliken, B., Joordens, S., Merikle. P. M.. & Seiffert, A. E. (1998). Selective attention: A reevaluation of the implications of negative priming. *Psychological Review*, *105*, 203–229.

Milliken, B., Tipper, S. P., & Weaver. B. (1994). Negative priming in a spatial localization task: Feature mismatching and distractor inhibition. *Journal of Experimental Psychology: Human Perception and Performance*, *20*, 624–646.

Milner. B. (1963). Effects of different brain lesions on card-sorting. *Archives of Neurology*, *9*, 90–100.

Müller. H. J.. & O'Grady, R. B. (2000). Dimension-based visual attention modulates dual-judgment accuracy in Duncan's (1984) one- versus two-object report paradigm. *Journal of Experimental Psychology: Human Perception and Performance*, *26*, 1332–1351.

Müller. H. J., Reimann, B., & Krummenacher. J. (2003). Visual search for singleton feature targets across dimensions: Stimulus- and expectancy-driven effects in dimensional weighting. *Journal of Experimental Psychology: Human Perception and Performance*, *29*, 1021–1035.

Neill. W. T. (1977). Inhibitory and facilitatory processes in selective attention. *Journal of Experimental Psychology: Human Perception and Performance*, *3*, 444–450.

Neill. W. T.. Lissner. L. S.. & Beck. J. L. (1990). Negative priming in same–different matching: Further evidence for a central locus of inhibition. *Perception and Psychophysics*, *48*, 398–400.

Neill. W. T., & Valdes. L. A. (1992). Persistence of negative priming: Steady state or decay? *Journal of Experimental Psychology: Learning, Memory and Cognition*, *18*, 565–576.

Neill. W. T.. & Valdes. L. A. (1996). Facilitatory and inhibitory aspects of attention. In A. F. Kramer. M. G. H. Coles. & G. D. Logan (Eds.). *Converging operations in the study of visual selective attention* (pp. 77–106). Washington. DC: American Psychological Association.

Neill. W. T., Valdes, L. A.. Terry. K. M.. & Gorfein. D. S. (1992). Persistence of negative priming: II. Evidence for episodic trace retrieval. *Journal of Experimental Psychology: Learning, Memory and Cognition*. *18*, 993–1000.

Neisser, U. (1967). *Cognitive psychology*. New York: Appleton-Century-Crofts.

Nissen, M. J. (1985). Accessing features and objects: Is location special? In M. I. Posner & O. S. M. Marin (Eds.), *Attention and performance: XI. Attention and neuropsychology* (pp. 205–219). Hillsdale, NJ: Lawrence Erlbaum Associates, Inc.

Nobre, A. C. (2001). The attentive homunculus: Now you see it. now you don't. *Neuroscience and Biobehavioural Reviews*, *25*, 477–496.

Paquet, L. (2001). Eliminating flanker effects and negative priming in the flankers task: Evidence for early selection. *Psychonomic Bulletin and Review, 8*, 301–306.

Park, J., & Kanwisher, N. (1994). Negative priming for spatial locations: Identity mismatching, not distractor inhibition. *Journal of Experimental Psychology: Human Perception and Performance, 20*, 613–623.

Posner, M. I., Snyder, C. R. R., & Davidson, B. J. (1980). Attention and the detection of signals. *Journal of Experimental Psychology: General, 109*, 160–174.

Remington, R. W., & Folk, C. L. (2001). A dissociation between attention and selection. *Psychological Science, 12*, 511–515.

Reynolds, J. H., & Chelazzi, L. (2004). Attentional modulation of visual processing. *Annual Review of Neuroscience, 27*, 611–647.

Rossi, A. F., & Paradiso, M. A. (1995). Feature-specific effects of selective visual attention. *Vision Research, 35*, 621–634.

Ruthruff, E., & Miller, J. (1995). Negative priming depends on ease of selection. *Perception and Psychophysics, 57*, 715–723.

Schneider, W. (1988). Micro experimental laboratory: An integrated system for IBM PC compatibles. *Behavior Research Methods Instruments and Computers, 20*, 206–217.

Shomstein, S., & Yantis, S. (2002). Object-based attention: Sensory modulation or priority setting? *Perception and Psychophysics, 64*, 41–51.

Stroop, J. R. (1935). Studies of interference in serial verbal reactions. *Journal of Experimental Psychology, 18*, 643–662.

Terry, K. M., Valdes, L. A., & Neill, W. T. (1994). Does "inhibition of return" occur in discrimination tasks? *Perception and Psychophysics, 55*, 279–286.

Tipper, S. P. (1985). The negative priming effect: Inhibitory priming by ignored objects. *Quarterly Journal of Experimental Psychology, 37A*, 571–590.

Tipper, S. P. (2001). Does negative priming reflect inhibitory mechanisms? A review and integration of conflicting views. *Quarterly Journal of Experimental Psychology, 54A*, 321–343.

Tipper, S. P., Brehaut, J. C., & Driver, J. (1990). Selection of moving and static objects for the control of spatially directed action. *Journal of Experimental Psychology: Human Perception and Performance, 16*, 492–504.

Tipper, S. P., MacQueen, G. M., & Brehaut, J. C. (1988). Negative priming between response modalities: Evidence for the central locus of inhibition in selective attention. *Perception and Psychophysics, 43*, 45–52.

Tipper, S. P., Weaver, B., & Houghton, G. (1994). Behavioural goals determine inhibitory mechanisms of selective attention. *Quarterly Journal of Experimental Psychology, 47A*, 809–840.

Treisman, A. (1969). Strategies and models of selective attention. *Psychological Review, 76*, 282–299.

Treisman, A., Kahneman, D., & Burkell, J. (1983). Perceptual objects and the cost of filtering. *Perception and Psychophysics, 6*, 527–532.

Treisman, A., & Sato, S. (1990). Conjunction search revisited. *Journal of Experimental Psychology: Human Perception and Performance, 16*, 459–478.

Treue, S., & Trujillo, J. C. M. (1999). Feature-based attention influences motion processing gain in macaque visual cortex. *Nature, 399*, 575–579.

Tsal, Y., & Lavie, N. (1988). Attending to color and shape: The special role of location in selective visual processing. *Perception and Psychophysics, 44*, 15–21.

Valdes-Sosa, M., Cobo, A., & Pinilla, T. (2000). Attention to object files defined by transparent motion. *Journal of Experimental Psychology: Human Perception and Performance, 26*, 488–505.

Vecera, S. P., & Farah, M. J. (1994). Does visual attention select objects or locations? *Journal of Experimental Psychology: General*, *123*, 146–160.

Weidner, R., Pollmann, S., Müller, H. J., & von Cramon, D. Y. (2002). Top-down controlled visual dimension weighting: An event-related fMRI study. *Cerebral Cortex*, *12*, 318–328.

Wolfe, J. M., Cave, K. R., & Franzel, S. L. (1989). Guided Search: An alternative to the feature integration model for visual search. *Journal of Experimental Psychology: Human Perception and Performance*, *15*, 419–433.

VISUAL COGNITION, 2006, 14 (4/5/6/7/8), 619–628

Ψ Psychology Press
Taylor & Francis Group

Colour as a Gestalt: Pop out with basic features and with conjunctions

James R. Pomerantz

Rice University, Houston, TX, USA

Gestalt phenomena are a cornerstone of perceptual psychology. Although some-times poorly understood, they are powerful and robust effects with significant implications for how we recognize objects and parse scenes. Traditionally, the study of Gestalts has focused on visual form perception, where parts combine in nonadditive ways to create wholes possessing novel emergent properties different from the "sum of their parts". Here I argue that colour perception meets the customary criteria applied to Gestalts at least well as shape perception does, in that colour emerges from nonadditive combination of wavelengths in the perceptual system and results in novel, emergent features. Regarding colour as a (and perhaps as *the* quintessential) Gestalt may help demystify Gestalts and help us better understand the role of colour in tasks such as visual search that are used to identify basic features in early vision. Colour should be thought of not as a basic feature or primitive property of the stimulus but rather as a complex conjunction of wavelengths that are integrated in perceptual processing. As a Gestalt, however, colour serves as a psychological primitive and so, as with Gestalts in form perception, it may lead to pop-out in visual search. Indeed, pop-out should be regarded as a prerequisite for claiming that a conjunction of features forms a Gestalt.

Students of psychology learn early on about Gestalts, beginning with the ubiquitous series of illustrations appearing in the early chapters of introductory textbooks. There we read attempts to translate this elusive German word into scientific terms, or at least into other languages, and we witness a spate of demonstrations showing various Gestalt laws of grouping and figure–ground segregation at work. As we read more deeply into the literature, including current research on Gestalt phenomena, we learn that despite significant progress towards understanding and operationalizing the concept (Beck, 1982; Kimchi, Behrmann, & Olson, 2003; Palmer, 1999; Pomerantz & Kubovy, 1981), in many respects it remains vague.

Please address all correspondence to James R. Pomerantz, Department of Psychology MS 25, PO Box 1982, Rice University, Houston, TX 77251-1892 USA. Email: pomeran@rice.edu

© 2006 Psychology Press Ltd
http://www.psypress.com/viscog
DOI: 10.1080/13506280500195052

WHAT IS A GESTALT?

Paraphrasing William James's famous pronouncement on attention, we might say that everybody knows what a Gestalt is. At least we all know one when we see one. Gestalts, most fundamentally, are patterns or higher order features that emerge when two or more perceptual elements are placed in close spatial or temporal proximity to one another, patterns or features that do not arise when only a single element is present. So when three disks are tossed onto a surface, one perceives not only the properties of each disk individually (its size, colour, and x-y coordinates) but also the configuration the three disks form, be it a triangle or a straight line. If each disk is shifted in the same direction and by the same distance, the configuration remains unchanged even though the x-y coordinates of all the disks have changed. In that sense, the "whole" created by the disks— the configuration or shape they form—is different from and independent of its parts. Should the three disks contain suitably placed notches, as in Kanizsa's (1979) well-known subjective contour figure, yet other Gestalts emerge. Likewise, should the three disks be enclosed within a circle, a face-like configuration might emerge, with individual disks serving as eyes or mouth.

GESTALTS OUTSIDE OF FORM PERCEPTION

Although Gestalts are not confined to visual form perception, that is where most examples are drawn and where most research has focused. We know, however, that Gestalts can arise in auditory perception, as when three tones played in sequence define a melody that remains invariant if each tone's frequency is changed proportionally or, when played simultaneously, define a chord. Apparently absent from the literature, however, is the notion that colours may be regarded as Gestalts, perhaps as quintessential Gestalts.

Of course colour does figure into the demonstration of other Gestalt principles, as when disks in Wertheimer's (1923, translated in part in Ellis, 1950) grids group into rows or columns based on colour similarity; or when colours divide into separate translucent layers following Metelli's (1974) scission phenomenon. Missing from mention, however, is the notion that colour itself is a Gestalt, an emergent phenomenon arising from the nonadditive combination of more primitive components. Upon reflection, I believe colour meets most, if not all, of the criteria that customarily define a Gestalt, and that by regarding colour as a Gestalt we may sharpen our yet-vague concept and perhaps peel away some of the mystery and confusion that always seems to bedevil discussions of Gestalts.

COLOUR VISION AS GESTALT PROCESSING

Although controversies remain in our understanding of human trichromatic vision, much of it is well understood. In particular, we know that at the earliest stages of coding, three separate receptor systems exist with overlapping spectral sensitivities—cones with overlapping tuning curves indicating their response to a range of wavelengths. At later stages of processing, these separate channels for short, medium, and long wavelengths are integrated via an opponent process network into signals representing a red–green axis, a yellow–blue axis, and a black–white (luminance) axis. Yet later stages of processing convert this representation into one that codes hue, brightness, and saturation (which are taken to be the three dimensions of conscious perceptual experience).

Does the recoding that takes place in colour vision resemble that which we observe with the perception of visual forms, with the whole being different from—having novel, emergent properties apart from—the sum of its parts? The nonlinear way in which wavelengths combine to produce subjectively experienced colours certainly seems Gestalt in nature. After all, not only do wavelengths mix to form colours quite different from the colours associated with the individual wavelengths alone, but those emergent colours do not appear as simple blends and often they are unpredictable, at least to perceivers not well-versed in colour vision theory. Many of the colours arising from wavelength mixtures are in no way similar to the colours perceived from their constituent wavelengths, and in fact these emergent colours often do not appear in the visible spectrum. A good example is white itself, which does not appear in the spectrum of a trichromat and could be viewed as every bit as much of a novel, emergent, and surprising feature as Kanizsa's (1979) subjective triangle. What is more, just as there is an infinite number of tonal sequences that can define the same melody, there is an infinite number of wavelength combinations that yield the perception of white.

WHOLES BEFORE PARTS

If colour can be viewed as a Gestalt, might an even stronger case be made that colour is *the* quintessential Gestalt? I believe that it can, for the following reason. One principal claim of Gestalt psychology is that, in perception, the whole precedes the parts. Although this argument can become complicated and has been framed in various ways, the central thesis is that the forest is seen before the trees, i.e., that global structures or wholes are perceived via a fast, primary ("preattentive") process, whereas local structures or parts are perceived only by a slow, secondary process that relies on focal attention. The evidence for this notion of global-first in form perception is mixed; in some cases it seems to apply (Navon, 1977), whereas in others it holds for only some of the time or not at all (Kinchla & Wolfe, 1979; Pomerantz, 1983; Pomerantz & Sager, 1975; for a review see Kimchi, 1992). Much depends on physical parameters of the stimulus such as spatial frequency and absolute size: If one looks at a newspaper photograph from a distance, one sees only the global scene and not the dots from which that scene emerges. If the stimulus is brought close enough to the eye, however, the dots prevail.

Does holistic perception dominate in the case of colour? The answer appears to be yes. Human vision, in fact, seems incapable of attending selectively to individual wavelengths or of recovering the underlying spectra of visual stimuli, a fact well attested to by the existence of metamers (identically appearing colours that arise from different underlying wavelength combinations). Unlike in form perception, where usually we can attend either to the parts or to the whole (albeit not with equal ease or efficiency), in colour perception, the parts—the constituent wavelengths— are not accessible to conscious perception or available for behavioural responses.

MULTISTABILITY

It may be that for just this last reason—the inaccessibility of the component parts—that colour is not usually thought of as a Gestalt. Most Gestalt effects involve multistability—the flip-flopping that accompanies our inspection of a Necker Cube, the Rubin faces–vase stimulus, the Bahnsen columns, Wertheimer's lattices, and other classic demonstrations. With most Gestalt effects, one can switch attention between the parts and the wholes and sometimes even from one component part to another. Much of the "gee-whiz" factor that makes Gestalt effects so compelling arises from this metaperceptual experience (Pomerantz & Kubovy, 1981) wherein observers are made aware of the workings of their own perceptual processes. With colour, we do not experience this multistability. Instead, we see only the end product of our visual system's combining parts automatically, involuntarily, and irreversibly into the perceptual wholes we experience as colours. I would argue that colour should nonetheless be regarded as a Gestalt despite its lack of multistability: Just as with other stimuli (such as real-world scenes viewed binocularly), with colour one perceptual organization of wavelengths proves so strong it simply dominates any alternatives and there is then no perceptual flip-flopping.

THE EXPERIENCE ERROR

Conceptualizing colour as a Gestalt may aid us in our understanding of holistic perception in other areas. As is recognized by many (see Palmer, 2003), the concept of Gestalt is now, as it has always been, somewhat confused and vague. Indeed, the very discussion of critical issues such as object perception is clouded by a lack of an operational definition of "object" (e.g., Wolfe & Bennett, 1997). When we conduct experiments and describe our stimuli, we often use terms like "stimulus", "item", "object", and so forth when, in truth, we would be hard pressed to defend ourselves in the face of claims that we are committing the "experience error".

In writing the methods section of a scientific paper on perception, if we refer to a stimulus as a "red" object, we are committing the experience error. This error was a concern for the Gestalt psychologists but has been widely ignored by contemporary researchers (save for Palmer, 1999). It was described by Wolfgang Köhler (1929/1947, p. 95) as follows:

> In psychology we have often been warned against the stimulus error, i.e., against the danger of confusing our knowledge of the physical conditions of sensory experience with this experience as such. As I see it, another mistake, which I propose to call the experience error, is just as unfortunate. This error occurs when certain characteristics of sensory experience are inadvertently attributed to the mosaic of stimuli.

In brief, we commit the experience error when we attribute a phenomenon that is a product of cognition—i.e., something in the head—to the stimulus—i.e., something in the outside world. Even though he knew nothing of the electromagnetic spectrum, Newton nonetheless knew that colour is not in the stimulus: "The rays, to speak properly, are not coloured. In them there is nothing else than a certain Power and Disposition to stir up a Sensation of this or that Colour" (Newton, 1704/1952, pp. 124–125). After all, radio waves, microwaves, and gamma rays lack colour to human eyes, so one might speculate what we might say in reply to an alien species that used colour terms for those portions of the total spectrum.

Instead of saying that a stimulus is red, we should say that is has a particular spectrum that is seen by human trichromats as red. This substitution would convey two benefits. The first is precision: To call a stimulus "red" vastly underspecifies the stimulus, given that there is potentially an infinite number of wavelength combinations that can produce the identical apparent shade of red. The second is explanatory power: To ascribe a perceptual outcome to the colour red is to explain one perceptual experience (or behaviour) in terms of another, and such perceptual causality quickly gets complex and hard to justify. The goal of cognitive science and psychophysics is, ultimately, to explain perception in terms of the stimulus, even though it may be—and often is the case—that cognitive mediation accounts for much of what we see.

IMPLICATIONS FOR PERCEPTUAL EXPERIMENTATION: VISUAL SEARCH

There are real and important implications of the experience error for ongoing perceptual research. Consider the burgeoning area of visual search, a field that holds the promise for understanding both the basic features underlying early vision and the features that guide later, attention-demanding visual processing (Treisman & Gelade, 1980; Wolfe, 1994; Wolfe & Horowitz, 2004).

One of the main tools in visual search studies is the calculated slope of the function relating reaction time (RT) to the number of items in a display to be searched. When searching for a red disk in a field of green disks, RTs to indicate whether the red target is present are largely independent of the number of green disks displayed. This indicates that colour is probably a basic feature, one that pops out of a display without having to be searched for sequentially. Targets defined by features such as colour, size, orientation, movement, and the like often pop out and so are thought to be primitives on which early vision is founded.

Targets defined by conjunctions of primitive features, by contrast, usually do not pop out and so must be detected through slow, inefficient search. Thus, searching for a red disk in a field of red squares and green disks is slow, presumably because it takes the second, attention-demanding step of feature integration to identify the target.

Thinking back to what has been noted above about colour and Gestalts, we must be careful in describing our stimuli to avoid committing the experience error. In calculating search slopes, for example, we divide RTs by the number of items in a display. In doing so, however, we must be sure we understand that number accurately, and that can prove tricky because, as noted above, we have no accepted definition for an "item" any more so than we have for an object, a stimulus, or even a "thing". If a display contains 32 disks that are spaced into pairs, do we say that the display contains 32 disks or 16 disk pairs?

Returning to colour, we must again consider that this feature resides in our heads and not in the stimulus. We should talk properly of wavelength combinations that lead to pop out, rather than speak of colours that pop out. The fact that we do not do so routinely, however, might not be so serious a matter. Talking about spectra can be cumbersome, after all, so in using the term "colour" might we simply be engaging in a universally understood shorthand?

Perhaps not. The point about colour, in terms of theories of visual search, is that basic features such as colour usually pop out, whereas conjunctions usually require focal attention. However, we must recall that colour itself is a conjunction of wavelengths! Thus, by taking our shorthand too literally, we run the risk of building contradictions into our theories.

If it is best to think of colour as a conjunction of wavelengths (or, taking it one step further into the language of sensory transduction, as a conjunction of the outputs of our short, medium, and long wavelength cone systems), would colour stand as the single exception to the principle that conjunctions do not lead to pop out? No, in part because there are other conjunctions that are detected quickly, such as Wolfe and Horowitz's (2004) example in which a black X will pop out from a field of white Xs and black Os. More directly relevant to the current argument, however, there are other instances of conjunction pop out that involve Gestalts. Consider, for example, the triple conjunction of the horizontal, vertical, and diagonal line segments that create arrows and triangles. As is shown in Figure 1, an arrow will pop out of a field of triangles as quickly as a black square pops out from a white background, even though the distinctive feature that makes an arrow differ from a triangle—an oppositely sloped diagonal line—often will not pop out from its mate (Pomerantz et al., 1977).

CONCLUSIONS

The primary conclusion to be drawn from these observations is that Gestalts are all about the integration of primitive elements into new units (or emergent features) that then become primitives in perceptual processing.

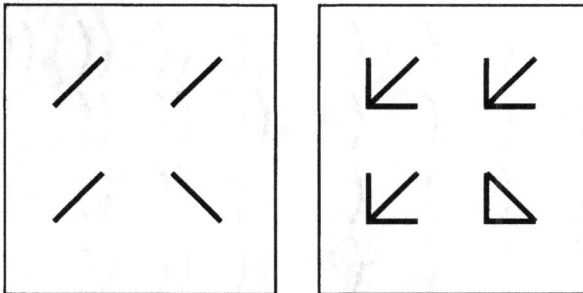

Figure 1.   In the left panel, RTs to locate the oddly sloped diagonal are long, indicating that it fails to pop out. In the right panel, identical L-shapes have been added to each diagonal, and now the triangle pops out from the arrows as quickly as a black square pops out from a white background (adapted with modifications from Pomerantz, Sager, & Stoever, 1977).

Unlike the integration of separable features that do not yield Gestalts (an integration that is slow and attention demanding), the integration of elements that yield Gestalts is fast and seemingly automatic in the sense of requiring no cognitive resources and being outside the reach of voluntary control.

In the case of wavelengths, the integration into perceived colours is also seemingly irreversible, with wavelength-specific information flowing through "sealed channels" (Pomerantz, 1978, 2003) that are not accessible to consciousness or available for response purposes. Functionally speaking, the whole of a colour such as white precedes the parts, i.e., the constituent wavelengths from which colour arises (cf. the reverse hierarchy notion of Hochstein & Ahissar, 2002; see also DiLollo, Kawahara, Zuvic, & Visser, 2001). So fast and complete is the perceptual integration of wavelengths that we are unaware that our visual system has created a Gestalt.

Should this line of reasoning prove correct, it suggests that whenever parts conjoin to form Gestalts, those conjunctions should give rise to very low or zero search slopes in RT experiments. There is good evidence of this from various configural superiority effects reported previously (Pomerantz et al., 1977). In fact, in some of those experiments where display elements group to create emergent features, doubling the number of homogeneous distractors drastically *reduced* RTs to localize the singleton target; see Figure 2. The result was *negative* search slopes, steeper than −200 ms/item. This illustrates again how powerful Gestalt contextual effects can be and how they can be measured using standard tools of cognitive psychology.

In any case, the strong argument here is that Gestalts must yield pop out if we are to regard them as proper Gestalts. Any jumble or conjunction of features could be proposed as a Gestalt, but for that claim to be credible, that conjunction should show pop out. In turn, this new and explicit criterion will help us clarify what is and is not a Gestalt.

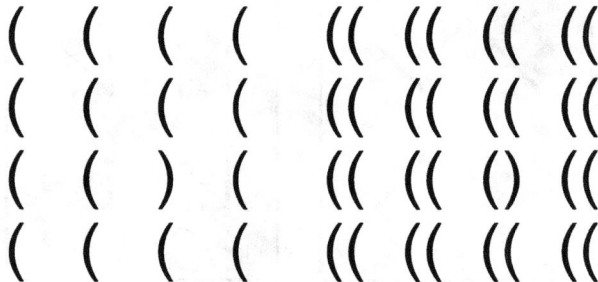

Figure 2.   Locating the rightward curving line segment takes longer in the left panel, where there are only 15 leftward curving distractors, than in the right panel, where there are 31 distractors (adapted with modifications from Pomerantz et al., 1977.) Under some conditions, the RT difference results in steeply negative search slopes exceeding −200 ms/line segment.

Gestalt phenomena are fascinating and important, but they have proven frustrating to study because of the difficulty of operationalizing them, in developing metrics for them, and in modelling them. By comparison with form perception, our understanding of colour perception is detailed and sophisticated. As Palmer (1999) has pointed out, colour can be seen as a useful microcosm of the entire perceptual system. If we regard colour as a Gestalt and approach the integration of elements of form into perceived shapes in ways analogous to how we model sensory integration of wavelength-specific information in the colour domain, we may strip away some of the vagueness that has accompanied Gestalt psychology and make significant progress towards understanding the perception of visual wholes.

REFERENCES

Beck, J. (1982). *Organization and representation in perception*. Hillsdale, NJ: Lawrence Erlbaum Associates, Inc.

DiLollo, V., Kawahara, J., Zuvic, S. M., & Visser, T. A. W. (2001). The preattentive emperor has no clothes: A dynamic redressing. *Journal of Experimental Psychology: General*, *130*, 479–492.

Ellis. W. D. (Ed.). (1950). *A sourcebook of Gestalt psychology*. New York: Humanities Press.

Hochstein, S., & Ahissar, M. (2002). View from the top: Hierarchies and reverse hierarchies in the visual system. *Neuron*, *36*, 791–804.

Kanizsa, G. (1979). *Organization in vision*. New York: Praeger.

Kimchi, R. (1992). Primacy of wholistic processing and global/local paradigm: A critical review. *Psychological Bulletin*, *112*, 24–38.

Kimchi, R., Behrmann, M., & Olson, C. R. (2003). *Perceptual organization in vision: Behavioral and neural perspectives*. Mahwah, NJ: Lawrence Erlbaum Associates, Inc.

Kinchla, R. A., & Wolfe, J. M. (1979). The order of visual processing: Top-down, bottom-up, or middle-out. *Perception and Psychophysics*, *25*, 225–231.

Köhler, W. (1947). *Gestalt psychology*. New York: Liveright. (Original work published 1929)

Metelli, F. (1974). The perception of transparency. *Scientific American*, *230*, 90–98.

Navon, D. (1977). Forest before trees: The precedence of global features in visual perception. *Cognitive Psychology*, *9*, 353–383.

Newton, I. (1952). *Opticks, or a treatise of the reflections, refractions, inflections, and colours of light* (4th ed.). New York: Dover. (Original work published 1704)

Palmer, S. E. (1999). *Vision science: Photons to phenomenology*. Cambridge, MA: MIT Press.

Palmer, S. E. (2003). Perceptual organization and grouping. In R. Kimchi, M. Behrmann, & C. R. Olson (Eds.), *Perceptual organization in vision: Behavioral and neural perspectives*. Mahwah, NJ: Lawrence Erlbaum Associates, Inc.

Pomerantz, J. R. (1978). Are complex visual features derived from simple ones? In E. L. J. Leeuwenberg & H. F. J. M. Buffart (Eds.), *Formal theories of visual perception* (pp. 217–229). Chichester, UK: John Wiley.

Pomerantz, J. R. (1983). Global and local precedence: Selective attention in form and motion perception. *Journal of Experimental Psychology: General*, *112*, 516–540.

Pomerantz, J. R. (2003). Wholes, holes, and basic features in vision. *Trends in Cognitive Sciences*, *7*(11), 471–473.

Pomerantz, J. R., & Kubovy, M. (1981). Perceptual organization: An overview. In M. Kubovy & J. R. Pomerantz (Eds.), *Perceptual organization* (pp. 423–456). Hillsdale, NJ: Lawrence Erlbaum Associates, Inc.

Pomerantz, J. R., & Sager. L. C. (1975). Asymmetric integrality with dimensions of visual pattern. *Perception and Psychophysics*, *18*, 460–466.

Pomerantz, J. R., Sager, L. C., & Stoever, R. J. (1977). Perception of wholes and of their compound parts: Some configural superiority effects. *Journal of Experimental Psychology: Human Perception and Performance*, *3*, 422–435.

Treisman, A., & Gelade, G. (1980). A feature-integration theory of attention. *Cognitive Psychology*, *12*, 97–136.

Wertheimer. M. (1923). Untersuchungen zur Lehre von der Gestalt, II. *Psychologische Forschung*, *4*, 301–350.

Wolfe, J. M. (1994). Guided Search 2.0: A revised model of visual search. *Psychonomic Bulletin and Review*, *1*, 202–238.

Wolfe, J. M., & Bennett, S. C. (1997). Preattentive object files: Shapeless bundles of basic features. *Vision Research*, *37*(1), 25–44.

Wolfe, J. M., & Horowitz, T. S. (2004). What attributes guide the deployment of visual attention and how do they do it? *Nature Reviews Neuroscience*, *5*, 1–7.

VISUAL COGNITION, 2006, 14 (4/5/6/7/8), 629–646

Ψ Psychology Press
Taylor & Francis Group

From searching for features to searching for threat: Drawing the boundary between preattentive and attentive vision

Kyle R. Cave

University of Massachusetts, Amherst, MA, USA

Martin J. Batty

University of Southampton, Southampton, UK

The distinction between preattentive and attentional processing has been a key element in many theories of attention, but there are conflicting claims as to which functions are performed preattentively, and which require attention. Recent studies suggest that stimuli associated with strong emotions or threat are effective at capturing and/or holding attention. Especially relevant for the question of preattentive vision are search experiments showing that emotional stimuli are sometimes found more quickly than neutral stimuli. An examination of these experiments indicates that there is no evidence that the threatening nature of stimuli is detected preattentively. There is evidence, however, that participants can learn to associate particular features, combinations of features, or configurations of lines with threat, and use them to guide search to threat-related targets. This debate highlights the importance of determining not only what information is encoded preattentively, but how target features that are used to guide search are specified.

A running theme through the last few decades of attentional research is the distinction between preattentive and attentional cognitive processes. In explaining auditory and speech perception, Broadbent (1958) proposed that the nervous system was a limited capacity channel. Only a subset of the inputs could be allowed to pass through the channel, and thus there had to be some means of selecting some inputs and filtering out the rest. For auditory stimuli, Broadbent proposed that physical properties such as

---

Please address all correspondence to Kyle R. Cave, University of Massachusetts, Department of Psychology, Tobin Hall, Amherst, MA 01003, USA. E-mail: kcave@psych.umass.edu

Thanks to Mark Auckland, Brendan Bradley, Nick Donnelly, Karin Mogg, Paul Pauli, Werner X. Schneider, Jim Stevenson, and an anonymous reviewer for helpful insights and useful advice.

http://www.psypress.com/viscog   DOI: 10.1080/13506280500193107

intensity, pitch, and location could be used to determine selection, which required a mechanism for detecting these properties before selection. In his textbook on *Cognitive Psychology*, Neisser (1967) applied similar principles to vision. He defined attention as "an allotment of analyzing mechanisms to a limited region of the field" (p. 88). This focal attention is preceded, in his account, by preattentive processes that are applied globally and holistically across the visual field. A similar distinction between preattentive and attentional processes has appeared in many other theories and models, including the influential Feature Integration Theory (Treisman & Gelade, 1980). These theories have triggered a large number of visual search experiments, with the search slopes from these experiments being used to distinguish between those visual processing tasks that can be accomplished by preattentive mechanisms and those that require attention.

IS THERE A BOUNDARY?

Drawing the line between preattentive and attentional processing has turned out to be difficult, and as a result the distinction has been blurred in some theories. In Guided Search (Wolfe. Cave, & Franzel, 1989; Cave & Wolfe, 1990; Wolfe, 1994; Wolfe & Gancarz. 1996), attentional mechanisms are still distinct from preattentive mechanisms, but part of the work in finding conjunction targets is moved from the attentional side to the preattentive side. In models with a hierarchical structure such as FeatureGate (Cave, 1999), selection occurs not all at once, but in a series of stages, which begins to blur the distinction between preattentive and attentional processes.

In models with a sharp distinction between preattentive and attentional mechanisms, this distinction between different types of visual properties becomes a question of which properties are detected by preattentive mechanisms, and which are left for attentional processing. Nakayama and Joseph (1998) argue that attention is used in identifying all stimuli, and they advocate dropping the distinction between properties that can be detected preattentively and properties that require attention. Their arguments suggest that the important distinction is between attention focused narrowly and attention focused widely to encompass a large region. Once again, this change blurs the boundary between preattentive vision and attentional vision. It is nonetheless clear that some visual properties can be detected with relatively simple computational mechanisms, and thus they can be detected and compared simultaneously over a wide area of the visual field more readily than other properties. Because these properties, or features, can be detected so easily and efficiently, they can effectively guide visual search. Thus, despite changes in theories of attention, it still makes sense to ask what counts as a feature, or at least what properties can effectively guide search.

The theoretical framework presented here will be described in terms of preattentive and attentional processing, but, if you prefer, you can translate all references to "preattentive processing" below into references to "processing during which attention is spread over a wide region containing many objects", and to translate "attentional processing" into "processing during which attention is narrowly focused". Under either translation, there are still questions about how attention is guided, especially in situations in which a number of objects or locations in the display have similar properties.

WHAT PROPERTIES CAN GUIDE SEARCH?

The early answers to the question of what properties can guide search came from Feature Integration Theory (Treisman & Gelade, 1980) and Texton Theory (Julesz, 1984, 1986; Julesz & Bergen, 1983), and included properties such as colour, orientation, direction and speed of motion, size, and stereoscopic depth. Later studies indicated that search could be guided by three-dimensional structure (Enns & Rensink, 1990a, 1990b, 1991), completed shapes (Rensink & Enns, 1998), and properties of surfaces (He & Nakayama, 1992). From these studies, it seems that salient differences involving most of the properties encoded in Marr's (1982) 2.5-D sketch can be used to guide search, as long as this includes information about grouping and uniform connectedness (see Wolfe & Cave, 1999).

Another line of research has demonstrated how extended practice with specific types of visual search can improve search performance for those particular targets (Schneider & Shiffrin, 1977; Shiffrin & Schneider, 1977). These experiments have generally included letters and digits, or other stimuli made up of relatively simple configurations of lines and curves, and they show effects of practice even for a single letter target in the standard single-frame presentation used in many visual search experiments (Kyllingsbaek, Schneider, & Bundesen, 2001). This ability to learn how to search may or may not occur with other types of stimuli, but it is certainly possible with consistent practice for simple configurations of lines and curves to guide search effectively.

These results are generally consistent with the assumption that the properties that can guide search are properties detected relatively early by the lower levels of the visual system. The early, parallel stage of Feature Integration Theory included modules for detecting properties such as colour, movement, and orientation, partly because of the discovery of individual neurons in visual cortex that were tuned to respond to these properties (Treisman & Gelade, 1980). Detecting 3-D structure and properties of surfaces requires more complex computations and more integration of information across different locations. Although this may be done later in the visual stream than the detection of colour and orientation, it can still be done relatively early, and thus it seems plausible that there will be parallel mechanisms for reconstructing these properties simultaneously at many locations across the visual field. Therefore preattentive processing can be equated with the parallel construction of a representation of the entire visual field that is something like a 2.5-D sketch (Marr, 1982), and information from this representation can guide search. Figure 1 shows a simple version of this type of theoretical framework, which is more or less the approach taken in Guided Search, FeatureGate, and later versions of Feature Integration Theory.

Under this guidance-by-features account, how does practice with search for a particular target improve search ability? One possible explanation is

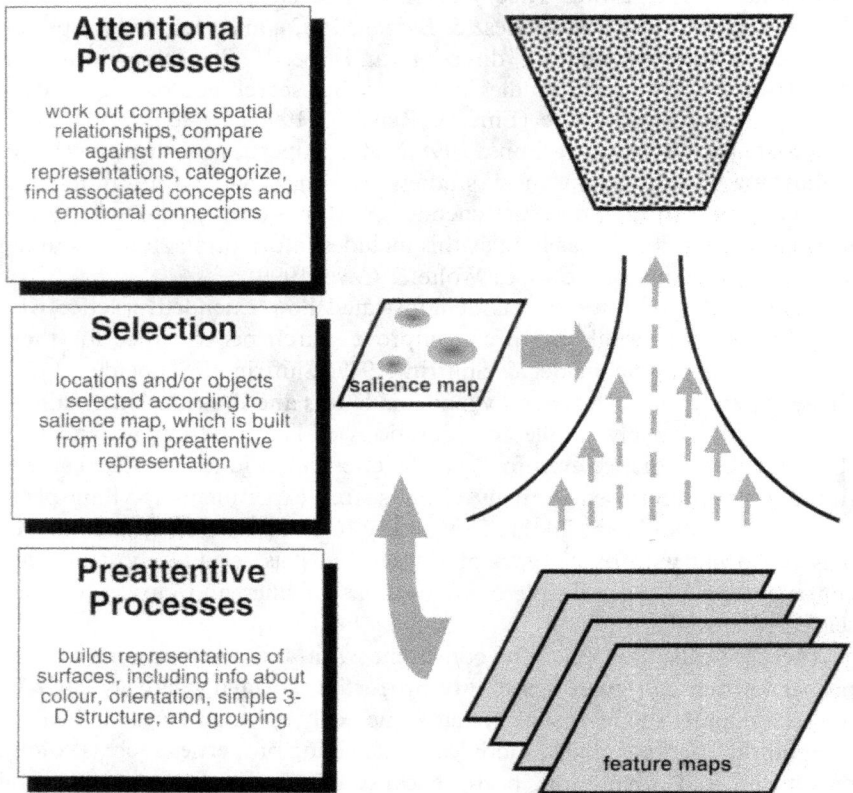

Attentional Processes

work out complex spatial relationships, compare against memory representations, categorize, find associated concepts and emotional connections

Selection

locations and/or objects selected according to salience map, which is built from info in preattentive representation

salience map

Preattentive Processes

builds representations of surfaces, including info about colour, orientation, simple 3-D structure, and grouping

feature maps

Figure 1. A theoretical framework for guidance of search by features. Attention is guided (via the saliency map) only by colour, orientation, motion, and the other simple surface properties encoded by preattentive processes.

that practice allows preattentive mechanisms to encode information about the presence of specific configurations of lines and curves. In other words, practice can produce new "feature" detectors for combinations of simple features. However, evidence against this account comes from Treisman, Vieira, and Hayes (1992), who found that the benefits from practice in visual search do not generalize to other visual discrimination tasks, as would be expected if new feature detectors had been formed. Another possible explanation is that the practice allows for the better use of information that was always available in the preattentive representation (see Figure 2). For instance, when first searching for the letter "R" among "H"s, "K"s, and "N"s, the participant may not know which feature or features best distinguish the target from the distractors, and search may be slow. With practice, the participant learns which of the features represented in the

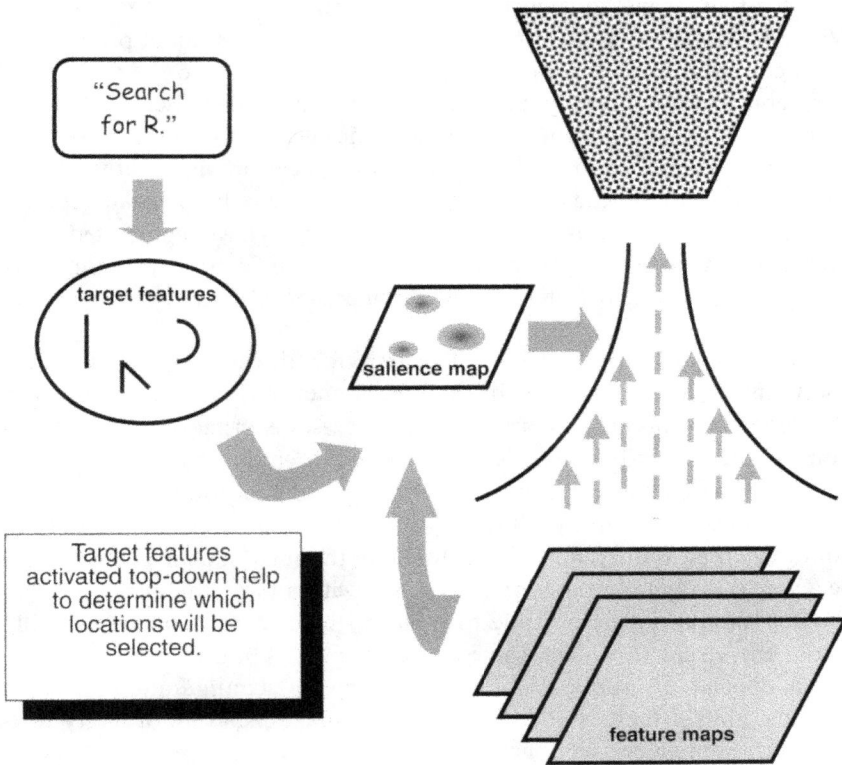

Figure 2. Before practice at searching for the letter "R", search is slow because the participant does not know which target features to activate to distinguish "R" from the distractor letters. Practice gives an opportunity to learn which target features work best.

preattentive representation can be used to find the target, and search performance improves. Effective guidance of search may require the use of a combination of features, and a long period of practice may be necessary to reach the optimal combination. Under this account, practice does not change the nature of the preattentive representation, but it improves the way this information is used to guide complex searches. This account preserves the idea that search can only be guided by properties detected relatively early on in visual processing.

ARE EMOTIONAL OR THREAT STIMULI DETECTED PREATTENTIVELY?

Recently a number of studies have tested the ability of emotionally laden or threatening stimuli to control the allocation of attention. These studies have used a variety of methods, including modifications of the Stroop task (e.g., Williams, Mathews, & MacLeod, 1996) and spatial attentional probes (e.g., MacLeod, Mathews, & Tata, 1986). Particularly relevant to the question of preattentive vision, however, are a set of studies using visual search that have been put forward to demonstrate the efficiency with which potentially threatening stimuli can be found when they appear among nonthreatening distractors. In these studies, the targets have generally been snakes, spiders, and angry faces, on the assumption that these stimuli have represented threat over a period of millions of years, which would provide the opportunity for evolutionary forces to foster the development of efficient visual detectors for them.

The claims about efficiency of search for threatening stimuli raises questions about the guidance-by-features framework outlined in Figure 1. The representation built by preattentive processes is primarily a representation of surfaces and simple visual properties. Identifying and categorizing objects as trees, houses, spiders, or snakes is presumably done after selection by attentional mechanisms. Distinguishing spiders and snakes from all the nonthreatening animals and objects found in the environment would seem to be a very complex computational task, and within the framework described above it should not be possible to perform these computations in parallel across the visual field. The same is true for extracting facial expressions, which depend on subtle changes in the spatial configuration of facial features. Thus if there is good evidence that snakes, spiders, or angry faces are detected preattentively, then the guidance-by-features framework would most likely break down. Consequently, the results from these visual search experiments must be examined carefully, with an eye on implications for theories of preattentive and attentional processing.

SEARCHING FOR SPIDERS AND SNAKES

Öhman, Flykt, and Esteves (2001) carried out a series of experiments with threat stimuli (photographs of snakes or spiders) and nonthreat stimuli (photographs of flowers or mushrooms). On each trial a group of four or nine of these photographs was presented, and the task was to determine if there was one photo that came from a different category than the others. Search slopes were lower for a threat target among nonthreat distractors (3 ms/item) than for a nonthreat target among threat distractors (15 ms/item). Thus search was more efficient for snakes and spiders than for flowers and mushrooms. However, there is no way of knowing whether this search asymmetry is due to the threatening nature of the snakes and spiders being identified preattentively, or whether search is instead guided by some simple visual feature or combination of features, such as a range of colours or spatial frequencies, that tends to appear more often or more strongly in the snake and spider photos than in the mushroom and flower photos. Search asymmetries of the type demonstrated here are fairly common (Treisman & Souther, 1985), even with simple abstract stimuli, so that result by itself does not indicate that threat is involved.

In a final experiment, Öhman, Flykt, and Esteves (2001) provide further evidence regarding the role of threat in search. In this experiment, participants were selected on the basis of high snake or spider fear or low snake/spider fear and carried out the same search task. Again, all participants were able to detect threat targets more efficiently than nonthreat targets. More importantly, fearful participants were faster to detect their feared than their nonfeared threat target (i.e., high spider-fear participants were faster to locate spider targets than snake targets, whereas high snake-fear participants were faster to detect snakes than spiders). Thus, although the possibility of feature differences between the stimulus groups leaves doubt as to whether threat is detected preattentively in these experiments, the results do show that the participant's attitude towards the stimulus can affect search performance.

It is not clear whether Öhman, Flykt, and Esteves (2001) interpret their results as fitting within the guidance-by-features framework described earlier. On the one hand, they argue that their results are "very hard to reconcile with a low-level physical confounding factor", and conclude instead that "the critical factor was a high-level one: the threat value of the stimulus" (p. 475), which seems to rule out an interpretation of search guidance by simple features. However, they also state that their results could be attributed to "elementary threat features" (p. 475) that have not yet been identified. It certainly seems possible to explain their results by assuming that there are features encoded in the preattentive representation that appear frequently in snakes and spiders and much less frequently in flowers and mushrooms. If so, then participants with strong fear must make better use of these features than others, either because they are more motivated to find targets that they fear, or because their fear has led them to search for these targets in the past and gives them the benefit of practice. Experiments in other types of visual search have shown that years of experience in searching for a particular class of targets can improve that type of search (Hoyer & Ingolfsdottir, 2003). Long-term spider phobia may cause people to become experts at finding spiders, presumably by strengthening connections between high-level spider representations and low-level visual features belonging to spiders.

This finding of faster search for threat targets was replicated by Tipples, Young, Quinlan, Broks, and Ellis (2002), who found faster search rates for threatening animals (snakes, bears, and dogs poised to attack) than for plants. In line with findings of Öhman Flykt, and Esteves (2001), when the display size of the search array was increased from four to nine items, RT's for the threatening animals increased at a rate of only 11 ms/item, whereas for plants, the increase was 28 ms/item. Whereas the former category falls close to the <10 ms/item search rate required for "quite efficient" searches (Wolfe, 1998), and "pop-out" (Treisman & Gelade, 1980), the search rate for plants is best described as "inefficient" (Wolfe, 1998). Although these data at first glance appear to provide firm evidence for enhanced attention to threat stimuli, doubts are raised by data from a second experiment, in which participants searched for pleasant animals (e.g., horses, kittens, "relaxed" dogs, etc.) hidden among plants, and vice versa. As in the first experiment, the smaller set size effect for animals than for plants was repeated, with a significantly faster rate of search for pleasant animals than plants (8 ms/item vs. 24 ms/item, respectively). As participants were able to search for both threatening and pleasant animals at a roughly equal rate, it appears that threat *per se* confers no advantage.

In a further experiment, pictures of fruit were added to the search matrices, and participants asked to search for both threatening and pleasant animals as a unified category in order to examine the possibility that *all* animals are seen as a potential threat. Once again, RTs to threatening and pleasant animals *and* fruit were roughly the same, whereas detection of flowers was significantly slower. Thus, although search for all animals was more rapid than for flowers, it was no more efficient than search for fruit. Perhaps evolution has produced efficient preattentive detectors for threatening animals and nonthreatening animals and fruit, or perhaps all of these categories tend to have simple features that are less likely to appear in flowers and mushrooms. Either way, threat itself, as opposed to features associated with threat, seems to be less of a factor in visual search than was first suggested.

SEARCHING FOR ANGRY OR SAD FACES

Angry faces have also been suggested as a stimulus that has indicated threat over an evolutionarily significant time period, and so searches for angry faces among neutral or happy faces have also been used to test for the effects of threat on search. One of the earliest studies was by Hansen and Hansen (1988), in which participants were required to find a discrepant face in a collection of pictures of human faces. Participants were significantly faster to detect a threatening face among friendly faces than vice versa, and the time taken to detect an angry face did not increase with set size. However, this experiment soon came under criticism, including some from the authors themselves (Hampton, Purcell, Bersine, Hansen, & Hansen, 1989). A number of explanations for their findings have since been offered, such as the possibility that friendly faces may be processed more efficiently than threatening faces because of their familiarity (Öhman, Lundqvist, & Esteves, 2001; Wolfe, 2001). In addition, the faster processing of threatening targets may reflect an ability to disregard nonthreatening faces more rapidly. Thus, participants should be faster to reject the ubiquitous smiling face than the less familiar angry face. The most damaging criticism, however, was the discovery of a low-level perceptual confound: Conspicuous dark areas were apparent on some parts of the threat faces (Purcell, Stewart, & Skov, 1996). Thus the more rapid response to identify the threatening faces could be attributed to unique features of these faces rather than affective expression.

The Hansen and Hansen (1988) study shows that in search experiments with photographs of faces, just as in experiments with photographs of snakes and mushrooms, it is almost impossible to eliminate the possibility of a simple featural difference between targets and distractors. Also, Öhman, Lundqvist, and Esteves (2001) argue that most individuals find it difficult to produce a convincing threatening face on demand, but have little problem in producing a reasonably convincing happy face. Most people have plenty of practice producing a smile on demand for social situations, but much less practice at producing angry faces. The individuals asked to generate angry faces for experimental stimuli may try a variety of different poses to convey anger, and thus produce a more heterogeneous set of angry faces than they will for happy faces. This difference in heterogeneity will bias experimental results, because heterogeneity of distractors reduces search performance (Duncan & Humphreys, 1989; Wolfe, 1998). These problems have led some researchers to use schematic or cartoon faces, which can be much more carefully controlled. The validity of this approach can be questioned, because evolution might not be expected to produce preattentive detectors for cartoon faces. However, most people are able to identify the affective expression of schematic faces accurately (Fox et al., 2000) and some of the results summarized below suggest that they may be effective search stimuli.

In one such study, by Öhman, Lundqvist, and Esteves (2001), the schematic faces were happy. angry, or neutral. Both happy and angry faces were easy to find among neutral distractors, with slopes for both below 10 ms/item. In these searches, the orientation of the lines representing the eyebrows provided a salient marker of the target's location: The eyebrows of the neutral faces were horizontal, whereas those of the happy and angry faces were oriented diagonally. Search slopes were steeper (~35 ms/item) with emotional distractors, i.e., an angry target appeared among happy distractors or a happy target appeared among angry distractors, presumably because eyebrow orientation no longer provided such a salient target feature. Thus, there is no suggestion that an angry face "pops out" (Treisman & Gelade, 1980) among happy faces. Nonetheless, angry targets were found somewhat more quickly than happy targets regardless of set size, whether the distractors were neutral or emotional. Interestingly, when emotional distractors were used, the threat advantage was only significant in experiments that used a longer exposure time (2 s rather than 1 s), which seems rather at odds with the idea that the detection of threat is very rapid to allow for quick reactions. Even larger doubts about the preattentive detection of threat are raised by the fact that the presence of threat did not affect the search slopes: The advantage for angry over happy targets did not increase with set size with either type of distractor.

One advantage of using faces as stimuli in these experiments is that many aspects of face perception, including the perception of emotional expression, are disrupted when faces are inverted (Yin, 1969). Thus, if affective expression is the critical factor in searching for angry faces, then the advantage for angry faces might lessen or disappear when faces are inverted. On the other hand, if participants are finding the angry faces by searching for relatively simple configurations of lines, then their performance will probably be similar whether the faces are inverted or upright. Öhman, Lundqvist, and Esteves (2001) included a condition with inverted faces, and found an equivalent anger superiority effect for both inverted and upright faces. Although this could be interpreted as evidence for a low-level explanation of the difference, Öhman, Lundqvist, and Esteves concluded that the attentional advantage for angry faces was so much stronger than other aspects of face perception that it applied even to inverted faces.

In a series of experiments by Fox et al. (2000), again using schematic faces, participants were again faster to detect an angry face amongst happy faces than vice versa. Their schematic faces were somewhat simpler than those of Öhman, Lundqvist, and Esteves (2001): In some conditions, each face was just an outline circle with two small circles for eyes, a short vertical line for a nose, and a curved or straight line for a mouth. This study produced a much stronger advantage for sad[1] faces over happy faces. The search slopes, although not indicating pop-out, showed a clear advantage for sad targets (16 ms/item) over happy targets (29 ms/item). In other experiments with no set size manipulation, Fox et al. found that the general RT advantage for sad/angry faces over happy faces disappeared when the faces were inverted, or when the eyes and nose were removed to leave just a mouth. Overall, Fox et al. were able to provide stronger evidence than Öhman, Lundqvist, and Esteves that facial expression, or some set of features associated with facial expression, played an important role in guiding search.

Similar evidence comes from another study with schematic faces by Eastwood, Smilek, and Merikle (2001). They used even simpler faces: Just two eyes and a mouth within a circle, with no nose. Their participants searched for happy or sad schematic faces embedded among neutral distractors. They used four different set sizes, ranging from 7 to 15 faces in each display. As in the previous experiments, participants were faster to detect sad faces compared to happy faces. Once again, sad faces did not pop out, but search slopes were lower for sad targets (13.0 ms/item) than for happy targets (20.5 ms/item).

Eastwood et al. (2001) also tested search for inverted faces to limit the recognition of affective expression. As in the earlier experiments, the inverted face search condition was used to provide a baseline, indicating the performance of lower level search mechanisms without the emotional labels. The slope difference between searches for angry and happy faces diminished with inversion (15.5 vs. 16.8 ms/item) and was no longer significant. Eastwood et al. interpreted this as evidence that the differences in search were due differences in affective valence between the stimuli rather than simple featural differences. A close look at the results reveals a puzzling pattern, however. The assumption of preattentive detection of threat predicts that a sad label on the target should make search faster than the baseline. Eastwood et al.'s data, however, indicate that happy targets are slowing search as much as (and perhaps more than) sad targets are speeding it up. Just why this should be is hard to explain; perhaps it has to do with the familiarity of the ubiquitous cartoon smiley face.

An experiment by Purcell and Stewart (2002) provides a useful insight into what information might be used to find the targets in these schematic face experiments. They used schematic faces modelled after those from Öhman, Lundqvist, and Esteves (2001), complete with eyebrow lines that sloped up towards the centre for happy faces, and down towards the centre for angry faces. As in all the schematic faces used in the experiments described above,

---

[1] Fox et al. (2000) concluded that the face with no eyebrows and a downturned mouth looked more sad than angry.

happy mouths were lines curving upwards, and angry mouths were lines curving downwards. Corresponding to the happy, sad, and neutral faces, Purcell and Stewart also created three different control faces, all with no eyebrows and small mouths so that they conveyed neutral expressions. These control faces included extra lines and curves on the forehead and cheeks so that they had configurations similar to those formed by the mouths and eyebrows on the emotional faces. On the "line-out" control face, the cheek lines ran from the centre of the face out towards to the edge, just as the eyebrow lines did on the angry face, and the ends of the curve on the forehead pointed up towards the top edge of the face, just as the angry mouth pointed down towards the bottom edge of the angry face. Likewise, on the "in-line" control face, the configurations made by the face outline and the cheek lines and forehead curve matched those in the happy face.

Purcell and Stewart (2002) presented arrays of nine faces, some with nine neutral distractors, and others with eight neutral distractors and a happy or angry target. They asked participants to press a key whenever they detected one face that was different than the others and to withhold their response when only distractors were present. They replicated Öhman, Lundqvist, and Esteves' (2001) finding, with faster responses to angry than to happy targets. The control condition used a similar task, with the line-in and line-out faces as targets, embedded in arrays of distractor faces with horizontal lines on the cheeks and forehead. The control results were virtually identical to the results with emotional faces: Responses were faster to the line-out faces, which had line configurations that were similar to those in the angry faces but did not signal any emotional expression.

This result suggests that the threat superiority effect evidenced in Öhman, Lundqvist, and Esteves' (2001) study is attributable to relatively simple configurations of lines rather than affective expression *per se*. Similar configural differences might also explain the slope differences found by Fox et al. (2000) and by Eastwood et al. (2001), although this is less clear because all of Purcell and Stewart's search arrays had the same number of items. Of course, evolution may have shaped a visual system in which lines pointing outward towards the edge of a circle are easily detected because they are often associated with angry faces. The experiment by Purcell and Stewart, however, indicates that it is the line configuration that makes the stimulus more salient, and not the emotional label attached to it.

Summary of face search results

Experiments from three different countries show better performance at finding angry or sad faces than at finding happy faces. There are advantages for both overall RT and search rate, although there is no indication that angry faces pop out from among other faces. The sad/angry advantage seems to depend at least in part on the stimuli being perceived as faces, because the advantage more or less disappears when the faces are inverted. Although it has not been tested systematically, comparisons across these experiments suggest that the sad/angry advantage becomes stronger as the schematic faces are made simpler. The controlled and balanced schematic stimuli, along with the experiments by Fox et al. (2000) with mouths alone, show that the advantage does not reflect the use of any single line or curve as a target. Instead, the advantage must be due to something about the configuration of different elements making up the face, although the results from Purcell and Stewart (2002) suggest that at least part of the effect could be due to something as simple as the spatial relationship between the circle outline and a few of the lines within it.

These results can fit within the guidance-by-features framework described above, but only if we make two assumptions. The first is that the preattentive representation includes not only information about each individual line and curve, but also some simple information about the configurations formed by lines and curves near one another. This assumption is necessary regardless of the face search data, in order to account for the ability to search for letters and digits after extended practice. The other assumption is that the semantic label attached to a configuration can make it easier to guide search to that configuration, and that with these faces an angry or sad label is more effective than a happy label.

In attentional theories such as Guided Search (Wolfe, Cave, & Franzel, 1989) and FeatureGate (Cave, 1999), complex searches require that features belonging to the target be specified through a top-down system, as shown in Figure 2. Perhaps these features are specified by activating a high-level semantic representation (e.g., "angry face"), which then activates lower level feature representations attached to it (e.g., junction formed by circle and inner lines pointing towards edge). Some high-level semantic representations may generally be more activated than others, perhaps because of their association with threat, and thus they produce more effective guidance of search. In this account, search can only be guided when there are features in the preattentive representation that distinguish between targets and distractors, but this featural information can only be used to guide search when there is a high-level semantic representation that can provide the correct activations.

SEARCHING FOR CONDITIONED THREAT STIMULI

If search guidance always depends on features and combinations of features that are identified preattentively, then search guidance should not be possible when there are no featural differences between targets and distractors. Batty, Cave, and Pauli (2005) tested this idea in a series of visual search experiments with abstract shapes that were linked to threat-related stimuli through a conditioning procedure. They created two target shapes and a distractor shape. Each was a square made up of a different configuration of four black and four white triangles. They were designed to be easy to discriminate when attended, but difficult to discriminate preattentively. Through a conditioning procedure, participants learned to associate one target with neutral pictures, and the other with threat-related pictures. People with a fear of snakes or spiders were selected as participants, and the threat stimuli were photographs of the animals that they feared. A similar experiment was done with other participants, for whom the threat stimuli were a variety of disturbing scenes such as mutilated bodies. In both experiments, the effectiveness of the conditioning was demonstrated with the Implicit Association Test (IAT).

On each trial, participants saw an array of distractor shapes, with one of the two targets included, and were asked to identify which target was present. The number of distractors varied from trial to trial. In all of the participant groups, search slopes for the threat-associated target were virtually identical to slopes for the neutral target. When there are no preattentive features available to distinguish between shapes, the association with threat does not lead to more efficient search.

WHAT IS ENCODED PREATTENTIVELY?

This review of preattentive vision started with a question on what properties can be used to guide search. The results described here from experiments on threat search require that this question be split into two separate questions. The first is this: What information is encoded preattentively in parallel across the visual field, or what counts as a feature? The results reviewed here have not changed the answer to this question very much. The preattentive representations that will be used to guide search, which we earlier described as composed of most of the information in Marr's 2.5-D sketch, must include information about simple line configurations. Based on the data available now, there seems to be no need to conclude that high-level conceptual information such as facial expressions, threat, or emotional associations are encoded preattentively.

HOW ARE SEARCH TARGETS SPECIFIED TOP-DOWN?

Just because there is information available preattentively that can distin-guish between targets and distractors does not guarantee that it will be used. The other half of the question, which perhaps has not been fully considered before, is this: What constraints are there on what can be specified top-down as a search target? Are there circumstances in which participants will not be able to specify the target features so that the target can be found efficiently, even when those features are encoded preattentively? (See Figure 3.)

Evidence relevant to this question comes from experiments on colour search. Hundreds of search experiments have demonstrated the ease of finding a target specified by a single colour, but searching for a target that has both red and yellow is very difficult (Wolfe et al., 1990), as is searching for a target that can be either red or yellow (Meneer, Barrett, Phillips, Cave, & Donnelly, 2003). However, searching for a red house with yellow windows is easier (Wolfe, Friedman-Hill, & Bilsky, 1994). Apparently, when two target colours must be activated simultaneously through top-down mechanisms to guide search, this can be done more effectively if it is done through

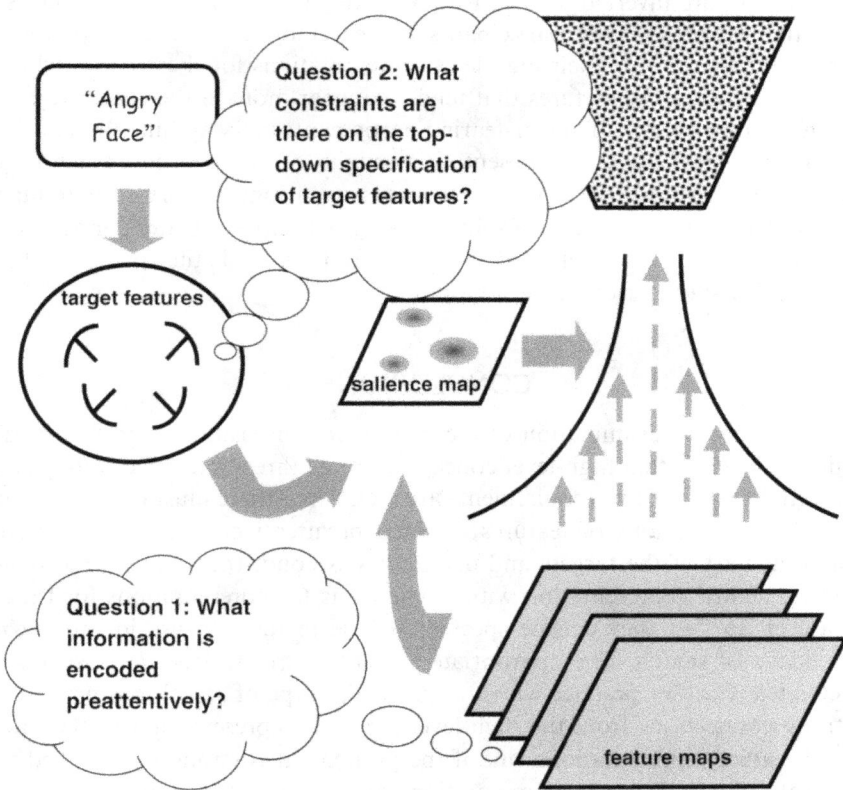

Figure 3.   Two separate questions about the guidance of search.

a single higher level representation, such as that for a red house with yellow windows. The featural information is always available preattentively, but can only be activated to guide search when the top-down links make it possible.

Within this account, practice at searching for letters improves search performance because it allows connections to be made between the high-level representations of the letters and the combinations of features that best distinguish them from the distractors. The necessary features were always represented preattentively, but before the practice, participants could not activate them in the appropriate combination for efficient search. In searches for schematic faces, participants can generate weak activation for the line configurations belonging to the targets by activating their representations for happy and angry faces. The angry face representations are generally somewhat more activated (perhaps because of the importance of detecting threat), which guides search more towards targets with those configurations. When faces are inverted, this activation through face representations is less effective. Likewise, when participants are searching for spiders, or puppies, or fruit, they activate their high-level representations for these items, which in turn activates the features that tend to appear more in the target objects than in other objects. If spider-fearing participants are searching for spiders, their high-level spider representation might always be more strongly activated than those for other participants, or a long history of searching for spiders may have given the spider-fearing participants better connections between their high-level spider representations and the features that distinguish spiders from other objects.

CONCLUSIONS

In summary, an examination of recent research on visual search for threat stimuli suggests that high-level concepts such as threat can effectively guide search, but only if two requirements are met. First, there must be features or simple combinations of features detected preattentively that appear more often as part of the targets and distractors. Second, there must be a high-level semantic representation with connections to representations for those features, so that they can be specified as the features to use in top-down guidance of search. The appropriate target features will be more strongly activated if earlier practice with this particular type of search has produced strong connections from the high-level semantic representation to the low-level feature representations, and if the participant is strongly motivated to activate the high-level representation because of strong fear or other emotional factors.

REFERENCES

Batty, M. J., Cave, K. R., & Pauli, P. (2005). Abstract stimuli associated with threat through conditioning cannot be detected preattentively. *Emotion*, *5*, 418–430.

Broadbent, D. E. (1958). *Perception and communication*. New York: Pergamon Press.

Cave, K. R. (1999). The FeatureGate Model of visual selection. *Psychological Research*. *62*, 182–194.

Duncan, J., & Humphreys, G. W. (1989). Visual search and stimulus similarity. *Psychological Review*, *96*, 433–458.

Eastwood, J. D., Smilek, D., & Merikle, P. M. (2001). Differential attentional guidance by unattended faces expressing positive and negative emotion. *Perception and Psychophysics*, *63*(6), 1004–1013.

Enns, J. T., & Rensink, R. A. (1990a). Scene-based properties influence visual search. *Science*, *247*, 721–723.

Enns, J. T., & Rensink, R. A. (1990b). Sensitivity to three-dimensional orientation in visual search. *Psychological Science*, *1*, 323–326.

Enns, J. T., & Rensink, R. A. (1991). Preattentive recovery of three-dimensional orientation from line drawings. *Psychological Review*, *98*, 335–351.

Fox, E., Lester, V., Russo, R., Bowles, R. J., Pichler, A., & Dutton, K. (2000). Facial expressions of emotion: Are angry faces detected more efficiently? *Cognition and Emotion*, *14*(1), 61–92.

Hampton, C., Purcell, D. G., Bersine, L., Hansen, C. H., & Hansen, R. D. (1989). Probing "pop-out": Another look at the face-in-the-crowd effect. *Bulletin of the Psychonomic Society*, *27*, 563–566.

Hansen, C., & Hansen, R. (1988). Finding the face in the crowd: An anger superiority effect. *Journal of Personality and Social Psychology*, *54*, 917–924.

He, Z. J., & Nakayama, K. (1992). Surface versus features in visual search. *Nature*, *359*, 231–233.

Hoyer, W. J., & Ingolfsdottir, D. (2003). Age, skill, and contextual cuing in target detection. *Psychology and Aging*, *18*, 210–218.

Julesz, B. (1984). A brief outline of the texton theory of human vision. *Trends in Neuroscience*, *7*, 41–45.

Julesz, B. (1986). Texton gradients: The texton theory revisited. *Biological Cybernetics*, *54*, 245–251.

Julesz, B., & Bergen, J. R. (1983). Textons, the fundamental elements in preattentive vision and perception of textures. *Bell System Technical Journal*, *62*(6.3), 1619–1645.

Kyllingsbaek, S., Schneider, W. X., & Bundesen, C. (2001). Automatic attraction of attention to former targets in visual displays of letters. *Perception and Psychophysics*, *63*, 85–98.

MacLeod, C., Mathews, A., & Tata, P. (1986). Attentional bias in emotional disorders. *Journal of Abnormal Psychology*, *95*(1), 15–20.

Marr, D. (1982). *Vision*. San Francisco: Freeman.

Menneer, T., Barrett, D. J., Phillips, L., Donnelly, N., & Cave, K. R. (2003). The breakdown of efficient search when either of two colour targets can appear. *Journal of Vision*, 3(9), 568a. Retrieved January 4, 2005, from http://journalofvision.org/3/9/568/

Nakayama, K., & Joseph, J. S. (1998). Attention, pattern recognition and popout in visual search. In R. Parasuraman (Ed.), *The attentive brain* (pp. 279–298). Cambridge, MA: MIT Press.

Neisser, U. (1967). *Cognitive psychology*. New York: Appleton-Century-Crofts.

Öhman, A., Flykt, A., & Esteves, F. (2001). Emotion drives attention: Detecting the snake in the grass. *Journal of Experimental Psychology: General*, *130*(3), 466–478.

Öhman, A., Lundqvist, D., & Esteves. F. (2001). The face in the crowd revisited: A threat advantage with schematic stimuli. *Journal of Personality and Social Psychology*, *80*, 381–396.

Purcell, D. J., & Stewart, A. (2002). *The face in the crowd: Yet another confound*. Poster presented at the 43rd annual meeting of the Psychonomic Society. Kansas City. Missouri.

Purcell, D. J., Stewart, A. L., & Skov. R. B. (1996). It takes a confounded face to pop out of a crowd. *Perception*, *25*, 1091–1108.

Rensink, R. A., & Enns, J. T. (1998). Early completion of occluded objects. *Vision Research*, *38*, 2489–2505.

Schneider, W., & Shiffrin. R. M. (1977). Controlled and automatic human information processing: I. Detection, search, and attention. *Psychological Review*. *84*. 1–66.

Shiffrin. R. M., & Schneider, W. (1977). Controlled and automatic human information processing: II. Perceptual learning, automatic attending and a general theory. *Psychological Review*. *84*, 127–190.

Tipples, J., Young, A. W., Quinlan, P., Broks. P. & Ellis. A. (2002). Searching for threat. *Quarterly Journal of Experimental Psychology*. *55A*(3). 1007–1026.

Treisman, A., & Gelade, G. (1980). A feature integration theory of attention. *Cognitive Psychology*, *12*, 97–136.

Treisman, A., & Souther, J. (1985). Search asymmetry: A diagnostic for preattentive processing of separable features. *Journal of Experimental Psychology: General*, *114*, 285–310.

Treisman, A., Vieira, A., & Hayes. A. (1992). Automaticity and preattentive processing. *American Journal of Psychology*. *105*. 341–362.

Williams. J. M., Mathews, A., & MacLeod. C. (1996). The Emotional Stroop task and psychopathology. *Psychological Bulletin*. *120*(1). 3–24.

Wolfe. J. M. (1994). Guided Search 2.0: A revised model of visual search. *Psychonomic Bulletin and Review*. *1*(2). 202–238.

Wolfe. J. M. (1998). Visual search. In H. Pashler (Ed.), *Attention* (pp. 13–73). Hove. UK: Psychology Press.

Wolfe, J. M. (2001). Asymmetries in visual search: An introduction. *Perception and Psychophysics*, *63*(3), 381–389.

Wolfe. J. M., & Cave, K. R. (1999). The psychophysical evidence for a binding problem in human vision. *Neuron*, *24*, 11–17.

Wolfe, J. M., Cave, K. R., & Franzel, S. L. (1989). Guided Search: An alternative to the Feature Integration model for visual search. *Journal of Experimental Psychology: Human Perception and Performance*, *15*, 419–433.

Wolfe. J. M., Friedman-Hill, S. R., & Bilsky. A. B. (1994). Parallel processing of part–whole information in visual search tasks. *Perception and Psychophysics*, *55*, 537–550.

Wolfe. J. M., & Gancarz, G. (1996). Guided Search 3.0: A model of visual search catches up with Jay Enoch 40 years later. In V. Lakshminarayanan (Ed.), *Basic and clinical applications of vision science* (pp. 189–192). Dordrecht. The Netherlands: Kluwer Academic.

Wolfe, J. M., Yu. K. P., Stewart. M. I., Shorter. A. D., Friedman-Hill, S. R., & Cave, K. R. (1990). Limitations on the parallel guidance of visual search: Color × color and orientation × orientation conjunctions. *Journal of Experimental Psychology: Human Perception and Performance*. *16*, 879–892.

Yin. R. K. (1969). Looking at upside down faces. *Journal of Experimental Psychology*. *81*(1). 141–145.

Section II.

The role of memory in the guidance of visual search

VISUAL COGNITION, 2006, 14 (4/5/6/7/8), 648–667

Ψ **Psychology Press**
Taylor & Francis Group

Does the inspector have a memory?

Raymond M. Klein and Kristie Dukewich

Dalhousie University, Halifax, Nova Scotia, Canada

Serial and parallel search strategies are distinguished and illustrated. Investigators are urged to explore when and how these strategies are used and combined in normal search rather than to focus on which one is "right". Although serial search would be more efficient if there were a system for discouraging wasteful reinspections, we should not be embarrassed by the possibility that serial search may be amnesic. A critical review and meta-analysis of studies exploring whether visual search is amnesic leads to the conclusion that it probably rarely is. In contrast, there is ample evidence for the existence of inhibitory tags (inhibition of return) that might discourage reinspections during search. Three strategies for linking these tags to increased search efficiency are described.

SERIAL, PARALLEL, AND HYBRID SEARCH STRATEGIES

Many everyday tasks involve searching through a set of items for a target. Broadly speaking, two classes of strategy have been distinguished: Serial and parallel. A serial search strategy involves sequential inspection of items in the set. In contrast, in a parallel strategy information about the "targetness" of each item in the set accumulates at the same time. Serial search can be self-terminating (a response is given once the target is found) or exhaustive (the set of items is inspected and then the response is given). If a serial search requires the same average inspection duration for items early as for items late in a search episode then the time to perform the target task (which might be to make a target present versus absent judgement; to indicate the location of the target; or to report some property of the target) will be a linear function of the number of items in the set. For this reason, among others, set size has become a ubiquitous independent variable in studies exploring search (Sternberg, 1970; Treisman & Gelade, 1980), and the slope of the linear function relating reaction time to set size (ms/item) is often used to generate an estimate of the inspection time per item. Under some conditions the time to find the target is unaffected by the number of items in the set. Such

---

Please address all correspondence to Raymond Klein, Department of Psychology, Dalhousie University, Halifax, Nova Scotia B3H 4J1, Canada. E-mail: ray.klein@dal.ca

http://www.psypress.com/viscog
DOI: 10.1080/13506280500194022

a "pop-out" effect suggests a parallel strategy in which a simultaneous comparison process rapidly reveals the target's distinctiveness from the other items.

Whereas serial search entails a linear, increasing function of set size upon RT, obtaining such a function is not sufficient to infer that the search strategy being used is, indeed, serial. The parallel strategy, despite its linkage to a null effect of set size (pop-out search), can also yield linearly increasing functions (Broadbent, 1987; Ratcliff, 1978; Townsend, 1971), though only in some regions of its parameter space.

It is a common information processing assumption that pattern recognition involves the accumulation of information over time. The examples below are presented both to illustrate this point and use it to help clarify the distinction between serial and parallel search.

Two-alternative forced choice single item identification

Suppose there are two kinds of urn, each containing an infinite number of stones. In one kind of urn 75% of the stones are white and 25% black; in the other kind of urn the proportions are 50:50. You would like to know if an urn is white (75:25) or grey (50:50), and the way you can find out is by looking at stones that you can sample one at a time. If you take one stone and it is white you now have some, admittedly a small bit of, information. Before taking this sample you would have been at chance guessing the urn's identity. Now you will be above chance if you guess "white", but because you haven't accumulated much evidence and the urn types are somewhat similar in composition, you will still make many errors. Now you have taken out 10 stones. If eight are white and two are black, a "white" guess is now much more likely to be right, but not always. With a sufficient number of samples you can be nearly certain of the urn's identity.

Searching for a target

Serial self-terminating strategy

Now imagine that the experimenter has arranged two types of display containing several urns: In one type of display all the urns are grey; in the other type, one urn is white while the remainder are grey. Your task is to determine whether or not there is a white urn in the display. In one search strategy, you inspect each urn, in turn taking a sufficient number of samples to be sufficiently confident to make the "white" versus "grey" identification. When you find the white urn you say "present"; when you find a grey one you try the next urn, and so on until all have been searched. Should you inspect all the urns without finding a white one you can confidently respond "absent". If you don't use a rigid search strategy, then having memory for which urns you've searched would be helpful. Perfect memory allows you to search without replacement, inspecting each urn only once. Using this serial self-terminating strategy, the slope on target absent trials would represent the duration of each inspection. Since the target, when present, will be found, on average, halfway through the items, the slope on present trials will be half that of the slope on absent trials. The use of the target-absent slope as a measure of inspection duration suggests that many investigators have assumed, implicitly at least, that in a typical search sampling is without replacement.[1] With no memory you would be in the amnesic world of Horowitz and Wolfe (1998; see below) where inspections of items would be with replacement. When sampling with replacement, the average time to find the target (finishing time) ought to be twice the time when sampling without replacement (see Horowitz & Wolfe. 2003. for a discussion). A decision that the target is not present can never be made with confidence, hence a decision rule (e.g., deadline) is needed to make an "absent" response in a reasonable amount of time, and the nature of this rule will affect the absent:present slope ratio.

Parallel accumulation

Now suppose that samples are still taken one at a time from an urn but that samples can be taken from all the urns at the same time. Information about each of the urns accumulates in parallel under this strategy, and once a sufficient number of samples are taken the observer might be able to make a confident judgement whether the set of urns does (present) or does not (absent) contain one white urn. Townsend (1971) and others (Broadbent, 1987; Ratcliff, 1978) have pointed out that because of noise in the sampling of evidence about each urn, each additional urn increases the chances of a mistaken response. To minimize the chances of an error as the number of urns increases, the criterion number of samples might be increased. With the right parameters this situation can yield linear functions of RT as a function of set size with a 2:1 slope ratio for target-absent versus target-present trials even though individual array items (urns) are not being inspected sequentially.

---

[1] A real-world search may include ad hoc mental processes not represented in the idealized strategies illustrated in our idealized "urn" examples. For example. when the searcher fails to find the target after one pass through the candidate items, some of these items may be rechecked. Such a strategy would artificially inflate the estimate of inspection time derived from the slope on target-absent trials.

When search is serial, does the inspector have a memory?

When there is more than one good strategy to solve a problem it seems reasonable to assume that nature may have figured out a way to take advantage of both. Serial and parallel strategies for searching a set for a target might be combined in several different ways (see Wolfe, Cave, & Franzel, 1989, for one hybrid model) to yield hybrid search strategies more efficient[2] than either component strategy alone. We recommend that future research seek to determine, rather than which strategy characterizes search, "when" and "how" the two strategies combine. Nevertheless, because of its intuitive appeal, the obviously sequential nature of scanning eye movements we often make when conducting real-world searches, and the subjective impression that search is sequential and stops when the target is found, the serial self-terminating search strategy has garnered considerable attention and, at least initially, will be the focus of this paper.

Accepting that sometimes search is sequential opens up the question, does the inspector avoid reexamining items, and if so how? One method is to use a rigid strategy such as always searching the visual array from left to right and top to bottom. Barring such a rigid search strategy, memory for which potential targets had been inspected and ruled out as such would make search more efficient (Horowitz & Wolfe, 2003; Klein, 1988). An explicit memory system (visual working memory) could be used to avoid reinspections, but this would impose a heavy cognitive load. An implicit and imperfect tagging system might work. Inhibition of return (IOR) has been touted as such a mechanism (Itti & Koch, 2001; Klein, 1988; Klein & MacInnes, 1999). In this paper we will present and critically evaluate the alternative hypothesis, that search is amnesic, and then we will describe the extant evidence supporting the proposal that IOR functions as a search or foraging facilitator by providing the search inspector with a memory, albeit imperfect, of previous inspections.

THE AMNESIC SEARCH HYPOTHESIS

In visual search experiments, slope is often reported as a measure of search efficiency. Typical slopes for attention-demanding search tasks in which the target is a spatial rearrangement of the distractors can produce a slope of

---

[2] Throughout this paper when we refer to the "efficiency" of search we are referring to the speed and accuracy of performance on the search task under discussion. The relative efficiency of different conditions (static and dynamic) or search strategies is assessed at each set size. Some investigators use the effect of set size upon performance (usually the slope of the RT/set size function) as the measure of search efficiency. We eschew this approach primarily because this measure overlooks the real-world consequences of relative slowness (or inaccuracy). That noted, it remains the case that if the slope is affected while the intercept remains the same, then there will be an efficiency difference in both senses.

20–30 ms/item. Horowitz and Wolfe (1998) argued that a model of amnesic search in which information about the target is continually disrupted can account for this number. In order to investigate this possibility, Horowitz and Wolfe designed a dynamic visual search condition in which memory for previously presented items was continually disrupted by moving the items in the display every 111 ms and compared it with a more traditional condition in which items remained in the same locations throughout the course of a trial (static condition). They reasoned that relocating the items during the course of a trial would disable location tagging if tagging existed and could be used. They found that target-present trials generated slopes that were similar in the static and dynamic conditions. Assuming that participants were using the same search strategy in the two conditions and relying primarily on these similar slopes to infer that search in the two conditions was equivalently efficient, Horowitz and Wolfe concluded that there is no memory for the locations of inspected items in the static condition because there is no possibility of using such a memory in the dynamic condition where items are moved around randomly. Horowitz and Wolfe's claim that visual search proceeds without memory was so counterintuitive that it inspired a backlash of studies investigating the role of memory in search (Khurana, Scheier, & Shimojo, 1999; Kristjansson, 2000; McCarley, Wang, Kramer, Irwin, & Peterson, 2003; Peterson, Kramer, Wang, Irwin, & McCarley, 2001; von Muhlenen, Müller, & Müller, 2003; see also Klein, Shore, MacInnes, Matheson, & Christie, 2000; Shore & Klein, 2000).

THE POSSIBILITY OF AMNESIC SEARCH NEEDN'T MAKE US UNCOMFORTABLE

Why do so many scholars experience discomfort when they consider the proposal that visual search is amnesic? We believe that the reason this proposal causes discomfort is that scholars naturally assume that the inefficiency this proposal seems to entail (inspecting and hence reinspecting items randomly) applies to us. Under this view, the individual is the search inspector, and it is disturbing to consider that we are behaving so inefficiently, randomly reinspecting array items. The history of research on search reveals an earlier, similar discomfort.

Exploring search through a set of items maintained in memory, Sternberg (1970) obtained target-present and target-absent functions that were parallel. From this pattern, he inferred a search mechanism that didn't terminate when the target was found, but instead exhaustively considered all the items and then delivered a target-present/absent result to a decision system.

When Sternberg (1970) first presented this pattern of results and his serial exhaustive search strategy to audiences of scholars, he found that psychologists experienced discomfort but engineers and computer scientists did not. The distress of the psychologists was rooted in the idea that "if I found the target, of course, I would respond; there would be no point in continuing the search". The engineers and computer scientists were not so quick to assume that they were searching. Because of the things they built (say cars and computer programs) the idea of delegation of responsibility to an automatic subroutine or servomotor was second nature to them.

We are disturbed by memoryless search at least in part because we think WE are searching. Why would WE be so "dumb"? Suppose, however, that WE launch a program that, guided by a saliency map, simply inspects candidates with replacement (i.e., with no memory), until the target is found. This automated subroutine returns an answer without the need for our conscious involvement during the search, just as does the machinery in Sternberg's (1970) model. It is not elegantly efficient (logically a search can proceed forever), but it will do at a pinch. Merely because it is possible (and possibly even plausible under some circumstances), does not mean that amnesic search is the typically used strategy.

Suppose that there is a low level (also automated) mechanism that—while imperfect and limited—can discourage reorienting towards already in-spected items. It might even do so by operating directly on the saliency map. Such a mechanism, namely IOR, could allow the other automated system to be more efficient or it could assist a conscious search agent by reducing the demands placed on working memory.

REPLICATIONS, EXTENSIONS, AND TESTS OF HOROWITZ AND WOLFE'S PROPOSAL

In Experiment 1 of Horowitz and Wolfe (1998) backward masking was used following each frame, with masks presented only at the locations that had contained items in the previous frame. Khurana et al. (1999) hypothesized that this type of "local" masking may have specifically disadvantaged performance in the static condition. According to Khurana et al., local masks might "reset" information accumulation at masked locations during each refresh, essentially "erasing" any inhibitory tags that might have been left behind there, which would significantly disadvantage performance in the static condition, while not much affecting performance in the dynamic condition (because items are more likely to be relocated to a previously unmasked location). To eliminate this possible difference, Khurana et al. included a global masking condition in which pre- and postmasks were presented in all the locations that could contain an item (whether or not these locations were occupied) in both the static and dynamic conditions. With local masks, Khurana et al. replicated Horowitz and Wolfe (1998),

Exp. 1); however, when global masks were used, they found that the target-present slope for the dynamic condition was approximately twice the target-present slope for the static condition—precisely the pattern predicted by a memory-driven inspection process without replacement in the static condition (Horowitz & Wolfe, 2003). Whereas the authors interpreted these results in terms of inhibitory tags that are susceptible to masking, Horowitz and Wolfe (1998) found similar slopes in the dynamic and static conditions when they got rid of masks between refreshes (Experiments 2 and 3). An alternative explanation is, therefore, offered for the Khurana et al. pattern. We suggest that more information is extracted when an object appears in a new location (Yantis & Hillstrom, 1994) than when an item is presented in a previously occupied location. Relative to the static condition, then, targets in the dynamic condition will benefit from these "new appearances" except when the global mask is used. Under global masking conditions no items will have the phenomenological status of new objects, and without the "new object" advantage on each frame the true inferiority of the dynamic condition emerges.

Converging evidence for the proposal that the dynamic condition affords a "new object" advantage over the static condition comes from two sources. First, by measuring accuracy while limiting processing time with pre- and postmasks, and parametrically manipulating exposure duration in a target identification task, Dukewich and Klein (2005) have demonstrated that the first hundred milliseconds of exposure to the array provides much more information than subsequent periods of equal duration. Second, Kristjansson (2000, Exp. 1) demonstrated that when objects in the dynamic condition change places, rather than appear in new locations, performance efficiency in the dynamic condition is inferior to that in the static condition. Of course, in this dynamic, but fixed location condition, after the first frame targets would not be appearing in "new" locations. We will discuss this study in further detail because Kristjansson conducted two experiments and our use of one of them to provide this converging evidence does not adequately reflect his rationale.

Kristjansson (2000) reasoned that if search proceeds without some mechanism to keep track of spatial locations that have already been inspected, then search efficiency should not be altered by relocating the target to previously occupied locations. On the other hand if, contrary to Horowitz and Wolfe (1998), already inspected locations were tagged as such, then search efficiency should be diminished on dynamic trials when the locations of the items remained the same while the identities were scrambled because now the target would regularly be relocated to locations that would frequently have been inspected. In order to limit the interpretation of results to the relevance of spatial location, Kristjansson randomly changed the orientation of array items during each display refresh in both static and dynamic conditions. Under these conditions it was found that search slope was significantly steeper in the dynamic condition than in the static condition (Kristjansson, Exp. 1). Noting that in a truly random condition, the probability that the target would move to a previously occupied location increases as the displayed set size approaches the total number of possible item locations, Kristjansson replicated Horowitz and Wolfe while using much greater set sizes. By the same logic that motivated Horowitz and Wolfe's dynamic, fixed location manipulation (Kristjansson's Exp. 1), as set size increases, IOR—if it were operating during dynamic visual search—becomes more likely to hurt performance. Providing converging evidence for his direct demonstration in Experiment 1, in Experiment 2 Kristjansson found much more efficient static than dynamic search for set sizes greater than 24.

Taken together, the results of Kristjansson's (2000) experiments are consistent with his proposal that inhibitory tags were being left behind at the locations of some of the items in Horowitz and Wolfe (1998) dynamic search task. For memory to be useful within an individual trial of visual search, the mechanism would have to exploit implicit memory so as to avoid overloading the capacity of the explicit memory system. IOR has certainly been suggested as a likely candidate for such a mechanism. Indeed, the action of IOR in Kristjansson's study would help to explain why relocating a target to a previously occupied location is detrimental to search performance. To the extent that IOR is implicit, observers may be unable to turn it off, even though IOR might hurt performance. Kristjansson's interpretation of his pattern of results (in terms of inhibitory tagging) is not as inconsistent with our interpretation (old object disadvantage/new object advantage) as it may, at first blush, appear. Consider the notion (see Christie & Klein, 2001) that IOR and a "new object" advantage may be two sides of the same coin. That noted, while an item presented in a previously occupied location will not derive a new object advantage, it also might not suffer from IOR unless the previous occupant of its location had been attended. Thus, in Kristjansson's study we think both mechanisms are operating. First, as in Khurana et al. (1999), the static and dynamic conditions have been put on a level playing field in that no items will benefit from the new object advantage. Second, it is possible that the targets in Kristjansson's dynamic condition have an increased chance of suffering from IOR laid down in previous frames.

Whether participants in the standard static and dynamic conditions are using the same strategy is a general issue that was initially raised by Klein and colleagues (Klein et al., 2000; Shore & Klein, 2000; see also Horowitz & Wolfe, 2003). Recently, von Muhlenen et al. (2003) explored one specific version of this proposal. They suggested that participants in the dynamic condition might adopt a "sit-and-wait" strategy, whereby they simply attend to a specific subregion of the display and wait for the target to appear there, might have been adopted by participants in Horowitz and Wolfe's (1998) dynamic condition. Horowitz and Wolfe were aware of this possibility and attempted to discourage their participants from adopting a "sit-and-wait" strategy. Von Muhlenen et al. suggest that the discouragement may not have been effective because it was based on a too narrow version of the strategy in which the inspected region was only as large as one item.

In contrast to Horowitz and Wolfe's (1998) approach, which was to attempt to discourage a "sit-and-wait" strategy, von Muhlenen et al. (2003) took a more direct approach: They forced such a strategy and compared the results to that obtained in the dynamic condition where they were hypothesizing such a strategy was in effect. The "sit-and-wait" strategy was forced by using an aperture condition in which participants could only view a restricted subregion of the display. As in Horowitz and Wolfe's original study, von Muhlenen et al. found that RTs for the static condition were faster than the RTs for the aperture and standard dynamic conditions. Search rates for the target-present trials revealed a striking similarity among all three conditions. Inspection of the target-absent data revealed a different pattern of results between the static condition on the one hand, and the standard dynamic and aperture conditions on the other. Moreover, the entire RT patterns from the aperture and dynamic conditions were indistinguishable. All of these findings seriously jeopardize Horowitz and Wolfe's assumption that participants were using the same strategies in their static and dynamic conditions. They also provide compelling evidence that participants in the dynamic search condition could have been using a "sit-and-wait" strategy.

META-ANALYTIC PRESENTATION OF HOROWITZ AND WOLFE'S STATIC/DYNAMIC COMPARISON

As noted above, Horowitz and Wolfe (1998) reasoned that if participants use the same search strategy in the static and dynamic conditions, and if search efficiency is equivalent in the two conditions, then it is unnecessary to assume that there is memory for the locations of inspected items in the static condition because there is no possibility of using such a memory in the dynamic condition. Klein and colleagues (Klein et al., 2000; Shore & Klein, 2000) pointed out that this logic depends on the veracity of two assumptions that, on the basis of Horowitz and Wolfe's own data pattern, seemed dubious: In the static and dynamic conditions participants must use the same strategy and their performance must be equally efficient in these two conditions. In the original study there were data patterns strongly indicating that participants had adopted different strategies in the two display conditions. Among these, present slopes were much shallower than absent slopes with static displays, whereas they were nearly the same with dynamic displays. When the data from the four experiments (see Table 1, P/A tasks) that have used the present/absent search task in combination with static and dynamic search are combined (using only data from set sizes between 8 and 18), the empirical robustness of this finding is demonstrated (static present = 22.775; static absent =47.025; dynamic present =19.475; dynamic absent = 23.125). Although this difference in pattern doesn't dictate a "different strategies" conclusion (cf. Broadbent, 1987), it certainly is consistent with one and warrants caution in asserting that identical strategies are used in these two conditions. With regard to search efficiency, the main points were that accuracy must be considered along with reaction time and that the entire decision must be considered, not just target-present trials.

A sufficient number of studies have been conducted using the static and dynamic conditions pioneered by Horowitz and Wolfe (1998) and with similar set sizes to permit us to conduct a meta-analysis. To be included in this analysis we required that the study use set sizes in the range from 8–18 items, that items be randomly assigned to locations in the dynamic condition ("free" but not "fixed" conditions were included), and that accuracy be reported for each important cell in the design. Studies using either an identification or present/absent task were included, and in the latter case, the data from present and absent trials were combined (averaged). The experiments satisfying these criteria are listed in Table 1.

Standard plots of performance as a function of condition (static/dynamic) and set size are shown for reaction time and accuracy in Figure 1a and b, respectively. Note that log (proportion correct) has been plotted instead of the more typical proportion correct. The log transformation was used because when independent, probabilities multiply. Since the log $(A*B) = \log (A) + \log (B)$, the use of this transform allows us to determine whether two factors are having additive or interactive effects on accuracy. A more detailed rationale can be found in Schweickert (1985). The overall RT

TABLE 1

Studies comparing search for targets using static and dynamic (à la Horowitz & Wolfe, 1998) displays (see text for further details)

Experiment	n	Set sizes in range	Task type[a]
Horowitz & Wolfe, 1998; E1	9	8, 12, 16	P/A
Horowitz & Wolfe, 1998; E2	9	8, 12, 16	P/A
Horowitz & Wolfe, 1998; E3	11	8, 12, 16	ID (E/N)
Kristjansson, 2000 E2	6	8, 12, 16	P/A
Von Muhlenen, Muller, & Muller, 2003	12	8, 12, 16	P/A
Horowitz & Wolfe, 2003	16	9, 12, 18	ID (E/N)

[a]P/A =tasks requiring a present/absent response; ID (E/N) =tasks requiring a discrimination of the target as "E" or "N".

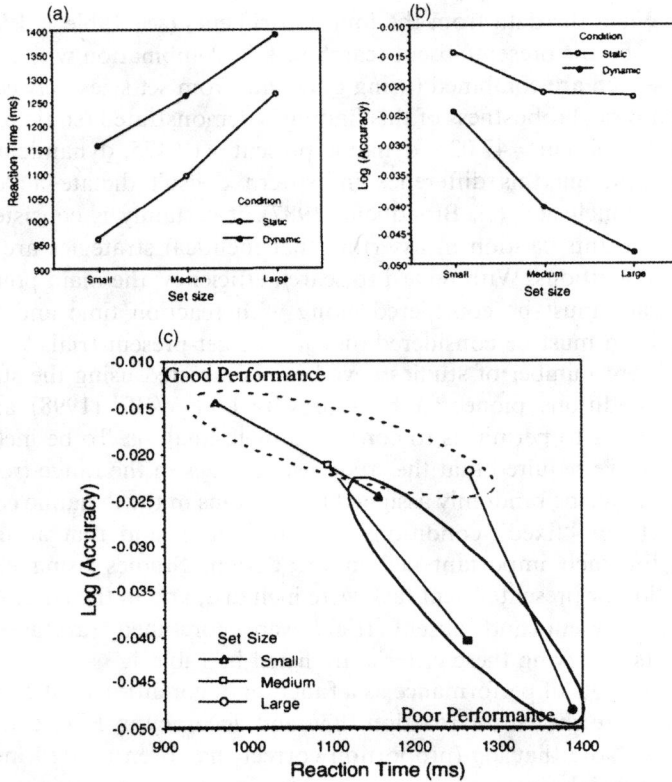

Figure 1. Results from a meta-analysis of six visual search studies using the static/dynamic search conditions, with target detection or target identification response criteria. Data from the static condition are plotted as open symbols; from the dynamic condition as filled: (a) Average RT for small, medium, and large set sizes for the static and dynamic conditions; (b) the log of accuracy for each of the categories of set size for the static and dynamic conditions; and (c) mean log(accuracy) plotted against mean RT for small, medium, and large set sizes. See text for details.

pattern (Figure 1a) is much like that reported by Horowitz and Wolfe (1998). RT increases with set size, $F(2, 10) = 37.1$, $p < .001$, and is faster in the static condition, $F(1, 5) = 9.466$, $p = .0276$. The slope in the static condition is not shallower than in the dynamic condition. Indeed, the reverse is nearly the case as indicated by the marginally significant interaction between condition and set size, $F(2, 10) = 3.646$, $p = .0647$. In the analysis of log accuracy (Figure 1b), there were significant effects of condition, with much lower accuracy in the dynamic condition, $F(1, 5) = 8.1$, $p = .036$, and set size, $F(2, 10) = 7.67$, $p = .0096$. The interaction between set size and condition was just significant, $F(2, 10) = 4.08$, $p = .0506$.

The efficiency of performance must take into consideration both reaction time and accuracy. By plotting the data with accuracy on the y-axis and reaction time on the x-axis, we can easily visualize whether performance in two conditions is equivalently efficient or different. Because speed can be traded for accuracy, it must be kept in mind that when two conditions fall along the positive diagonal they might be drawn from the same speed–accuracy tradeoff function, hence representing a difference in relative emphasis on speed versus accuracy rather than a difference in information processing efficiency. Horizontal and vertical shifts are likely to reflect efficiency differences, but they could be confused with shifts along the asymptote at ceiling or shifts along the most steeply rising portion of the curve. In contrast, differences along the negative diagonal represent unambiguous efficiency differences. As can be seen in Figure 1c, for each set size processing is more efficient in the static than in the dynamic condition.

It is agreed that location tags could not contribute helpfully to search performance in the dynamic condition and consequently that the relatively high levels of performance achievable in this condition must arise because of a search strategy that does not rely on such tags. That noted, the possibility that participants are using different strategies in the dynamic and static search conditions, as noted in the preceding section, warrants caution when drawing conclusions from the similar RT slopes in the two conditions. Moreover, as shown in this section, considering reaction time and accuracy jointly, it is clear that performance in the dynamic condition is not as efficient as performance in the static condition, and this efficiency difference seems to increase with set size. We therefore suggest that the static versus dynamic comparison has failed as a method for determining whether memory operates when we search static displays, To determine whether the search inspector has a memory, we recommend a more direct approach: Look for evidence of memory during static search.

DIRECT EVIDENCE FOR INHIBITORY TAGS DURING SEARCH

Inhibition of return was discovered (Posner & Cohen, 1984), and has been most intensively explored, using a cue–target paradigm (for a review see Klein, 2000). Typically, at short intervals following an uninformative peripheral cue, performance at the cued location is better than at an equivalent uncued location, an advantage usually attributed to the exogenous capture of attention by the cue. At longer intervals, presumably after attention has been disengaged from the cue and recentred at fixation, performance at the originally cued and attended location often becomes worse than performance at an uncued location. Reflecting the proposal that after being removed from a location in space attention is inhibited from returning there, this performance decrement has been called "inhibition of return". Whereas the idea that IOR functions to direct orienting toward new items was first put forward in Posner and Cohen's (1984) seminal paper, Klein (1988) was the first to specifically suggest that by doing so IOR might operate to facilitate difficult search for targets that do not pop out.

IOR possesses a number of characteristics that are necessary for it to serve as a "foraging facilitator", in other words, to serve as a within-trial memory mechanism useful in visual search (see Klein, 2004, for a review): (1) IOR is encoded in environmental rather than retinal coordinates (Maylor & Hockey, 1985). When, as would be the case outside the laboratory, eye movements are used to search an array, this property allows tags to remain within the array while gaze is shifted from one array element to another. (2) When a moving object is inhibited the inhibition may move with the object (Tipper, Driver, & Weaver, 1991). This object-coding of IOR would be needed when we search a dynamic scene in which some candidate targets are in motion. (3) IOR is able to tag multiple locations (Snyder & Kingstone, 2000), which is necessary in visual search in order to keep track of previously inspected objects determined not to be the target or regions determined not to contain the target. (4) Observations at a neural level suggest that IOR begins immediately following the exogenous deployment of attention (see Klein, 2004, for a review) though it is usually not seen in cue–target paradigms because it is masked by facilitation (Danziger & Kingstone, 1999. (5) Finally, IOR can last for over 3 s (Samuel & Kat, 2003), a time course that makes it useful for a typical search episode.

Klein (1988) tested the foraging facilitator proposal by combining search with a probe detection task. On half of the trials, 60 ms following the search task response, a probe appeared in a location that had been previously occupied or previously empty. Following a difficult search, participants were slower to respond when the probe appeared in a previously occupied location than when it appeared in a previous empty location, suggesting that during the search for the target, searched locations were being tagged by an inhibitory mechanism in order to prevent reinspection of those locations.

When Wolfe and Pokorny (1990) failed to replicate Klein (1988), the involvement of IOR in visual search was called into question (Klein & Taylor, 1994). Despite this challenge, Tipper, Weaver, and Jerreat (1994) suggested that, given the importance of objects in IOR and visual search, perhaps the removal of the search array before the presentation of the luminance probe might clear the inhibitory tags. In support of this idea, Müller and von Mühlenen (2000) and Takeda and Yagi (2000), using the search-and-probe paradigm developed by Klein, found evidence for inhibitory tags after search only if the display remained on the screen.

Klein and MacInnes (1999), aware of the likelihood that IOR is generated in the oculomotor system (Rafal, Calabresi, Brennan, & Sciolto, 1989; Taylor & Klein, 1998), looked for IOR using a gaze-contingent probe while monitoring eye movements during search for a camouflaged target. In their first experiment, Klein and MacInnes had participants search for Waldo or the Wizard in pictures from the "Where's Waldo?" series of books by Martin Hanford. Following several voluntary search saccades, a probe was presented and the participant task was asked to overtly orient to the probe as soon as it was detected.[3] Consistent with Müller and von Mühlenen (2000) and Takeda and Yagi (2000), Klein and MacInnes found no evidence of IOR when the search array was removed. However, when the search array remained visible, participants were slower to respond to the probe when it appeared in a previously fixated location compared to when it appeared at a location further away. Reaction time to saccade to the probe was longer when the scene was removed than when it remained, a curious finding considering that in the former condition the probe was presented on a blank background. This unanticipated pattern was tentatively attributed to the fact that probes were delivered unexpectedly while the participant was searching for "Waldo", and that perhaps removal of the scene coordinates, which would be used to plan the next search saccade, resulted in a refractoriness within the saccadic system. In part to test this idea, MacInnes and Klein (2003) conducted a similar experiment in which they asked participants to search for "something interesting" in the same "Where's Waldo?" displays used by Klein and MacInnes (1999). Once a participant had fixated a region or object of interest for 500 ms, either the probe was presented and the participant was required to saccade to it, or a tone was presented indicating that the participant should continue searching the display. In this context, it was expected that the participant would not be in a high state of saccadic programming at the time of the probe, because—by having stopped for 500 ms—they had indicated a temporary cessation of search. This is in stark contrast to Klein and MacInnes (1999), who presented probes within 20 ms of the start of a fixation during an ongoing search. Once again, participants were slower to foveate the probe when it appeared at a location near the previous fixation, and once again, this effect was eliminated if the search array was removed. Consistent with the temporary refractoriness explanation presented above, in this experiment saccadic RT was faster when the scene was removed than when it remained present.

---

[3] We refer the reader to the following paper (Thomas et al., in press) of which we just became aware. Participants were foraging for fruit while being on the lookout for flashing leaves in a virtual-reality display. Methodologically, the study is a combination of Klein's (1988) manual detection probe and Klein & MacInnes's (1999) oculomotor search tasks. The results strongly support the foraging facilitator role attributed to IOR.

Kramer and his colleagues (for a study not reviewed here, see McCarley, Kramer, Boot, Peterson, Wang, & Irwin, 2006 this issue) have conducted a number of studies that provide converging evidence for the proposal that inhibitory tags left behind following overt orienting operate as an implicit memory system that guides future orienting towards new as opposed to already inspected objects. Peterson et al. (2001) monitored eye movements during search in order to calculate the number of refixations during a visual search trial. The relatively low rate of refixation was inconsistent with the predictions of a memory-less search model. Moreover, a large proportion of refixations were directed to the target, suggesting that participants were verifying the target identity. McCarley et al. (2003) used a dynamic gaze-contingent visual search task to investigate patterns of attentional orienting. Participants were guided through a sequence of items in a sort of saccadic "follow the dots" task. Occasionally, following the fixation of an item, two items became visible as possible saccade targets: One of these was new, and one was in a previously inspected location. Participants were more likely to fixate the new item than the previously inspected. Although this new object preference weakened with increases in the number of saccades since the old location had been fixated, it remained significant for up to four intervening saccades. Boot, McCarley, Kramer, and Peterson (2004) provide an important follow-up to McCarley et al. Using a similar task they compared performance when participants were instructed to fixate the old and the new item in displays with two items. Participants found it easy to fixate new items (achieving 77% in the one-back condition) and difficult to fixate old ones (only achieving 33% in the one-back condition). Saccade latencies were also longer when participants were instructed to fixate old items than when they were instructed to orient towards new items or when they were free to fixate either item, suggesting orienting to new items was relatively automatic. In addition, the rate of refixation of old items when participants were instructed to go-to-new items was only 10%, and was statistically indistinguishable from the go-to-either item condition. Taken together, these studies provide evidence for a low-level, automatic mechanism that biases inspections toward novel stimuli, an idea that is entirely consistent with the proposal that IOR is a search facilitator.

We would like to conclude this section with a few comments and caveats. To the extent that IOR might tag inspected items in a difficult search task, it would be unrealistic to think that the tags left behind would enable the inspector to sample entirely without replacement—as if "memory" for inspected items were perfect. The main reason is that the number of inhibitory tags available for this purpose seems to be between three and six (e.g., Snyder & Kingstone, 2000; but see Takeda, 2004, for a much higher estimate). In this regard, and in agreement with Horowitz (2006 this issue), it makes more sense to ask "How much memory does the search inspector have?" than to dwell on whether it has any memory at all. It should also be kept in mind that many searches can be successfully completed by directing attention (or gaze) towards regions of space. Under these conditions, the likely limited number of inhibitory tags may actually suffice to avoid regional reinspections. When overt orienting during search is shown to avoid reinspections, this may reflect memory (implicit or explicit) for previous inspection behaviours, but this might also be the result of a deliberate strategy, generated in advance, that guides search through the array (see Gilchrist & Harvey, 2006 this issue; but see MacInnes & Klein, 2003). Innovative methods, like the "follow the dots" technique pioneered by McCarley et al. (2003), however, provide evidence that orienting is inhibited from returning to previously inspected regions even when a deliberate search strategy is not possible.

SEARCHING FOR CONVERGING EVIDENCE

As discussed in the preceding section, there is now a substantial body of evidence suggesting that there is an inhibitory aftermath of orienting, evidence of which can be seen following a search episode. Although these findings provide a foundation for the proposal that the inhibitory tags left behind at previously attended locations might serve as a foraging facilitator by discouraging reinspections, converging evidence would be desirable.

Here we suggest a general strategy for generating converging evidence and we will exemplify it with three specific suggestions. The general strategy is rooted in the following reasoning: If IOR plays a role in serial search by discouraging reinspections, then factors that interfere with IOR should result in decreased serial search efficiency; and, conversely, factors that enhance IOR should increase serial search efficiency. Three specific methods that may yield IOR differences suitable for testing this proposal are: experimental, neuropsychological, and correlational (individual differences).

One experimental manipulation, described by Smilek, Enns, Eastwood, and Merikle, (2006 this issue), that increased search efficiency, may have done so by increasing the efficacy of the inhibitory tags hypothesized to discourage reinspections.[4] Smilek et al. demonstrated that encouraging participants to adopt a more passive attitude improved search efficiency when search was difficult, but not when it was easy. An IOR-based explanation for this finding would be viable under the following assump-

---

[4] This is not the only explanation. Such an improvement might have been accomplished if the passive instructions increased reliance upon the parallel strategy described earlier and if that strategy turned out to be more efficient than the serial strategy for the search displays used by Smilek et al. This differential strategy–emphasis explanation and the IOR explanation described in the text are not mutually exclusive.

tions: (1) A relatively automatically accessed spatial working memory system stores the tags generated by our previous orienting behaviour, (2) unless we need to explicitly remember this behaviour these tags will have a negative valence, and (3) it is this negative valence that is reflected as IOR in spatial cuing and search studies. The Smilek et al. finding could then be explained if it were further assumed that: (1) There is a tendency for these tags to gain some positive valence when participants begin to think about them of their own volition and, (2) the passive instructions reduce or eliminate this tendency. Since any tendency for the tags to acquire a positive valence would interfere with the foraging facilitator role attributed to them (Klein, 2000), the passive instructions used by Smilek et al. could have increased search efficiency by optimizing the efficacy of the hypothetical inhibitory tagging system. One way to directly test this suggestion would be to use postsearch probes (Klein, 1988) while maintaining the search array (Müller & von Mühlenen, 2000; Takeda & Yagi, 2000) to see if there is greater IOR in the passive than in the active condition. There is converging evidence for the aforementioned assumptions that IOR is laid down without the need for "cognitive control" but in a limited capacity spatial working memory system. Firstly, IOR can be generated by cues of which we are unaware (Ivanoff & Klein, 2003). Secondly, imposing a working memory load after an uninformative peripheral cue has no effect on IOR, unless the load is placed upon *spatial* working memory (Castel, Pratt, & Craik, 2003). It has similarly been shown that visual search interferes with a spatial working memory task (Oh & Kim, 2004) but not with a *verbal* working memory task. Together these findings show that cognitive control is not needed for visual search or for IOR, whereas, in contrast, a spatial working memory system is required for both.

Recent technological advances might allow for a direct experimental disruption of IOR via transcranial magnetic stimulation (Walsh & Pascual-Leone, 2003). Were it possible to use this technique to selectively interfere with IOR (see Ro, Farnez, & Chang, 2003, for a possible demonstration; but see Klein, 2004, for a critique) then one could see whether difficult but not easy search were also disrupted. In such a situation, were it possible to measure the frequency of revisitations, then a more specific prediction could be tested: Not only will search become less efficient during IOR disruption, but it would also become more likely that distractors would be reexamined during a search episode.

A second, neuropsychological, approach requires finding a patient group for whom IOR is unusually strong or weak. The foraging facilitator proposal predicts that such groups would be unusually superior or inferior (respectively) at difficult (nonpop-out) search. Separate studies of search (O'Riordan, Plaisted, Driver, & Baron-Cohen, 2001) and IOR (Brian, 2001) in autistic individuals appear to confirm one half of this expectation.

O'Riordan et al. (2001) found shallower slopes than controls when a difficult search was performed and Brian (2001) found larger magnitudes of IOR in autistic than in control participants. Because this latter finding was not replicated in a subsequent study (McConnell, 2003), the suggested linkage should be regarded cautiously. In all likelihood, discrepancies like this one are rooted in the fact that performance in a cue–target or target–target task is influenced by a myriad of facilitatory and inhibitory effects. Methodological variations from one study to the next are, therefore, likely to impact on the degree to which a measure of IOR reflects its true magnitude in the tested group of individuals. One suggestion we would make to ameliorate this difficulty is that the strategy be implemented using a measure of IOR that is collected in the aftermath of a search episode (as in Klein, 1988).

Finally, a similar approach can be used to look at individual differences in a normal population. As hypothesized for patients, if the foraging facilitator hypothesis is correct then individuals who show a large amount of IOR should also show more efficient search (and conversely).

REFERENCES

Boot, W. R., McCarley, J. S., Kramer, A. F., & Peterson, M. S. (2004). Automatic and intentional memory processes in visual search. *Psychonomic Bulletin and Review, 11*, 854–861.

Brian, J. A. (2001). Inhibition in autism: Evidence of excessive inhibition-of-return. *Dissertation Abstracts International: Section B. The Sciences and Engineering, 61*(12B), 6733.

Broadbent, D. (1987). Simple models for experimentable situations. In P. Morris (Ed.), *Modelling cognition* (pp. 169–185). Chichester, UK: John Wiley.

Castel, A. D., Pratt, J., & Craik, F. I. M. (2003). The role of spatial working memory in inhibition of return: Evidence from divided attention tasks. *Perception and Psychophysics, 65*, 970–981.

Christie, J., & Klein, R. M. (2001). Negative priming for spatial location? *Canadian Journal of Experimental Psychology, 55*(1), 24–38.

Danziger, S., & Kingstone, A. (1999). Unmasking the inhibition of return phenomenon. *Perception and Psychophysics, 61*, 1024–1037.

Dukewich, K. R., & Klein, R. M. (2005). Implications of search accuracy for serial self-terminating models of search. *Visual Cognition, 12*, 1386–1403.

Gilchrist, I. D., & Harvey, M. (2006). Evidence for a systematic component within scan paths in visual search. *Visual Cognition, 14*, 704–715.

Hillstrom, A. P., & Yantis, S. (1994). Visual motion and attentional capture. *Perception and Psychophysics, 55*(4), 399–411.

Horowitz, T. S. (2006). Revisiting the variable memory model of visual search. *Visual Cognition, 14*, 668–684.

Horowitz, T. S., & Wolfe, J. M. (1998). Visual search has no memory. *Nature, 394*(6693), 575–576.

Horowitz, T. S., & Wolfe, J. M. (2003). Memory for rejected distractors in visual search? *Visual Cognition, 10*(3), 257–298.

Itti, L., & Koch, C. (2001). Computational modeling of visual attention. *Nature Reviews Neuroscience*, *2*, 194–203.

Ivanoff, J., & Klein, R. M. (2003). Orienting of attention without awareness is affected by measurement-induced attentional control settings. *Journal of Vision*, *3*(1), 32–40. Retrieved from http://journalofvision.org/3/1/4/

Khurana, B., Scheier, C., & Shimojo, S. (1999). *Global masking reveals memory in visual search*. Unpublished manuscript.

Klein, R. M. (1988). Inhibitory tagging system facilitates visual search. *Nature*, *334*, 430–431.

Klein, R. M. (2000). Inhibition of return. *Trends in Cognitive Sciences*, *4*(4), 138–147.

Klein, R. M. (2004). Orienting and inhibition of return. In M. S. Gazzaniga (Ed.), *The cognitive neurosciences* (3rd ed., pp. 545–560). Cambridge, MA: MIT Press.

Klein, R. M., & MacInnes, J. (1999). Inhibition of return is a foraging facilitator in visual search. *Psychological Science*, *10*(4), 347–352.

Klein, R. M., Shore, D. I., MacInnes, W. J., Matheson, W. R., & Christie, J. (2000). *Remember that memoryless theory of visual search? Well, forget it!* Unpublished manuscript.

Klein, R. M., & Taylor, T. L. (1994). Categories of cognitive inhibition with reference to attention. In D. Dagenbach & T. H. Carr (Eds.), *Inhibitory processes in attention, memory, and language* (pp. 113–150). New York: Academic Press.

Kristjansson, A. (2000). In search of remembrance: Evidence for memory in visual search. *Psychological Science*, *11*(4), 328–332.

MacInnes, J., & Klein, R. (2003). Inhibition of return biases orienting during the search of complex scenes. *Scientific World Journal*, *3*(3), 75–86.

Maylor, E. A., & Hockey, R. (1985). Inhibitory component of externally controlled covert orienting in visual space. *Journal of Experimental Psychology: Human Perception and Performance*, *11*(6), 777–787.

McCarley, J. S., Kramer, A. F., Boot, W. R., Peterson, M. S., Wang, R. F., & Irwin, D. E. (2006). Oculomotor behaviour in visual search for multiple targets. *Visual Cognition*, *14*, 685–703.

McCarley, J. S., Wang, R. F., Kramer, A. R., Irwin, D. E., & Peterson, M. S. (2003). How much memory does oculomotor search have? *Psychological Science*, *14*(5), 422–426.

McConnell, B. A. (2003). *Inhibition of return in individuals with autistic spectrum disorders: Evidence for excessive facilitation and delayed inhibition*. Unpublished doctoral dissertation, York University, Toronto, Ontario, Canada.

Müller, H. J., & von Muhlenen, A. (2000). Probing distractor inhibition in visual search: Inhibition of return. *Journal of Experimental Psychology: Human Perception and Performance*, *26*(5), 1591–1605.

Oh, S.-H., & Kim, M.-S. (2004). The role of spatial working memory in visual search efficiency. *Psychonomic Bulletin and Review*, *11*, 275–281.

O'Riordan, M. A., Plaisted, K. C., Driver, J., & Baron-Cohen, S. (2001). Superior visual search in autism. *Journal of Experimental Psychology: Human Perception and Performance*, *27*(3), 719–730.

Peterson, M. S., Kramer, A. F., Wang, R. F., Irwin, D. E., & McCarley, J. S. (2001). Visual search has memory. *Psychological Science*, *12*(4), 287–292.

Posner, M. I., & Cohen, Y. (1984). Components of visual orienting. In H. Bouma & D. G. Bouwhuis (Eds.), *Attention and performance: X. Control of language processes* (pp. 551–556). Hove, UK: Lawrence Erlbaum Associates Ltd.

Rafal, R. D., Calabresi, P. A., Brennan, C. W., & Sciolto, T. K. (1989). Saccade preparation inhibits reorienting to recently attended locations. *Journal of Experimental Psychology: Human Perception and Performance*, *15*(4), 673–685.

Ratcliff, R. (1978). A theory of memory retrieval. *Psychological Review*, *85*, 59–108.

Ro, T., Farnez, A., & Chang, E. (2003). Inhibition of return and the human frontal eye fields. *Experimental Brain Research*, *150*, 290–296.

Samuel, A. G., & Kat, D. (2003). Inhibition of return: A graphical meta-analysis of its timecourse, and an empirical test of its temporal and spatial properties. *Psychonomic Bulletin and Review*, *10*(4), 897–906.

Schweickert, R. (1985). Separable effects of factors on speed and accuracy: Memory scanning, lexical decision, and choice tasks. *Psychological Bulletin*, *97*, 530–546.

Shore, D. I., & Klein, R. M. (2000). On the manifestations of memory in visual search. *Spatial Vision*, *14*, 59–76.

Smilek, D., Enns, J. T., Eastwood, J. D., & Merikle, P. M. (2006). Relax! Cognitive strategy influences visual search. *Visual Cognition*, *14*, 543–564.

Snyder, J. J., & Kingstone, A. (2000). Inhibition of return and visual search: How many separate loci are inhibited? *Perception and Psychophysics*, *62*(3), 452–458.

Sternberg, S. (1970). Memory-scanning: Mental processes revealed by reaction-time experiments. In J. S. Antrobus (Ed.), *Cognition and affect* (pp. 13–58). Boston, MA: Little, Brown.

Takeda, Y. (2004). Search for multiple targets: Evidence for memory-based control of attention. *Psychonomic Bulletin and Review*, *11*, 71–76.

Takeda, Y., & Yagi, A. (2000). Inhibitory tagging in visual search can be found if search stimuli remain visible. *Perception and Psychophysics*, *62*(5), 927–934.

Taylor, T. L., & Klein, R. M. (1998). On the causes and effects of inhibition of return. *Psychonomic Bulletin and Review*, *5*(4), 625–643.

Thomas, L. E., Ambinder, M. A., Hsieh, B., Levinthal, B., Crowell, J. A., Irwin, D. E., et al. (in press). Fruitful visual search: Inhibition of return in a virtual foraging task. *Psychonomic Bulletin & Review*.

Tipper, S. B., Driver, J., & Weaver, B. (1991). Object-centered inhibition of return of visual attention. *Quarterly Journal of Experimental Psychology*, *43A*(2), 289–298.

Tipper, S. P., Weaver, B., & Jerreat, L. M. (1994). Object-based and environment-based inhibition of return of visual attention. *Journal of Experimental Psychology: Human Perception and Performance*, *20*(3), 478–499.

Townsend, J. T. (1971). A note of the identifiability of parallel and serial processes. *Perception and Psychophysics*, *10*, 161–163.

Treisman, A. M., & Gelade, G. (1980). A feature-integration theory of attention. *Cognitive Psychology*, *12*, 97–136.

Von Muhlenen, A., Müller, H., & Müller, D. (2003). Sit-and-wait strategies in dynamic visual search. *Psychological Science*, *14*(4), 309–314.

Walsh, V., & Pascual-Leone, A. (2003). *Transcranial magnetic stimulation: A neurochronometrics of mind*. Cambridge, MA: MIT Press.

Wolfe, J. M., Cave, K. R., & Franzel, S. L. (1989). Guided Search: An alternative to the feature integration model for visual search. *Journal of Experimental Psychology: Human Perception and Performance*, *15*(3), 419–433.

Wolfe, J. M., & Pokorny, C. W. (1990). Inhibitory tagging in visual search: A failure to replicate. *Perception and Psychophysics*, *48*, 357–362.

Yantis, S., & Hillstrom, A. P. (1994). Stimulus-driven attentional capture: Evidence from equiluminant visual objects. *Journal of Experimental Psychology: Human Perception and Performance*, *20*, 95–107.

VISUAL COGNITION, 2006, 14 (4/5/6/7/8), 668–684

ᴪ Psychology Press
Taylor & Francis Group

Revisiting the variable memory model of visual search

Todd S. Horowitz

Visual Attention Laboratory, Brigham & Women's Hospital and Harvard Medical School, Cambridge, MA, USA

How much memory does visual search have? A number of recent papers have explored this question from various points of view. In this paper, I propose a formal framework for comparing answers across different experimental paradigms. This framework is based on the "variable memory model" (Arani, Karwan, & Drury, 1984). This model has three parameters: Encoding probability (θ), recall probability (ϕ), and target identification probability (p'). The model can be used to generate cumulative distribution functions for reaction time (RT) or saccades. I compare the model to a dataset of RTs collected on a standard inefficient search for block 2s among block 5s. Assuming perfect identification ($p' = 1$), I found that mean encoding probability was .33, and mean recall probability .71. The variable memory model provides a common metric for characterizing the behaviour of observers in different laboratories, in terms that are easy to relate to the memory literature.

Does visual search have memory? After years of neglect, this question has recently become prominent in the literature. The goal of this paper is less to find a definitive answer to this question than to redefine and clarify the terms of the debate. I propose that the proper question should be "How much memory does visual search have?", and I will suggest a formal framework for comparing answers across experimental paradigms. First, however, I will define what I mean by "memory". I am not asking whether or not memory processes are involved in visual search. It is self-evident that a variety of memory systems are critical to successful visual search, in or out of the laboratory. At a minimum, the observer must remember what the target is, and what the appropriate response is. Following Shore and Klein (2000), I will outline three levels of memory in visual search, defined by the timescale of the experimental trial or session. At the longest timescale, we can investigate long-term perceptual learning in search, which occurs over

Please address all correspondence to Todd S. Horowitz, Visual Attention Laboratory, 64 Sidney Street, Suite 170, Cambridge, MA 02139, USA. E-mail: toddh@search.bwh.harvard.edu

I would like to thank David Fencsik, Steven Flusberg, Sarah Klieger, Melina Kunar, Evan Palmer, Ken Sobel, Adrian von Mühlenen, Jeremy Wolfe, and an anonymous reviewer for helpful comments on the manuscript, and Megan Hyle for data collection.

http://www.psypress.com/viscog   DOI: 10.1080/13506280500193958

many sessions (e.g., Ahissar & Hochstein, 2000; Chua & Chun, 2003; Leonards, Rettenbach, Nase, & Sireteanu, 2002). At shorter timescales, we can look at trial-to-trial priming (Goolsby & Suzuki, 2001; Hillstrom, 2000; Kumada & Humphreys, 2002; Maljkovic & Nakayama, 1994, 1996). Finally, at the shortest timescale, we can ask to what extent the visual system remembers which objects have already been examined during a trial, and which have yet to be attended. This is the type of memory I will address in this paper. Note that I am not asking whether the observer actually forms a memory of items examined during the search. The question I am interested in here is whether there is a memory for rejected distractors that is used to prevent attention from returning to those distractors during the course of a single search trial. So, an observer might remember seeing a particular distractor, or a distractor might prime (negatively or positively) a later response, but that same distractor might still be revisited once or more by attention during a search. In fact, items that are attended more than once might actually leave a stronger trace in memory.

For ease of exposition, I will assume that visual search proceeds by selecting one item at a time, and that, at least at the start of a trial, all items are equally likely to be selected. Such a straight serial model is an oversimplification. There may be cases where multiple items are processed simultaneously, and certainly there is a gradient of salience for all but the most carefully constructed stimulus arrays (see Itti 2006 this issue). Some would argue that the serial model is entirely wrong, and that search proceeds simultaneously on all items at the same time (Eckstein, Thomas, Palmer, & Shimozaki, 2000; Palmer & McLean, 1995). This debate is somewhat orthogonal to the question of memory in search as I define it. The arguments I put forward here can be easily generalized to any model in which capacity is limited and can be reallocated dynamically during search.

RESEARCH ON MEMORY IN VISUAL SEARCH

The question of memory in visual search can be divided empirically into two domains, concerning covert and overt deployments of attention respectively. The answer may prove to be the same for both eye movements and attentional deployments, but it may not.

We have developed two paradigms for addressing the question of memory for covert deployments of attention. The randomized search paradigm (Horowitz & Wolfe, 1998, 2003) employs a logic akin to lesion studies: If we prevent observers from keeping track of rejected distractors, does that harm search performance? In the *dynamic* condition, each trial consists of a series of frames. The stimuli in each frame are identical, except that their locations are shuffled randomly from frame to frame. The target is present in every frame. This manipulation enforces memoryless search, because remembering where a distractor was at time t_1 does not tell you where that same distractor ends up at t_2. The *static* control condition resembles a typical search trial in which a single static frame is presented. Here, observers could use memory if they had it. In both cases we vary set size and measure reaction time (RT). The RT × Set slope from the static condition measures how efficiently observers can locate the target under normal circumstances. The size slope from the dynamic condition reflects how efficiently they can find the target without keeping track of the locations of rejected distractors. If observers have perfect memory, then they will be substantially impaired in the dynamic condition, when that memory becomes useless. In this case, the dynamic slope will be twice the static slope, because memoryless search is half as efficient as search with memory (for the mathematical derivation of this statement, see Horowitz & Wolfe, 2001). On the other hand, if observers do not use memory even in the static condition, then disabling this memory will have no effect, and the two conditions will have the same slope. Across a number of experiments with varying stimulus conditions, we found little evidence for steeper slopes in the dynamic condition, and clear evidence against a doubling of the slope from static to dynamic conditions. These findings have been replicated in other laboratories (Gibson, Li, Skow, Salvagni, & Cooke, 2000; but see Kristjánsson, 2000; von Muhlenen, Müller, & Müller, 2003). In short, all evidence from these experiments points to the conclusion that search in the static condition is just as memoryless as search in the dynamic condition.

In the second paradigm (Horowitz & Wolfe, 2001), we sought a signature of memory within a single stimulus condition. Here we relied on the mathematics of sampling distributions. Perfect memory corresponds to sampling without replacement from the search array, while no memory corresponds to sampling with replacement. Varying set size with search for a single target is ambiguous, because both sampling modes will produce a linear increase in RT. However, when there are multiple targets in a single display, the two modes make qualitatively different predictions. The time to find successive targets is constant under sampling without replacement. As each target is found, the pool of available targets left to find shrinks, but the pool of distractors which have not been attended yet shrinks proportionately. Under sampling with replacement, however, the pool of distractors is constant, while the number of available targets shrinks, leading to an accelerating function. Of course, it is methodologically difficult to measure RTs to successive targets, since the times between target detection might be smaller than the minimum time required to raise a finger and put it down again. However, we devised a method that allowed us to measure the lag between locating successive targets in a multiple-target display.

In this paradigm (Horowitz & Wolfe, 2001), the number of targets in a display (of fixed display set size) is varied within a block of trials, and observers are asked to determine whether or not there are at least n targets in the display, where the value of n is varied between blocks. We assume that the RT on "yes" trials measures the time to find the nth target in such a display. By averaging data from trials with the same number of targets in the display across different blocks of trials, we can plot the RT to find the nth target of some fixed number of targets across a range of n. In our experiments, we varied n from 2 to 5 and analysed data when there were five targets. We found highly accelerated functions, consistent with sampling with replacement (memoryless search). However, Takeda (2004) has argued that this pattern is due to an increased memory load with increasing values of n. We have shown that this increase in search rate with memory load is at least partially due to Takeda's choice of stimuli (Horowitz, Wolfe, & Birnkrant, 2003), but the debate has not yet been resolved (see also McCarley, Kramer, Boot, & Peterson, 2006 this issue).

The question of sampling with or without replacement would seem easier to resolve in the domain of overt attention, or eye movements, where one can actually measure directly where the eyes are directed and determine if any refixation occurs. However, there is surprisingly little agreement in this literature. Peterson, Kramer, Wang, Irwin, and McCarley (2001) reported perfect memory for eye movements, while Gilchrist and Harvey (2000) measured the rate of refixation to be around 50%, and suggested that they may have underestimated the true value (see also Gilchrist & Harvey, 2006 this issue).

HOW MUCH MEMORY DOES VISUAL SEARCH HAVE?

Rather than continuing to argue about whether visual search has no memory or perfect memory, the premise of this paper is that it is time to ask a more nuanced question: How much memory does visual search have? The question acknowledges that the assumption of perfect, infinite memory for all distractors is unrealistic. However, abandoning this assumption does not require us to assume pure amnesia, or "visual search in the eternal present", as we once put it (Horowitz & Wolfe, 1997). Instead, it is likely that the deployment of attention is guided by its own history to some extent—by how much of its history becomes the empirical question.

This is not an entirely new framing of the question. Horowitz and Wolfe (2001) fit a set of limited-capacity memory models to their data, estimating that observers could avoid revisiting the last three to five rejected distractors (see also Alvarez, Horowitz, Wong, & Wolfe, 1999). Takeda's (2004) data produced much larger estimates of 20–25 rejected distractors. In the oculomotor domain, McCarley, Wang, Kramer, Irwin, and Peterson (2003), using an innovative saccadic choice procedure, estimated that there was a memory for the previous three eye movements (see also Klein & MacInnes, 1999).

If we want to know how much memory visual search has, we need to know what the metric is. How do we quantify memory? The work described above has employed what I will call a "stack model". This model assumes that the last few deployments of attention are recorded, so that if the observer is currently attending to the nth item in the sequence, the $n + 1$th deployment of attention can avoid the $n - 1$th, $n - 2$th ... $n - c$th items, where c represents the hypothesized capacity. Once deployment $n + 1$ is completed, however, the nth item is placed on the stack, and the $n - c$th item drops out. After the first c items have been attended, the model enters a steady state in which the number of potential targets for attention is the number of total objects minus the capacity. If we adopt the stack model, then the metric c is capacity. How many previous items are remembered?

A variant of the stack model might be called the "decay model". Working from the premise that inhibition of return (IOR) serves as the mechanism for implementing memory in visual search (Klein, 1988; Posner & Cohen, 1984), several researchers have claimed that if attention is directed to several locations via a sequence of cues, an inhibitory trace can be observed at those locations. This inhibition decays over time such that the most recently cued location shows the strongest inhibition, and the first cued location the weakest (Dodd, Castel, & Pratt, 2003; Pratt & Abrams, 1995; Wright & Richard, 1996). The important parameter for decay models is obviously the decay rate. However, results are usually translated into a capacity estimate by assuming a rate of deployment and computing how many inhibitory traces are still above threshold when the model reaches the steady state (e.g., McCarley et al., 2003; Wright & Richard, 1996).

Here I reintroduce a third option, the "variable memory model" (Arani, Karwan, & Drury, 1984). While models of visual search have implicitly assumed perfect memory for some time (e.g., Schneider & Shiffrin, 1977; Treisman & Gelade, 1980), the term "memory" was not employed in this context in the cognitive psychology literature until our 1998 paper (Horowitz & Wolfe, 1998). The assumed mechanism for preventing attention from returning to rejected distractors was IOR (Klein, 1988; Posner & Cohen, 1984), which is not generally conceived of as a memory system, and models which asserted that rejected distractors were "marked off" (Grossberg, Mingolla, & Ross, 1994; Wolfe, Cave, & Franzel, 1989) were vague about exactly how this marking off might have been implemented. Our claim that "visual search has no memory" was a sort of pun, since sampling with replacement is referred to in the probability literature as "memoryless" (Johnson & Kotz, 1977).

The variable memory model describes memory in visual search in terms drawn from the study of memory in other contexts. The model assumes that when an item is attended, the location of that item is encoded into memory or not with some probability; subsequently, each time attention is shifted again, there is some probability that the location of that item will be recalled. So the key parameters of the variable memory model are encoding and recall probability. Furthermore, the model also acknowledges that perception is imperfect by including a parameter describing the probability that the target is attended but not recognized as such.

THE VARIABLE MEMORY MODEL

The variable memory model was developed by Arani et al. (1984) to describe memory for eye movements. This model has a number of advantages over stack and decay models. First, it predicts latency distributions, rather than just means. Second, data can be characterized along two or three psychologically interesting dimensions. Finally, since it was originally developed to model eye movements, it can allow us to compare data from eye movement studies and RT studies primarily aimed at covert attention. In this section, I will describe the model more formally, and then compare the model to some data collected in our laboratory.

The model has three free parameters: θ, φ, and p'. θ represents encoding probability, φ recall probability, and p' the probability of correctly identifying a target.[1] Assume that each epoch of the model represents a single deployment of attention. The heart of the model is the memory term, describing the probability ($P_{i,k}$) that on the ith epoch, the system will remember that a particular item was attended during the kth epoch:

$$P_{i,k} = \theta \varphi^{i-k} \tag{1}$$

Thus, the system is more likely to forget that a particular item was attended as the trial goes on. If both φ and θ are set to 1.0, then the system has perfect memory. If either parameter is 0.0, the system is amnesic. The interesting cases are in between the two extremes.

The cumulative distribution function is obtained by computing the probability of detecting the target during a given epoch, then summing over epochs. The probability P_i of detecting a target in epoch i, is a function of three factors: (1) The probability that the target has not been detected in a

---

[1] One weakness of the model is the assumption that only misses are possible, and not false alarms. However, in RT studies of search, with near-unlimited exposure durations, false alarms are quite rare.

previous epoch: (2) the number of items in the display: and (3) the memory parameters.

If we assume perfect perception ($p' = 1.0$), then computing P_i is fairly straightforward. Given a display set size of M items, the probability of detecting the target in epoch 1 is always $\frac{1}{M}$. For epoch 2, there are two possible outcomes. Either the location of the item examined on epoch 1 is remembered, in which case the probability of detecting the target is $\frac{1}{M-1}$, or it is not, in which case the probability is again $\frac{1}{M}$. The probability of successfully recalling the location of the item examined on epoch 1 can be computed from Equation 1 as $\theta\varphi$, and the probability of not recalling the location is therefore $1 - \theta\varphi$. The probability of detecting the target given each outcome is multiplied by the probability of each outcome, and the resulting probabilities are summed. Of course, if the target had been detected in the first epoch, then by definition it cannot be detected in the second epoch, so we also have to multiply by the probability that the target was not detected in epoch 1.

$$P_2 = (1 - P_1)\left[\theta\varphi\frac{1}{M-1} + (1 - \theta o)\frac{1}{M}\right] \tag{2}$$

The probability of detecting the target in epoch 3 is computed in a similar manner, except that there are four possible outcomes to consider. The number of possible outcomes increases exponentially as 2^{i-1}, until $i > M$. At this point, certain outcomes can be eliminated. For example, assume $M = 6$. The seventh deployment of attention will only occur if at least one of the first five had been forgotten. If the first five were all remembered, then the probability of finding the target on the sixth deployment would have been 1.0.[2] Therefore, the set of outcomes for $i \geq M$ is always the same as the set of outcomes for $i = M - 1$. We can generalize Equation 2 as Equation 3, where p_j is the probability of the jth possible outcome, d_j the probability of detecting the target given that outcome, and $\delta = i$ for $i < M$ and $\delta = M - 1$ for $i \geq M$:

$$P_i = \left(1 - \sum_{k=1}^{i-1} P_k\right)\left(\sum_{j=1}^{2^{\delta-1}} p_j d_j\right) \tag{3}$$

The cumulative distribution function is then simply:

$$f(i) = \sum_{i=1}^{i_{max}} P_i \tag{4}$$

where i_{max} is however many attentional deployments you wish to compute.

---

[2] We assume $p' = 1.0$, and also that once a particular deployment is forgotten, it was not remembered again. Arani et al. (1984) claimed that model output did not change significantly if a deployment that was not recalled in one epoch was allowed to be recalled in a later epoch.

The choice of i_{max} is not, however, a matter of whim. The exponential increase in the number of possible outcomes for each epoch quickly imposes serious costs in terms of computing time. After deriving the model, Arani et al. (1984) turned to simulations to compare their model with data. Advances in computing technology over the last two decades have made this less of an issue for contemporary researchers. In this paper, I will present illustrative output from the analytic model, as opposed to simulations. However, I have chosen examples where I can keep i_{max} fairly low, and I have not actually fit the model to data. Instead, the model was run with representative values of the two key memory parameters and compared to a dataset.

DATASET

Since the model assumes serial deployment of attention, the most straightforward thing to do is to compare its output to data from a visual search task which is held to have a strong serial component. Spatial configuration searches (Wolfe, 1998b), in which the targets and distractors differ only in the spatial arrangement of their components, are typically assumed to require serial search (Wolfe, 1998a). Here I use data from a search for 2s among 5s. The digits were constructed from the same set of five line segments, two vertical and three horizontal, differing only in being mirror images of one another (see Figure 1).

The data come from a larger experiment, which will be described in detail elsewhere, designed to provide data for modelling search RT distributions. There were 10 observers in this experiment. Display set sizes of three, six, twelve, and eighteen items were used. Targets were present on 50% of trials. Set size and target presence or absence were mixed within blocks of trials. Observers completed 500 trials per cell for a total of 4000 trials per observer. Error trials, as well as those with RTs > 5000 ms or < 150 ms, were excluded from the RT analysis. The average median RT × Set size functions are shown in Figure 2A, while Figure 2B presents the error rates. The average median RT × set size slopes for these observers were 42.9 ms/item for target-present trials and 99.9 ms/item for target-absent trials. Both the magnitude of these slopes and the 1:2.33 ratio between them are typical of this search task.

Was this a serial search? Inferring the type of search from the slope value is a notoriously tricky business (Wolfe, 1998b). Bricolo, Gianesini, Fanini, Bundesen, and Chelazzi (2002) defined a more stringent set of criteria to establish that the data are at least consistent with serial search. First, the minimum RTs should be independent of set size for target-present trials, but increase with set size for target-absent trials. Second, variance (normalized by mean RT) should be independent of set size for target-absent trials, but

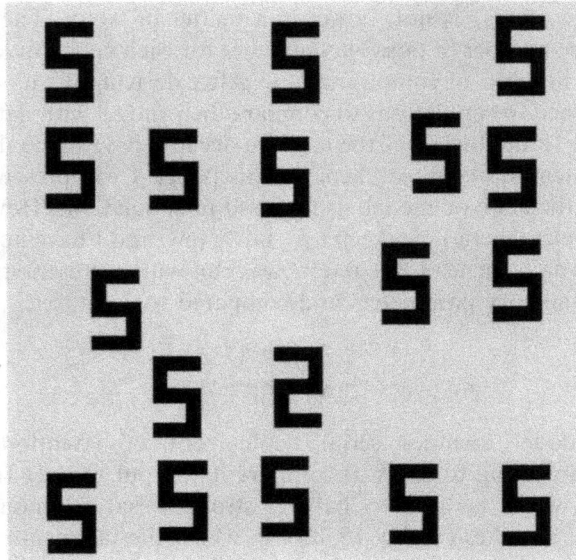

Figure 1. Sample display used in collection of the dataset. Observers searched for the "2" among "5" distractors.

increase with set size for target-present trials. Panels C and D of Figure 2 demonstrate that these data are roughly consistent with both criteria.

Minimum RT increased with set size, $F(3, 27) = 14.85$, $p < .001$, and was greater for target-present trials than target-absent trials, $F(1, 9) = 20.80$, $p < .005$. However, the two factors interacted, $F(3, 27) = 8.89$, $p < .001$. Analysis of simple effects showed that minimum RT increased with set size for both target-absent trials, $F(3, 27) = 12.17$, $p < .001$, and for target-present trials, $F(3, 27) = 10.66$, $p < .001$. However, the slope of the minimum RT × Set size function was much shallower for target-present trials than for target-absent trials (4.3 ms/item vs. 26.9 ms/item), $t(9) = 4.12$, $p < .005$. This pattern is similar to what Bricolo et al. (2002) observed. They attributed the small but significant increase in minimum RT with set to the fact that the probability of locating the target in the first epoch decreases with set size, thus reducing the probability of observing the minimum possible RT.

Variance data conform more strictly to the criteria. Normalized standard deviation increased with set size, $F(3, 27) = 4.59$, $p < .05$, and was greater for target-present trials than target-absent trials, $F(1, 9) = 65.25$, $p < .00005$. Again, the two factors interacted, $F(3, 27) = 26.66$, $p < .001$. Analysis of simple effects showed that normalized standard deviation increased with set size for target-present trials, $F(3, 27) = 19.72$, $p < .001$, but not for target-absent trials, $F(3, 27) < 1$.

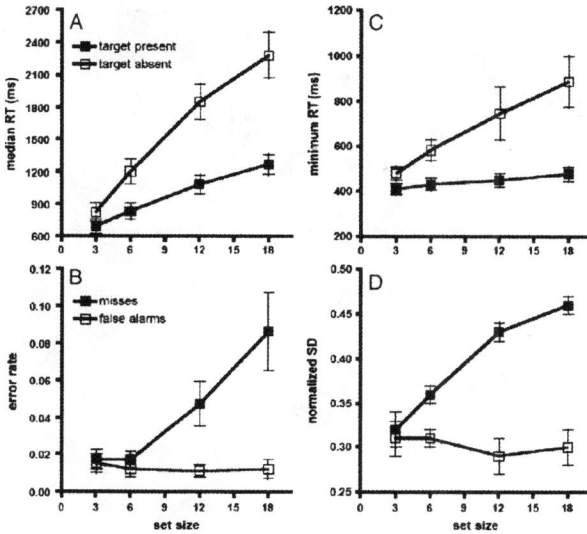

Figure 2. Summary statistics from the dataset as a function of set size and target presence/absence. In all panels, filled symbols represent data from target present trials, open symbols data from target absent trials. Error bars indicate the standard error of the mean. Panel A shows median RT data; panel B shows error rates; panel C shows the minimum RT; and panel D shows standard deviation normalized by mean RT.

BEHAVIOUR OF THE MODEL

The model uses Equation 3 to compute P_i and Equation 4 to compute the cumulative distribution function. The model was implemented in Matlab version 6.5, Release 13 (Mathworks) and run on an Apple PowerMacintosh G4 desktop computer with dual 1.25 GHz processors using Mac OS 10.3.2.

Two competing factors determined which subset of the data would be compared to the model. On the one hand, the more items in the display, the greater the range of possible outcomes. In the extreme, for example, changing the memory parameters will have no effect on a search with set size 1. On the other hand, the exponential increase in computing time would make modelling the set size 18 data prohibitively time consuming. I therefore settled on the set size 6 data for illustrative purposes. I chose a value of 50 for I_{max}, because the cumulative distribution for a pure memoryless model ($\theta = \varphi = 0.0$) will exceed the 99.5% point by then.

Given M and I_{max}, I then generated model predictions by varying the encoding probability θ and recall probability φ from 0 to 1 in increments of 0.1, yielding 121 cumulative distribution functions. Not all of these are unique, of course, since all cases where either θ or φ is 0.0 are identical memoryless cumulative distribution functions. Figure 3 shows three slices

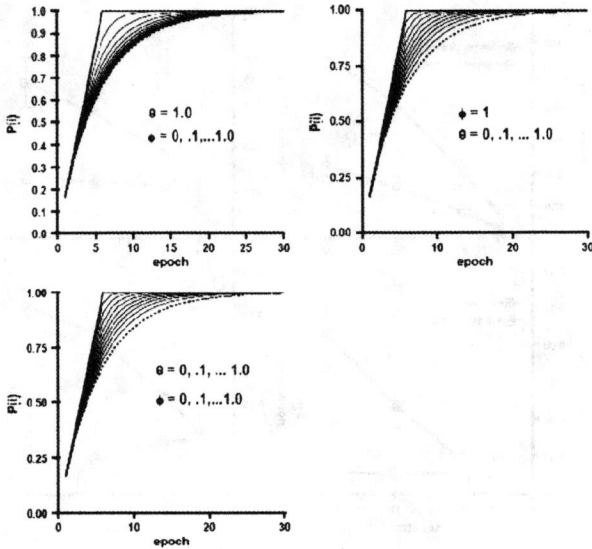

Figure 3. Selected cumulative distributions functions produced by the model. In all panels, the dotted lines indicate the purely memoryless case where at least one parameter is set to 0.0. Subsequent solid curves moving upwards indicate incremental changes in the critical variable, until the slightly thicker solid curve indicates the perfect memory case where both parameters are set to 1.0. Panel A demonstrates the effect of holding θ constant at 1.0 and varying φ; panel B holds φ constant and varies θ; and panel C is a diagonal cut through the parameter space, in which encoding and recall probabilities are always equal.

through the resulting parameter space. In all panels, the dotted lines indicate the purely memoryless case where at least one parameter is set to 0.0. Subsequent solid curves moving upward indicate incremental changes in the critical variable, until the slightly thicker solid curve indicates the perfect memory case where both parameters are set to 1.0. Panel A demonstrates the effect of holding θ constant at 1.0 and varying φ. Small changes in the recall probability rapidly move the functions away from the perfect memory curve. Panel B holds φ constant and varies θ. Changes in encoding probability have a less dramatic effect on the shape of the function. This is because encoding happens only once for a given location, while recall is repeated in each successive epoch. Panel C is a diagonal cut through the parameter space, in which encoding and recall probabilities are always equal.

Cumulative distribution functions for all ten observers are shown in Figure 4. Upon even a cursory inspection of the data, it is clear that these distributions depart from the ideal perfect memory predictions (illustrated as the thick curves in Figure 3). Quantifying this intuition is of course more difficult, and the purpose of this paper.

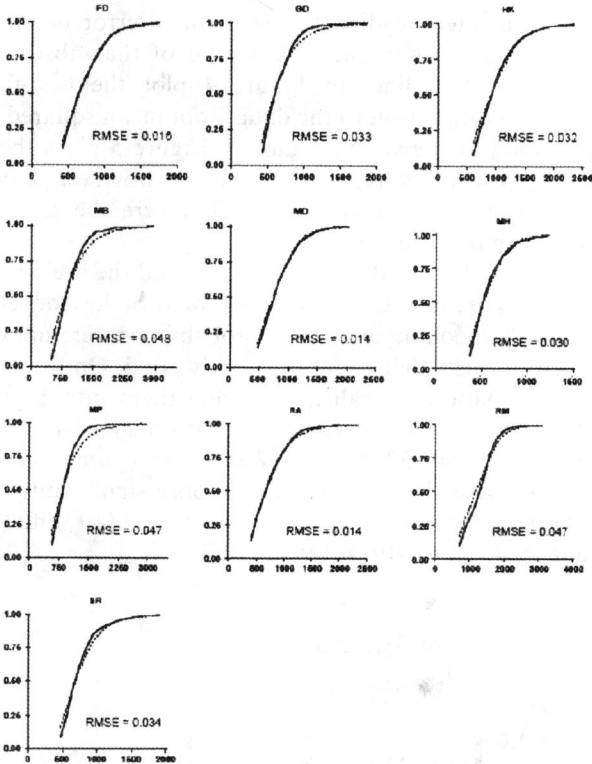

Figure 4. Cumulative distribution functions of RT for each of the 10 observers. RT is on the x-axis and cumulative proportion of trials on the y-axis. Solid lines represent data. Dotted lines represent the best-fitting model. Root mean square error (*RMSE*) between data and model is listed on each panel.

I compared the data from each subject to each of 101 model functions (100 functions generated by crossing a vector of 10 φ values from 0.1 to 1.0 in steps of 0.1 with the identical vector of θ values, plus the φ = θ = 0.0 function) by converting the data to a cumulative histogram with as many bins as there were epochs in the model. The upper tails presented a dilemma for two reasons. First, they are poorly sampled in the data, so that a single long RT in an individual observer's dataset would radically change the size of the bins relative to other observers. Second, while the higher memory models usually reached 1.0 well before the I_{max}th bin, the low memory models did not. Therefore, I trimmed both models and data at the .995 level. Root mean squared error between the data and model was computed for each case. Since the parameters represent rates that can vary only between 0 and 1, statistical analysis was performed on arcsin-transformed values. *T*-tests against 0 and 1 were evaluated as one-tailed tests.

The pair of parameters leading to the minimal error between data and model were taken as a rough characterization of that observer's memory performance. The dotted lines in Figure 4 plot the best-fitting model functions for direct comparison to the data. Root mean squared error values for these models are also given in Figure 4. Figure 5 plots the best-fitting parameter values. Each dot represents a single observer, except for two points ($\varphi = 0.9$, $\theta = 0.9$, and $\varphi = 0.8$, $\theta = 0.7$) where the same parameters were obtained for multiple observers.

The average value of θ was 0.82 ($SEM = .04$), and the average φ value was 0.86 ($SEM = .03$). Whether these values are high or low depends on your point of view. Both encoding and recall probabilities were above .50 for all observers, which suggests that memory is fairly good. On the other hand, if we take the mean parameter values and plug them into Equation 1, the average observer would only have a .71 probability of recalling the last location attended, and a .33 chance of recalling a location attended six epochs ago. In any case, the mean values are both significantly greater than 0.0: θ, $t(9) = 18.04$, $p < .00001$; φ, $t(9) = 18.06$, $p < .00001$, and less than 1.0: θ, $t(9) = 6.28$, $p < .0001$; φ, $t(9) = 4.94$, $p < .0005$.

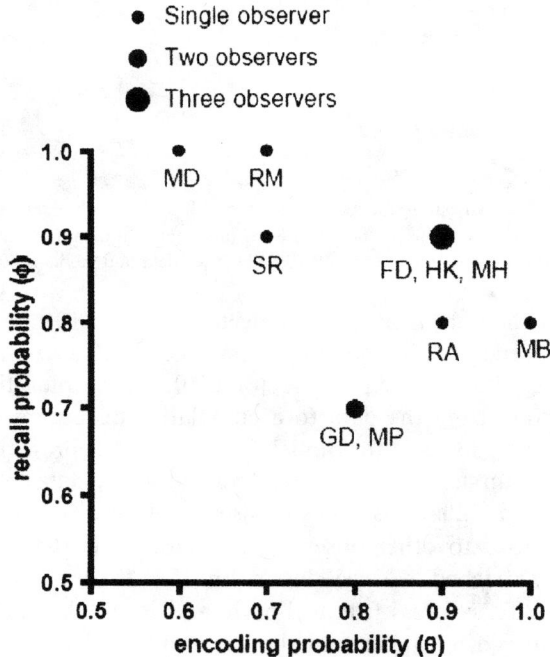

Figure 5.   Closest-fitting model parameters for each of the 10 observers. θ (encoding probability) values are plotted on the x-axis; and φ (recall probability) on the y-axis. Size of the symbol indicates how many observers are represented at that point. Observers' initials are indicated below each point.

Looking at the individual results in Figure 5, it is clear that there are substantial differences among observers. The three observers in the upper left portion of the graph have relatively poor encoding, but are quite good at recalling what they do manage to encode. Observers GD and MP are better at encoding locations, but more likely to forget them. There is also a cluster of three "eidetic" observers who are quite efficient at both encoding and recall.

While Figure 5 illustrates the spread of parameter values across the space, the model parameters did not predict search performance. The two parameters exhibited a modest, but nonsignificant, negative correlation with one another ($r = .52$, $p > .10$). I tested the correlation between both parameter values and seven performance measures: Target-present slope, target-absent slope, slope ratio (target-absent:target-present), target-present intercept, target-absent intercept, mean target-present RT, and mean target-absent RT. In general, encoding probability was negatively related to slope and RT measures, while recall probability was positively related. However, none of these correlations reached significance. Nor did the combination of the two parameters predict variation in any of the dependent measures in a regression analysis. This may be due in part to the coarse quantization of parameter values; only five different values of each parameter were observed.

DISCUSSION

These analyses are meant to illustrate the potential for this class of model to illuminate results from visual search experiments. The exact parameter values should be taken with a pinch of salt, since I did not perform finely tuned model fitting. Further explorations with this dataset are necessary. For instance, it would be important to show that the model parameters derived across different conditions (such as set size) showed some within-observer correlations, and it would be interesting to see if the parameters varied systematically with set size.

One aspect of the model that I have not yet implemented (partly because of the combinatorial explosion of terms, see Arani et al., 1984) is the parameter p'. Perception (and decision) is not perfect, so it is likely that even with suprathreshold, highly visible displays, the visual system will on occasion mistake a target for a distractor or (more rarely; Zenger & Fahle, 1997) a distractor for a target. Simulation work indicates that when memory is perfect, varying p' produces distributions quite unlike those observed in these data. However, this may not be true for stimuli that are perceptually more confusable or degraded.

The variable memory model provides a useful way to characterize the behaviour of observers in terms that are easy to relate to the memory literature. Certain applications suggest themselves naturally. For instance, manipulating the display with "landmarks" (Peterson, Boot, Kramer, & McCarley, 2004) might be expected to affect the encoding parameter θ, while varying memory load should affect recall probability φ. While the memory parameters did not predict global performance measures such as slope or RT in these data, I suspect that they might predict performance differences between conditions that rely on memory, such as in our randomized search experiments (Horowitz & Wolfe, 2003). One obvious application is to return the model to its native environment, the study of eye movements. In this context, several aspects of the model can be extracted directly from the data. Epochs are fixations, and epoch duration is fixation time. While the model was originally designed to accommodate eye movement data, as far as I can tell it has not been applied in the two decades since its original publication, possibly because computing power was inadequate to implement the model when it was first published. This is less of an issue today, and will be even less so in the future.

When introducing the topic, I suggested that we move on from the question of whether visual search has memory to the question of how much memory. The answer, I suspect, will depend a great deal on task demands. My suggestion now is that we should start asking more sophisticated questions altogether, exploring the conditions governing memory performance in visual search tasks. The variable memory model can be a useful tool in this exploration.

REFERENCES

Ahissar. M., & Hochstein, S. (2000). The spread of attention and learning in feature search: Effects of target distribution and task difficulty. *Vision Research*, 40(10–12), 1349–1364.

Alvarez. G. A.. Horowitz, T. S., Wong. A., & Wolfe. J. M. (1999). New evidence against global accumulation of information in visual search. *Investigative Ophthalmology & Visual Science*, 40(4). S344.

Arani. T.. Karwan. M. H.. & Drury. C. G. (1984). A variable-memory model of search. *Human Factors*. 26(6). 631–639.

Bricolo. E.. Gianesini, T., Fanini, A.. Bundesen. C.. & Chelazzi, L. (2002). Serial attention mechanisms in visual search: A direct behavioral demonstration. *Journal of Cognitive Neuroscience*, 14(7), 980–993.

Chua. K. P.. & Chun. M. M. (2003). Implicit scene learning is viewpoint dependent. *Perception and Psychophysics*, 65(1). 72–80.

Dodd. M. D.. Castel. A. D.. & Pratt. J. (2003). Inhibition of return with rapid serial shifts of attention: Implications for memory and visual search. *Perception and Psychophysics*, 65(7), 1126–1135.

Eckstein. M. P.. Thomas. J. P.. Palmer. J.. & Shimozaki. S. S. (2000). A signal detection model predicts the effects of set size on visual search accuracy for feature. conjunction. triple conjunction. and disjunction displays. *Perception and Psychophysics*, 62(3). 425–451.

Gibson. B. S., Li, L., Skow, E., Salvagni, K., & Cooke, L. (2000). Memory-based tagging of targets during visual search for one versus two identical targets. *Psychological Science*. *11*(4), 324–328.

Gilchrist, I. D., & Harvey, M. (2000). Refixation frequency and memory mechanisms in visual search. *Current Biology*, *10*(19), 1209–1212.

Gilchrist, I. D., & Harvey, M. (2006). Evidence for a systematic component within scan paths in visual search. *Visual Cognition*, *14*, 704–715.

Goolsby, B. A., & Suzuki, S. (2001). Understanding priming of color-singleton search: Roles of attention at encoding and "retrieval". *Perception and Psychophysics*, *63*(6), 929–944.

Grossberg, S., Mingolla, E., & Ross, W. D. (1994). A neural theory of attentive visual search: Interactions of boundary, surface, spatial, and object representations. *Psychological Review*, *101*(3), 470–489.

Hillstrom, A. P. (2000). Repetition effects in visual search. *Perception and Psychophysics*, *62*(4), 800–817.

Horowitz, T. S., & Wolfe, J. M. (1997). Visual search in the eternal present. *Abstracts of the Psychonomic Society*, *2*, 26.

Horowitz, T. S., & Wolfe, J. M. (1998). Visual search has no memory. *Nature*, *394*(6693), 575–577.

Horowitz, T. S., & Wolfe, J. M. (2001). Search for multiple targets: Remember the targets, forget the search. *Perception and Psychophysics*, *63*(2), 272–285.

Horowitz, T. S., & Wolfe, J. M. (2003). Memory for rejected distractors in visual search? *Visual Cognition*, *10*(3), 257–298.

Horowitz, T. S., Wolfe, J. M., & Birnkrant, R. S. (2003). Search for multiple targets: Search rate depends on what is being remembered. *Abstracts of the Psychonomic Society*, *8*, 11.

Itti, L. (2006). Quantitative modelling of perceptual salience at human eye position. *Visual Cognition*, *14*, 959–984.

Johnson, N. L., & Kotz, S. (1977). *Urn models and their applications*. New York: John Wiley.

Klein, R. (1988). Inhibitory tagging system facilitates visual search. *Nature*, *334*, 430–431.

Klein, R. M., & MacInnes, W. J. (1999). Inhibition of return is a foraging facilitator in visual search. *Psychological Science*, *10*(4), 346–352.

Kristjánsson, A. (2000). In search of remembrance: Evidence for memory in visual search. *Psychological Science*, *11*(4), 328–332.

Kumada, T., & Humphreys, G. W. (2002). Cross-dimensional interference and cross-trial inhibition. *Perception and Psychophysics*, *64*(3), 493–503.

Leonards, U., Rettenbach, R., Nase, G., & Sireteanu, R. (2002). Perceptual learning of highly demanding visual search tasks. *Vision Research*, *42*(18), 2193–2204.

Maljkovic, V., & Nakayama, K. (1994). Priming of pop-out: I. Role of features. *Memory and Cognition*, *22*(6), 657–672.

Maljkovic, V., & Nakayama, K. (1996). Priming of pop-out II: Role of position. *Perception and Psychophysics*, *58*(7), 977–991.

McCarley, J. S., Kramer, A. F., Boot, W. R., Peterson, M. S., Wang, R. F., & Irwin, D. E. (2006). Oculomotor behaviour in visual search for multiple targets. *Visual Cognition*, *14*, 685–703.

McCarley, J. S., Wang, R. F., Kramer, A., Irwin, D. E., & Peterson, M. S. (2003). How much memory does oculomotor search have? *Psychological Science*, *14*(5), 422–426.

Palmer, J., & McLean, J. (1995). *Imperfect, unlimited-capacity, parallel search yields large set-size effects*. Paper presented at the meeting of the Society of Mathematical Psychology, Irvine, CA, USA.

Peterson, M. S., Boot, W. R., Kramer, A. F., & McCarley, J. S. (2004). Landmarks help guide attention during visual search. *Spatial Vision*, *17*, 497–510.

Peterson, M. S., Kramer, A. F., Wang, R. F., Irwin, D. E., & McCarley, J. S. (2001). Visual search has memory. *Psychological Science*, *12*(4), 287–292.

Posner, M. I., & Cohen, Y. (1984). Components of attention. In H. Bouma & D. G. Bouwhuis (Eds.), *Attention and performance X: Control of language processes* (pp. 55–66). Hove, UK: Lawrence Erlbaum Associates Ltd.

Pratt, J., & Abrams, R. A. (1995). Inhibition of return to successively cued spatial locations. *Journal of Experimental Psychology: Human Perception and Performance, 21*(6), 1343–1353.

Schneider, W., & Shiffrin. R. M. (1977). Controlled and automatic human information processing: I. Detection. search, and attention. *Psychological Review, 84*(1), 1–66.

Shore, D. I., & Klein. R. M. (2000). On the manifestations of memory in visual search. *Spatial Vision, 14,* 59–75.

Takeda, Y. (2004). Search for multiple targets: Evidence for memory-based control of attention. *Psychonomic Bulletin and Review, 11,* 71–76.

Treisman, A., & Gelade. G. (1980). A feature-integration theory of attention. *Cognitive Psychology, 12,* 97–136.

Von Muhlenen, A., Müller. H. J., & Müller, D. (2003). Sit-and-wait strategies in dynamic visual search. *Psychological Science, 14*(4), 309–314.

Wolfe, J. M. (1998a). Visual search. In H. Pashler (Ed.). *Attention* (pp. 13–73). Hove, UK: Psychology Press.

Wolfe, J. M. (1998b). What can 1 million trials tell us about visual search? *Psychological Science, 9*(1), 33–39.

Wolfe, J. M., Cave. K. R., & Franzel, S. L. (1989). Guided Search: An alternative to the feature integration model for visual search. *Journal of Experimental Psychology: Human Perception and Performance, 15*(3), 419–433.

Wright. R. D., & Richard, C. M. (1996). Inhibition of return at multiple locations in visual space. *Canadian Journal of Experimental Psychology, 50*(3), 324–327.

Zenger. B., & Fahle, M. (1997). Missed targets are more frequent than false alarms: A model for error rates in visual search. *Journal of Experimental Psychology: Human Perception and Performance, 23*(6), 1783–1791.

VISUAL COGNITION, 2006, 14 (4/5/6/7/8), 685–703

Ψ Psychology Press
Taylor & Francis Group

Oculomotor behaviour in visual search for multiple targets

Jason S. McCarley, Arthur F. Kramer, and Walter R. Boot

University of Illinois at Urbana-Champaign, IL, USA

Matthew S. Peterson

George Mason University, Fairfax, VA, USA

Ranxiao F. Wang and David E. Irwin

University of Illinois at Urbana-Champaign, IL, USA

Analysing response time (RT) data from a novel, multiple-target visual search task, Horowitz and Wolfe (2001) found evidence to suggest that the control of attention during visual search is not guided by memory for which of the items or locations within a display have already been inspected. Here, analysis of eye movement data from a similar experiment suggests that RT effects in the multiple-target search task are primarily due to changes in eye movements, and that effects which appeared to reveal memory-free search were actually produced by changes in oculomotor sampling behaviour.

With a series of recent reports, Horowitz and Wolfe (Horowitz & Wolfe, 1998, 2001, 2003; Wolfe, Alvarez, & Horowitz, 2000) have raised a surprising challenge for theorists of visual search. Models of search have largely converged on a common framework, postulating a hybrid architecture in which parallel preprocessing across the visual field guides the attentional selection of potential target items (e.g., Chelazzi, 1999; Duncan & Humphreys, 1989; Itti & Koch, 2000; Treisman & Sato, 1990; Wolfe, 1994; Wolfe, Cave, & Franzel, 1989). Efficiency of search is determined by the facility with which parallel mechanisms can steer attention toward the appropriate item.

Please address all correspondence to Jason S. McCarley, University of Illinois at Urbana-Champaign Institute of Aviation, Aviation Human Factors Division, 1 Airport Road, Savoy, IL 61874, USA. E-mail: mccarley@uiuc.edu

We thank J. Krummenacher, T.S. Horowitz, and C. Olivers for helpful comments on an earlier draft. This work was supported by a National Institute of Health grant to MSP (R01 MH64505).

DOI: 10.1080/13506280500194147

Search times will vary with the number of distractors in a display either when competition between target and distractors increases the time necessary for parallel processes to resolve the target's location (Chelazzi, 1999; Duncan & Humphreys, 1989) or when a unique target candidate cannot be identified by parallel processes and must be located through serial attentional scanning (Treisman & Sato, 1990; Wolfe, 1994). Otherwise, search times will be independent of distractors.

An assumption common to many of these models is that mechanisms exist to "cross off" items or locations as they are attended in the course of serial inspection, preventing wasteful revisits of attention to known distractors. Calculations of search rate in serial self-terminating models, for example, generally assume that no item is attended more than once; without this assumption, search rates as they are typically calculated would considerably overestimate the performance cost of each distractor (Horowitz & Wolfe, 1998). Klein and others (Klein, 1988; Müller & von Mühlenen, 2000; Takeda & Yagi, 2000; Tipper, Weaver, & Watson, 1996) have argued that revisits are prevented by inhibitory tags that are attached to stimuli as they are attended. Without some such trace, needless revisits to nontargets items would presumably hinder search dramatically. Horowitz and Wolfe, however, have questioned this assumption. Serial deployments of attention, they suggest, may be guided by bottom-up analysis of a visual display or by knowledge-driven facilitation of stimuli with known target features, but are not influenced by memory for where attention has already been. Visual search is not *memory-driven*, but *memory-free* or *amnesic*.

One apparent piece of evidence for memory-free search has come from a novel form of search task. Horowitz and Wolfe (2001) modified the traditional search paradigm by asking observers to search for multiple targets within a single display. The observer's task was to determine if a specified minimum number targets was present each trial. Digits and letters, respectively, served as targets and distractors. The total number of items present (targets plus distractors) was held constant across displays. The number of targets varied from trial to trial. Analogizing the task to an urn game, the authors described different patterns their reaction time (RT) data might take, one of which would provide evidence of memory-guided search and the other of which would suggest memory-free search. Mathematically, memory-guided serial search is a process of sampling without replacement from a pool of targets and distractors. Assuming that items are sampled one at a time, the expected value of S, the number of attentional samples needed to draw a criterion number n targets from a display containing t targets and d distractors, is a linear function of n (Johnson & Kotz, 1977): Solid lines in Figure 1 present the predicted numbers of samples necessary to find a criterion number of targets assuming a display of 15 items total containing either four or five targets present. Given a linear relationship between the

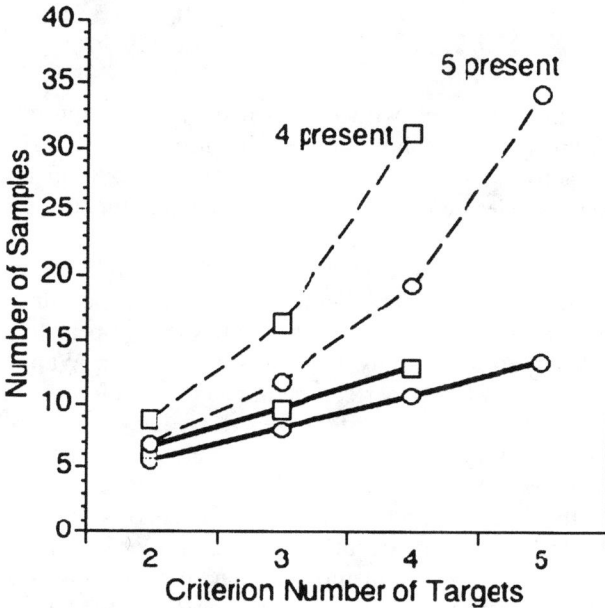

Figure 1. Data patterns for positive responses predicted by the memory-driven (solid lines) and memory-free (dashed lines) visual search models described by Horowitz and Wolfe (2001). Labels indicate number of targets present.

number of items sampled prior to a response and RT for that response, the RTs for correct positive responses under this model, holding the total display size constant, should therefore vary linearly with the criterion number of targets. Conversely, amnesic serial search in the multiple-target task is a process of sampling with replacement from a pool of targets and distractors. Again assuming that items are sampled singly, the expected value of S is given by the negative binomial distribution (Johnson & Kotz, 1977):

$$E[S] = \frac{n(t + d + 1)}{t + 1}$$

$$E(S) = 1 + \frac{d}{t}$$

Given that the pool of available targets decreases by one item and the pool of distractors increases by one following the discovery of each new target, the expected number of samples necessary to locate a criterion number n targets is given by:

$$E[S] = \sum_{i=1}^{n} \left(1 + \frac{d + i - 1}{t - i + 1} \right)$$

Predictions are presented with the dashed lines of Figure 1. Assuming once more a linear relationship between the number of items sampled and RT, RT for positive responses, holding total display size constant, will vary as a positively accelerated function of n. The RT functions reported by Horowitz and Wolfe (2001) were in fact positively accelerated, consistent with the predictions of the memory-free search model.

Evidence suggesting amnesic search, however, is puzzling in light of results from a number of eye movement studies that appear to demonstrate memory-guided search. A study by Peterson, Kramer, Wang, Irwin, and McCarley (2001) found near perfect memory in an oculomotor search task; fixations on previously inspected items were infrequent, and rarely appeared to result from memory lapses. As discussed elsewhere (McCarley, Wang, Kramer, Irwin, & Peterson, 2003), this impressive level of performance seems likely to have resulted in part from observers' use of mnemonic scanning strategies. Several other studies, however, have also found corroborating evidence for memory-driven oculomotor search, giving indication of two- to four-item memory capacity (Boot, McCarley, Kramer, & Peterson, 2004; Gilchrist & Harvey, 2000; Klein & MacInnes, 1999; MacInnes & Klein, 2003; McCarley et al., 2003). These effects appear attributable largely to *inhibition of return* (IOR; Boot et al., 2004; Klein & MacInnes, 1999; see Paul & Tipper, 2003, for discussion of relationship between IOR in cuing tasks and IOR in oculomotor search tasks), the tendency for observers to briefly inhibit a location from which attention has recently been withdrawn (Klein, 2000; Posner & Cohen, 1984). Interestingly, IOR is also known to affect the control of covert attention shifts— attentional shifts in the absence of eye or head movements—but appears to emerge only following activation of collicular mechanisms involved in saccade preparation (Rafal, Calabresi, Brennan, & Sciolto, 1989; Sapir, Soroker, Berger, & Henik, 1999). In light of these findings, Horowitz and Wolfe (2001) speculated that findings of memory-free attentional guidance might hold only in covert search. Eye movements may be memory-guided during visual search, in other words, while attentional processes operating within the course of a gaze are not.

Interestingly, the multiple-target search task provides a useful way to test the possibility that covert attention is memory free but overt attention is memory guided. The speculation that amnesic covert processing is responsible for deviations from linearity in the RT data for multiple-target search entails a clear assumption about oculomotor behaviour during task performance. Following Zelinsky and Sheinberg (1997), we can express the RT for a single trial of a visual search task as the sum $g_0 + g_1 + g_2 + \ldots + g_n$, where g_0 is initial saccade latency within a trial, g_i is the duration of the ith gaze thereafter (including the time needed for the saccade execution), and n is the total number of gazes executed in the course of search.[1] By definition, an overt attention shift is an eye and/or head movement, and a covert shift is a repositioning of attention in the absence of an eye or head movement (Posner, 1980). To ascribe an RT effect to covert attentional processes, then, is to assert that the effect was produced by a change in oculomotor gaze durations, not by a change in gaze frequency. In the present case, the hypothesis that overt but not covert search is memory guided amounts to a claim that the number of gazes executed per trial should increase as a linear function of the criterion number, and that nonlinearity in the manual RT data should be the result of concomitant increases in gaze duration.

It is possible, of course, that data will not conform to these predictions. In particular, it may be that curvilinearity in RT functions for multiple-target search is produced by changes in gaze frequency. How might we account for this pattern of effects? Such results might be taken as evidence of memory-free oculomotor search, counter to the reports noted above. Such a result would indicate that findings of memory-guided oculomotor search do not generalize to the multiple-target task, and would help to establish boundary conditions on the role of memory in guiding search. Alternatively, deviations from linearity might attributable to factors aside from lapses of memory for where the eyes have been. A straightforward way to test these possibilities is to assess the effects of criterion number on the frequency of *first-pass* gazes. First-pass gaze frequency indicates the number of different or unique stimuli gazed at each trial, ignoring return gazes on items that have already been looked at. If curvilinearity in overall gaze frequency functions is produced solely by a tendency for observers to revisit previously inspected items, then first-pass gaze frequency functions should match the predictions of a memory-driven model. After subtracting revisits, that is, we should be left with linear gaze frequency functions. Positively accelerated first-pass gaze frequency functions would therefore implicate changes in oculomotor sampling behaviour, unrelated to failures of memory-guided attention, as the source of deviations from linearity in RT and total gaze frequency functions.

The present experiment thus had two goals. The first was to determine whether deviations from linearity in the RT functions for multiple-target

---

[1] Nomenclature here differs slightly from that of Zelinsky and Sheinberg (1997), who discussed their data in terms of fixation durations rather than gaze durations. Analysis is focused on gazes rather than fixations in the current work, as gaze was deemed a more appropriate measure of a single oculomotor sample of given object. It seemed inappropriate, for example, to treat the fixation following a corrective saccade as a distinct attentional sample of the fixated object.

search are attributable solely to changes in gaze duration, as predicted by the memory-free covert/memory-guided overt search hypothesis, or whether they can be traced instead to changes in gaze frequency. The second was to determine whether curvilinear performance functions are the result of amnesic search processes, or might instead reflect changes in some other aspect of oculomotor behaviour as a function of criterion number. Toward that end, eye movement and manual response data were collected while observers performed a multiple-target search task similar to that of Horowitz and Wolfe (2001). Targets were Ts rotated 0°, 90°, 180°, or 270° from upright. To ensure generalizability of results, two variants of the experiment were conducted, one using plusses (+) as distractors and the other using crosses (X). On the basis of target distractor similarity, search in the former condition should be noticeably more difficult than in the latter.

METHOD

Observers

Observers were fifteen young adults recruited from the community of the University of Illinois at Urbana-Champaign. All had normal or corrected to normal visual acuity.

Apparatus

Stimuli were presented on a 21-inch monitor with resolution of 1024×768 pixels and 85 Hz refresh rate. Eye movements were recorded with an Eyelink eye tracker (SR Research Ltd) with temporal resolution of 500 Hz and spatial resolution of 0.2 degrees. An eye movement was classified as a saccade either when its distance exceeded 0.2 degrees and its velocity reached 30 deg/s, or its distance exceeded 0.2 degrees and its acceleration reached 9500 deg/s^2. Observers viewed displays from a distance of 72 cm, with viewing distance controlled by a chinrest.

Stimuli

Targets were 0.64° $\times$ 0.64° Ts randomly rotated 0°, 90°, 180°, or 270° degrees from upright. For one group of observers ($n = 7$) distractors were size-matched plusses. For another group ($n = 8$), distractors were size-matched Xs. Stimulus items were placed within the cells of a 5×5 grid with a centre-to-centre spacing of 4.78° between neighbouring cells. Within its cell each item was randomly jittered by up to 0.48° vertically and horizontally.

Procedure

Observers were asked to search displays for the presence of a criterion number of target items. The total number of stimulus items (target plus distractors) within a display was always 15, with the number of targets t varying between 1 and 5. The observer's task each trial was to determine whether a specified minimum number n of targets was present within the display. If the criterion number of targets or more was present, the observer was to respond by pressing the "F" on the experimental computer's keyboard. If fewer than the criterion number was present, the observer was to respond by pressing "J". Values of criterion number ranged from 2 to 5. A positive response was appropriate for half the trials within each block. For a given trial type, positive or negative, the number of targets present was selected at random from the appropriate range of values (0 to $n-1$ for negative trials; n to 5 for positive trials).

Each observer completed eight blocks of trials, two for each value of criterion number tested. Note that as criterion number increases, the set of values of t which qualify for a positive response decreases. When the criterion number is 2, for example, a positive response is appropriate for displays containing two, three, four, or five targets. When the criterion number is 5, on the other hand, a positive response is merited only when there are exactly five targets present. To obtain roughly equal numbers of trials for each combination of n and t demanding a positive response, therefore, it is necessary either to vary the proportion of positive responses within a block, or to include larger numbers of trials in some blocks than in others. Given that changes in the proportion of positive responses seemed likely to induce changes in observers' response criteria, we opted for the latter tactic. For values 2, 3, 4, and 5 of t, more specifically, there were, respectively, 20, 40, 60, 80, and 100 trials per block. Each block began with three randomly chosen practice trials. A text message to indicate the current criterion number was presented prior to each of the first four trials of a block, and a reminder message was presented every tenth trial thereafter. Order of blocks 1–4 was randomized for each observer under the constraint that each value of criterion number be used once. Order of blocks 5–8 was the same as that of blocks 1–4.

RESULTS

Presentation will centre on analysis of the four targets-present and five targets-present conditions in which a positive response was merited, since only these provide the data needed to distinguish between the models of interest. Data for conditions meriting a negative response are presented and discussed briefly below. Data for the two targets and three targets-present conditions in which a positive response was appropriate showed no effects inconsistent with the reported findings and are not discussed further. For analysis, data were submitted to one-way ANOVAs with the criterion number of targets (2, 3, or 4 for the four targets-present conditions, 2, 3, 4, or 5 for the five targets-present conditions) as a within-subjects factor. Data for the four and five targets-present conditions, and for the plus-shaped distractor and X-shaped distractor conditions, were analysed separately. Given the very specific predictions made by the competing models under consideration, presentation will focus on the results of linear and quadratic trend analyses rather than on the results of the omnibus ANOVAs. More specifically, linear trend analyses will be used to test for increases in dependent variables as a function of n, and quadratic trend analyses will be used to test the possibility that these increases were positively accelerated. Data for trials ending in an incorrect response are omitted from analyses of RT and eye movement data. Error rates were low (under 5%) in all positive response conditions and were positively correlated with RTs ($rs > .9$), mitigating concerns about speed–accuracy tradeoffs, and therefore are not discussed further. Statistical results for the remaining dependent variables of interest are presented in Table 1 (plus-shaped distractors) and Table 2 (X-shaped distractors).

TABLE 1

Trend analyses of data for search among plus-shaped distractors (degrees of freedom = 1, 6 for all analyses)

	Linear trend		Quadratic trend	
	F	P	F	P
Response times				
4 targets present	59.757	<.001	68.388	<.001
5 targets present	44.423	.001	89.117	<.001
Gaze frequencies				
4 targets present	55.065	<.001	19.066	.005
5 targets present	52.454	<.001	43.987	.001
Gaze durations				
4 targets present	14.013	.010	1.108	.333
5 targets present	7.682	.032	.477	.516
First-pass gazes				
4 targets present	59.570	<.001	10.209	.019
5 targets present	68.534	<.001	22.619	.003

TABLE 2
Trend analyses of data for search among X-shaped distractors (degrees of freedom = 1, 7 for all analyses)

	Linear trend		Quadratic trend	
	F	P	F	P
Response times				
4 targets present	24.699	.002	33.491	.001
5 targets present	38.783	<.001	17.583	.004
Gaze frequencies				
4 targets present	18.325	.004	29.819	.001
5 targets present	33.452	.001	20.434	.003
Gaze durations				
4 targets present	1.020	.345	2.280	.175
5 targets present	1.295	.293	7.281	.031
First-pass gazes				
4 targets present	22.506	.002	28.065	.001
5 targets present	43.676	<.001	25.864	.001

RTs and gaze frequencies

Figure 2 presents mean RTs (solid lines) and gaze frequencies (dashed lines) for trials ending in a correct positive response. Data for search among plus-shaped distractors are presented in panel A, data for search among X-shaped distractors in panel B. Each oculomotor fixation was classified as being on one object within the display, with the assignment of a fixation to an object determined by a nearest neighbour algorithm. In cases where the point of regard did not fall directly on an item, that is, the fixation was classified as being on the object nearest to the point of regard. Analysis using an alternative criterion, whereby a fixation was classified as being on a given object if the object fell within a 2° radius of the current point of regard, produced a pattern of results similar to that reported below. A gaze was defined as any number of consecutive oculomotor fixations on a single object. The fixation ongoing at the time of stimulus onset (i.e., preceding the first saccade of the trial) was not included in the gaze count.

As expected, search was faster in general among X-shaped distractors than among plus-shaped distractors. Patterns of effects, however, were similar across the two tasks. For search among either form of distractor, RTs and gaze frequencies both increased as the number of targets being sought increased. More importantly, changes in both measures were positively accelerated, inconsistent with the predictions of a model in which overt but not covert search is memory guided. The correlations between mean RT and mean gaze frequency were near perfect across both forms of distractors and

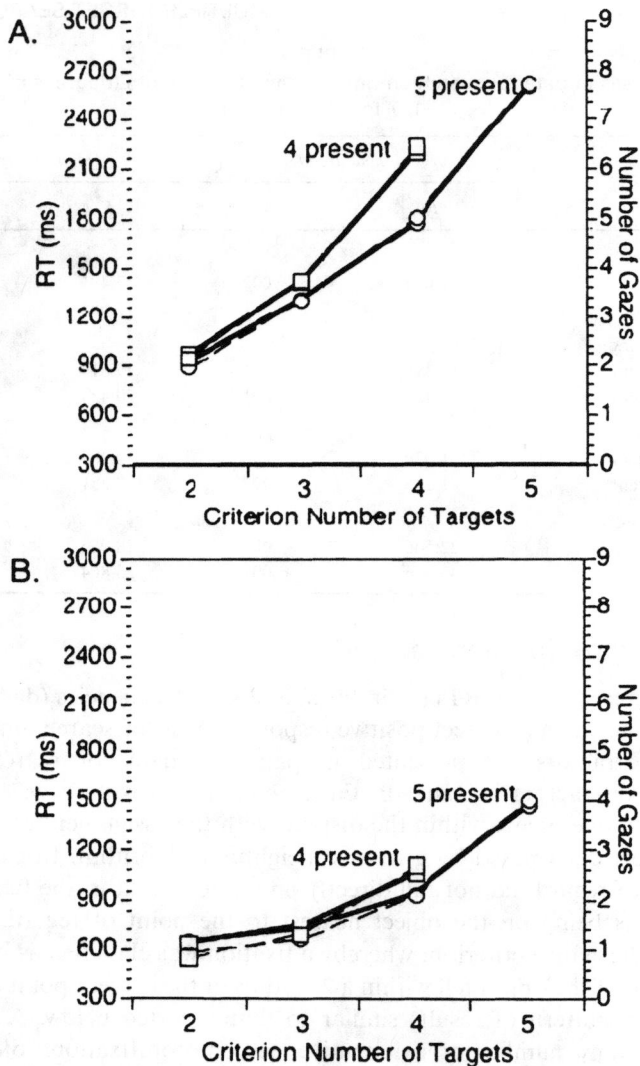

Figure 2. RTs and gaze frequencies for trials ending in a correct positive response for search among plus-shaped distractors (A) and X-shaped distractors (B).

both values of t, all rs $> .99$. RT data thus replicated the pattern of effects reported by Horowitz and Wolfe (2001), but contrary to the speculation that curvilinearity in the RT functions was produced by amnesic covert attention, nearly all of the variance in the RT data was accounted for by increases in numbers of gazes per trial.

694

Gaze durations

Figure 3 presents mean gaze durations for trials ending in a correct positive response. Durations for search among plus-shaped distractors increased reliably as a function of criterion number, as evidenced by significant linear trends in both the four targets-present and five targets-present data. Relative to the changes in RT, however, increases in gaze durations were modest. In the five targets-present condition, for example, an increase in criterion number from 2 to 5 produced a 25 ms increase in gaze duration. Given a concomitant increase of 5.7 gazes per trial, this change contributed only 142 ms to an overall increase of almost 1700 ms in RT. Data for search among X-shaped distractors showed no significant linear trend, suggesting little if any increase in gaze duration as an function of n. Consistent with the analyses of RTs and gaze frequencies described above, changes in gaze durations thus contributed very little to the steep increases in RT as a function of criterion number.

First-pass and return gazes

The above data indicate that curvilinearity in RT functions was produced almost entirely by changes in gaze frequency, contrary to the predictions of a visual search model in which covert but not overt attention is amnesic. To determine whether nonlinear gaze frequency data were evidence of memory-free overt search, data were divided into first-pass and return (i.e., second-pass and later) gazes. Solid lines in Figure 4 present mean numbers of first-pass gazes for trials ending in a correct positive response. Dashed lines present mean numbers of return gazes. The frequency of returns to previously inspected items did trend higher as criterion number increased, as would be predicted by a memory-free model of oculomotor search. Under no conditions, however, did the mean number of return gazes per trial exceed 1. Oculomotor revisits thus contributed only minimally to the increases in gaze frequency produced by an increase in n. Corroborating this conclusion, first-pass gaze frequency functions were positively accelerated, despite the fact that they included no revisits to earlier fixated stimuli. These results suggest that changes in oculomotor sampling behaviour, rather than a tendency to revisit previously attended items, were responsible for deviations from linearity in gaze frequency data.

RTs and gaze frequencies for negative responses

Figure 5 presents mean RTs and gaze frequencies for correct negative responses. Not surprisingly, the values of both measures tended to increase

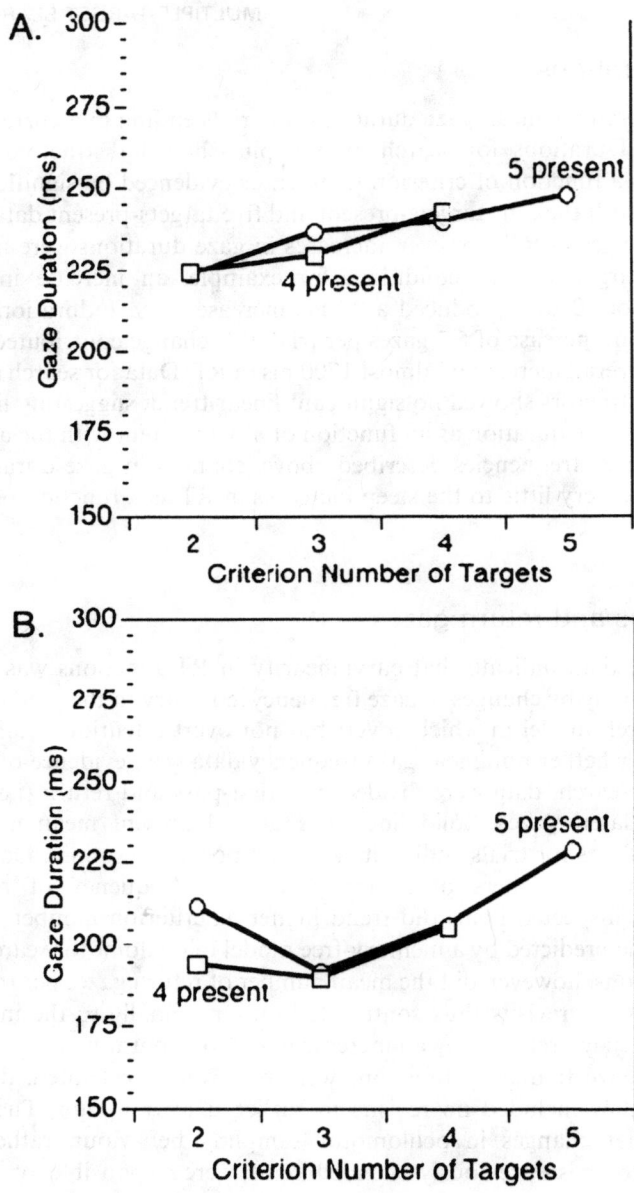

Figure 3. Gaze durations for trials ending in a correct positive response for search among plus-shaped distractors (A) and X-shaped distractors (B).

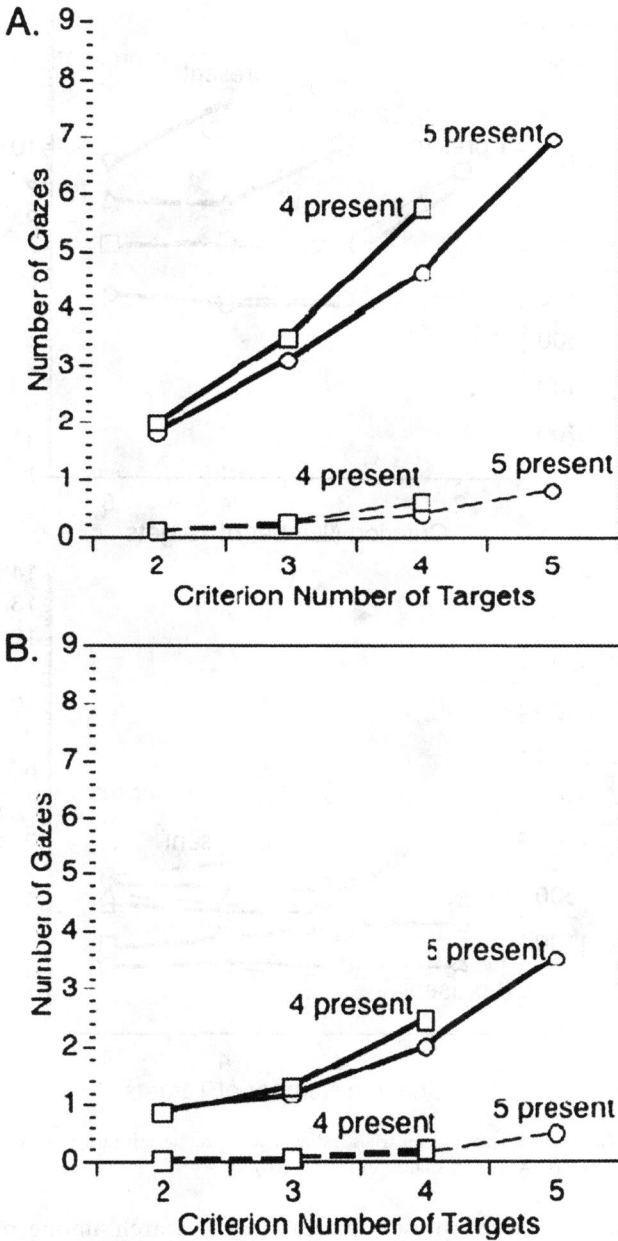

Figure 4. First-pass gaze frequencies (solid lines) and return gaze frequencies (dashed lines) for trials ending in a correct positive response for search among plus-shaped distractors (A) and X-shaped distractors (B).

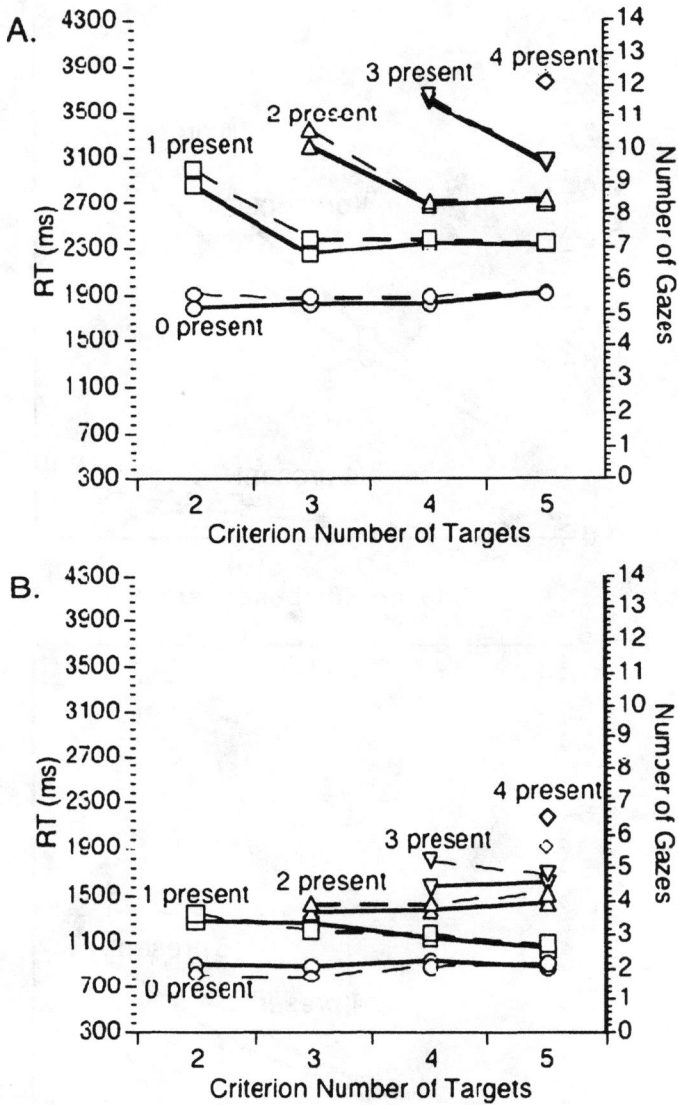

Figure 5. RTs and gaze frequencies for trials ending in a correct negative response for search among plus-shaped distractors (A) and X-shaped distractors (B).

as the number of targets present increased. For search among plus-shaped distractors, values tended to decrease as a function of n, while for search among X-shaped distractors, values were generally independent of n. Mean error rates ranged from 0% to 10%, but showed no significant effects of

698

criterion number. Negative response data thus showed no effects to contradict any of the conclusions drawn from analysis of the positive response data above.

DISCUSSION

Consistent with earlier reports (Horowitz & Wolfe, 2001), RTs in the present experiment rose according to a positively accelerated function as the criterion number of targets increased. Contrary to the hypothesis that curvilinear RT functions might be evidence of memory-free covert search, however, changes in RT were produced almost entirely by changes in the number of gazes executed each trial, and not by changes in gaze duration. In turn, gaze frequency functions were curvilinear even after removing redundant gazes on items that had been previously inspected, indicating that deviations from linearity were not caused primarily by oculomotor revisits as would be predicted by a memory-free model of overt search. Results indicate that curvilinear RT and gaze frequency functions were not produced by amnesic attentional guidance, but by changes in oculomotor behaviour as a function of criterion number.[2]

Interestingly, the present data accord nicely with the findings of Takeda (2004), who incorporated a manipulation of total set size (number of targets plus distractors) within a multiple-target search task like that employed here. Data showed a slowing of behavioural search rates as the number of targets being sought increased. Takeda concluded that the data were fit well by a memory-driven model in which search rates declined as a function of criterion number, mimicking the predictions of a memory-free model. The current results are consistent with this conclusion, and suggest more specifically that variations in search rate across criterion number are produced by changes in oculomotor sampling behaviour.

One possible explanation for these changes is that they reflect variations in the *perceptual span* with which observers search. Eye movement researchers have defined the perceptual span as the region of the visual field from which information is extracted during the course of an oculomotor fixation (Rayner, 1998). This region is not fixed within observers, but can vary with stimulus properties and cognitive load (e.g., Bertera & Rayner, 2000; Pomplun, Reingold, & Shen, 2001; Rayner & Fisher, 1987). When high target–distractor similarity (Rayner & Fisher, 1987) or increased cognitive task demands (Pomplun et al., 2001) make

---

[2] See Kristjánsson (2000), Müller and von Mühlenen (2000), Shore and Klein (2000), and von Mühlenen, Müller, and Müller (2003) for methodological discussion of other evidence offered for the memory-free search hypothesis.

search more difficult, for example, the perceptual span constricts. Notably, the qualitative pattern of effects predicted by the memory-driven and memory-free models described in the introduction (linear vs. positively accelerated functions) holds even if multiple items are processed in parallel with a single attentional sample. The prediction of linear gaze frequency functions from memory-driven search, however, is contingent on the assumption that the average number of items processed with each gaze is constant across changes in the number of targets sought. If the number of items sampled per gaze decreases as the criterion number increases, the number of gazes per trial will increase faster than predicted by a model that assumes a constant sample size, even if search is in fact memory driven. These considerations suggest that gaze frequencies might increase as a positively accelerated function of criterion number because of a tendency for observers to shift from processing many items per gaze over a wide perceptual span to processing fewer items per gaze over a narrow span. Such a change would be consistent with Takeda's (2004) conclusion that variations in search rate are responsible for deviations from linearity in RT data for multiple-target search; a contracting perceptual span would provide a mechanism to explain the decline in search rate that occurs as criterion number increases. The suggestion that observers were in general searching with a perceptual span of larger than 1 is confirmed by the finding that gaze frequencies were consistently lower than the number of attentional samples predicted by a model in which a single item is processed per sample (compare the gaze frequency data of Figure 2 to the predictions plotted in Figure 1). In other words, observers did appear to be processing multiple stimuli per gaze.

Why might the perceptual span narrow as a function of criterion number? One possibility is that decreases in span at larger values of n are the result of increased cognitive load. To perform the multiple-target search task, it is necessary for the subject to keep a mental record of which items have already been enumerated so as to avoid counting them more than once. As noted by Takeda (2004), an increase in criterion number therefore entails an increase in the number of items that must be remembered. This change in mental load might well constrict the perceptual span.[3] Another possibility is that narrowing of the span reflects a change in performance strategy, analogous to the shift from *subitizing* to *counting* that occurs when subjects are asked to enumerate varying numbers of items within a display (e.g., Jensen, Reese, & Reese, 1950; Trick & Pylyshyn, 1994). Subitizing, the ability to rapidly enumerate small numbers of items, appears to involve a parallel visual

---

[3] It possible that the strength of this effect varies by the form of working memory load—visuospatial, verbal, or executive (Baddeley, 1986)—imposed by the search task (Han & Kim, 2004; Oh & Kim, 2004; Woodman & Luck, 2004).

analysis over a diffusely attended area; counting, which becomes necessary when enumerating a larger number of items, appears to reflect the process of shifting a narrow attentional focus in serial between small groups of items. Within the multiple-target search task, it may be relatively easy even with a broad perceptual span to determine that the number of targets present exceeds a small criterion number. When the criterion number is larger, conversely, it may be necessary to narrow the perceptual span so that target items may be individuated and enumerated more carefully. Consistent with this possibility is the finding in the current data that deviations from linearity were more pronounced in the RT and gaze frequency functions for search among plus-shaped distractors than for search among X-shaped distractors. Given the higher target–distractor similarity of the former condition, attentional breadth may have been relatively narrow even when criterion number was small (Rayner & Fisher, 1987). Further research will be necessary, however, to test these various possibilities.

REFERENCES

Baddeley, A. D. (1986). *Working memory*. Oxford, UK: Oxford University Press.

Bertera, J. H., & Rayner, K. (2000). Eye movements and the span of the effective visual stimulus in visual search. *Perception and Psychophysics, 62*, 576–585.

Boot, W. R., McCarley, J. S., Kramer, A. F., & Peterson, M. S. (2004). Automatic and intentional memory processes in visual search. *Psychonomic Bulletin and Review, 11*, 854–861.

Chelazzi, L. (1999). Serial attention mechanisms in visual search: A critical look at the evidence. *Psychological Research, 62*, 195–219.

Duncan, J., & Humphreys, G. W. (1989). Visual search and stimulus similarity. *Psychological Review, 96*, 433–458.

Gilchrist, I. D., & Harvey, M. (2000). Refixation frequency and memory mechanisms in visual search. *Current Biology, 10*, 1209–1212.

Han, S. H., & Kim, M. S. (2004). Visual search does not remain efficient when executive working memory is working. *Psychological Science, 15*, 623–628.

Horowitz, T. S., & Wolfe, J. M. (1998). Visual search has no memory. *Nature, 394*, 575–577.

Horowitz, T. S., & Wolfe, J. M. (2001). Search for multiple targets: Remember the targets, forget the search. *Perception and Psychophysics, 63*, 272–285.

Horowitz, T. S., & Wolfe, J. M. (2003). Memory for rejected distractors in visual search? *Visual Cognition, 10*, 257–298.

Itti, L., & Koch, C. (2000). A saliency-based search mechanism for overt and covert shifts of visual attention. *Vision Research, 40*, 1489–1506.

Jensen, E., Reese, E., & Reese, T. (1950). The subitizing and counting of visually presented fields of dots. *Journal of Psychology, 30*, 363–392.

Johnson, N. L., & Kotz, S. (1977). *Urn models and their applications*. New York: Wiley.

Klein, R. M. (1988). Inhibitory tagging facilitates visual search. *Nature, 334*, 430–431.

Klein, R. M. (2000). Inhibition of return. *Trends in Cognitive Science*, 138–147.

Klein, R. M., & MacInnes, W. J. (1999). Inhibition of return is a foraging facilitator in visual search. *Psychological Science, 10*, 346–352.

Kristjánsson, Á. (2000). In search of remembrance: Evidence for memory in visual search. *Psychological Science*, *11*, 328–332.

MacInnes, W. J., & Klein, R. M. (2003). Inhibition of return biases orienting during the search of complex scenes. *The Scientific World*, *3*, 75–86.

McCarley, J. S., Wang, R. F., Kramer, A. F., Irwin, D. E., & Peterson, M. S. (2003). How much memory does oculomotor search have? *Psychological Science*, *14*, 422–426.

Müller, H. J., & von Mühlenen, A. (2000). Probing distractor inhibition in visual search: Inhibition of return. *Journal of Experimental Psychology: Human Perception and Performance*, *26*, 1591–1605.

Oh, S. H., & Kim, M. S. (2004). The role of spatial working memory in visual search efficiency. *Psychonomic Bulletin and Review*, *11*, 275–281.

Paul, M. A., & Tipper, S. P. (2003). Object-based representations facilitate memory for inhibitory processes. *Experimental Brain Research*, *148*, 283–289.

Peterson, M. S., Kramer, A. F., Wang, R. F., Irwin, D. E., & McCarley, J. S. (2001). Visual search has memory. *Psychological Science*, *12*, 287–292.

Pomplun, M., Reingold, E. M., & Shen, J. (2001). Investigating the visual span in comparative search: The effects of task difficulty and divided attention. *Cognition*, *81*, B57–B67.

Posner, M. I. (1980). Orienting of attention. *Quarterly Journal of Experimental Psychology*, *32*, 3–25.

Posner, M. I., & Cohen, Y. (1984). Components of visual orienting. In H. Bouma & D. G. Bouwhuis (Eds.), *Attention and performance X: Control of language processes* (pp. 531–556). Hove, UK: Lawrence Erlbaum Associates Ltd.

Rafal, R. D., Calabresi, P. A., Brennan, C. W., & Sciolto, T. K. (1989). Saccade preparation inhibits reorienting to recently attended locations. *Journal of Experimental Psychology: Human Perception and Performance*, *15*, 673–685.

Rayner, K. (1998). Eye movements in reading and information processing: 20 years of research. *Psychological Bulletin*, *124*, 372–422.

Rayner, K., & Fisher, D. L. (1987). Eye movements and the perceptual span during visual search. In J. K. O'Regan & A. Levy-Schoens (Eds.), *Eye movements: From physiology to cognition* (pp. 293–302). Amsterdam: North-Holland.

Sapir, A., Soroker, N., Berger, A., & Henik, A. (1999). Inhibition of return in spatial attention: Direct evidence for collicular generation. *Nature Neuroscience*, *2*, 1053–1054.

Shore, D. I., & Klein, R. M. (2000). On the manifestations of memory in visual search. *Spatial Vision*, *14*, 59–75.

Takeda, Y. (2004). Search for multiple targets: Evidence for memory-based control of attention. *Psychonomic Bulletin and Review*, *11*, 71–76.

Takeda, Y., & Yagi, A. (2000). Inhibitory tagging in visual search can be found if search stimuli remain visible. *Perception and Psychophysics*, *62*, 927–934.

Tipper, S. P., Weaver, B., & Watson, F. L. (1996). Inhibition of return to successively cued spatial locations: Commentary on Pratt and Abrams (1995). *Journal of Experimental Psychology: Human Perception and Performance*, *22*, 1289–1293.

Treisman, A., & Sato, S. (1990). Conjunction search revisited. *Journal of Experimental Psychology: Human Perception and Performance*, *16*, 459–478.

Trick, L. M., & Pylyshyn, Z. W. (1994). Why are small and large numbers enumerated differently? A limited-capacity preattentive stage in vision. *Psychological Review*, *101*, 80–102.

Von Mühlenen, A., Müller, H. J., & Müller, D. (2003). Sit-and-wait strategies in dynamic visual search. *Psychological Science*, *14*, 309–314.

Wolfe, J. M. (1994). Guided Search 2.0: A revised model of visual search. *Psychonomic Bulletin and Review*, *1*, 202–238.

Wolfe, J. M., Alvarez, G. A., & Horowitz, T. S. (2000). Attention is fast but volition is slow. *Nature*, *406*, 691.

Wolfe, J. M., Cave, K. R., & Franzel, S. L. (1989). Guided Search: An alternative to feature integration model for visual search. *Journal of Experimental Psychology: Human Perception and Performance*, *15*, 419–433.

Woodman, G. F., & Luck, S. J. (2004). Visual search is slowed when visuospatial working memory is occupied. *Psychonomic Bulletin and Review*, *11*, 269–274.

Zelinsky, G. J., & Sheinberg, D. L. (1997). Eye movements during parallel-serial visual search. *Journal of Experimental Psychology: Human Perception and Performance*, *23*, 244–262.

VISUAL COGNITION, 2006, 14 (4/5/6/7/8), 704–715

Ψ Psychology Press
Taylor & Francis Group

Evidence for a systematic component within scan paths in visual search

Iain D. Gilchrist

Department of Psychology, University of Bristol, UK

Monika Harvey

Department of Psychology, University of Glasgow, UK

We present evidence that scan paths in visual search can include a systematic component. The task for subjects in the experiment was to search for a target that was either present or absent. With regular grid-like displays, participants generated more horizontal saccades than vertical saccades. Disruption of the grid structure in the display modulated but did not eliminate the systematic component. This is consistent with the scan path being partly determined by a cognitive strategy. We discuss the implications of this finding for studies that use refixation to investigate memory mechanisms in visual search.

Monitoring eye movements during visual search has become an important method for investigating the processes that mediate between display onset and the manual response (e.g., Findlay, 1997; Hooge & Erkelens, 1996, 1999; Zelinsky & Sheinberg, 1997). Models of visual search and particularly ones that include the programming of saccades, have tended to focus on bottom up salience driven mechanisms for saccade allocation to items in the display (e.g., Itti & Koch, 2000). At the centre of most of these models is a salience map of one form or another. The salience of items is determined by the strength of the visual input to the system and by the characteristics of the target. So, for example if the target is a green vertical bar then green items and vertical items will have enhanced salience. This is the mechanism by which attention (Wolfe, 1994; Wolfe, Cave, & Franzel, 1989) or saccades (Findlay & Walker, 1999; Itti & Koch, 2000; Wolfe & Gancarz, 1996) are deployed to items that are more similar to the target. Over and above these

Please address all correspondence to I. D. Gilchrist, Department of Psychology, University of Bristol, Bristol BS8 1TN, UK. E-mail: I.D.Gilchrist@bristol.ac.uk

This work was supported by a grant from the EPSRC UK (grant no: GR/M37295). We would like to thank Casimir Ludwig for help with data collection.

DOI: 10.1080/13506280500193719

salience-based processes it is assumed that the location to be fixated next is determined by a random process (Itti & Koch, 2000; Scinto, Pillalamarri, & Karsh, 1986). However, four decades ago Williams (1966) suggested that there was often a bias in the direction of saccades in search and that these biases reflected a systematic process rather than the action of a random process (see also Norton & Stark, 1971a, 1971b; Yarbus, 1967). This observation is of course consistent with introspection. When search becomes difficult we tend to start in one place and work systematically through the display. In this paper we have used Williams' (1966) term "systematic" to describe this nonrandom component in the scan path. Although there have been qualitative reports of a systematic component in scanning (e.g., Hooge & Erkelens, 1996), it has not been studied quantitively. Indeed early attempts to quantify scan paths in visual search lead to the conclusion that random-walk models best characterized the allocation of fixations in search (Scinto et al., 1986). More recently, Motter and Belky (1998) investigated the extent to which the previous saccade influenced the characteristics of the subsequent saccade. They found no evidence for either the length or the direction of the previous saccade having a large influence on the subsequent saccade, except for a slight bias for the next saccade to avoid the area just crossed by the saccade. One of the reasons for the lack of evidence for systematic scanning in visual search may be that although scanning could be purely systematic, such a process will often operate alongside other salience-based processes to determine which item is fixated next. If systematic scanning is not the sole factor determining the structure of the scan path it may not be easy to detect its presence. In this paper we report an experiment in which we record eye movements in visual search. The purpose of this report is to (1) describe a method by which systematic patterns in scan path structure can be identified, (2) demonstrate that systematic scanning does occur in visual search, and (3) show that the extent of this behaviour is modulated by, but relatively robust to, substantial disruption of display structure.

One of the difficulties of detecting the presence of systematic scanning behaviour is developing methods by which it can be detected both across trials and across participants and then analysed using statistical techniques. Following Williams' (1966) claim that there is often a directionality to successive fixations, in the current experiment we analysed the frequency of saccade directions. Analysis of saccade direction has the potential to reveal systematic patterns, even when they are combined with other mechanisms to determine the final scan path.

In the current experiment, across three conditions, we manipulated the regularity of the display while keeping display size and the display elements constant and analysed the frequency of saccades in each direction across conditions.

EXPERIMENT

In all three conditions the target was an upright triangle, and the distractor items were downward pointing triangles and leftward pointing triangles. In Condition 1 the items were completely regular, less regular in Condition 2, and even less so in Condition 3.

Method

Participants.   Twelve adults (9 female and 3 male, age range 19–45 years) took part in the study. All were from the University of Bristol and were paid, or received course credit, for their time.

Design and procedure.   The experiment was a repeated measures design, with the order of condition presentation presented in separate blocks and counterbalanced across the participants. Viewing distance was 57 cm. The participants were instructed to make a present/absent response using a button box.

At the beginning of each trial, a small white disc with a black dot in its centre appeared in the middle of the screen. Online compensation for any spatial offset in the calculated eye position was made at this point before each trial.

The display was then presented until a manual response was made and, when appropriate, this was followed by an error message presented centrally on the screen. Participants were given verbal instructions describing the task and asked to respond as quickly and accurately as possible.

Displays were presented on a 17-inch SVGA monitor with 800×600 pixel resolution. A chinrest was used to minimise head movements. In all conditions the target was an upright triangle and the distractor items were triangles pointing downwards and pointing to the left (see Figure 1), display size was 25 items. In trials where the target was not present, the target was replaced with one of the distractor types.

Each of the three blocks contained 98 trials. Participants were given a break of approximately 3 minutes between blocks of trials. In Condition 1 the 25 items were placed randomly on the junctions of an imaginary 5×5 grid resulting in a spatially regular display. In Condition 2 the same 25 display items were placed randomly on the junctions of an imaginary 6×6 grid leaving 12 randomly selected locations blank in each trial. And in Condition 3, the display items were placed randomly on the junctions of an imaginary 7×7 grid, leaving 24 randomly selected locations blank in each trial. Across all three conditions the overall display size was kept constant (12×12 deg). As a result, Condition 1 was the most spatially structured

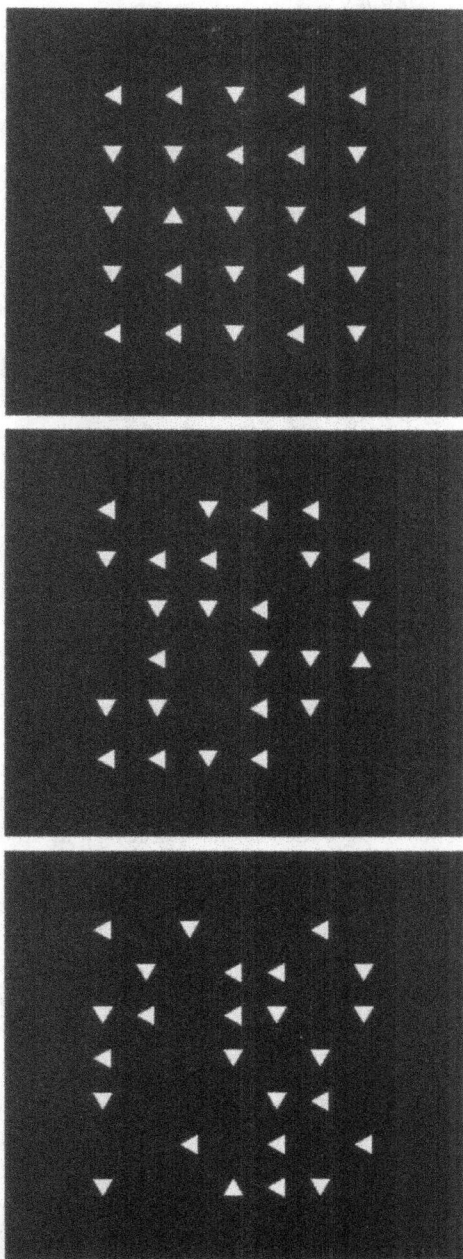

Figure 1. Example displays: Condition 1 (upper panel), Condition 2 (middle panel). and Condition 3 (lower panel).

707

display and Condition 3 was the least structured display. Example displays can be seen in Figure 1.

Eye movement recording and analysis. Two dimensional, binocular eye movements were recorded using an SMI Eye-Link eyetracker (SensoMotoric Instruments GmbH, Berlin, Germany). The Eye-Link system uses an infrared video technique sampling at 250 Hz, and features a head movement compensation mechanism. Displays were presented on one PC (subject PC), while a second PC (operator PC) recorded the eye position data online. Each block of trials was preceded by a nine-point calibration and validation procedure.

The eye position data were analysed off line by an automatic saccade detection procedure. For each participant, the data were analysed only from the eye that produced the best spatial resolution, which in this experiment was typically 0.20 deg.

A fixation was defined as having ended when the eye velocity exceeded 30 deg/s. A fixation began after the velocity fell below this value for five successive samples (20 ms). This rather stringent criterion excludes the interval of ocular instability just after the saccade and so leads to a more accurate calculation of fixation location which is an important measure in the current experiment. However, as a result the fixation durations reported in this paper may be shorter (by approximately 15 ms) than those typically reported elsewhere. The absolute direction of all the saccades larger than 1 degree was analysed. Saccades were coded for direction in degrees with saccades in a vertical direction coded as zero. For each participant, in each condition, the frequency of saccades in each direction in 10 degree frequency bins was calculated. As the total number of saccades was large, even for a single participant, these data could be analysed using standard parametric tests. The percentage of fixations outside the display area was 3.3% in Condition 1, 4.5% in Condition 2, and 6.1% in Condition 3. These fixations were excluded for subsequent analyses.

Results

Errors. The percentages of manual response error trials per condition were 6.72%, 7.14%, and 6.38%, for Conditions 1, 2, and 3 respectively. Most errors occurred on target-present trials (13.3%) rather than target-absent trials (0.68%). Error trials were excluded from later analyses.

Reaction times. Mean reaction times in the three conditions are shown in Table 1. A repeated measures ANOVA was carried out on these data. Reaction times were slower for target-absent (4665 ms) than for target-present (2549 ms), $F(1, 11) = 63.7$, $p < .001$; but there was no reliable effect

TABLE 1

The mean reaction times (in ms), fixation duration (in ms), and number of fixations in the experiment; values are given for target-present and target-absent trials by condition, with standard deviations in parentheses

Measure	Condition 1		Condition 2		Condition 3	
	Present	Absent	Present	Absent	Present	Absent
Mean reaction time (ms)	2443	4596	2752	4723	2453	4676
SD	(755)	(1663)	(849)	(1626)	(650)	(1604)
Mean fixation duration (ms)	225	217	221	213	221	214
SD	(29)	(23)	(22)	(20)	(21)	(19)
Mean number of fixations	10.7	18.5	11.6	18.3	11.0	19.0
SD	(3.0)	(6.2)	(3.2)	(5.9)	(2.8)	(6.10)

of Condition, $F(2, 22) < 1$. There was also no significant interaction between condition and target presence, $F(2, 22) < 1$. Inspection of Table 1 revealed that numerically there were only very small differences between the conditions.

Fixation duration and fixation number. The total number of fixations examined in each condition were 17,196 in Condition 1, 17,619 in Condition 2, and 17,635 in Condition 3. Mean fixation duration and the number of fixations per trial are shown in Table 1. A repeated measures ANOVAs revealed a significant effect of target presence on fixation duration, with fixations in target present trials being longer (222 ms) than fixations in target absent trials (215 ms), $F(1, 11) = 12.7$, $p < .01$. However, there was no significant effect of condition, $F(2, 22) = 2.15$, $p = .140$, nor a significant interaction, $F(2, 22) < 1$. For the number of fixations per trial there was again a significant effect of target presence in that there were, on average, more fixations in the target absent trials (18.6 fixations) than the target present trials (11.1 fixations), $F(1, 11) = 58.9$, $p < .001$. There were no reliable effects of condition, $F(2, 22) < 1$. The interaction did not reach significance but was marginal, $F(2, 22) = 2.90$, *ns. p* = .08. For fixation duration and fixation number, there was no evidence for reliable differences between conditions.

Saccade direction. The distribution of saccade directions in the three conditions is shown in Figure 2.

A repeated measures ANOVA was carried out on saccade direction frequency. There was no significant effect of condition, $F(2, 22) < 1$. However, there was a significant effect of direction, $F(35, 385) = 15.5$,

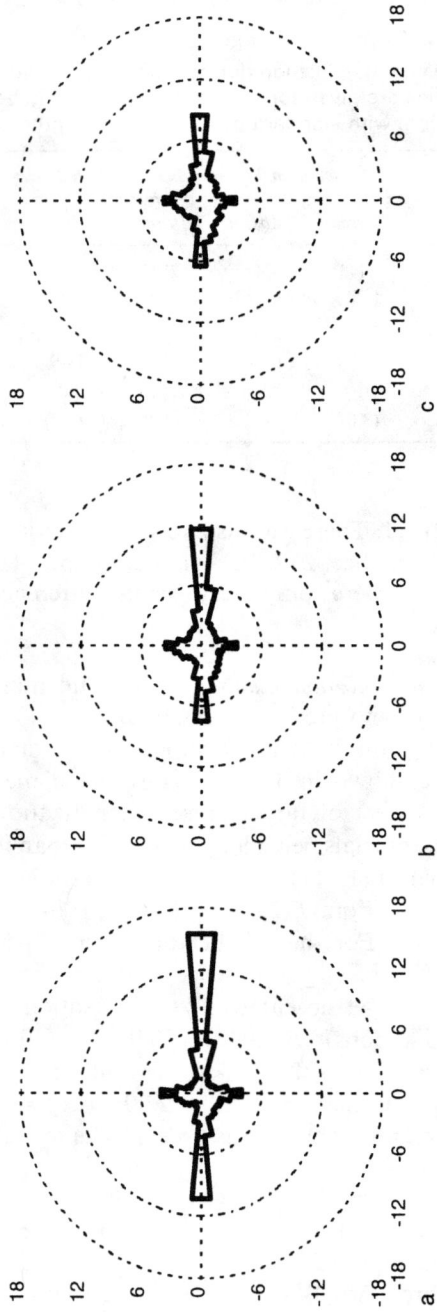

Figure 2. The distribution of the angle of movement of each saccade in Condition 1 (panel a), Condition 2 (panel b), and Condition 3 (panel c).

$p < .001$, indicating a reliable increase in the number of saccades generated in a specific direction consistent with a systematic component in the scan paths. In addition there was a significant interaction, $F(70, 770) = 5.75$, $p < .001$. Pairwise comparisons between each of the three conditions showed a significant interaction in all cases: Conditions 1 and 2, $F(35, 385) = 4.56$, $p < .001$; Conditions 2 and 3, $F(35, 385) = 3.25$, $p < .001$; Conditions 1 and 3, $F(35, 385) = 7.73$, $p < .001$. These interactions reflect a decreasing asymmetry in the saccade direction distributions from Conditions 1 to 3.

There was evidence for systematic scanning in all three conditions as reflected in the main effect of direction. The systematic scanning effect took the form of more horizontal saccades than other directions. In addition this effect was strongest for the more structured displays. These effects on saccade direction were not apparent from simple inspection of single scan paths, and it certainly was not possible to differentiate the extent of these effects between conditions by inspection alone.

Discussion

In the current experiment we found strong evidence for systematic scanning in visual search. The method introduced allowed the detection of properties of the scanning that were consistent across participants and across conditions. The extent of systematic scanning was modulated by display structure: As the display became less regular across conditions so the asymmetries in the directions of the saccades produced was reduced. However, there was even evidence for such asymmetries in Condition 3 where the regularity of the display had been significantly disrupted. One possibility is that the asymmetries in the directions of the saccades produced here simply reflect low-level oculomotor biases. For example, even the organization of oculomotor muscles may lead to biases in the number of saccades in each direction. However, here we have shown that the extent of these asymmetries differs across different display conditions. If the effect was a result of low-level oculomotor factors we would expect it to be constant across condition. In a comparison between the conditions, we found no reliable differences between reaction time and number of fixations. This suggests that task difficulty was relatively well matched across conditions. However, as the distribution of saccade direction shows, the manipulation of display regularity had a systematic and reliable effect on the nature of the scanning. The experiment also allows an important additional conclusion to be drawn. Although systematic scanning was modulated by display regularity, the results from Conditions 2 and 3 confirm that systematic scanning occurs even for displays that are not perfectly regular. Indeed the results suggest that these effects are relatively robust to quite large disruptions of the regularity of the structure as can be seen in Condition 3. If the regularity of the display structure were reduced further the presence of any detectable systematic behaviour may be further reduced and even disappear. The current experiment did not investigate this change in detail. Instead it demonstrated that systematic scanning does not depend solely on a completely regular display and is not dependent solely on task difficulty. However, most naturalist visual scenes do contain an extensive complex spatial structure (Marr, 1982). In these more visually complex conditions it may be that this structure shapes systematic scanning. The form that the systematic scanning took in this experiment was almost certainly a function of the type of structure that was imposed on the displays: specifically the display items were placed randomly on the intersections of a grid. However, previous work by Hooge and Erkelens (1996) has shown that participants will systematically scan around circular displays, suggesting that systematic scanning is not a behaviour restricted only to grid based displays.

Memory processes have an influence on search behaviour at a number of levels (Shore & Klein, 2000). However, one contentious issue is the extent to which visual search relies on memory mechanisms to prevent items that have been inspected from being reinspected. Estimates of the capacity for this type of memory have ranged from no memory at all (Horowitz & Wolfe, 1998) to a limited memory capacity (Gilchrist & Harvey, 2000), and to a more extensive memory capacity (Peterson, Kramer, Wang, Irwin, & McCarley, 2001). One approach to this question has been to record eye movements in order to get a more direct measure of where attention is allocated at any one time. The key measure here has been the extent of refixation of distractors. The logic is that when no refixation occurs then the items have been remembered. A number of groups have modelled this kind of data to obtain an estimate of the capacity of the memory store (Gilchrist & Harvey, 2000; Peterson et al., 2001). This leads to two key, interrelated, questions. The first is what does it mean when an item is refixated? And the second is, what does is mean when an item is not refixated? The answer to neither of these questions is straightforward. What does it mean when an item is refixated? Refixating a distractor item in visual search appears to suggest that the subject has forgotten that the item has been visited and so is returning to reinspect it. However, as Gilchrist and Harvey (2000) pointed out, refixations can also occur because the participant moved away from the fixated item before the processing of that item was completed. The refixation in this case simply reflects a return to the item to complete processing. Indeed such deadline limiting of fixation duration is part of the influential model of saccade control developed by Henderson (1992). What does it mean when an item is not fixated? One possibility is that visual processing in the periphery has ruled out that item as a possible target. This process of visual guidance is an important determinant of saccadic selection in search (e.g., Findlay, 1997). However, a number of researches in this field have ruled out guidance by using display items that are very small, or very similar to that target (e.g., Peterson et al., 2001), so that it is impossible to distinguish the target from distractors without fixating. It would appear then that if the stimuli in the search task are correctly selected, an item not being fixated is evidence for memory. However, the story may not be that simple. The evidence presented here suggests that saccades in visual search can be systematic. If the saccades generated by participants are not random, but instead have a systematic component, then this itself can reduce refixations. In the most extreme case, where participants follow a fixed route thorough the display no refixations will occur. The lack of refixations would not be a product of remembering specifically which items had been visited but instead would reflect the consequence of following a predictable route. If such a mechanism does influence scan paths then a lack of refixations in a task may not be a hallmark of memory in search. In turn this suggests that when the display has a structure that can drive systematic scanning it is possible that systematic scanning can substitute for memory. If participants follow broadly the same scan path on each trial this would allow them to eliminate part of the display simply because it occurred earlier in the search. In the current experiment there is a decrease in the extent of strategic scanning across conditions. If the above argument is correct, then we would expect a concurrent increase in task difficulty because participants were less able to rely on systematic scanning to support efficient search. This increase in task difficulty should be reflected in an increase in the number of fixations and an increase in the overall response time: We found neither in the current experiment. There are a number of possible explanations for this apparent anomaly. Various authors have suggested that memory capacity in search is quite large (e.g., Peterson et al., 2001); however, the deployment of this memory might in itself require effort (Gilchrist, North, & Hood, 2001). In the current experiment what may have occurred is a tradeoff between memory deployment and systematic behaviour resulting in approximately equivalent overall search performance. Another possibly is that, in the less regular displays, participants were still engaging in the same amount of systematic scanning but that the particular form of scanning adopted varied either across subjects or even trial-to-trial. If the form of the systematic scanning is inconsistent then the method presented in this paper is unable to detect its presence—instead the method presented here detects systematic scanning that is consistent across trials and participants. Further work would clearly be needed to disentangle these possibilities. However, whatever the explanation, the current experiment demonstrates the presence of systematic scanning in search. The presence of systematic scanning does not rule out memory processes as being important in search. However, what is clear is that a number of mechanisms appear to structure scan paths in more difficult visual search. Understanding the relationships between these mechanisms and developing methods to detect and quantify their effects is an important step in understanding the search process. As a step towards this, the present paper presents a method for detecting and statistically analysing systematic components in scan paths.

REFERENCES

Findlay, J. M. (1997). Saccade target selection during visual search. *Vision Research*, *37*, 617–631.

Findlay, J. M., & Walker, R. (1999). A model of saccade generation based on parallel processing and competitive inhibition. *Behavioral and Brain Science*, *22*, 661–721.

Gilchrist, I. D., & Harvey, M. (2000). Refixation frequency and memory mechanisms in visual search. *Current Biology*, *10*, 1209–1212.

Gilchrist, I. D., North, A., & Hood, B. (2001). Is visual search really like foraging? *Perception*, *30*, 1459–1464.

Henderson, J. M. (1992). Visual attention and eye movement control during reading and picture viewing. In K. Rayner (Ed.), *Eye movements and visual cognition* (pp. 261–283). Berlin: Springer-Verlag.

Hooge, L. T. C., & Erkelens, C. J. (1996). Control of fixation duration in a simple search task. *Perception and Psychophysics*, *58*, 969–976.

Hooge, I. T. C., & Erkelens, C. J. (1999). Peripheral vision and oculomotor control during visual search. *Vision Research*, *39*, 1567–1575.

Horowitz, T. S., & Wolfe, J. M. (1998). Visual search has no memory. *Nature*, *394*, 575–577.

Itti, L., & Koch, C. (2000). A saliency-based search mechanism for overt and covert shifts of visual attention. *Vision Research*, *40*, 1489–1506.

Marr, D. (1982). *Vision*. San Francisco: W. H. Freeman.

Motter, B. C., & Belky, E. J. (1998). The guidance of eye movements during active visual search. *Vision Research*, *38*, 1805–1815.

Norton, D., & Stark, L. (1971a). Eye movements in visual perception. *Scientific American*, *224*, 34–43.

Norton, D., & Stark, L. (1971b). Scanpaths in saccadic eye movements while viewing and recognising patterns. *Vision Research*, *11*, 929–942.

Peterson, M. S., Kramer, A. F., Wang, R. X. F., Irwin, D. E., & McCarley, J. S. (2001). Visual search has memory. *Psychological Science*, *12*, 287–292.

Scinto, L. F. M., Pillalamarri, R., & Karsh, R. (1986). Cognitive strategies for visual search. *Acta Psychologica*, *62*, 263–292.

Shore, D. I., & Klein, R. M. (2000). On the manifestations of memory in visual search. *Spatial Vision*, *14*, 59–75.

Williams, L. G. (1966). The effect of target specification on objects fixated during visual search. *Perception and Psychophysics*, *1*, 315–318.

Wolfe, J. M. (1994). Guided Search 2.0: A revised model of visual search. *Psychonomic Bulletin and Review*, *1*, 202–238.

Wolfe, J. M., Cave, K. R., & Franzel, S. L. (1989). Guided Search: An alternative to the feature integration model for visual search. *Journal of Experimental Psychology: Human Perception and Performance*, *15*, 419–433.

Wolfe, J. M., & Gancarz, G. (1996). Guided Search 3.0: A model of visual search catches up with Jay Enoch 40 years later. In V. Lakshminarayanan (Ed.), *Basic and clinical applications of vision science* (pp. 189–192). Berkeley, CA: Kluwer Academic Publishers.

Yarbus, A. L. (1967). *Eye movements and vision*. New York: Plenum Press.

Zelinsky, G. J., & Sheinberg, D. L. (1997). Eye movements during parallel-serial visual search. *Journal of Experimental Psychology: Human Perception and Performance*, *23*, 244–262.

VISUAL COGNITION, 2006, 14 (4/5/6/7/8), 716–735

Ψ **Psychology Press**
Taylor & Francis Group

The preview search task: Evidence for visual marking

Christian N. L. Olivers

Vrije Universiteit Amsterdam, The Netherlands

Glyn W. Humphreys and Jason J. Braithwaite

University of Birmingham, UK

A series of experiments are reviewed providing evidence for the idea that when new visual objects are prioritized, old objects are inhibited by a top-down controlled suppression mechanism—a process referred to as visual marking. Evidence for the top-down aspect of visual marking is presented, by showing that new object prioritization, as measured in the preview paradigm, depends on task settings and available attentional resources. Evidence for the inhibitory aspect is presented, by showing that selection of new items is impaired when these items share features with the old items. Such negative carryover effects occur within as well as between trials. Alternative accounts and the evidence for them is discussed. It is concluded that the various accounts are not mutually exclusive and that the data is best explained by a combination of mechanisms.

There has been much debate on how new object onsets are prioritized in visual search. That they can be prioritized is now beyond reasonable doubt, as numerous researchers have found either advantages in search when the target is defined (or cued) by a new onset, or disadvantages when one of the distractors is defined (or cued) by a new onset (e.g., Folk, Remington, & Johnston, 1992; Remington, Johnston, & Yantis, 1992; Theeuwes, Kramer, Hahn, & Irwin, 1998b; Todd & Kramer, 1994; Yantis & Jonides, 1984). Debates have centred on whether onsets have a special status in this respect (Jonides & Yantis, 1988; Miller, 1989), whether they capture attention in an automatic, bottom-up manner or are subject to top-down control (Atchley, Jones, & Hoffman, 2003; Donk & Theeuwes, 2003; Folk et al., 1992; Gibson & Kelsey, 1998; Peterson, Belopolsky, & Kramer, 2003; Theeuwes, 1991;

Please address all correspondence to Chris Olivers, Cognitive Psychology, Van der Boechorststraat 1, 1081 BT Amsterdam, The Netherlands. Email: cnl.olivers@psy.vu.nl

The work reviewed here was supported by grants from the Medical Research Council (UK) and a PhD studentship from the School of Psychology, University of Birmingham, awarded to J.B.

DOI: 10.1080/13506280500194188

Watson & Humphreys, 2000; Yantis & Jonides, 1984, 1990), and whether new onset prioritization merely involves activation of the new elements or also inhibition of the old elements (Donk & Theeuwes, 2001, 2003; Donk & Verburg, 2004; Olivers & Humphreys, 2003; Watson & Humphreys, 1997; Watson, Humphreys, & Olivers, 2003; see also Jiang, Chun, & Marks, 2002, for an account in terms of temporal grouping). The present paper focuses on the latter two debates. We review existing as well as new evidence in favour of the hypothesized mechanism we have called visual marking. Visual marking is the top-down inhibition of irrelevant old information, in anticipation of the appearance of relevant new information. We propose that this mechanism operates together with (but is not the same as) bottom-up attentional activation by new onsets and grouping by common onset.

THE PREVIEW BENEFIT AND VISUAL MARKING

Watson and Humphreys introduced the preview paradigm to investigate further the mechanisms underlying the selection of new objects (Watson & Humphreys, 1997). Figure 1 illustrates the crucial conditions behind this paradigm, together with idealized results. Typically participants may be given a 1000 ms preview of a set of distractors (e.g., green Hs), before adding a second set of items to the display (e.g., blue A distractors and a blue H target). Once the second set is presented, the display conforms to that used in standard conjunction search tasks. However, in this preview condition, search is much more efficient than in the standard conjunction baseline, in which both green and blue distractors appear simultaneously. In fact, search slopes are often no higher than in a standard single feature baseline, in which only the second set (the blue items) is present. Apparently, participants can use the preview period to ignore the old items and limit their search to the new items only. Thus, although the physical appearance of the distractors does not change, the fact that they appear earlier in time and at different locations than targets reduces their influence on selection (see also Treisman, Kahneman, & Burkell, 1983).

In explaining the preview benefit, Watson and Humphreys (1997) proposed that the old items are inhibited in anticipation of the new items—a mechanism referred to as visual marking. They further found that the preview benefit was disrupted when participants performed a secondary task during the preview period. Consequently, visual marking was envisaged as a top-down process: The inhibition is only applied when necessary and when there are sufficient attentional resources.

The present paper consists of three parts. In the first part, we summarize evidence for the top-down aspect of new object prioritization, showing that the preview benefit depends on task requirements and attentional resources.

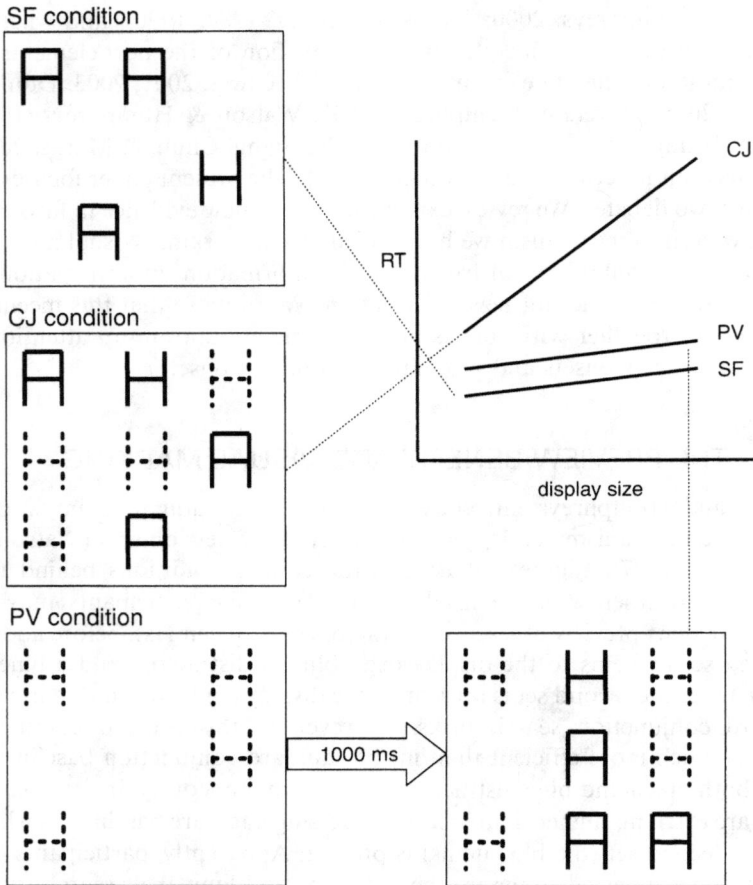

Figure 1. Schematic representation of the preview paradigm and its typical results. In the single feature (SF) condition, the target is a blue H amongst blue A distractors. In the conjunction (CJ) condition the target is a blue H amongst blue As and green Hs. In the preview (PV) condition, the green Hs are presented first for 1000 ms, followed by the addition of the blue set. Note that the PV search slope resembles that of the SF rather than the CJ condition. The results here are idealized for illustration purposes.

In the second part, we summarize evidence for the inhibitory aspect of new object prioritization, showing that ignoring old items may have negative effects on new items when they share a feature or location with the old items. Together, the evidence supports the visual marking hypothesis. In the third and final part we discuss alternative accounts of the preview benefit, such as the automatic onset capture account (Donk & Theeuwes, 2001), and the temporal grouping account (Jiang et al., 2002).

SELECTION OF NEW ONSETS IS SUBJECT TO TOP-DOWN CONTROL

The study of new onset prioritization was kickstarted by the work of Yantis and Jonides (1984), who found that, in visual search, items defined by an abrupt new onset received priority over items defined by an offset, even when the target was unlikely to be defined by an onset. Yantis and Jonides concluded that the abrupt onsets captured attention automatically. However, later studies have suggested that abrupt onset capture may at least partly be subject to top-down control (e.g., Folk et al., 1992; Gibson & Kelsey, 1998). For instance, Yantis and Jonides (1990) themselves showed that abrupt onsets do not capture attention if observers are focused on a specific location.

Several studies have now shown that the prioritization of new objects in the preview paradigm is similarly under the influence of top-down control. In one of the first experiments, Watson and Humphreys (1997) showed that the preview benefit was disrupted when participants performed the additional task of shadowing a series of digits presented at the centre of the preview display. Apparently, the secondary task required attentional resources that were otherwise used to prioritize the new items. This goes against the idea that new items are prioritized completely automatically. One potential problem with this study was that there was not only an additional task during the preview period, but there were also additional visual stimuli in the display. This may have disrupted the preview on a lower, more sensoric level, rather than on a more central attentional resource level. To control for this, Olivers and Humphreys (2002) presented the secondary task before rather than during the preview period, manipulating available resources by inducing an attentional blink (i.e., the unavailability of attention for about 500 ms due to the processing of an earlier target; Raymond, Shapiro, & Arnell, 1992). They found that the preview benefit was completely abolished when the previewed items were presented inside the attentional blink period. Similarly, Humphreys, Watson, and Jolicoeur (2002) have found disruptions of new object prioritization not only with a visual, but also with an auditory secondary task, which suggests again that more central attentional resources are required during the preview.

Additional evidence for top-down control in preview search comes from studies showing that the prioritization of new items is task dependent. In one experiment, Watson and Humphreys (2000) occasionally presented a probe dot on either one of the old or one of the new items and the participant's task was to detect this probe. On the remaining trials the task was to find a visual search target in the new set. As expected, dot detection accuracy for probes presented on old items was worse than on new items, indicating that the latter were prioritized. Interestingly, the difference between old and new items almost disappeared when the task changed so that probe dots were to be detected on all trials (and the visual search target became irrelevant). This provides direct support for the idea that new onset prioritization is task-dependent. Similar results for both response times (RTs) and accuracy data have been reported by Olivers and Humphreys (2002) and Humphreys, Jung-Stalmann, and Olivers (2004). Finally, Olivers, Humphreys, Heinke, and Cooper (2002) found that new onsets were less strongly (or not at all) prioritized when the old items had just previously been relevant to the observer, either because a target was possibly hidden among the old items, or because these items were required for another task such as estimating their number. Together, these results support the idea that new onset prioritization is subject to intentional, and attentional, control.

SELECTION OF NEW ONSETS IS SUBJECT TO INHIBITORY CARRYOVER EFFECTS

Another line of evidence in favour of the visual marking account involves inhibitory carryover effects from one stimulus to the other. Several studies now show that the selection of new items is hampered if they share features such as colour, orientation, location, and possibly other properties, with previewed distractors. The findings suggest that visual marking makes use of these features to effectively ignore irrelevant information. The approach is very much reminiscent of the negative priming paradigm, in which a distractor presented on one trial becomes the target on the next. The typical finding is that processing of this target is delayed relative to targets that are unrelated to previous trials (e.g., Tipper, 1985), suggesting its representation is inhibited. Here we will review evidence for carryover effects between trials as well as between old and new sets within a trial.

Between-trial carryover effects

Direct evidence for an inhibitory mechanism comes from a study by Olivers and Humphreys (2002, Exp. 4). Figure 2 shows a schematic representation of the tasks involved. The participant's first task was to identify a target letter from a stream of letters presented rapidly and serially at fixation (a so-called RSVP stream). This task typically induces an attentional blink, a temporary lapse of attention of up to about 500 ms (Raymond et al., 1992). Immediately following the RSVP stream, a preview of green H distractors was presented for 450 ms, followed by a set of blue items. The second task was to search for a blue H target in this second set. Crucially, by presenting the RSVP target either early or late in the stream, the previewed distractors could be moved either outside or inside the attentional blink period. We

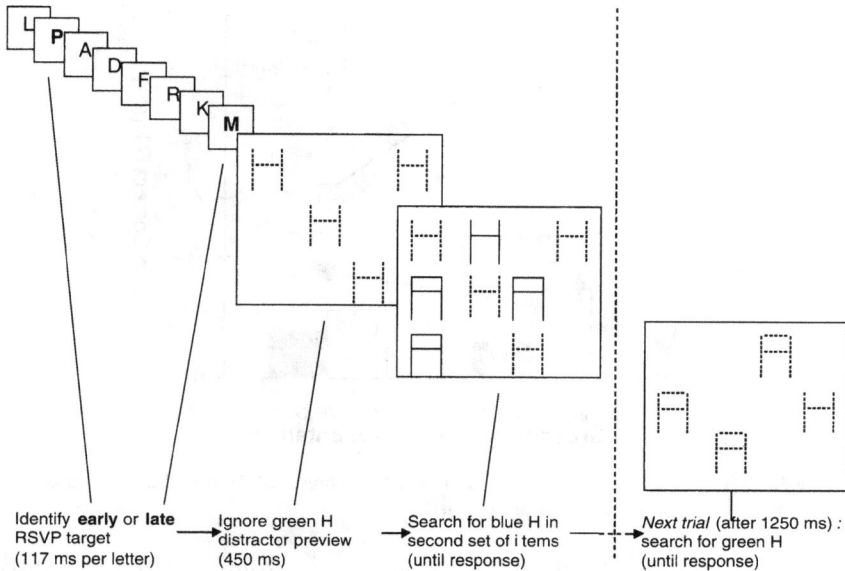

Figure 2. Schematic representation of the combined rapid serial visual presentation (RSVP) and preview task used in Experiment 4 of Olivers and Humphreys (2002). Adapted from Olivers and Humphreys (2002) with permission from Elsevier.

hypothesized that the attentional blink, when induced late in the stream, would take away vital attentional resources from the top-down inhibition mechanism applied to the previewed green Hs. Consequently, the search for the blue H would be slowed by the presence of unsuppressed distractors. This was exactly the result, as is shown by the top line in Figure 3: RTs to blue H targets were longer when green H distractors had been presented inside the blink compared to outside the blink. More important in the present context however was the effect on the next trial. This trial never involved an RSVP task, but instead a simple search for a green H target amongst green A distractors. Note that the target on this task was the same as the previewed distractors on the previous trial. The argument was again that when the green H distractors were presented outside the blink on the previous trial, they received stronger inhibition than when presented inside the blink. If so, turning them into the target on the subsequent trial might slow down search relative to when there were insufficient resources to suppress them in the first place. The results confirmed this hypothesis, as shown by the bottom line in Figure 3. Search was slower for green H targets when green H distractors had previously been presented outside the blink. This finding suggests some suppression was carried over from one trial to the next, on the basis of shared colour, or perhaps shared form. Taken

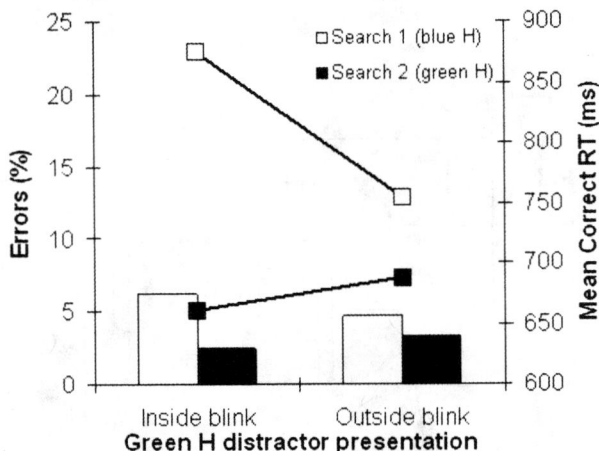

Figure 3.   Results from Experiment 4 of Olivers and Humphreys (2002). Adapted from Olivers and Humphreys (2002) with permission from Elsevier.

together the results provide direct evidence for a resource-limited inhibitory mechanism applied to old items, as proposed under the visual marking hypothesis. They also indicate that this mechanism is at least in part feature based.

Similar conclusions can be drawn from a previously unpublished experiment. In this experiment, 58 participants (mean age 22.8 years, range 18–39) previewed one set of items for 300 ms, and searched a second set of items on each trial. The two sets differed in both colour and orientation, and the target was defined by the direction of an arrow (left/right) on one of the new bars (see Figure 4 for some example displays). The crucial factor was the relationship between two consecutive trials. In the unrelated condition, the two sets on any trial n would differ in both colour and orientation from the two sets on trial $n-1$. In the repeat first set condition, the first set of trial n was the same as the first set of trial $n-1$ (in colour and orientation, but not necessarily location, as bars were randomly repositioned). In the first set becomes second condition, the second set on trial n was the same as the first set of trial $n-1$ (again, in colour and orientation, not location). We hypothesized that, if the first set is being inhibited and some of this inhibition persists across trials, repeating the first set would result in a benefit relative to unrelated trials, since the same information is inhibited again. In contrast, when the inhibited items become the to-be-searched items, we may expect a cost relative to unrelated trials. Figure 5 shows the mean RTs for correct trials of each trial type (unrelated, repeat first set, first set becomes second). An ANOVA revealed that RTs varied significantly with trial type, $F(2, 114) = 7.87$, $MSE = 3622.9$, $p = .001$. Importantly, RTs were

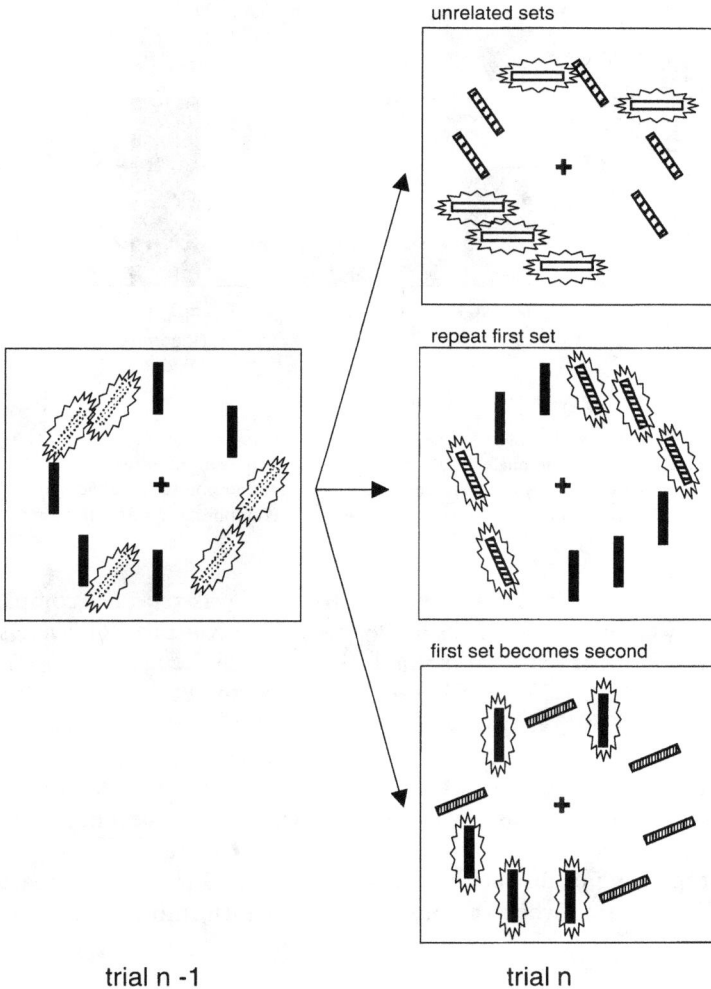

unrelated sets

repeat first set

first set becomes second

trial n -1   trial n

Figure 4. Schematic representation of the different conditions of Experiment 1. The "bangs" represent the new bars. Not drawn here are the small arrows that were present on the centres of the bars. The target bar contained a left- or right-pointing arrow, the other new bars up- or down-pointing arrows. The previewed bars also contained left- or right-pointing arrows. Each trial started with a grey fixation dot followed after 500 ms by two sets of six bars, one presented for 300 ms, before the other was added. The trial ended with a 500 ms blank screen. The bars measured 0.18 degrees wide ×0.72 degrees tall and their centres were randomly placed on the perimeter of a virtual circle with a radius of 3.80 degrees from fixation. The two sets differed in colour (red, green, blue, yellow, pink, grey, which were isoluminant for the first author) as well as orientation (starting from vertical, rotated 0, 22.5, 45, 67.5, 90, 112.5, 135, and 157.5 degrees). Colour and orientation were selected pseudorandomly depending on the intertrial relationship.

723

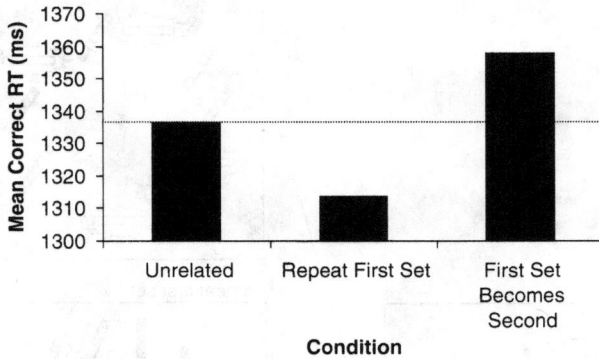

Figure 5. RT results of the intertrial carryover experiment reported in the main text. when item colour and orientation were unrelated to the previous trial. when items in the first set were the same as items in the first set of the previous trial. and when items in the second set were the same as items in the first set of the previous trial. Adapted from Olivers and Humphreys (2003) with permission from Elsevier.

indeed faster. by 23 ms, when the first (old) set was repeated compared to when sets were unrelated, $t(57) = 2.06$. $p < .05$. In contrast, RTs were slower, by 21 ms, when the searched (second) set had been the ignored (first) set on the previous trial. $t(57) = 2.01$. $p < .05$. The error rates were stable across conditions. as 3.50% errors were made in the unrelated condition, 3.55% in the repeat first set condition, and 3.44% in the first set becomes second condition. These results provide further evidence for the idea that previewed items are inhibited, as is put forward by the visual marking hypothesis. Apparently, some of this inhibition persists across trials, resulting in more efficient ignoring of distractors when the previewed items are repeated, but less efficient search when the previewed items turn into the to-be-searched items.

Within-trial carryover effects

In addition to the between-trial carryover effects, other work indicates that similar carryover effects occur between sets within a trial. Braithwaite and colleagues (Braithwaite & Humphreys, 2003; Braithwaite. Humphreys, & Hodsoll, 2003: see also Gibson & Jiang, 2001) had participants search for either one of two target letters ("N" or "Z") amongst a set of random distractor letters. all of which could appear in various colours. This is typically a slow and inefficient task. However, in line with previous work (e.g., Kaptein, Theeuwes, & van der Heijden, 1995). search was much improved by giving the participant information on the target's colour (even though it was not the only item in the display sporting that colour). Search also improved by presenting a preview of distractors, as observers could limit their search to the new set. In fact, search was most efficient when there was a preview and knowledge about the target's colour, indicating that observers made use of both types of information at the same time. However, search efficiency suffered when the target had the same colour as the previewed items relative to when it had a different colour. This was true regardless of whether or not the participant knew the target's colour, that is, the beneficial effects of target colour knowledge and the detrimental effects of target—distractor colour sharing were additive. Braithwaite et al. (2003) therefore concluded that observers may employ two types of attentional set: A "positive" (excitatory) set for the to-be-searched target colour, and a "negative" (inhibitory) set for the to-be-ignored distractor colour. When an item carries a to-be-ignored as well as a to-be-found feature, the net result may be that the two sets cancel each other out.

Similar ideas were put forward by Olivers and Humphreys (2003) on the basis of the effects distractor previews had on the attentional capture by unique targets and distractors (often called singletons; Pashler, 1988). Olivers and Humphreys (2003) presented participants with preview tasks in which, as before, one set of distractors was shown first, followed by the addition of another set of distractors, including a target. Either the target or one of the new distractors could be a singleton, carrying a salient colour and/or orientation. Figure 6 illustrates some of the conditions. Note that the singleton was always in the second set, and it was also always unique relative to this second set. Olivers and Humphreys argued that if the second (new) set is simply prioritized directly, without observers having to inhibit the preview, the singleton should retain its attention-guiding capacity and lead to benefits in search when it is a target, and to costs when it is a distractor. If, however, previewed items are suppressed, and some of this suppression is carried over to the new display on the basis of feature similarity, then we should expect reduced effects from singletons that share features with the old items. Figure 7 shows the typical costs when the singleton was a distractor, for conditions in which there was no preview (i.e., the single feature condition), in which there was a preview of 1000 ms which stayed on, in which there was a 1000 ms preview but one that switched off when the new items appeared, and in which there was a 100ms preview, again switching off as soon as the new items appeared. Singletons possessing a different colour than the previewed items retained their attention capturing capacity, as costs remained constant across the conditions. In contrast, singleton costs were much reduced when the singleton shared its colour with the previewed items—even when the previewed items had already been switched off by the time the singleton appeared. Similar effects were found for singleton targets (not shown here).

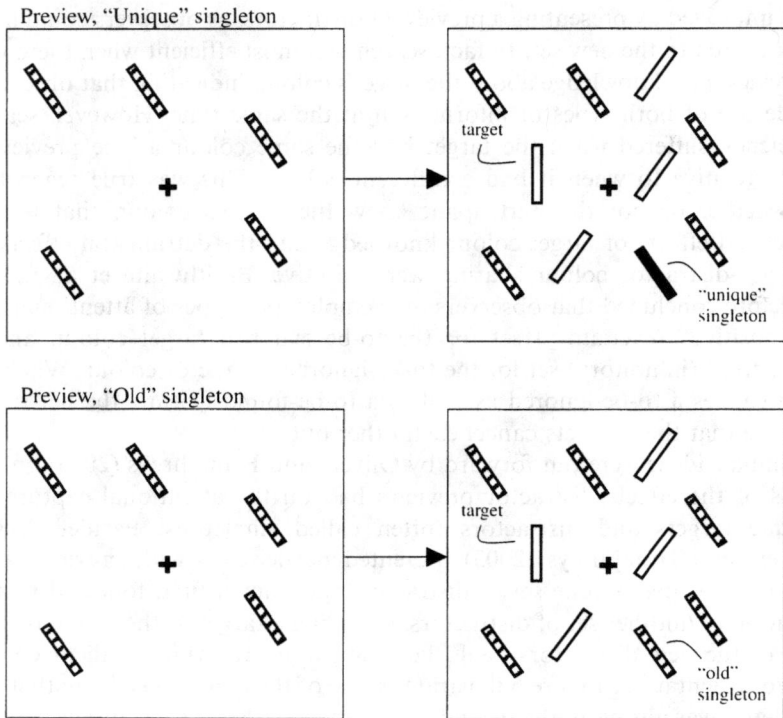

Figure 6. Stimulus examples from the singleton inhibition paradigm of Olivers and Humphreys (2003). Adapted from Olivers and Humphreys (2003) with permission from Elsevier.

The idea of two attentional sets, one for the target information, one for the distractor information, was also proposed by Theeuwes and Burger (1998). They found that in an inefficient search task, a singleton distractor could be ignored, but only when both the target and distractor colour were known from trial to trial. When either of the two varied, the singleton interfered with search. Theeuwes and Burger concluded that singleton distractors capture attention due to strong bottom-up activation. Only when observers know what to attend to and know what to inhibit can they exert maximum top-down control over selection and eliminate this bottom-up activation caused by singleton distractors.

A final study worth pointing out in this section is one of the first preview experiments looking at within-trial carryover effects, and which actually found no such effects. In this experiment, Watson and Humphreys (1997), Exp. 7) presented an initial preview set of green distractors, followed by a mainly blue target set that also included some additional green distractors. The number of green items in the first and second set was varied, but always

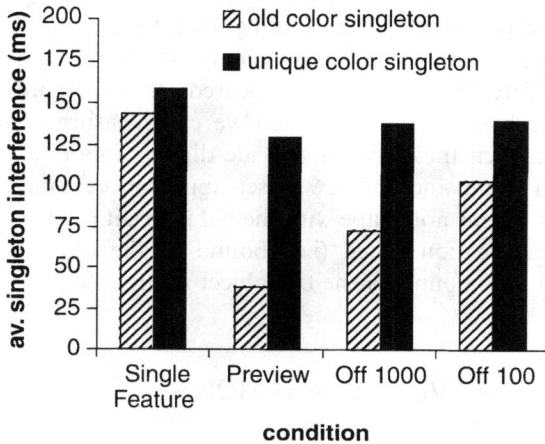

Figure 7. Results for the singleton distractor conditions of Experiment 4 of Olivers and Humphreys (2003). Shown is the average interference caused by singleton distractors in the new (second) set, when this singleton shares its colour with the old items (in the preview conditions) or has a unique colour.

added up to a constant number, so that the more green items there were in the first, the fewer there were in the second. The rationale behind the experiment was that if the old green items are inhibited through their distinguishing feature (i.e., green), the new green items should also be inhibited and therefore not affect search. However, Watson and Humphreys found a systematic effect on search rates of the number of green items in the new set. They concluded that the inhibition was not feature based. Note though that an increase of the number of green items in the new set was confounded with a decrease in the number of green items in the old set. It is possible that the strength of the inhibition depends on the number of items that need to be inhibited. For example, it may be easier to ignore one new green item after having ignored seven old green items than to ignore seven new items after having ignored only one old green item. Moreover, even though the new green items may have been suppressed, this does not mean they could not compete at all in search. Any inhibition may have been counteracted by onset-related activation (either top down or bottom up).

Location- or object-based carryover effects

So far, we have discussed between- and within-trial carryover effects on the basis of feature similarity. In a way, the probe dot studies referred to earlier provide another version of these effects. Of special interest is the study by Humphreys et al. (2004). They found that the detection of dots occasionally presented on old items not only suffered relative to new items, but also relative to dots presented on an empty background grid (the grid was present to control for luminance masking). These costs relative to the background were already present before the new items appeared. If we regard the background as a suitable baseline against which we can measure relative activation and inhibition, then these results provide direct support for the suppression of old items in advance of new onset appearances. Since the probe dots shared neither colour nor shape with the old items, it is likely that this inhibition was either location based (i.e., bound to the old object's location) or object based (i.e., bound to the old object itself).

ALTERNATIVE EXPLANATIONS

Automatic capture by new onsets

Donk and Theeuwes (2001; see also Belopolsky, Theeuwes, & Kramer, 2005; Donk, 2006 this issue; Peterson et al., 2003) have claimed that the preview benefit is not due to the top-down inhibition of old items, but merely the result of the automatic activation of the new items, caused by their abrupt luminance transients (cf. Todd & van Gelder, 1979). Initial support for this claim comes from three experiments in which Donk and Theeuwes (2001) varied the relative luminance of the items to their background. In their first experiment both old and new items were green on an equiluminant grey background. It was found that the number of old items had a substantial effect on search, indicating that they could not be excluded from selection. In the second experiment, the old items were initially presented in green on a (nonequiluminant) black background. The background luminance was then gradually increased so that by the time they appeared, the new elements were equiluminant with the background. Again it was found that the old items affected search efficiency anew items could not be fully prioritized. In the third experiment, the old items were presented on an equiluminant grey background. The background luminance was then gradually lowered, so that by the time they appeared, the new elements were defined by a luminance difference relative to this background. Now the old elements did not affect search and the new elements were completely prioritized. Donk and Theeuwes interpreted these findings as evidence that a luminance onset is required for new items to be prioritized, whereas the relative luminance of the old items does not matter. Furthermore, in a follow-up study, Donk and Theeuwes (2003) showed that new items received priority over old items even when the target was equally likely (or even more likely) to appear in the old set (cf. Yantis & Jonides, 1984), suggesting that the new object priority was automatic rather than top-down controlled.

A number of remarks can be made here. First, although we believe there is sound evidence for the idea that old visual information can be inhibited, we do not take this to imply that the influence of attentional capture by abrupt new onsets should be excluded. We do not wish to deny that capture by new onsets plays an important role, especially when the new onsets are relevant to the task. We simply believe that this mechanism can be augmented by the top-down inhibition of old items. Second, recent studies have suggested that luminance information is not that crucial to obtain a preview benefit. Humphreys et al. (in press) found a preview benefit even though in their displays all items were, on average, equiluminant with each other and with the background grid, while random dynamic luminance noise was added to these displays to further mask any overall luminance differences between items. Furthermore, a recent study by Braithwaite, Humphreys, Watson, and Hulleman (2005) indicates that a preview benefit may be found with equiluminant stimuli if the preview period is extended to 3 s (rather than the typical 1 s), suggesting that the representation (and subsequent inhibition) of equiluminant information may need time to build up. Why Donk and Theeuwes (2001) did not find a preview benefit with their displays remains an open question, but one possibility is that the items were generally quite difficult to distinguish (as is the case with green items on a grey background), or that the gradual ramping up of the background luminance disrupted the preview.

A third remark is that even if new items are prioritized through their onset, it is unlikely that this is a completely stimulus-driven process as proposed by Donk and Theeuwes. As we have outlined above, whether old items are inhibited or not, prioritization of new items is subject to task settings as well as to the availability of attentional resources, indicating a strong top-down component. The fact that Donk and Theeuwes (2003) found that new objects were prioritized even when the target was more likely to be in the old set does not negate a top-down explanation. In their study, the target always appeared together with the new set (even when the target was in the old set; it was then defined by an equiluminant colour change of one of the old items, simultaneous with the appearance of the new set), and the onset capture may thus have been contingent upon the active anticipation of this new set, because this set indicated the beginning of the search task (see Gibson & Kelsey, 1998, for the same argument). In contrast, when participants start searching the old set before the new set appears, prioritization of the new items is disrupted, as was found by Olivers et al. (2002).

Temporal grouping

Jiang, Chun, and Marks (2002) have proposed that the preview benefit is the result of temporal grouping. The old distractors are grouped on the basis of their common temporal dynamics (i.e., their common onset), as are the new items. The two groups may thus be separated (and searched) on the basis of their asynchrony. Jiang and Wang (2004) later extended this account by proposing that search through the new items is aided by two mechanisms: One quickly decaying memory for the temporal asynchrony of the new items relative to the old items, and a more persistent visual short-term memory for about four to five new items. Interestingly, several neuroimaging studies have now indicated that bilateral superior (and also inferior) parietal areas play an important role in the preview task relative to single set and full set baseline search tasks (Humphreys, Kyllingsbæk, Watson, Olivers, & Paulson, 2004; Olivers, Smith, Matthews, & Humphreys, 2005; Pollmann et al., 2003). These areas have been thought to be part of a top-down frontoparietal attention and short-term memory network (see for reviews, Corbetta, 1998; Kanwisher & Wojciulik, 2000; Kastner & Ungerleider, 2000), but also to play a role in the spatiotemporal dynamics of stimuli (Coull, Frackowiak, & Frith, 1998; Gottlieb, Kusunoki, & Goldberg, 1998). Recently, we have found additional evidence that the parietal lobe plays a crucial role in distinguishing new from old items (Olivers & Humphreys, 2004). We presented patients suffering from posterior parietal damage with a preview task and compared them to age-matched controls. Whereas the control participants could effectively ignore the old items and prioritize the new set (resulting in a preview benefit), the patients had severe difficulties in detecting the new target, to the extent that there was no benefit and sometimes even a cost relative to a full set baseline in which all items were presented simultaneously. This result held even when search was made easier or when segregation between old and new was promoted by an outline shape drawn around the old items. We concluded that this group of patients has difficulties either with segmenting new from old, or with disengaging from old information after possibly successful segmentation (cf. Petersen, Robinson, & Currie, 1989; Posner, Walker, Friedrich, & Rafal, 1984).

As has been indicated before (e.g., Jiang & Wang, 2004), the (spatio)temporal segmentation account and inhibition account (and also the onset account) are not mutually exclusive. The spatiotemporal segmentation of old and new may be maximized by inhibiting the old group and prioritizing (either automatically or top-down) the new group.

Feature-based inhibition

Most results reviewed here show that visual marking can be feature based, in that it uses colour or orientation to suppress the old information. Other results show it does not have to be feature based. Both Olivers, Watson, and Humphreys (1999) and Theeuwes, Kramer, & Atchley (1998a) demonstrated preview benefits for sets of items that did not differ in colour, or indeed in any basic feature. Under the visual marking account, this could be explained by invoking location-based inhibition mechanisms (see Watson & Humphreys, 1997). It therefore seems that previewed items are suppressed through whatever representation is available, whether features, locations, or both. In contrast, if neither feature nor location information is available, visual marking fails (as shown by Olivers et al., 1999). An alternative explanation, as is proposed by Donk (2006) this issue, is that the feature-based inhibition we found is part of a more general mechanism that operates during various types of attentional selection tasks (e.g., Cepeda, Cave, Bichot, & Kim, 1998) and is therefore not special to the preview. Note that, in this respect, the feature-based carryover effects reviewed here are also reminiscent of the negative priming phenomenon (e.g., Neill, 1977; Tipper, 1985). According to Donk's view, feature-based inhibition operates during, but is not crucial to obtaining, a preview benefit. For a preview benefit, attentional capture by new onsets is sufficient, and feature-based inhibition is merely an additional possibility to refine selection. The prediction then is that when there are no feature differences, there will be no inhibition, just onset capture. Existing studies provide little resolution on this issue, as indeed most studies claiming to provide direct evidence for inhibition also employ feature differences between old and new sets. A number of probe dot studies may come closest to a solution to this matter (Humphreys et al., 2004; Olivers & Humphreys, 2002; Watson & Humphreys, 2000). These studies show that detection of small dots suffers when presented on old (previewed) items relative to new items, and also relative to a (presumably neutral) background. Since the probe dots do not share features with the previewed objects, and performance is contingent on the positions of the probes (close to old vs. new distractors), one may argue that the inhibition is location based, and not just a byproduct of more general feature-based selection mechanisms. However, it needs to be pointed out that, so far, the probe studies too have used displays containing colour and/or orientation differences between old and new sets, thus allowing feature-based effects back in. A stronger test would be to present probes on old items that cannot be distinguished from new items except for their moment of onset. The visual marking account predicts that probe detection should still suffer. Finally, the idea that visual marking is just another case of a more general inhibitory mechanism is not an unattractive proposal. It would mean that the mechanism behind visual marking does not represent a special case solely applicable to previews, but instead reflects a universal top-down inhibitory process that can be applied to distracting information presented at any moment in time, whether simultaneous with or in advance of the target information (see Peterson et al., 2003). Such a mechanism would make sense in an efficient yet flexible cognitive system.

CONCLUSION

We have reviewed evidence showing that previewing certain items affects the selection of other items presented later in time. These effects occur between, as well as within trials, and depend on the feature similarity between old and new items. We have also reviewed evidence showing that presenting an additional task either before or during the preview affects the selection of the new items, showing that prioritization of new items requires limited resources. Finally, we have reviewed evidence showing that deprioritization of the old, and prioritization of the new, is dependent on overall task settings. Taken together, we interpret these findings as evidence for an inhibitory process applied to old visual information, which may augment more automatic attentional capture mechanisms, as well as temporal segmentation processes. We propose that the attention system may employ two attentional sets; one positive set for target properties, one negative set for distractor properties. Future studies will need to address further how these attentional sets interact across features, space, and time.

REFERENCES

Atchley, P., Jones, S. E., & Hoffman, L. (2003). Visual marking: A convergence of goal- and stimulus-driven processes during visual search. *Perception and Psychophysics, 65*(5), 667–677.

Belopolsky, A. V., Theeuwes, J., & Kramer, A. F. (2005). Prioritization by transients in visual search. *Psychonomic Bulletin and Review, 12*, 93–99.

Braithwaite, J. J., & Humphreys, G. W. (2003). Inhibition and anticipation in visual search: Evidence from effects of color foreknowledge on preview search. *Perception and Psychophysics, 65*(2), 213–237.

Braithwaite, J. J., Humphreys, G. W., & Hodsoll, J. (2003). Ignoring color over time: The selective effects of color on preview-based visual search of static items. *Journal of Experimental Psychology: Human Perception and Performance, 29*, 758–778.

Braithwaite, J. J., Humphreys, G. W., Watson, D. G., & Hulleman, J. (2005). Revisiting preview search at isoluminance: New onsets are not necessary for the preview advantage. *Perception & Psychophysics, 67*, 1214–1228.

Cepeda, N. J., Cave, K. R., Bichot, N. P., & Kim, M. S. (1998). Spatial selection via feature driven inhibition of distractor locations. *Perception and Psychophysics, 60*, 727–746.

Corbetta, M. (1998). Frontoparietal cortical networks for directing attention and the eye to visual locations: Identical, independent, or overlapping neural systems? *Proceedings of the National Academy of Sciences, USA, 95*, 831–838.

Coull, J. T., Frackowiak, R. S. J., & Frith, C. D. (1998). Monitoring for target objects: Activation of right frontal and parietal cortices with increasing time on task. *Neuropsychologia, 36*(12), 1325–1334.

Donk, M. (2006). The preview benefit: Visual marking, feature-based inhibition, temporal segregation, or onset capture? *Visual Cognition, 14*, 736–748.

Donk, M., & Theeuwes, J. (2001). Visual marking beside the mark: Prioritizing selection by abrupt onsets. *Perception and Psychophysics, 63*(5), 891–900.

Donk, M., & Theeuwes, J. (2003). Prioritizing selection of new elements: Bottom-up versus top-down control. *Perception and Psychophysics*, 65(8), 1231–1242.

Donk, M., & Verburg, R. C. (2004). Prioritizing new elements with a brief preview period: Evidence against visual marking. *Psychonomic Bulletin and Review*, 11, 282–288.

Folk, C., Remington, R. W., & Johnston, J. C. (1992). Involuntary covert orienting is contingent on attentional control settings. *Journal of Experimental Psychology: Human Perception and Performance*, 18, 1030–1044.

Gibson, B. S., & Jiang, Y. (2001). Visual marking and the perception of salience in visual search. *Perception and Psychophysics*, 63, 59–73.

Gibson, B. S., & Kelsey, E. M. (1998). Stimulus-driven attentional capture is contingent on attentional set for displaywide visual features. *Perception and Psychophysics*, 24(3), 699–706.

Gottlieb, J. P., Kusunoki, M., & Goldberg, M. E. (1998). The representation of visual salience in monkey parietal cortex. *Nature*, 391, 481–484.

Humphreys, G. W., Jung-Stalmann, B., & Olivers, C. N. L. (2004). An analysis of the time course of attention in preview search. *Perception and Psychophysics*, 66, 713–730.

Humphreys, G. W., Kyllingsbæk, S., Watson, D. G., Olivers, C. N. L., & Paulson, X. (2004). Parieto-occipital areas involved in efficient filtering in search: A time course analysis of visual marking using behavioral and functional imaging procedures. *Quarterly Journal of Experimental Psychology*, 57A, 610–635.

Humphreys, G. W., Watson, D. G., & Jolicoeur, P. (2002). Fractionating the preview benefit in search: Dual task decomposition of visual marking by timing and modality. *Journal of Experimental Psychology: Human Perception and Performance*, 28(3), 640–660.

Jiang, Y., Chun, M. M., & Marks, L. E. (2002). Visual marking: Selective attention to asynchronous temporal groups. *Journal of Experimental Psychology: Human Perception and Performance*, 28, 717–730.

Jiang, Y., & Wang, S. W. (2004). What kind of memory supports visual marking? *Journal of Experimental Psychology: Human Perception and Performance*, 30(1), 79–91.

Jonides, J., & Yantis, S. (1988). Uniqueness of abrupt visual onset in capturing attention. *Perception and Psychophysics*, 43, 346–354.

Kanwisher, N., & Wojciulik, E. (2000). Visual attention: Insights from brain imaging. *Nature Reviews: Neuroscience*, 1, 91–100.

Kaptein, N. A., Theeuwes, J., & van der Heijden, A. H. C. (1995). Search for a conjunctively defined target can be selectively limited to a color-defined subset of elements. *Journal of Experimental Psychology: Human Perception and Performance*, 21, 1053–1069.

Kastner, S., & Ungerleider, L. G. (2000). Mechanisms of visual attention in the human cortex. *Annual Review of Neuroscience*, 23, 315–341.

Miller, J. (1989). The control of attention by abrupt visual onsets and offsets. *Perception and Psychophysics*, 45, 567–571.

Neill, W. T. (1977). Inhibitory and facilitatory processes in selective attention. *Journal of Experimental Psychology: Human Perception and Performance*, 3, 444–450.

Olivers, C. N. L., & Humphreys, G. W. (2002). When visual marking meets the attentional blink: More evidence for top-down, limited capacity inhibition. *Journal of Experimental Psychology: Human Perception and Performance*, 28(1), 22–42.

Olivers, C. N. L., & Humphreys, G. W. (2003). Visual marking inhibits singleton capture. *Cognitive Psychology*, 47, 1–42.

Olivers, C. N. L., & Humphreys, G. W. (2004). Spatiotemporal segregation in visual search: Evidence from parietal lesions. *Journal of Experimental Psychology: Human Perception and Performance*, 30, 667–688.

Olivers, C. N. L., Humphreys. G. W.. Heinke. D.. & Cooper, A. C. G. (2002). Prioritization in visual search: Visual marking is not dependent on a mnemonic search. *Perception and Psychophysics*, *64*(4), 540–560.

Olivers, C. N. L., Smith, S., Matthews. P.. & Humphreys, G. W. (2005). Prioritizing new over old: An fMRI study of the preview search task. *Human Brain Mapping*. *24*. 69–78.

Olivers, C. N. L., Watson, D. G., & Humphreys. G. W. (1999). Visual marking of locations and feature maps: Evidence from within-dimension defined conjunctions. *Quarterly Journal of Experimental Psychology*, *52A*, 679–715.

Pashler, H. (1988). Cross-dimensional interaction and texture segregation. *Perception and Psychophysics*, *43*, 307–318.

Petersen. S. E.. Robinson, D. L., & Currie. J. N. (1989). Influences of lesions of parietal cortex on visual spatial attention in humans. *Experimental Brain Research*, *76*, 267–280.

Peterson, M. S., Belopolsky, A. V., & Kramer. A. F. (2003). Contingent visual marking by transients. *Perception and Psychophysics*. *65*(5). 695–710.

Pollmann, S., Weidner, R., Humphreys. G. W.. Olivers. C. N. L., Müller, K., Lohmann, G., et al. (2003). Separating segmentation and target detection in posterior parietal cortex: An event-related fMRI study of visual marking. *NeuroImage*, *18*, 310–323.

Posner, M. I., Walker, J. A., Friedrich. F. J.. & Rafal. R. D. (1984). Effects of parietal injury on covert orienting of attention. *Journal of Neuroscience*, *4*, 1863–1874.

Raymond, J. E., Shapiro, K. L., & Arnell. K. M. (1992). Temporary suppression of visual processing in an RSVP task: An attentional blink? *Journal of Experimental Psychology: Human Perception and Performance*. *18*. 849–860.

Remington. R. W., Johnston, J. C., & Yantis. S. (1992). Involuntary attentional capture by abrupt onsets. *Perception and Psychophysics*. *51*. 279–290.

Theeuwes. J. (1991). Exogeneous and endogeneous control of attention: The effect of visual onsets and offsets. *Perception and Psychophysics*. *49*. 83–90.

Theeuwes. J., & Burger. R. (1998). Attentional control during visual search: The effect of irrelevant singletons. *Journal of Experimental Psychology: Human Perception and Performance*. *24*(5), 1342–1353.

Theeuwes, J., Kramer. A. F., & Atchley. P. (1998a). Visual marking of old objects. *Psychonomic Bulletin and Review*, *5*, 130–134.

Theeuwes. J., Kramer. A. F.. Hahn. S.. & Irwin. D. E. (1998b). Our eyes do not always go where we want them to go: Capture of eyes by new objects. *Psychological Science*, *9*, 379–385.

Tipper. S. P. (1985). The negative priming effect: Inhibitory priming by ignored objects. *Quarterly Journal of Experimental Psychology*. *37A*. 571–590.

Todd. J. T.. & van Gelder. P. (1979). Implications of a transient-sustained dichotomy for the measurement of human performance. *Journal of Experimental Psychology: Human Perception and Performance*. *5*. 625–638.

Todd. S., & Kramer. A. F. (1994). Attentional misguidance in visual search. *Perception and Psychophysics*, *56*, 198–210.

Treisman, A., Kahneman. D.. & Burkell. J. (1983). Perceptual objects and the cost of filtering. *Perception and Psychophysics*. *33*. 527–532.

Watson, D. G., & Humphreys. G. W. (1997). Visual marking: Prioritizing selection for new objects by top-down attentional inhibition of old objects. *Psychological Review*. *104*, 90–122.

Watson, D. G., & Humphreys. G. W. (2000). Visual marking: Evidence for inhibition using a probe-dot paradigm. *Perception and Psychophysics*. *62*. 471–481.

Watson. D. G.. Humphreys. G. W.. & Olivers. C. N. L. (2003). Visual marking: Using time in visual selection. *Trends in Cognitive Sciences*, *7*(4). 180–186.

Yantis, S., & Jonides, J. (1984). Abrupt visual onsets and selective attention: Evidence from visual search. *Journal of Experimental Psychology: Human Perception and Performance, 10,* 601–621.

Yantis, S., & Jonides, J. (1990). Abrupt visual onsets and selective attention: Voluntary versus automatic allocation. *Journal of Experimental Psychology: Human Perception and Performance, 16,* 121–134.

VISUAL COGNITION, 2006, 14 (4/5/6/7/8), 736–748

Ψ Psychology Press
Taylor & Francis Group

The preview benefit: Visual marking, feature-based inhibition, temporal segregation, or onset capture?

Mieke Donk

Department of Cognitive Psychology, Vrije Universiteit, Amsterdam, The Netherlands

The preview effect demonstrates that if observers in a visual search task are allowed a preview of a subset of elements before another subset of elements is added to the display, the first subset of elements no longer competes for attentional selection in the search process. Watson and Humphreys (1997) explained this effect by proposing that the locations of previewed elements are top down inhibited during the preview by a process they refer to as visual marking. The results of recent studies cannot easily be explained by the original visual marking account. As a consequence, three alternative views have emerged. According to one notion, a feature-based inhibition account, the preview benefit is mediated by inhibition applied at the level of feature maps in addition to location-based inhibition. A second view, the temporal segregation hypothesis, assumes that prioritized selection of new elements results from observers being able to selectively attend to one group of elements that can be perceptually segregated from another group on the basis of temporal asynchrony. A third view assumes that the preview benefit is caused by onset capture mediated by the appearance of the new elements. The present paper reviews the key findings concerning the preview benefit with the aim to resolve some of the controversies about how observers prioritize selection of new over old elements.

We live in a continuously changing visual world offering an almost infinite number of stimuli to process. Yet, the human information processing capacity is limited. To behave efficiently, visual selection is required to distinguish relevant from irrelevant stimuli. One way in which people select visual information is through the prioritization of new over old information. That is, people tend to attend to new objects at the expense of objects already present in the visual field (e.g., Donk & Theeuwes, 2001; Jonides & Yantis,

Please address all correspondence to Mieke Donk, Department of Cognitive Psychology, Vrije Universiteit, van der Boechorststraat 1, 1081 BT Amsterdam, The Netherlands. E-mail: w.donk@psy.vu.nl

I thank Chris Olivers, and an anonymous reviewer for comments on an earlier version of this paper.

 DOI: 10.1080/13506280500193230

1988; Kahneman, Treisman, & Burkell, 1983; Theeuwes, 1991, 1994; Watson & Humphreys, 1997; Yantis & Hillstrom, 1994; Yantis & Johnson, 1990; Yantis & Jones, 1991; Yantis & Jonides, 1984, 1990). The present paper aims to provide an overview of the research concerning the mechanisms underlying prioritized selection of multiple new objects.

Scientific evidence for prioritized selection of new over old objects was initially provided by Kahneman et al. (1983), who demonstrated a reduced distractor interference effect when distractors were displayed prior to the appearance of the imperative stimulus. More recently, Watson and Humphreys (1997) also demonstrated that previewing a set of elements reduces their effect on reaction time (RT). In this study, observers were presented with one set of elements (old elements) for at least 400 ms before another set of elements (new elements) was added to the display. The task of observers was to indicate the presence or absence of a prespecified target element that could only appear among the new elements. Search performance in this preview condition was compared to that in a condition in which all elements were presented simultaneously and a condition in which only the new elements were presented. The results of Watson and Humphreys demonstrated a preview benefit, i.e., a higher search efficiency in the preview condition than in the condition in which all elements were simultaneously presented. In fact, observers were able to selectively ignore the old elements so that search efficiency in the preview condition was equal to that in the condition in which only the new elements were presented. The results indicated that observers were able to selectively assign priority to the new over old elements. To explain the results, Watson and Humphreys proposed that observers are able to selectively inhibit the locations of the old elements in anticipation of the new elements, a process they referred to as visual marking. Visual marking presumably occurs in a top-down fashion: Observers are assumed to inhibit the locations of the old elements during the preview only if it is advantageous for them to do so. The top-down goal-based inhibition of the locations of the old elements biases selection towards the new elements upon their appearance (see also Humphreys, Jung-Stalmann, & Olivers, 2004; Kunar, Humphreys, Smith, & Watson, 2003c; Watson & Humphreys, 1997, 2000).

Even though visual marking can account for much of the data obtained with the preview paradigm, the results of many recent studies cannot be easily explained by it (e.g., Donk & Theeuwes, 2001; Jiang, Chun, & Marks, 2002b; Watson & Humphreys, 1998). This development led to a differentiation along three theoretical lines.

First, various authors adhere to the basic idea that observers use a top-down inhibitory mechanism to prevent old elements from being processed. However, in contrast to the initial visual marking account, nowadays many authors assume that the inhibition may also be applied at the level of whole feature maps (Braithwaite & Humphreys, 2003; Braithwaite, Humphreys, & Hodsoll, 2003; Kunar, Humphreys, & Smith, 2003a; Olivers & Humphreys, 2002, 2003; Olivers, Watson, & Humphreys, 1999; Watson & Humphreys, 1998). This view will be referred to in terms of a feature-based inhibition account to discriminate it from the original visual marking account.

Second, it has been proposed that prioritized selection is based on the presence of temporal segregation cues (Jiang et al., 2002b). According to this view, new elements are prioritized over old ones because new and old elements can be segregated into two perceptual groups due to their temporal asynchrony. Subsequently, attention can selectively enhance the processing of one group over the other. Even though this temporal segregation account of prioritized selection was put forward as an alternative to the visual marking account, it bears some resemblance to this theory. Most importantly, according to the temporal segregation hypothesis, prioritized selection is assumed to be based on a top-down process.

Finally, others have completely refuted the idea that observers prioritize new over old elements by top-down processing. Instead, it is assumed that prioritizing new elements occurs because the luminance onsets accompanying the appearance of the new elements automatically attract attention in a bottom-up fashion (Belopolsky, Theeuwes, & Kramer, 2005; Donk & Theeuwes, 2001, 2003; Donk & Verburg, 2004). This view will be referred to as the onset account. Because the preview benefit is assumed to be caused by a bottom-up process, the onset account contrasts strongly with the other accounts of the preview benefit.

The present paper reviews the key findings on the preview benefit with the aim to resolve some of the controversies about how observers prioritize selection of new over old elements. The first section presents results from recent experiments using the preview paradigm as it was originally introduced by Watson and Humphreys (1997). The results of these recent studies tend to favour a feature-based inhibition account over the original visual marking account. Neither a temporal segregation account nor an onset account can appropriately explain the results presented in this section. The second section describes findings that cannot be explained on the basis of visual marking and feature-based inhibition. The results presented in this section primarily support the onset account. The final section aims to reconcile the alternative theoretical accounts and provides concluding remarks.

THE RELEVANCE OF FEATURE DIFFERENCES IN PREVIEW SEARCH

Since Watson and Humphreys (1997) introduced the idea of visual marking, a number of authors have been involved with the question how old elements are inhibited or, as expressed by Kunar, Humphreys, Smith, & Hulleman (2003b) in their title, "What is 'marked' in visual marking?" (Braithwaite & Humphreys, 2003; Braithwaite et al., 2003; Kunar et al., 2003a; Olivers & Humphreys, 2002, 2003; Olivers et al., 1999; Watson & Humphreys, 1998).

Initially, Watson and Humphreys (1997) proposed that observers actively inhibit the locations of old elements to prevent them from being processed. In their Experiment 7, observers searched for a blue letter "H" among green "H"s and blue "A"s. The preview display consisted of one, four, or seven green "H"s followed after 1000 ms by the addition of seven, four, or one green "H"s, respectively, along with eight blue items. The results demonstrated that varying the proportion of old to new green distractors substantially affected search efficiency. According to Watson and Humphreys, this suggests that inhibition of the old green distractors was location based and not feature based, as in the latter case the proportion of old to new green distractors should not have mattered. However, Experiment 7 did not allow a comparison between the effects of the number of new green and new blue elements. As a consequence, it is unclear whether there really was no colour-based inhibition at all.

Evidence for the idea that prioritization of new elements can also be based on inhibition applied at the level of whole feature maps, stems from a later study. In six experiments, Watson and Humphreys (1998) showed that observers can prioritize new elements even when old elements are moving. To account for this finding, they proposed that observers may use one of two different ways to inhibit the processing of old elements. They argued that with static old elements, inhibition is location based, whereas with dynamic old elements, inhibition is feature based. That is, to prevent old moving elements from being processed, inhibition is assumed to be applied to a common property of those elements such as their colour.

Since Watson and Humphreys (1998), the feature-based inhibition hypothesis gained much credit, not only to account for results obtained with moving displays but also with static displays (see also Olivers, Humphreys, and Braithwaite, 2006 this issue). For example, Olivers and Humphreys (2002) performed an experiment (Experiment 4) in which observers had to localize a blue "H" target among previewed green "H"s and new blue "A"s. After the preview task, an additional search display was presented consisting of green "A"s and one green "H" target that also had to be localized. The results showed that if search for the blue "H" target in the preview task was inefficient (as induced by an attentional blink), search for the green "H" target in the second search task was efficient. If preview search was efficient, search performance in the second search task was less efficient. Olivers and Humphreys (2002) concluded that the preview benefit is at least partly due to feature-based inhibition. On the one hand, failures to successful inhibit the colour of the old elements lead to relative good performance in a subsequent search task in which the target shares the colour with the previously previewed elements. On the other hand, if observers are successful in inhibiting the previewed elements, subsequent search for a target sharing its colour with the previewed elements is hampered due to nonspatial inhibition of the colour of the previewed elements.

Braithwaite et al. (2003) also provided evidence for inhibitory carryover effects in preview search based on colour (see also Braithwaite & Humphreys, 2003). In a sequence of five experiments, Braithwaite et al. demonstrated that colour similarity between old and new elements has a profound effect on search efficiency in a preview task. For instance, when the target in the search display shared its colour with the majority of the previewed elements, search efficiency was seriously hampered in comparison to when this was not the case. Braithwaite et al. attributed this effect to feature-based inhibition. That is, colour-based inhibition of the old elements was assumed to be carried over to the target if it had the same colour.[1]

Finally, Olivers and Humphreys (2003) combined the preview paradigm with the presence of a feature singleton in the search display. For example in Experiment 2, observers had a preview task in which they had to search for a target among previewed old elements and new elements. Among the new elements, a singleton could be presented which was always unique in a simple feature dimension relative to the new elements. The singleton presented could share one or more features with the previewed old elements. Olivers and Humphreys reasoned that if the previewed old elements are inhibited and if this inhibition is feature based, the extent to which the singleton captures attention should be modulated as a function of its similarity to the previewed elements. The results demonstrated that if a singleton was similar to the previewed elements, the effects of singleton presence were less than if the singleton was dissimilar to the previewed old elements. These results again provide evidence for the idea that the preview benefit is caused by feature-based inhibition.

In sum, recent studies have provided cumulative evidence for feature-based inhibition as an explanation for the preview benefit. Whereas initially, feature-based inhibition was discarded as a viable explanation for the preview benefit (in Watson & Humphreys, 1997), increasingly more studies are demonstrating that feature-based inhibition does play a role in the preview paradigm. The role of feature-based inhibition in the preview benefit has gained much credit not only to account for findings with moving stimuli (Watson & Humphreys, 1998), but also to explain results obtained with

---

[1] In addition to colour-based inhibition, Braithwaite et al. (2003) as well as Braithwaite and Humphreys (2003) also assume that the prioritization of new elements can be further supported by the possibility to use an anticipatory set for a known target colour.

static displays (Braithwaite & Humphreys, 2003; Braithwaite et al., 2003; Kunar et al., 2003a; Olivers & Humphreys, 2002, 2003; Olivers et al., 1999).

At this point, it is important to note that in the preview paradigm used in the above studies, old elements were always different from new elements in a simple feature-dimension. Theeuwes, Kramer, and Atchley (1998) were the first to point this out. They argued that the original findings of Watson and Humphreys (1997) might not be unique to preview search but instead represent another demonstration of subset selective search by colour (e.g., Egeth, Virzi, & Garbart, 1984; Kaptein, Theeuwes, & van der Heijden, 1995). To investigate this issue, Theeuwes et al. had observers search for a white "H" among a variable number of old and new other white letters. Numbers of old and new letters were independently manipulated permitting a direct comparison between the effect of the number of old elements and the effect of the number of new elements on search performance. The results showed that even though there was no colour difference between old and new elements, observers were perfectly able to prioritize the selection of new over old elements as evident from the finding that only the number of new elements affected search performance whereas the number of old elements did not. Theeuwes et al. concluded that prioritized selection of new over old elements was not just another demonstration of subset selective search by colour.

Even though the results of Theeuwes et al. (1998) are in line with the original visual marking account of Watson and Humphreys (1987), they cannot be explained by a feature-based inhibition account. In fact, old and new elements were indistinguishable from each other except for the moment in time at which they were presented. When old and new elements share all their features, observers cannot use a mechanism of feature-based inhibition to prioritize selection of one over another subset of elements. The next section will be concerned with research in which old and new elements only differ in their temporal onset.

INHIBITION, TEMPORAL SEGREGATION, OR ONSET CAPTURE?

As noted in the previous section, the results of studies in which the old elements carried a different colour than the new elements are in line with the idea that the preview benefit is caused by feature-based inhibition. However, studies in which old and new elements cannot be discriminated on the basis of a simple feature have generally led to completely different views on how observers prioritize selection of new over old elements (but see Theeuwes et al., 1998).

For example, Jiang et al. (2002b) had observers search for a rotated "T" among rotated L-shaped objects. Old and new elements could not be distinguished from each other on the basis of one simple feature. The results showed that the preview benefit disappeared if the old elements changed shape or luminance at the onset of the new elements, whereas preview search was not disrupted when the old elements changed shape and luminance prior to the presentation of the new elements. Moreover, preview search was also unaffected when the background changed. According to both a visual marking account and a feature-based inhibition account the preview benefit should have been disrupted by asynchronous as well as synchronous changes in the old elements. Watson and Humphreys (1997) postulated that any dynamic change should be disruptive for the preview benefit because dynamic changes are assumed to reset the inhibition process. In contrast, according to a temporal segregation account, the temporal asynchrony is critical in determining whether or not a preview benefit occurs. The results therefore provided evidence favouring the temporal segregation account and against the inhibition accounts.

Quite different were the conclusions of Donk and Theeuwes (2001). They had observers search for a green target letter "H" among a variable number of green old and new letters on a grey background. The numbers of old and new elements were independently manipulated (see also Jiang, Chun, & Marks, 2002a; Theeuwes et al., 1998). Old and new elements could not be distinguished from each other on the basis of a simple feature. The presentations of the old and new elements were or were not accompanied by a luminance change. The results showed that prioritizing selection of new elements was critically dependent on whether or not the appearance of new elements was accompanied by an abrupt luminance onset. Search performance was only independent of the number of old elements if new elements were presented with abrupt luminance onsets. If there was no luminance onset of new elements, search performance depended on both the number of new elements and the number of old elements. The results did not depend on the onset characteristics of the old elements. In other words, for a preview benefit to occur, new elements were required to appear with luminance onset irrespective of the onset characteristics of the old elements. These results cannot easily be explained by the original visual marking account, nor by the feature-based inhibition notion. In fact, to explain the results of Donk and Theeuwes a visual marking account should include the idea that luminance onsets are crucial for prioritized selection. One might, for example, argue that the effect of inhibiting the locations of the old elements is to enable new onsets to enhance activation in an attentional system responsive to dynamic change in the visual environment. If the new elements do not activate this system (i.e., when they are equiluminant with the background) then effective prioritization should not occur. A feature-based inhibition account cannot explain the results of Donk and Theeuwes, since there were no feature differences between old and new elements. Because there were no variations in the temporal properties of the stimuli over conditions, a temporal segregation account (Jiang et al., 2002b) can neither explain the results. If one assumes that other forms of perceptual grouping play a role in the preview benefit, one would have expected that it should have been relatively easy to segregate two groups of elements if they had different onset characteristics, i.e., when the old elements appeared with onset whereas the new elements did not. The results of Donk and Theeuwes showed that this is not the case. To explain their results, Donk and Theeuwes (see also Donk & Theeuwes, 2003; Donk & Verburg, 2004) proposed that prioritized selection is caused by luminance onset capture (e.g., Theeuwes, 1991; Yantis & Johnson, 1990; Yantis & Jones, 1991; Yantis & Jonides, 1984, 1990). According to this onset account, new elements are assumed to be automatically prioritized over old elements because the abrupt luminance onsets accompanying the appearance of the new elements generate a large bottom-up activation biasing observers to prioritize the processing of new elements over old ones. Although Donk and Theeuwes' original study did not allow one to conclude that prioritized selection is based on a bottom-up process, the results of a more recent study (Donk & Theeuwes, 2003) suggest that this is indeed the case.

In Donk and Theeuwes (2003), observers were presented with displays containing one set of elements consisting of green "H"s and blue "A"s (old elements) followed after a certain time interval by a second set of elements also consisting of green "H"s and blue "A"s (new elements). Observers were instructed to search for the presence of a blue "H" target, which was presented on 50% of the trials with equal probability among the old and new elements (Experiments 1 and 2) or twice as often among the old elements than among the new elements (Experiment 3). If the target was presented among the old elements, upon presentation of the new elements, one of the previously presented green "H"s turned blue. The colour change from green to blue was not accompanied by a luminance change, i.e., the colours green and blue were equiluminant to each other. If the target was presented among the new elements, one of the new elements was the blue "H" target. The results showed that if the target was presented among the new elements, search performance only depended on the number of new elements, whereas if the target was presented among the old elements, search depended on both the number of old and the number of new elements. These results demonstrated that new elements were prioritized for selection over old ones even though observers had no incentive to do so. These results provide strong evidence against any notion assuming that prioritized selection of new over old elements is based on a top-down process. According to both a visual marking account and a feature-based inhibition account, prioritized selection is contingent on the maintenance of an appropriate goal state. The temporal segregation hypothesis also assumes prioritized selection to be goal driven. In fact, according to Jiang et al. (2002b), an observer may allocate attention to whatever group of elements (i.e., the old or the new elements) is known to contain the target.[2] The results of Donk and Theeuwes (2003) showed that this is not the case. Observers do not seem to be able to prioritize selection for old over new elements.

More recently, Atchley, Jones, and Hoffman (2003) also reported results indicating that prioritized selection of new over old elements is based on a bottom-up process. They too found that if observers search for a target that appears with equal probability among the old and new elements, observers prioritized selection of new over old elements. In their Experiment 1, observers searched for a target letter "H" among distractor letters "A". In one condition, the target was presented with equal probability among the old elements (through the offset of the top-line segment of an old distractor "A" upon the appearance of the new elements) and among the new elements. The results showed that search efficiency was always higher if the target occurred among the new elements compared to if it occurred among the old elements. These results are consistent with the idea that the preview benefit is due to the operation of a bottom-up process.[3]

Recently, Donk and Verburg (2004) provided further evidence favouring the onset account. They allowed observers only a very brief preview of the old elements (i.e., 50 ms). They used the preview paradigm in which the number of old and new elements were independently manipulated. Observers searched for a target that could only occur among the new elements. In one condition, old elements were presented equiluminant with the background followed after 50 ms by the addition of the new elements. New elements were presented with luminance onset. Upon presentation, the luminance of the new elements was higher than that of the background. After another 50 ms the luminance of the new elements was set off to the luminance level of the

---

[2] In Experiment 4, Jiang et al. (2002b) had participants to indicate whether the rotation of a target "T" was up, down, left, or right. The target was always presented among the old elements containing multiple L-shaped objects. New elements consisting of multiple rotated "T"s were added to the display after 150 ms. The results indicated that participants were able to correctly report the identity of the target in about 65% of the trials. Jiang et al. inferred on the basis of these results that observers can prioritize the selection of old over new elements. However, it should be noted that if prioritized selection for old elements had been perfect, performance should have been close to 100%.

[3] It is important to note that the results of several other studies (Humphreys, Watson, & Jolicoeur, 2002; Olivers & Humphreys, 2002; Watson & Humphreys, 1997, 2000) suggest that prioritized selection is based on top-down processing. These studies have, however, generally utilized a preview task in which old and new elements not only differed in their temporal onset, but also in colour. If there is, however, no colour difference, as in Atchley et al. (2003) and Donk and Theeuwes (2003), prioritized selection seems to be completely bottom-up driven.

background and that of the old elements. In the other condition, both old and new elements appeared with an initial higher luminance. The results indicated that participants were able to prioritize selection of new over old elements when new elements were presented with luminance onset whereas old elements were not. New elements could not be prioritized if both old and new elements appeared with luminance onset. Donk and Verburg concluded that new elements can be prioritized over old elements, even with a very brief preview. However, if the presentation of the old elements is accompanied by luminance onset, attention might be captured by these onsets (Theeuwes, 1991; Yantis & Jonides, 1990). It might take a certain amount of time before attention can be completely disengaged from the locations of the old elements (Duncan, Ward, & Shapiro, 1994). As a consequence, during this interval new elements may fail to capture attention. The results of Donk and Verburg provided evidence for the onset account: Prioritization of new elements seems to be based on an instantaneous process rather than on a time-consuming process. If prioritized selection would have been caused by inhibition or segregation, prioritization should not have occurred in the present experiment. Both, the inhibition accounts and the temporal segregation account assume that observers need time to prioritize selection of new elements.[4] Recently, Belopolsky et al. (2005) demonstrated that, even without a preview interval, elements that appear with luminance onset can be perfectly prioritized over elements that appear without luminance onset. These results suggest again that the mechanism responsible for prioritized selection is not based on a time-consuming process of inhibition. Further-more, these results demonstrate that a temporal separation between two groups of elements is not crucial for prioritized selection. These findings argue therefore against both inhibition accounts as well as the temporal segregation account.

Together the above findings provide evidence for the view that if old and new elements cannot be discriminated on the basis of a simple feature, the preview benefit appears to be caused by onset capture (Donk & Theeuwes, 2001). According to this account, new elements receive attentional priority in a purely stimulus-driven manner. It seems as if the abrupt onsets accompanying the appearance of the new elements generate a large bottom-up activation biasing observers to prioritize the processing of new elements over old ones. At this point it is important to note that even though the above results cannot be explained by visual marking, feature-based inhibition, or the temporal segregation hypothesis, it is conceivable that

---

[4] Jiang et al. (2002b) remark that the interval between the presentation of the old and new elements should be "long enough for attention to be deployed to one group and not the other" (p. 719). They suggested that the required length of this interval should be at least 200 ms.

other mechanisms play an additional role. The extent to which this occurs is a question for further research.

CONCLUSIONS

The above sections aimed to provide an overview of research on how people prioritize the selection of new over old objects. The first section provided a review of studies using the preview paradigm of Watson and Humphreys (1997). The results of these studies demonstrated that if old and new elements differ in a simple feature value, people apply feature-based inhibition in prioritizing selection of new over old elements. It is important to note that the demonstration of feature-based inhibition in the preview paradigm does not imply that the preview benefit is necessarily *caused* by feature-based inhibition. In fact, the results discussed in that section (e.g., Braithwaite & Humphreys, 2003; Braithwaite et al., 2003; Olivers & Humphreys, 2002, 2003) are also compatible with the idea that prioritized selection is caused by another mechanism while observers apply colour-based inhibition to optimize selection of the relevant subgroup. Indeed, as outlined in the second section, if old and new elements share their basic features, the preview benefit does not seem to be caused by inhibition. The results presented in that section suggest that prioritization of new over old elements seems to be primarily caused by onset capture (Donk, 2005; Donk & Theeuwes, 2001, 2003; Donk & Verburg, 2004). It was shown that prioritized selection of new over old elements: (1) Depends on the luminance onset characteristics of the new elements, (2) is mediated by a bottom-up process, and (3) occurs instantaneously upon the presentation of the new elements. Together, the results presented in this second section provide evidence favouring the onset account. Nevertheless, other mechanisms, such as inhibition or temporal segregation, may play an additional role to optimize selection of the relevant subset of elements.

Recently, Donk (2005) had observers search for a target that was presented at variable intervals after the presentation of the new elements. Old and new elements could not be discriminated on the basis of a simple feature. The results demonstrated that the preview benefit decreased as the interval between the presentation of the new elements and the target increased. It is conceivable that, in order to prioritize selection of new over old elements, onset capture is effective during the first several hundred milliseconds after the presentation of the new elements. To optimize subset selective search afterwards, observers may use other mechanisms. The extent to which such another mechanism plays role may depend on the exact stimulus configuration and instructions. Currently, it remains to be seen how the alternative mechanisms put forward to account for the preview benefit can work in concert. A major challenge for future research is to determine how these different mechanisms act in concert to achieve prioritized selection for new elements.

REFERENCES

Atchley, P., Jones, S. E., & Hoffman, L. (2003). Visual marking: A convergence of goal- and stimulus-driven processes during visual search. *Perception and Psychophysics*, *65*, 667–677.

Belopolsky, A. V., Theeuwes, J., & Kramer, A. F. (2005). Prioritization by visual transients in search: Evidence against the visual marking account of the preview benefit. *Psychonomic Bulletin and Review*, *12*, 93–99.

Braithwaite, J. J., & Humphreys, G. W. (2003). Inhibition and anticipation in visual search: Evidence from effects of color foreknowledge on preview search. *Perception and Psychophysics*, *65*, 213–237.

Braithwaite, J. J., Humphreys, G. W., & Hodsoll, J. (2003). Color grouping in space and time: Evidence from negative color-based carryover effects in preview search. *Journal of Experimental Psychology: Human Perception and Performance*, *29*, 758–778.

Donk, M. (2006). Prioritizing selection of new elements: On the time-course of the preview effect. *Visual Cognition*, *12*, 1373–1385.

Donk, M., & Theeuwes, J. (2001). Visual marking beside the mark: Prioritizing selection by abrupt onsets. *Perception and Psychophysics*, *63*, 891–900.

Donk, M., & Theeuwes, J. (2003). Prioritizing selection of new elements: Bottom-up versus top-down control. *Perception and Psychophysics*, *65*, 1231–1242.

Donk, M., & Verburg, R. C. (2004) Prioritizing new elements with a brief preview period: Evidence against visual marking. *Psychonomic Bulletin and Review*, *11*, 282–288.

Duncan, J., Ward, R., & Shapiro, K. (1994). Direct measurement of attentional dwell time in human vision. *Nature*, *369*, 313–315.

Egeth, H. E., Virzi, R. A., & Garbart, H. (1984). Searching for conjunctively defined targets. *Journal of Experimental Psychology: Human Perception and Performance*, *10*, 32–39.

Humphreys, G. W., Jung-Stalmann, B., & Olivers, C. (2004). An analysis of the time-course of visual marking using a probe dot procedure. *Perception & Psychophysics*, *66*, 713–730.

Humphreys, G. W., Watson, D. G., & Jolicoeur, P. (2002). Fractionating the preview benefit in search: Dual-task decomposition of visual marking by timing and modality. *Journal of Experimental Psychology: Human Perception and Performance*, *28*, 640–660.

Jiang, Y., Chun, M. M., & Marks, L. E. (2002a). Visual marking: Dissociating effects of new and old set size. *Journal of Experimental Psychology: Human Perception and Performance*, *28*, 293–302.

Jiang, Y., Chun, M. M., & Marks, L. E. (2002b). Visual marking: Selective attention to asynchronous temporal groups. *Journal of Experimental Psychology: Human Perception and Performance*, *28*, 717–730.

Jonides, J., & Yantis, S. (1988). Uniqueness of abrupt visual onset in capturing attention. *Perception and Psychophysics*, *43*, 346–354.

Kahneman, D., Treisman, A., & Burkell, J. (1983). The cost of visual filtering. *Journal of Experimental Psychology: Human Perception and Performance*, *9*, 510–522.

Kaptein, N. A., Theeuwes, J., & van der Heijden, A. H. C. (1995). Search for a conjunctively defined target can be selectively limited to a color defined subset of elements. *Journal of Experimental Psychology: Human Perception and Performance*, *21*, 1053–1069.

Kunar, M. A., Humphreys, G. W., & Smith. K. J. (2003a). Visual change with moving displays: More evidence for color feature map inhibition during preview search. *Journal of Experimental Psychology: Human Perception and Performance, 29.* 779–792.

Kunar, M. A., Humphreys, G. W., Smith. K. J., & Hulleman, J. (2003b). What is "marked" in visual marking? Evidence for effects of configuration in preview search. *Perception & Psychophysics, 65,* 982–996.

Kunar, M. A., Humphreys. G. W., Smith. K. J., & Watson, D. G. (2003c). When a reappearance is old news: Visual marking survives occlusion. *Journal of Experimental Psychology: Human Perception and Performance. 29,* 185–198.

Olivers, C. N. L., & Humphreys. G. W. (2002). When visual marking meets the attentional blink: More evidence for top-down. limited-capacity inhibition. *Journal of Experimental Psychology: Human Perception and Performance, 28,* 22–42.

Olivers, C. N. L., & Humphreys. G. W. (2003). Visual marking inhibits singleton capture. *Cognitive Psychology, 47,* 1–42.

Olivers, C. N. L., Humphreys. G. W., & Braithwaite. J. J. (2006). The preview search task: Evidence for visual marking. *Visual Cognition. 14,* 716–735.

Olivers, C. N. L., Watson, D. G., & Humphreys. G. W. (1999). Visual marking of locations versus feature maps: Evidence from within-dimension defined conjunctions. *Quarterly Journal of Experimental Psychology. 52A.* 679–715.

Theeuwes, J. (1991). Exogenous and endogenous control of attention: The effect of visual onsets and offsets. *Perception and Psychophysics, 49,* 83–90.

Theeuwes, J. (1994). Stimulus-driven capture and attentional set: Selective search for color and visual abrupt onsets. *Journal of Experimental Psychology: Human Perception and Performance, 20,* 799–806.

Theeuwes. J., Kramer, A. F., & Atchley. P. (1998). Visual marking of old objects. *Psychonomic Bulletin and Review, 5,* 130–134.

Watson. D. G., & Humphreys. G. W. (1997). Visual marking: Prioritizing selection for new objects by top-down attentional inhibition of old objects. *Psychological Review. 104,* 90–122.

Watson, D. G., & Humphreys, G. W. (1998). Visual marking of moving objects: A role for top-down feature based attentional inhibition. *Journal of Experimental Psychology: Human Perception and Performance, 24,* 946–962.

Watson, D. G., & Humphreys, G. W. (2000). Visual marking: Evidence for inhibition using a probe-dot detection paradigm. *Perception and Psychophysics, 62,* 471–481.

Yantis. S., & Hillstrom, A. P. (1994). Stimulus-driven attentional capture: Evidence from equiluminant visual objects. *Journal of Experimental Psychology: Human Perception and Performance, 20,* 95–107.

Yantis. S., & Johnson, D. N. (1990). Mechanisms of attentional priority. *Journal of Experimental Psychology: Human Perception and Performance, 16,* 812–825.

Yantis. S., & Jones, E. (1991). Mechanisms of attentional selection: Temporally modulated priority tags. *Perception and Psychophysics, 50,* 166–178.

Yantis. S., & Jonides, J. (1984). Abrupt visual onsets and selective attention: Evidence from visual search. *Journal of Experimental Psychology: Human Perception and Performance, 10,* 601–621.

Yantis, S., & Jonides, J. (1990). Abrupt visual onsets and selective attention: Voluntary versus automatic allocation. *Journal of Experimental Psychology: Human Perception and Performance, 16,* 121–134.

VISUAL COGNITION, 2006, 14 (4/5/6/7/8), 749–780

Ψ Psychology Press
Taylor & Francis Group

Why don't we see changes? The role of attentional bottlenecks and limited visual memory

Jeremy M. Wolfe

Visual Attention Lab, Brigham and Women's Hospital and Harvard Medical School, Boston, MA, USA

Andrea Reinecke

Dresden University of Technology, General Psychology, FR Germany

Peter Brawn

Access Testing Centre, Sydney, NSW Australia

Seven experiments explore the role of bottlenecks in selective attention and access to visual short-term memory (VSTM) in the failure of observers to identify clearly visible changes in otherwise stable visual displays. Experiment 1 shows that observers fail to register a colour change in an object even if they are cued to the location of the object by a transient at that location as the change is occurring. Experiment 2 shows the same for orientation change. In Experiments 3 and 4, attention is directed to specific objects prior to making changes in those objects. Observers have only a very limited memory for the status of recently attended items. Experiment 5 reveals that observers have no ability to detect changes that happen after attention has been directed to an object and before attention returns to that object. In Experiment 6, attention is cued at rates that more closely resemble natural rates and Experiment 7 uses natural images. Memory capacity remains very small (<4 items).

If you ask typical observers, outside of a vision research laboratory, what they are seeing right now, they will probably tell you that they are seeing a large number of objects placed in a spatially continuous scene. If you ask them if they are seeing *all* of that at the same time, they will look at you

Please address all correspondence to Jeremy M Wolfe, Visual Attention Lab, Brigham and Women's Hospital, 64 Sidney St., Suite 170, Cambridge, MA 02139, USA. Email: wolfe@search.bwh.harvard.edu

We thank Ron Rensink, Dan Simons, Melina Kunar, and Kristin Michod for comments on earlier drafts of this paper. Support was provided by a grant from the National Institute of Mental Health, MH56020.

http://www.psypress.com/viscog
DOI: 10.1080/13506280500195292

quizzically but they will agree that all of the objects seem to be visually present in the present instant of time. It hardly seems like much of a question. However, if you ask atypical observers, those who have been studying the question over the past 20 years or so, the answers may be quite different. A range of phenomena suggest that human observers are unable to perform tasks that would seem to be quite trivial if we could see what was in front of our eyes in the uncomplicated manner suggested by naïve introspection.

Change blindness is one of the most striking of these phenomena. In a typical change blindness paradigm, the observer is told to monitor an image for a change. As long as transients are masked and as long as the observer is not attending to the object that is changing, observers will be very poor at detecting quite substantial changes. These can range from changes to significant objects in natural scenes to changes in "basic features" like colour (Phillips, 1974; Rensink, O'Regan, & Clark, 1997; Simons, 2000; Simons & Levin, 1997).

Similar failures to report what is in front of the eyes occur when observers are attending to one aspect of a display and subsequently queried about another. Thus, Mack and Rock (1998) found that observers who were answering a question about a pair of lines would fail to report salient stimuli presented at fixation ("inattentional blindness"). Simons and his colleagues (following on Neisser & Becklen, 1975) have shown that observers who were monitoring one set of actors would fail to notice other actors (e.g., a woman in a gorilla suit) as they entered and left a scene (Simons & Chabris, 1999).

Some have argued that these results demonstrate that we only "see" the current object of attention and that the rest of the apparent perceptual world is a "grand illusion" (Noë, Pessoa, & Thompson, 2000). An alternative approach to effects like change blindness and inattentional blindness has been to argue that these are not blindness—failures of vision, but amnesias—failures of memory. Of necessity, experimenters need to ask about the change, the coloured spot, or the gorilla after it is gone. Perhaps observers simply forget what they do not attend ("inattentional amnesia"— Wolfe, 1999) or, in the case of change blindness, perhaps the second, changed image wipes out the memory for the first image. Apparent support for this view can be gleaned from "repeated search" experiments in which observers search hundreds of times through an unchanging visual display. On each trial, the object of search changes but the scene would remain constant. In numerous versions of this task, observers show little or no change in search efficiency with repetition (Wolfe, Klempen, & Dahlen, 2000; Wolfe, Oliva, Butcher, & Arsenio, 2002). It is as if each search begins *de novo* with no benefit for having performed the same search over the same stimuli many times.

In spite of our close connections to the author of the inattentional amnesia hypothesis, it must be admitted that it does not really work as a complete account for the range of phenomena. First, there are problems from within the change blindness literature. For example, it is possible to show good memory for the previous state of a scene if the question is asked correctly. Even if an observer did not notice the disappearance of an object like a basketball, that observer might be able to report the original colour of the ball (Simons, Chabris, Schnur, & Levin, 2002). Perhaps more importantly, it is clear that observers have excellent memories for some material even after very limited exposure. Picture recognition studies have shown that brief exposures are all that is needed to produce good recognition memory for hundreds, even thousands of pictures (Potter & Levy, 1969; Shepard, 1967; Standing, 1973). More recently, Hollingworth and Henderson have developed a task that can be considered to be a hybrid of picture recognition memory and change blindness paradigms (Henderson & Hollingworth, 2003; Hollingworth, 2004; Hollingworth & Henderson, 2002). Observers view a computer-generated scene filled with objects. As they saccade from item to item, an item can be changed. When asked later (including *much* later after several scenes have been viewed), observers are good at determining if a previously fixated (and, presumably attended) item has been changed or not. Henderson and Hollingworth (2003, p. 58) conclude that, far from being a grand illusion, there is a "rich scene representation" that is "retained across saccades and stored in visual memory".

In some ways, this is an odd debate. We have long known that the proximal stimulus on the retina is not the distal stimulus in the world and we have known that our perception is nothing like a direct experience of the proximal stimulus on the retina. What we experience must be some creation of our visual system. The fact that a change in the distal stimulus does not necessarily produce the experience of change in our representation of the world is not, in itself, surprising. The surprise lies in the nature of the changes that we miss or fail to identify.

In this paper, we argue that the changes we fail to notice or fail to identify and our surprise at these errors arise because visual awareness is the product of two pathways from visual input to visual experience. One pathway—call it the "selective" pathway—is responsible for object recognition and other operations that are limited to one item or to a small group of items at any one time (e.g., Is the red region to the left or right of the green?; Logan, 1995). The other pathway—call it the "nonselective pathway"—supports visual experience throughout the visual field but is capable of only a limited analysis of the input. For instance, the existence of objects may be noted in this pathway, but not their identity. This two pathway conception has some similarities to Ron Rensink's "triadic architecture" (2000b, 2000c).

Change blindness phenomena arise out of two bottlenecks in processing. The first of these is inherent in the selective pathway. The visual search literature indicates that we recognize objects at a rate of, at most 20–30 objects/second (Wolfe, 1998) and that it is necessary to selectively attend to an object in order to recognize it (Wolfe & Bennett, 1997). Imagine that a scene has been examined and its salient objects registered. If one of those objects is changed and changed back without being selected by attention, the change will go unnoticed.

Moreover, our memory for visual stimuli is limited. That is the second bottleneck. Visual short-term memory is limited to perhaps four items (Luck & Vogel, 1997). Like other aspects of long-term memory, visual long-term memory must be vast in order to accommodate the picture recognition memory results. Nevertheless, that memory is neither precise nor unlimited. A classic textbook illustration is the poor performance of observers asked to state if Lincoln faces left or right on the US penny (Nickerson & Adams, 1979). Returning to change blindness: again imagine that a scene has been examined and its salient objects registered. If one of those objects is changed and *not* changed back, that change will go unnoticed if the item is not attended during the change (bottleneck 1) and if the change fails to produce a just noticeable difference within the memory for the changed scene (bottleneck 2). (Note that in the Hollingworth and Henderson task, observers are asked if a specific and unique item has changed. This turns the task from a recall to a recognition task, making it somewhat easier.)

The element of surprise in change blindness is produced by the nonselective pathway and by long-term visual memory. The nonselective pathway gives us *some* visual experience at all locations in the field. Memory for what has recently been selected and for what we know about visual stimuli allows us to give meaning to this experience. We are lulled into the belief that we fully see and understand what is in front of us and, as a result, we are surprised when it is proven not to be the case. Thus, faced with a brief array of letters, the nonselective pathway delivers a set of objects to visual experience. The selective pathway delivers the identity of a few of these. We infer a screen full of identified letters and are, perhaps, surprised to find that we do not know what was in the top row if asked shortly after the letters vanish (Sperling, 1960).

The most compelling illustrations of change blindness involve gorillas and vanishing airplane engines. In the experiments reported here, we illustrate the relationship of change blindness to bottlenecks in selective attention and to limits on visual memory by using very minimal displays. In most of these experiments, stimuli are simply arrays of coloured dots. In six experiments, a partial-report technique was used to investigate observers' memory for simple display scenes. Experiment 1 shows that observers, faced with an array of coloured dots do not have the ability to tell if one of those dots changed colour. Experiment 2 makes the same point for orientation. Observers do not detect a change unless they happen to attend to the item. In Experiments 3 and 4, we arrange for attention to be directed to specific dots prior to a change. We can show that observers attended to specific dots. At least, they could report the colour of these dots. Nevertheless, the ability to describe the colour of a recently attended item is poor—consistent with the limited nature of visual memory. Experiment 5 demonstrates that attention to an object gives observers some memory for the state of the object at the time when it was attended, but no memory for subsequent changes to that same object once attention has gone elsewhere. Experiment 6 directs attention at rates comparable to natural deployments of attention without improving the immediate memory for the colour of a cued spot. Experiment 7 shows that this result is obtained with real world images.

EXPERIMENT 1: A FAILURE OF IMMEDIATE VISUAL MEMORY FOR COLOUR

As noted, the most striking apparent failures of immediate visual memory are the change blindness experiments in which observers fail to report changes in something dramatic like the identity of a speaker (Simons & Levin, 1998). These failures do not require semantically complex stimuli. Rensink (2000a) had participants search for a change in a display of coloured and oriented bars. The display alternated between frames with a single change in just one bar. A blank screen masked the transient that would have otherwise identified the location of the change. Rensink's results suggested that participants could monitor the colour or orientation of about four objects (cf. Luck & Vogel, 1997). In the Rensink study, observers knew the nature of the change but not its locus. Perhaps change blindness is critically dependent on this spatial uncertainty. In Experiment 1, in order to eliminate that difficulty, the locus of change was cued at the time of the change. The observers merely had to report whether a change had occurred at the cued locus. The display was otherwise unchanged. There was no intervening blank screen and no distracting transient (e.g., a "mudsplash"; O'Regan, Rensink, & Clark, 1999). Can observers report the presence or absence of a colour change that occurs "right before their eyes"?

Method

Participants. Ten participants, 18–55 years, of age were tested. All participants gave informed consent and were paid for their participation. All participants passed the Ishihara colour screen and had at least 20/25 acuity with best correction.

Stimuli. The experiments were run on Apple Power Macintosh controlled by MATLAB software using the Psychophysics Toolbox extensions (Brainard, 1997; Pelli, 1997). Stimuli were displayed on Mitsubishi Diamond Pro and Raster Ops Superscan MC*001 monitors running at a frame rate of 75 Hz. Responses were recorded via the keyboard. As illustrated schematically in Figure 1, there were 20 display elements, randomly divided between red and green circles, on a black background. The luminances of the stimuli were equated to a mean of 6 cd/m². To further guard against the brightness of the elements affecting their salience we introduced a random variation of $\pm 10\%$ into the luminance of each element. The cue consisted of a luminance increment in one of the elements by 50% of its original luminance. From the viewing distance of 57 cm each element had a diameter of 1.5 deg. Elements were randomly assigned positions on the basis of a 10×10 grid of possible locations within a display area of 33 deg $\times$ 26 deg.

Procedure. For each trial, the elements of the array were displayed for a period randomly chosen between 500 and 1000 ms. During this period, observers simply looked at the static display. At the end of this time, the luminance of a single, target element was increased. On 50% of trials, this luminance increment was simultaneously accompanied by a change in colour (from either red to green or green to red). Note that the remainder of the display was unchanged. Observers made an unspeeded response naming the colour of the circle *before* the luminance cue. Feedback in the form of beeps informed participants as to when they responded correctly or incorrectly. The intertrial interval was 1000 ms. Each subject completed one block of 200 trials. Participants were allowed breaks whenever requested. A new display was presented on each trial. The luminance increment might act as a weak mask. However, if attention is directed to an item, it is completely trivial to determine if the colour of the item after the luminance increment is the same as the colour prior to the increment. For instance, in pilot work we found

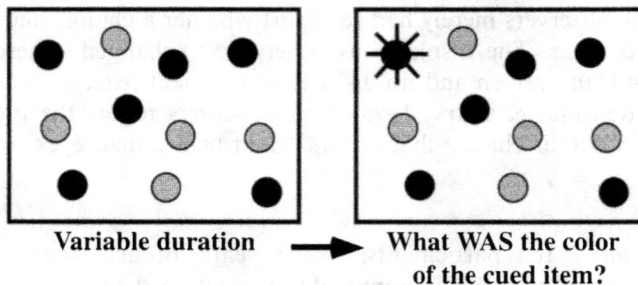

Variable duration ➡ **What WAS the color of the cued item?**

Figure 1. Schematic representation of the stimuli used in Experiment 1. Here, black stands for red and hatched for green.

that performance was essentially perfect if the critical item is precued by 200 ms.

Results and discussion

The average percentage correct was 55.2%. This is significantly above 50%, $t(9) = 3.7$, $p = .005$. As noted, if the subject is attending to an item, performance on the task is essentially perfect. If we assume that observers could accurately report the colour change for one item and would have to guess about the change at any other location, then performance should be 52.5% correct. The 55.2% average performance does not differ from this level, $t(9) = 1.9$, $p > .05$. Indeed, the 95% confidence interval for these data runs from 52% to 58% correct; performance that would be consistent with an ability to monitor or remember the colour of one to three of the stimuli. A regression analysis indicated no increase in performance over the course of the 200 trials, $F(1, 9) = 1.035$, $p > .05$.

The results of Experiment 1 suggest that colour information is available for recall from only a very few of the items in the display, even though all items are clearly visible. Observers knew the task and might be expected to deploy all available resources to its performance. In this case, the available resource would seem to be a VSTM that could encode one to three items in the 500–1000 ms of exposure. What is important about this result is that observers show little ability to detect a change in colour even when there is no uncertainty about the location of the change and even though the only transient in the display serves to attract attention to the locus of change rather than away.

Note that this is not "change blindness" is the usual sense. Observers are aware of the change and its location. They are largely unable to describe the nature of the change. Did the changed item change its colour and luminance or just its luminance? Experiment 2 shows a similar inability to describe the orientation of visible but unattended items.

EXPERIMENT 2: ORIENTATIONAL AMNESIA

The experimental design, illustrated in Figure 2, is very similar to that of Experiment 1, except that here observers are asked to describe the orientation of an item immediately after that item is hidden by a mask. Thus, Figure 2 shows the display that an observer would see after the target item was replaced by the square mask.

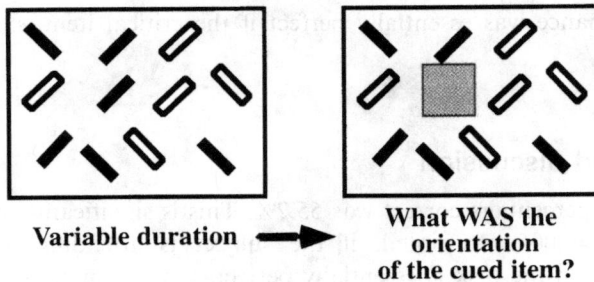

Figure 2. Stimuli from Experiment 2. Observers would report on the orientation of the line segment now hidden by the square mask.

Method

Participants. Eight participants were recruited for this experiment under the same conditions as in Experiment 1.

Stimuli. In this experiment, the stimuli were red and green bars (2 deg × 0.5 deg). Thirty-two bars were presented on an irregular 6 × 6 grid. Elements could be tilted 45 deg clockwise or 45 deg counterclockwise, with no relationship between element tilt and colour. A grey rectangle served as a cue to the location of the relevant item and as a mask of the orientation of that item.

Procedure. The procedure was identical to Experiment 1, except instead of using a luminance change to cue participants, target elements were masked by being replaced with a grey rectangle. Using exactly the same method as in Experiment 1 fails because an orientation change produces an apparent motion signal. Observers reported the orientation of the masked bar. Each subject completed one block of 200 trials.

Results and discussion

Mean percentage correct for this task was 48.9%. This was not significantly different from 50%, $t(7) = 0.6$, $p > .05$. In this experiment, there was no evidence for retention of the orientations of even a small handful of items as there was in Experiment 1. This might reflect some difference between the processing of unattended orientation and colour. For instance, it might be difficult to code left and right tilt into VSTM (Wolfe & Friedman-Hill, 1992). Alternatively, it might be that the square mask acted as a new object, knocking the old item out of VSTM if it happened to be in VSTM (a form of object substitution masking; DiLollo, Enns, & Rensink, 2000). In any case, the slight difference between colour and orientation is not directly germane to this paper. What is important is that, in either case, the features of clearly visible stimuli are not reportable immediately after those features are obscured. Neither feedback nor 200 trials of practice helped. Once again a regression analysis showed no increase in performance over the course of the 200 trials, $F(1, 7) = 1.05$, $p > .05$.

EXPERIMENT 3: DOES PRIOR ATTENTION HELP?

In Experiments 1 and 2 observers are unable to describe the colour or orientation of items the instant after those items had been removed or changed. Those items had been visible for some length of time and there was no uncertainty as to the location of the item to be reported. Is this a reflection of the limits on VSTM or, perhaps, did observers fail to pay attention in Experiments 1 and 2? In Experiment 1, there was some evidence that observers had attended to and could report the colour of one to three items. In Experiment 2, the data did not even provide evidence for that level of effort on the part of the observers. Even though items can be identified at a rate of 20–30 items per second, perhaps our observers just did not bother. We do not know because the deployment of attention was not under any experimental control. Observers were free to attend or not attend to stimuli prior to the cue. In Experiment 3, deployment of attention was manipulated by inducing observers to attend to specific items. We asked if some memory for the basic features of attended items survives the hiding of those features.

Method

Experiment 3 used a simple extension of the methods of Experiment 1 as illustrated in Figure 3. A set of coloured disks was presented on the screen. A specific disk was cued by increasing its brightness. Observers were asked to identify the *current* colour of that cued stimulus ("What IS the colour?"; henceforth, an IS response). After a variable number of IS responses to disks in the same, otherwise static display, one item was cued and masked and the observer was asked "What WAS the colour?" (henceforth, WAS responses). The item cued for a WAS response might or might not have been cued for a previous IS decision. Moreover, the number of intervening responses between an IS response to an item and a subsequent WAS decision about the same item could be systematically varied in order examine the time course of any benefits of prior attention.

Participants.   Nine participants were recruited for this experiment under the same conditions as in Experiment 1.

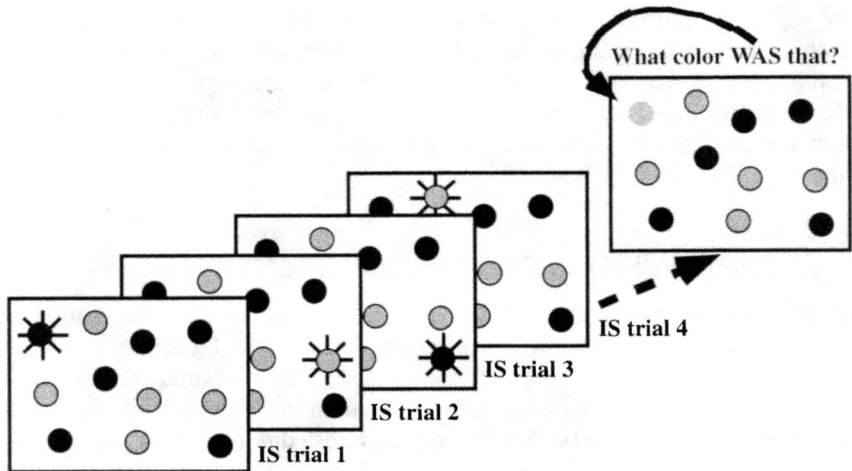

Figure 3. Sample sequence for Experiment 3. Observers make decisions about the current colour of cued items. On critical trials, they try to identify the colour of an item that may or may not have been previously cued.

Stimuli. Stimuli were the red and green circles of Experiment 1. A luminance increment of 75% cued observers on IS trials. The final WAS target was cued by changing one of the items from red or green to blue. Since blue was not otherwise displayed, the appearance of the blue disk told the observer that it was time for a WAS response. Thus, in this version of the experiment, observers knew the locus of the change. They knew that a change (to blue) had occurred. All they needed to do was to report on the colour that had been present the instant before the change. This is a completely trivial task if just a single item is displayed.

Procedure. At the start of a trial, the elements of the array were displayed for a period randomly chosen between 1500 and 2000 ms. After this initial period, one element was cued by an increment in luminance. Observers made an unspeeded response naming the colour of this element as red or green. As soon as a response was made, a different element was cued at random. This process continued for anywhere from 2 to 14 such IS responses. At the end of the sequence of IS responses, a final target element turned blue. On 80% of trials, this element had previously been cued for an IS response. If so, it had been cued either 2, 4, 8 or 12 responses prior to the WAS response. On 20% of the trials, the item cued for the WAS response had not been cued for an IS response. After the WAS response, the screen was blanked. A 1000 ms intertrial interval preceded the next stimulus array. Each

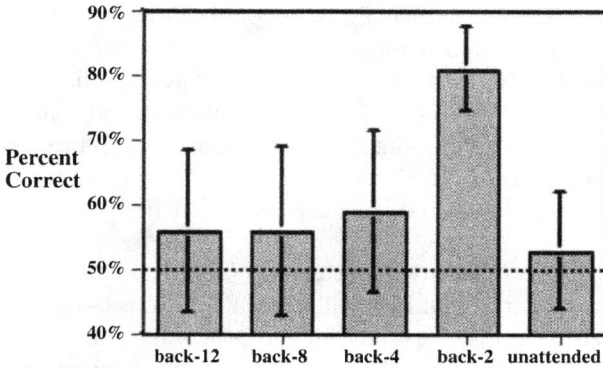

Figure 4. Mean percentage correct for the five types of WAS trials in Experiment 3. Error bars show the 95% confidence intervals around the mean. Note that "back-12" is the most distantly probed in time and "back-2" the most recent. Thus time runs from left to right.

observer completed two blocks of 200 WAS trials and an average of 4240 IS trials. Observers were allowed breaks whenever requested.

Results and discussion

Average percent correct as a function of IS–WAS interval is shown in Figure 4. Confidence intervals and t-test of the hypothesis that performance is above the 50% level are shown in Table 1.

The baseline (uncued) condition produced 53% correct responses. This serves as a replication of Experiment 1 though in this case performance did not differ significantly from chance, $t(8) = 2.01$, $p > .05$. Turning to the cued conditions, there is a clear effect of prior IS responses on the accuracy of a subsequent WAS response. Observers perform quite well on WAS responses that are made to an item that had been the subject of an IS

TABLE 1

Testing the hypothesis that performance on WAS trials in Experiment 3 differs from chance (50%)

	Mean	DF	t-Value	P-Value	95% Lower	95% Upper
unattended	.528	8	.728	.4876	.440	.616
back-2	.806	8	10.727	<.0001	.7 40	.871
back-4	.592	8	1.685	.1304	.466	.718
back-8	.558	8	1.010	.3420	.426	.690
back-12	.556	8	1.002	.3456	.428	.683

response two responses earlier. From 80% correct in the 2-back condition, performance falls to a roughly constant level for the three other cued conditions (4-, 8-, and 12-back). Performance is not significantly above 50% for any of these conditions (see Table 1), though we might imagine that the small elevation above 50% might rise to statistical significance with more participants or more trials. Participants were 95% correct on the IS trials. They tended to be slower and less accurate on the first trial in a series of IS responses.

The results show that attending to and naming an item makes it more likely that the colour of that item will be available immediately after the item is masked. The effect is clear only for the 2-back data. It is, at best weakly suggestive for the 4-back condition. Note that this suggests a very limited role for any VSTM in this task. The last two to four items might be remembered and even that paltry number could be the result of verbal recoding. Experiment 4 replicates this result with some variation in methods.

Hollingworth (2004) used a similar method with more natural scene images. He also found a small recency effect. However, he found evidence for substantial longer term memory for attended items. As discussed above, his methods allow observers to use whatever processes support picture recognition memory (Did this unique wrench change orientation?), whereas our method did not (Was this decidedly nonunique red dot previously green?).

EXPERIMENT 4: PRIOR ATTENTION TO A
WELL-LEARNED DISPLAY

In Experiment 3, an array of stimuli was presented for up to 14 IS responses and for a single WAS response. In Experiment 4, a single array was presented for 100 WAS trials. Observers made a series of IS responses and a smaller number of WAS responses. Some items were never cued for IS responses. Items that were cued could be cued many times. As in Experiment 3, one critical variable was the number of IS decisions lying between a WAS response and the most recent IS response to the same stimulus. This method also makes it possible to examine effects of extended exposure to the stimulus.

With prolonged exposure to a static display, we worried that observers might be able to use various undesirable strategies to arrive at a correct response. For example, in this unspeeded task participants might simply count the number of circles of each colour and note a change in number. To thwart this sort of strategy, a subset of irrelevant stimuli changed colour on each trial. Observers were never queried about these items.

Method

Participants.   Ten participants were recruited for this experiment under the same conditions as in Experiment 1.

Stimuli.   The stimuli in this experiment were again made up of coloured circular elements on a black background. Experiment 4 used four colours— red, green, cyan, and purple, changing the chance level to 25%. There were 30 items in the stimulus array. Twenty of these were task-relevant. The remaining 10 irrelevant (never cued) items changed colour with each response. To avoid confusion with the irrelevant colour changes, the nature of the cue was changed in this experiment. For IS responses, a small white dot appeared in the centre of probed items. For WAS responses, the entire item turned white.

Procedure.   At the start of a trial, the elements of the array were displayed for a period randomly chosen between 1500 and 2000 ms. At this point one element was cued by a small white dot appearing in its centre. Observers made an unspeeded IS response, giving the colour of the cued item. As soon as a response was made, a different element would be cued at random and the 10 irrelevant elements would all change colour at random. After 2 to 14 such IS responses, an item would turn entirely white and the observer was instructed to make a WAS response about the now-hidden colour of that item. Note that this item was the same colour at the moment it was hidden that it had been throughout the preceding run of IS responses. As was the case with Experiment 3, this element could have been one that had been previously attended (either 2-, 4-, 8- or 12-back in the sequence of response), or one that had not (i.e., a disk that had remained constant in its colour but about which no IS judgement had been made). After the WAS trial, the process would start again, with an element being probed for an IS decision. The critical difference between Experiments 3 and 4 was that, in Experiment 3 a new array was presented after each WAS response, while in Experiment 4 the same array was used for an entire block of trials. Each subject completed two blocks of 200 WAS trials and an average of 2120 IS trials. Participants were allowed breaks whenever requested. Two participants completed only one block of 200 WAS trials ($\sim$2100 IS trials). Their data follow the same pattern as the more practiced participants and are included in the analysis.

Results and discussion

Figure 5 shows the mean percentage correct for the five conditions. As was the case with Experiment 3, inspection of this figure shows an effect of

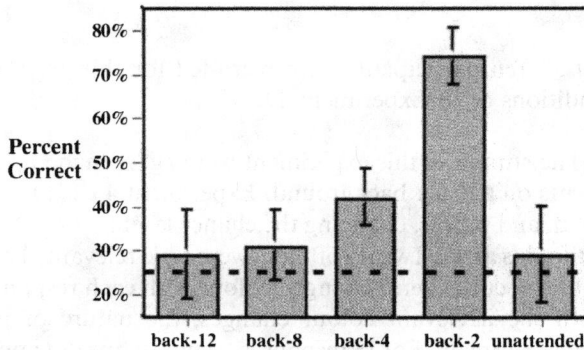

Figure 5. Results for Experiment 4. The dotted line shows the 25% chance level. Error bars show the 95% confidence intervals.

condition on percentage correct such that performance was the highest for the attended 2-back condition and lowest for the unattended condition. There appears to be a trend of decreasing performance levels as we go from 2-back towards 12-back. With four possible colours to choose from, chance performance is 25%. Table 2 shows 95% confidence intervals and t-test results, testing the hypothesis that performance differs from the 25% level.

In this experiment, the 2- and 4-back conditions show evidence for memory. The 8- and 12-back results are a bit above the 25% level but not significantly so. It might seem surprising that steady exposure to the same set of stimuli in Experiment 4 did not produce more evidence for memory. Recall that participants were responding to a set of 20 disks that did not change during the block of 200 WAS and approximately 2100 IS trials. Thus, even disks that had not been the subject of an IS decision might have been cued multiple times during the course of the extended block of trials for a WAS decision. There is a hint of a developing memory for these unattended disks. Performance on unattended disks rises from an average of 20% in the first quarter of the trials to 33% in the last quarter. This improvement is

TABLE 2
Testing the hypothesis that performance on WAS trials in Experiment 4 differs from chance (25%)

	Mean	DF	t-Value	P-Value	95% Lower	95% Upper
unattended	.289	9	.792	.4490	.178	.400
2-back	.742	9	16.781	<.0001	.676	.808
4-back	.416	9	5.772	.0003	.351	.481
8-back	.310	9	1.687	.1258	.230	.390
12-back	.292	9	.931	.3764	.190	.394

significant: Paired t-test, $t(9) = 2.6$, $p = .015$. However, there is no similar evidence for a developing memory for the 8- and 12-back stimuli. Perhaps this weak evidence for memory beyond a recent memory for IS responses is not surprising. The demand characteristics of this task might not push participants toward memorization of the display. Recall that 10 of the 30 disks change colour at random so the overall configuration of the display changes from moment to moment. These results suggest that detailed memory for a display may not develop passively even if an observer is looking at unchanging objects. While this task presents an unnatural situation, it is not an unreasonable approximation to real-world situations. Imagine the view from a pavement cafe. The fact that many objects (cars, pedestrians, pigeons) are changing does not make it impossible for you to learn something about the static objects in the field (fountain, pavement, streetlight). As noted, in approximations to natural scenes, Hollingworth and Henderson (2002; Hollingworth, 2004) found evidence for memory for previously fixated objects. Their experiments show that you can remember something of what you have seen. This, of course, is hardly surprising. Our experiments show how little is remembered of simple stimuli that remain visible up until the moment that the memory is probed.

EXPERIMENT 5: WHEN IS THE SCENE MEMORY UPDATED?

At the outset of this paper, we proposed two factors limiting the ability to detect changes in scenes. First, objects are selected by attention and recognized at a rate of 20–30 items per second and a change can be detected only if the object is attended at the right time. Second, there are profound limits on the capacities of short- and longer term visual memories. The first four experiments are consistent with this view. Performance is very poor. The only exceptions can be attributed to the role of a limited capacity VSTM (with a possible longer term contribution in Experiment 4). The presence of a limited memory for attended items allows a more direct test of the hypothesis that *only* changes to attended items can be detected. In Experiment 5, we exploit this limited memory in order to test the role of selective attention. Consider the case in which the observer successfully recalled the colour of an item that had been cued two trials previously (a 2-back IS response). What is the basis of the successful WAS response? There are, at least, two possibilities. Our hypothesis states that the representation of the scene and the memory for that representation were updated at the time of the IS response. The effects of attention to that particular item would end when attention was directed to the next item. Alternatively, attention to the item at the time of the IS response might produce some ongoing change in the processing of the attended item such that its information about its

Trial 1   **Trial 2**   **Trial N**

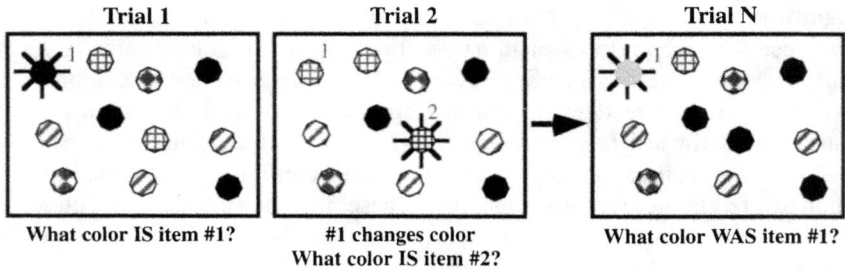

What color IS item #1?   #1 changes color   What color WAS item #1?
                         What color IS item #2?

Figure 6. Sample sequence for Experiment 5. After an IS response, the item might change its colour. Thus, item 1 is queried for an IS response on Trial 1. Its colour is changed at the time of Trial 2 when another item is attended. On the critical WAS trial (Trial *N*), observers try to identify the colour of that item just prior to the mask. Are they more likely to give the "true" colour (that shown in Trial 2) or the colour from the IS response on Trial 1?

current colour would be available even after attention had been deployed elsewhere. Experiment 5 is designed to distinguish between these possibilities.

Figure 6 illustrates the design of the experiment. As in Experiment 4, observers make a series of IS responses, followed by a WAS response. In Experiment 5, however, the colour of a cued item was changed immediately at the time of the cueing of the next IS response. Thus, in Figure 7, the item labelled "1" is cued for an IS response on Trial 1. Item "2" is cued on Trial 2. Note that item "1" changes colour at this time. Later, on some Trial *N*, item

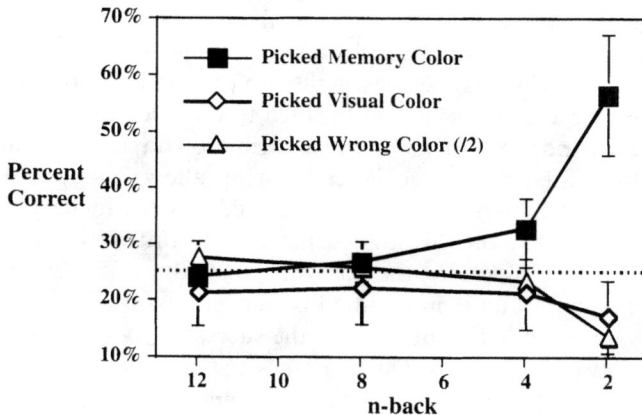

Figure 7. Results of Experiment 5. Because chance level for wrong responses is 50%, wrong response rates are divided by 2 to make them comparable to the memory and visual responses, each of which has a chance probability of 25%. Error bars are 95% confidence intervals. As before, the most recently cued items are to the right of the graph.

1 is cued again, now for a WAS response. There are three types of answers to the question "What colour WAS item 1?"

1. If observers only gain information about the object at the time when the object is attended, then, assuming that they remembered it, they would provide the colour *remembered* from the trial when that item was last cued.
2. If attention to the object changes the processing of the object in a manner that makes continuous monitoring of the colour possible, then, assuming that they remembered it, observers could respond with the newer colour that was *visible* just prior to the mask that cued a WAS response.
3. Finally, of course, observers might simply guess. Given that there are four colours in this experiment, they would have a 50% chance of producing an entirely *wrong* response.

Chance responding would yield 25% *memory colour* responses, 25% *visual colour* responses, and 50% responses giving one of the two remaining colours (*wrong colour* responses).

Method

Participants.   Ten participants were recruited for this experiment under the same conditions as in Experiment 1.

Stimuli.   The stimuli in this experiment were the same as in Experiment 4 but with no task-irrelevant items. Except for the change in the colour after an IS response, the display remained completely static. Set size was 20 items.

Procedure.   At the start of a trial, the elements of the array were displayed for a period randomly chosen between 1500 and 2000 ms. At this point one element was cued by a small white dot appearing in its centre. Observers named the colour of the element (IS response). As soon as a response was made, the colour of the cued item switched to one of the three other possible colours and a new item was cued at random for the next IS. This process continued for 2–14 such responses, whereupon one element turned entirely white and the observer was asked to report what colour it had been before it turned white (WAS response). As was the case with Experiment 4, this element could have been one that had been previously attended (either 2, 4, 8, or 12 responses ago), or one that had not (i.e., a disk about which no IS judgement had been made). After this WAS decision, the process would start again, with elements being probed for IS decisions. Note that observers were instructed to give the colour of the disk immediately prior to the WAS cue, but they were not informed about possible changes in the colour of the previously cued items. Thus, for the observer, the newer, visible colour of the disk was the truly "correct" response. Indeed, observers were given trial-by-trial feedback in which only correct visual colour responses were labelled as "correct" in order to push observers to give the visual colour response if possible. Each observer completed two blocks of 100 WAS trials. These were accompanied by approximately 2100 IS responses per block.

Results and discussion

Figure 7 and Table 3 show mean percentage correct for visual colour and memory colour responses. Each of these has a chance probability of 25%. Wrong colour responses have a chance probability of 50% so Figure 7 shows wrong colour rates divided by two to make them directly comparable to the correct response rates. Table 3 shows the results of t-tests testing for significant deviation from the 25% chance level. As in Experiment 4, actual performance deviates from chance performance only for the WAS responses made to items that were the subject of IS responses 2 or 4 responses previously. The observers are producing memory colour responses, reporting on the colour that *was* present when they were last queried about a specific disk. They show no evidence of an ability to make correct visible colour responses. Visible colour and wrong colour responses differ from chance

TABLE 3
Testing the hypothesis that rates of different types of responses in Experiment 5 differ from chance (25%). Note that italicized conditions are significantly below chance

	Mean	DF	t-Value	P-Value	95% Lower	95% Upper
VIS back2	*.171*	9	*−2.847*	*.0192*	*.108*	*.234*
VIS back 4	.215	9	−1.282	.2318	.153	.277
VIS back8	.227	9	−.842	.4218	.165	.289
VIS Back12	.211	9	−1.562	.1527	.155	.267
MEM back 2	**.565**	9	**6.634**	**<.0001**	**.457**	**.672**
MEM back 4	**.325**	9	**3.197**	**.0109**	**.272**	**.379**
MEM back8	.268	9	1.137	.2847	.232	.304
MEM back 12	.241	9	−.795	.4470	.216	.266
WRONG back2/2	*.133*	9	*−7.382*	*<.0001*	*.097*	*.169*
WRONG back4/2	.231	9	−1.606	.1426	.204	.258
WRONG back8/2	.254	9	.305	.7673	.228	.279
WRONG back12/2	.274	9	1.888	.0916	.245	.303
Unattended	.301	9	1.809	.1039	.237	.364

levels for the 2-back condition but only because they fall significantly *below* chance levels.

WAS responses to unattended items produced a 30% accuracy rate. This was not significantly different from the 25% level expected by chance.

The results of Experiment 5 replicate the results of Experiments 3 and 4. A few recently attended items get into some sort of memory and are available for recall. However, consistent with the hypothesis that object information is updated only while an item is selected, there is no evidence that attention to an item makes it possible to detect or remember subsequent changes to that item. Assuming that the memory being probed is VSTM, this result shows that the maintenance of items in VSTM is not based on reference to information about those object, retained in the earliest stages of visual processing. Early representations of the objects presumably reflect changes in the colour of even unattended items. For example, one would expect the negative afterimage of the dot to reflect a colour change even if the observer was unaware of the change.

EXPERIMENT 6: RAPID CUEING

The argument of this paper is that failures to detect change and/or failures to recognize the nature of a change occur because we only update the identity of objects when we selectively attend to them and that this updating of the visual representation is subject to memory capacity limitations. The method of Experiments 3–5 has been to control the updating process by having observers make IS responses prior to making a critical WAS response. While this allows us to be sure that observers have attended to specific items, these putative updating events are occurring at a rate much slower than anyone's estimate of the rates of object recognition in tasks like visual search or in scene analysis. In Experiment 6, a series of items is cued very rapidly, at rates comparable to object processing rates estimated from other tasks. At these speeds, we cannot collect the IS responses that assured us that observers were complying by attending to our selection of items. However, we can collect WAS responses and seek evidence for an effect of the cueing.

Rapid presentation of cues addresses another concern. The fairly slow, self-paced nature of Experiments 3, 4, and 5 might have encouraged verbal recoding. Note that fully reliable verbal memory is not likely to have governed responses because the task would have been dauntingly complex. First, the observer would need to have remembered a set of colour terms in order (e.g., red, blue, red, green). When an item was cued for a WAS response, the observer would have to have known that the item cued for the WAS response was, for example, the 4-back item. Then the observer could read out the correct item from the list. This seems unlikely. It does seem possible that observers might improve over chance performance by remembering the last two or three colours and using those colour names to guess about the WAS response, especially for 2-back items. Any sort of verbal recoding will be made more difficult if the stimulus onset asynchrony (SOA) between cues is short.

Method

Participants. Twelve participants were recruited for this experiment under the same conditions as in Experiment 1.

Stimuli. Visual stimuli were 20 coloured squares subtending 1 deg on a side at the 57 cm viewing distance. On each trial, items occupied randomly chosen locations on an invisible 5×5 grid subtending 17 deg on a side. Squares could be yellow, blue, green, purple, or red. Colours were randomly chosen with the constraint that there be at least one item of each colour in a display. To cue an item, its luminance increased briefly by 50% and its area increased briefly by 75%. This luminance and size change should serve as an effective exogenous cue to attract attention (Brawn & Snowden, 1999).

The WAS response was cued by a grey cross subtending 1.7×1.7 deg. This served to hide the underlying square and, thus, mask the colour of the cued item. It also served as a clear cue for a "WAS" response. Stimuli and their experimental configuration are illustrated schematically in Figure 8.

Procedure. An experimental trial started with the presentation of a white fixation cross. After 500 ms the display of 20 squares of randomly chosen colours and positions appeared. After another 500 ms the cueing sequence started. Depending on the block, either three, six, or eight elements were

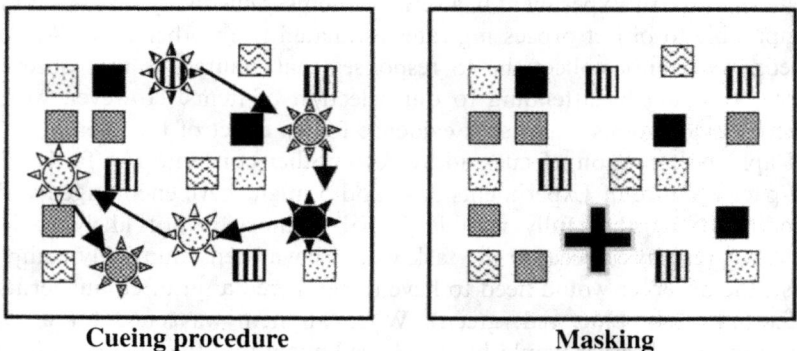

Cueing procedure   **Masking**

Figure 8.   Stimuli are 20 coloured squares. After rapid cueing of three, six, or eight items, one item is hidden and probed for the memory test. What colour was presented on the position of the cross?

cued, one after another, at one of three SOAs: 50, 150, or 300 ms. These rates are comparable to estimates of the rate of deployment of covert attention. After the end of the cue sequence, a single item was masked by a grey cross, and observers made the unspeeded 5 AFC colour choice by pressing one of five keys with colour words inscribed on the keyboard buttons. On 90% of trials, the probed item was chosen from the cued set. We assume these to be the "attended items". The other 10% of cues were used to measure baseline levels of recall for previously uncued items. The position of the masked item in the previously cued set was randomized. The cue length and SOA variables were blocked. Observers were tested for an average of 50 trials at each n-back position plus 10% trials at uncued locations. All told, observers performed 2550 trials.

On screen feedback was provided after each trial and a brief computer-generated tone marked incorrect decisions. Participants initiated each trial with a key press and could take breaks whenever requested. Volunteers were instructed to attend to the cue string to prepare for a memory test and then make an unspeeded decision to indicate the target colour. The importance of accuracy was emphasized.

Results and discussion

The first interesting aspect of these results is that observers perform at better than chance levels even for the uncued items. The accuracy for those items is shown in Table 4.

This is almost undoubtedly an unintended side effect of the experimental design. Colours were chosen randomly in each display with the constraint that all colours had to be present. That means, in the extreme, that a display could have consisted of one red, one blue, one, green, one purple, and sixteen

TABLE 4

Accuracy for test items that had not been pre-cued. Note that all are above the nominal 20% "chance" level and that most are significantly above that level by a paired t-test

Cue String	SOA	% correct	$t(11)$	P-Value
3 items	50 msec	27%	1.78	0.103
3 items	150 msec	27%	2.77	0.018
3 items	300 msec	30%	2.30	0.042
6 items	50 msec	30%	3.99	0.002
6 items	150 msec	29%	2.88	0.015
6 items	300 msec	24%	1.81	0.098
8 items	50 msec	28%	2.33	0.040
8 items	150 msec	28%	2.88	0.015
8 items	300 msec	24%	1.38	0.196

yellow items. Under these circumstances, an observer who was guessing about the colour of a now hidden item, would do well to guess "yellow". This works only if observers can base an estimate of the relative frequencies of colours on information gathered while selective attention is occupied elsewhere. There is evidence that this is the case (Braun & Julesz, 1998; Wolfe, Klempen, & Horowitz, 1997). Given these displays, an ideal observer could achieve 30% correct by always guessing the most common colour in the display. Our observers fall just a bit short of that ideal (27% on average across all conditions).

For the purposes of the present studies, this result merely means that accuracy on cued items should be tested against the empirical "chance" level averaging 27% and not against the theoretical 20% level. One could test against the ideal 30% correct level but this assumes that human observers could ascertain the most common colour on every trial. That seems too conservative (though the change would not alter the analysis very much).

Figure 9 shows accuracy as a function of order in the precue list for each cue SOA and for lists of three, six, and eight items. As in the other figures, time runs from left to right so that the item cued most recently is on the right side of the figure. The dotted line in each graph shows the empirical chance performance for uncued items (averaged across cue string length).

Tables 5–7 show the results of paired t-tests comparing performance at each n-back position to the appropriate, empirical chance level for that set of trials.

Note that these tests of accuracy levels against a baseline are planned comparisons. Thus the p-values in Tables 5–7 are not corrected for multiple comparisons. Nevertheless, one might want to be cautious about the significance of conditions with p-values near .05. Several conclusions can be drawn from these results. First, there is clear evidence for better performance for cued items than for uncued. Second, this evidence is strongest for the most recently cued items (n-back, 0, 1, or 2). Third, there is a hint of a primacy effect: String length 3, SOA $= 50$; string lengths 6 and 8, SOA $= 150$ and 300. For the longer strings and slower SOAs, a primacy effect could be taken as an indication of some form of verbal recoding. Recency is more consistent with the actions of a limited-capacity VSTM.

We can estimate the capacity of the memory from these data by assuming that, at each position in the list ...

1. Accuracy $=$ P(remembering the item)$+(1-$P(remembering))*the empirical chance level.
2. P(remembering) $=$ capacity/string length.

Solving for capacity, we find that

3. Capacity $= \Sigma^{list}(\dfrac{Acc - Ch}{1 - Ch})$

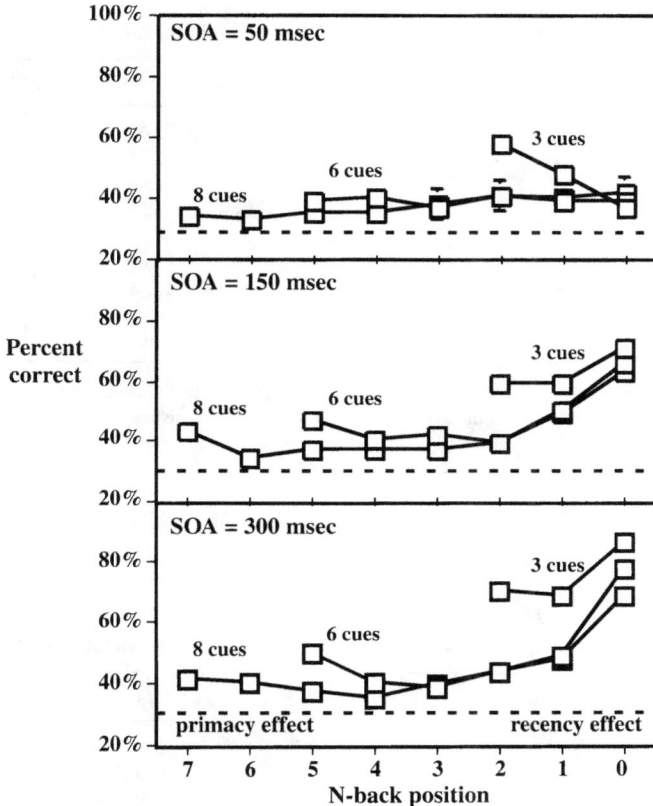

Figure 9. Accuracy as a function of position in the precue list for each SOA and each cue string length. Items cued most recently are plotted at the right of this figure.

where "Acc" is the accuracy for each item in the list and "Ch" is the empirical chance level.

The results of this calculation are shown in Figure 10.

Note that SOA is the determining feature. Given more time, the capacity rises from about one item to about two. Interestingly, this is little affected by the number of items cued. We cannot perform identical calculations for the other experiments because observers may have attended to more positions than we cued and because we did not test all list positions as we did here. However, the results of previous experiments are consistent with the notion that observers have only a limited capacity to remember attended items.

The results of this experiment are consistent with the hypothesis that a very limited capacity VSTM allows observers to recover the identity of a very

TABLE 5

Testing the significance of deviation from chance levels for cue strings of length 3

nback	SOA	Mean Diff.	t(11)	P-Value
0	50 msec	10%	2.69	0.021
1	50 msec	22%	7.11	<.0001
2	50 msec	31%	8.97	<.0001
0	150 msec	44%	6.31	<.0001
1	150 msec	32%	4.88	0.0005
2	150 msec	32%	4.67	0.0007
0	300 msec	56%	13.38	<.0001
1	300 msec	38%	6.95	<.0001
2	300 msec	40%	6.66	<.0001

"Mean difference" is the difference between the average empirical chance level and the average performance for that position in the list. Even with a concern for statistical significance raised by the problem of multiple comparisons, it is clear that observers perform better than chance.

TABLE 6

Testing the significance of deviation from chance levels for cue strings of length 6

n-back	SOA	Mean Diff.	t(11)	P-Value
0	50	10%	2.43	0.0334
1	50	9%	2.43	0.0334
2	50	11%	3.09	0.0103
3	50	8%	2.58	0.0257
4	50	10%	2.55	0.0271
5	50	10%	2.58	0.0258
0	150	37%	7.09	<.0001
1	150	21%	4.90	0.0005
2	150	10%	2.80	0.0174
3	150	13%	2.98	0.0125
4	150	11%	2.78	0.018
5	150	18%	2.58	0.0257
0	300	53%	14.37	<.0001
1	300	24%	6.39	<.0001
2	300	19%	4.40	0.0011
3	300	14%	3.03	0.0114
4	300	16%	4.16	0.0016
5	300	25%	4.39	0.0011

Given a concern for statistical significance raised by the problem of multiple comparisons, the strongest evidence for above chance performance lies at the longer SOAs and the most recent positions in the list (n-back 0,1, 2).

TABLE 7
Testing the significance of deviation from chance levels for cue strings of length 8

nback	SOA	Mean Diff.	t(11)	P-Value
0	50	13%	2.46	0.0314
1	50	11%	2.84	0.0162
2	50	13%	2.08	0.0619
3	50	9%	2.14	0.0554
4	50	7%	1.64	0.1284
5	50	6%	1.88	0.0869
6	50	5%	1.22	0.249
7	50	6%	1.74	0.1091
0	150	35%	6.56	<.0001
1	150	22%	5.32	0.0002
2	150	11%	2.58	0.0255
3	150	9%	2.41	0.0347
4	150	10%	2.54	0.0274
5	150	9%	2.29	0.043
6	150	7%	1.95	0.0773
7	150	16%	2.62	0.024
0	300	45%	10.52	<.0001
1	300	24%	8.08	<.0001
2	300	19%	7.69	<.0001
3	300	16%	5.88	0.0001
4	300	12%	3.00	0.012
5	300	13%	4.26	0.0013
6	300	17%	4.70	0.0007
7	300	18%	4.59	0.0008

The strongest evidence for above chance performance lies at the longer SOAs and the most recent positions in the list (n-back 0,1, 2). At SOA 200, there is some evidence for a weak primacy effect as well as a recency effect.

few recently attended items. In spite of the differences in method, the results are broadly similar to the results of the previous experiments: Good memory for the most recently cued item with rapidly declining memory thereafter. Given the rapid rate of cueing in this experiment, it seems unlikely that verbal recoding accounts for the results in this case.

EXPERIMENT 7: NATURAL SCENES

In a final experiment, we return to the more naturalistic stimuli used in the more striking change blindness demonstrations. Our goal is to see if the addition of a rich, meaningful context would make a substantial change in the results of experiment like the previous one.

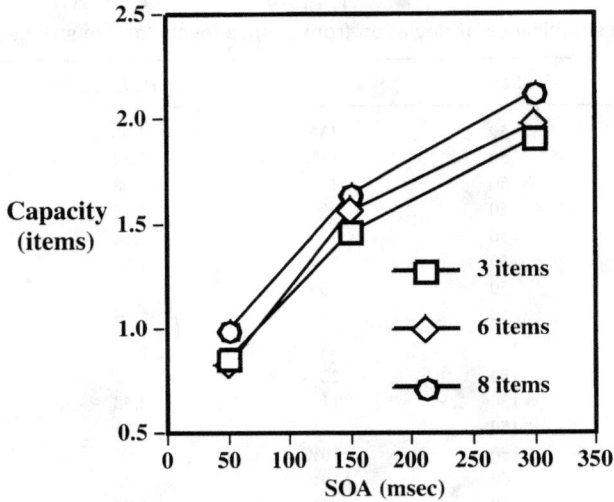

Figure 10.   Capacity as a function of SOA for different cue list lengths.

Method

In Experiment 7, observers looked at scenes like that shown in Figure 11.

Actual stimuli were full colour. There were four background scenes. Associated with each scene was a set of 36 plausible items (meaning, for example, that the lamppost appeared in the courtyard scene of Figure 11 but not in the kitchen scene). On any given trial, 12 of the items were placed in plausible locations on the background (e.g.. the lamppost appeared on the

Figure 11.   Observers viewed a scene like the one on the left of this figure. Twelve objects like those on the left (but proportionally smaller) were seeded into plausible locations in the image. Actual images were full colour.

street level, not in mid-air or on a roof). The background occupied an area of about 30 ×20 deg. Each object fitted into a 2.6 ×2.6 deg region (note that objects were not always appropriately size scaled but were not ridiculous in context).

After viewing a fixation stimulus for 1000 ms, observers viewed the scene passively for 500 ms. Then either three or six items were cued at SOAs of 150 or 300 ms in different blocks. At the end of the cue string, one item was hidden by a yellow box. The set of all 36 objects was presented as a response screen and the observer indicated which of the 36 items had been present at the location of the yellow square. As in the previous experiment, 10% of trials queried the identity of an uncued item. The other items were picked at random from the cued list. Feedback was given on each trial. After practice, observers were tested for 920 trials.

Ten observers between 18 and 40 were tested under the same conditions as in prior experiments.

Results

Accuracy as a function of position in the cue list is shown in Figure 12.

The first feature of the results that bears notice is baseline performance. Given that observers are picking from a set of 36 items, chance would seem to be 1/36 or 2.8%. Performance is far in excess of that level. If we assume that four or five items are held in VSTM, then chance would be higher—the chance of having the item in VSTM plus the chance of picking it at random (14–16%). Performance is above this level, too. Clearly, observers are

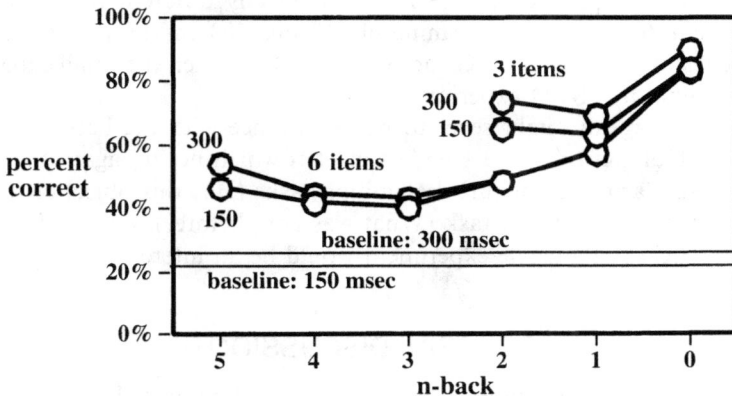

Figure 12.   Accuracy as a function of position in the cue list for SOAs of 150 and 300 and cue list lengths of 3 and 6 items. "Baseline" accuracy is accuracy for uncued items.

TABLE 8
Capacity estimates for Experiment 7

	"Empirical" guessing level		theoretical guessing level	
	SOA 150	SOA 300	SOA 150	SOA 300
3 items	1.8	2.2	2.1	2.3
6 items	2.1	2.4	3.1	3.2

learning something about even the uncued items. The most likely source of information, as in the prior experiment, is the colour of the items. Red stop signs, blue baby carriages, and so forth, appeared consistently throughout the experiment. If an observer noted that there was less red in the cued display, then the set of possible target items would be greatly reduced.

Accuracy for the cued items is modestly higher than the comparable results in Experiment 6 but the overall impression is that use of realistic stimuli does not markedly change the results. This is borne out in the capacity estimates. One can ask, as in the previous experiment, how much additional information is available about the cued items than about the uncued. To answer this question, we use the empirical chance levels of around 25% shown on the figure. Alternatively, one can ask how many of the 12 objects are available to the observer in any manner. In this case, we use the theoretical chance level of 2.8%. The estimates are shown in Table 8.

The capacity estimates are a bit larger than those in the previous experiment. However, as with the accuracy data, the interesting fact is that the results of Experiment 7 are not dramatically different from those of Experiment 6. Even with meaningful stimuli, 500 ms of preview and a relatively slow, 300 ms SOA, capacity doesn't even reach the small capacities usually found in VSTM experiments.

While this result might seem to be at variance with the better memory shown in Hollingworth and Henderson, it is worth noting again that their task has similarities to picture recognition tasks (Has this object changed?) while ours is a cued recall task (What was here before?). Comparing these two approaches in a single experiment would be an interesting project.

GENERAL DISCUSSION

The results of these seven experiments help to illuminate the relationships between change blindness, VSTM, and visual experience. To briefly review the implications of the specific experiments:

1. Experiment 1 shows that observers are very poor at describing a change (or its absence) even when very simple stimuli are used, even when there is no uncertainty as to the location of the change and even when no effort made to hide the change signal or divert attention away from that change. It may be a little unfair to call this "change blindness" in that the observer is perfectly aware that something happened at the locus of interest. However, the observer is generally blind to the nature of the change.

2. Experiment 2 shows that this is not an oddity of changes in colour. The same result is obtained with orientation.

3. Experiments 3 and 4 demonstrate that there is some memory for recently attended items in the display but that this is very limited, either in time or in capacity. Observers are quite good at giving the colour of a recently cued item and quite poor when asked about items earlier in the cued list.

4. Experiment 5 shows that attention to an item at one moment in time conveys no benefit if the observer must note a change in that item after attention has been diverted elsewhere. When there is an accessible representation of the features of an object, it appears that the available features are those that were noted when the object was last attended. Subsequent changes in the object are not available for explicit recall, though beyond doubt, it would be the changed colour that would determine implicit measures of visual processing such as the colour of a negative afterimage at that location.

5. Experiment 6 shows that little changes when the cueing rate is speeded up. There is still evidence for a very limited capacity memory for cued items. This makes it unlikely that the results of Experiments 1–5 involved verbal recoding. At the same time, the lack of improvement in performance suggests there is no perfect "iconic" memory of the image, available to be read out at the end of a swiftly presented cue sequence.

6. Finally, Experiment 7 shows that the meaning and structure of real-world scenes produces only modest increases in the estimates of the capacity of the memory that limits performance in these tasks.

We hold that these results are consistent with the two pathways account offered at the start of this paper. In Experiment 5, for example, observers spend a long time looking at a relatively stable scene. If asked, no doubt, they would tell you that they were looking at a collection of coloured dots. They would have some notion of the statistical properties of the display—colours, sizes, etc. (Ariely, 2001; Chong & Treisman, 2003). In the present experiments, this is illustrated by the ability to perform at above chance levels when guessing the colour of an uncued dot in Experiment 6. The nonselective pathway would deliver an experience of colour at specific loci in the field. The series of IS responses would make it clear to the observers that they could identify the colour of any specific spot, if asked. All of this would give rise to the compelling impression of a visual world, filled with identifiable objects. Given that rapid speed of identification, observers may be forgiven for the impression that all of this information is instantaneously available. However, when asked for the colour of a spot at the instant it vanishes, observers' responses reveal the limits imposed by two bottlenecks. First, they are only able to report on the colour of targets that have been recently selected (the subject of recent IS responses). Second, even for those items, accuracy is limited by a memory with a capacity of something less than four items. In this manner, observers can see and yet be blind.

Other work on VSTM has pointed to a capacity of four objects (Luck & Vogel, 1997). It is interesting that the capacity estimates here are even lower. Studies like the Luck and Vogel study typically use smaller set sizes than we used here. It is possible that we spread the limited capacity so thinly that our method could not see all of it. Alternatively, looking at Figure 10, for example, we can imagine that capacity might have been larger with longer interstimulus intervals. In any case, it is quite clear that the capacity of the memory required for this task is extremely limited. Other, seemingly similar tasks appear to show a larger memory. For example, inhibition of return (IOR) is a phenomenon in which responses are slowed or less accurate at loci that have been recently visited by attention (Klein, 2000). Several experiments have used a paradigm similar to ours. A series of items are cued in sequence and then IOR is assessed as a function of position in the cue (Danziger, Kingstone, & Snyder, 1998; Dodd, Castel, & Pratt, 2003; Snyder & Kingstone, 2000). Results vary but there are credible claims for IOR for six or more positions. This might be considered to be an illustration of the distinction between implicit and explicit memories. Observers do not know that IOR is present or absent at a locus. It is revealed by RT lags or reduced accuracy. While it may serve a useful function (Klein & MacInnes, 1999), it does not have an impact on visual experience. In the present context, the dissociation between IOR and VSTM is reminiscent of our discussion of the results of Experiment 5. In Experiment 5, participants were unable to report on a change in colour of a dot if that change happened *after* the dot had been attended and before it was attended again. Nevertheless, we could have found implicit evidence that some parts of the visual system had registered the change (e.g., with an afterimage measure). For present purposes, IOR can be considered to be similarly implicit evidence that attention had visited a locus even if that information is not helpful in the task of identifying change at the once-attended locus.

REFERENCES

Ariely, D. (2001). Seeing sets: Representation by statistical properties. *Psychological Science*, *12*(2), 157–162.

Brainard, D. H. (1997). The Psychophysics Toolbox. *Spatial Vision*, *10*, 443–446.

Braun, J., & Julesz, B. (1998). Dividing attention at little cost: Detection and discrimination tasks. *Perception and Psychophysics*, *60*(1), 1–23.

Brawn, P., & Snowden, R. J. (1999). Can one pay attention to a particular color? *Perception and Psychophysics*, *61*(5), 860–873.

Chong, S. C., & Treisman, A. (2003). Representation of statistical properties. *Vision Research*, *43*(4), 393–404.

Danziger, S., Kingstone, A., & Snyder, J. J. (1998). Inhibition of return to successively stimulated locations in a sequential visual search paradigm. *Journal of Experimental Psychology: Human Perception and Performance*, *24*(5), 1467–1475.

Di Lollo, V., Enns, J. T., & Rensink, R. A. (2000). Competition for consciousness among visual events: The psychophysics of reentrant visual processes. *Journal of Experimental Psychology: General*, *129*(4), 481–507.

Dodd, M. D., Castel, A. D., & Pratt, J. (2003). Inhibition of return with rapid serial shifts of attention: Implications for memory and visual search. *Perception and Psychophysics*, *65*(7), 1126–1135.

Henderson, J. M., & Hollingworth, A. (2003). Eye movements and visual memory: Detecting changes to saccade targets in scenes. *Perception and Psychophysics*, *65*(1), 58–71.

Hollingworth, A. (2004). Constructing visual representations of natural scenes: The roles of short- and long-term visual memory. *Journal of Experimental Psychology: Human Perception and Performance*, 30(3), 519–537.

Hollingworth, A., & Henderson, J. M. (2002). Accurate visual memory for previously attended objects in natural scenes. *Journal of Experimental Psychology: Human Perception and Performance*, *28*(1), 113–136.

Klein, R. M. (2000). Inhibition of return. *Trends in Cognitive Sciences*, *4*(4), 138–147.

Klein, R. M., & MacInnes, W. J. (1999). Inhibition of return is a foraging facilitator in visual search. *Psychological Science*, *10*(July), 346–352.

Logan, G. (1995). Linguistic and conceptual control of visual spatial attention. *Cognitive Psychology*, *28*, 103–174.

Luck, S. J., & Vogel, E. K. (1997). The capacity of visual working memory for features and conjunctions. *Nature*, *390*(20 Nov.), 279–281.

Mack, A., & Rock, I. (1998). *Inattentional blindness*. Cambridge, MA: MIT Press.

Neisser, U., & Becklen, R. (1975). Selective looking: Attending to visual significant events. *Cognitive Psychology*, *7*, 480–494.

Nickerson, R., & Adams, M. J. (1979). Long-term memory for a common object. *Cognitive Psychology*, *11*, 287–307.

Noë, A., Pessoa, L., & Thompson, E. (2000). Beyond the grand illusion: What change blindness really teaches us about vision. *Visual Cognition*, *7*, 93–106.

O'Regan, J. K., Rensink, R. A., & Clark, J. J. (1999). Change blindness as a result of "mudsplashes". *Nature*, *398*, 34.

Pelli, D. G. (1997). The VideoToolbox software for visual psychophysics: Transforming numbers into movies. *Spatial Vision*, *10*(4), 437–442.

Phillips, W. A. (1974). On the distinction between sensory storage and short-term visual memory. *Perception and Psychophysics*, *16*(2), 283–290.

Potter, M. C., & Levy, E. I. (1969). Recognition memory for a rapid sequence of pictures. *Journal of Experimental Psychology*, *81*, 10–15.

Rensink, R. A. (2000a). The dynamic representation of scenes. *Visual Cognition*, *7*(1), 17–42.

Rensink, R. A. (2000b). Seeing, sensing, and scrutinizing. *Vision Research*, *40*(10–12), 1469–1487.

Rensink, R. A. (2000c). Visual search for change: A probe into the nature of attentional processing. *Visual Cognition*, *7*, 345–376.

Rensink, R. A., O'Regan, J. K., & Clark, J. J. (1997). To see or not to see: The need for attention to perceive changes in scenes. *Psychological Science*, *8*, 368–373.

Shepard, R. N. (1967). Recognition memory for words, sentences, and pictures. *Journal Verbal Learning and Verbal Behavior*, *6*, 156–163.

Simons, D. J. (2000). Current approaches to change blindness. *Visual Cognition*, *7*(1–3), 1–15.

Simons, D. J., & Chabris, C. F. (1999). Gorillas in our midst: Sustained inattentional blindness for dynamic events. *Perception*, *28*(9), 1059–1074.

Simons, D. J., Chabris, C. F., Schnur, T. T., & Levin, D. T. (2002). Evidence for preserved representations in change blindness. *Consciousness and Cognition*, *11*, 78–97.

Simons, D. J., & Levin, D. T. (1997). Change blindness. *Trends in Cognitive Sciences*, *1*(7), 261–267.

Simons, D. J., & Levin, D. T. (1998). Failure to detect changes to people in a real-world interaction. *Psychonomic Bulletin and Review*, *5*(4), 644–649.

Snyder, J. J., & Kingstone, A. (2000). Inhibition of return and visual search: How many separate loci are inhibited? *Perception and Psychophysics*, *62*(3), 452–458.

Sperling, G. (1960). The information available in brief visual presentations. *Psychological Monographs*, *15*, 201–293.

Standing, L. (1973). Learning 10,000 pictures. *Quarterly Journal of Experimental Psychology*, *25*, 207–222.

Wolfe, J. M. (1998). Visual search. In H. Pashler (Ed.), *Attention* (pp. 13–74). Hove, UK: Psychology Press.

Wolfe, J. M. (1999). Inattentional amnesia. In V. Coltheart (Ed.), *Fleeting memories* (pp. 71–94). Cambridge, MA: MIT Press.

Wolfe, J. M., & Bennett, S. C. (1997). Preattentive object files: Shapeless bundles of basic features. *Vision Research*, *37*(1), 25–43.

Wolfe, J. M., & Friedman-Hill, S. R. (1992). On the role of symmetry in visual search. *Psychological Science*, *3*(3), 194–198.

Wolfe, J. M., Klempen, N., & Dahlen, K. (2000). Post-attentive vision. *Journal of Experimental Psychology: Human Perception and Performance*, *26*(2), 693–716.

Wolfe, J. M., Klempen, N. L., & Horowitz, T. S. (1997). The gist of the meaningless: Is scene recognition a type of visual search. *Investigative Ophthalmology and Visual Science*, *38*(4), S488.

Wolfe, J. M., Oliva, A., Butcher, S. J., & Arsenio, H. C. (2002). An unbinding problem? The disintegration of visible, previously attended objects does not attract attention. *Journal of Vision*, *2*(3), 256–271.

VISUAL COGNITION, 2006, 14 (4/5/6/7/8), 781–807

Ψ Psychology Press
Taylor & Francis Group

Visual memory for natural scenes: Evidence from change detection and visual search

Andrew Hollingworth

University of Iowa, Iowa City, IA, USA

This paper reviews research examining the role of visual memory in scene perception and visual search. Recent theories in these literatures have held that coherent object representations in visual memory are fleeting, disintegrating upon the withdrawal of attention from an object. I discuss evidence demonstrating that, far from being transient, visual memory supports the accumulation of information from scores of individual objects in scenes, utilizing both visual short-term memory and visual long-term memory. In addition, I review evidence that memory for the spatial layout of a scene and memory for specific object positions can efficiently guide search within natural scenes.

In the past decade, the interaction between perception and memory has received a great deal of attention from cognitive scientists. Much of this interest has originated from increased understanding that perception is a dynamic, serial process, extended over space and time. In this paper, I will discuss two related lines of research in which the relationship between perception and memory has come to the fore: Scene perception and visual search. While viewing natural scenes, the eyes shift (via saccadic eye movements) approximately three times each second to bring different scene regions onto the fovea, where visual acuity is highest (see Henderson & Hollingworth, 1998, for a review). Across saccades, visual encoding is suppressed (Matin, 1974), dividing visual input into discrete episodes. Given the discrete, serial nature of scene perception, memory is required to retain and accumulate visual information from local objects as the eyes and attention are oriented from object-to-object within a scene. Similarly, visual search typically requires the serial allocation of attention to individual objects in the course of finding a target and rejecting distractors (Woodman & Luck, 2003). Roles for memory in search include keeping track of objects

---

Please address all correspondence to Andrew Hollingworth, Department of Psychology, University of Iowa, 11 Seashore Hall E, Iowa City, IA 52242-1407, USA.
E-mail: andrew-hollingworth@uiowa.edu
This research was supported by National Institute of Health Grant R03 MH65456.

 DOI: 10.1080/13506280500193818

that have already been examined (e.g., Klein, 1988) and guiding attention to targets that appear in predictable locations (e.g., Chun & Jiang, 1998).

The following discussion of scene perception, search, and visual memory will be placed within the context of recent claims that visual memory is transient, playing little or no role in the representation of natural scenes or in search (Rensink, 2000; Wolfe, 1999). I will review evidence that, contrary to these claims, visual memory supports robust accumulation of visual information from scores of individual objects in scenes and that visual memory can efficiently guide search within real-world environments.

SCENE PERCEPTION, CHANGE BLINDNESS, AND VISUAL MEMORY

The phenomenon of change blindness has shaped recent thinking on the role of visual memory in scene perception. In change blindness studies, participants often fail to detect otherwise salient changes when detection depends on visual memory. Dependence on memory has been achieved either by introducing an interstimulus interval (ISI) between differing images (e.g., Rensink, O'Regan, & Clark, 1997), by introducing a change to an image during an eye movement (e.g., Grimes, 1996; Henderson & Hollingworth, 1999, 2003c), or by occluding a change with a physical object (e.g., Simons & Levin, 1998). In perhaps the most well-known change blindness paper, Rensink et al. (1997) presented photographs of real-world scenes and introduced a change to a portion of the image on each trial, such as the deletion of an airplane's engine in an airport scene. Each image in this *flicker paradigm* was presented for 240 ms, with an 80 ms neutral grey ISI. The change was repeated by alternating the two images until the participant detected the change (i.e., the airplane's engine would disappear, then reappear, then disappear, and so on). Rensink et al. found that for many changes, participants required extended viewing (often more than 30 s) before they detected the change. Researchers have concluded from such effects that very little visual information (at an extreme, no visual information, O'Regan, 1992; O'Regan & Noë, 2001) is retained from one view of a scene to the next, and therefore that visual representations of complex, natural scenes must be impoverished (Becker & Pashler, 2002; Irwin & Andrews, 1996; Rensink, 2000, 2002; Rensink et al., 1997; Simons, 1996; Simons & Levin, 1997; Wheeler & Treisman, 2002; Wolfe, 1999).

Rensink (2000, 2002) has provided the most theoretically elaborated account of this *visual transience* hypothesis. Rensink's view, which he terms *coherence theory*, provides a broad account of vision, attention, and memory. Coherence theory can be distilled into the following set of claims. First, low-level vision produces a description of the visual field in terms of *proto-objects*. Proto-objects, according to Rensink, are the earliest form of object representation in the visual system, in which local regions of the visual field are parsed, and sensory features corresponding to individual objects are loosely assembled. Proto-objects are computed in a bottom-up fashion, in parallel across the visual field, and independently of attention. They are also highly volatile: Proto-objects decay very quickly after visual stimulation is removed and are highly susceptible to interference from new sensory information (i.e., they are susceptible to backward masking, which Rensink terms *overwriting*). In the context of change detection, proto-objects are not by themselves sufficient to detect a change, because they will typically have decayed prior to the appearance of the changed image, or if they have not yet decayed, sensory processing of the new image will mask them (overwrite them), leaving the visual system with no informational basis upon which to detect the change.

Further, coherence theory holds that visual attention is critical to the consolidation of proto-objects into a coherent, robust representation that does not immediately decay and is not susceptible to backward masking. When attention selects a set of proto-objects that correspond to an object in the visual field, the object's features, which were only loosely assembled prior to the allocation of attention, are bound into a coherent object representation (which Rensink terms a *nexus*). Activation from the nexus feeds back to the proto-objects, and this recurrent flow of information to the proto-object level allows proto-objects to be maintained robustly across delays and to resist masking from subsequent sensory input. Rensink terms the nexus plus stabilized proto-objects a *coherence field*. Under coherence theory, it is the continued maintenance of these proto-objects in the coherence field that allows one to perceive a change to an attended object in a scene across disruptions such as a brief ISI or eye movement.

Finally, coherence theory holds that once attention is removed from an object, the coherent object representation (the nexus) comes unbound, the recurrent activation from the nexus to the proto-objects is lost, and the proto-objects return to their original state as fleeting and susceptible to masking. Thus, perceiving a change to a previously attended object is equivalent to perceiving a change to an object that has never been attended. In neither case is there a coherent representation to support change detection: "After focused attention is released, the object loses its coherence and dissolves back into its constituent proto-objects. There is little or no 'after effect' of having been attended" (Rensink, 2000, p. 20). Although Rensink claims that coherent visual representation is limited to the currently attended object, he does allow that other forms of representation may be retained robustly from a complex scene. In particular, the gist (or basic identity of a scene, such as "kitchen" or "airport") is remembered robustly, as well as the abstract spatial organization of the scene, or layout. But neither of these representations preserves information about the visual details of individual objects in the scene.

In summary, coherence theory claims that a coherent visual representation sufficient to support change detection is available only for the currently attended object. When attention is withdrawn from an object, feature binding comes undone, and any coherent object representation dissolves back into its constituent features. As a result, visual representations do not accumulate as attention is oriented from object-to-object within a scene, and visual scene representations are therefore impoverished, leading to change blindness. These claims are not unique to coherence theory. Many other researchers have made similar proposals regarding the transience of visual memory. Some prominent examples include the following.

- "Binding information [in memory] can be lost when new visual objects are presented and attention is withdrawn, causing bound objects to fall apart. Bound visual objects may survive in memory across distraction only when they are recoded into a nonvisual form, such as a verbal label." (Wheeler & Treisman, 2002, p. 62)
- "... when a scene is viewed, observers create two representations. One contains the gist, or meaning, of a scene, and the other represents the visual details of a small portion of the scene. The gist representation is thought to be relatively stable, and more conceptual than visual in nature (Wolfe, 1998). By contrast, the representation of visual details is thought to be volatile and fleeting. At any instant, observers represent only the small portion of the visual observer's attention shifts, so do the contents of VSTM [visual short-term memory], leaving no memory or representation of the previously attended visual stimuli ...." (Becker & Pashler, 2002, p. 744)
- "During any fixation, we have a rich visual experience. From that visual experience, we abstract the meaning or gist of a scene. During the next visual fixation, we again have a rich visual experience, and if the gist is the same, our perceptual system assumes the details are the same." (Simons & Levin, 1997, p. 267)
- "When attention is deployed elsewhere, the visual representation of an object appears to revert to its preattentive state." (Wolfe, 1999, p. 78)

As is evident from these statements, the concept of visual transience and its consequences (such as visually impoverished representations of scenes) have been highly influential in recent thinking on vision and memory. Thus, the visual transience view deserves close scrutiny. My discussion will focus on Rensink's coherence theory, because it is the most prominent and most clearly specified visual transience theory, but coherence theory stands for a larger class of theory that has been widely accepted within the vision community.

Visual memory systems

Before discussing whether visual memory is indeed transient, it is necessary to briefly review current knowledge regarding the properties of visual memory. Visual memory appears to be composed of four different memory stores: Visible persistence, informational persistence, visual short-term memory (VSTM), and visual long-term memory (VLTM) (see Irwin, 1992b, for an excellent review). Visible and informational persistence are often grouped together as *iconic memory* or, preferably, *sensory persistence* (Coltheart, 1980). Visible persistence and informational persistence preserve a precise, high-capacity, sensory trace that is generated across the visual field but is highly volatile. Visible persistence, as the name suggests, is phenomenologically visible (that is, one sees a stimulus as visibly persisting after it has been removed). The duration of visible persistence is extraordinarily brief, decaying within approximately 80–100 ms after the *onset* of a stimulus (Di Lollo, 1980). Informational persistence is a nonvisible sensory trace that persists for approximately 150–300 ms after stimulus offset (Irwin & Yeomans, 1986). Both visible persistence and informational persistence are highly susceptible to interference from new sensory processing; they are susceptible to backward masking. VSTM maintains visual representations abstracted away from precise sensory information. It has a limited capacity of 3–4 objects (Irwin, 1992a; Luck & Vogel, 1997; Pashler, 1988) and less spatial precision than point-by-point sensory persistence (Irwin, 1991; Phillips, 1974). However, VSTM is not significantly disrupted by backward masking (Pashler, 1988; Phillips, 1974) and can be maintained over durations on the order of seconds (Phillips, 1974) and across saccades (Irwin, 1992a). VLTM appears to maintain visual representations similar to those maintained in VSTM (see Hollingworth, 2004) but with the capability to accumulate visual information from scores of individual objects (Hollingworth, 2004, 2005b). Note that of the four visual memory stores, only visible persistence directly supports visual phenomenology. Other forms of visual memory certainly maintain visual information, but they do not directly support visual experience. With the exception of extraordinarily brief visible persistence, visual memory is nonvisible.

Aligning coherence theory with the visual memory literature, it is clear that proto-objects in coherence theory map onto sensory persistence (i.e., visible persistence and/or informational persistence). Both proto-objects and sensory persistence are low-level visual representations generated in parallel across the visual field independently of attention, both are highly volatile, and both are susceptible to backward masking. Further, the coherence field (the nexus plus the stabilized proto-objects) directly maps onto VSTM (Rensink, 2000).[1] Thus, coherence theory can be rephrased in the following manner using terminology from the visual memory literature. When looking at a visual image, low-level sensory representations are generated across the visual field. When the image is removed, low-level sensory (iconic) persistence is fleeting and is highly susceptible to masking. However, the visual system can consolidate a small number of visual objects into a more stable store, VSTM, which can then be maintained in the service of explicit report or comparison in a change detection task.

From this perspective, visual transience theories are perfectly consistent with existing visual memory research. Early research on sensory memory (Averbach & Coriell, 1961; Sperling, 1960) found that for briefly presented arrays of letters, low-level sensory representations were generated across the visual field, but after stimulus removal, these low-level representations were fleeting and highly susceptible to masking. Approximately three or four letters, however, could be attended and consolidated into a more stable memory store (which we now term VSTM) that could support letter report at longer delays. The transience of sensory representations has been a background assumption in the visual memory literature for the last 40 years. Thus, the novelty of visual transience theories lies not in the claim that sensory representations are fleeting, but rather in the claim that after an object is attended and consolidated into VSTM, that object representation comes unbound when attention is withdrawn, leaving no trace of the coherent object representation that had been previously formed. Under visual transience theories, it is this absence of visual accumulation that explains poor detection in change blindness studies. One must be attending the object that changes in order to detect the change, because a coherent object representation is maintained only for the currently attended object.

From this review of visual memory systems, it is clear that the only plausible candidates for the accumulation of visual information during scene viewing are VSTM and VLTM: visible and informational persistence decay too quickly and are highly susceptible to masking. The critical question,

---

[1] The coherence theory view of VSTM differs from standard models in that coherence theory claims low-level sensory representations (proto-objects) constitute a component of VSTM; attention allows the continued maintenance of proto-objects for the attended object in VSTM (Rensink, 2000). However, a great deal of evidence demonstrates that even for attended objects, VSTM is abstracted away from precise sensory information (Henderson, 1997; Henderson & Hollingworth, 2003b; Irwin, 1991; Phillips, 1974). For example, Phillips (1974) presented single, checkerboard objects at fixation in a change detection task. The checkerboard object was clearly attended, since it was the only stimulus on display. Yet, Phillips found that high-capacity sensory persistence was fleeting, and that VSTM maintained representations abstracted away from sensory persistence, even for an attended object.

then, is whether VSTM and VLTM are indeed used to accumulate visual information from individual objects as the eye and attention are oriented from object-to-object within a scene, or whether visual object representations come unbound upon the withdrawal of attention, with little or no accumulation of visual information.

Robust visual memory for objects in natural scenes

My colleagues and I have conducted a series of studies to answer this question (see Henderson & Hollingworth, 2003b, for an earlier review). Hollingworth and Henderson (2002; Hollingworth, Williams, & Henderson, 2001b) examined the basic issue of whether coherent visual object representations can be maintained after the withdrawal of attention. In these experiments, eye movements were monitored while participants viewed computer-generated depictions of real-world scenes. Figure 1 shows a sample scene. The computer waited until the participant had directly fixated a target object in the scene (to ensure it had been attended). Subsequently, the target object was changed during a saccade to a different (nontarget) object in the scene. Because visual attention is automatically and exclusively allocated to the goal of a saccade prior to the initiation of that eye movement (e.g., Hoffman & Subramaniam, 1995), the target object was no longer attended when the change occurred; attention had shifted to the nontarget object that was the goal of the saccade. The target object was changed either by rotating it 90° in depth or by replacing it with another object from the same basic-level category (token change). Rotation change detection, in particular, required memory for the visual details of the target, since the changed target differed from the original target only in orientation. Coherence theory predicts that these object changes should not have been

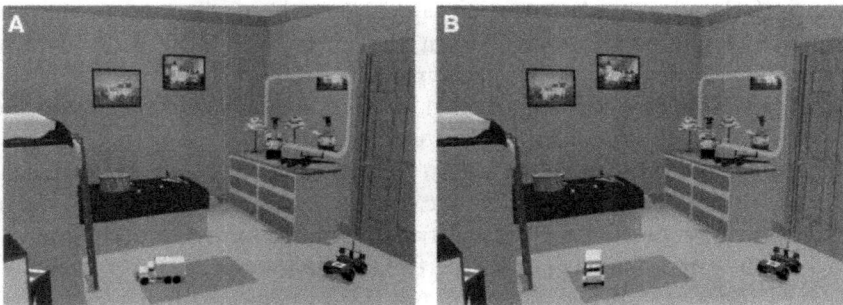

Figure 1. Sample stimuli from studies of visual memory and scene perception (Hollingworth, 2003a, 2004, 2005b; Hollingworth & Henderson, 2002). Panel A shows the initial scene. Panel B shows an object change (rotation in depth of the toy truck).

detectable, because attention had been withdrawn from the target object prior to the change. Yet, participants were able to successfully detect token and rotation changes on a significant proportion of trials, demonstrating that visual memory accumulates visual representations from previously attended objects in scenes.

In a converging experiment (Hollingworth & Henderson, 2002), a previously attended target object was masked during a saccade to a different object in the scene. Two object alternatives were then displayed sequentially within the scene. One was the original target, and the other was either a different token or different orientation distractor. Despite the fact that attention was no longer directed to the target when it was masked, participants performed the discrimination tasks at rates above 80% correct. Further, accurate discrimination performance was observed even when many fixations on other objects intervened between target fixation and test. When more than nine fixations on other objects intervened between target fixation and test, token discrimination performance was 85.3% correct and orientation discrimination performance was 92.3% correct. Memory for the visual details of previously attended objects was clearly robust across shifts of attention and of the eyes.

The experiments in Hollingworth and Henderson (2002) depended on the relationship between eye position and attention (that attention covertly precedes the eyes to a saccade target) to ensure that tested objects were not currently attended at test. Hollingworth (2003a) used a converging method to control the allocation of attention. Participants viewed a scene for 20 s. Then, a bright green dot appeared abruptly in the scene at a location different from that of the target object. The target object was then masked, and the mask was removed to reveal either the target object changed (rotation or token change) or unchanged. The task was change detection. Given evidence that abruptly appearing objects capture attention (e.g., Yantis & Jonides, 1984), attention should have been allocated to the dot onset, and not to the target, when the target was masked. A control experiment demonstrated that participants did indeed shift attention to the onset dot. Finally, a four-digit verbal working memory load minimized the possibility of verbal encoding. Despite the fact that the target was not currently attended, change detection performance was very high indeed. Percentage correct data were used to calculate A', a signal detection measure that models proportion correct in a two-alternative forced choice paradigm and varies from .5 (chance) to 1.0 (perfect sensitivity) (Grier, 1971). Mean A' was .91 for token change detection and .87 for rotation change detection, consistent with the results of Hollingworth and Henderson. Again, visual representations sufficient to make subtle judgements were retained reliably after the withdrawal of attention.

Accurate memory for the visual form of objects in these studies was almost certainly due to the retention of abstracted visual representations in VSTM, in VLTM, or in both. To examine the relative contributions of VSTM and VLTM to the online visual representation of natural scenes, Hollingworth (2004) used a serial position manipulation to control the sequence of objects fixated and attended within a scene. On each trial of this *follow-the-dot* paradigm, participants followed a small, bright green dot as it visited a series of objects in a scene, shifting gaze to fixate the object most recently visited by the dot. Each object in a scene was visited once, and the sequence of objects was designed to mimic a natural eye movement scan path on the scene. The serial position of a target object in the sequence was manipulated. The dot could appear on the target relatively early in viewing or relatively late. After the sequence was completed, the target object was masked, and the mask was then removed to reveal either the original target object or a different object token.[2] Again, the task was change detection.

If VSTM contributes to online scene representation, then one would expect the objects attended most recently before the test to be remembered most accurately, a recency effect characteristic of retention in short-term memory (Murdock, 1962; Phillips & Christie, 1977). If VLTM contributes to online scene representation, then one would expect memory for objects fixated early in viewing to be consistently above chance and to reflect retention beyond typical 3–4 object estimates of VSTM capacity. This is exactly what was found. The basic pattern of results from Hollingworth (2004) is depicted in Figure 2. Object memory was consistently superior for the two objects fixated most recently before the test. This recency advantage indicates a VSTM component to online scene representation, apparently limited to two objects.[3] Objects examined earlier than two-objects before the test were nonetheless remembered at rates well above chance ($A' = \sim.80$), and there was no evidence of further forgetting with more intervening objects. That is, performance was equivalent for objects fixated between three objects before the test and ten objects before the test. At ten objects before the test, memory capacity easily exceeded 3–4 object estimates of VSTM capacity. This robust prerecency performance therefore indicates a VLTM component to online scene representation. Irwin and Zelinsky (2002; see also Zelinsky & Loschky, 1998) have found similar effects for object position memory. Thus, VSTM appears to support memory for the visual form of the last two objects fixated and attended in a scene, with memory for objects attended earlier supported by VLTM.

---

[2] Memory for object orientation was also tested in a two-alternative forced-choice task and produced the same serial position effects as token change detection.

[3] This estimate is consistent with independent estimates of VSTM capacity for complex objects (Alvarez & Cavanagh, 2004).

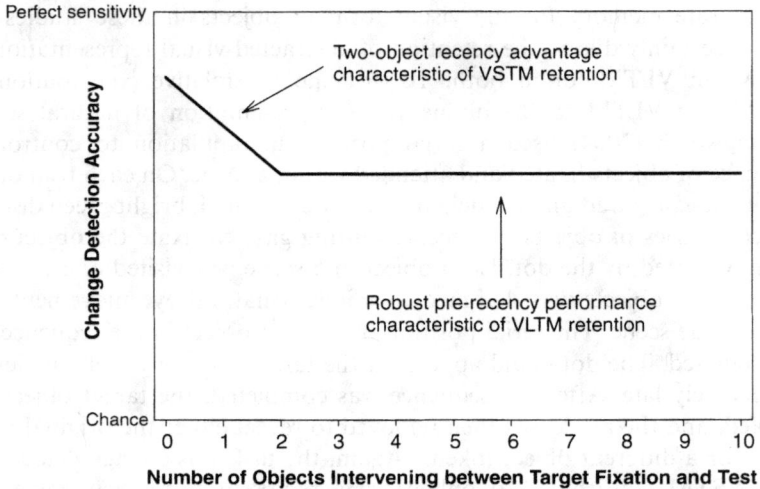

Figure 2. Stylized depiction of the serial position results from Hollingworth (2004), plotting change detection accuracy against the number of objects fixated between target fixation and test. Zero objects indicate that the last object attended in the scene was tested.

Given this significant role for VLTM in the online representation of natural scenes, how robustly are the visual details of individual objects retained in long-term memory (LTM)? In the 1960s and 1970s, studies of picture memory found that LTM could support the retention of multiple thousands of individual photographs (Nickerson, 1965; Shepard, 1967; Standing, 1973; Standing, Conezio, & Haber, 1970). The distractor pictures used in these experiments, however, were typically chosen to be highly different from studied images, making it difficult to identify the type of memory supporting recognition. Based in part on change blindness effects, recent discussions of this literature have tended to ascribe accurate long-term picture memory to retention of scene gist rather than to retention of the visual details of the photographs (Chun. 2003; Potter, Staub, & O'Connor, 2004; Simons, 1996).

To examine the capacity of LTM for the visual details of individual objects in natural scenes. Hollingworth (2004) used the follow-the-dot method but delayed the change detection test until the end of the session, after all scenes had been viewed. In this condition, more than 400 objects, on average, were examined between target examination and test. Of course, participants did not know which of these objects would be tested until the test occurred. Despite these considerable memory demands. participants performed the token change detection task at a rate well above chance ($A' = .75$), which was only moderately lower than change detection performance when object memory was tested during scene viewing. We have recently delayed object change detection tests (both token and orientation changes) for 24 hours (Hollingworth, 2005b), and change detection performance was still above chance ($A' = \sim .70$). To put this in concrete terms, after having viewed 48 different scenes and hundreds of individual objects, and after a delay of 24 hours, participants can still detect that the toy truck in the bedroom scene (Figure 1) has changed orientation. Clearly, VLTM is not limited to scene gist.

These results are in striking contrast to visual transience claims in the change blindness literature. For example, Simons and Levin (1997) speculated that only the basic meaning of a scene (the gist, such as *bedroom*) may be retained across a saccade from one eye fixation on a scene to the next, a delay of only 20–60 ms. Instead, participants are capable of retaining the visual details of hundreds of individual objects (Hollingworth, 2004) across delays of at least 24 hours (Hollingworth, 2005b).

Understanding change blindness

Evidence of robust visual memory for the visual details of individual objects in scenes naturally leads one to consider why change blindness would ever be observed in the first place. Change blindness is a relative phenomenon. Rarely are subjects entirely insensitive to changes.[4] For example, in the first demonstration of change detection failure within real-world scenes, Grimes (1996) and McConkie (1991) found that some changes were detected by only 25% of participants, whereas others were detected by as much as 80% of participants. Similarly, in a prominent example of an incidental, real-world change paradigm, Simons and Levin (1998) found that approximately 50% of participants failed to detect the replacement of one person for another.

Failures of change detection are typically juxtaposed with an ideal of error-free change detection. But what would be necessary to ensure error-free change detection? Error-free change detection across temporal disruptions such as saccades and brief ISIs requires (at least) two representations and a comparison operation. First, the initial image must be represented in visual memory across the disruption. Second, the perceptual information available in the second image must be represented after the change has been introduced. Third, a comparison process must operate to detect discrepancies between the two representations. To ensure error-free change detection performance, the memory representation would need to be a precise and complete record of the visual information available in the initial image. Similarly, the perceptual representation from the test image also would need

---

[4] See Henderson and Hollingworth (2003b) for one of the few cases in which change blindness is apparently absolute.

to be precise and complete. Finally, the comparison process would need to operate over the entire extent of both representations.

But this model of error-free change detection performance has little a priori plausibility. The human retina encodes high-resolution visual information only over a very small region of the visual field (Riggs, 1965). Consider the case in which a participant is provided a single fixation on a scene before the introduction of a change. Even if the memory representation of the initial image has perfect fidelity, with no visual information loss across the delay, a change could be missed because the changing object lay in the periphery of the visual field and information of sufficient resolution had not been available.

To rescue our model of error-free change detection, we might propose that if participants were allowed multiple fixations on the initial image prior to the change, high-resolution, sensory information from foveated regions might be integrated to form a composite representation retaining precise information across much of the visual field. This type of composite global image model was proposed in the 1970s (e.g., McConkie & Rayner, 1976), primarily to explain the phenomenology of seeing a complete and detailed visual world across eye movements. Such a model has typically been considered to predict error-free change detection (that is, change blindness has been taken as evidence against this model). However, even with the ability to construct a composite image, changes may go undetected if the changing region has not been fixated prior to the change. Since a composite image would require fixation of many local scene regions, its construction would take a significant amount of time (on the order of seconds), and many regions of a scene are not fixated even given extended viewing of 20 s or longer (Henderson & Hollingworth, 1998). And, even if the critical region had been fixated prior to the change, if the critical region is not fixated in the test image, then the change could go undetected despite the retention of precise sensory information in memory. Thus, the physical structure of the eye and the serial nature of foveal object processing makes it highly unlikely that one could ever achieve error-free change detection performance, even with the most generous model of visual memory and comparison processes.

Things get worse for change detection, because we have known for many years that the visual system does not build up precise representations of scenes by integrating high-resolution, foveal information from fixated regions. As reviewed above, precise sensory memory is fleeting (Averbach & Coriell, 1961; Di Lollo, 1980; Sperling, 1960) and simply does not last long enough to support sensory integration across multiple fixations. In the early 1980s, researchers directly tested whether visible persistence is integrated from one fixation to the next, as would be needed to construct a visible, composite sensory image of a scene (Bridgeman & Mayer, 1983; Irwin, Yantis, & Jonides, 1983; McConkie & Zola, 1979; O'Regan & Lévy-

Schoen, 1983; Rayner & Pollatsek, 1983; see also Henderson, 1997; Henderson & Hollingworth, 2003c; Irwin, 1991). For example, Irwin et al. (1983) found that participants could not integrate two complementary patterns of dots when the dots were presented in the same spatial position but on subsequent fixations, demonstrating that the type of sensory integration possible within a fixation at short SOAs (Di Lollo, 1980) does not occur across separate fixations.

Recently, Henderson and Hollingworth (2003c) sought to put the issue of sensory accumulation across eye movements to rest. Participants were shown images of common environments, with each image partially occluded by a set of vertical grey bars (as if viewing the scene from behind a picket fence). During eye movements, the occluded and visible portions of the image were reversed, so that all previously occluded regions of the scene became visible and all previously visible regions occluded. This change drastically altered the low-level content of the entire image (the value of every single pixel changed) but preserved more abstract visual information, such as the general shape of objects and the spatial relationships between objects. Participants were almost entirely insensitive to these changes, demonstrating that visual memory across eye movements is abstracted away from precise sensory information. If sensory representations are not retained and integrated across an eye movement, then sensory information could not be accumulated across multiple fixations to form a composite, global image of a scene.

Actually, one can easily demonstrate that high-resolution, foveal information is not integrated across saccades to form a visible, composite image. Choose two smallish objects (any two objects will do) and place them at two different positions about a foot apart on a nearby surface. Fixate object 1, and without removing fixation, attend to the quality of visual experience for object 2. Object 2 will be projecting to a region of the retina with relatively low resolution, so it should appear fuzzy and indistinct. Now, shift fixation to object 2 and fixate it as long as you care to. Shift fixation back to object 1, and again attend to the quality of perceptual experience for object 2. It should still appear fuzzy and indistinct, precisely as it did before it was directly fixated. The high-resolution foveal information encoded during the fixation on object 2 was not retained to support subsequent detailed perceptual experience of that object: No composite sensory image was formed.

This demonstration illustrates an additional point about visual experience and change detection. Change blindness is often thought to be surprising given the fact that we see a detailed visual world across the visual field. But, in fact, we do not see detail across the visual field, even for previously fixated objects. People see a complete and detailed visual world only in the loose sense that they are not typically aware of the fact that they are not experiencing detail across the visual field (see Dennett, 1991). But it takes only a modicum of effort to realize that peripheral vision is sketchy and indistinct. It would be more accurate to say that we perceive the visual world *as being* complete and detailed. This is a perfectly valid inference (Cohen, 2002), because the world itself is indeed complete and detailed, even if we do not see all of that detail at once.

To summarize, there is simply no plausible model of visual memory and comparison that would produce error-free change detection in change blindness paradigms. Some degree of change blindness is inevitable. But that still leaves open the question of why, given evidence of robust memory for the visual form of objects (Hollingworth, 2003a, 2004, 2005b; Hollingworth & Henderson, 2002), change detection can be as poor as it often is. For example, the appearance and disappearance of the engine on an aeroplane in a flicker paradigm should certainly be detectable by the retention of a higher level visual representation in VSTM or VLTM. Why, then, do participants often fail to notice this sort of change?

Failures of encoding.   Change blindness may occur in many circumstances because the local information from the target region has yet to be encoded when a change occurs. Hollingworth and Henderson (2002; see also Hollingworth, Schrock, & Henderson, 2001a) examined change detection performance as a function of whether the target object had been fixated prior to the change. Changes to previously fixated objects were detected at rates well above chance. However, changes to unfixated objects were detected at a rate no higher than the false alarm rate, suggesting that without direct fixation, information sufficient to detect a change was rarely encoded. It may take participants many seconds to fixate each of the potentially changing objects in a scene, explaining delays in detection of repeating changes, such as those in the flicker paradigm. These observations are consistent with the general claim that attention is important for change detection (Rensink et al., 1997), especially when one considers that fixation position and the spatial allocation of visual attention are tightly linked. Although attention may be critical for forming a visual memory representation sufficient to detect most changes, that does not imply that visual representations come unbound after the withdrawal of attention, however.

Failures of retrieval and comparison.   Even if one forms a visual memory representation of sufficient accuracy to detect a change, it may be no trivial matter retrieving that representation and comparing it with current perceptual information in order to detect a change. Early change blindness studies assumed that explicit change detection provided an exhaustive measure of visual memory. A number of converging sources of evidence, however, demonstrate that explicit change detection significantly underestimates visual memory and that retrieval and comparison failures are a significant cause of change blindness.

First, changes may go undetected despite accurate memory, because the changed object is not attended or fixated after the change. In Hollingworth and Henderson (2002), single changes to objects in scenes often went undetected until the object happened to be refixated later in viewing. Such a delay, if it had been observed in a flicker paradigm, would have been considered extended change blindness, yet the ultimate detection of the change demonstrated that participants had a memory representation of the relevant object; that representation just was not retrieved and compared to current perceptual information until attention and the eyes were directed back to the target.

Hollingworth (2003a) directly examined the role of retrieval and comparison failure in change blindness using a change detection paradigm in which a scene was viewed for 20 s, followed by a brief mask and a test scene. The target object in the test scene was either the same, rotated, or replaced by a different token. In addition, the target object in the test scene was either postcued by a green arrow or not postcued. The latter method is typical of change blindness experiments. Without a postcue, participants had to decide whether any object in the scene had changed. With a postcue, participants only needed to determine whether the cued object had changed. If change blindness is caused, at least in part, by failed retrieval and comparison, then change detection should be improved when retrieval and comparison demands are minimized by the postcue. This was indeed the case, with significantly higher change detection performance in the postcue condition. In addition, with the benefit of a postcue, change detection performance approached ceiling, both for token and orientation change detection; change blindness was largely eliminated.

Converging evidence that explicit change detection underestimates visual memory comes from three studies conducted by Simons, Levin, and colleagues. In Simons, Chabris, Schnur, and Levin (2002), a naïve participant engaged in conversation with a person carrying a basketball. The basketball was covertly removed during a disruption, and the participant was then asked to report any odd events or changes. If such general questions did not yield report of the removed basketball, the participant was asked specifically about the basketball. With a direct retrieval cue, participants could then often report specific perceptual details of the basketball, even though they did not notice that it had been removed. Similarly, Angelone, Levin, and Simons (2003) found that when participants failed to detect the replacement of one person for another, they could still choose the original person in a forced-choice test at levels above chance. Mitroff, Simons, and Levin (2004), using a computer-based object change detection task, found that on some miss trials, participants had sufficient pre- and postchange information to detect a change but had not adequately compared those representations.

Finally, evidence of preserved memory in the face of change blindness is observed using measures more sensitive than explicit report of change (Fernandez-Duque & Thornton, 2000; see Thornton & Fernandez-Duque, 2002, for a review). When a change is not reported, participants are slower to incorrectly report "same" for an object that changed than to correctly report "same" for an object that did not change (Williams & Simons, 2000). And when a change is not reported, fixation durations on a changed object are longer than on the same object when it has not changed (Hayhoe, Bensinger, & Ballard, 1998; Henderson & Hollingworth, 2003a; Hollingworth et al., 2001b; Ryan, Althoff, Whitlow, & Cohen, 2000). There is currently debate about whether these effects indicate that there are multiple change detection mechanisms (i.e., an implicit mechanism and an explicit mechanism), or whether the data can be accounted for by a single change detection mechanism (Fernandez-Duque, Grossi, Thornton, & Neville, 2003; Fernandez-Duque & Thornton, 2003; Mitroff, Simons, & Franconeri, 2002). Regardless of the resolution of this debate, effects of change on indirect measures (such as RT and fixation duration) in the absence of explicit report of change demonstrate that explicit change detection underestimates visual memory.

Effects of unreported change on indirect measures may be generated by threshold mechanisms for signalling change in the world. Dynamic vision often introduces perceptual discrepancies that could be attributed either to internal error or to external change. For example, when making a saccade to an object, the eyes often fall short of the target of the eye movement. After the completion of such an eye movement, the saccade target object does not lie at the centre of gaze. This circumstance could be due to the inaccuracy of the eye movement (internal error), but it could also be due to the movement of the target object during the saccade (external change). By actually shifting saccade targets during saccades, researchers have revealed that the visual system sets a threshold for attributing position discrepancy to a change in the world. If the displacement of the saccade target is greater than approximately one-third of the distance of the saccade, participants are likely to perceive the target to have moved, attributing the discrepancy to change in the world (e.g., Bridgeman, Hendry, & Stark, 1975; McConkie & Currie, 1996). Below that threshold, the visual system remains sensitive to the displacement (a corrective saccade is executed to bring the saccade target onto the fovea), but participants are rarely aware of the displacement or of the corrective saccade. Thus, for small discrepancies that are likely to have been caused by motor error, the visual system does not attribute the discrepancy to a change in the world, and participants do not perceive the target object to have moved. Despite sensitivity to the discrepancy and appropriate correction, participants are "blind" to the change. Further, if external change is made clearly evident by blanking the target briefly after the eye movement, participants are more likely to attribute the discrepancy to a shift of the target, and explicit awareness of the shift is dramatically improved (Deubel, Schneider, & Bridgeman, 1996).

Threshold mechanisms can also be observed in the phenomenon of insensitivity to incremental change (Hollingworth & Henderson, 2004). In a version of the flicker paradigm, Hollingworth and Henderson gradually rotated an entire scene, with each image incremented by 1 degree of orientation. Participants were remarkably insensitive to these gradual changes, often coming to treat significantly different views of a room (i.e., ones in which many of the original objects had rotated out of view) as unchanged continuations of the initial view. Despite failure to detect the incremental rotation, memory was nevertheless sensitive to the difference between views. With incremental rotation, scene memory came to reflect the recent, changed state of the environment rather than the initial state. This implicit updating of memory to reflect the most recent state of the environment meant that comparison typically operated over similar representations: The currently visible image was compared to memory for the most recent image(s). Thus, the discrepancy between perceptual information and memory tended to be very small, falling below threshold for explicit detection of change, despite the fact that both representations were highly different from the initial image. Even though memory was sensitive to the fact that the image had changed, individual comparisons rarely exceeded threshold for explicit awareness of change, yielding change blindness.

The original explanations for change blindness were highly attractive in their parsimony: Changes were missed because coherent visual representations disintegrate upon the withdrawal of attention (Rensink et al., 1997). It is clear that visual sensory memory is indeed transient (Sperling, 1960), and participants would certainly detect changes more accurately if sensory information was retained and integrated across disruptions such as eye movements, but we have long known that such integration does not occur (e.g., Irwin et al., 1983). Although sensory memory is transient, higher level visual representations are retained robustly in VSTM and in VLTM (Hollingworth, 2003a, 2004, 2005b; Hollingworth & Henderson, 2002): Coherent visual representations do not necessarily disintegrate upon the withdrawal of attention. Recent evidence suggests that despite the ability to accumulate visual representations in VSTM and VLTM, participants fail to detect changes (1) because they have not fixated and attended the changing object prior to the change and thus have not had an opportunity to encode information sufficient to detect a change, (2) because they have not retrieved or adequately compared a memory representation to current perceptual information, and (3) because. for many comparisons. evidence of discrepancy falls below threshold for signalling a change in the world.

VISUAL SEARCH AND THE REPRESENTATION OF NATURAL SCENES

Simultaneously with work on change blindness, Horowitz and Wolfe (1998) reported a phenomenon they termed *memory-free* search, which led to a theoretical account of perception. attention, and memory very similar to Rensink's (2000) coherence theory. Horowitz and Wolfe used a search task in which they either kept the positions of search elements static or scrambled the locations of search elements every 111 ms. If search has a memory component, e.g., one that keeps track of which objects and locations have already been examined (Klein. 1988). then search should have been less efficient when scrambling eliminated the utility of memory. Yet, Horowitz and Wolfe found that search efficiency. as measured by the slope relating reaction time to set size, was no different for scrambled search and static search. They concluded that visual search does not rely on memory. Converging evidence came from a paradigm in which participants repeatedly searched for a different target over a static search array (Wolfe, Klempen, & Dahlen. 2000). Wolfe et al. found that search efficiency did not improve with array repetition, suggesting that participants did not form a memory representation of the array that could influence dynamic visual search.

To account for these findings. Wolfe (1999) proposed that early vision produces loose assemblages of visual features (which Wolfe & Bennett. 1997, termed *preattentive object files* and which appear to be essentially the same concept as Rensink's proto-objects). Attention serves to bind features into a coherent object representation (Wolfe. 1999, p. 77):

> When the eyes first open on a new scene, preattentive processes extract features and assign them. loosely. to preattentive objects. Typically, attention will be deployed to one object. The act of attention allows the features of the object to be organized and processed in a way that permits object recognition. The attended object is perceived differently than the not-yet-attended objects in the scene. Assuming this is to be the case, what happens when attention is to be deployed to the next object? Does the visual representation have a *memory* for the work of attention?

Based on the evidence from search paradigms, Wolfe concluded, as did Rensink (2000), that visual representations dissolve into their elementary features after the withdrawal of attention.

Wolfe's (1999) proposals primarily concern conscious vision. Whatever effects attention has on conscious perception are lost as soon as attention is withdrawn from an object. Put in slightly different terms, Wolfe proposes that the visual system does not accumulate *visible*, coherent object representations as attention is oriented from one object to another. But is there a plausible model that could produce visible accumulation across shifts of attention? The only visual memory store that preserves visible representations is visible persistence, and visible persistence decays within 80–100 ms after the onset of a stimulus, providing no plausible basis for accumulation. Thus, the Wolfe claim appears entirely consistent with early research demonstrating that visible, sensory memory is transient (Averbach & Coriell, 1961; Di Lollo, 1980; Sperling, 1960) and that visible representations do not accumulate during viewing (e.g., Irwin et al., 1983).[5]

Leaving issues of phenomenology aside, the more general claim that memory plays no role in search (Horowitz & Wolfe, 1998) has generated a great deal of research demonstrating that memory does indeed play an important role in visual search paradigms. Memory supports search both within a trial, as the visual system keeps track of which objects have been examined (Gibson, Li, Skow, Brown, & Cooke, 2000; Klein, 1988; Klein & MacInnes, 1999; Kristjánsson, 2000; Müller & von Mühlenen, 2000; Peterson, Kramer, Wang, Irwin, & McCarley, 2001; Takeda & Yagi, 2000; von Mühlenen, Müller, & Müller, 2003), and across trials, as memory for previous searches guides attention to a target object (Chun & Jiang, 1998, 1999). I will not discuss this work in detail, as it has been reviewed comprehensively elsewhere (Shore & Klein, 2000; Woodman & Chun, 2006 this issue). I will, however, briefly review studies conducted in my laboratory designed to investigate the role of memory in real-world search, linking research on visual search to research on scene perception and change detection.

To provide a direct test of the role of memory in search over natural scenes, I developed a search paradigm in which previous exposure to a search scene was controlled (Hollingworth, 2003b). Participants either saw a preview of a scene prior to search through that scene, or they did not see a preview. Figure 3 shows the key events in a trial. Each trial in the preview condition began with a preview display of a real-world scene for 10 s

---

[5] If visible object representations were to accumulate as attention shifts from object to object in a scene, then the following should occur. When first gazing upon a new environment, perceptual experience should be quite impoverished, since few objects would yet have been attended. However, visual experience should get progressively richer as more objects are attended and visible representations are accumulated. The fact that this does not happen—the world looks equivalently rich whether one has been looking at a scene for a few hundred ms or a few minutes—provides further, intuitive evidence that visible information does not accumulate during viewing, whether across shifts of attention or shifts of the eyes.

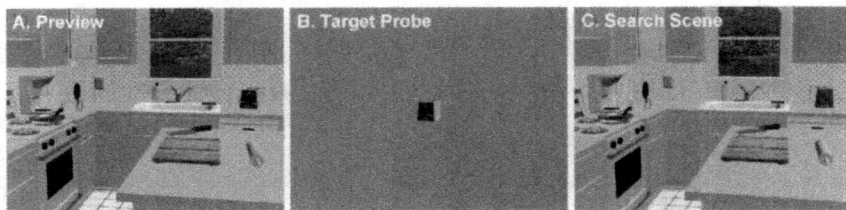

Figure 3. Key stimuli in a preview condition trial of Hollingworth (2003b). In the search scene, the target object has been mirror reversed.

(Figure 3, panel A). The object that would later be the search target was present in the preview, but participants did not know which of the objects in the preview would be the target. The target was then displayed in isolation in the centre of the screen (the *target probe*, Figure 3, panel B) to indicate which object should be found in the search scene. The target probe was identical to the target object that had appeared in the preview scene. Next, a search scene was displayed (Figure 3, panel C). The target object was always present in the search scene in the same location as it had appeared in the preview. However, the target in the search scene was either identical to the target in the preview scene (and thus identical to the target probe), or it was mirror reversed. Participants' task was to find the target in the search scene and respond to indicate whether it was the same as the target probe or mirror reversed. Note that memory for the orientation of the target in the preview could not facilitate search, since the target orientations in the preview and search scenes were uncorrelated. Only memory for spatial properties of the scene (such as target position) could facilitate search. The no-preview condition was identical to the preview condition, except no scene preview was displayed. Search efficiency was assessed by collecting reaction time data and by monitoring eye movements.

If search were more efficient with a scene preview, this would provide a straightforward demonstration that memory for the spatial structure of a scene can dynamically influence search. First, mean correct RT was reliably faster with a preview (1232 ms) than without (1487 ms), a difference of 255 ms. Second, mean elapsed time from the onset of the search scene to the first eye fixation on the target object was shorter in the preview condition (374 ms) than in the no preview condition (586 ms). With a 10 s preview, participants came to fixate the target object only 374 ms after the onset of the search scene. On most trials in the preview condition, there was only one or two fixations intervening between search onset and target fixation. In these cases, either the very first saccade or the second saccade on the search scene brought the eyes to the target object. These data actually underestimate how efficiently the eyes were oriented to the target; for many of the trials with two intervening fixations, the first saccade during search was directed to the target but landed just short, leading to a quick fixation and a corrective saccade. Memory typically guided attention directly to the target.

These results are consistent with work by Chun and Jiang (1998) showing benefits for search when the spatial configuration of elements is repeated. Chun and Jiang used a search task with randomly configured simple stimuli (rotated "T"s and "L"s). Throughout the session, some spatial configurations of search elements were repeated. Specifically, the locations of distractors and the target were held constant, but the identities of the distractors and target were randomly varied. After just a handful of repetitions, search over repeated configurations was faster than search over novel configurations, suggesting that participants had learned that a particular spatial configuration predicted a particular target location and had used this knowledge to guide attention efficiently to that target location. This learning appeared to be implicit, because participants could not recognize repeated configurations at the end of the session.

The scene preview results described above (Hollingworth, 2003b) complement the Chun and Jiang (1998) findings and extend our knowledge of how memory influences search. First, repeated exposures to a search environment are not necessary to produce memory effects; memory can guide search even after a single exposure. Second, repeated search and target localization are not necessary to produce memory effects; search was facilitated by memory even though participants had never searched for the target object before. Finally, memory representations supporting search need not be implicit in nature. After a 10 s preview, participants can explicitly recall the locations of objects in scenes and can estimate target position quite accurately (Hollingworth, 2005a).

What type of spatial memory supported search in the scene preview experiment? There appear to be two main possibilities. First, memory for the spatial configuration of contextual surfaces and objects in the scene could have guided attention to a location where the target object was likely to be found. For example, if one remembered the spatial position of a kitchen counter from the preview image, followed by a toaster target, one could bias search towards the likely location of the toaster on the counter (see Henderson, Weeks, & Hollingworth, 1999; Oliva, Torralba, Castelhano, & Henderson, 2003). Second, participants might remember the specific location of the target object and direct attention to that remembered location. Memory for the configuration of contextual surfaces and objects is broadly consistent with visual transience theories of scene representation (Rensink, 2000; Simons, 1996), because these views hold that abstract spatial layout is encoded and retained robustly without attention. However, memory for the specific locations of objects requires maintaining binding between object representations and scene locations (Irwin & Zelinsky, 2002).

Evidence that search can be facilitated by memory for specific target location would bolster the claim that visual memory supports the retention and accumulation of local object information in scenes (Hollingworth, 2003a, 2004, 2005b; Hollingworth & Henderson, 2002) and would extend those claims to the domain of spatial memory.

To examine the contributions of memory for contextual information and memory for specific target location, Hollingworth (2003b) added a third preview condition to the scene preview paradigm. In this target-absent preview condition, the scene preview was identical to the standard preview condition, except the target object was not present in the preview. If search were more efficient in the standard preview condition than in the target-absent preview condition, this would demonstrate that memory for the specific position of the target object facilitates search, as the two conditions differed only in the presence of the target in the preview scene. If search were more efficient in the target-absent preview condition than in the no preview condition, this would demonstrate that memory for the layout of contextual objects and surfaces facilitates search. Indeed, search was more efficient in the standard preview condition than in the target-absent preview condition, which in turn was more efficient than search in the no-preview condition, both for correct RT and for elapsed time to target fixation. In summary, scene memory can exert a strong influence on dynamic visual search, guiding attention and the eyes to a search target. Scene representations supporting search include memory for the layout of contextual objects and surfaces and memory for the positions of individual objects.

CONCLUSION

When looking upon a complex scene. visual sensory representations are generated across the visual field. If the scene is removed or perceptual processing otherwise interrupted (e.g., across an eye movement), sensory persistence decays very quickly (Averbach & Coriell, 1961; Di Lollo, 1980; Sperling, 1960) and is not integrated from one view of the scene to the next (Henderson & Hollingworth, 2003c; Irwin et al., 1983). However, directing attention to an object allows the formation of a coherent visual representation (Treisman, 1988) and the consolidation of that representation into more stable VSTM (Averbach & Coriell, 1961; Irwin, 1992a; Schmidt, Vogel, Woodman, & Luck, 2002; Sperling, 1960), which maintains visual representations abstracted away from precise sensory information (Irwin, 1991; Phillips, 1974). After attention is withdrawn from an object, abstracted visual representations persist (Hollingworth, 2003a; Hollingworth & Henderson, 2002), and they accumulate in memory as attention and the eyes are oriented from object-to-object within a scene (Hollingworth, 2004), supported both by VSTM (for the last two objects attended) and by VLTM (for objects attended earlier) (Hollingworth, 2004). VLTM then supports the retention of scores of individual object representations over relatively long periods of time (Hollingworth, 2004, 2005b). Scene representations retain information not only about the visual form of individual objects but also about the locations of objects and the configuration of objects and surfaces within a scene (Hollingworth, 2005a). Memory for the spatial properties of a scene can interact dynamically with perceptual processing during visual search, efficiently guiding attention and the eyes to target locations (Chun & Jiang, 1998; Hollingworth, 2003b).

REFERENCES

Alvarez, G. A., & Cavanagh, P. (2004). The capacity of visual short-term memory is set both by visual information load and by number of objects. *Psychological Science*, *15*, 106–111.

Angelone, B. L., Levin, D. T., & Simons, D. J. (2003). The relationship between change detection and recognition of centrally attended objects in motion pictures. *Perception*, *32*, 947–962.

Averbach, E., & Coriell, A. S. (1961). Short-term memory in vision. *The Bell System Technical Journal*, *40*, 309–328.

Becker, M. W., & Pashler, H. (2002). Volatile visual representations: Failing to detect changes in recently processed information. *Psychonomic Bulletin and Review*, *9*, 744–750.

Bridgeman, B., Hendry, D., & Stark, L. (1975). Failure to detect displacement of the visual world during saccadic eye movements. *Vision Research*, *15*, 719–722.

Bridgeman, B., & Mayer, M. (1983). Failure to integrate visual information from successive fixations. *Bulletin of the Psychonomic Society*, *21*, 285–286.

Chun, M. M. (2003). Scene perception and memory. *Psychology of Learning and Motivation*, *42*, 79–108.

Chun, M. M., & Jiang, Y. (1998). Contextual cueing: Implicit learning and memory of visual context guides spatial attention. *Cognitive Psychology*, *36*, 28–71.

Chun, M. M., & Jiang, Y. (1999). Top-down attentional guidance based on implicit learning of visual covariation. *Psychological Science*, *10*, 360–365.

Cohen, J. (2002). The grand grand illusion illusion. *Journal of Consciousness Studies*, *9*, 141–157.

Coltheart, M. (1980). The persistences of vision. Philosophical Transactions of the Royal Society of London. *Series B*, *290*, 269–294.

Dennett, D. C. (1991). *Consciousness explained*. Boston: Little, Brown.

Deubel, H., Schneider, W. X., & Bridgeman, B. (1996). Post-saccadic target blanking prevents saccadic suppression of image displacement. *Vision Research, 36*, 985–996.

Di Lollo, V. (1980). Temporal integration in visual memory. *Journal of Experimental Psychology: General*, *109*, 75–97.

Fernandez-Duque, D., Grossi, G., Thornton, I. M., & Neville, H. J. (2003). Representation of change: Separate electrophysiological markers of attention, awareness, and implicit processing. *Journal of Cognitive Neuroscience*, *15*, 1–17.

Fernandez-Duque, D., & Thornton, I. M. (2000). Change detection without awareness: Do explicit reports underestimate the representation of change in the visual system? *Visual Cognition*, *7*, 323–344.

Fernandez-Duque, D., & Thornton, I. M. (2003). Explicit mechanisms do not account for implicit localization and identification of change: A reply to Mitroff et al. (2002). *Journal of Experimental Psychology: Human Perception and Performance, 29,* 846–858.

Gibson, B. S., Li, L., Skow, E., Brown, K., & Cooke, L. (2000). Searching for one versus two identical targets: When visual search has memory. *Psychological Science, 11,* 324–327.

Grier, J. B. (1971). Nonparametric indexes for sensitivity and bias: Computing formulas. *Psychological Bulletin, 75,* 424–429.

Grimes, J. (1996). On the failure to detect changes in scenes across saccades. In K. Akins (Ed.), *Vancouver studies in cognitive science: Vol. 5. Perception* (pp. 89–110). Oxford, UK: Oxford University Press.

Hayhoe, M. M., Bensinger, D. G., & Ballard, D. H. (1998). Task constraints in visual working memory. *Vision Research, 38,* 125–137.

Henderson, J. M. (1997). Transsaccadic memory and integration during real-world object perception. *Psychological Science, 8,* 51–55.

Henderson, J. M., & Hollingworth, A. (1998). Eye movements during scene viewing: An overview. In G. Underwood (Ed.), *Eye guidance in reading and scene perception* (pp. 269–283). Oxford, UK: Elsevier.

Henderson, J. M., & Hollingworth, A. (1999). The role of fixation position in detecting scene changes across saccades. *Psychological Science, 10,* 438–443.

Henderson, J. M., & Hollingworth, A. (2003a). Eye movements and visual memory: Detecting changes to saccade targets in scenes. *Perception and Psychophysics, 65,* 58–71.

Henderson, J. M., & Hollingworth, A. (2003b). Eye movements, visual memory, and scene representation. In M. A. Peterson & G. Rhodes (Eds.), *Perception of faces, objects, and scenes: Analytic and holistic processes* (pp. 356–383). New York: Oxford University Press.

Henderson, J. M., & Hollingworth, A. (2003c). Global transsaccadic change blindness during scene perception. *Psychological Science, 14,* 493–497.

Henderson, J. M., Weeks, P. A., Jr., & Hollingworth, A. (1999). The effects of semantic consistency on eye movements during complex scene viewing. *Journal of Experimental Psychology: Human Perception and Performance, 25,* 210–228.

Hoffman, J. E., & Subramaniam, B. (1995). The role of visual attention in saccadic eye movements. *Perception and Psychophysics, 57,* 787–795.

Hollingworth, A. (2003a). Failures of retrieval and comparison constrain change detection in natural scenes. *Journal of Experimental Psychology: Human Perception and Performance, 29,* 388–403.

Hollingworth, A. (2003b). *Visual memory and the online representation of complex scenes.* Paper presented at the Munich Visual Search symposium. Munich, Germany.

Hollingworth, A. (2004). Constructing visual representations of natural scenes: The roles of short- and long-term visual memory. *Journal of Experimental Psychology: Human Perception and Performance, 30,* 519–537.

Hollingworth, A. (2005a). Memory for object position in natural scenes. *Visual Cognition, 12,* 1003–1016.

Hollingworth, A. (2005b). The relationship between online visual representation of a scene and long-term scene memory. *Journal of Experimental Psychology: Learning, Memory, and Cognition, 31,* 396–411.

Hollingworth, A., & Henderson, J. M. (2002). Accurate visual memory for previously attended objects in natural scenes. *Journal of Experimental Psychology: Human Perception and Performance, 28,* 113–136.

Hollingworth, A., & Henderson, J. M. (2004). Sustained change blindness to incremental scene rotation: A dissociation between explicit change detection and visual memory. *Perception and Psychophysics, 66,* 800–807.

Hollingworth, A., Schrock, G., & Henderson, J. M. (2001a). Change detection in the flicker paradigm: The role of fixation position within the scene. *Memory and Cognition*, *29*, 296–304.

Hollingworth, A., Williams, C. C., & Henderson, J. M. (2001b). To see and remember: Visually specific information is retained in memory from previously attended objects in natural scenes. *Psychonomic Bulletin and Review*, *8*, 761–768.

Horowitz, T. S., & Wolfe, J. M. (1998). Visual search has no memory. *Nature*, *394*, 575–577.

Irwin, D. E. (1991). Information integration across saccadic eye movements. *Cognitive Psychology*, *23*, 420–456.

Irwin, D. E. (1992a). Memory for position and identity across eye movements. *Journal of Experimental Psychology: Learning, Memory, and Cognition*, *18*, 307–317.

Irwin, D. E. (1992b). Visual memory within and across fixations. In K. Rayner (Ed.), *Eye movements and visual cognition: Scene perception and reading* (pp. 146–165). New York: Springer-Verlag.

Irwin, D. E., & Andrews, R. (1996). Integration and accumulation of information across saccadic eye movements. In T. Inui & J. L. McClelland (Eds.), *Attention and performance XVI: Information integration in perception and communication* (pp. 125–155). Cambridge, MA: MIT Press.

Irwin, D. E., Yantis, S., & Jonides, J. (1983). Evidence against visual integration across saccadic eye movements. *Perception and Psychophysics*, *34*, 35–46.

Irwin, D. E., & Yeomans, J. M. (1986). Sensory registration and informational persistence. *Journal of Experimental Psychology: Human Perception and Performance*, *12*, 343–360.

Irwin, D. E., & Zelinsky, G. J. (2002). Eye movements and scene perception: Memory for things observed. *Perception and Psychophysics*, *64*, 882–895.

Klein, R. (1988). Inhibitory tagging system facilitates visual search. *Nature*, *334*, 430–431.

Klein, R. M., & MacInnes, W. J. (1999). Inhibition of return is a foraging facilitator in visual search. *Psychological Science*, *10*, 346–352.

Kristjánsson, A. (2000). In search of remembrance: Evidence for memory in visual search. *Psychological Science*, *11*, 328–332.

Luck, S. J., & Vogel, E. K. (1997). The capacity of visual working memory for features and conjunctions. *Nature*, *390*, 279–281.

Matin, E. (1974). Saccadic suppression: A review and an analysis. *Psychological Bulletin*, *81*, 899–917.

McConkie, G. W. (1991). *Where vision and cognition meet*. Paper presented at the Human Frontier Science Program workshop on Object and Scene Perception, Leuven, Belgium.

McConkie, G. W., & Currie, C. B. (1996). Visual stability across saccades while viewing complex pictures. *Journal of Experimental Psychology: Human Perception and Performance*, *22*, 563–581.

McConkie, G. W., & Rayner, K. (1976). Identifying the span of the effective stimulus in reading: Literature review and theories of reading. In H. Singer & R. B Ruddell (Eds.), *Theoretical models and processes in reading* (pp. 137–162). Newark, DE: International Reading Association.

McConkie, G. W., & Zola, D. (1979). Is visual information integrated across successive fixations in reading? *Perception and Psychophysics*, *25*, 221–224.

Mitroff, S. R., Simons, D. J., & Franconeri, S. L. (2002). The Siren Song of implicit change detection. *Journal of Experimental Psychology: Human Perception and Performance*, *28*, 798–815.

Mitroff, S. R., & Simons, D. J., & Levin, D. T. (2004). Nothing compares 2 views: Change blindness results from failures to compare retained information. *Perception and Psychophysics*, *66*, 1268–1281.

Murdock, B. B. (1962). The serial position effect of free recall. *Journal of Experimental Psychology*, *64*, 482–488.

Müller, H. J., & von Mühlenen. A. (2000). Probing distracter inhibition in visual search: Inhibition of return. *Journal of Experimental Psychology: Human Perception and Performance*, *26*, 1591–1605.

Nickerson, R. S. (1965). Short-term memory for complex meaningful visual configurations: A demonstration of capacity. *Canadian Journal of Psychology*, *19*, 155–160.

Oliva, A., Torralba. A.. Castelhano. M. S.. & Henderson, J. M. (2003). Top down control of visual attention in object detection. *IEEE Proceedings of the International Conference on Image Processing*, *1*, 253–256.

O'Regan. J. K. (1992). Solving the "real" mysteries of visual perception: The world as an outside memory. *Canadian Journal of Psychology*, *46*, 461–488.

O'Regan. J. K.. & Lévy-Schoen. A. (1983). Integrating visual information from successive fixations: Does trans-saccadic fusion exist? *Vision Research*, *23*, 765–768.

O'Regan. J. K.. & Noë, A. (2001). A sensorimotor account of vision and visual consciousness. *Behavioral and Brain Sciences*, *24*, 939–1011.

Pashler. H. (1988). Familiarity and the detection of change in visual displays. *Perception and Psychophysics*, *44*, 369–378.

Peterson, M. S., Kramer, A. F., Wang, R. F.. Irwin. D. E., & McCarley, J. S. (2001). Visual search has memory. *Psychological Science*, *12*, 287–292.

Phillips, W. A. (1974). On the distinction between sensory storage and short-term visual memory. *Perception and Psychophysics*, *16*, 283–290.

Phillips. W. A., & Christie. D. F. M. (1977). Components of visual memory. *Quarterly Journal of Experimental Psychology*, *29*, 117–133.

Potter. M. C.. Staub. A., & O'Connor. D. H. (2004). Pictorial and conceptual representation of glimpsed pictures. *Journal of Experimental Psychology: Human Perception and Performance*, *30*, 478–489.

Rayner. K., & Pollatsek, A. (1983). Is visual information integrated across saccades? *Perception and Psychophysics*, *34*, 39–48.

Rensink, R. A. (2000). The dynamic representation of scenes. *Visual Cognition*, *7*, 17–42.

Rensink, R. A. (2002). Change detection. *Annual Review of Psychology*, *53*, 245–277.

Rensink, R. A., O'Regan, J. K., & Clark. J. J. (1997). To see or not to see: The need for attention to perceive changes in scenes. *Psychological Science*, *8*, 368–373.

Riggs, L. A. (1965). Visual acuity. In C. H. Graham (Ed.). *Vision and visual perception* (pp. 321–349). New York: Wiley.

Ryan. J. D.. Althoff. R. R.. Whitlow. S.. & Cohen. N. J. (2000). Amnesia is a deficit in relational memory. *Psychological Science*, *8*, 368–373.

Schmidt. B. K.. Vogel. E. K.. Woodman. G. F., & Luck. S. J. (2002). Voluntary and automatic attentional control of visual working memory. *Perception and Psychophysics*, *64*, 754–763.

Shepard. R. N. (1967). Recognition memory for words, sentences, and pictures. *Journal of Verbal Learning and Verbal Behavior*, *6*, 156–163.

Shore. D. I.. & Klein. R. M. (2000). On the manifestations of memory in visual search. *Spatial Vision*, *14*, 59–75.

Simons. D. J. (1996). In sight. out of mind: When object representations fail. *Psychological Science*, *7*, 301–305.

Simons. D. J.. Chabris. C. F.. Schnur. T. T.. & Levin, D. T. (2002). Evidence for preserved representations in change blindness. *Consciousness and Cognition*, *11*, 78–97.

Simons. D. J., & Levin. D. T. (1997). Change blindness. *Trends in Cognitive Sciences*, *1*, 261–267.

Simons. D. J., & Levin. D. T. (1998). Failure to detect changes to people during a real-world interaction. *Psychonomic Bulletin and Review*, *5*, 644–649.

Sperling. G. (1960). The information available in brief visual presentations. *Psychological Monographs*, *74*(11, Whole no. 498).

Standing, L. (1973). Learning 10,000 pictures. *Quarterly Journal of Experimental Psychology*, *25*, 207–222.

Standing, L., Conezio, J., & Haber, R. N. (1970). Perception and memory for pictures: Single-trial learning of 2500 visual stimuli. *Psychonomic Science*, *19*, 73–74.

Takeda, Y., & Yagi, A. (2000). Inhibitory tagging in visual search can be found if search stimuli remain visible. *Perception and Psychophysics*, *62*, 927–934.

Thornton, I. M., & Fernandez-Duque, D. (2002). Converging evidence for the detection of change without awareness. In J. Hyönä, et al. (Eds.), *The brain's eyes: Neurobiological and clinical aspects of oculomotor research* (pp. 99–118). Amsterdam: Elsevier Science.

Treisman, A. (1988). Features and objects: The fourteenth Bartlett memorial lecture. *Quarterly Journal of Experimental Psychology*, *40A*, 201–237.

Von Mühlenen, A., Müller, H. J., & Müller, D. (2003). Sit-and-wait strategies in dynamic visual search. *Psychological Science*, *14*, 309–314.

Wheeler, M. E., & Treisman, A. M. (2002). Binding in short-term visual memory. *Journal of Experimental Psychology: General*, *131*, 48–64.

Williams, P., & Simons, D. J. (2000). Detecting changes in novel 3D objects: Effects of change magnitude, spatiotemporal continuity, and stimulus familiarity. *Visual Cognition*, *7*, 297–322.

Wolfe, J. M. (1998). Visual memory: What do you know about what you saw? *Current Biology*, *8*, R303–R304.

Wolfe, J. M. (1999). Inattentional amnesia. In V. Coltheart (Ed.), *Fleeting memories* (pp. 71–94). Cambridge, MA: MIT Press.

Wolfe, J. M., & Bennett, S. C. (1997). Preattentive object files: Shapeless bundles of basic features. *Vision Research*, *37*, 25–44.

Wolfe, J. M., Klempen, N., & Dahlen, K. (2000). Postattentive vision. *Journal of Experimental Psychology: Human Perception and Performance*, *26*, 693–716.

Woodman, G. F., & Chun, M. M. (2006). The role of working memory and long-term memory in visual search. *Visual Cognition*, *14*, 808–830.

Woodman, G. F., & Luck, S. J. (2003). Serial deployment of attention during visual search. *Journal of Experimental Psychology: Human Perception and Performance*, *29*, 121–138.

Yantis, S., & Jonides, J. (1984). Abrupt visual onsets and selective attention: Evidence from visual search. *Journal of Experimental Psychology: Human Perception and Performance*, *10*, 601–621.

Zelinsky, G., & Loschky, L. (1998). Toward a realistic assessment of visual working memory. *Investigative Ophthalmology and Visual Science*, *39*, S224.

VISUAL COGNITION, 2006, 14 (4/5/6/7/8), 808–830

Ψ **Psychology Press**
Taylor & Francis Group

The role of working memory and long-term memory in visual search

Geoffrey F. Woodman

Vanderbilt University, Nashville, TN, USA

Marvin M. Chun

Yale University, New Haven, CT, USA

Models of attentional deployment in visual search commonly specify that the short-term, or working memory, system plays a central role in biasing attention mechanisms to select task relevant information. In contrast, the role of long-term memory in guiding search is rarely articulated. Our review of recent studies calls for the need to revisit how existing models explain the role of working memory and long-term memory in search. First, the role of working memory in guiding attentional selection and search is much more complex than many current theories propose. Second, both explicit and implicit long-term memory representations have such clear influences on visual search performance that they deserve more prominent treatment in theoretical models. These new findings in the literature should stir the conception of new models of visual search.

Visual search tasks have long been used by cognitive scientists to study the deployment of attention to targets within complex arrays of distractor stimuli (Green & Anderson, 1956; Green, McGill, & Jenkins, 1953; Neisser, 1964). An attractive feature of the visual search task is that it taxes perceptual processing while presumably placing minimal demands on memory in contrast to other paradigms popularized during the same period (e.g., Sternberg, 1966). Technically speaking, a subject only needs to remember what to search for and how to respond to its presence or absence. Such considerations may have helped make visual search such a popular tool for

Please address all correspondence to Geoffrey F. Woodman, Department of Psychology, Wilson Hall, 111 21st Avenue South, Vanderbilt University, Nashville, TN 37240-1103, USA. E-mail: geoffrey.f.woodman@vanderbilt.edu

We thank Steve Luck, Gordon Logan, Andrew Rossi, and Andrew Hollingworth for valuable discussions regarding the issues addressed in this paper. GFW is supported by an individual NRSA from the National Institute of Health (F32 EY015043) and MMC is supported by a grant from the National Eye Institute (R01 EY014193).

http://www.psypress.com/viscog   DOI: 10.1080/13506280500197397

studying perceptual processing of features and objects (e.g., Treisman, 1988; Wolfe, 1994, 1998; Yantis & Jonides, 1984). Ironically, however, the field has begun to shift its focus from perceptual processing to an increased appreciation for the role of memory in visual search. For example, one may ask whether a memory representation of the target is formed after it is detected. In addition, do observers encode distractors that were attended during a visual search trial? More specifically, researchers have recently vigorously debated whether distractor locations are tagged by memory representations or not during visual search (e.g., Horowitz & Wolfe, 1998, 2003; Kristjánsson, 2000; von Mühlenen, Müller, & Müller, 2003). If memory for targets and or distractors exists, what types of memory stores are involved (e.g., Shore & Klein, 2000)? Although these issues are far from being resolved, recent research has shed light upon how memory representations of targets and nontarget objects guide attention during visual search. This paper will survey the most current research on how different memory systems impact visual search. Several unifying themes emerge from this review.

Memory representations exert their effects on visual search both within trials and across trials, and so we organize our discussion accordingly. Within a single trial of visual search, short-term, or working memory, representations of targets and distractors contribute to efficient processing. Across trials, long-term memory representations of targets and distractors also influence search. This scheme of organizing memory effects on search is the same as that introduced in Shore and Klein's excellent review of this issue (2000).[1] Our discussion will focus on the many new studies that have emerged since their review to further clarify how different memory systems represent targets and distractors to guide search. We note an increasing need to update models of visual search in light of recent new findings in the literature. For example, models of visual search often propose that target representations, or templates, are maintained in visual working memory and guide attention to select similar items from the currently available visual

---

[1] Because visual search tasks are typically comprised of discrete trials, it is useful to distinguish different roles of memory according to how memory influences performance within or across trials. We assume that within-trial effects are best subserved by working memory that has limited-capacity and requires active maintenance to perform a task at hand. Because target and distractor locations typically change unpredictably from trial to trial, the system should reset itself on each new trial to minimize debilitating proactive interference. Such resetting is naturally performed by the working memory system, according to theories of memory and models of visual search. Across-trial influences appear to be best explained by LTM processes that have larger capacity and less susceptibility to interference and erasure, serving to extract useful regularities that may occur over time. Although we will discuss this distinction in more detail later, we acknowledge that the distinction between working memory and LTM is a simplification, and in fact, we will conclude that visual search benefits from both working memory and long-term memory systems.

information (Bundesen, 1990: Desimone & Duncan, 1995; Duncan & Humphreys, 1989). However. the relationship between working memory and search is more complicated than suggested by these models. In contrast, models of attentional deployment during search offer scant treatment of how long-term memory representations of targets and distractors influence the efficiency of visual search, but a growing body of studies point to a prominent role for long-term memory.

VISUAL WORKING MEMORY AND SEARCH

Virtually every general model of cognitive processing posits that temporary memory (i.e., working memory) storage is essential for complex information processing (e.g., Anderson, 1993: Meyer & Kieras, 1997). Working memory is believed to support our ability to retain, accrue, and manipulate information over short periods of time. For example, it has been proposed that our working memory capabilities support sentence construction during language use (e.g., Just & Carpenter. 1980), the integration of information across blinks and saccades (e.g., Irwin. 1992: Irwin & Andrews, 1996), and complex problem solving by representing possible solutions (e.g., Newell & Simon, 1972). We have focused the current discussion on theoretical proposals and empirical studies of the involvement of working memory in visual search. Because the capacity of the visual working memory store appears to be limited to a small number of items (e.g., Irwin & Andrews, 1996; Lee & Chun, 2001; Luck & Vogel. 1997; Simons, 1996; Vogel, Woodman, & Luck, 2001) it requires careful utilization when the visual system is overloaded with information. as it is during demanding visual search tasks.

In visual search, researchers have proposed two ways that working memory may be vital. One proposed use is that each attended item may be transferred into working memory while search is performed (Bundesen, 1990: Duncan & Humphreys, 1989; Treisman, 1988). According to such an account, a stimulus that draws attention to its self (e.g., a waving sports fanatic) will automatically enter the visual working memory of an observer (e.g., a basketball player preparing to shoot a free throw). The majority of these models propose that attended items need to be entered into visual working memory to compare with a target representation that is maintained in visual working memory (Bundesen, 1990; Duncan & Humphreys, 1989). The second related proposal is that representations stored in visual working memory during search serve to bias the deployment of attention to similar items. In this way, the maintenance of an object representation in visual working memory largely determines what inputs are selected during search (Bundesen, 1990; Desimone & Duncan, 1995; Duncan & Humphreys, 1989).

We first provide a brief review of several of the most influential models of selective processing during visual search.

One of the first theories proposed to explain the differences that exist between efficient and inefficient visual search tasks was the Feature Integration Theory (FIT) of Treisman and colleagues (Treisman, 1988; Treisman & Gelade, 1980; Treisman & Sato, 1990; Treisman, Sykes, & Gelade, 1977). FIT proposes that certain visual search tasks are inefficient because the individual objects in the arrays require focused perceptual attention in order for their features to be bound into object representations. Specifically, FIT proposes that the deployment of focused attention to an object location serves to bind the features of that object together. After an object's features are bound, that representation is stored as an *object file*. One possible interpretation of an object file is that it is a representation in visual working memory. Thus, one interpretation of FIT leads to the prediction that focusing attention on an object leads to its encoding into visual working memory.

Duncan and Humphreys (1989) proposed an alternative account of processing during visual search. They hypothesize that there is a limited amount of attention that can be distributed across multiple items in the visual field. The more attention allocated to a given object, the greater the chance that a perceptual representation of this item will enter working memory, thereby allowing a behavioural response about that object to be made. What determines how much resource is allocated to each item? Duncan and Humphreys propose that resource allocation depends upon the match between each perceptual representation and a target template maintained in visual working memory. This and other models of visual search do not fully specify what constitutes a target template, however, it can be assumed to be either a picture-like representation or an abstract representation that defines features. For example, when the task requires searching for a red square, it is proposed that observers store a red square (or an abstract description of a red square) in working memory, and the priority of each perceptual representation for transfer into visual working memory is therefore greatest for red items, square items, and especially red-square items. In this manner, the current contents of visual working memory are posited to bias the transfer of similar perceptual representations into working memory. Specifically, Duncan and Humphreys go on to propose that if during search visual working memory "... is filled it must be flushed before the entry of new information can begin" (p. 446). Thus, Duncan and Humphreys' model of attention makes very explicit claims about how visual working memory is utilized during visual search.

Duncan and Humphreys (1989) are not the only theorists to propose that visual working memory is essential for efficiently processing complex arrays of objects. For example, Bundesen (1990) proposed a powerful computational model of visual attention that shares several conceptual characteristics with the model of Duncan and Humphreys. Bundesen's Theory of Visual Attention (TVA) is a flexible computational model in which representations are entered into visual working memory, and at the same time categorized, based on their similarity to a target representation also maintained in visual working memory. Yet another influential model of attentional selection is the biased competition account of Desimone and Duncan (1995). The biased competition account proposes that representations compete for access to limited-capacity mechanisms of the brain. Examples of scarce resources for which representations might compete are the receptive field of cells, representational space in working memory, and access to response execution mechanisms. This account has been applied to visual search tasks in considerable detail. The biased competition account proposes that the visual system becomes biased to process target-like objects by maintaining a representation of the expected target in visual working memory. This will tend to strengthen matching representations, allowing them to compete more effectively for limited resources. The strongest evidence for the maintenance of target templates during search comes from single-unit recording studies.

Chelazzi, Miller, Duncan, and Desimone (1993) recorded from neurons in the temporal lobe of macaque monkeys while they performed a delayed match-to-sample (DMS) task. In this task, a sample item was presented, and after a delay interval an array of several items was shown. The subject then made a motor response indicating whether the sample item (the target) was present or where it was located. Chelazzi et al. found that the neurons that coded for the target maintained an elevated firing rate during the delay intervals. This elevated firing rate was interpreted as evidence that a working memory representation of the target was being maintained during the retention interval. In addition, it was hypothesized that this memory representation provides a bias signal to the neurons that perform perceptual analysis. This bias signal in turn increases the baseline firing rate and therefore induces a competitive advantage for neurons that selectively respond to the target.

The importance of visual working memory representations during visual search in the biased competition account is emphasized by this quote: "Visual search simply appears to be a variant of a working memory task, in which the distractors are distributed in space rather than time" (Desimone & Duncan, 1995, p. 207). Although the findings of the single-unit studies provide valuable insight regarding how DMS tasks are performed, it is quite possible that visual search is performed differently when the task does not explicitly require visual working memory storage of the target. For example, in typical visual search tasks with human observers, the target remains constant for many minutes or even throughout the entire experiment. It is possible that when the identity of the searched-for target is stable across many trials that task performance becomes automated and can be driven by long-term memory representations (e.g., Logan, 1988). Thus, it will be important to confirm that human and nonhuman primate subjects rely upon the same mechanisms when performing identical cognitive tasks.

In summary, we have discussed the theoretical underpinnings of two types of interactions between perception and working memory. First, several theories of attention propose that attended items are obligatorily transferred into visual working memory during each trial of visual search (Bundesen, 1990; Duncan & Humphreys, 1989; Treisman, 1988). The second type of posited interaction between perception and working memory is that working memory representations are maintained throughout each trial of visual search to influence perceptual mechanisms in a top down manner, such that items similar to those represented in visual working memory are automatically selected for preferential processing (Desimone & Duncan, 1995; Duncan & Humphreys, 1989). These models make specific predictions that can be empirically tested, as we shall review below.

Are all attended objects represented in visual working memory during a visual search trial?

It is very difficult to determine what is being stored in visual working memory during the performance of a task such as visual search. However, several recent studies have sought to determine whether representations of items in a search array are stored in visual working memory, or in any type of memory store, during a visual search trial. In particular, a recent debate in the literature surrounds the proposal that visual search requires no visual working memory resources at all. Specifically, Horowitz and Wolfe (1998) have proposed that no information about the identity or location of objects is accrued in visual working memory during search. In two different conditions, subjects searched for rotated "T"s embedded in arrays of rotated "L"s. In one condition, the search arrays were static (as in most visual search experiments). In the other condition, the locations of the objects changed every 100 ms during the 2.3 s trial. They reasoned that if information about the location of the target accrues slowly over time in memory, then subjects should be less efficient at finding the target when the object locations change every 100 ms because the accrual process would have to restart with every change. Horowitz and Wolfe found that the slopes of the search functions did not differ between the static and the changing displays, indicating that subjects were just as efficient at finding targets in the changing as in the static condition. From these results, Horowitz and Wolfe argued that visual search does not rely on information that accrues in visual working memory or any other memory store.

The claim for amnesic search has triggered an intense debate in which several researchers have argued that the conclusion may apply only to the task and set of conditions employed by Horowitz and Wolfe (Gibson, Li, Skow, Brown, & Cooke, 2000; Horowitz & Wolfe, 2001, 2003; Kristjánsson, 2000; Shore & Klein, 2000). For example, Shore and Klein (2000) suggest that the results obtained by Horowitz and Wolfe were due to subjects trading off accuracy for speed in the dynamic condition in which the locations of the items changed during each trial. Other researchers have proposed that performance in the dynamic condition becomes less efficient when larger search arrays are used (Kristjánsson, 2000), or performance in the dynamic condition could be due to observers adopting a strategy of statically attending to one quadrant and waiting for the target to appear there (von Mühlenen et al., 2003).

Beyond the Horowitz and Wolfe paradigm, the necessity of working memory in search can be tested with a dual-task interference approach. Woodman, Vogel, and Luck (2001) tested whether visual working memory was needed during a search task that required serial shifts of attention (Woodman & Luck, 1999, 2003). The logic of the approach was as follows. If attended representations are encoded into visual working memory during search, then filling the visual store to capacity with irrelevant information should decrease search efficiency and possibly even prohibit the performance of visual search. Thus, they required observers to remember up to four colours or shapes while performing a demanding visual search task and compared visual search efficiency to a condition in which subjects performed the same visual search task in isolation. They found that the efficiency of search, as measured by the slope of the RT × Set size functions, did not differ between the dual-task and single-task conditions (Figure 1B). Several models (e.g., Bundesen, 1990; Duncan & Humphreys, 1989) predict the opposite result because nontarget items not held in visual working memory are likely to be reselected by attention and therefore decrease the efficiency with which the target object can be processed.

A related prediction is that if working memory is necessary for search, then subjects should be less accurate at the working memory task when more items in the search array need to be processed. In contrast, Woodman et al. (2001) found that regardless of the set size of the search array the same amount of information could be maintained in visual working memory. That is, performing search displaced approximately the same amount of information from visual working memory across the set sizes tested (for example see Figure 1C). This result runs counter to predictions made by models that propose the contents of visual working memory are expelled if the visual store is full when search is performed (e.g., Duncan & Humphreys,

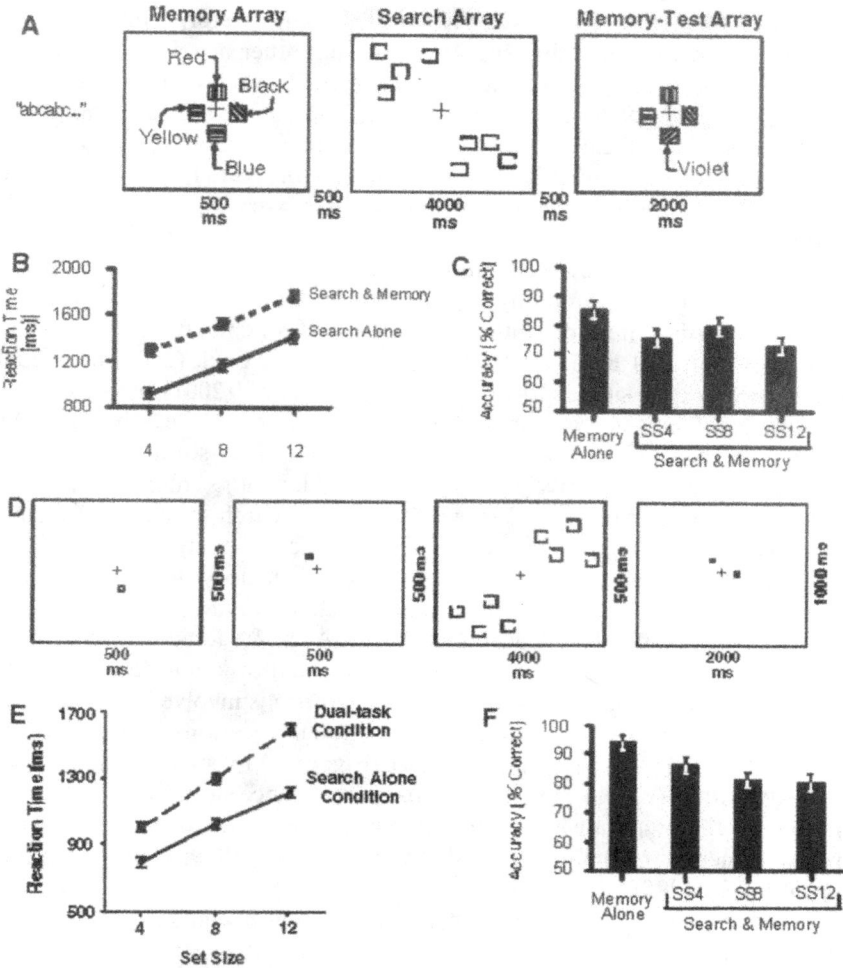

Figure 1. Example stimuli and findings from Woodman and Luck (2004) and Woodman et al. (2001). Sequence of stimuli presented in Experiment 2 of Woodman et al. (2001) (A). Visual search reaction time with and without an object working memory load (B). Performance on the visual working memory task with and without search during the retention interval (C). Example of the stimulus sequence used in Woodman and Luck (in press) (D). Visual search RT data in the search alone and search-plus-spatial-memory task (E). Spatial change-detection accuracy when the two locations were maintained in isolation compared to during visual search at different set sizes.

1989). In summary, this study found little evidence that supports the idea that representations of searched-for objects need to be maintained in visual working memory during each trial.

An interesting and important aspect of visuospatial working memory is that it not only represents objects, but it also can also maintain spatial location information. Moreover, the working memory stores for objects and for spatial locations may be separate from each other or rely upon different aspects of the visuospatial subsystem (e.g., Baddeley & Logie, 1999; Goldman-Rakic, 1996; Logie, 1995). Visual search requires attention to be shifted from one location to another (Treisman & Gelade, 1980; Wolfe, 1994), and it may also benefit from tracking of visited locations (Klein, 1988). This raises the possibility that spatial working memory may be necessary for visual search.

Accordingly, two research groups independently tested the hypothesis that concurrently maintaining representations of spatial locations during each search trial interferes with the efficiency of a demanding visual search task. Both Oh and Kim (2004) and Woodman and Luck (2004) used dual-task methodology similar to that of Woodman et al. (2001) but, instead of requiring subjects to remember objects during visual search, observers needed to remember several spatial locations. The studies found that maintaining even a relatively small number of locations interfered with the efficiency of search compared to when the same search task was performed in isolation, see Figure 1E. These findings are consistent with existing research demonstrating that spatial working memory tasks tax spatial attention mechanisms presumably because spatial attention is being focused on the to-be-remembered locations (e.g., Awh & Jonides, 1998; Awh, Jonides, & Reuter-Lorenz, 1998). Thus, the dual-task interference results indicate that the same spatial attention mechanism is involved in both visual search and the active maintenance of spatial locations. Moreover, the differential effects of maintaining object (Figure 1A) versus spatial location representations (Figure 1D) provides further evidence supporting theoretical proposals that separate stores or mechanisms exist for object and spatial working memory functions (e.g., Baddeley & Logie, 1999; Goldman-Rakic, 1996; Logie, 1995).[2]

A growing number of studies also suggest that visual search tasks that require eye movements to the search elements are supported by a memory system that retains the locations of the last four or so foveated locations. Specifically, Peterson, Kramer, Wang, Irwin, and McCarley (2001) recorded eye movements while subjects performed visual search for a small form-defined target. They found that subjects very rarely made eye movements back to an object if it had recently been foveated; however, the probability of refixation increased dramatically if four other objects were fixated since the

---

[2] The majority of evidence supports a distinction between spatial and object working memory stores, but this does not mean that object and spatial working memory representations cannot be linked (e.g., Jiang, Olson, & Chun, 2000; Rao, Rainer, & Miller, 1997). In fact, it is likely that one role of attention is to bind information across such separate working memory stores (e.g., Wheeler & Treisman, 2002).

fixation of any given object. These findings seem closely tied to the inhibition of return (IOR) phenomenon in which subjects are slower to respond to a target presented at a previously attended location than at a previously unattended location (for a thorough discussion see Shore & Klein, 2000). Interestingly, some recent findings suggest that IOR is most reliably observed during visual search when the search task involves eye movements to objects in search arrays that remain visible while items were probed for inhibition (Klein & MacInnes, 1999; Müller & von Mühlenen, 2000). Finally, Castel, Pratt, and Craik (2003) found that performing tasks that demanded the use of spatial working memory prevented subjects from showing the IOR effect. This suggests that spatial working memory may play an important role in maintaining representations that contribute to the IOR phenomenon.

We draw three general conclusions from the studies discussed above. First, empirical results do not support theories that propose that a target must be represented in visual object working memory for attention to be efficiently deployed to that object in a search array. Second, actively maintaining *spatial locations* appears to draw upon the same mechanisms that are taxed during demanding visual search tasks, unlike maintaining *objects* in working memory. Finally, visual search tasks that require subjects to make eye movements may engage memory for tagging visited items that is less reliably recruited in visual search paradigms where covert selection plays the dominant role. Further research will be needed to clarify this issue among others, such as the involvement of the central executive component of working memory during a visual search trial (de Fockert, Rees, Frith, & Lavie, 2001). For example, a recent study demonstrated that occupying central executive processes severely impaired the efficiency of visual search (Han & Kim, 2004).

Is attention automatically drawn to items that match the contents of working memory during visual search?

A central tenant of many models of visual search is that target template representations are maintained in visual working memory to bias attention to select similar items (Desimone & Duncan, 1995; Duncan & Humphreys, 1989). This proposal assumes that attention is automatically biased to select incoming information that is similar to that stored in visual working memory. Some evidence supporting this assumption has been found using delayed-match-to-sample tasks with monkeys (Chelazzi et al., 1993), and attentional blink (Pashler & Shiu, 1999) and cueing studies (Downing, 2000; Pratt & Hommel, 2003) with human subjects. However, several recent studies with monkey and human observers suggest that the contents of working memory can be used flexibly to bias attention mechanisms and in some cases working memory resources may not be needed at all for efficient search.

In several experiments, Woodman and Luck (in press; see also Downing & Dodds, 2004; Woodman, 2002) extended the logic of previous studies (i.e., Downing, 2000; Pashler & Shiu, 1999) to the domain of visual search. Specifically, they tested the hypothesis that attention is automatically deployed to items that match those stored in visual working memory during a visual search trial. The experiments were designed so that subjects had no reason to strategically shift attention to items that are similar to those represented in visual working memory. That is, the subjects were provided with an incentive for not attending to items that match those in working memory because the matching search item was never the target in the search task (for use of similar logic see Folk, Remington, & Johnston, 1992). Moreover, an item matching the representation held in visual working memory as not present in the visual search array on every trial. If the distractors that match the contents of visual working memory do not interfere with visual search, this would indicate that items matching those in visual working memory do not capture attention in a strongly automatic manner. They consistently found that subjects were not slower to find the target when a distractor matched an object represented in visual working memory. These findings suggest that attention is not automatically deployed to items simply because they are similar to an object in memory, but instead the contents of visual working memory can be used adaptively to guide attention away from items that are known to be nontargets. A highly flexible model such as TVA (Bundesen, 1990) could account for these findings because the contents of working memory could be used to set the appropriate bias terms to zero so attention would never be deployed to similar items.

One may question whether working memory representations are ever used to guide attention during visual search. However, several recent studies suggest that working memory may be crucial for efficient visual search when the identity of the target changes from trial to trial. In an elegant lesion study, Rossi, Harris, Bichot, Desimone, and Ungerleider (2001) had monkeys perform a visual search task in which the identity of the target changed frequently (i.e., every several trials) or infrequently (i.e., the target was the same for an entire day of search trials). The corpus callosum of each monkey was cut and essentially all prefrontal cortex aspirated from one hemisphere. By separating the hemispheres of the brain the researchers had the unlesioned hemisphere of the monkeys serve as a within subject control for the lesioned side. The prefrontal cortex is believed to be the part of the brain that implements working memory functions (e.g., Goldman-Rakic, 1996; Miller, 1999). Thus, stimuli presented to the lesioned hemisphere are processed without the benefit of working memory mechanisms. However, they found that when the identity of the search target remained the same across many trials search efficiency was the same whether performed by the intact or lesioned hemisphere. In contrast, when the searched-for target changed frequently across trials the lesioned hemisphere performed search extremely inefficiently compared to the intact hemisphere. A behavioural study in which human observers concurrently performed a visual working memory task and visual search has yielded a similar pattern of results (Woodman, 2002). Concurrently maintaining information in visual working memory did not interfere with visual search when the identity of the target did not change across an entire block of trials, but interference occurred when the identity of the target was different on each trial.

In fact, even without a concurrent working memory load, search performance is markedly slower when target identity changes from trial to trial within blocks (Bravo & Nakayama, 1992). Two factors appear responsible. First, the need to reconfigure the visual system to search for a new target on each trial requires time (Di Lollo, Kawahara, Zuvic, & Visser, 2001; Kawahara, Zuvic, Enns, & Di Lollo, 2003). The findings described in the previous paragraph suggest that working memory plays a critical role in such reconfiguration. When the target does not switch within a block, observers may rely on long-term representations of the target. A second reason that search is faster when the target identity is constant is that when the same target feature repeats across trials, search benefits from feature priming. Maljkovic and Nakayama (1994, 1996, 2000) required subjects to discriminate the shape of the target that was a different colour than the distractors in the search array, commonly known as a *pop-out* search task. In addition, the specific colour of the target could change from trial to trial although it was always different from the colour of the distractors. They found that when the target was the same colour on consecutive trials subjects were faster at discriminating the target's shape. Moreover, this facilitation for target colour repetition lasted across several intervening trials. This effect, known as priming of pop-out, may reflect an implicit memory representation of the attended target. This memory representation causes attention mechanisms to select similar items and inhibit items that do not match it during a number of subsequent search trials. These memory representations significantly influence the efficiency of pop-out search for approximately 30 s regardless of whether subjects attempt to use them or not (Maljkovic & Nakayama, 1994), suggesting that the representations are maintained in a short-term implicit memory system. A related observation made by Müller and colleagues (Found & Müller, 1996; Krummenacher, Müller, & Heller, 2001; Müller, Heller, & Ziegler, 1995) is that observers are also faster to detect pop-out targets when they can predict along what feature dimension (e.g., colour or orientation) the target will differ from the distractors. This suggests that priming of pop-out may spread within a feature dimension or that search can be facilitated by actively configuring the visual system to process features of the relevant dimension (e.g., Müller et al., 1995).

Thus, object working memory may be needed for reconfiguration when targets change from trial to trial, but not when observers may rely on long-term memory representations for targets that do not change within blocks. In contrast, the spatial selection mechanism that maintains spatial working memory representations appears to be necessary for all search tasks. The phenomenon of priming of pop-out shows that perceptual traces of attended targets facilitate search in subsequent trials. These findings provide a nice lead into the following section that will review many other demonstrations of how memory representations of both targets and distractors affect visual search from trial to trial.

LONG-TERM MEMORY AND SEARCH

Visual search can benefit from memory representations of previously attended targets as well as distractors. We begin by examining the evidence for the retention of target information across many trials, and then turn to the issue of whether information about the distractor objects is remembered across trials.

Is information about attended items stored in long-term memory across trials?

Whereas the working memory system is believed to be severely limited in its capacity to store information, long-term memory stores appear to be vast if not unlimited in capacity (Standing. 1973; Standing, Conezio, & Haber, 1970). Therefore, one might predict that an item that was attended during search would be remembered beyond the time of presentation. This is exactly the type of evidence that Hollingworth recently reported (2004). He required subjects to perform a dot-following task in which a dot was shifted between objects in a computer rendered scene followed by a memory probe at the end of the trial. The objects in the search array were small enough to require that they be foveated to be discriminated. He then tested subjects' recognition memory for an item that they foveated some number of fixations ago. He found that subjects could discriminate items that they had previously fixated during search from visually similar foils. Moreover, subjects' change-detection accuracy remained high, i.e., an A' of approximately .75, even when over 400 objects had been fixated between the fixation of the to-be-tested object and the testing event. Hollingworth obtained a similar type of result using a visual search task in which subjects previewed the search scene before being cued as to what the target object would be on that trial. During both the preview and active search of the scene subjects' eye movements were recorded. Using this paradigm, he found that observers could fixate the target significantly faster if they had received a preview on that trial compared to those trials in which they did not. Surprisingly, this benefit was observed even when the target object had not appeared in the preview of the scene, although the size of the facilitation was reduced compared to when the target object was actually present. This suggests that subjects do not just remember the target location from the preview but that a representation of the contextual objects and surfaces is built up and stored in memory. These results suggest that the visual system accumulates information about the spatial layout and specific locations of objects in complex scenes. Similar conclusions were drawn by Castelhano and Henderson (2005), using a paradigm in which observers' memory for distractors was tested. Their subjects demonstrated above-chance recognition for the distractors even though they had only been attended in order to reject them as nontargets. In summary, these findings suggest that our memory for items that are fixated during search is quite robust even after processing a large number of other objects within the session (e.g., Hollingworth & Henderson, 2002).

In contrast to the conclusions drawn using these overt measures of selective processing, other approaches to this question have yielded the opposite conclusion. For example, one may try to have subjects commit a visual search array to memory by repeating the same display over many search trials to see how overlearning may affect the efficiency of search. This was the approach taken by Wolfe, Klempen, and Dahlen (2000) in a series of experiments. They required subjects to perform visual search in several conditions. In the repeated search condition subjects where shown exactly the same array for up to a thousand trials and were simply asked to search for a different target on each trial. In the comparison condition the visual search arrays were composed of randomly selected elements on each trial. Wolfe et al. predicted that if information about the search array accrues in long-term memory then across trials search should become increasingly efficient (i.e., exhibit shallower search slopes) in the repeated search condition relative to the condition in which a new search array was presented on each trial. However, the slopes of the search functions did not differ between conditions. These data suggest that subjects continue to perform visual search using the same visual strategies even though a more efficient memory search algorithm is available to them. The findings of Wolfe et al. are surprising given previous reports of increased search efficiency with practice (Schneider & Shiffrin, 1977; Shiffrin & Schneider, 1977). Although the methods differed greatly, an explanation for the lack of learning in Wolfe et al.'s task is that they employed a variable mapping task in which the target changes from trial to trial, a task condition that leads to inefficient learning, according to Shiffrin and Schneider. Nevertheless, the lack of benefit from repeated searches through the same display in Wolfe et al.'s study remains impressive.

Do memory representations of distractors influence search efficiency across trials?

Another approach for studying the relation between visual search and long-term memory is through the effects of learned semantic relatedness. Returning to Shiffrin and Schneider's studies (Schneider & Shiffrin, 1977; Shiffrin & Schneider, 1977), they classically demonstrated that target recognition is facilitated if there is a consistent mapping (association) between the target and distractor set. In addition, Chun and Jiang (1999) showed that target detection was facilitated when the target shape always appeared together with the same set of distractor shapes, compared to a condition in which the target shape was not correlated with the background distractor shapes.

Real-world associations facilitate search as well. Recently, Moores, Laiti, and Chelazzi (2003) demonstrated that distractor objects that are semantically related to a searched-for target influence the speed and accuracy with which visual search can be performed. Although the presence of an object (e.g., a hammer) that is semantically related to the target being searched for (e.g., nails) did not significantly influence the speed and accuracy of finding the target when it was present, on target absent trials subjects were significantly more likely to respond incorrectly or slowly to an array that contained a related distractor than one that did not. Moores et al. propose that distractors that are semantically related to the target attract attention to themselves. Supporting this proposal, subjects were more likely to make a saccade to the related distractor than unrelated control items. Attention researchers have tended to study visual search using stimuli that lack strong semantic associations so that experimental results are easier to interpret. Nevertheless, the Moores et al. study shows that the inherent structure of long-term memory is likely to be ecologically important for everyday vision, which undoubtedly benefits from visual knowledge accumulated over the lifetime of an observer.

Although the study described above proposes that some distractors may attract attention to themselves based on their associations to targets in long-term memory, other research suggests that memory representations of ignored distractors can cause similar items to be processed less efficiently. For example, when observers discriminate the identity of a target word (or shape) superimposed upon a distractor word (or shape) of a different colour, target discrimination time is increased if that target was shown previously as a distractor. This effect known as *negative priming* is commonly thought to result because the suppression of the distractor is necessary for target selection (DeSchepper & Treisman, 1996; Tipper, 1985). However, debate has raged over the time course of this effect (Neill & Valdes, 1992) and the underlying mechanism that causes it (Moore, 1996). The modal paradigm for studying negative priming involves presenting a single target and distractor that essentially share the same spatial location. Therefore, the processing demands differ significantly from visual search paradigms in which many distractors are distributed around a target with each occupying a unique location. Supporting this distinction is ample evidence that representations of distractor objects are stored in memory during search and that these representations have the opposite effect of facilitating search in familiar environments.

One way for our visual systems to find target objects more efficiently is for it to take advantage of statistical regularities present in the world that surrounds us. For example, if you could store a representation of the context in which you find a specific target object then you should be able to find the target more quickly the next time you encounter that same context. Recent studies have provided evidence for such learning of contextual information that serves to guide attention to embedded target items. Chun and Jiang (1998, 1999) had subjects perform a fairly demanding visual search task (e.g., a left or right rotated target "T" among rotated distractor "L's") across many blocks of trials. During the first block of trials the subjects discriminated the identity of each target in randomly generated spatial configurations of distractor objects. However, on each subsequent block of trials, half of trials presented configurations of distractors that were repeated from the first block. The old, repeated display trials were interleaved with trials that presented new randomly generated spatial configurations of distractors. The target was always in the same location in these repeated configurations of distractors although the target identity, and therefore the required response, was not correlated with the presence of a specific configuration. As shown in Figure 2, Chun and Jiang (1998, 2003) found that subjects generally became faster at discriminating targets across blocks of trials. In addition to this general learning of the task, observers became even faster at discriminating targets embedded in repeated configurations relative to targets in the novel distractor configurations. Chun and Jiang (1998, 1999) termed this effect *contextual cueing* based on the idea that subjects' memory representations of the repeated contexts of distractors were guiding attention to the target location.

The remarkable aspect of the learning that underlies contextual cueing is that it appears to occur implicitly. That is, although subjects become significantly faster at finding targets in repeated arrays compared to novel arrays they report being completely unaware that such repetitions occurred.

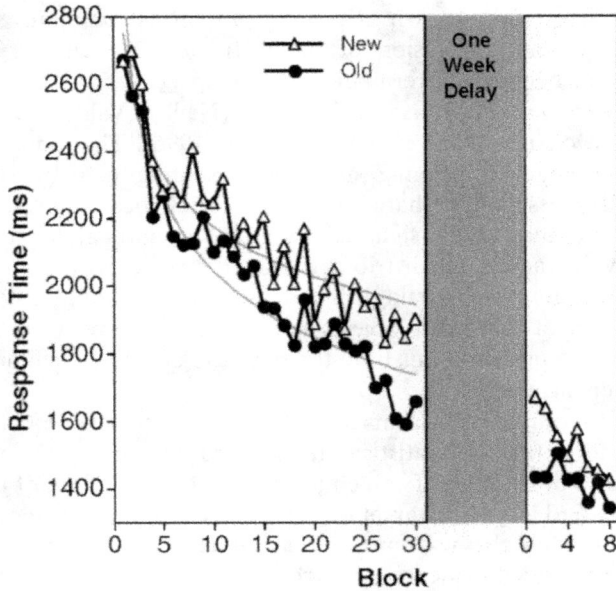

Figure 2.   Targets appearing in repeated (old) scenes were detected more quickly than in new scenes. The learning persisted up to at least 1 week (Exp. 3. Chun & Jiang. 2003).

Moreover, the few participants who did report being aware that such repetitions were occurring produced contextual cueing effects of similar magnitude to those produced by subjects who were unaware of the repetitions (Chun & Jiang, 1998). When subjects were tested with an old–new forced-choice discrimination task following the visual search session, they were at chance at discriminating distractor contexts they had seen 30 times from novel displays they had never seen before. Other explicit tests of subjects' memory for the repeated contexts yielded similar results. For example, observers did not perform better than chance when shown the repeated configurations of distractors without the targets and required to choose the quadrant in each array that they believed should contain the target item (Chun & Jiang, 2003). In addition to the implicit nature of contextual learning. the representations of the learned distractor configurations appear to last a long time. Specifically, subjects who were retested on the visual search task 1 week after originally learning the set of repeated contexts were still significantly faster at searching for targets in the repeated contexts (see Figure 2) (Chun & Jiang, 2003). Finally, this type of implicit learning is not specific to spatial contexts of distractors but is also observed when target identity covaries with the identity of the distractors. when the trajectory of a moving target is predictable based on the trajectories of the moving distractors (Chun & Jiang, 1999), and when the temporal position of a target is predictable from the temporal sequence of distractor stimuli shown in a RSVP paradigm (Olson & Chun, 2001).

Thus, our visual systems are extremely sensitive to statistical regularities that may be present in visual search arrays. This sensitivity to statistical relationships between stimuli not only facilitates visual search performance but also appears to be important for learning scene structure (Fiser & Aslin, 2001), visual event structure (Fiser & Aslin, 2002a, 2002b), as well as other types of learning, such as word boundary learning in infants (Saffran, Aslin, & Newport, 1996).

CONCLUSIONS

In this paper we reviewed theoretical proposals on the roles that memory representations play in the efficient processing of stimuli during search. After weighing the evidence we can draw two general conclusions regarding the relationship between memory and search.

The first is that working memory representations of targets might be essential in guiding attention only when the identity of the target changes frequently from trial-to-trial. Nearly every model of visual search makes explicit claims that visual working memory is required to find targets and reject distractors in any search task. However, recent findings suggest that object working memory is not required when subjects search for the same target across trials within a session. Subjects may rely on long-term representations of targets instead. When the target changes on each trial, however, object working memory is needed to update the target template representations. In contrast to the task-dependent effects of object working memory, spatial working memory is always required in visual search. It is likely that spatial working memory is used to tag distractor locations as attention shifts from one object to another until the target is detected. Existing visual search models require revision to incorporate the different roles of object working memory and spatial working memory.

Our second conclusion is that long-term memory representations of targets, distractors, and the relations between the two play a significant role in biasing how attention is deployed in visual search. Theories have typically ignored the role of long-term memory in order to focus on bottom-up visual factors and within-trial top-down effects. However, to increase the ecological validity of visual search, models must begin to articulate how long-term visual knowledge biases attention. We suggest that such knowledge derives from statistical learning of regularities that undeniably exist in the visual environment. Simply put, memory traces of attended targets and target contexts facilitate the viewing of similar scenes in future encounters.

We opened this review by stating that an advantage of the visual search task is that it appears to require minimal memory requirements. So it is ironic to see that the role of memory in visual search has become such a major focus of study and debate in modern research.

REFERENCES

Anderson. J. R. (1993). *Rules of the mind*. Hillsdale. NJ: Lawrence Erlbaum Associates. Inc.

Awh, E.. & Jonides. J. (1998). Spatial working memory and spatial selective attention. In R. Parasuraman (Ed.), *The attentive brain* (pp. 353–380). Cambridge. MA: Mit Press.

Awh. E.. Jonides. J.. & Reuter-Lorenz. P. A. (1998). Rehearsal in spatial working memory. *Journal of Experimental Psychology: Human Perception and Performance*, *24*(3), 780–790.

Baddeley. A. D.. & Logie. R. H. (1999). Working memory: The multiple component model. In P. Shah & A. Miyake (Eds.). *Models of working memory* (pp. 28–61). Cambridge. UK: Cambridge University Press.

Bravo. M. J.. & Nakayama. K. (1992). The role of attention in different visual-search tasks. *Perception and Psychophysics, 51*(5). 465–472.

Bundesen. C. (1990). A theory of visual attention. *Psychological Review, 97*, 523–547.

Castel, A., Pratt, J., & Craik, F. I. M. (2003). The role of spatial working memory in inhibition of return: Evidence from divided attention tasks. *Perception and Psychophysics, 65*, 970–981.

Castelhano, M. S., & Henderson, J. M. (2005). Incidental visual memory for objects in scenes. *Visual Cognition, 12*, 1017–1040.

Chelazzi. L.. Miller, E. K., Duncan. J., & Desimone. R. (1993). A neural basis for visual search in inferior temporal cortex. *Nature. 363*. 345–347.

Chun. M. M.. & Jiang. Y. (1998). Contextual cueing: Implicit learning and memory of visual context guides spatial attention. *Cognitive Psychology. 36*(1). 28–71.

Chun. M. M.. & Jiang. Y. (1999). Top-down attentional guidance based on implicit learning of visual covariation. *Psychological Science. 10*. 360–365.

Chun. M. M.. & Jiang. Y. (2003). Implicit. long-term spatial contextual memory. *Journal of Experimental Psychology: Learning, Memory. and Cognition, 29*, 224–234.

De Fockert. J. W.. Rees. G., Frith. C. D.. & Lavie. N. (2001). The role of working memory in visual selective attention. *Science, 291*(5509). 1803–1806.

DeSchepper, B., & Treisman, A. (1996). Visual memory for novel shapes: Implicit coding without attention. *Journal of Experimental Psychology: Learning, Memory, and Cognition, 22*(1). 27–47.

Desimone. R.. & Duncan. J. (1995). Neural mechanisms of selective visual attention. *Annual Review of Neuroscience. 18*. 193–222.

Di Lollo. V.. Kawahara. J.. Zuvic. S. M.. & Visser. T. A. W. (2001). The preattentive emperor has no clothes: A dynamic redressing. *Journal of Experimental Psychology: General. 130*. 479–492.

Downing. P. E. (2000). Interactions between visual working memory and selective attention. *Psychological Science. 11*. 467–473.

Downing. P. E.. & Dodds. C. M. (2004). Competition in visual working memory for control of search. *Visual Cognition. 11*. 689–703.

Duncan. J.. & Humphreys, G. W. (1989). Visual search and stimulus similarity. *Psychological Review, 96*(3), 433–458.

Fiser. J.. & Aslin. R. N. (2001). Unsupervised statistical learning of higher-order spatial structures from visual scenes. *Psychological Science. 12*(6). 499–504.

Fiser. J.. & Aslin. R. N. (2002a). Statistical learning of higher-order temporal structure from visual shape sequences. Journal of Experimental Psychology: Learning. Memory. *and Cognition, 28*(3). 458–467.

Fiser. J.. & Aslin, R. N. (2002b). Statistical learning of new visual feature combinations by infants. *Proceedings of the National Academy of Science, 99*, 15822–15826.

Folk, C. L., Remington, R. W., & Johnston, J. C. (1992). Involuntary covert orienting is contingent on attentional control settings. *Journal of Experimental Psychology: Human Perception and Performance, 18*, 1030–1044.

Found, A., & Müller, H. J. (1996). Searching for unknown feature targets on more than one dimension: Investigating a "dimension-weighting" account. *Perception and Psychophysics, 58*, 88–101.

Gibson, B. S., Li, L., Skow, E., Brown, K., & Cooke, L. (2000). Searching for one or two identical targets: When visual search has a memory. *Psychological Science, 11*, 324–327.

Goldman-Rakic, P. S. (1996). Regional and cellular fractionation of working memory. *Proceedings of the National Academy of Sciences of the USA, 93*(24). 13473–13480.

Green, B. F., & Anderson, L. K. (1956). Color coding in a visual search task. *Journal of Experimental Psychology, 51*(1), 19–24.

Green, B. F., McGill, W. J., & Jenkins, H. M. (1953). *The time required to search for numbers on large visual displays* [Tech. Rep. No. 36]. Lincoln Laboratory, Massachusetts Institute of Technology, Cambridge, MA.

Han, S.-H., & Kim, M.-S. (2004). Visual search does not remain efficient when executive working memory is working. *Psychological Science, 15*(9), 623–628.

Hollingworth, A. (2004). Constructing visual representations of natural scenes: The roles of short- and long-term visual memory. *Journal of Experimental Psychology: Human Performance and Perception, 30*, 519–557.

Hollingworth, A., & Henderson, J. M. (2002). Accurate visual memory for previously attended objects in natural scenes. *Journal of Experimental Psychology: Human Perception and Performance, 28*, 113–136.

Horowitz, T. S., & Wolfe, J. M. (1998). Visual search has no memory. *Nature, 394*, 575–577.

Horowitz, T. S., & Wolfe, J. M. (2001). Search for multiple targets: Remember the targets, forget the search. *Perception and Psychophysics, 63*, 272–285.

Horowitz, T. S., & Wolfe, J. M. (2003). Memory for rejected distractors in visual search? *Visual Cognition, 10*, 257–298.

Irwin, D. E. (1992). Memory for position and identity across eye movements. Journal of Experimental Psychology: Learning, Memory. *and Cognition, 18*, 307–317.

Irwin, D. E., & Andrews, R. V. (1996). Integration and accumulation of information across saccadic eye movements. In T. Inui & J. L. McClelland (Eds.), *Attention and performance XVI: Information integration in perception and communication* (pp. 125–155). Cambridge, MA: MIT Press.

Jiang, Y., Olson, I. R., & Chun, M. M. (2000). Organization of visual short-term memory. *Journal of Experimental Psychology: Learning, Memory, and Cognition, 2*, 683–702.

Just, M. A., & Carpenter, P. A. (1980). A theory of reading: From eye fixations to comprehension. *Psychological Review, 87*, 329–354.

Kawahara, J., Zuvic, S. M., Enns, J. T., & Di Lollo, V. (2003). Task switching mediates the attentional blink even without backward masking. *Perception and Psychophysics, 65*, 339–351.

Klein, R. (1988). Inhibitory tagging system facilitates visual search. *Nature, 334*, 430–431.

Klein, R. M., & MacInnes, W. J. (1999). Inhibition of return is a foraging facilitator in visual search. *Psychological Science, 10*, 346–352.

Kristjánsson, Á. (2000). In search of remembrance: Evidence for memory in visual search. *Psychological Science, 11*, 328–332.

Krummenacher, J., Müller, H. J., & Heller, D. (2001). Visual search for dimensionally redundant pop-out targets: Evidence for parallel-coactive processing of dimensions. *Perception and Psychophysics, 63*, 901–917.

Lee, D., & Chun, M. M. (2001). What are the units of visual short-term memory, objects or spatial locations? *Perception and Psychophysics, 63*, 253–257.

Logan, G. D. (1988). Toward an instance theory of automatization. *Psychological Review, 95*, 492–527.

Logie, R. H. (1995). *Visuo-spatial working memory*. Hove, UK: Lawrence Erlbaum Associates Ltd.

Luck, S. J., & Vogel, E. K. (1997). The capacity of visual working memory for features and conjunctions. *Nature, 390*, 279–281.

Maljkovic, V., & Nakayama, K. (1994). Priming of pop-out: I. Role of features. *Memory and Cognition, 22*(6), 657–672.

Maljkovic, V., & Nakayama, K. (1996). Priming of pop-out: II. The role of position. *Perception and Psychophysics, 58*(7), 977–991.

Maljkovic, V., & Nakayama, K. (2000). Priming of pop-out: III. A short-term implicit memory system beneficial for rapid target selection. *Visual Cognition, 7*(5), 571–595.

Meyer, D. E., & Kieras, D. E. (1997). A computational theory of executive cognitive processes and multiple-task performance: Part 1. Basic mechanisms. *Psychological Review, 104*, 3–65.

Miller, E. K. (1999). Prefrontal cortex and the neural basis of executive functions. In G. W. Humphreys & J. Duncan (Eds.), *Attention, space, and action: Studies in cognitive neuroscience* (pp. 250–272). New York: Oxford University Press.

Moore, C. M. (1996). Does negative priming imply preselective identification of irrelevant stimuli? *Psychonomic Bulletin and Review, 3*(1), 91–94.

Moores, E., Laiti, L., & Chelazzi, L. (2003). Associative knowledge controls deployment of visual selective attention. *Nature Neuroscience, 6*, 182–185.

Müller, H. J., Heller, D., & Ziegler, J. (1995). Visual search for singleton feature targets within and across feature dimensions. *Perception and Psychophysics, 57*, 1–17.

Müller, H. J., & von Mühlenen, A. (2000). Probing distractor inhibition in visual search: Inhibition of return (IOR). *Journal of Experimental Psychology: Human Perception and Performance, 26*, 1591–1605.

Neill, W. T., & Valdes, L. A. (1992). Persistence of negative priming: Steady state or decay? *Journal of Experimental Psychology: Human Perception and Performance, 18*, 565–576.

Neisser, U. (1964). Visual search. *Scientific American, 210*(6), 94–102.

Newell, A., & Simon, H. A. (1972). *Human problem solving*. Englewood Cliffs, NJ: Prentice Hall.

Oh, S.-H., & Kim, M.-S. (2004). The role of spatial working memory in visual search efficiency. *Psychonomic Bulletin and Review, 11*(2), 275–281.

Olson, I. R., & Chun, M. M. (2001). Temporal contextual cueing of visual attention. *Journal of Experimental Psychology: Learning, Memory, and Cognition, 27*, 1299–1313.

Pashler, H., & Shiu, L. P. (1999). Do images involuntarily trigger search? A test of Pillsbury's hypothesis. *Psychonomic Bulletin and Review, 6*(3), 445–448.

Peterson, M. S., Kramer, A. F., Wang, R. F., Irwin, D. E., & McCarley, J. S. (2001). Visual search has memory. *Psychological Science, 12*, 287–292.

Pratt, J., & Hommel, B. (2003). Symbolic control of visual attention: The role of working memory and attentional control settings. *Journal of Experimental Psychology: Human Perception and Performance, 29*, 835–845.

Rao, S. C., Rainer, G., & Miller, E. K. (1997). Integration of what and where in the primate prefrontal cortex. *Science, 276*(5313), 821–824.

Rossi, A. F., Harris, B. J., Bichot, N. P., Desimone, R., & Ungerleider, L. G. (2001). Deficits in target selection in monkeys with prefrontal lesions. *Society for Neuroscience Abstracts*, 574–579.

Saffran, J. R., Aslin, R. N., & Newport, E. L. (1996). Statistical learning by 8-month-old infants. *Science*, 274(5294), 1926–1928.

Schneider, W., & Shiffrin, R. M. (1977). Controlled and automatic human information processing: I. Detection, search and attention. *Psychology Review*, 84, 1–66.

Shiffrin, R. M., & Schneider, W. (1977). Controlled and automatic human information processing: II. Perceptual learning, automatic attending, and a general theory. *Psychological Review*, 84, 127–190.

Shore, D. I., & Klein, R. M. (2000). On the manifestations of memory in visual search. *Spatial Vision*, 14, 59–75.

Simons, D. J. (1996). In sight, out of mind: When object representations fail. *Psychological Science*, 7(5), 301–305.

Standing, L. (1973). Learning 10,000 pictures. *Quarterly Journal of Experimental Psychology*, 25, 207–222.

Standing, L., Conezio, J., & Haber, R. N. (1970). Perception and memory for picture: Single-trial learning of 2500 visual stimuli. *Psychonomic Science*, 19, 73–74.

Sternberg, S. (1966). High-speed scanning in human memory. *Science*, 153, 652–654.

Tipper, S. P. (1985). The negative priming effect: Inhibitory priming by ignored objects. *Quarterly Journal of Experimental Psychology: Human Experimental Psychology*, 37A, 571–590.

Treisman, A. M. (1988). Features and objects: The Fourteenth Bartlett Memorial Lecture. *Quarterly Journal of Experimental Psychology*, 40, 201–237.

Treisman, A. M., & Gelade, G. (1980). A feature-integration theory of attention. *Cognitive Psychology*, 12, 97–136.

Treisman, A. M., & Sato, S. (1990). Conjunction search revisited. *Journal of Experimental Psychology: Human Perception and Performance*, 16, 459–478.

Treisman, A. M., Sykes, M., & Gelade, G. (1977). Selective attention and stimulus integration. In S. Dornič (Ed.), *Attention and performance VI* (pp. 333–363). Hillsdale, NJ: Lawrence Erlbaum Associates, Inc.

Vogel, E. K., Woodman, G. F., & Luck, S. J. (2001). Storage of features, conjunctions, and objects in visual working memory. *Journal of Experimental Psychology: Human Perception and Performance*, 27, 92–114.

Von Mühlenen, A., Müller, H. J., & Müller, D. (2003). Sit-and-wait strategies in dynamic search. *Psychological Science*, 14, 309–314.

Wheeler, M., & Treisman, A. M. (2002). Binding in short-term visual memory. *Journal of Experimental Psychology: General*, 131, 48–64.

Wolfe, J., Klempen, N. L., & Dahlen, K. (2000). Postattentive vision. *Journal of Experimental Psychology: Human Perception and Performance*, 26, 693–716.

Wolfe, J. M. (1994). Guided Search 2.0: A revised model of visual search. *Psychonomic Bulletin and Review*, 1, 202–238.

Wolfe, J. M. (1998). Visual search. In H. Pashler (Ed.), *Attention* (pp. 13–73). Hove, UK: Psychology Press.

Woodman, G. F. (2002). *The involvement of visual working memory in visual search*. Unpublished dissertation, University of Iowa, Iowa City, IA.

Woodman, G. F., & Luck, S. J. (in press). Do the contents of visual working memory automatically influence attentional selection during visual search? *Journal of Experimental Psychology: Human Perception and Performance*.

Woodman, G. F., & Luck, S. J. (1999). Electrophysiological measurement of rapid shifts of attention during visual search. *Nature*, 400, 867–869.

Woodman, G. F., & Luck, S. J. (2003). Serial deployment of attention during visual search. *Journal of Experimental Psychology: Human Perception and Performance*, *29*, 121–138.

Woodman, G. F., & Luck, S. J. (2004). Visual search is slowed when visuospatial working memory is occupied. *Psychonomic Bulletin and Review*, *11*(2), 269–274.

Woodman, G. F., Vogel, E. K., & Luck, S. J. (2001). Visual search remains efficient when visual working memory is full. *Psychological Science*, *12*, 219–224.

Yantis, S., & Jonides, J. (1984). Abrupt visual onsets and selective attention: Evidence from visual search. *Journal of Experimental Psychology: Human Perception and Performance*, *10*, 601–621.

Section III.

Brain mechanisms of visual search

VISUAL COGNITION, 2006, 14 (4/5/6/7/8), 832–850

ψ Psychology Press
Taylor & Francis Group

Contributions from cognitive neuroscience to understanding functional mechanisms of visual search

Glyn W. Humphreys and John Hodsoll

Behavioural Brain Sciences, School of Psychology, University of Birmingham, Birmingham, UK

Chris N. L. Olivers

Department of Cognitive Psychology, Vrije Universiteit, Amsterdam, The Netherlands

Eun Young Yoon

Behavioural Brain Sciences, School of Psychology, University of Birmingham, Birmingham, UK

We argue that cognitive neuroscience can contribute not only information about the neural localization of processes underlying visual search, but also information about the functional nature of these processes. First we present an overview of recent work on whether search for form–colour conjunctions is constrained by processes involved in binding across the two dimensions. Patients with parietal lesions show a selective problem with form–colour conjunctive search relative to a more difficult search task not requiring cross-dimensional binding. This is consistent with an additional process—cross-dimensional binding—being involved in the conjunctive search task. We then review evidence from preview search using electrophysiological, brain imaging, and neuropsychological techniques suggesting preview benefits in search are not simply due to onset capture. Taken together the results highlight the value of using converging evidence from behavioural studies of normal observers and studies using neuroscientific methods.

Over the past decade there has been a substantial growth in the number of studies that use methods from cognitive neuroscience to analyse cognitive processes. These methods either use measures of brain activity (e.g., the

Please address all correspondence to Glyn W. Humphreys, Behavioural Brain Sciences, School of Psychology, University of Birmingham, Birmingham B15 2TT, UK. E-mail: g.w.humphreys@bham.ac.uk

This work was supported by grants from the BBSRC and MRC UK and by the British Council/NWO.

http://www.psypress.com/viscog
DOI: 10.1080/13506280500195516

magnitude of the BOLD response in fMRI, the magnitude of a specific component of a stimulus-evoked response potential in ERP recordings), or procedures that intervene with processing at a neural level (e.g., transcranial magnetic stimulation or effects of brain lesions), to provide new data on the neural substrates of cognition. Studies using these techniques to assess visual search have provided important new data on both which neural systems mediate search, and on their time course of operation. For example, experiments using functional brain imaging in humans have consistently demonstrated that search is dependent on a frontoparietal network that overlaps with the neural circuitry involved in the control of eye movements (e.g., Corbetta & Shulman, 1998, 2002). The processes that direct search can also be complemented by the top-down preactivation of other brain areas, from those mediating high-level pattern recognition (e.g., Chelazzi, Duncan, Miller, & Desimone, 1998; Chelazzi, Miller, Duncan, & Desimone, 1993), to the priming of early visual areas when spatial expectancies for targets can be developed (Ress, Backus, & Heeger, 2000; see Kanwisher & Wojciulik, 2000, for a review). However, in addition to throwing light on which brain regions are engaged during search, do such studies provide constraints on under-standing the *functional* mechanisms of search—how search might operate in terms of *algorithms* as well as neural processes? This is the question that we review here. We address the issue through studies of two issues—whether the need to "bind" information from different visual dimensions constrains search (e.g., in search for conjunctive targets; cf. Treisman & Gelade, 1980), and whether the benefit from previewing distractors in search is due solely to the capture of attention by new items (cf. Donk & Theeuwes, 2001, with Watson, Humphreys, & Olivers, 2003). In both cases, we argue that data derived from cognitive neuroscientific studies contribute to our under-standing of the functional mechanisms of search.

BINDING AND VISUAL SEARCH

In 1980, Treisman and Gelade published a now classic paper demonstrating a clear difference between search for targets defined by a feature contrast relative to distractors (a difference in shape or colour) and search for targets defined by a conjunction of features from different dimensions (for example, both their shape and their colour, e.g., a red circle target presented amongst red squares and blue circles). Although search for targets defined by single features was little affected by the number of distractors present (and so was likely based on spatially parallel processing), search for form–colour conjunctions was linearly affected (consistent with spatially serial, attentive processing). This result was the foundation for one of the central tenets of Feature Integration Theory (FIT), that search is constrained by the need to bind together visual features that are processed independently (form and colour, in this instance). According to FIT, the binding of independently processed features is dependent on attention being allocated to the locations of stimuli, effectively filtering out irrelevant features (from other stimuli) from the binding process. This assertion has received support from physiological studies showing that attention modulates the receptive fields of cells in area V4, which appear to contract around the location of an attended stimulus (Moran & Desimone, 1985).

Although FIT provides a functional account of the difference between so-called feature- and conjunction-defined targets, it is by no means the only theory put forward to explain the behavioural data. For example, Guided Search (Wolfe, 1994), like FIT, holds that search is constrained by the need to bind independently processed features, but it allows for search to be guided in a top-down fashion to salient features defining a particular conjunction. This provides an explanation of why search for form–colour conjunctions can be efficient when feature values defining the stimuli are very different from one another (e.g., Wolfe, Cave, & Franzel, 1989). Other theories, though, make no qualitative distinction between the processing of independent features and of feature conjunctions. Attentional Engagement Theory (AET; Duncan & Humphreys, 1989, 1992) holds that both independent features and conjunctions of features are processed in parallel, but search is constrained by the similarity relations between (1) the target and the distractors, and (2) the distractors themselves. High target–distractor similarity slows search, whereas high distractor–distractor similarity can facilitate search by enabling distractors to be grouped and rejected together. In terms of their similarity relations, conjunctive targets may be difficult to select in search because they share features with distractors, whereas distractors can have different features from one another. When conjunctive targets are presented amongst homogeneous distractors, however, distractor–distractor grouping may be stronger than target–distractor grouping, with efficient search emerging from the parallel rejection of distractors (e.g., Duncan & Humphreys, 1989; Humphreys, Quinlan, & Riddoch, 1989). For AET the processes leading to the selection of feature- and conjunction-defined targets may differ quantitatively but they are not necessarily qualitatively different.

These contrasting theoretical accounts have been extremely difficult to separate from behavioural data alone. For example, although the finding of linear effects of the number of distractors on search is consistent with FIT's position that conjunctive search should involve serial attention to each item, the data can also be accommodated by models in which conjunctions are coded in parallel (e.g., Heinke, Humphreys, & Tweed, 2006 this issue; Humphreys & Müller, 1993; Townsend, 1971). Likewise, effects of grouping on search match the predictions of AET, but they can also be explained by

FIT if additional processes are allowed to contribute to search, such as the inhibition of feature maps common to distractor but not target features (e.g., Treisman & Sato, 1990). Can data from cognitive neuroscience help here— for instance, by indicating that an additional process of binding is involved when participants search for form–colour conjunctions rather than feature-defined targets?

There have been several attempts made to address this question. For example, Donner et al. (2002) measured brain activity using fMRI when participants searched either for form–colour conjunctions or for feature-defined targets that were as difficult to detect as the conjunctions. In this case, any enhanced activity in the conjunction search task should not simply reflect the increased difficulty of conjunction search. They found that there were areas of overlap across the conjunction and hard feature-search tasks, relative to an easy feature-search baseline (e.g., in posterior regions of the intraparietal sulcus; IPS), along with some areas where activity was greater in one task than the other. For example, the area joining the IPS to the transverse occipital sulcus, plus also the frontal eye fields, showed greater activation in the conjunction than in the hard feature-search task. On the other hand, there was greater activation in the hard feature-search task, relative to the conjunction task, in the anterior IPS. Given that search difficulty was matched in the hard-feature and conjunction conditions, these differences suggest that some distinct processes were recruited in the two tasks. Nevertheless, it is unclear what these processes might be. For example, areas showing increased activation in the conjunction task may reflect the unique need for feature binding in this condition. Alternatively, however, they might reflect greater top-down guidance of search (e.g., guiding search to items of the target's colour; Wolfe, 1994). If there was top-down guidance of conjunction search, then areas showing increased activity in the hard feature-search task might reflect additional serial scanning of attention in that condition relative to the (guided) conjunction search condition.

Somewhat different imaging results were reported by Nobre, Coull, Walsh, and Frith (2003). They orthogonally manipulated search difficulty with whether the target was defined by a single feature or a conjunction of features (including both hard and easy versions of both feature and conjunction search). They found that, in general, activation increased in the hard search conditions irrespective of whether search was for a feature- or a conjunction-defined target (particularly in the superior parietal lobule and the right IPS). In contrast, there were only sparse increases in activity in the conjunction tasks relative to the feature search tasks, and these took place in regions of parietal cortex that also showed sensitivity to search difficulty (i.e., that showed increased activity in hard search tasks relative to easy search tasks). These results suggest that feature and conjunction search tasks may not differ qualitatively, but there are quantitative effects of search difficulty, perhaps reflecting increased competition for selection when targets and distractors are similar (cf. Duncan & Humphreys, 1989, 1992). On the other hand, null effects are typically difficult to interpret. Also, it is possible that the need for binding was not stressed in these conjunction search tasks. For example, in different, difficult conjunction searches targets were defined by colour and motion direction, and by velocity and form; there is behavioural evidence that participants may employ parallel filtering of motion-defined targets in visual search (e.g., McLeod, Driver, & Crisp, 1988; Nakayama & Silverman, 1986). If one set of distractors can be filtered in parallel, then it might not be necessary to bind all features to find the target amongst the remaining subset of distractors.

A different approach is to examine the behavioural consequences when brain activity is disrupted in regions putatively involved in binding and search. Several studies have demonstrated that damage to parietal cortex can lead to problems in feature binding, so that patients make abnormal numbers of illusory conjunction responses, where they appear to bind attributes belonging to different stimuli (see Friedman-Hill, Robertson, & Treisman, 1995; Humphreys, Cinel, Wolfe, Olson, & Klempen, 2000, for evidence from effects of bilateral parietal lesions; see Cohen & Rafal, 1997, for evidence from effects of unilateral parietal damage). Parietal patients are also frequently worse at conjunction search than at search for feature-defined targets, consistent with their problem in binding having a differential impact on conjunction search (e.g., Eglin, Robertson, & Rafal, 1989; Friedman-Hill et al., 1995; Riddoch & Humphreys, 1987). However, it is also the case that parietal patients can manifest abnormal effects of search difficulty even for feature-defined targets, as the saliency of such targets is decreased (Humphreys & Price, 1994; Humphreys & Riddoch, 1993). Studies where conjunction and feature searches have been directly compared in neuropsychological patients have not matched the conditions for search difficulty, making it impossible to assess whether the effects of parietal lesions are due specifically to impaired binding or to more general problems associated with difficult search.

Other intervention studies have used transcranial magnetic stimulation (TMS) to assess temporary effects of parietal stimulation on feature and conjunction search tasks. Ashbridge, Walsh, and Cowey (1997) first reported that TMS applied to the right IPS disrupted conjunction search more than feature search, but again search difficulty was not equated. More recently Ellison, Rushworth, and Walsh (2003) contrasted TMS effects on both easy and hard versions of both feature and conjunction search tasks (cf. Nobre et al., 2003). They found the TMS applied to right posterior parietal cortex selectively disrupted the conjunction relative to the feature search tasks. This fits with the idea that some extra process, such as feature binding, might be modulated by the posterior parietal cortex and might play a selective role in conjunction search. However, the hard feature task was more difficult than either conjunction task, so that an additional process, such as top-down guidance of search, might have influenced performance with conjunctions. This additional process (rather than binding) could have been disrupted by TMS. Furthermore, the difficulty of the hard feature task could have effectively limited any further disruptive effects on search.[1]

Hence, prior cognitive neuroscience research on this issue has been suggestive but inconclusive. Recently we (Humphreys & Hodsoll, 2006) investigated the same issue using a neuropsychological approach, comparing a small group of five patients with inferior parietal lesions with age-matched control. Search for a (relatively easy) form–colour conjunction target (a green "X" amongst green "O"s and red "X"s) was assessed in comparison with a more difficult feature search task (the target was a white shallow line, sloped 33° either up or down from the horizontal; the distractors were steeper white lines, sloped 66° either up or down from the horizontal). The target was either present or absent, and when present it fell either in the left or right visual field. The backgrounds were always black and there was a single display size of 16 items (8 in the left field and 8 in the right; see Figure 1 for examples of the displays). In order to avoid ceiling or floor effects, and the difficulty in interpreting the slow RTs that can be found with neuropsychological patients, the stimulus exposure was limited with the durations set to generate a level of about 80% correct performance across the feature and conjunction search tasks (for the patients and controls alike). On trials where the subject decided that the target was present, they were asked to state whether it fell in the left or right field. Performance was scored as correct when both the present/absent decision and the localization decision were accurate.

The data for target present trials are shown in Figure 2. For both the controls and the patients performance on absent trials was around 90% correct, for both tasks (control mean = 91% for conjunction search and 87% for feature search; patient mean = 90% for conjunction search and 88% for feature search). When incorrect, the controls had no bias to report a target in the right versus the left field (46% vs. 54% of the false alarms, averaged across the tasks). The patients had a bias to their contralesional field (72% of the false alarms were localized in the contralesional field, averaged across the tasks). On present trials the overwhelming numbers of errors were target misses rather than mislocalizations (95% for controls, 94% for patients). For

---

[1] Reaction times (RTs) were measured. When there are slow RTs in search, there may be some rate-limiting factor (e.g., the ability to discriminate the target from a distractor) that constrains performance even if TMS had an effect on other processes (e.g., the speed of serially selecting each stimulus for subsequent discrimination). For example, if the time to discriminate the target from the distractor is sufficiently long and variable, then there may be negligible effects due to changing the speed of selecting each item for discrimination.

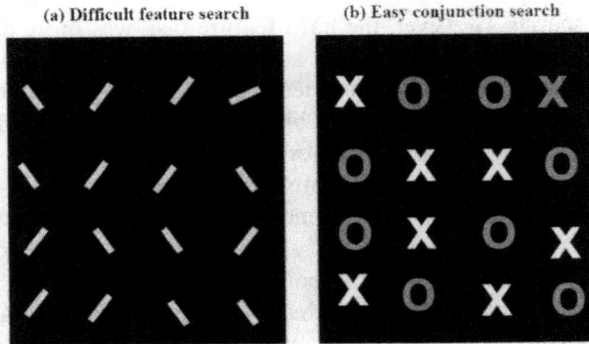

Figure 1. Example displays used by Humphreys and Hodsoll (2006). (a) Hard feature search (target = shallow, distractors = steep); (b) easy conjunction search (grey = green in the displays, and white = red; target = green "X"). For each type of search we depict a "present" trial with the target in the top right location.

the controls there was an overall advantage on present trials for the (easy) conjunction task over the (difficult) feature search task, and this held irrespective of whether the target appeared in the left or right visual fields (Figure 2a). This advantage could reflect any of several processes: (1) Easier matching to memory, since there was only a single conjunction target but two possible feature targets (shallow line oriented either right or left); (2) greater feature-based guidance of search in the conjunction condition, since the features making up the conjunction target were relatively salient

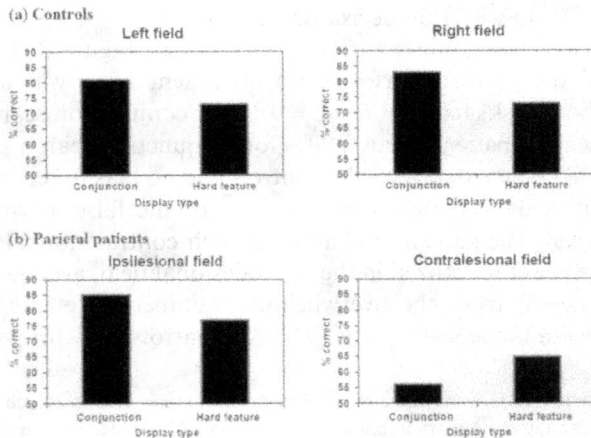

Figure 2. The percentage correct target detections for control participants ($N = 5$) and patients with unilateral parietal lesions ($N = 5$). The mean duration for the control participants was 300 ms; the mean duration for the patients was 800 ms.

compared with the distractor features along each dimension; (3) effects of increased competition in selecting the feature-based target, due to the greater similarity of the feature distractors to targets. For the patients, however, quite different effects occurred on present trials according to the field where the target appeared (Figure 2b). When the target fell in the ipsilesional field, the pattern of performance followed that of the controls (better discrimination for conjunction over feature-defined targets). When the target appeared in the contralesional field performance was worse for both conditions compared with when the target fell in the ipsilesional field. However, the discrimination of contralesional conjunction targets was particularly poor, with performance now being better for the hard feature over the conjunction stimuli. The poor conjunction search was not simply due to poor colour discrimination in the contralesional field. The patients performed perfectly at discriminating the green "X" target when single items were presented in either the ipsi- or contralesional fields. This reversal of the "conjunction advantage" found with controls rules out various interpretations of the data. For example, the effects with the contralesional target cannot be attributed to general search difficulty (increased costs due to distractor similarity or to having two "templates" for feature targets), since an effect of difficulty would simply enhance the "conjunction advantage". It also cannot be attributed to patients being unable to use guided search in their contralesional field. If a guided search process was disrupted for conjunction targets then both conjunction and feature search should rely on serial search and comparison of each item relative to the memory template for the target (cf. Duncan & Humphreys, 1989). Note that guided search is typically contingent on the features of targets and distractors being relatively discriminable (Wolfe, 1994). Thus it is unlikely that any serial comparison with a memory template would be harder for such conjunctions than for difficult (low discriminability) stimuli in feature search. The conjunction search task should not become *more* difficult than the feature search task. Instead, the observed reversal of the normal pattern of performance suggests that parietal damage selectively disrupted a process necessary for conjunction but not for feature search—the most likely candidate being the binding of form and colour in the contralesional field. This is also supported by the biased false alarms generated by patients on target-absent trials. We suggest that the stable binding of form and colour properties of stimuli is modulated by the parietal lobe, and that this binding process operates as one constraint on search for targets defined by the conjunction of features from across different visual dimensions (form and colour in this case).

One account of this pattern of results is provided by FIT, which proposes that binding is contingent on a spotlight of attention (controlled through the parietal lobe) filtering out competing features in the visual field (Treisman, 1998). Parietal damage may prevent the application of the "spotlight" to the contralesional field, so that incorrect bindings are formed. Alternatively it may be that the parietal system provides top-down feedback in a spatially parallel manner to earlier visual regions coding form and colour, stabilizing conjoint activity at common locations (cf. Humphreys et al., 2000). If the parietal lesion impairs feedback to the contralesional field, bindings may be unstable. In either case, this "binding" process is more important for detecting cross-dimension conjunctions than for detecting targets defined by a feature difference within a single dimension.

THE PREVIEW BENEFIT IN SEARCH

In the real world, visual search does not only operate across space but also across time, as we deal with new information coming into the environment and ignore old stimuli that may no longer be critical to action. Watson and Humphreys (1997) examined search across time as well as space by presenting a variation of form–colour conjunction search in which they presented one set of distractors (the preview) prior to the second set of distractors plus the target (when present) (e.g., green "H" distractors followed by blue "A" distractors + blue "H" target). Although the final display was identical to the display in a standard form–colour conjunction task, Watson and Humphreys found that there was no impact of the old items on the efficiency of search; search rates were equivalent to those obtained when just the blue items were presented (the single feature baseline condition). There was also a time course to this effect. To generate optimal performance, the old items had to have been presented at least 400 ms before the new (see also Humphreys, Kyllinsbæk, Watson, Olivers, Law, & Paulson, 2004b). There is thus a "preview benefit" in search, where only new items influence search efficiency provided old items have been in the field for some time.

Watson and Humphreys (1997) argued that at least part of the preview benefit was due to observers inhibiting a representation of the old stimuli. Evidence consistent with this inhibitory account comes from studies using probe detection procedures to examine the allocation of visual attention during search. Probes that fall at the location of old items are difficult to detect relative to probes falling on new stimuli (Olivers & Humphreys, 2002; Watson & Humphreys, 2000), and relative to probes that appear in neutral locations (Humphreys, Jung-Stalmann, & Olivers, 2004a). Other evidence suggests that there can be inhibition of the features as well as the locations of old items, so that it is difficult to detect targets that carry the same features as ignored old items (e.g., if the target has the same colour as ignored old distractors; Braithwaite & Humphreys, 2003; Olivers & Humphreys, 2002; Olivers, Humphreys, & Braithwaite, 2006 this issue). This feature-based carryover effect even modulates the detection of targets that are defined by a salient singleton feature relative to the new distractors (Olivers & Humphreys, 2003).

Other accounts of the preview advantage have also been proposed. Jiang, Chun, and Marks (2002), for example, hold that it reflects temporal grouping and segmentation of the old and new displays, without necessarily involving inhibition of the old items. Donk and Theeuwes (2001) propose that the advantage is due purely to the capture of attention by the new onsets in the second (search) display. In many studies, these different functional accounts make similar predictions. For example, differences in probe detection at the locations of old and new items could be caused by attention being prioritized to new stimuli rather than being deprioritized away from old items. Nevertheless, differences between detection at old and neutral locations, which can occur even when probes precede the new stimuli, are less easy to explain without recourse to the notion that old locations are suppressed (Humphreys et al., 2004a).

There are now several studies of preview search that have taken a cognitive neuroscience perspective, using direct measures of brain activation during both preview and search displays. Jacobsen, Humphreys, Schröger, and Roeber (2002) measured evoked potential responses to stimuli and reported an increased and sustained negative potential that occurred prior to the search display and that was associated with participants actively ignoring the preview. This activation was most pronounced at frontal and parietal sites. Humphreys et al. (2004b) used PET to measure brain activity across blocks of search where the duration of the preview display varied. Search for the target became easier as the preview was presented for longer durations, but activity in the superior parietal lobe increased. Pollmann et al. (2003) also found increased and earlier activation in the superior parietal lobe in the preview relative to single feature and conjunction search conditions, and this was present even on "dummy" trials on which no search displays were presented after the preview. These last two studies suggest that subjects in preview search encode and possibly also inhibit a representation of the old items in the superior parietal lobes, which likely contain a spatial map of occupied areas of visual field (cf. Ungerleider & Haxby, 1994; Ungerleider & Mishkin, 1982). Pollmann et al. also found earlier and increased activation in a second site, the temporal-parietal junction (TPJ), that was associated with the ease of search rather than the presence of the preview—thus activity in the TPJ was enhanced in the single feature and the preview conditions when compared with the conjunction baseline. This TPJ activity likely reflects the allocation of attention to a salient new target, a process common to the single feature and preview search conditions.

Watson et al. (2003) note that there may be multiple factors that contribute to the preview benefit, with effects due to temporal segmentation and suppression of old items supplemented by attentional capture to new onsets. But having new items defined by onsets may not be crucial. Donk and Theeuwes (2001) argued for the importance of new onsets because they found that old items did have an impact on search when new stimuli were isoluminant with their background (i.e., when new items were not defined by onsets). On the other hand, the locations of stimuli that are isoluminant with their background may be coded relatively coarsely, making it difficult both to inhibit old locations and to allocate attention efficiently to the locations of new stimuli. Humphreys et al. (2004a) presented search stimuli by making a colour change to the elements of a background grid. Every 16 ms, all the elements (in the search stimuli and the background grid) randomly and independently changed slightly in luminance so that, on average, the luminance was equal between the search items and the remaining contours of the grid. This way the new search items were well-defined against their background (as at any moment in time there were some random luminance differences between grid elements), without them being defined by a luminance onset (indeed some elements were defined by a luminance offset). A robust preview advantage was observed, suggesting that defining a target by its onset is not critical.

A further way to assess whether attentional capture by new onsets is necessarily a part of the preview advantage is to test whether patients who are selectively impaired in preview search can nevertheless show efficient allocation of attention to onsets. If this is the case, then efficient allocation of attention to onsets cannot be sufficient to generate the preview advantage. Olivers and Humphreys (2004) tested patients with posterior parietal damage (typically involving the inferior parietal lobe, but in some cases extending into the intraparietal sulcus). As a whole this group did not show marked neglect, but did tend to have extinction under brief stimulus presentation conditions. Olivers and Humphreys found that preview search was selectively disrupted in patients with parietal damage (especially for targets falling contralateral to their lesion—search in the preview condition could then be less efficient than in a single feature baseline and no more efficient than a conjunction search baseline). Recently we (Humphreys, Olivers, & Yoon, 2006) have built on this result by examining the performance of patients with unilateral parietal damage in paradigms where, respectively, a preview advantage and an advantage for selecting onset targets are normally observed. In both tasks, participants searched for a yellow "H" target that appeared along with a set of random letters, all also presented in yellow. In the preview study, one set of distractors was presented first for 1000 ms before the second set of distractors appeared along with the target. Display sizes of 4 old + 4 new or 8 old + 8 new items were used. Performance was compared with a half set baseline in which only the new items appeared (display sizes 4 and 8), or a full set baseline in which the full set of distractors appeared along with the target (display sizes 8 and 16). In the onset-capture study, the letters were preceded by a set of premasks (for 1000 ms). Contours in the premasks were then offset to create letters. and simultaneously another letter appeared in a previously unoccupied location in the display (the onset target). The target was again a yellow "H". and the distractors were other random letters drawn in yellow. There were either 3 offset letters + 1 onset letter, or 7 offset letters + 1 onset letter. The target was equally likely to be the onset stimulus or one of the stimuli created by offsetting contours in a premask. When tested under these conditions. normal participants show an advantage in responding to a target defined by an onset relative to one defined by an offset (although the onset is then irrelevant; Yantis & Jones, 1991; Yantis & Jonides, 1984). In both the preview and the onset-capture studies, the target was always present and the participants' task was to localize it. Performance was assessed in seven patients, three with unilateral left and four with unilateral right lesions involving the parietal lobe. Example displays are shown in Figure 3.

Data from the preview search task are shown in Figure 4. The results reveal that the patients had relatively normal performance in the preview condition when the target fell in their ipsilesional visual field. Search was more efficient (i.e., there was a reduced effect of the display size) in the

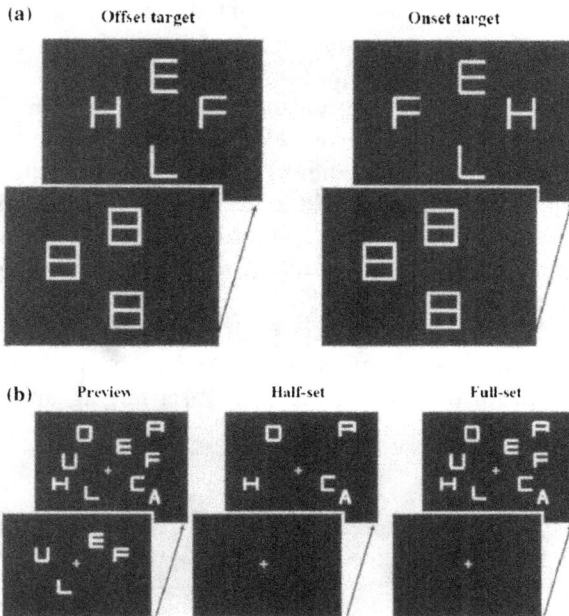

Figure 3. (a) Example displays from the offset and onset conditions; (b) example displays for the preview, half set and full set search conditions. In all cases the target is an "H".

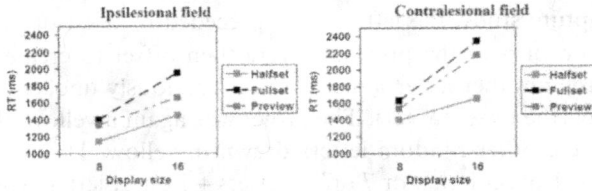

Figure 4. Visual search latencies for 7 patients with unilateral parietal damage in the half set. full set and preview search conditions. for targets falling in the ipsilesional or contralesional fields.

preview condition than in the full set baseline, and the slope of the search function was no greater in the preview condition than in the half set baseline (when only the new letters were presented). In contrast, performance was selectively poor in the preview condition when targets were presented contralateral to the lesion. With contralesional targets, there was no difference between the preview condition and the full set baseline (neither in terms of overall reaction times or in terms of the slope of the search functions). and the slope for the preview condition was reliably greater than the slope of the search function in the half set condition. Interestingly, search was slowed for both the preview and full set conditions when the target fell in the contralesional field, but there was no effect on the slope of the function in the half set baseline. This suggests that the patients remained able to attend relatively efficiently to a target in their contralesional field when it was one of a small number of new items presented in an otherwise empty display (with up to four items appearing in their contralesional and four in their ipsilesional fields). However, they were impaired when there were old items also present (in the preview condition) and when larger numbers of items were presented simultaneously (eight items in their contralesional field and eight in the ipsilesional field, in the full set baseline). The selective deficit in selecting targets in the preview condition replicates the findings of Olivers and Humphreys (2004).

The results from the onset-capture study are depicted in Figure 5. These data contrast with those from preview search. The patients showed an overall advantage for detecting onset over offset targets, and, importantly,

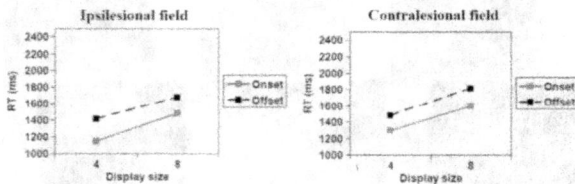

Figure 5. RTs to detect an onset or offset defined target presented in the ipsilesional or contralesional fields of patients with unilateral parietal lesions.

this did not differ for targets appearing in the contra- and ipsilesional fields (there was no interaction between field and the onset advantage). The onset advantage was apparent in the intercept rather than the slope of the search function. This may be because there was approximately equal competition for selection from the (multiple) offset distractors when the target was an onset, and from the onset + offset distractors when the target was an offset;[2] Battelli, Cavanagh, Martini, and Barton (2003) have recently reported that parietal patients have difficulty distinguishing between onsets and offset stimuli, suggesting some decreased sensitivity to onsets. Nevertheless the intercept effect does indicate that the patients could set a lower threshold for onset relative to offsets, so producing a general advantage for onset targets. If prioritized selection of onsets was sufficient to generate a preview advantage, then such a lowered threshold for responding to onset compared to offset stimuli should have led to an advantage for the preview condition over the full set baseline (and note that the old distractors remained in the field rather than offsetting, in the preview search condition, and so should have competed even less than the offset distractors in the onset condition). Also this advantage should have been equal across the fields, as the onset advantage did not interact with field. Clearly this was not the case. This in turn indicates that factors other than prioritized attention to onsets contribute to preview search, and these other factors are impaired following damage to the parietal lobe.

One possible reason for the reduced preview benefit is that parietal patients have impaired temporal segmentation (cf. Jiang et al., 2002), and so are insensitive to the staggered presentation of stimuli in preview displays. However, this fails to explain why the problem is confined to contralesional targets in the preview condition. Alternatively, there may be impaired spatial disengagement of attention from the old items falling in the patients' ipsilesional fields (cf. Posner, Walker, Friedrich, & Rafal, 1984), which selectively disrupts attentional allocation to new, contralesional, search stimuli. Olivers and Humphreys (2004) examined this last argument by orthogonally manipulating the spatial locations of old and new items in preview search, while keeping the temporal relations between the displays constant. They found that performance was worst when both the old and the new items fell in the same visual field, and that performance was improved if the old items appeared in one field and the new items in the other (even when the old items fell in the ipsilesional field and the new in the contralesional field, when poor spatial disengagement of attention from the old stimuli should have been maximized). This result indicates that the

---

[2] We have also found this same pattern, of an onset advantage in terms of an intercept rather than a slope effect, in controls matched in age to the patients. It may be that competition from onsets and offsets becomes closer as participants age.

spatial as well as the temporal relations between the stimuli are important for search, but that processes concerned with the spatial segmentation of old and new items, rather than spatial disengagement of attention, are particularly problematic for the patients. The difficulty of spatial segmentation is increased when old and new items overlap compared with when they fall in the same visual field, and the posterior parietal patients had particular problems under this condition. It may be that the patients have an impaired visual-spatial working memory and so fail to maintain (and inhibit) a representation of the old items (Wojciulik, Hussain, Clarke, & Driver, 2001). Due to this failure in maintenance, old items compete for selection with the new items, with the competition being particularly strong when the items fall in the same area of field. However, we found no correlation between a measure of visual spatial working memory (the Corsi block span) and the size of the average cost in the preview condition relative to the half set baseline for contralesional targets, $r(5) = -.266$, $p > .565$. Rather than impaired visual spatial working memory *per se*, Olivers and Humphreys proposed that the parietal patients have poor spatiotemporal segmentation in vision, with parietal damage leading to a reduced ability to segment old from new items based on both their temporal and their spatial codes (particularly when the spatial codes for old and new items overlap). This spatiotemporal segmentation process may normally be enhanced by inhibition of the old items, modulated through the parietal lobe (cf. Watson & Humphreys, 1997). In any case, the neuropsychological data advance prior behavioural studies of preview search by demonstrating that prioritized attention to onsets is not sufficient to generate a preview benefit in visual search.

CONCLUSIONS

The evidence we have presented has highlighted that data from cognitive neuroscience can contribute not only to an understanding of the neural substrates of visual search, but also to an understanding of the functional mechanisms involved. We have reviewed recent neuropsychological data indicating that:

1. Patients with posterior parietal lesions can have problems with search for form–colour conjunctions that cannot be accounted for in terms of overall search difficulty or in terms of the loss of top-down guidance of search, which might take place in conjunction but not in hard feature search tasks (Humphreys & Hodsoll, 2006). This selective problem is consistent with form–colour conjunctions requiring a unique binding

process that is not required in search for low-salient targets defined within a single feature dimension.

2. Parietal patients can show an advantage in detecting targets defined by an onset over those defined by an offset, both in their contra- and their ipsilesional fields, whereas there is a selective loss of the preview benefit in search in the contralesional field (Humphreys et al., 2006). This result reveals that a maintained ability to prioritize attention to onset stimuli is not sufficient to generate the preview benefit in search, at least when other processes are impaired by the brain lesion. Other recent behavioural data reveal that a preview advantage can be observed when new stimuli are defined by a colour change rather than an onset, provided that the stimuli are well-defined relative to the background (in Humphreys et al., 2004a, but not in Donk & Theeuwes, 2001). Taken together the results indicate that prioritized attention to onsets is neither necessary (data with normal participants) nor sufficient (neuropsychological data) to produce the preview advantage. Of course this does not mean that onsets cannot contribute to preview search, and they may do so when new stimuli are defined by onsets and when other impairments do not reduce the effectiveness of onsets for selection (e.g., when there is a failure in the inhibition of old items). However, the data do show that an onset-capture account cannot provide a complete explanation of preview effects in search. The neuropsychological data, on impaired preview search, also complement evidence from electrophysiological studies (Jacobsen et al., 2002) and brain imaging (Humphreys et al., 2004b; Pollmann et al., 2003) that indicate that old items are differentially coded (and presumably deprioritized for selection) under preview search relative to baseline conditions.

As well as providing evidence on some of the functional processes that modulate search (e.g., cross-dimension binding of features, spatiotemporal prioritization, and deprioritization of selection), the data also help to reveal the role played in search by particular brain regions. For instance, the evidence on conjunction search highlights the role of the posterior parietal lobe in cross-dimension binding (Treisman, 1998). Data from brain imaging studies of preview search differentiate between the superior parietal lobe (selectively activated by previews) and the temporal-parietal junction (sensitive to the ease of search). For example, the former may hold a spatial representation of the old items, which forms the basis for their subsequent deprioritization in selection; the latter may be involved in generating a rapid orienting response to a target. Finally, the neuropsychological data on deficits in preview search (e.g., Olivers & Humphreys, 2004) suggest that parietal regions modulate the spatiotemporal segmentation of visual stimuli, and not simply the disengagement of spatial attention or the ability to segment stimuli on the basis of temporal signals alone. One possibility is that both spatial and temporal segmentation processes are served by the selective inhibition of parietal neurons, over time, responsive to particular spatial locations.

REFERENCES

Ashbridge. E.. Walsh. V.. & Cowey. A. (1997). Temporal aspects of visual search studied by transcranial magnetic stimulation. *Neuropsychologia*, *35*, 1121–1131.

Battelli, L., Cavanagh. P.. Martini. P.. & Barton, J. J. S. (2003). Bilateral deficits of transient visual attention in right parietal patients. *Brain*, *126*, 2164–2174.

Braithwaite, J. J., & Humphreys. G. W. (2003). Inhibition and anticipation in visual search: Evidence from effects of color foreknowledge on preview search. *Perception and Psychophysics*, *65*, 213–237.

Chelazzi, L., Duncan, J., Miller, E. K.. & Desimone. R. (1998). Responses of neurons in inferior temporal cortex during memory-guided visual search. *Journal of Neurophysiology*. *80*, 2918–2940.

Chelazzi, L., Miller, E. K., Duncan. J.. & Desimone. R. (1993). A neural basis for visual search in inferior temporal cortex. *Nature*. *363*. 345–347.

Cohen. A.. & Rafal, R. D. (1991). Attention and feature integration: Illusory conjunctions in a patient with a parietal lobe lesion. *Psychological Science*, *2*, 106–110.

Corbetta. M., & Shulman. G. L. (1998). Human cortical mechanisms of visual attention during orienting and search. *Philosophical Transactions of the Royal Society, London, Series B, 353*. 1353–1362.

Corbetta. M., & Shulman, G. L. (2002). Control of goal directed and stimulus-driven attention in the brain. *Nature Reviews Neuroscience*. *3*. 201–215.

Donk, M., & Theeuwes, J. (2001). Visual marking beside the mark: Prioritizing selection by abrupt onsets. *Perception and Psychophysics*. *93*. 891–900.

Donner, T. H., Kettermann, A., Diesch. E.. Ostendorf. F.. Villringer, A., & Brandt, S. A. (2002). Visual feature and conjunction searches of equal difficulty engage only partially overlapping frontoparietal networks. *NeuroImage*. *15*. 16–25.

Duncan. J.. & Humphreys. G. W. (1989). Visual search and stimulus similarity. *Psychological Review*. *96*. 433–458.

Duncan. J.. & Humphreys. G. W. (1992). Beyond the search surface: Visual search and attentional engagement. *Journal of Experimental Psychology: Human Perception and Performance*. *18*. 578–588.

Eglin. M.. Robertson. L. C.. & Rafal. R. D. (1989). Visual search performance in the neglect syndrome. *Journal of Cognitive Neuroscience*. *1*. 372–385.

Ellison, A., Rushworth. M.. & Walsh. V. (2003). The parietal cortex in visual search: A visuomotor hypothesis. In W. Paulus. F. Tergau. M. A. Nitsche. J. C. Rothwell. U. Ziemann, & M. Hallen (Eds.). *Transcranial magnetic stimulation and transcranial direct current stimulation* (Suppl. to Clinical Neurophysiology. Vol. 56). Amsterdam: North-Holland.

Friedman-Hill, S. R., Robertson, L. C., & Treisman. A. (1995). Parietal contributions to visual feature binding: Evidence from a patient with bilateral lesions. *Science*. *269*. 853–855.

Heinke. D.. Humphreys. G. W.. & Tweed. C. L. (2006). Top-down guidance of visual search: A computational account. *Visual Cognition*, *14*, 985–1005.

Humphreys, G. W., Cinel, C., Wolfe, J., Olson, A., & Klempen, N. (2000). Fractionating the binding process: Neuropsychological evidence distinguishing binding of form from binding of surface features. *Vision Research*, *40*, 1569–1596.

Humphreys, G. W., & Hodsoll, J. (2006). The role of the parietal lobe in cross-dimension binding. *Manuscript submitted for publication*.

Humphreys, G. W., Jung-Stalmann, B., & Olivers, C. N. L. (2004a). An analysis of the time course of attention in preview search. *Perception and Psychophysics*, *66*, 713–730.

Humphreys, G. W., Kyllinsbæk, S., Watson, D. G., Olivers, C. N. L., Law, I., & Paulson, O. (2004b). Parieto-occipital areas involved in efficient filtering in search: A time course analysis of visual marking using behavioural and functional imaging procedures. *Quarterly Journal of Experimental Psychology*, *57A*, 610–635.

Humphreys, G. W., & Müller, H. M. (1993). SEarch via Recursive Rejection (SERR): A connectionist model of visual search. *Cognitive Psychology*, *25*, 43–110.

Humphreys, G. W., Olivers, C. N. L., & Yoon, E. Y. (2006). An onset advantage without a preview benefit: Neuropsychological evidence separating onset and preview effects in search. *Journal of Cognitive Neuroscience*, *18*, 110–120.

Humphreys, G. W., & Price, C. J. (1994). Visual feature discrimination in simultanagnosia: A study of two cases. *Cognitive Neuropsychology*, *11*, 393–434.

Humphreys, G. W., Quinlan, P. T., & Riddoch, M. J. (1989). Grouping effects in visual search: Effects with single- and combined-feature targets. *Journal of Experimental Psychology: General*, *118*, 258–279.

Humphreys, G. W., & Riddoch, M. J. (1993). Interactions between object and space vision revealed through neuropsychology. In D. E. Meyer & S. Kornblum (Eds.), *Attention and performance XIV: Synergies in experimental psychology, artificial intelligence, and cognitive neuroscience* (pp. 143–162). Cambridge, MA: MIT Press.

Jacobsen, T., Humphreys, G. W., Schröger, E., & Roeber, U. (2002). Visual marking for search: Behavioral and event-related brain potential analyses. *Cognitive Brain Research*, *14*, 410–421.

Jiang, Y., Chun, M. M., & Marks, L. E. (2002). Visual marking: Selective attention to asynchronous temporal groups. *Journal of Experimental Psychology: Human Perception and Performance*, *28*, 717–730.

Kanwisher, N., & Wojciulik, E. (2000). Visual attention: Insights from brain imaging. *Nature Reviews (Neuroscience)*, *1*, 91–100.

McLeod, P., Driver, J., & Crisp, J. (1988). Visual search for conjunctions of movement and form in parallel. *Nature*, *332*, 154–155.

Moran, J., & Desimone, R. (1985). Selective attention gates visual processing in the extra-striate cortex. *Science*, *229*, 782–784.

Nakayama, K., & Silverman, G. H. (1986). Serial and parallel processing of visual feature conjunctions. *Nature*, *320*, 264–265.

Nobre, A. C., Coull, J. T., Walsh, V., & Frith, C. D. (2003). Brain activations during visual search: Contributions of search efficiency vs. feature binding. *NeuroImage*, *18*, 91–103.

Olivers, C., & Humphreys, G. W. (2002). When visual marking meets the attentional blink: More evidence for top-down limited capacity inhibition. *Journal of Experimental Psychology: Human Perception and Performance*, *28*, 22–42.

Olivers, C. N. L., & Humphreys, G. W. (2003). Visual marking and singleton capture: Fractionating the unitary nature of visual selection. *Cognitive Psychology*, *47*, 1–42.

Olivers, C. N. L., & Humphreys, G. W. (2004). Spatio-temporal segregation in visual search: Evidence from parietal lesions. *Journal of Experimental Psychology: Human Perception and Performance*, *30*, 661–687.

Olivers, C. N. L., Humphreys, G. W., & Braithwaite, J. J. (2006). The preview search task: Evidence for visual marking. *Visual Cognition*, *14*, 716–735.

Pollmann, S., Weidner, R., Humphreys, G. W., Olivers, C. N. L., Muller, K., Lohmann, G., et al. (2003). Separating segmentation and target detection in posterior parietal cortex: An event-related fMRI study of visual marking. *NeuroImage*, *18*, 310–323.

Posner, M. I., Walker, J. A., Friedrich, F. J., & Rafal, R. D. (1984). Effects of parietal injury on covert orienting of attention. *Journal of Neuroscience*, *4*, 1863–1874.

Ress, D., Backus, B., & Heeger, D. (2000). Activity in primary visual cortex predicts performance in a visual detection task. *Nature Neuroscience*, *3*, 940–945.

Riddoch, M. J., & Humphreys, G. W. (1987). Perceptual and action systems in unilateral neglect. In M. Jeannerod (Ed.), *Neurophysiological and neuropsychological aspects of spatial neglect* (pp. 151–182). Amsterdam: Elsevier Science.

Townsend, J. T. (1971). A note on the identification of parallel and serial processes. *Perception and Psychophysics*, *10*, 161–163.

Treisman, A. (1998). Feature binding, attention and object perception. *Philosophical Transactions of the Royal Society*, *353*, 1295–1306.

Treisman, A., & Gelade, G. (1980). A feature-integration theory of attention. *Cognitive Psychology*, *12*, 97–136.

Treisman, A., & Sato, S. (1990). Conjunction search revisited. *Journal of Experimental Psychology: Human Perception and Performance*, *16*, 459–478.

Ungerleider, L. G., & Haxby, J. V. (1994). "What" and "where" in the human brain. *Current Opinions in Neurobiology*, *4*, 157–165.

Ungerleider, L. G., & Mishkin, M. (1982). Two cortical visual systems. In D. J. Ingle, M. A. Goodale, & R. J. W. Mansfield (Eds.), *Analysis of visual behaviour* (pp. 549–586). Cambridge, MA: MIT Press.

Watson, D. G., & Humphreys, G. W. (1997). Visual marking: Prioritising selection for new objects by top-down attentional inhibition. *Psychological Review*, *104*, 90–122.

Watson, D. G., & Humphreys, G. W. (2000). Visual marking: Evidence for inhibition using a probe-dot detection paradigm. *Perception and Psychophysics*, *62*, 471–481.

Watson, D. G., Humphreys, G. W., & Olivers, C. N. L. (2003). Visual marking: Using time in visual selection. *Trends in Cognitive Sciences*, *7*, 180–186.

Wojciulik, E., Hussain, M., Clarke, K., & Driver, J. (2001). Spatial working memory deficit in unilateral neglect. *Neuropsychologia*, *39*, 390–396.

Wolfe, J. M. (1994). Guided Search 2.0: A revised model of visual search. *Psychonomic Bulletin and Review*, *1*, 202–238.

Wolfe, J. M., Cave, K. R., & Franzel, S. L. (1989). Guided Search: An alternative to the feature integration model for visual search. *Journal of Experimental Psychology: Human Perception and Performance*, *15*, 419–433.

Yantis, S., & Jones, E. (1991). Mechanisms of attentional selection: Temporally modulated priority tags. *Perception and Psychophysics*, *50*, 166–178.

Yantis, S., & Jonides, J. (1984). Abrupt visual onsets and selective attention: Evidence from visual search. *Journal of Experimental Psychology: Human Perception and Performance*, *10*, 601–621.

VISUAL COGNITION, 2006, 14 (4/5/6/7/8), 851–862

Ψ Psychology Press
Taylor & Francis Group

Visual search and spatial deficits

Lynn C. Robertson

Veterans Affairs Medical Research, Martinez, CA, USA

Joseph L. Brooks

University of California, Berkeley, CA, USA

Studies of visual search with patients with spatial attentional deficits have shown that the ability to bind basic features properly and thus to search for the conjunction of two spatially contiguous features is compromised. However, the effect of spatial deficits on feature search is more controversial. Here, we explore questions raised by the neuropsychological literature regarding feature processing and demonstrate that features "pop out" in the affected visual field, albeit more slowly. The implications for feature processing and selection as well as the relevance for understanding spatial deficits are discussed.

The neuropsychological literature has demonstrated that visual search for conjunctions becomes more difficult when visual spatial deficits are present, whereas feature search remains relatively intact. Perhaps the most dramatic example of this difference has been reported in patients with Balint's syndrome produced by *bilateral* damage to the dorsal (occipital-parietal) processing stream of the cortex (see Balint, 1909/1995; Freidman-Hill, Robertson, & Treisman, 1995). When symptoms are severe, these patients see only one object at a time (simultanagnosia) and lose the ability to control which object will pop into view next. Another striking symptom is that they are unable to locate even the objects they do see (see Rafal, 2001; Robertson, 2004, for a more complete description of the syndrome). When forced to guess the object's location, they may protest or perform at chance levels (Friedman-Hill et al., 1995). When asked to point to the object, they are unable to do so correctly, and their errors in spatial reports are unsystematic. These problems are isolated to space external to the body: Locating sensation on the body is typically intact, as is the ability to move body

Please address all correspondence to Lynn C. Robertson, Veterans Affairs Medical Research, 150 Muir Rd, Martinez, CA 94553, USA. E-mail: lynnrob@berkeley.socrates.edu

http://www.psypress.com/viscog   DOI: 10.1080/13506280500196324

parts in one direction or another on command (Robertson, Treisman, Friedman-Hill, & Grabowecky, 1997).

Accompanying the spatial deficits are problems in properly binding features in perception such as colour, size, or motion and shape, producing illusory conjunctions (Bernstein & Robertson, 1998; Friedman-Hill et al., 1995; Humphreys, Cinel, Wolfe, Olson, & Klempen, 2000; Robertson, 2003). For instance, a red "O" and blue "T" might be perceived as a blue "O" and red "T". These illusory conjunctions, which can be found in normal perceivers under data limited or controlled laboratory conditions (Treisman & Schmidt, 1982), are prevalent even under free viewing conditions in patients with Balint's syndrome. When spatial attention is compromised, whether by laboratory manipulations or by neurological insult, correctly binding surface features together is also compromised.

It has been argued that a binding problem that produces illusory conjunctions should also affect conjunction search (Feature Integration Theory—Treisman & Gelade, 1980; although see Desimone & Duncan, 1995, and Duncan & Humphreys, 1989, for alternative accounts). Indeed, this is the case. Robertson et al. (1997) asked a patient with Balint's syndrome (RM) to report whether or not a red "X" was present in two-, four-, or six-item displays (Figure 1), a trivial task for normal perceivers with such small set sizes. The target was presented either with red "O" and blue "X" distractors (conjunction search) or with all "O"s or blue "X"s (feature search). RM's responses were painfully slow when looking for conjunctions (up to 6 s), even in these small set size displays, and RT was quite variable. He made numerous errors, and the pattern of errors for feature and conjunction search was most revealing. His miss and false alarm rates for feature search were similar (Table 1) and close to that of his miss rate (target

Feature Search   Conjunction Search

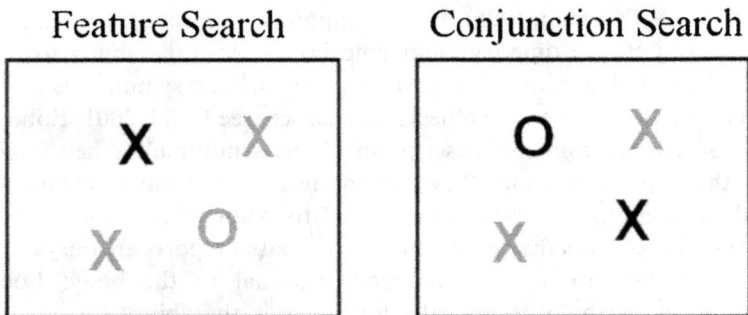

Figure 1.   Example of search displays with the target present that was used to study feature search (left) and conjunction search (right) in a patient with Balint's syndrome. Displays were chromatic and the patient was asked to detect the presence or absence of the red "X" (black represents red and grey represents blue).

TABLE 1
Percentage misses and false alarms for feature and
conjunction search for patient RM with Balint's syndrome

	Percent errors	
	Feature	Conjunction
Misses	4.0%	4.0%
False Alarms	1.3%	38.3%

present displays) for conjunction search. Consistent with his high number of illusory conjunctions, he made 38.3% false alarms in conjunction search (target absent displays). When the display contained red and blue and "X"s and "O"s but no red "X", he miscombined colour and letter and reported seeing a red "X" on over a third of the trials. When asked if this is what he actually saw, he replied that it was.

Patients with unilateral damage resulting in unilateral neglect[1] also have special difficulty searching for conjunctions,[2] especially when the target is in their contralesional field (Eglin, Robertson, & Knight, 1989; Eglin, Robertson, Knight, & Brugger, 1994; Esterman, McGlinchey-Berroth, & Milberg, 2000; Riddoch & Humphreys, 1987). This can occur even when difficulty or saliency between conjunction and feature search is equated (Humphreys, 2003). This problem need not affect the rate of search on the contralesional side *per se* (see Figure 2), and can be attributed to a "contralateral delay" (up to 20 s or more) to begin searching the neglected side. The difference between intercepts for search functions on the spared[3] and neglected sides increases as the number of distractors on the spared side increases. This difference can decrease when the distractors on the spared side are grouped (Robertson, Eglin, & Knight, 2003). In other words, perceptual organization that reduces the number of functionally integrated items in the spared field can change the magnitude of the contralateral delay.

Another important aspect of search with this patient population is that the contralateral delay does not reflect a simple bias to start search at a more ipsilesional point than normal and then scan continuously in the

---

[1] Unilateral visual neglect as defined clinically does not necessarily mean that a patient *never* attends to the contralesional side of space. They typically can be cued to attend to this side, and rehabilitation measures often include training patients to cue themselves accordingly.

[2] Also see Cohen and Rafal (1991) for evidence of illusory conjunctions on the neglected side of space in a patient with unilateral right neglect from left hemisphere damage.

[3] We will refer to the ipsilesional, non-neglected side as the "spared" side, but this is not quite correct. Search rates were slower on both the ipsi- and contralesional sides than normal, age-matched participants in the data reported by Eglin et al. (1989). Search in the ipsilesional side occurred first with a disproportionate delay to begin search on the contralesional side.

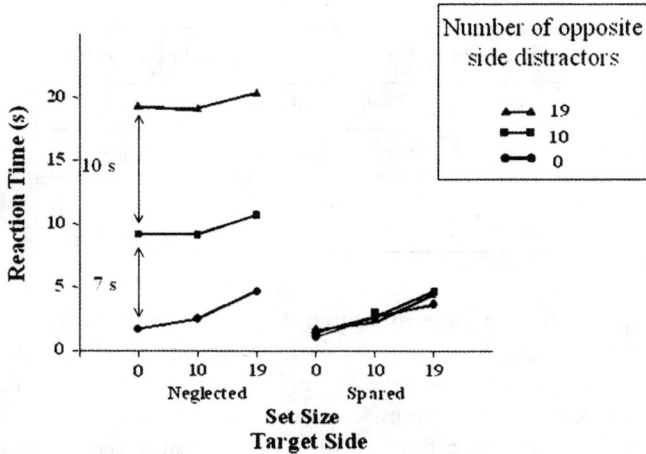

Figure 2.   Mean response time (in seconds) for a group of patients with unilateral neglect to detect a conjunction target on the neglected and spared side of a search display as a function of the number of distractors on the target side and the number on the opposite side (adapted from Eglin et al., 1989).

contralesional direction. There is something special about the midline that delays searching the neglected side. For instance, the search rate on the *spared* side in Figure 2 was estimated to be nearly 300 ms per item (slower than normal but systematically linear). At this rate, it should take about 3 s to begin searching the neglected side when 10 distractors appear on the spared side opposite the target, but instead it took over 7 s to do so. Even when patients knew there would *always* be a target in the display, they did not start searching the neglected side until scanning items on the spared side more than once. Critically, whether the intercepts between spared and neglected sides changed or not, serial search patterns for conjunctions were present. Response times increased linearly as a function of the number of distractors on the same side as the target in a group of patients with unilateral neglect (Eglin et al., 1989, 1994; Esterman et al., 2000; Robertson et al., 2003).

Feature search is different. When patients with unilateral parietal and/or frontal damage and neglect are asked to detect the presence or absence of a target with a unique feature, response times on the neglected side can be flat over set size, consistent with parallel search (Brooks, Wong, & Robertson, 2005; Esterman et al., 2000, Laeng, Brennen, & Espeseth, 2002; Riddoch & Humphreys, 1987). If these patients are asked to *locate* the target instead of giving a yes/no answer, nonzero slopes may appear, but the slopes are nowhere near as steep as those for conjunction search (Eglin et al., 1989, 1994). Nevertheless, whether there is a shallow or flat slope, intercepts on the neglected side are generally elevated relative to intercepts on the spared side. Despite this elevation, search rates can be similar to those observed in normal perceivers (Figure 3). These findings together suggest that features can be processed in parallel (pop-out) in the neglected field but reach detection threshold later than features in the spared field. The intercept differences between the spared and neglected sides in feature search suggest that dorsal damage also affects ventral processing. These findings are consistent with a proposal by Humphreys (1998) that in normal visual search intact parallel processing of item locations by the dorsal system gives a boost to parallel processing of features by the ventral stream through early interactions between dorsal and ventral pathways (Humphreys, 1998). The claim is that the spatial locations and colours of search items in the display are each processed in parallel through interacting dorsal and ventral streams, increasing the signal and speeding feature detection. If this is the case, then feature selection within the ventral stream should be slowed when spatial inputs are compromised. Parallel feature processing should still occur, but reach the threshold of awareness later.

FEATURES POP OUT WITH OR WITHOUT INTACT SPATIAL ABILITIES

We directly tested the hypothesis that features are processed in parallel but that the time required to reach detection threshold is delayed in a patient (SV) with unilateral visual neglect due to right hemisphere damage.

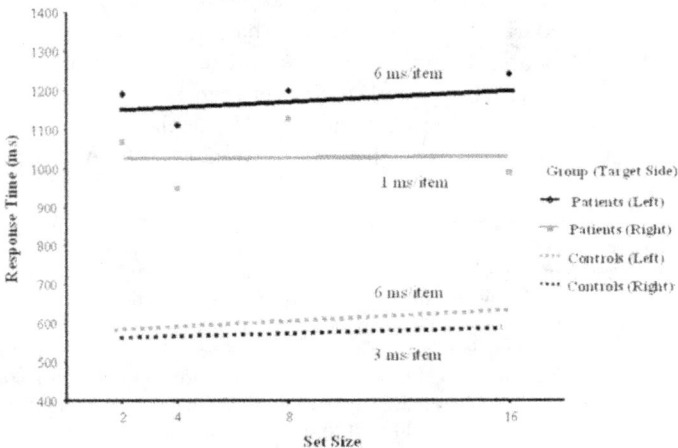

Figure 3.   Feature search for a group of patients with left neglect and right hemisphere damage and a group of normal controls when searching for a "Q" among "O"s (i.e., the presence of the tail of the "Q"). Mean response time for feature search in the contralesional (left) and ipsilesional (right) sides of a display as a function of set size. (Figure provided by Michael Esterman, based on data reported in Esterman et al., 2000.)

SV showed mild chronic neglect and extinction on standard neuropsychological tests[4] even several years post stroke. Unlike previous studies using reaction time measures, we adopted a psychophysical staircase method to estimate the stimulus presentation time needed for SV to reach 75% correct detection (Kaernbach, 2000).

SV suffered a middle cerebral artery infarct in the right hemisphere affecting dorsolateral frontal areas and most of the lateral parietal lobe with extension into temporal-parietal junction and superior temporal plain. The lesion spared the ventral temporal areas, including areas that code colour (e.g., V4/V8). Consistently, she had normal colour vision as assessed by Dvorine Pseudo-Isochromatic plates. In addition, a computerized perimetry test showed that SV's visual fields were intact well within the visual angle of the displays.

The displays either contained four or eight items presented on one side of fixation or the other (unilateral) or eight or sixteen items presented on both sides (bilateral). The search items were 1° in diameter "O"s presented equidistant from a central fixation cross (Figure 4), approximately 7.3° in the periphery (eye movements were monitored and trials when movements occurred did not contribute to the staircase threshold calculation). The probability of a target being present on any given trial was 50%. The subject's task was to report whether a target appeared or not in an unspeeded manner. Each trial was preceded by a 1000 ms fixation point in the centre of the display, and the examiner sat opposite SV behind the computer to watch for eye movements and keyed in a code for those trials on which they occurred. These trials were less than 1%.

Unilateral and bilateral conditions were blocked in six different sessions. Condition order was counterbalanced between sessions, and separate thresholds were estimated for each side of the display for each condition in each block.[5] The staircases for the two sides of the display were

---

[4] SV showed symptoms of visual neglect since the time of her stroke several years prior to testing in the present experiment. She was again administered a standard battery for neglect shortly before the present experiment was run. She bisected horizontal lines an average of 5 cm to the right of centre, extinguished all the left items in a two-item display and missed three-quarters of the left items when only one item appeared either to the left or right of centre. She also demonstrated visual extinction and neglect on standard bedside confrontation testing. Due to travel limitations, a perimetry test of visual fields was performed on a laptop computer by presenting a 0.3 blue circle briefly on a white background. The circle only appeared after she responded to a central mark that was difficult to detect unless fixated. This procedure assured central eye fixation. SV sat approximately 60 cm from the screen, and was asked to press a key on the mouse as soon as she detected a target. The target could appear in one of a total of 44 locations spanning the monitor screen, 10 times in each location.

[5] Presentation time was adjusted in increments of $\Delta T = 6 - [(r+1) - \mathrm{mod}((r+1),2)]/2$ screen frames, where $r =$ the number of reversals encountered and $\mathrm{mod}(a,b)$ is the remainder after division of a by b.

Unilateral displays

Bilateral display

Unilateral displays

Bilateral display

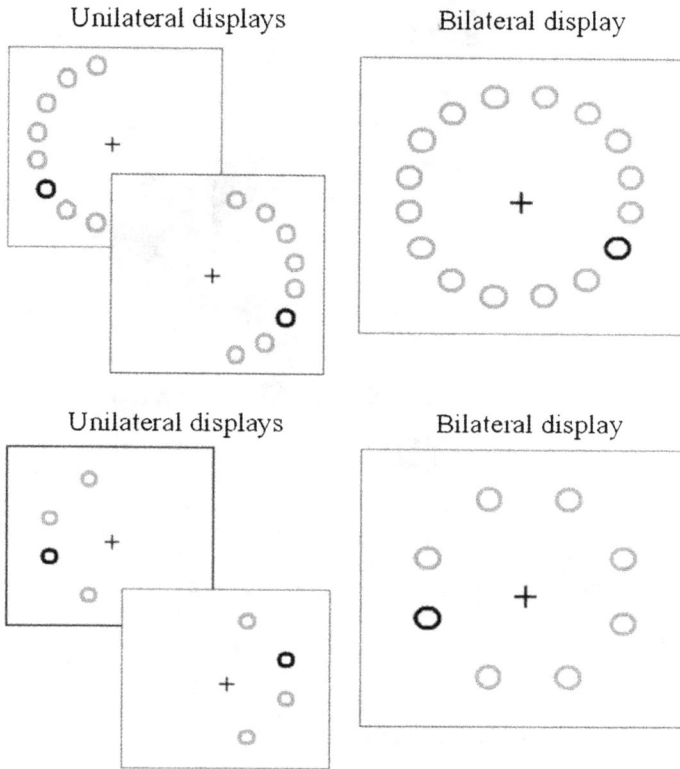

Figure 4.   Example of unilateral and bilateral displays. The target was a green (black) circle among red (grey) circles. Displays were either dense (top) or sparse (bottom).

interleaved so that the probability of a target on the two sides was equal within each block. The display at the start of each block was presented for 800 ms, the time decreasing or increasing over trials contingent on SV's response until 10 reversals occurred for each side of the display. Threshold estimates were recorded for each session and based on the last eight reversals for each side independently. The computer refresh rate limited the minimum threshold and the time increments and decrements to 10 ms. Each block lasted between 5 and 10 min.

As shown in Figure 5, the hypothesis was confirmed: The number of distractors on the same side as the target made virtually no difference in threshold presentation time. Consistent with SV's left neglect, threshold presentation times for unilateral displays were longer when the target was in the affected field (left visual field or LVF) than when it was in the right visual field (RVF), and bilateral displays increased thresholds for the LVF even

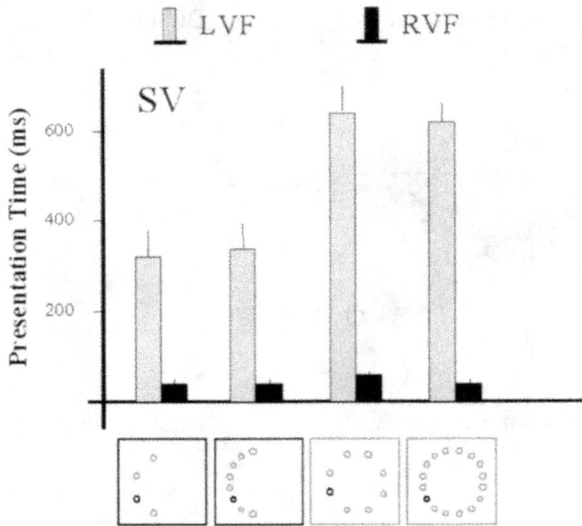

Figure 5.   Mean threshold stimulus presentation times to produce 75% correct feature detection for patient SV. Thresholds are shown for left visual field (LVF) and right visual field (RVF) for unilateral and bilateral displays. Patterns at the bottom are cartoons that represent displays with a LVF target.

more (an extinction-like pattern). The number of distractors in the RVF made virtually no difference in the magnitude of this increase. Displays had to be presented for over 200 ms longer when the display was bilateral and targets were in the LVF than when targets and distractors were presented in the LVF alone.

IMPLICATIONS FOR NEGLECT AND EXTINCTION

Unilateral neglect is generally defined as missing information on the contralesional side of space even when stimulation is confined to only that side, and extinction as missing information on the contralesional side only under double simultaneous stimulation. For instance, a patient might be asked to point to the side or sides of stimulation when they see an examiner move something in the patient's right and/or left visual field (such as the examiner's fingers). These effects are seldom all or none (as long as primary visual areas are intact). That is, patients may miss 60% of contralesional stimulation on unilateral trials and 90% on bilateral trials. In this way, a patient can be said to suffer from both neglect and extinction. SV's clinical profile conformed to this pattern, and her thresholds in our study did as well. Distractors increased LVF thresholds even when there was no evidence for a serial scan through displays. Perhaps surprisingly, improved grouping by proximity (created by doubling the number of distractors) had no effect on these thresholds. The effect of proximity on grouping is well known and has been shown many times (see Palmer, 1999, for a thorough discussion). Even though bilateral displays with 16 distractors formed a better circular configuration than those with 8, proximity (density) of the items in the display had no effect on threshold detection time.[6] RVF distractors increased threshold, but again it did not matter whether they were sparsely or densely packed. Thus, the amount of colour (i.e., red) in the RVF was not as important as its mere presence, and items that grouped into a better circle made no difference.

SV's lesion did not extend into primary visual areas or into ventral areas associated with colour processing. Nevertheless, more dorsal lesions appeared to compromise the function of these ventral areas. In SV's case it directly affected feature encoding on the same hemisphere as the lesion, slowing feature detection overall, consistent with her neglect.

IMPLICATIONS FOR VISUAL SEARCH

The thresholds observed with SV are consistent with reaction time studies reported in the neuropsychological literature suggesting that features can be processed in parallel on the neglected/extinguished side, although speed of processing might be slowed. An important new finding is derived from the difference in thresholds between unilateral and bilateral displays. Feature displays limited to the LVF (and thus projected to the damaged right hemisphere) were slowed in reaching target detection threshold. But even longer display presentations were required when distractors were added to the RVF. This pattern was evident despite the fact that cortical areas associated with colour perception (Zeki, 1980) were spared and were anatomically and functionally intact in SV.

One could argue that distractors on the right attracted attention, slowing attentional allocation to the left side, and thus the feature target did not truly "pop out". But there are reasons to reject this argument. First, there was no evidence that increasing the colour signal (i.e., number of distractors) within a visual field affected LVF thresholds (compare the two left bars and the two right bars for LUV in Figure 5). These results are consistent with parallel feature processing in specialized colour processing areas within the ventral stream of the contralateral hemisphere that is simply slower to reach

---

[6] Eight naïve individuals were asked to judge which of the bilateral figures created the better circle or whether both were the same. All eight chose the dense patterns over the sparse patterns without hesitation.

threshold. Second, when the number of distractors was the same (compare the two middle LUF bars), their distribution across the two fields decreased detection in the LVF dramatically, which would not be expected with a serial search or even an inefficient parallel search for features. However, the results are consistent with feature processing interactions between the two hemispheres. The fact that there are specialized areas for colour processing in each hemisphere suggests the existence of two colour maps that under normal circumstances communicate without a spatial bias. In fact, there is clear fMRI evidence that ipsilateral stimulation activates V4, although less than contralateral stimulation (Tootell, Mendola, Hadjikhani, Liu, & Dale, 1998), providing ample evidence in normal perceivers for this type of interaction.

In the case of SV the items projected to the left hemisphere (RVF) inhibited feature detection in the LVF. This does not mean that spatial selection was necessary for feature detection, but rather that the fidelity or speed of the information processed by the intact ventral stream of the damaged hemisphere can be decreased by both a reduced spatial signal due to dorsal damage of the same hemisphere and a change in the feature signal from the opposite hemisphere. The prior entry of RVF items slowed detection of LVF targets, presumably through callosal interactions.

Invoking a serial search for the target (even a global serial search from one side to the other) is not required to account for these findings. Rather, we can expand on Humphreys' (1998) claim that, in normal feature search, parallel spatial and feature processing in dorsal and ventral streams respectively interact to "boost" the strength of search items. In this model, there is mutual facilitation. The present findings add an additional influence from the opposite hemisphere that appears to be inhibitory. In the case of SV, right dorsal damage would produce an overall disruption in this system by reducing the normal boost in feature processing in the same hemisphere, which in turn would reduce the strength of the signal across the callosum. This would lead to an imbalance between right and left signals that are normally mutually inhibitory.

Note that both these models are consistent with parallel feature processing and the predictions of feature integration theory that spatial or focal attention is not necessary for feature detection (Treisman & Gelade, 1980). They are also at least partly consistent with biased competition models of visual search (Desimone & Duncan, 1995), at least at the spatial resolution of competition between hemispheres for processing resources. In this case, the competition is for a specialized population of neurons (presumably in the temporal lobe) that encode colour features on the left and right of a visual display.

CONCLUSIONS

There has been much speculation about whether spatial attention is involved in feature search. Are search slopes shallow because a fast scan can be made when targets are salient? The neuropsychological literature on visual search in patients with spatial deficits suggests that the answer is "No". In fact, features (but not conjunctions) can be detected with nearly complete loss of spatial information of the external world (e.g., Balint's syndrome). However, feature processing is not entirely normal in these cases even when ventral processing streams are intact. We have shown that thresholds for feature detection do not increase within each visual field with added distractors for a patient with chronic neglect and extinction. However, such displays must be presented longer to reach contralateral thresholds and longer still when bilateral displays are presented. Clearly, spatial information is not required for feature search to occur in parallel. However, spatial information does influence the amount of time that it takes to resolve feature processing independently of the number of distractors present.

These findings are consistent with early dorsal interactions with parallel feature processing in ventral streams as well as with strong interactions between specialized feature processing areas across hemispheres. When unilateral damage and neglect are present, the normal interactions between these areas are compromised.

REFERENCES

Balint, R. (1909). Seelenlahmung des "Schauens", optische Ataxie, raumliche Storung der Aufmerksamkeit. *Monatshrift fur Psychiatrie und Neurologie, 25*, 5–81. (Translated in *Cognitive Neuropsychology*, 1995, *12*, 265–281)

Bernstein, L. J., & Robertson, L. C. (1998). Independence between illusory conjunctions of color and motion with shape following bilateral parietal lesions. *Psychological Science, 9*, 167–175.

Brooks, J. L., Wong, Y., & Robertson, L. C. (2005). Crossing the midline: Reducing visual extinction by re-establishing hemispheric balance. *Neuropsychologia, 43*, 572–582.

Cohen, A., & Rafal, R. (1991). Attention and feature integration: Illusory conjunctions in a patient with parietal lobe lesions. *Psychological Science, 2*, 106–110.

Desimone, R., & Duncan, J. (1995). Neural mechanisms of selective visual attention. *Annual Review of Neuroscience, 18*, 193–222.

Duncan, J., & Humphreys, G. (1989). Visual search and stimulus similarity. *Psychological Review, 96*, 433–458.

Eglin, M., Robertson, L. C., & Knight, R. T. (1989). Visual search performance in the neglect syndrome. *Journal of Cognitive Neuroscience, 4*, 372–381.

Eglin, M., Robertson, L. C., Knight, R. T., & Brugger, P. (1994). Search deficits in neglect patients are dependent on size of the visual scene. *Neuropsychology, 4*, 451–463.

Esterman, M., McGlinchey-Berroth, R., & Milberg, W. P. (2000). Parallel and serial search in hemispatial neglect: Evidence for preserved preattentive but impaired attentive processing. *Neuropsychology, 14*, 599–611.

Friedman-Hill, S., Robertson, L. C., & Treisman. A. (1995). Parietal contributions to visual feature binding: Evidence from a patient with bilateral lesions. *Science*, *269*, 853–855.

Humphreys, G. W. (1998). Neural representation of objects in space: A dual coding account. *Philosophical Transactions Royal Society of London, Series B*, *353*, 1341–1351.

Humphreys, G. W. (2003, June). *Brain mechanisms of search: Grouping, filtering and searching*. Paper presented at the Munich Visual Search symposium, Holzhausen am Ammersee, Germany.

Humphreys, G. W., Cinel, C., Wolfe, J., Olson, A., & Klempen, N. (2000). Fractionating the binding process: Neuropsychological evidence distinguishing binding of form from binding of surface features. *Vision Research*, *40*, 1569–1596.

Kaernbach, C. J. (1990). A single-interval adjustment-matrix (SIAM) procedure for unbiased adaptive testing. *Journal of the Acoustical Society of America*, *88*, 2645–2655.

Laeng, B., Brennen, T., & Espeseth, T. (2002). Fast responses to neglected targets in visual search reflect pre-attentive processes: An exploration of response times in visual neglect. *Neuropsychologia*, *40*, 1622–1636.

Palmer, S. E. (1999). *Vision sciences*. Cambridge, MA: MIT Press.

Rafal, R. (2001). Balint's syndrome. In M. Behrmann (Ed.), *Disorders of visual behaviour* (Vol. 4, pp. 121–141). Amsterdam: Elsevier Science.

Riddoch, M. J., & Humphreys, G. W. (1987). Perceptual and action systems in unilateral visual neglect. In M. Jeannerod (Ed.). *Neuropsychological and neurophysiological aspects of spatial neglect* (pp. 151–181). Amsterdam: North-Holland/Elsevier Science.

Robertson, L. C. (2003). Binding, spatial attention and perceptual awareness. *Nature Reviews Neuroscience*, *4*, 93–102.

Robertson, L. C. (2004). *Space, objects, minds and brains*. New York: Psychology Press.

Robertson, L. C., Eglin, M., & Knight, R. T. (2003). Grouping influences in unilateral visual neglect. *Journal of Clinical and Experimental Neuropsychology*, *25*, 297–307.

Robertson, L. C., Treisman, A., Friedman-Hill, S., & Grabowecky, M. (1997). The interaction of spatial and object pathways: Evidence from Balint's syndrome. *Journal of Cognitive Neuroscience*, *9*, 295–317.

Tootell, R. B. H., Mendola, J. D., Hadjikhani, N. K., Liu, A. K., & Dale, A. M. (1998). The representation of the ipsilateral visual field in human cerebral cortex. *Proceedings of the National Academy of Sciences*, *95*, 818–824.

Treisman, A. M., & Gelade, G. (1980). A feature-integration theory of attention. *Cognitive Psychology*, *12*, 97–136.

Treisman, A. M., & Schmidt, H. (1982). Illusory conjunctions in perception of objects. *Cognitive Psychology*, *14*, 107–141.

Zeki, S. M. (1980). The representations of color in the cerebral cortex. *Nature*, *284*, 412–418.

VISUAL COGNITION, 2006, 14 (4/5/6/7/8), 863–876

Ψ Psychology Press
Taylor & Francis Group

Frontal control of attentional capture in visual search

Nilli Lavie

Department of Psychology, University College London, UK

Jan de Fockert

Department of Psychology, Goldsmiths College, University of London, UK

Lavie and colleagues recently suggested that cognitive control functions that are mediated by frontal cortex provide goal-directed control of selective attention, serving to minimize interference by goal-irrelevant distractors. Here we provide new evidence for this claim from an attentional capture paradigm. An event-related fMRI experiment shows that the presence (vs. absence) of an irrelevant colour singleton distractor in a visual search task was not only associated with activity in superior parietal cortex, in line with a psychological attentional capture account, but was also associated with frontal cortex activity. Moreover, behavioural interference by the singleton was negatively correlated with frontal activity, suggesting that frontal cortex is involved in control of singleton interference. Behavioural tests confirmed that singleton interference depends on availability of cognitive control to the search task: Singleton interference was significantly increased by high working memory load. These results demonstrate the important role of frontal cognitive control of attention by working memory in minimizing distraction.

Focused goal-directed behaviour depends on top-down control of attention, so that attention is allocated to stimuli in accordance with current priorities. Lavie and colleagues (de Fockert, Rees, Frith, & Lavie, 2001; Lavie, 2000; Lavie, Hirst, de Fockert, & Viding, 2004) have recently suggested that cognitive control functions mediated by the frontal lobe, such as working memory, provide such goal-directed control of visual selective attention. Specifically, Lavie and colleagues proposed that working memory serves to actively maintain current processing priorities during task performance, and thus that availability of working memory for a selective attention task is critical for minimizing interference by goal-irrelevant distractors.

Please address all correspondence to Nilli Lavie, Department of Psychology, University College London, Gower St, London WC1E 6BT, UK. E-mail: n.lavie@ucl.ac.uk

This work was supported by a Medical Research Council grant to the first author.

DOI: 10.1080/13506280500195953

In support of this hypothesis, Lavie (2000; Lavie et al., 2004) showed that response competition effects produced by an irrelevant distractor in a selective attention task (consisting of a central target letter and a flanking distractor letter) are increased under conditions of high working memory load, when subjects were required to rehearse a set of six digits during performance of the selective attention task, compared to conditions of low working memory load when subjects had to rehearse just one digit or none. Moreover, in an fMRI study, de Fockert et al. (2001) manipulated working memory load during a Stroop-like selective attention task in which subjects were required to classify famous names while ignoring distractor faces (that could be either response-congruent with the target name, i.e., the face of the person named, or incongruent with the target, i.e., a face of a person from an opposite category). They found that working memory load was not only associated with increased activity in frontal cortex (a main effect), but also with increased activity related to the presence (vs. absence) of a distractor face in visual cortex (an interaction of working memory load and distractor face conditions), and with greater distractor interference effects on behaviour.

However, although the convergence of behavioural findings with neuro-imaging results seems to make an appealing case for the role of frontal cognitive control functions, such as working memory, in preventing interference by goal-irrelevant distractors, the evidence described so far was confined to flanker and Stroop-like tasks. In this paper we present new evidence from functional imaging and behavioural experiments using the paradigm of attentional capture in visual search, in support of the claim that the extent to which an irrelevant singleton distractor captures attention and produces interference effects on visual search performance depends on the availability of frontal control functions to the search task.

Previous visual search studies have demonstrated that the presence of an irrelevant distractor with a unique feature that makes it a singleton in the visual search display (e.g., an irrelevant red distractor among green objects) will typically distract attention from focusing on the search target, producing the phenomenon of attentional capture (see Folk & Remington, 2006 this issue; Theeuwes, Reimann, & Mortier, 2006 this issue; Yantis, 2000). Such interruption of goal-driven attention is found even when the distractor object forms a singleton on a dimension that is never relevant to the task (e.g., a colour singleton will interfere with search on the basis of other features, such as search for a curved target among angular shapes), suggesting that the singleton distractor has captured attention, rather than that attention was allocated to the distractor at will (e.g., Theeuwes, 1996).

FUNCTIONAL IMAGING STUDY

The behavioural studies on attentional capture have led us to the following hypotheses about the neural correlates of attentional capture in visual search. First, as the singleton distractor attracts attention, we hypothesized that neural systems known to be involved in the allocation of attention to goal-relevant stimuli may also be associated with attentional capture by goal-irrelevant singleton distractors. Specifically, activity in parietal cortex has been previously associated with the allocation of attention in a wide variety of tasks, including visual search (Corbetta, Shulman, Miezin, & Petersen, 1995) and spatial cueing (e.g., Corbetta, Miezin, Shulman, & Petersen, 1993; for reviews see Corbetta & Shulman, 2002; Wojciulik & Kanwisher, 1999). We therefore expected that capture of attention by an irrelevant singleton distractor during visual search would also be associated with parietal activity. Second, because attention was captured by a goal-irrelevant distractor, the competition between the target and the irrelevant singleton distractor was expected to impose a greater demand on top-down control mechanisms typically associated with the frontal lobe in order to resolve the competition (for review see Duncan & Owen, 2000). We thus anticipated that attentional capture by an irrelevant singleton would also implicate activity in frontal cortices associated with such top-down control. We tested these hypotheses in an fMRI study (de Fockert, Rees, Frith, & Lavie 2004), in which we scanned subjects during performance in Theeuwes's (1991, 1992) task of visual search in the presence of an irrelevant colour singleton.

Method

Subjects. Ten young adults with normal vision and normal colour vision gave informed consent and participated in the study.

Stimuli and procedure. Subjects searched for a unique shape target (circle) among distractors of a different shape (diamonds) and were required to indicate the orientation (horizontal or vertical) of the line segment in the target by a speeded key press (see Figure 1A). We compared search performance and brain activity between conditions of presence and absence of an irrelevant colour singleton distractor. Since these conditions also vary the presence or absence of an odd colour in the array, we added another condition in which the colour singleton was present on the target shape. Comparing activity in the presence (vs. absence) of a colour singleton distractor to activity in the presence (vs. absence) of a colour singleton target (i.e., an interaction) would allow us to identify specifically the neural correlates of attentional capture by an irrelevant distractor. In order to produce a factorial design (as required for examining the interaction), we

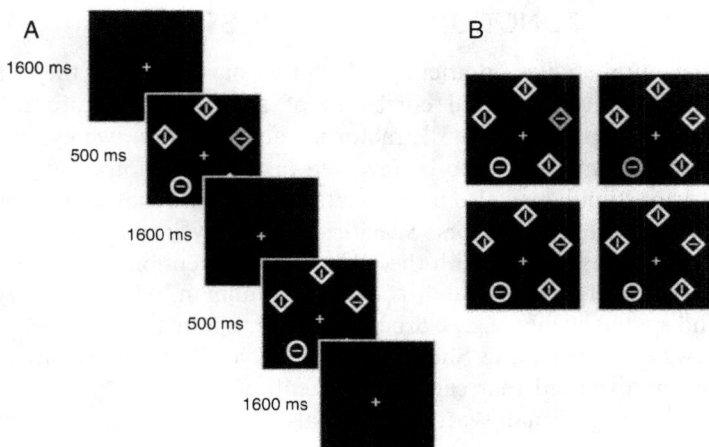

Figure 1. (A) Trial sequence. The example shows a colour singleton distractor present display and a colour singleton distractor absent display. (B) Colour singleton present (top row) and absent (bottom row) conditions were combined with distractor singleton (left column) and target singleton (right column) conditions to produce four display types. The colour singleton absent conditions included a reduced size (by 20%) singleton on the target or distractor. These displays, together with null events (fixation), were presented in equal proportions, in a random order during the experiment. In the figure, red colour singletons are printed in grey.

assigned colour singleton absent trials to a distractor condition or a target condition by presenting either one of the distractors or the target with a nonsalient but noticeable reduced size (by 20%) singleton, to produce colour singleton distractor absent or colour singleton target absent conditions, respectively (Figure 1B). In a behavioural pilot experiment we established that these size singleton distractors indeed do not produce any interference effects on response times (RTs) or errors. One fifth of all trials were null events, on which the fixation point was presented for the duration of a trial.

Data acquisition and analysis. A 2T Siemens VISION system was used to acquire both T1 anatomical volume images and T2*-weighted echoplanar (EPI) images with blood oxygenation level dependent (BOLD) contrast. Each participant completed two blocks of 240 trials, chosen at random from the five trial categories, while being scanned. The MRI data acquired during these two blocks consisted of 216 volumes in each block, of which the first six volumes per run were discarded to allow for T1 equilibration effects. Volumes were acquired continuously with an effective repetition time (TR) of 2.4 s/volume. Prior to the scanning sessions, participants completed a practice block consisting of 20 trials.

Statistical Parametric Mapping (SPM99: Wellcome Department of Imaging Neuroscience, University College London) was used for temporal and spatial data preprocessing, and data analysis. Data were time-corrected for slice acquisition times (using the middle slice as a reference). All volumes were then realigned to the first volume, and normalized to a standard EPI template volume (based on the MNI reference brain; Cocosco, Kollokian, Kwan, & Evans, 1997) in the space of Talairach and Tournoux (1988). These EPI volumes were then smoothed with an isotropic 10-mm FWHM Gaussian kernel.

Statistical results were based on a fixed effects model with a $p < .05$ height threshold (corrected for the whole brain volume examined) for report of regions of significant activation. For the interaction contrast, we used a small-volume correction with spheres of 10 mm radius around the peak voxels in the areas of significant activity related to the simple main effect (presence vs. absence of colour singleton distractors). For the ANOVA with subjects as the random factor, the BOLD signal was extracted for all voxels contained within the three clusters of significant activation (at $t > 4.54$, corresponding to $p < .05$, corrected for multiple comparisons) in the presence (vs. absence) of distractor singletons. Next, for each participant, the averages BOLD signal across all voxels in each of the three clusters was entered into ANOVAs with colour singleton presence (present, absent) and singleton stimulus (target, distractor) as within-subjects factors and participants as the random factor.

Results and discussion

Behavioural responses. The behavioural data collected during the scanning sessions showed that the presence of a colour singleton distractor produced significant interference ($M = 809$ ms and 10% errors, for colour singleton distractor present trials compared with $M = 713$ ms and 6% errors for colour singleton distractor absent trials, with a size distractor present instead), $F(1, 9) = 38.4$, $p < .001$ for the RTs. This result is consistent with previous behavioural findings in similar visual search studies of attentional capture (e.g., Theeuwes, 1991, 1992, 1994). Interestingly, the size of the attentional capture effect is larger than the attentional capture effects in previous experiments using this task (these average less than 20 ms in Theeuwes's, 1992, experiments) and appears in the range of attentional capture effects found in tasks in which on some trials or on some blocks the singleton feature is used to define the target (Theeuwes, 1991). The greater interference effect in our experiment is therefore likely to be due to the fact that we incorporated trials in which the target was also presented with the colour singleton. The presence of a colour singleton on the target only led to a small and nonsignificant trend for facilitation ($M = 730$, 7% errors for colour singleton target present trials compared with $M = 739$, 7% errors for colour target singleton absent trials, with a size singleton target instead),

$F < 1$ for the RTs. This may be attributed to a floor effect, given that the target was a shape singleton so could pop out without the additional colour singleton on it.

Imaging data.   Brain activity time-locked to the individual trials was determined using an event-related analysis of the fMRI data. Figure 2 shows that activity associated with the presence (vs. absence) of a colour singleton distractor was found in bilateral superior parietal cortex (Brodmann area 7) and in left lateral precentral gyrus (BA 6) of the frontal cortex. Moreover, parietal and frontal cortices also showed significant interactions, such that activity in the presence (vs. absence) of a colour singleton distractor was greater than activity in the presence (vs. absence) of a colour singleton target. These interactions were consistent across subjects and were replicated in an ANOVA with participants as the random factor (see Figure 3). These findings confirm that activity in parietal and frontal cortices related to the presence (vs. absence) of a colour singleton distractor could not be attributed to the mere presence of an odd colour in the array.

Parietal activation.   As superior parietal cortex has been previously associated with spatial shifts of attention (see Corbetta & Shulman, 2002, for review), the present findings suggest that spatial attention was allocated to the singleton distractor, consistent with an attentional capture account of the behavioural interference effects.[1] Specifically, many previous behavioural studies have shown that capture of attention by an irrelevant singleton involves spatial shifts of attention to the singleton position (e.g., Yantis & Jonides, 1990; see Yantis, 2000, for review). Although it has been shown that attentional set can under some conditions eliminate spatial cueing effects (e.g., Folk, Remington, & Johnston, 1992), this has only been shown in tasks that are very different from the task used in the present study (e.g., the singleton is presented before the search array and thus does not directly compete with the target).

---

[1] It is worth noting that, although serial spatial shifts of attention may not be required for the search process in this feature-search task (Treisman, 1988), shifts of focused attention to the target position are required for the orientation discrimination aspect of this task (in order to discriminate the orientation of the small line (0.5 of visual angle) within the target shape, among the competing orientations in the nontarget shapes). Thus, in the absence of a singleton distractor, although the target will initially pop out, focused attention will be shifted to it in order to perform the orientation discrimination task. When the singleton distractor is present, however, it will pop out more readily than the target (due to its greater salience, see Theeuwes, 1992), and thus may be wrongly selected for a spatial shift of attention. Thus, the presence of a singleton distractor should involve an extra shift of spatial attention (as attention has to be shifted once more from the distractor to the target).

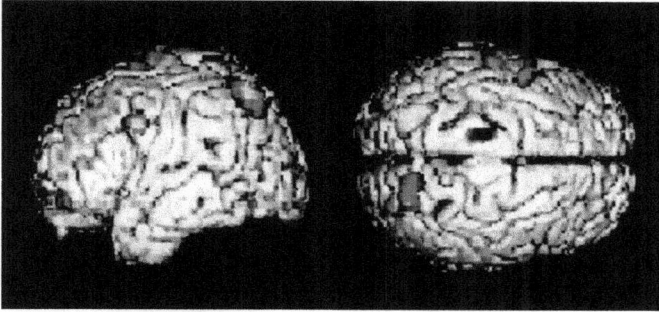

Figure 2. Activity related to the presence (vs. absence) of a colour singleton distractor. Shown are left lateral (left panel) and dorsal (right panel) views of a T1-weighted anatomical template image in Talairach space (Talairach & Tournoux, 1988). For display purposes, activity is shown at $p < .001$, uncorrected, with an extent threshold of 200 voxels. Areas of significant activation (at $p < .05$, corrected) were left superior parietal cortex (peak activation: -24, -66, 50, $t = 5.85$, $p < .001$), right superior parietal cortex (peak activation: 26, -68, 50, $t = 4.67$, $p < .030$), and left lateral precentral gyrus (peak activation: -46, 4, 36, $t = 4.79$, $p < .018$).

It is important to note that although the superior parietal cortex has been associated with both covert shifts of attention (that do not involve eye movements) and overt shifts of attention (that involve eye movements as well, see Corbetta, 1998; Corbetta et al., 1998), the activations found in the present study cannot be attributed to eye movements since eye position was monitored during scanning, and eye position results confirmed that there were no significant differences in eye position between any of the experimental conditions: Fixation was consistently maintained within two

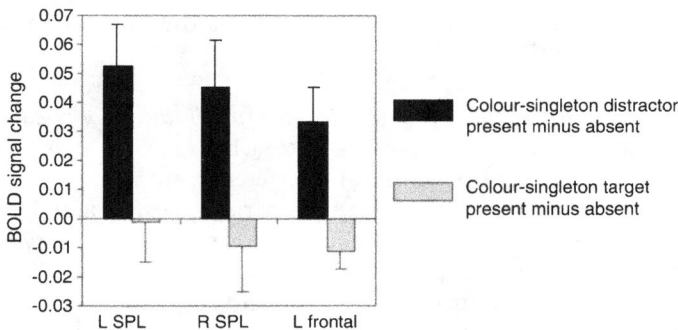

Figure 3. Activity associated with the interaction between colour singleton presence (present, absent) and singleton stimulus (distractor, target). Bars represent BOLD signal change, averaged across voxels in each cluster, and across participants. Shown is the difference in mean activity between colour singleton present vs. absent, plotted separately for left superior parietal cortex (L SPL), right superior parietal cortex (R SPL), and left lateral precentral gyrus, and for distractor and target singletons. Error bars represent interparticipant standard error.

degrees of fixation, less than the eccentricity of the search array (which subtended 3.1° from fixation to the centre of each display item).

Frontal activation. The frontal activity found is in line with our expectation that target selection in the presence of a competing, attention-capturing, singleton distractor would place a greater demand on top-down frontal control functions, as these are needed to resolve the competition between the target and capturing singleton distractor. Indeed, activity in BA 6 has often been implicated in attentional selection for action (e.g., Deiber et al., 1991; van Oostende, van Hecke, Sunaert, Nuttin, & Marchal, 1997) and in competition for responses in Stroop-like tasks (e.g., Hazeltine, Bunge, Scanlon, & Gabrieli, 2003; Schumacher & D'Esposito, 2002; Zysset, Müller, Lohmann, & von Cramon, 2001).

Moreover, we found a significant negative correlation between activity in left frontal cortex (percentage signal change in the presence vs. absence of singleton distractor calculated as a proportion of the average fMRI signal per each individual) and the magnitude of the interference effect in RT (also calculated as a proportion of the average RT per individual), $r = -.712$, $p = .021$ (two-tailed). Whereas activity in the two clusters of activation in the bilateral superior parietal cortex showed no significant correlation with the RT effect, $r = .247$, $p = .49$, and $r = -.103$, $p = .78$ for the left and right superior parietal cortex, respectively, there was a significant negative correlation between activity in the left frontal cortex and the magnitude of the RT interference effect: Greater activity in frontal cortex (when a colour distractor was present vs. absent) was associated with smaller interference effects by the irrelevant distractor. This finding suggests that top down control functions mediated by frontal cortex serve to control against interference by irrelevant distractors. We discuss this suggestion in greater detail below.

Contrast between parietal role and frontal role in attentional capture. In contrast with the strong negative correlation between the signal in frontal cortex and magnitude of behavioural interference, there was no significant correlation between activity in superior parietal cortex and behavioural interference. This contrast may indicate that these structures serve different functions in attentional capture. The activity in superior parietal cortex may reflect stimulus-driven shifts of attention towards the irrelevant distractor, as the irrelevant colour singleton we used was more salient than the shape target (see Theeuwes, 1996). As such, attention may always be captured by the more salient distractor, with little variation in the extent of attentional shifts and the strength of the associated signal in superior parietal cortex, thus precluding any correlation with behavioural interference effects. The extent to which the irrelevant singleton distractor (that has nevertheless captured spatial attention) will produce interference on behaviour, however, may be determined by the extent to which frontal cortex exerts a strong or weak top-down control signal (in order to resolve the competition between the target and the capturing distractor).

Functional imaging conclusions. We conclude that the neural correlates of attentional capture by an irrelevant singleton during visual search are in parietal and frontal cortex. The superior parietal activity suggests allocation of spatial attention to the singleton distractor, in line with an attentional capture account for the singleton interference effects. The finding of a negative correlation between frontal activity and behavioural interference suggests a role for frontal cortex in control of interference by the irrelevant (yet attentional capturing) singleton.

Top-down control of attentional capture by working memory: Behavioural tests. The suggestion of the correlation between fMRI signal and behaviour that attentional capture by an irrelevant singleton is controlled by frontal cortex is limited by the fact that correlations cannot inform about any causal role. We therefore examined the role of frontal cognitive control functions in attentional capture in new behavioural experiments (Lavie & de Fockert, 2005).

As discussed in the introduction, Lavie and colleagues (e.g., Lavie et al., 2004) have recently suggested that top-down control of selective attention by frontal cortex involves active maintenance of priorities between goal-relevant targets and goal-irrelevant distractors in working memory through-out task performance. Importantly, the frontal areas involved in such control in de Fockert et al.'s (2001) study (i.e., areas associated with the main effect of working memory load) included the frontal area implicated in control against singleton distractor interference in the present study. However, these previous studies assessed distractor interference effects within a Stroop-like task. The hypothesis that working memory serves to provide goal-directed control of visual attention, allowing to prevent interference by goal-irrelevant distractors, suggests that the extent to which goal-irrelevant singletons will capture attention, and thus interfere with search for the goal-relevant target, should also depend on the availability of working memory to control goal-directed performance of the visual search task. We therefore predicted that high working memory load during performance of a visual search task in the presence of an irrelevant singleton would result in greater attentional capture by the irrelevant singleton compared with no, or low, working memory load.

We tested these predictions in experiments in which we interleaved a task of attentional capture in visual search (based on Theeuwes', 1992, study) with a working memory task. The visual search task was very similar to that used in the imaging study except for the following changes: We did not include a condition of colour singleton on the shape target; instead a colour singleton distractor was present on 50% of the trials and absent on the remaining 50% of trials. We did not include a size singleton in the singleton absent condition conditions and we presented displays for 200 ms in order to prevent eye movements during search.

High load on working memory was manipulated by requesting subjects to rehearse a set of six digits (Experiment 1) or four digits in exact order (Experiment 2) in order to recognize whether a memory probe following the visual search task was present or absent in the memory set of that trial

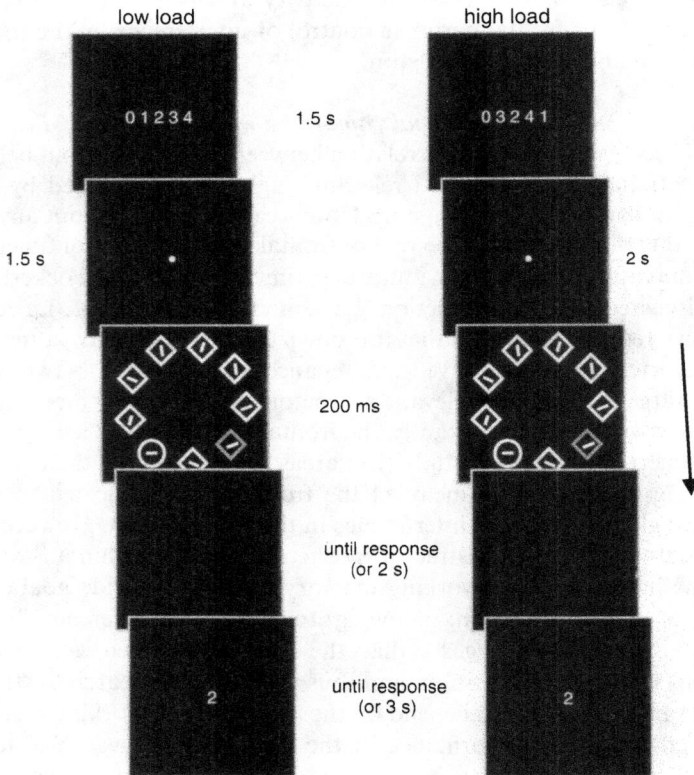

Figure 4. Examples of a low load (left panel) and high load (right panel) trial. The memory set always consisted of the digits 0, 1, 2, 3, 4, which were either presented in sequential order on each trial (low working memory load), or in a different random order on each trial (high load). The digit 0 always occurred at the start of each memory set to ensure that both conditions of load had four possible memory probe responses (1, 2, 3, 4). In the visual search task, the target and all the nontarget shapes were green (white in the figure), except for the singleton distractor, which was presented in red (grey in the figure). This example shows colour singleton present displays. On half the trials (picked up at random) the singleton was absent.

(Experiment 1) or in order to recall a digit that followed the probe digit in the memory set (Experiment 2). The interference effects produced by a colour singleton in the visual search task were compared between these high load conditions and a no load condition in which subjects did not perform the working memory task (Experiment 1), or a low load condition in which the memory set was always in the same order (the digit sequence "0, 1, 2, 3, 4" was always presented as the memory set; Experiment 2) (see Figure 4).

Our hypothesis that the interference on visual search by an irrelevant singleton distractor depends on availability of working memory to control performance in the visual search task lead to the prediction of greater singleton interference effects in conditions of high working memory load than in conditions with no or low working memory load. The results provided support for this prediction: both in Experiment 1 and Experiment 2 we found that singleton interference effects were significantly greater (at $p < .02$) in conditions of high working memory load (mean singleton interference effects were 51 ms in Experiment 1 and 88 ms in Experiment 2) compared to no working memory load (the mean interference effect under no load was 15 ms in Experiment 1) or low working memory load (the mean interference effect under low load was 52 ms in Experiment 2). These results provide support for the hypothesis that attentional capture by task-irrelevant singletons in a visual search task depends on the availability of working memory for the search task.

GENERAL DISCUSSION

The present experiments demonstrate that the extent to which an irrelevant colour singleton interferes with performance in a shaped-based visual search task depends on top-down cognitive control functions that are known to be mediated by frontal cortex. Our functional imaging study revealed that the presence (vs. absence) of such colour singleton distractors in the visual search display is not only associated with neural activity in bilateral superior parietal cortex, in line with the idea that the singleton captured spatial attention, but was also associated with activity in left precentral gyrus of the frontal cortex. Moreover, the strength of the neural signal in left frontal cortex was negatively correlated with the magnitude of singleton interference effects on behaviour. This finding suggests that frontal cortex is involved in control of interference by an irrelevant singleton distractor.

An important cognitive control function that is mediated by frontal cortex is working memory. Behavioural tests confirmed a causal role for working memory in the control of singleton interference effects on visual search. Singleton interference on visual search was significantly increased under conditions of high working memory load compared with conditions of low or no working memory load. These experiments provide direct support for the hypothesis that goal-directed control of visual selective attention is mediated by frontal cognitive control functions such as working memory.

The present findings may also enhance our understanding of the mechanism of attentional capture, specifically whether attentional capture is purely stimulus driven or may also be subject to top-down control. The finding that singleton interference is negatively correlated with neural signal strength in frontal cortex and is modulated by working memory load suggests that capture by the singleton is subject to top-down control. The finding, however, that an irrelevant colour singleton always captured attention in our task, and produced interference on behaviour and activity in superior parietal cortex (an area known to mediate spatial shifts of attention) even under conditions of low or no working memory load, when top-down control functions are fully available to the task, points to a stimulus-driven component of attentional capture. The feature differences we used for the target and singleton distractor meant that the irrelevant colour singleton was more salient than the shape target. Under these conditions, the singleton disrupted visual search despite being goal-irrelevant, in line with stimulus-driven accounts for attentional capture (e.g., Theeuwes, 1996). It is important to note, however, that the stimulus-driven component of capture is dictated by the relative stimulus salience not the exact feature used. Thus it is highly likely that presenting a singleton with a very distinct shape or size differences during search for a target defined by a less distinct colour difference would produce similar effects of capture, with similar activations and similar effects of working memory load to those currently found. This could be an interesting question for further study.

Regarding the role of top-down cognitive control of attentional capture, it is important to note that the present results converge on the same conclusion as that made following previous experiments using Stroop-like tasks (e.g., de Fockert et al., 2001; Lavie, 2000; Lavie et al., 2004). Since Stroop-like tasks measure distractor interference via effects of response-congruency on target RTs, whereas attentional capture in visual search is measured via the RT cost produced by the presence (vs. absence) of an irrelevant singleton, the convergence of these different measures on the same conclusion suggests a general role for frontal cognitive control functions in goal-directed control of visual selective attention.

REFERENCES

Cocosco, C. A., Kollokian, V., Kwan. R. K.-S., & Evans, A. C. (1997). BrainWeb: Online interface to a 3D MRI simulated brain database. *Neuroimage*. *5*(Part 2/4), S425.

Corbetta, M. (1998). Fronto-parietal cortical networks for directing attention and the eye to visual locations: Identical, independent, or overlapping neural systems? *Proceedings of the National Academy of Sciences of the United States of America*, *95*, 831–838.

Corbetta, M., Akbudak, E., Conturo, T. E., Drury, H. A., Linenweber, M., Ollinger. J. M., et al. (1998). A common network of functional areas for attention and eye movements. *Neuron*, *21*, 761–773.

Corbetta, M., Miezin, F. M., Shulman, G. L., & Petersen, S. E. (1993). A PET study of visuospatial attention. *Journal of Neuroscience*, *13*, 1202–1226.

Corbetta, M., & Shulman, G. L. (2002). Control of goal-directed and stimulus-driven attention in the brain. *Nature Reviews Neuroscience*, *3*, 201–215.

Corbetta, M., Shulman, G. L., Miezin, F. M., & Petersen, S. E. (1995). Superior parietal cortex activation during spatial attention shifts and visual feature conjunction. *Science*, *270*, 802–805.

De Fockert, J. W., Rees, G., Frith, C. D., & Lavie, N. (2001). The role of working memory in visual selective attention. *Science*, *291*, 1803–1806.

De Fockert, J. W., Rees, G., Frith, C. D., & Lavie, N. (2004). Neural correlates of attentional capture in visual search. *Journal of Cognitive Neuroscience*, *16*, 751–759.

Deiber, M. P., Passingham, R. E., Colebatch, J. G., Friston, K. J., Nixon, P. D., & Frackowiak, R. S. (1991). Cortical areas and the selection of movement: A study with positron emission tomography. *Experimental Brain Research*, *84*, 393–402.

Duncan, J., & Owen, A. M. (2000). Common regions of the human frontal lobe recruited by diverse cognitive demands. *Trends Neuroscience*, *23*, 475–483.

Folk, C. L., & Remington, R. (2006). Top-down modulation of preattentive processing: Testing the recovery account of contingent capture. *Visual Cognition*, *14*, 445–465.

Folk, C. L., Remington, R. W., & Johnston, J. C. (1992). Involuntary covert orienting is contingent on attentional control settings. *Journal of Experimental Psychology: Human Perception and Performance*, *18*, 1030–1044.

Hazeltine, E., Bunge, S. A., Scanlon, M. D., & Gabrieli, J. D. E. (2003). Material-dependent and material-independent selection processes in the frontal and parietal lobes: An event-related fMRI investigation of response competition. *Neuropsychologia*, *41*, 1208–1217.

Lavie, N. (2000). Selective attention and cognitive control: Dissociating attentional functions through different types of load. In S. Monsell & J. Driver (Eds.), *Attention and performance XVIII: Control of cognitive performance* (pp. 175–194). Cambridge, MA: MIT Press.

Lavie, N & de Fockert, J. (2005). The role of working memory in attentional capture. *Psychonomic Bulletin and Review*, *12*, 669–674.

Lavie, N., Hirst, A., de Fockert, J., & Viding, E. (2004). Load theory of selective attention and cognitive control. *Journal of Experimental Psychology: General*, *133*, 339–354.

Schumacher, E. H., & D'Esposito, M. (2002). Neural implementation of response selection in humans as revealed by localized effects of stimulus–response compatibility on brain activation. *Human Brain Mapping*, *17*, 193–201.

Talairach, J., & Tournoux, P. (1988). *Co-planar stereotaxic atlas of the human brain*. New York: Thieme Medical.

Theeuwes, J. (1991). Cross-dimensional perceptual selectivity. *Perception and Psychophysics*, *50*, 184–193.

Theeuwes, J. (1992). Perceptual selectivity for color and form. *Perception and Psychophysics*, *51*, 599–606.

Theeuwes, J. (1994). Stimulus-driven capture and attentional set: Selective search for color and visual abrupt onsets. *Journal of Experimental Psychology: Human Perception and Performance*, *20*, 799–806.

Theeuwes, J. (1996). Perceptual selectivity for color and form: On the nature of the interference effect. In A. Kramer, M. Coles, & G. Logan (Eds.), *Converging operations in the study of selective visual attention* (pp. 297–314). Washington, DC: American Psychological Association.

Theeuwes, J., Reimann, B., & Mortier, K. (2006). Visual search for featural singletons: No top-down modulation, only bottom-up priming. *Visual Cognition, 14,* 466–489.

Treisman, A. (1988). Features and objects: The fourteenth Bartlett Memorial Lecture. *Quarterly Journal of Experimental Psychology, 40A,* 201–237.

Van Oostende, S., van Hecke, P., Sunaert, S., Nuttin, B., & Marchal, G. (1997). FMRI studies of the supplementary motor area and the premotor cortex. *NeuroImage, 6,* 181–190.

Wojciulik, E., & Kanwisher, N. (1999). The generality of parietal involvement in visual attention. *Neuron, 23,* 747–764.

Yantis, S. (2000). Control of visual attention. In S. Monsell & J. Driver (Eds.), *Attention and performance XVIII: Control of cognitive performance* (pp. 71–208). Cambridge, MA: MIT Press.

Yantis, S., & Jonides, J. (1990). Abrupt visual onsets and selective attention: Voluntary versus automatic allocation. *Journal of Experimental Psychology: Human Perception and Performance, 16,* 121–134.

Zysset, S., Müller, K., Lohmann, G., & von Cramon, D. Y. (2001). Color–word matching Stroop task: Separating interference and response conflict. *NeuroImage, 13,* 29–36.

VISUAL COGNITION, 2006, 14 (4/5/6/7/8), 877–897

Ψ **Psychology** Press
Taylor & Francis Group

Neural correlates of visual dimension weighting

Stefan Pollmann

Universität Leipzig, Tagesklinik für Kognitive Neurologie, Leipzig, Germany

Ralph Weidner

Forschungszentrum Jülich, Institut für Medizin, Jülich, Germany

Hermann J. Müller

Department Psychologie, Ludwig-Maximilians-Universität München, Munich, Germany

D. Yves von Cramon

Universität Leipzig, Tagesklinik für Kognitive Neurologie, and Max-Planck-Institute for Human Cognitive and Brain Sciences, Leipzig, Germany

In a series of functional magnetic resonance experiments, we have investigated the neural basis of attentional dimension weighting in crossdimensional singleton search. Previous studies led to the characterization of a frontoposterior network of brain areas, which in part overlaps with the frontoparietal network supporting overt and covert attention shifts, but also involves anterior prefrontal components, which are likely to be involved in the detection of change and the initiation and control of attention shifts. Although this frontoposterior network is characterized by transient dimension change-related activation, we present new evidence that the effect of attentional weighting of a target-defining dimension is a modulation of the visual input areas processing the attended dimension.

In visual search for salient singleton-feature items, search costs are observed when the feature by which the target differs from the nontarget objects on a given trial is defined in a different visual dimension to that on

Please address all correspondence to Prof. Dr. Stefan Pollmann, Otto-von-Guericke-Universität Magdeburg, Institut für Psychologie II, PF 4120, 39016 Magdeburg, Germany. E-mail: stefan.pollmann@nat.uni-magdeburg.de

This study was supported by the Deutsche Forschungsgemeinschaft (DFG grant FOR 309/3-1). We thank two anonymous reviewers for their helpful comments.

http://www.psypress.com/viscog   DOI: 10.1080/13506280500196142

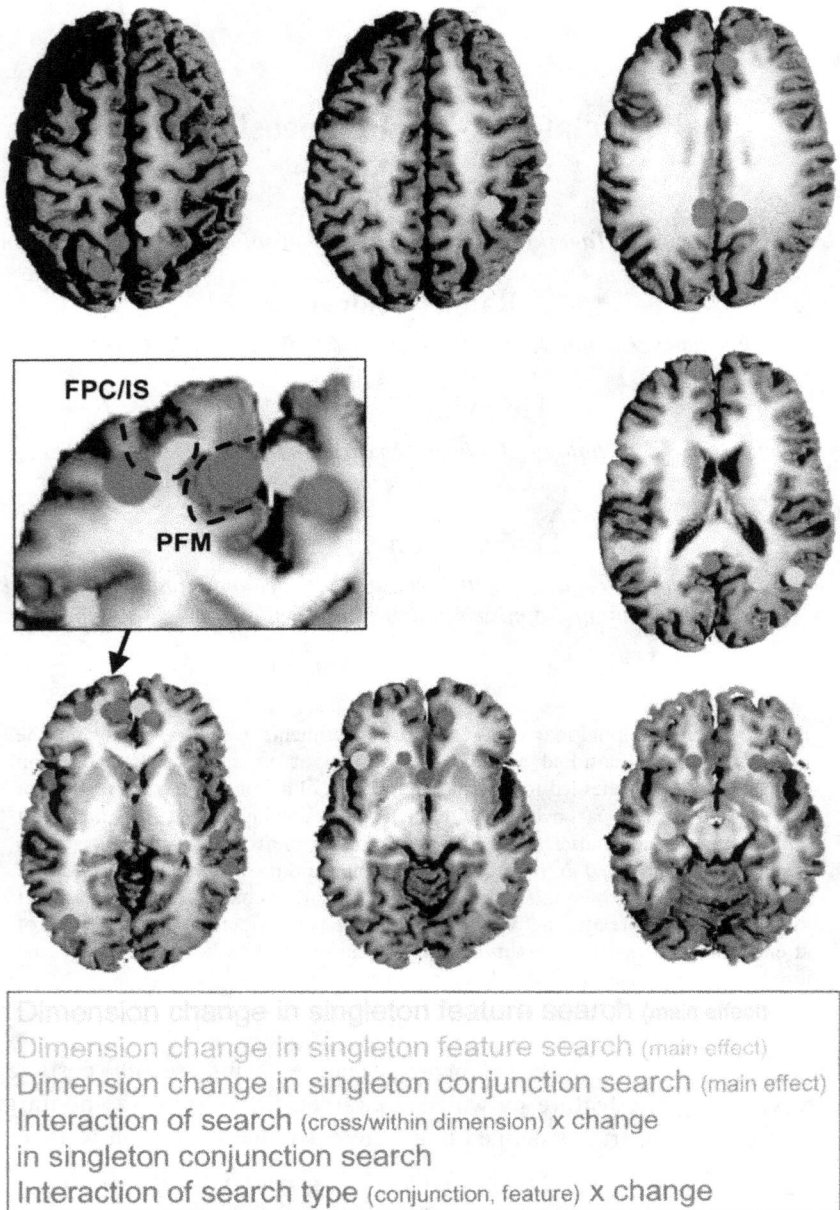

Dimension change in singleton feature search (main effect)
Dimension change in singleton feature search (main effect)
Dimension change in singleton conjunction search (main effect)
Interaction of search (cross/within dimension) x change
in singleton conjunction search
Interaction of search type (conjunction, feature) x change

Figure 1. (See opposite for caption).

the preceding trial (e.g., a colour-defined target following a motion-defined target; Found & Müller, 1996). In contrast, no such change costs are observed when the target is defined by a different feature within the same dimension (e.g., a red target following a blue target). To explain this pattern of results, Müller, Heller, and Ziegler (1995) proposed a "dimension-weighting" account, according to which there is a limit to the total amount of attention, or attentional weight (cf. Duncan & Humphreys, 1989), available to be allocated to objects' dimensions. Potential target-defining dimensions (i.e., dimensions in which the target might differ from the nontarget objects) are assigned weight in accordance with their variability across trials. Target detection is facilitated when attentional weight is allocated to the target-defining dimension to amplify the target's saliency signal generated within this dimension (cf. Cave & Wolfe, 1990; Wolfe, 1994). In the case of salient targets defined by a deviant single feature (as described above), the allocation of attention weight to the target-defining dimension is largely stimulus driven. Dimension changes incur a cost because they involve a shift of attention weight from the old to the new dimension. A more detailed account of the behavioural research on visual dimension weighting is presented by Müller and Krummenacher (2006 this issue).

Functional imaging of visual dimension weighting. In a series of event-related functional magnetic resonance imaging (fMRI) studies, we have investigated the neural basis of attentional changes between visual dimensions (Pollmann, Weidner, Müller, & von Cramon, 2000, 2006; Weidner, Pollmann, Müller, & von Cramon, 2002). In this paper, we review the central findings from these studies and present new data on the attentional modulation of dimension-specific visual input areas during visual singleton-feature search across target-defining dimensions. Figure 1 gives an overview of the dimension change-related activation patterns.

Figure 1 (opposite). Overview of activation patterns obtained in our series of event-related fMRI experiments on visual dimension weighting. For singleton feature searches, the main effect of dimension change is represented by yellow (Pollmann et al., 2000) and, respectively, blue spots (Pollmann et al., 2006). For singleton conjunction search, the main effect of dimension change is represented by green spots and the interaction Dimension change (present, absent) × Search type (cross-dimension, within-dimension) by purple spots (Weidner et al., 2002, Exp. 1). The interaction Search task (singleton feature, singleton conjunction) × Dimension change (present, absent) is represented by red spots (Weidner et al., Exp. 2). The spots are centred on the points of maximum activation. The maximum is set to a standard value for all loci, rather than representing the actual activation strengths. Inserted is an enlarged view of left anterior prefrontal cortex (FPC/IS: Frontopolar cortex/intermediate sulcus; PFM: Pregenual frontomedian cortex).

FRONTOPOSTERIOR NETWORK ACTIVATED DURING DIMENSION CHANGES

In our first fMRI study on visual dimension weighting, we investigated the network of brain areas involved in visual dimension changes (Pollmann et al., 2000). Participants performed visual singleton-feature searches while lying in the magnetic resonance tomograph. One goal of this study was to measure phasic activation increases related to changes in the target-defining dimension from the previous to the current trial. Such phasic dimension change-related increases in the blood-oxygenation-level-dependent (BOLD) response were observed in a number of brain areas across the cerebral cortex. This network consisted of many areas that have consistently been reported to be involved in visual search or shifts of visual attention, including visual areas of the occipital lobe in fusiform gyrus, lateral occipital gyri, and cuneus; precuneus, superior parietal lobule, and supramarginal gyrus in the parietal lobe; and middle temporal gyrus and posterior superior temporal sulcus in the temporal lobe. One major component of the frontoparietal network, the frontal eye fields, though displaying activity in comparison of search trials versus fixation, has consistently failed to show dimension change-related activation in our studies. This may indicate that FEF supports visuospatial, rather than dimensional, attention changes. In addition, we found change-related activation in left frontopolar cortex and, less pronounced, in pregenual frontomedian cortex at the rostral border of anterior cingulate cortex.

These data indicated that a large part of the network that supports visual search and covert as well as overt visual attention shifts (e.g., Corbetta et al., 1998; Donner et al., 2002; Gitelman et al., 1999; Kastner, Pinsk, de Weerd, Desimone, & Ungerleider, 1999; Müller et al. 2003; Nobre et al., 1997; Pollmann & von Cramon, 2000) was phasically involved in visual dimension changes. In addition, anterior prefrontal areas, which were not typically found to be involved in visual attention shifts, were also involved in visual dimension changes (see Pollmann, 2001, 2004, for a detailed discussion of the contribution of anterior prefrontal cortex to visual dimension weighting). The finding that a large-scale network, particularly including prefrontal cortex, which is usually related to executive functions, was activated by visual dimension changes was nontrivial, as the task to be performed was efficient, "pop-out", search of singleton-feature targets. However, the increased neural change-related activity indirectly measured by the change-related BOLD-signal increases paralleled the increased search reaction times (RTs) manifest when the target-defining dimension changed (rather than remaining the same) from the previous to the current trial.

These dimension change costs occurred despite the fact that the target-defining dimension was irrelevant for the response, which was simply to elicit a speeded target-present versus target-absent reaction regardless of the target-defining dimension. Furthermore, the costs occurred despite the targets being highly salient, so that attentional weighting of the target-defining dimension may not have been strictly necessary for detection (although weighting did make search more efficient when the target dimension remained the same across successive trials). In this situation, changes in the attentional weight setting are likely to be driven externally by changes in the target-defining dimension, rather than internally by intention. In two further experiments, we examined a task that involved endogenously controlled changes in dimensional weighting, and compared the neural networks supporting endogenously and exogenously driven changes (Weidner et al., 2002).

ENDOGENOUSLY CONTROLLED VISUAL DIMENSION WEIGHTING

Endogenously controlled dimension weighting was investigated in a singleton conjunction search task that followed the same logic as the singleton feature search used by Pollmann et al. (2000). The target was defined by the conjunction of a feature in a constant, primary dimension (always size) and a feature in a variable, secondary dimension (colour or motion). In contrast to singleton feature search, singleton conjunction search was inefficient, indicated by slow search RTs. Singleton conjunction search led, again in contrast to singleton feature search, to increased activation along the superior frontal sulcus, dominantly in the right hemisphere. The major difference in the change-related activation elicited by both experiments was a double dissociation between a change-related increase of frontopolar activation in singleton feature, but not singleton conjunction search, and the reverse, a selective dimension change-related activation in singleton conjunction, but not singleton feature search, in pregenual frontomedian cortex (Weidner et al., 2002; indicated by the red spots in Figure 1). In more posterior brain areas, dimension change-related activation was elicited mostly within the same anatomical structures in both types of task. Posterior parietal activation, however, reflected more general (rather than specifically dimension) change-related processes, evidenced by comparable activations related to dimension changes and intradimensional feature changes (Weidner et al., 2002).

We hypothesized that the prefrontal areas activated following dimension changes, the left frontopolar cortex and the pregenual frontomedian cortex, were involved in the control of attentional weight shifting between visual dimensions and that high-level "visual" areas in parietal and temporal cortices mediate these attention shifts via feedback to dimension-specific visual input areas.

MODULATION OF DIMENSION-SPECIFIC VISUAL INPUT AREAS

The dimension-weighting account postulates that a change in the target-defining dimension initiates a shift in the allocation of attention from the old to the new dimension (Found & Müller, 1996). Accordingly, we expected to see a modulation of the activation in visual input modules for the target-defining dimensions colour and motion. In our first experiment, we observed such an attentional modulation in that the activation increased in bilateral fusiform foci when the participants attended to colour as the target-defining dimension (Pollmann et al., 2000). The location of the activation focus was concordant with previous reports of area V4, which is involved in colour processing (e.g., McKeefry & Zeki, 1997; for a review, see Bartels & Zeki, 2000). When targets were instead defined by motion direction, an increase in activation was observed in lateral occipital cortex (dominantly on the right) at locations in the vicinity of the human MT + complex (hMT +),[1] which responds to moving stimuli (e.g., Beauchamp, Cox, & DeYoe, 1997). Thus, attending to colour or motion led to increased activation in brain areas that are involved in processing the respective target-defining visual dimension.

These attentional modulations of V4 and hMT + activity were obtained in a comparison of experimental blocks in which the targets were constantly defined within a given visual dimension: Colour in one block, motion in the other (see also Corbetta, Miezin, Dobmeier, Shulman, & Petersen, 1991). The dimension-weighting account, however, assumes a shift of attentional weight from the old to the new dimension, which starts with a change in the target-defining dimension (e.g., from colour to motion) and then persists across trials until the next dimension change (from motion to colour). To investigate attentional dimension weighting in crossdimensional search, the data of a new fMRI experiment were analysed for evidence of attentional modulation in dimension-specific visual input modules. Unlike the previous studies, the present experiment used a "compound" search task in which participants had to detect the presence of a singleton colour or, respectively, motion target in the display, but give a two-alternative forced-choice response based on a form feature of the target (i.e., the information required for the response was independent of that required for detecting the target).

---

[1] The term hMT + indicates that the human activation data may represent area MT or other motion processing areas, such as MST, hence MT +.

Krummenacher, Müller, and Heller (2002) had shown that the typical dimension change effects (cf. Found & Müller, 1996) are also obtained in compound tasks, although they are reduced relative to simple detection tasks. The advantage of using a compound task for the purposes of the present experiment was that no target-absent trials were required. This permitted not only an event-related analysis of target dimension change versus no-change trials, but also an analysis of trial "epochs" (uninterrupted by target-absent events) with colour targets versus "epochs" with motion targets.

METHODS

Participants

Twenty-one observers (nine female) took part in a single fMRI experimental session. They ranged between 21 and 37 years in age, with a mean age of 26.4 years. All observers were right-handed, as assessed by the Edinburgh Handedness Inventory (Oldfield, 1971). The fMRI procedures were approved by the University of Leipzig ethics committee. All observers gave prior written informed consent according to the guidelines of the Max Planck Institute.

Stimuli, task, design, and procedure

Stimuli were displayed by an LCD projector on a back-projection screen mounted in the bore of the magnet behind the participant's head. Participants viewed the screen wearing mirror glasses, which were equipped with corrective lenses if necessary.

The fMRI session began with the presentation of a 30 s fixation period, followed by the presentation of 624 experimental trials, and ending with a 30 s fixation period. Trial duration was 1.5 s. Each trial began with the presentation of a search display. The display was terminated by the participant's response or after a maximum duration of 1.5 s. A white fixation cross was displayed during the intertrial interval, which was, variably, 0, 500, or 1000 ms in duration. The experiment used a 2×2 factorial design, with the factors dimension change (yes/no) and response change (yes/no). Trials from each of the four cells of the design matrix were presented with a probability of .2, the remaining trials were null events, that is, fixation periods of the same length as the experimental trials. The order of events, including null events, was determined using maximum-length shift register sequences (m-sequences; for a detailed description, see Buracas & Boynton, 2002), which counterbalance subsequences of a given length in order to ensure that trials from each condition were preceded equally often by trials from each of the other conditions.

The visual search displays consisted of 25 triangles on a black background. The stimuli were arranged in a grid-like pattern, covering an area of $13° \times 13°$ of visual angle. Each triangle pointed randomly in one of two directions, equally often to the left and the right (Figure 2). All stimuli moved sinusoidally along the horizontal axis (maximum amplitude $=0.2°$, speed $=1.2°/s$). Each search display contained a singleton pop-out target, which was equally likely to be defined by a unique colour relative to the nontargets (a red horizontally moving triangle among green horizontally moving triangles) or by a unique motion direction (a green triangle moving along an oblique axis tilted oriented $+45°$ from the horizontal among horizontally moving green triangles).

Participants were asked to give a speeded forced-choice response, indicating the pointing direction of the target triangle, using their right-hand index (left button) or middle finger (right button).

fMRI measurement.

Functional images were collected at 3T by a Bruker 30/100 Medspec system (Bruker Medizintechnik, Ettlingen, Germany), using a gradient echo EPI sequence (TR $=2000$ ms, TE $=30$ ms, flip angle $=90°$). Twenty axial slices were acquired parallel to the AC-PC plane, allowing for whole brain coverage. Slice thickness was 4 mm and interslice distance 1 mm, with a 19.2 cm FOV and a 64×64 image matrix. Data were analysed using the LIPSIA software package (Lohmann et al., 2001). Slice acquisition time differences were corrected by sinc interpolation. Movement artefacts were corrected using a matching metric based on linear correlation. Baseline drifts were corrected by high-pass filtering, implemented using a discrete Fourier transform with an individually tailored cutoff period of five times the mean temporal distance between trials of the same experimental condition. In the spatial domain, the data were filtered using a Gaussian filter with FWHM $=$ 7 mm. Following this preprocessing, the functional data sets were coregistered with the individual participants' high-resolution anatomical data sets and normalized by linear scaling. Data were analysed using the general linear model (Friston et al., 1995). Epoch-based analyses were performed using a half-sine fixed response model. The beginning of colour epochs was defined by a change from motion to colour as the target-defining dimension (i.e., the onset of a search display containing a colour-defined target when the previous trial contained a motion-defined target). Colour epochs ended at the next change from colour to motion (i.e., the onset of a display with a motion-defined target following a display with a colour-defined target).

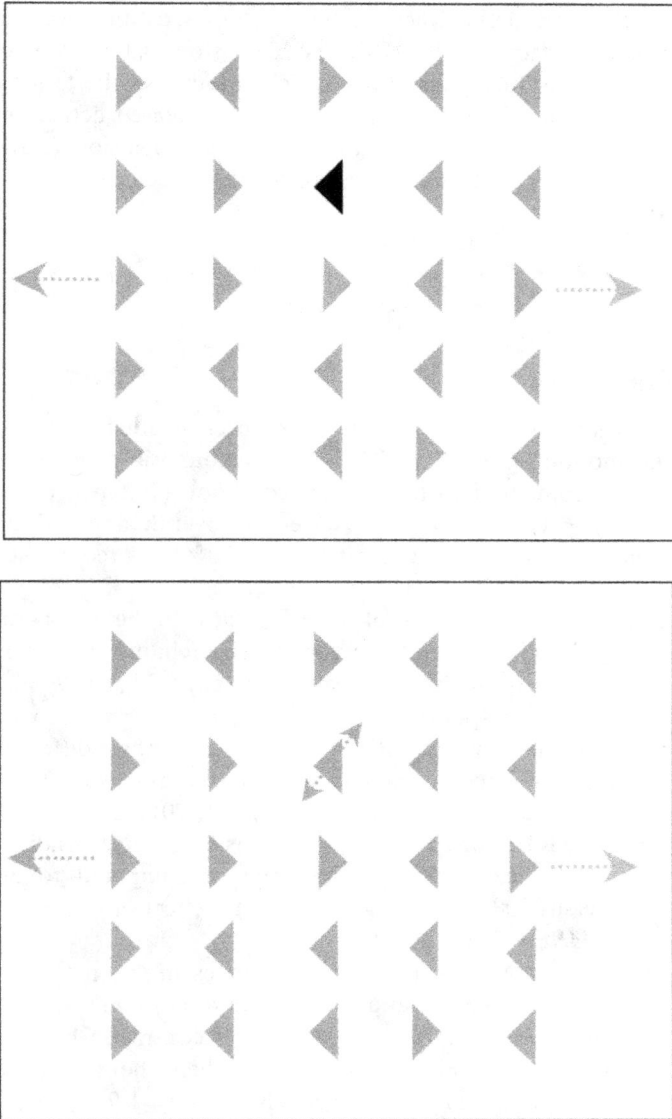

Figure 2. Search displays. Search displays consisted of a matrix of 25 (i.e., 5 × 5) triangles that pointed randomly to the left or right. In each display, one triangle, the target, differed from the others, the distractors, either by its colour (red, indicated by black in the figure, as compared to green, indicated by grey) or its direction (axis) of sinusoidal motion (45° oblique as compared to horizontal). Participants had to detect the odd-one-out target triangle and make a button press response indicating the target's pointing direction (left or right).

Motion epochs were defined accordingly. Group activation was calculated using a random-effects model (Holmes & Friston, 1998). We tested for increased activation during epochs in which colour was the target-defining dimension in the posterior fusiform gyrus and increased activation during epochs in which motion was the target-defining dimension in the lateral occipital gyrus. The significance criterion for these region-of-interest (ROI) analyses was $\alpha = .01$.

RESULTS

Behavioural data

Reaction times (RTs) and error rates have been evaluated separately for colour- and motion-target trials. RTs for the colour trials were significantly faster (700 ms) compared to the motion condition (722 ms); paired t-test: $t(2) = 4.0831$, $p < .001$. Error rates were low overall and did not differ between conditions (colour = 3.5%; motion = 3.1%); paired t-test: $t(20) = -0.4295$, ns.

A repeated-measures ANOVA of the RT data, with the factors dimension change (change, no change) and response change (change, no change), only revealed the interaction to be significant, $F(1, 20) = 7.6$, $MSE = 2366$, $p < .05$. Collapsed across response change conditions, there was no significant RT increase for trials on which the target dimension changed (relative to the preceding trial) compared to no-change trials, 713 versus 709 ms (non-significant main effect of dimension change), $F(1, 20) = 2.8$, $MSE = 278.55$, $p > .05$. Likewise, RTs, collapsed across dimension change conditions, were not significantly increased for response change compared to no-change trials, 714 ms versus 708 ms (nonsignificant main effect of response change), $F(1, 20) = 3.3$, $MSE = 722.3$, $p > .05$.

In the absence of a response change, changes in the target dimension significantly slowed RTs (715 and 701 ms for dimension change and no-change trials, respectively), $t(20) = 2.8$, $p < .05$; in contrast, when there was a response change, RTs tended to be faster when the target dimension changed, too (710 and 717 ms, respectively), $t(20) = 1.97$, $p = .06$. In the absence of a dimension change, changes in the response significantly slowed RTs (717 and 701 ms for response change and no-change trials, respectively), $t(20) = 3.3$, $p < .01$; however, when there was a dimension change, RTs were somewhat, though not significantly faster when the response changed as well (710 and 715 ms for response change and no-change trials, respectively), $t(19) = 0.93$, $p > .05$. This interactive pattern of dimension change and response change effects is robust: The same pattern was observed in a reanalysis of the compound-task RT data of Krummenacher et al. (2002; see Müller & Krummenacher, 2006 this issue).

Error rates were low overall (3.2%). In order to rule out that the RT effects were due to speed–accuracy tradeoffs, the error data were examined by an analogous, Dimension change (change, no change) × Response change (change, no change), ANOVA. This ANOVA revealed only the interaction to be significant: Dimension change, $F(1, 20) = 0.63$, $MSE = 0.01$, ns; response change, $F(1, 20) = 0.031$, $MSE = 0.004$, ns; Dimension change × Response change, $F(1, 20) = 7.46$, $MSE = 0.21$, $p < .05$. In the absence of a response change, there was a trend towards higher error rates on dimension change compared to no-change trials (3.5% vs. 2.8%), $t(20) = 1.78$, $p = .9$; in the presence of response change, there were significantly lower error rates on dimension change trials (2.7% vs. 3.9%), $t(20) = 2.51$, $p < .05$. This pattern of error effects reinforces the RT effects.

Functional-imaging data

In order to investigate the attentional modulation in extrastriate visual areas processing colour and motion, we compared the activation in epochs with colour as the target-defining dimension to the activation in epochs with motion as the target dimension. To increase the power of the comparisons, we focused on two regions of interest (ROIs) that we had previously observed to exhibit attentional modulation in singleton feature search (Pollmann et al., 2000). One of these areas was the posterior fusiform gyrus, which contains the human area V4 (our previous activations for sustained attention at $x = -23$, $y = -64$, $z = -7$, and $x = 22$, $y = -76$, $z = -16$, corresponding to the location of posterior V4, according to Bartels & Zeki, 2000); the other one was an area in lateral occipital cortex, around the bifurcation of the inferior temporal sulcus in its ascending and posterior descending limbs, which contains the hMT+ complex (Dumoulin et al., 2000). Previously, we found activations for sustained attention to motion somewhat more anteriorly at $x = 41$, $y = -52$, $z = -2$ (Pollmann et al., 2000). Note, though, that Beauchamp et al. (1997), reviewing fMRI studies of motion processing, reported a more posterior average location of hMT+ at $x = +/-42$, $y = -70$, $z = -3$.

We expected increased activation during colour epochs in posterior fusiform gyrus and increased activation during motion epochs in lateral occipital cortex. In line with our expectations, we found a significantly increased activation during colour epochs compared to motion epochs in the right posterior fusiform gyrus bordering the collateral sulcus ($x = 13$, $y = -89$, $z = -3$; $Z_{max} = 2.58$; Figure 3). Motion epochs exhibited increased

Colour - Motion:

a)

Motion – Colour:

b)

2 ▬▬ 4

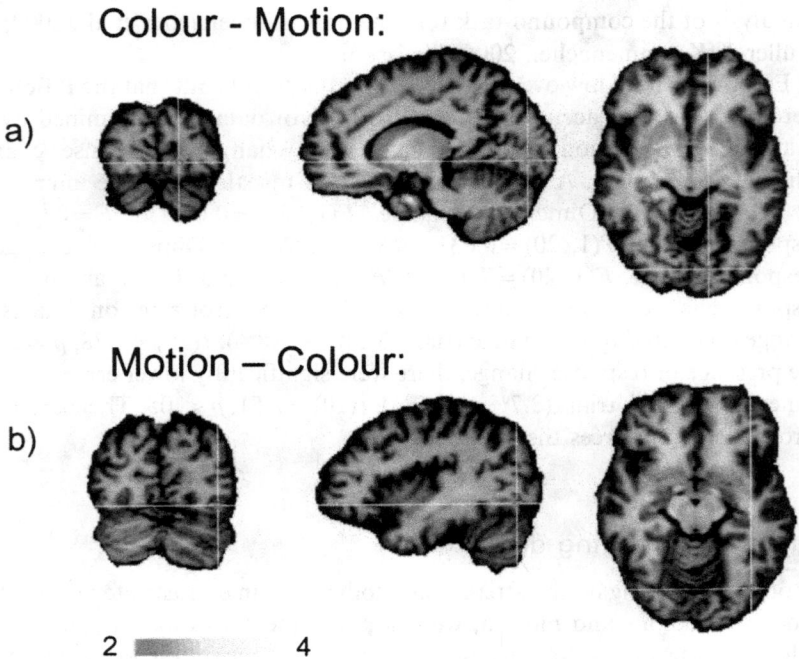

Figure 3. (a) Increased activation for epochs with colour as the target-defining dimension compared to motion as the target-defining dimension in right fusiform gyrus ($x = 13$, $y = -89$, $z = -3$: coordinates of Talairach & Tournoux, 1998). (b) Increased activation for epochs with motion as the target-defining dimension compared to colour as the target-defining dimension in right lateral occipital gyrus ($x = 37$, $y = -78$, $z = -8$). The colour scale of the activation overlays represents z-values. Left hemisphere is on the left.

activation compared to colour epochs in lateral occipital cortex at $x = 37$, $y = -78$, $z = -8$ ($Z_{max} = 2.41$).

The analyses of dimension-change versus response-change-related imaging data are presented in a separate paper (Pollmann et al., 2006).

DISCUSSION

The interaction of anterior prefrontal cortices and visual posterior areas, presumably mediated by frontoparietal and frontotemporal back projections, is of great interest for understanding the neural basis of visual attention. In previous studies, we described a frontoposterior network of brain areas that was phasically active during changes of the target-defining dimension in visual singleton search. In the following sections, we will discuss the evidence revealed in the present study on visual dimension weighting in occipital areas for colour and motion processing, and go on to consider the frontoposterior network involved in visual dimension weighting and possible contributions of its component structures. A schematic representation of this network is given in Figure 4, and Figure 1 provides a summary of our imaging data on visual dimension weighting.

One central finding of our previous studies was that, in addition to the frontoparietal network supporting visual search and covert visual attention shifts, frontopolar areas exhibited dimension change-related activation. Specifically, in singleton feature search, dimension changes were associated with increased left lateral frontopolar activation in the vicinity of the intermediate frontal/frontomarginal sulcus; in contrast, in singleton conjunction search, dimension changes were associated with pregenually located frontomedian activation. In both types of search task, dimension changes resulted in RT costs, which, on the dimension-weighting account, reflect the reallocation of attentional weight from the old to the new target-defining dimension. However, these weight shifts are induced in different ways in the two tasks. In singleton feature search, the change in the target-defining dimension is triggered by the salient target itself. By contrast, in singleton conjunction search, the dimension change proceeds under top-down control, when the search process fails to discern the presence of a target in the previously weighted (secondary) dimension.

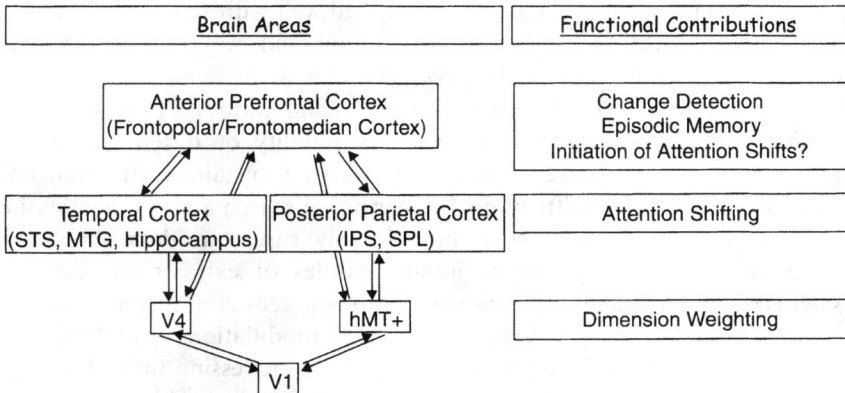

Figure 4. Schematic illustration of the dimension-weighting network. Core anatomical structures activated during visual dimension changes are shown on the left, putative associated functions on the right. The arrows between boxes indicate potential bottom-up and recurrent connections between areas. Due to the complexity of the network, the indicated connectivity is unlikely to be complete. STS: Superior temporal sulcus; MTG: Middle temporal gyrus; IPS: Intraparietal sulcus; SPL: Superior parietal lobule; hMT+: Human MT+ complex.

The present study

The present results provide further evidence for the dimension-weighting account. Both electrophysiological work in the monkey and human imaging studies have shown that attending to a location, stimulus feature, or object may lead to a modulation of activity in visual cortex (for a recent review, see Treue, 2003). In our previous experiments, we have observed a signal increase in the fusiform gyri at the location of human posterior V4 when colour was the target-defining dimension throughout a block of trials, and in lateral occipital gyrus, somewhat anterior to the human MT+ complex, when motion was the target-defining dimension (Pollmann et al., 2000).

These modulations of activation, however, may have been due to sustained attention over whole blocks of trials, rather than shifts of attention from the old to the new target-defining dimension in crossdimensional search, as postulated by the dimension weighting account. Therefore, in the present experiment, we compared the activation obtained during epochs in crossdimensional search in which successive targets were defined in the colour versus the motion dimension. We observed increased activation in right posterior fusiform gyrus when colour, rather than motion, was the target-defining dimension. The reverse pattern, increased activation during motion epochs compared to colour epochs, was observed in right lateral occipital gyrus. The fusiform signal increase during colour epochs was located slightly posterior to the location of posterior V4 according to a review of colour processing studies (Bartels & Zeki, 2000). The signal increase during motion-defined epochs agreed well with previous reports of the location of hMT+. However, both colour and motion-related activations were located more posteriorly than the activations we previously observed for sustained attention to colour and motion. It is not clear whether this merely reflects anatomical variability or differences in the experimental design between studies, or whether sustained attention and attentional dimension shifts in crossdimensional search activate neighbouring, but distinct neuronal ensembles. In any case, our data show that activation in dimension-specific input modules of extrastriate cortex is systematically modulated depending on the target-defining dimension in crossdimensional singleton feature search. The modulations were dimension specific and did not reflect general influences of processing time. Although responses were overall faster to colour than to motion targets, the signal increases for colour targets in the fusiform and for motion targets in the lateral occipital gyri were symmetric. This pattern of modulations is may be taken to support the dimension-weighting account, according to which a change in the target-defining dimension entails a shift of attention from the old to the new target-defining dimension.

One possible objection is that, in principle, the activation differences between colour and motion epochs may reflect bottom-up effects resulting from the presence of colour and, respectively, motion singletons in the two types of epoch. This is unlikely, however, because the search displays used in the present experiment provided strong inputs into both colour and motion processing areas: Participants were exposed to the onset of 25 coloured triangles (all green, except for one possible red singleton) that were all moving sinusoidally (all oscillating along the horizontal axis, except for one possible diagonally moving singleton). Given the massive colour and motion signals produced by the 25 display elements, it is unlikely that the presence of a colour or motion singleton exerted a major impact on the bottom-up activation of V4 or hMT+. This reasoning is supported by the fact that we failed to observe any change-related activation differences when we investigated different singleton targets within the same dimension, although the target colour or motion changed (red and blue targets in the presence of green distractors and left and right diagonally moving targets in the presence of horizontally moving distractors; Pollmann et al., 2000) which might have led to stimulus-induced activation changes in V4 or hMT+.

Each trial contained a target, either defined by a singleton colour or motion. This means that, according to the dimension-weighting account, attention was constantly allocated either to the colour or motion dimension. This means that we cannot distinguish whether increased activation in V4 and hMT+ was due to signal increase when attention was allocated to the preferred dimension, signal decreases when attention was directed at the alternative dimension, or a mixture of both. Future experiments may clarify this issue by introducing a third condition, e.g., orientation-defined targets, in which attention is withdrawn from both colour and motion.

Anatomical connectivity and recurrent processing

Neuroanatomical connectivity studies have revealed long connections from the prefrontal cortex to reach the posterior parietal cortex, the temporal lobe (superior, inferior temporal regions, and the superior temporal sulcus) and the paralimbic areas (Pandya, Dye, & Butters, 1971). In monkeys, ventral BA10 (which includes the site of frontopolar dimension change-related activation in our studies with humans) is connected with visual association area VA2 (Pandya & Yeterian, 1985). Since the human homologue of VA2 is not known, one can only speculate that the posterior fusiform and lateral occipital gyri are part of it and target sites of back projections from the frontopolar region. It is, at least, plausible that back projections from frontopolar regions are targeted to second- and third-order, rather than first-order, visual association cortices.

It is well established that long association connections from frontal and parietal cortices to extrastriate visual areas are involved in visual attention (Felleman & van Essen, 1991; Lewis & van Essen, 2000). Electrophysiological and human imaging studies have shown these reciprocal connections to be used for both bottom-up and top-down processing within the context of selective attention (Hochstein & Ahissar, 2002; Lamme & Roelfsema, 2000; Noesselt et al., 2002). The rapid interplay between bottom-up and top-down processes is difficult to analyse noninvasively in the human brain, because of temporal limitations with fMRI and uncertainties with localizing the sources of electrical and magnetic encephalographic signals.

Dimension change processes and dimension-specific processing

However, in our fMRI studies of visual dimension weighting, we found two temporally distinct response patterns. A large frontoposterior network, extending from frontopolar cortex via higher order visual association cortices to extrastriate visual cortex, was phasically activated following visual dimension changes. This dimension change-related activation pattern (which is accompanied by an increase in search RTs) indicates a transient increase in neural activity that, according to the dimension-weighting account, reflects a process of reallocating attention from the old to the new dimension. The second activation pattern, revealed in the present study, varies on a slower timescale, in that activation increased when colour became the target-defining dimension and remained at an increased level until the next motion-defined target was presented. This activation was observed in posterior fusiform and lateral occipital gyri and is likely to reflect the outcome of the dimension-weighting process: Increased activation in a colour-sensitive visual area for the duration of the period in which colour was the target-defining, attended dimension and increased activation in a motion-sensitive area when motion was the target-defining dimension.

It is more difficult to distinguish the contributions of the component areas within the dimension change-related network. However, among the areas with a change-related signal increase, one can distinguish between those areas that belong to the well-described frontoparietal network subserving shifts of visual attention and visual search (Corbetta et al. 1998; Donner et al., 2002; Gitelman et al., 1999; Müller et al., 2003; Nobre et al., 1997; Pollmann & von Cramon, 2000; Pollmann et al., 2000; Weidner et al., 2002) and those that do not belong to this network. It is likely that the former areas, in particular, those along the intraparietal sulcus and in the superior parietal lobule, are involved in executing shifts of attention between visual dimensions (Corbetta & Shulman, 2002; Yantis et al., 2002), which give rise to increased activation in visual input areas that analyse the attended dimension.

Role of anterior prefrontal cortex in dimension weighting

One question remains: What is the functional significance of the dimension change-related activation in those areas that do not belong to the traditional frontoparietal network subserving visual attention, specifically the left frontopolar cortex in the case of stimulus-triggered dimension changes and pregenual frontomedian cortex in the case of top-down controlled changes?

A potential contribution of frontopolar cortex to visual dimension weighting may be the detection of task-relevant changes under conditions of stimulus ambiguity. Anterior prefrontal activation has also been observed in other paradigms that involve a component of uncertainty, for example, with ambiguous target-defining dimensions in the Wisconsin Card Sorting Test (WCST; Grant & Berg, 1948; Rogers, Andrews, Grasby, Brooks, & Robbins, 2000; see also Nagahama et al., 2001, who differentiated changes related to the stimulus dimension, which involved anterior prefrontal cortex, from switches of stimulus–response associations, which activated posterior prefrontal cortex) and ambiguous word primes in cued recall (Henson, Shallice, Josephs, & Dolan., 2002). Taken together, this evidence suggests that anterior prefrontal cortex is involved in the search for relevant information under conditions of uncertainty. Selection of relevant information under uncertainty may also be a contributing factor to the real-world problems in planning and execution of multiple task sequences (Burgess, Veitch, de Lacy Costello, & Shallice, 2000; Goel, Grafman, Tajik, Gana, & Danto, 1997) and prospective memory (Burgess, Quayle, & Frith, 2001) in patients with anterior prefrontal lesions.

Note that our participants were not explicitly instructed to switch attention or respond in any specific way to visual dimension changes. Rather, dimension weighting seems to take place implicitly when the target-defining dimension changes (see also Müller, Krummenacher, & Heller, in press). Shifting attentional weight from the old to the new target-defining dimension may not be strictly necessary, given the "pop-out" character of the targets. But such weight shifts can be advantageous, expediting detection RTs on dimension repetition, relative to dimension change, trials. However, in order to initiate an attention shift, the task-relevant change in the display, in our case, in the target-defining dimension, must be registered first, and this requires the (episodic) comparison of stimulus attributes, in our case, the colour and movement direction of the singleton, between the current trial and the previous trial. There is evidence that frontopolar cortex plays a role in this process.

Frontopolar cortex is reliably activated during retrieval from long-term memory (Christoff & Gabrieli, 2000; Rugg & Wilding, 2000), which is an important prerequisite for an episodic comparison of present and past trials. A comparison between previous and current stimulus attributes may be especially important in tasks that permit (semi-)automatic processing, in order to maintain the flexibility to respond adequately to changes in the environment. Such a comparison depends on what has been termed "source memory"—the memory under what circumstances a particular item was encoded. Recently, Dobbins, Foley, Schacter, and Wagner (2002) reported left frontopolar cortex (though more lateral and inferior than the activations reviewed above) to support source memory selectively, whereas more posterior left inferior frontal areas exhibited activations related to both source and item memory. However, the task of Dobbins et al. required explicit recollection of the circumstances of encoding, in contrast to present visual singleton search task, which may be a reason for the differential locations of activation in frontopolar cortex between the two tasks. Nevertheless, the distinction between anterior inferior frontal activation (extending into frontopolar cortex) associated with source memory, and more posterior inferior frontal activation associated with both source and item memory is potentially important. It suggests that left anterior prefrontal cortex may have a specific role in episodic memory, which may be utilized for the control of attention whenever the task requires search for an ambiguously defined target, involving shifts of attention between visual dimensions.

CONCLUSION

Changes in the target-defining dimension in visual singleton search lead to a transient activation in an extensive frontoposterior network of brain areas. This network consists of areas in parietal and temporal cortex, that are known to support shifts of attention, and of anterior prefrontal areas, particularly the lateral frontopolar cortex ant the pregenual frontomedian cortex, that may be involved in the detection of change and the initiation and control of attention shifts. These attention shifts express themselves in terms of modulations in dimension-specific visual input areas, which take the form of an elevated activation that is maintained over trials as long as the target-defining dimension remains constant.

REFERENCES

Bartels, A., & Zeki, S. (2000). The architecture of the colour centre in the human visual brain: New results and a review. *European Journal of Neuroscience*, *12*, 172–193.

Beauchamp, M. S., Cox, R. W., & DeYoe, E. A. (1997). Graded effects of spatial and featural attention on human area MT and associated motion processing areas. *Journal of Neurophysiology*, *78*(1), 516–520.

Buracas, G. T., & Boynton, G. M. (2002). Efficient design of event-related fMRI experiments using M-sequences. *Neuroimage*, *16*(3, Pt 1), 801–813.

Burgess, P. W., Quayle, A., & Frith, C. D. (2001). Brain regions involved in prospective memory as determined by positron emission tomography. *Neuropsychologia*, *39*(6), 545–555.

Burgess, P. W., Veitch, E., de Lacy Costello, A., & Shallice, T. (2000). The cognitive and neuroanatomical correlates of multitasking. *Neuropsychologia*, *38*, 848–863.

Cave, K. R., & Wolfe, J. M. (1990). Modelling the role of parallel processing in visual search. *Cognitive Psychology*, *22*, 225–271.

Christoff, K., & Gabrieli, J. D. E. (2000). The frontopolar cortex and human cognition: Evidence for a rostrocaudal hierarchical organization within the human prefrontal cortex. *Psychobiology*, *28*(2), 168–186.

Corbetta, M., Akbudak, E., Conturo, T. E., Snyder, A. Z., Ollinger, J. M., Drury, H. A., et al. (1998). A common network of functional areas for attention and eye movements. *Neuron*, *21*, 761–773.

Corbetta, M., Miezin, F. M., Dobmeier, S., Shulman, G. L., & Petersen, S. E. (1991). Selective and divided attention during visual discriminations of shape, colour, and speed: Functional anatomy by positron emission tomography. *Journal of Neuroscience*, *11*, 2383–2402.

Corbetta, M., & Shulman, G. L. (2002). Control of goal-directed and stimulus-driven attention in the brain. *Nature Reviews Neuroscience*, *3*, 201–215.

Dobbins, I. G., Foley, H., Schacter, D. L., & Wagner, A. D. (2002). Executive control during episodic retrieval: Multiple prefrontal processes subserve source memory. *Neuron*, *35*(5), 989–996.

Donner, T. H., Kettermann, A., Diesch, E., Ostendorf, F., Villringer, A., & Brandt, S. A. (2002). Visual feature and conjunction searches of equal difficulty engage only partially overlapping frontoparietal networks. *NeuroImage*, *15*, 16–25.

Dumoulin, S. O., Bittar, R. G., Kabani, N. J., Baker, C. L., Jr., Le Goualher, G., Bruce Pike, G., & Evans, A.C. (2000). A new anatomical landmark for reliable identification of human area V5/MT: A quantitative analysis of sulcal patterning. *Cerebral Cortex*, *10*, 454–463.

Duncan, J., & Humphreys, G. W. (1989). Visual search and stimulus similarity. *Psychological Review*, *96*, 433–458.

Felleman, D. J., & van Essen, D. C. (1991). Distributed hierarchical processing in the primate cerebral cortex. *Cerebral Cortex*, *1*, 1–47.

Found, A., & Müller, H. J. (1996). Searching for unknown feature targets on more than one dimension: Investigating a "dimension-weighting" account. *Perception and Psychophysics*, *58*, 88–101.

Friston, K. J., Holmes, A. P., Worsley, K. J., Poline, J. B., Frith, C. D., & Frackowiak, R. S. J. (1995). Statistical parametric maps in functional imaging: A general linear approach. *Human Brain Mapping*, *2*, 189–210.

Gitelman, D. I., Nobre, A. C., Parrish, T. B., LaBar, K. S., Kim, Y.-H., Meyer, J. R., & Mesulam, M. M. (1999). A large-scale distributed network for covert spatial attention. *Brain*, *122*, 1093–1106.

Goel, V., Grafman, J., Tajik, J., Gana, S., & Danto, D. (1997). A study of patients with frontal lobe lesions in a financial planning task. *Brain*, *120*, 1805–1822.

Grant, D. A., & Berg, E. A. (1948). A behavioural analysis of degree of reinforcement and ease of shifting to new responses in a Weigl-type card sorting problem. *Journal of Experimental Psychology*, *38*, 404–411.

Henson, R. N. A., Shallice, T., Josephs, O., & Dolan, R. J. (2002). Functional magnetic resonance imaging of proactive interference during spoken cued recall. *NeuroImage*, *17*, 543–558.

Hochstein, S., & Ahissar, M. (2002). View from the top: Hierarchies and reverse hierarchies in the visual system. *Neuron*, *36*, 791–804.

Holmes, A. P., & Friston, K. J. (1998). Generalizability, random effects, and population interference. *NeuroImage*, *7*, S754.

Kastner, S., Pinsk, M. A., de Weerd, P., Desimone, R., & Ungerleider, L. G. (1999). Increased activity in human visual cortex during directed attention in the absence of visual stimulation. *Neuron*, *22*, 751–761.

Krummenacher, J., Müller, H. J., & Heller, D. (2002). Visual search for dimensionally redundant pop-out targets: Redundancy gains in compound tasks. *Visual Cognition*, *9*, 801–837.

Lamme, V. A., & Roelfsema, P. R. (2000). The distinct modes of vision offered by feedforward and recurrent processing. *Trends in Neurosciences*, *23*, 571–579.

Lewis, J. W., & van Essen, D. C. (2000). Corticocortical connections of visual, sensorimotor, and multimodal processing areas in the parietal lobe of the macaque monkey. *Journal of Comparative Neurology*, *428*, 112–137.

Lohmann, G., Mueller, K., Bosch, V., Mentzel, H., Hessler, S., Chen, L., & von Cramon, D. Y. (2001). Lipsia: A new software system for the evaluation of functional magnetic resonance images of the human brain. *Computerized Medical Imaging and Graphics*, *25*(6), 449–457.

McKeefry, D. J., & Zeki, S. (1997). The position and topography of the human colour centre as revealed by functional magnetic resonance imaging. *Brain*, *120*, 2229–2242.

Müller, H. J., Heller, D., & Ziegler, J. (1995). Visual search for singleton feature targets within and across feature dimensions. *Perception and Psychophysics*, *57*, 1–17.

Müller, H. J., & Krummenacher, J. (2006). Locus of dimension weighting: Preattentive or postselective? *Visual Cognition*, *14*, 490–513.

Müller, H. J., Krummenacher, J., & Heller, D. (2004). Dimension-specific intertrial facilitation in visual search for pop-out targets: Evidence for a top-down modulable visual short-term memory effect. *Visual Cognition*, *11*, 577–602.

Müller, N., Donner, T. H., Bartelt, O. A., Brandt, S. A., Villringer, A., & Kleinschmidt, A. (2003). The functional neuroanatomy of visual conjunction search. *NeuroImage*, *20*, 1578–1590.

Nagahama, Y., Tomohisa, O., Katsumi, Y., Hayashi, T., Yamauchi, H., Oyanagi, C., et al. (2001). Dissociable mechanisms of attentional control within the human prefrontal cortex. *Cerebral Cortex*, *11*, 85–92.

Nobre, A. C., Sebestyen, G. N., Gitelman, D. R., Mesulam, M. M., Frackowiak, R. S., & Frith, C. D. (1997). Functional localization of the system for visuospatial attention using positron emission tomography. *Brain*, *120*, 515–533.

Noesselt, T., Hillyard, S. A., Woldorff, M. G., Schoenfeld, A., Hagner, T., Jäncke, L., et al. (2002). Delayed striate cortical activation during spatial attention. *Neuron*, *35*, 575–587.

Oldfield, R. C. (1971). The assessment and analysis of handedness: The Edinburgh inventory. *Neuropsychologia*, *9*, 97–113.

Pandya, D. N., Dye, P., & Butters, N. (1971). Efferent cortico-cortical projections of the prefrontal cortex of the rhesus monkey. *Brain Research*, *31*, 35–46.

Pandya, D. N., & Yeterian, E. H. (1985). Architecture and connections of cortical association areas. In A. Peters & E. G. Jones (Eds.), *Cerebral cortex: Vol. 4. Association and auditory cortices* (pp. 1–61). New York: Plenum Press.

Pollmann. S. (2001). Switching between dimensions, locations, and responses: The role of the left frontopolar cortex. *NeuroImage*, *14*, S118–S124.

Pollmann, S. (2004). Anterior prefrontal cortex contributions to attention control. *Experimental Psychology*, *51*, 270–278.

Pollmann, S., & von Cramon, D. Y. (2000). Object working memory and visuospatial processing: Functional neuroanatomy analyzed by event-related fMRI. *Experimental Brain Research*, *133*, 12–22.

Pollmann, S., Weidner, R., Müller, H. J., & von Cramon, D. Y. (2000). A fronto-posterior network involved in visual dimension changes. *Journal of Cognitive Neuroscience*, *12*, 480–494.

Pollmann, S., Weidner, R., Müller, H. J., & von Cramon, D. Y. (2006). Selective and interactive neural correlates of visual dimension changes and response changes. *NeuroImage*, *30*, 254–265.

Rogers, R. D., Andrews, T. C., Grasby, P. M., Brooks, D. J., & Robbins, T. W. (2000). Contrasting cortical and subcortical activations produced by attentional-set shifting and reversal learning in humans. *Journal of Cognitive Neuroscience*, *12*, 142–162.

Rugg, M. D., & Wilding, E. L. (2000). Retrieval processing and episodic memory. *Trends in Cognitive Sciences*, *4*(3), 108–115.

Talairach, J., & Tournoux, P. (1988). *Co-planar stereotactic atlas of the human brain*. Stuttgart, Germany: Thieme.

Treue, S. (2003). Visual attention: The where, what, how and why of saliency. *Current Opinion in Neurobiology*, *13*, 428–432.

Weidner, R., Pollmann, S., Müller, H. J., & von Cramon, D. Y. (2002). Top-down controlled visual dimension weighting: An event-related fMRI study. *Cerebral Cortex*, *12*, 318–328.

Wolfe, J. M. (1994). Guided Search 2.0: A revised model of visual search. *Psychonomic Bulletin and Review*, *1*, 202–238.

Yantis, S., Schwarzbach, J., Serences, J. T., Carlson, R. L., Steinmetz, M. A., Pekar, J. J., & Courtney, S. M. (2002). Transient neural activity in human parietal cortex during spatial attention shifts. *Nature Neuroscience*, *5*, 995–1002.

VISUAL COGNITION, 2006, 14 (4/5/6/7/8), 898–910

Ψ Psychology Press
Taylor & Francis Group

Visual search and single-cell electrophysiology of attention: Area MT, from sensation to perception

Stefan Treue

Cognitive Neuroscience Laboratory, German Primate Centre, Göttingen, Germany

Julio Cesar Martinez-Trujillo

Department of Physiology, McGill University, Montreal, Quebec, Canada

Evolution has equipped the visual system of primates with sophisticated features that allow the concentration of neuronal processing resources on a small subset of the incoming information. Here we review evidence, concentrating on recordings from area MT in the extrastriate cortex of macaque monkeys trained to perform visual tasks, that these "bottom-up" filtering processes are tightly integrated with "top-down" attentional mechanisms that together they create an integrated saliency map. This topographic representation emphasizes behavioural relevance of the sensory input at the expense of an accurate and complete representation of the external world.

The visual system of humans and many other primates is an evolutionary success story. As much as half of the cortical surface of the primate brain is dedicated to the processing of visual information. However, despite this strong bias towards visual processing, the sensory end of the system (i.e., the retina) collects an amount of information that far exceeds the processing capacity of even human cortex. To resolve this conundrum we harvest the enormous information provided by the photoreceptors of the eye in a very specific manner. The structure of the visual system is therefore a fascinating collection of aspects that allows the concentration of processing resources on what the organism considers the currently most interesting and/or relevant information. These aspects include: (1) The development of a fovea (i.e., a central portion of the retina with particularly high spatial resolution and colour processing abilities), (2) the existence of a specialized eye movement system with the ability to precisely orient the eyes (i.e., the fovea) in space

Please address all correspondence to Prof. Dr. Stefan Treue. German Primate Center, Kellnerweg 4, Göttingen, Germany. E-mail: treue@gwdg.de

http://www.psypress.com/viscog   DOI: 10.1080/13506280500197256

towards relevant visual targets, and (3) an uneven allocation of processing resources biased towards foveal processing throughout the visual system.

But to fully utilize the advantages of high resolution foveal processing the organism needs to serially direct its gaze at all portions of the visual field potentially containing relevant information in the high spatial frequency spectrum. This serial scanning process is demanding not only because of the need for an efficient occulomotor system but foremost because the system is faced with the problem of deciding where to direct its gaze next, based on the limited information available from the peripheral visual field. Again, the visual system has strategies to address this issue. One is to represent the visual field in cortex as a saliency map, i.e., as a topographic representation that indicates local feature contrast across the whole visual field (Itti & Koch, 2001) and that is used for deciding where to look next (Koch & Ullman, 1985; Parkhurst, Law, & Niebur, 2002; Treue & Martinez-Trujillo, 2003). This is a very powerful approach to the selection of potentially interesting parts since these are often characterized by being different from their immediate vicinity, i.e., by their salience. The other approach is to use nonsensory information to guide the scanning process. This is usually a priori information about the environment (e.g., knowledge of how letters are placed on a page when making saccades during reading) or information that reflects the consequences of the behavioural state of the organism regarding the relative importance of various portions of the environment (e.g., when searching for different items in the same visual scene the organisms creates different scanning patterns). The use of this nonsensory information to guide visual search is a high level process developed by cognitive brain systems and is commonly known as visual attention. In the interest of brevity we will focus this review on the results of studies investigating the effects of visual attention on the processing of motion information in primate visual cortex.

A fast and accurate analysis of motion information is of central importance to organisms that move through the environment and that are either predators or potential preys for others. It is therefore not surprising that sensitivity to motion is present in almost all animals. Higher mammals, especially primates have a devoted specialized cortical pathway (e.g., the "dorsal" or "where" pathway) and cortical areas within this pathway to the processing of motion information. The central such cortical region is the middle temporal area (MT) located in the rhesus monkey in the fundus of the superior temporal sulcus. Since its first description in the owl monkey area MT has become the most intensively studied extrastriate visual area. Many studies in past decades have concentrated on bottom-up (sensory) processing within the area (i.e., the encoding of sensory properties of visual motion by MT neurons) and its contribution to perception (Britten, Shadlen, Newsome, & Movhson, 1996; Parker & Newsome, 1998); more recent studies have focused on top-down modulation of sensory processing in MT by attention, not only in electrophysiological studies in monkeys (Cook & Maunsell, 2002; Dodd, Krug, Cumming, & Parker, 2001; Martinez-Trujillo & Treue, 2002, 2004; Recanzone & Wurtz, 2000; Reynolds & Desimone, 2003; Seidemann & Newsome, 1999; Treue & Martinez-Trujillo, 1999; Treue & Maunsell, 1996) but also in fMRI experiments in the presumed human homologue (Beauchamp, Cox, & DeYoe, 1997; Berman & Colby, 2002; Büchel, Josephs, Rees, Turner, Frith, & Friston, 1998; O'Craven, Rosen, Kwong, Treisman, & Savoy, 1997; Shulman, Ollinger, Akbudak, Conturo, Snyder, Petersen, & Corbetta, 1999). Here we will provide an overview of the main electrophysiological findings by first reviewing studies of spatial attention and then will turn to studies investigating nonspatial, feature-based attentional modulation of sensory signals in area MT.

NEURAL BASIS OF TOP-DOWN INFLUENCES ON THE SALIENCY MAP BASED ON THE LOCATION OF SPATIAL ATTENTION

Amongst the first studies of attentional modulation of sensory information processing in visual cortex is the work of Moran and Desimone (1985). They demonstrated that directing attention to one of two stimuli inside the receptive field of a neuron in extrastriate area V4 reduces the unattended stimulus' influence on the cell's activity. Later work extended these findings (Luck, Chelazzi, Hillyard, & Desimone, 1997; Reynolds, Chelazzi, & Desimone, 1999). While these studies demonstrated top-down influences on sensory information processing in early areas of the temporal pathway (such as V4), early areas of the dorsal pathway, such as MT were long considered immune to such modulation (Treue, 2001).

As we will show below this view did not hold up to closer inspection. In fact, the available data suggest a high degree of similarity, down to quantitative aspects between the attentional influences of neuronal responses in areas V4 and MT (McAdams & Maunsell, 2000; Treue & Martinez-Trujillo, 1999). As in area V4 the effect of directing spatial attention to one of two stimuli in the receptive field causes a response modulation that can be thought of as an enhanced influence of the attended and a reduced influence of the unattended stimulus (Treue & Martinez-Trujillo, 1999; Treue & Maunsell, 1996) (Figure 1a).

However, the studies that have used two stimuli located inside the receptive field of a visual neuron and demonstrated a response bias toward the attended stimulus failed to answer an important question. Is this response bias due to the effects of attending to the spatial location or to nonspatial features of the relevant stimulus? Since the two stimuli used in

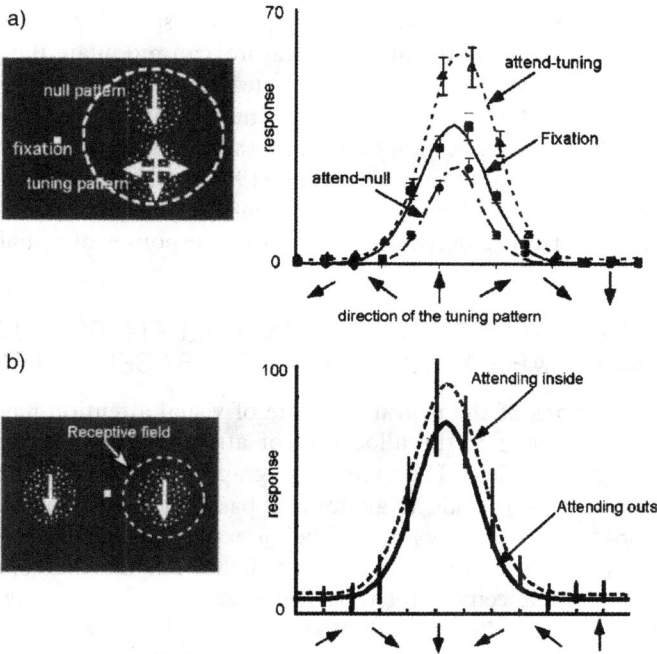

Figure 1. (a) Attentional modulation with two stimuli inside the receptive field. The left panel is a schematic representation of the experimental design. Two random dot patterns (RDPs) were presented inside the receptive field (RF), the "null pattern" always moving in the neuron's antipreferred direction (here downwards), whereas the "tuning pattern" moved in one of 12 possible directions. The right panel shows the response modulation evoked by the various directions of the tuning pattern for the three behavioural conditions (attend-tuning, fixation, and attend-null). (b) Attentional modulation with one stimulus inside the receptive field. The left panel is a schematic representation of the experimental design. Two random dot patterns (RDPs) were presented, one inside and one outside the RF. In a given trial both moved in the same direction, picked from 12 possible directions. The right panel shows the response modulation evoked by the various directions inside the RF for the two behavioural conditions (attending inside and attending outside the RF).

such studies differed in both location and nonspatial features (e.g., colour, orientation, motion direction) it was not possible to discriminate between these two alternatives. We have used identical stimuli located inside and outside the receptive field of visual neurons to determine the attentional modulation of neuronal responses as a function of the allocation of spatial attention in the absence of changes in feature-based attention. In agreement with results from area V4 (McAdams & Maunsell, 1999), directing attention inside the receptive field of an MT neuron increases the response in a multiplicative fashion (i.e., the response to all stimuli is increase by the same proportion, independently of the cells' selectivity for the attended stimulus) (Figure 1b).

Although these findings have demonstrated that spatial attention, even in the absence of changes in the attended feature, can modulate the responses of neurons in the visual cortex of primates it does not clarify whether attending to nonspatial features of visual stimuli can also evoked a response modulation. In fact the question of whether the response modulation seen in the initial study of Moran and Desimone (1985) is due to spatial attention remains to be answered. Next, we will concentrate on experiments searching for the effects of feature-based attention on the responses of visual neurons.

NEURAL BASIS OF TOP-DOWN INFLUENCES ON THE SALIENCY MAP BASED ON FEATURE-BASED ATTENTION

Early investigations of the neural correlate of visual attention have focused on spatial attention, i.e., the allocation of attention based on the spatial location in the visual field. The spatial topography of most of the extrastriate visual areas seems to provide an anatomical basis for attentional modulation based on spatial location as neurons being exposed to similar modulation (i.e., suppression for those with receptive fields outside the "spotlight of attention" and enhancement for those with receptive fields overlapping the attentional focus) are close to each other in cortex. More recent studies have manipulated the allocation of attention to nonspatial stimulus features (e.g., Von Mühlenen & Müller. 1999) while keeping the spatial allocation of attention constant. We used such an approach to investigate feature-based attentional modulation in area MT. Two rhesus monkeys were trained to attend to a stimulus placed far outside the receptive field of a given neuron being recorded from. A stimulus inside the receptive field provided a sensory input and could either move in the preferred or antipreferred direction of the cell. The attentional modulation was induced by varying the direction of motion of the attended stimulus outside the receptive field, which in a given trial could move in either the cell's preferred or antipreferred direction. The task for the animal was to detect and respond to a subtle change in the motion direction of the attended stimulus. Note that the two attentional conditions did not differ in the location of attention as in both types of trials the animal was directing attention to the stimulus outside the receptive field, always at the same location. Furthermore in both types of trial the sensory response of the cell was to an unattended stimulus.

Nevertheless we observed that across the sampled population of MT neurons the response to the preferred direction inside the receptive field was on average 15% higher when the attended stimulus outside the receptive field was moving in the preferred rather than the antipreferred direction (Figure 2a). This effect can be interpreted in two ways. Either the response of MT neurons is enhanced whenever attention is allocated to a stimulus moving in

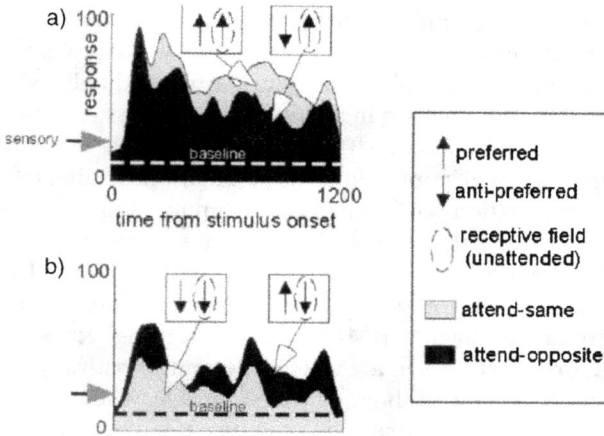

Figure 2. Feature-based attentional modulation of an example MT neuron. The two panels plot the response of the neuron to a stimulus inside the RF moving in the neuron's preferred (top panel) or antipreferred direction (bottom panel) when attention was directed at the stimulus outside the RF moving in the same (grey spike density function) or opposite (black spike density function) direction. The dashed lines indicate the response in the absence of any stimulus and the arrow marks the response level to the respective stimulus inside the RF when attention was simply directed at the fixation point.

the same direction as the one inside the receptive field. Such an effect could represent object-based attention if one interprets it as an expression of the grouping of the two stimuli according to the Gestalt principle of common fate. Alternatively, the modulation could represent feature-based attention in that a cell's response would be enhanced by attention to the neuron's preferred direction anywhere in the visual field. When the unattended stimulus inside the receptive field moves in the preferred direction both accounts predict the same modulation, namely an enhanced response when attention is directed at the preferred direction.

This issue can be resolved by determining the modulation of the responses to the antipreferred direction inside the receptive field when switching attention between the same preferred and antipreferred directions of the stimulus outside. Under these circumstances, the object-based account would predict an enhanced response when attention was directed to the antipreferred motion, whereas the feature-based would predict a lower response when attention is directed to the antipreferred direction stimulus. Our data clearly support the feature-based hypothesis as we find a stronger response with attention on the preferred direction even when the cell's sensory responses is elicited by an antipreferred direction stimulus inside the receptive field (Figure 2b; Martinez-Trujillo & Treue, 2004).

In summary, if the attended stimulus more closely matches the preferred feature of the neuron, e.g., is moving in the cell's preferred direction, attention will increase the cell's firing rate. Correspondingly, when attention is directed to a stimulus moving in a direction that is less preferred by the cell the response will be reduced. Attention therefore has a push-pull effect, enhancing the neuronal population's representation of attended and reducing the representation of unattended stimuli. Using a very similar experimental design, Saenz and colleagues have been able to demonstrate feature-based attentional modulation of both, psychophysical performance (Saenz, Buracas, & Boynton, 2003) and brain activity, using functional magnetic resonance imaging (fMRI: Saenz, Buracas, & Boynton, 2002). Single-cell recording studies in area V4 of the ventral pathway have reported feature-based attentional modulation (McAdams & Maunsell, 2000; Motter, 1994) supporting the view that this phenomenon is used throughout the visual cortex.

SIMILARITY OF TOP-DOWN AND BOTTOM-UP INFLUENCES OF ATTENTION ON STIMULUS SALIENCE

Both the space and feature-based attentional influences we have observed in MT will enhance the influence of attended stimuli at the expense of those currently unattended. While this will provide the organism with an improved representation of stimuli inside the spatial focus and those matching the attended features it is less obvious how attention will influence the saliency map that has been suggested to underlie the serial scanning of the visual field by saccadic eye movements (Itti & Koch, 2000). Although the saliency map is assumed to represent stimulus saliency across a number of dimensions (e.g., orientation, direction of motion, spatial frequency, and luminance contrast; Itti & Koch, 2001), the feature most directly linked to the response strength across neurons in visual cortex is luminance contrast. Except for a small subpopulation of neurons (Motter, personal communication) all stimulus-responsive cells in both the temporal and dorsal cortical pathway show a monotonic increase in responses to increased stimulus contrast.

It is therefore an appealing possibility that attention manipulates the saliency map (which collates sensory information) by modulating neuronal responses, creating an integrated saliency map that combines bottom-up with top-down saliency (Treue, 2003; Weidner, Pollmann, Müller, & von Cramon, 2002). Such integration could be achieved if attention exerts the same influence on neuronal responses as changed luminance contrast does. Some evidence in favour of this hypothesis is provided by the finding that both contrast and attention multiply neuronal tuning curves. Neuronal tuning curves derived using attended stimuli are scaled versions of those tuning curves derived from unattended stimuli. Similarly tuning curves based on high contrast stimuli are scaled versions of those measured using low contrast stimuli. But this similarity might simply reflect that both stimulus contrast and attention have similar but separate multiplicative underlying mechanisms.

We approached this issue by determining if stimulus contrast and stimulus attention have more deeply routed similarities that are likely not accidental but could reflect a common underlying physiological mechanism. To this purpose we trained rhesus monkeys to attend to a stimulus outside the receptive field while presenting a preferred direction and an antipreferred direction stimulus inside the receptive field. Across trials we widely varied the luminance contrast of the preferred direction stimulus. This latter sensory manipulation allowed us to determine the neuron's contrast-response function expressed in the dependence of neuronal firing rates on the contrast of the preferred motion stimulus (Figure 3a). As expected this contrast response function has a sigmoidal shape, i.e., a central quasilinear

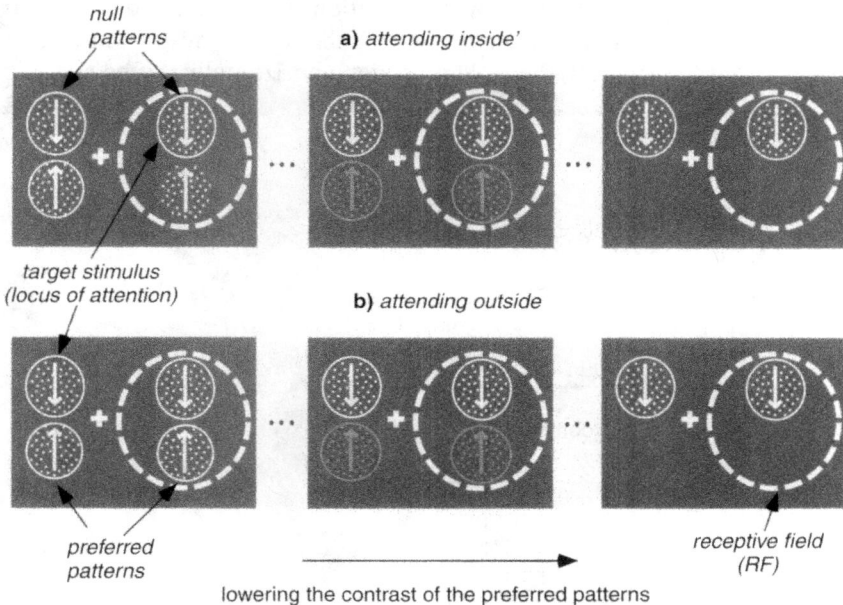

Figure 3. Experimental design investigating the modulation of the contrast response function by attention. Four stimuli were presented, two inside the receptive field (dashed ellipse) and two in the opposite hemifield. The animals were cued to attend either to the upper stimulus inside the RF (top row) or outside the RF (bottom row), both moving in the cell's antipreferred direction. The luminance of the lower stimuli (moving in the preferred direction) was systematically varied between trials.

modulation of neuronal responses with contrast variations is flanked by asymptotic regions at both low and high contrast. If the multiplicative modulation by attention observed in other experiments is assumed to be imposed on this contrast response function by top-down influences a similar vertical stretching of the contrast response function should result as was observed for direction and orientation tuning curves. Alternatively if stimulus contrast and stimulus attention are just various aspects of a unified system reflecting overall stimulus saliency, changes in attention should have the same effect as changes in stimulus contrast, i.e., attentional modulation should shift the contrast response function horizontally. To determine the attentional modulation of the contrast response function we again established the contrast response function but this time with the attention of the animal directed at the full-contrast antipreferred direction stimulus inside the receptive field (Figure 3b). As described above this allocation of attention to the less preferred of two stimuli inside the receptive field should lower responses. Figure 4 shows that this is indeed what happens. More interestingly though, the magnitude of this reduction is neither a constant reduction in the absolute response across the wide luminance contrasts tested nor a constant multiplicative modulation. Rather the modulation is strongest in the central quasilinear portion of the contrast response function and peters off towards both ends. This creates a horizontally shifted contrast

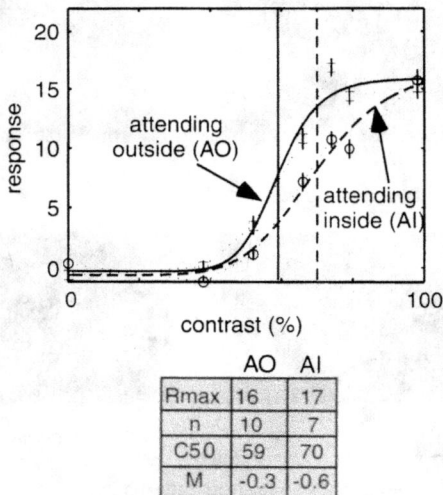

	AO	AI
Rmax	16	17
n	10	7
C50	59	70
M	-0.3	-0.6

Figure 4. Modulation of the contrast response function of one neuron The plot shows the response of an example neuron to the stimulus conditions shown in Figure 3. The square symbols are responses when attention was on the antipreferred direction RDP outside the RF (lower panels in Figure 3), whereas the circular symbols indicate responses when attention was on the antipreferred direction RDP inside the RF. The table shows the parameters of the best fit to the two data sets.

response function indicating than attention and contrast modulation share the same nonlinearity. This provides support for the hypothesis that bottom-up and top-down effects share a common neural hardware. This would make it difficult for perception to disentangle increases of stimulus salience from the effects of allocating attention to a particular stimulus or stimulus feature. Furthermore, this should cause attended stimuli to have an increased perceived contrast, a prediction confirmed by an elegant recent study by Carrasco, Ling, and Read (2004).

THE FEATURE-SIMILARITY GAIN MODEL OF ATTENTION

The similarity of effects of spatial and feature-based attention in MT, but also in other areas of visual cortex suggest that they reflect a unified attentional system in which the spatial location of a stimulus is simply another feature, such as its colour or direction of motion. We have proposed a *feature-similarity gain model of attention*, which predicts the sign and magnitude of attentional modulation of sensory responses by the similarity between the attended feature (e.g., stimulus location, colour, direction of motion) and a given cell's preference for this feature (Martinez-Trujillo, 2004; Treue & Martinez-Trujillo, 1999). In accordance with our findings the model predicts particularly strong response enhancement in cases where an attended stimulus is within the receptive field (high feature-similarity between the location of attention and the cell's preference, i.e., receptive field location) and is moving in the cell's preferred direction (high feature-similarity between the animal's attended direction of motion and the cell's directional preference). The feature-similarity gain model (FSM) of attention differs from the biased-competition model (BCM) of Desimone and colleagues (Desimone & Duncan, 1995; Reynolds et al., 1999) in that the BCM sees attention as a mechanism to influence the competition between various objects in a visual scene for neural representation, whereas the FSM interprets attention as a mechanism that changes the distribution of response gains of neurons across a whole population of neurons, independently of the stimuli that might be present in the visual field. However, both models have been able to account for the known electrophysiological effects of attention in visual cortex. Further research and computational modelling is needed to assess their relative validity in different experimental settings.

OVERALL EFFECTS OF ATTENTION ON THE ACTIVITY OF NEURONAL POPULATIONS IN VISUAL CORTEX

It is important to point out that although the attentional modulation observed in MT seems to be multiplicative, the actual factor not only differs between cells but also as a function of the similarity of the attended stimulus property to the cell's preference. This has important consequences for the attentional modulation across a population of neurons that are activated by a stimulus inside their receptive field. Because these cells all differ in their preferred direction or other relevant stimulus property, their individual attentional modulation is different even though they all might be responding to the same physical stimulus. Those cells with a preference close to the attended features are going to experience an enhanced response gain; those for which the attended features are far from the cell's preference will be reduced in their firing rate (Martinez-Trujillo & Treue, 2004). This creates a push-pull effect across the population that will increase the signal-to-noise ratio of the population response to stimuli that match the attended features. This effect will selectively enhance the salience of potential targets in a search situation, where feature-based attention can be allocated (since the relevant feature is known), whereas spatial attention plays no role (since the location of the target item is unknown).

In summary, what is known about attentional modulation of the visual information processing in area MT of the dorsal cortical pathway indicates that bottom-up (sensory) and top-down (attentional) processes in vision are joined in a system that seems to contribute to the creation of an integrated saliency map. This topographic representation of the visual world is used to identify those items in the visual scene that are potentially most relevant for the organism's survival and deserve further scrutiny. In this system a lack of attentional allocation can be compensated by a high sensory saliency ("pop-out") and vice versa (Nothdurft, 2000). The integrated saliency map also reflects an internal representation of the visual world that is more concerned with enhancing the perceptual strength (saliency) of relevant stimuli and the suppression of irrelevant aspects than with the creation of an accurate and complete internal representation of the external world.

REFERENCES

Beauchamp. M. S.. Cox. R. W.. & DeYoe. E. A. (1997). Graded effects of spatial and featural attention on human area MT and associated motion processing areas. *Journal of Neurophysiology*. *78*. 516–520.

Berman, R. A., & Colby, C. L. (2002). Auditory and visual attention modulate motion processing in area MT+. *Cognitive Brain Research*. *14*. 64–74.

Britten, K. H., Shadlen, M. N.. Newsome. W. T.. & Movshon, J. A. (1992). The analysis of visual motion: A comparison of neuronal and psychophysical performance. *Journal of Neuroscience*, *12*, 4745–4765.

Büchel. C.. Josephs, O., Rees, G., Turner, R., Frith. C. D., & Friston, K. J. (1998). The functional anatomy of attention to visual motion: A functional MRI study. *Brain*. *121*. 1281–1294.

Carrasco, M., Ling, S., & Read, S. (2004). Attention alters appearance. *Nature Neuroscience*, *7*, 308–313.

Cook, E. P., & Maunsell, J. H. R. (2002). Attentional modulation of behavioral performance and neuronal responses in middle temporal and ventral intraparietal areas of macaque monkey. *Journal of Neuroscience*, *22*, 1994–2004.

Desimone, R., & Duncan, J. (1995). Neural mechanisms of selective visual attention. *Annual Review of Neuroscience*, *18*, 193–222.

Dodd, J. V., Krug, K., Cumming, B. G., & Parker, A. J. (2001). Perceptually bistable three-dimensional figures evoke high choice probabilities in cortical area MT. *Journal of Neuroscience*, *21*, 4809–4821.

Itti, L., & Koch, C. (2000). A saliency-based search mechanism for overt and covert shifts of visual attention. *Vision Research*, *40*, 1489–1506.

Itti, L., & Koch, C. (2001). Computational modelling of visual attention. *Nature Reviews Neuroscience*, *2*, 194–203.

Koch, C., & Ullman, S. (1985). Shifts in selective visual attention: Towards the underlying neural circuitry. *Human Neurobiology*, *4*, 219–227.

Luck, S. J., Chelazzi, L., Hillyard, S. A., & Desimone, R. (1997). Neural mechanisms of spatial selective attention in areas V1, V2, and V4 of macaque visual cortex. *Journal of Neurophysiology*, *77*, 24–42.

Martinez-Trujillo, J. C., & Treue, S. (2002). Attentional modulation strength in cortical area MT depends on stimulus contrast. *Neuron*, *35*, 365–370.

Martinez-Trujillo, J. C., & Treue, S. (2004). Feature-based attention increases the selectivity of population responses in primate visual cortex. *Current Biology*, *14*, 744–751.

McAdams, C. J., & Maunsell, J. H. R. (1999). Effects of attention on orientation-tuning functions of single neurons in Macaque cortical area V4. *Journal of Neuroscience*, *19*, 431–441.

McAdams, C. J., & Maunsell, J. H. R. (2000). Attention to both space and feature modulates neuronal responses in macaque area V4. *Journal of Neurophysiology*, *83*, 1751–1755.

Moran, J., & Desimone, R. (1985). Selective attention gates visual processing in the extrastriate cortex. *Science*, *229*, 782–784.

Motter, B. C. (1994). Neural correlates of attentive selection for color or luminance in extrastriate area V4. *Journal of Neuroscience*, *14*, 2178–2189.

Nothdurft, H. C. (2000). Salience from feature contrast: Additivity across dimensions. *Vision Research*, *40*, 1183–1201.

O'Craven, K. M., Rosen, B. R., Kwong, K. K., Treisman, A., & Savoy, R. L. (1997). Voluntary attention modulates fMRI activity in human MT-MST. *Neuron*, *18*, 591–598.

Parker, A. J., & Newsome, W. T. (1998). Sense and the single neuron: Probing the physiology of perception. *Annual Review of Neuroscience*, *21*, 227–277.

Parkhurst, D., Law, K., & Niebur, E. (2002). Modeling the role of salience in the allocation of overt visual attention. *Vision Research*, *42*, 107–123.

Recanzone, G. H., & Wurtz, R. H. (2000). Effects of attention on MT and MST neuronal activity during pursuit initiation. *Journal of Neurophysiology*, *83*, 777–790.

Reynolds, J. H., Chelazzi, L., & Desimone, R. (1999). Competitive mechanisms subserve attention in macaque areas V2 and V4. *Journal of Neuroscience*, *19*, 1736–1753.

Reynolds, J. H., & Desimone, R. (2003). Interacting roles of attention and visual salience in V4. *Neuron*, *37*, 853–863.

Saenz, M., Buracas, G. T., & Boynton, G. M. (2002). Global effects of feature-based attention in human visual cortex. *Nature Neuroscience*, *5*, 631–632.

Saenz, M., Buracas, G. T., & Boynton, G. M. (2003). Global feature-based attention for motion and color. *Vision Research*, *43*, 629–637. ·

Seidemann, E., & Newsome, W. T. (1999). Effect of spatial attention on the responses of area MT. *Journal of Neurophysiology*, *81*, 1783–1794.

Shulman, G. L., Ollinger, J. M., Akbudak. E., Conturo, T. E., Snyder. A. Z., Petersen, S. E., & Corbetta, M. (1999). Areas involved in encoding and applying directional expectations to moving objects. *Journal of Neuroscience*, *19*, 9480–9496.

Treue, S. (2001). Neural correlates of attention in primate visual cortex. *Trends in Neurosciences*, *24*, 295–300.

Treue, S. (2003). Visual attention: The where. what, how and why of saliency. *Current Opinion in Neurobiology*, *13*, 428–432.

Treue, S., & Martinez-Trujillo. J. C. (1999). Feature-based attention influences motion processing gain in macaque visual cortex. *Nature*, *399*, 575–579.

Treue. S.. & Martinez-Trujillo, J. C. (2003). Moving the mind's eye before the head's eye. *Current Biology*, *13*, R442–R444.

Treue. S.. & Maunsell, J. H. R. (1996). Attentional modulation of visual motion processing in cortical areas MT and MST. *Nature*, *382*, 539–541.

Von Mühlenen, A., & Müller, H. J. (1999). Visual search for motion-form conjunctions: Selective attention to movement direction. *Journal of General Psychology*, *126*, 289–317.

Weidner. R.. Pollmann, S., Müller, H. J.. & von Cramon, D. Y. (2002). Top-down controlled visual dimension weighting: An event-related fMRI study. *Cerebral Cortex*, *12*, 318–328.

VISUAL COGNITION, 2006, 14 (4/5/6/7/8), 911–933

Ψ Psychology Press
Taylor & Francis Group

A theory of a saliency map in primary visual cortex (V1) tested by psychophysics of colour–orientation interference in texture segmentation

Li Zhaoping

Department of Psychology, University College London, London, UK

Robert J. Snowden

School of Psychology, Cardiff University, Cardiff, UK

It has been proposed that V1 creates a bottom-up saliency map, where saliency of any location increases with the firing rate of the most active V1 output cell responding to it, regardless the feature selectivity of the cell. Thus, a red vertical bar may have its saliency signalled by a cell tuned to red colour, or one tuned to vertical orientation, whichever cell is the most active. This theory predicts interference between colour and orientation features in texture segmentation tasks where bottom-up processes are significant. The theory not only explains existing data, but also provides a prediction. A subsequent psychophysical test confirmed the prediction by showing that segmentation of textures of oriented bars became more difficult as the colours of the bars were randomly drawn from more colour categories.

A saliency map aids the selection of visual inputs for further processing given limited computational resources. To better understand the selection, we separate bottom-up from top-down mechanisms (Cave, 1999; Wolfe, Cave, & Franzel, 1989), and consider a saliency map of the visual field constructed by bottom-up mechanisms only, such that a location with a higher scalar value in this map is more likely to attract attention and be further processed. It has been proposed (Li, 1999a, 2002) that the primary visual cortex creates a saliency map from direct visual input defined mainly by contrast, and that the saliency of a visual location increases with the firing rate of the most responsive V1 output cell to that location, regardless of the feature tuning of the cell. The primary visual cortex receives many top-down

Please address all correspondence to Li Zhaoping, Dept. of Psychology, University College London, London WC1E 6BT, UK. E-mail: z.li@ucl.ac.uk

This work is supported in part (LZ) by the Gatsby Charitable Foundation.

   DOI: 10.1080/13506280500196035

inputs from higher visual areas. Hence, the proposed bottom-up saliency map in V1 is an idealization when the top-down influences are ineffective, such as very shortly after visual presentation onset and without specific top-down knowledge, or when the animal is under anaesthesia. The condition of "shortly after stimulus onset" should not be viewed as a severe restriction, since, computationally, bottom-up selections must be fast, and should be less necessary after the initial selection or long after the corresponding stimulus onset. Furthermore, the saliency value should be such that it is regardless of the visual features like colour and orientation (Treisman & Gelade, 1980) such that, for example, the saliency of a red dot can be compared with that of a vertical moving bar (Nothdurft, 2000). This desirable property may have led to a common belief, as implicitly or explicitly expressed in previous works (Itti & Koch, 2000; Koch & Ullman, 1985; Treisman & Gelade, 1980; Wolfe et al., 1989) on saliency maps, that saliency must be signalled by cells untuned to features, such as cells in parietal cortex (Gottlieb, Kusunoki, & Goldberg, 1998; Itti & Koch, 2001) and that the saliency map must be outside V1 whose cells are feature tuned. However, just as the purchasing power of UK sterling is regardless of the holder's nationality or gender, the firing rate of V1 cells could be an universal currency for saliency with or without simultaneously decoding the input features from them. Thus, in principle, the read-out from the bottom-up saliency signal could be feature blind.

Indeed, V1 sends outputs directly to superior colliculus, which is involved in generating saccades (Shipp, 2004) and could be viewed as reading out the V1 saliency map. It has recently been shown that electrical microstimulation of neurons in V1, with currents as low as $2 \mu A$, can evoke saccades by monkeys towards the receptive field locations of the stimulated cells (Tehovnik, Slocum, & Carvey, 2003). V1's role for bottom up saliency does not preclude it from serving other roles such as contributing to object recognition.

Physiologically, the response of a V1 cell to inputs within its classical receptive field (CRF) can be influenced by contextual inputs near but outside the CRF, due to the long but finite range intracortical interactions linking nearby cells (Kapadia, Ito, Gilbert, & Westheime, 1995; Knierim & van Essen, 1992; Sillito, Grieve, Jones, Cudeiro, & Davis, 1995). Hence, by our proposal that the V1 response dictates saliency, the saliency of a location is determined by *both* the input strength (or contrast) at that location and its context, as expected (Nothdurft, 2000). For instance, a vertical bar will pop out of a background of horizontal bars, but not from a background of vertical bars. This is because the evoked response to the vertical bar (in a cell tuned to vertical orientation) would be much higher than responses to the background horizontal bars (in cells tuned to horizontal orientation), making the vertical bar most salient in the input image. The contextual influence processes most responsible in this case is iso-orientation suppression (Knierim & van Essen, 1992), the observation that a cell's response to the optimally oriented bar within its CRF is suppressed by up to 80% when the bar is surrounded by bars of the same orientation outside the CRF. Cells tuned to the horizontal orientation responding to the horizontal bars in the background experience iso-orientation suppression, whereas the cell tuned to vertical bar responding to the single vertical bar does not (Li, 1999a, 1999b; Sillito et al., 1995). Hence, iso-feature suppression is the neural basis for pop-out. Long-range connections indeed tend to link cells tuned to similar features (Li & Li, 1994). In particular, iso-colour suppression has also been physiologically observed (Wachtler, Sejnowski, & Albright, 2003), and, from the analysis above, should be responsible for colour pop-out, say a red among greens.

Physiologically, a visual location containing one or more (overlapping) visual items can evoke responses from many V1 cells whose CRFs overlap. For instance, a small vertical red bar may excite cells tuned to vertical orientation, or cells tuned to red but untuned to orientation, or cells whose optimal orientation is 5 degrees from vertical and whose tuning width is 15°, etc. According to our theory (Li, 2002), the saliency of a location is determined by the firing rate of the most responsive V1 output cell to it, regardless of the cell's optimal feature value. Hence, the saliency of the red vertical bar are likely signalled by a cell tuned to vertical, or a cell tuned to red, but less likely by a cell tuned to 10 degrees from vertical. (For simplicity of our argument without loss of generality, we ignore cells simultaneously or conjunctively tuned to both colour and orientation in most of this paper. We will show later that including the conjunction cells does not change our main conclusions qualitatively.) Which cell will be the most active to signal the saliency of this red vertical bar will depend on the contextual stimuli of this bar. For instance, if this red vertical bar is surrounded by a background of green vertical bars, the bar will pop out psychophysically due to its unique colour. Physiologically, this bar would excite a cell tuned to red colour much more than it does to a cell tuned to vertical orientation at the same CRF location, assuming that the activity levels are comparable in colour tuned and orientation tuned cells responding to the background bars (otherwise, when the colour signals are too weak, colour pop-out ceases anyway). This is because the responding cell tuned to vertical orientation would experience iso-orientation suppression (due to a background of vertical bars) while the cell tuned to red colour would not experience iso-colour suppression (the background has only green but not red bars). Analogously, a red vertical bar in a background of red horizontal bars will pop out by its unique orientation, and would have its saliency signalled by a cell tuned to vertical orientation.

In this paper, we will apply our theory of the V1 saliency map to understand and predict the phenomena of colour–orientation interference in texture segmentation. It is common knowledge that visual search for a target bar of unique orientation, i.e., orientation singleton, oriented at 45° among 135° distractor bars is easy, so is the segmentation between two textures of uniformly oriented bars at 45° and 135° respectively. Snowden (1998) observed that the texture segmentation became difficult when each stimulus bar was randomly assigned a colour from two choices (say red and green), whereas the orientation singleton search remained easy under the same colour randomization (see Figure 2A–D). Note that in both tasks only orientation feature should matter for the task decision. Nevertheless, colour feature seems to interfere in the performance. (Nothdurft, 1997, also observed interference of luminance variations on orientation based texture segmentation.) Although the tasks, often performed under brief visual presentation and/or under time pressure, require final decisions based on the orientation feature, they also require an initial and presumably dominant task component, namely selection (of the orientation singleton or border) by bottom-up saliency, which is feature blind. The observed colour interference is comprehensible in our framework by noting the changes in the saliencies of the orientation singleton or the texture border under the colour randomization. It essentially arises because (1) saliency of a coloured bar may be signalled by a colour tuned cell or an orientation tuned cell depending on the stimulus context, and (2) the saliency of one coloured bar signalled by a colour tuned cell can be compared with the saliency of another signalled by an orientation tuned cell to judge which bar is more salient to compete for visual selection. In this paper, a V1 model is used to implement the saliency map theory to account for such colour interference. Furthermore, we show a theoretical prediction that colour interference in orientation texture segmentation should increase with more colour categories in the colour randomization (see Figure 2B, D, and F). A psychophysical experiment is then carried out to test and confirm the prediction.

There have been previous models of saliency maps, in particular, those by Itti and Koch (2000) and by Koch and Ullman (1985). These works differ from our theory (and model) in the following ways. First, previous works either do not specify the cortical area for the saliency map, or presume explicitly or implicitly that the saliency map is outside V1, whereas our theory explicitly states V1 as the locus of the map. Second, the previous works require separate feature maps that extract local spatial discontinuities in the features such as colour and orientation. So for instance, a colour feature map can help to extract the colour pop-out features. These separate feature maps are then combined by summation or weighted summation of their outputs to a master saliency map so that the saliency of a visual location is encoded irrespective of the particular feature which is responsible for this location to be salient. In contrast, our theory (to signal saliency by the activity of the most responsive cell to a visual location regardless of its feature tunings) does not require separate feature maps, nor any subsequent combinations of them. Indeed many V1 cells are known to be tuned simultaneously to different features such as orientation and motion direction, they could also signal saliency and it would be impossible to have separate feature maps unless cells tuned to the conjunctive feature form yet another, e.g., an orientation–motion conjunction feature map—in which case the arguments for the single feature maps become weaker. Furthermore, not requiring combinations of any maps gets rid of a computational complexity. After all, physiologically, numerous V1 cells respond to a single visual item; many overlapping but nonidentical and unequal-sized receptive fields cover a single visual location. It is computationally complex and expensive, perhaps too complex and expensive for the initial bottom up selection purpose before object recognition, to decide which cells should contribute in which way to the saliency of a visual location. To select a location to attend to, it is computationally cheap (perhaps cheapest) to simply attend to the receptive field location of the most responsive output cell in V1, no matter which features the cell is tuned to and which other cells respond (though less vigorously) to the same visual location. In this sense, saliency signals in V1 are represented by a field of neural activity levels from all V1 output cells, from which the location of the highest single cell activity is selected for further visual processing.

If each V1 cell is tuned to no more than one feature dimension, and one cell's response to one feature value does not affect another's response to another feature, then V1 may be viewed as composed of separate cell groups, each is defined by their common preferred feature value and forms a single feature map. In this case, our proposed selection process may be viewed as a maximum operation over *both* feature maps and spatial locations. This is in contrast to the (weighted) *summation* operation over feature maps and maximum operation over spatial locations in traditional saliency models (Itti & Koch, 2000; Koch & Ullman, 1985; Krummenacher, Müller, & Heller, 2001; Müller, Heller, & Ziegler, 1995; Treisman & Gelade, 1980; Wolfe et al., 1989). Note that the selection process of maximum operation over both feature maps and spatial locations means a maximum operation over all cells, thereby rendering the feature maps irrelevant for bottom-up saliency computation even if they exist. This also means that, it is not necessary to separately represent or replicate (in V1 or elsewhere) the maximum response over feature maps or cell groups for a given visual location. (Within V1, it is doubtful that separate feature maps exist since there is interaction between cells responding to different features via mechanisms of feature unspecific surround suppression between nearby neurons regardless of their feature preferences, see Heeger, 1992, and lateral connections linking cells tuned to nonidentical feature values, see Kapadia et al., 1995; Knierim & van Essen, 1992.) However, for simplicity of presentation (as used sometimes in this paper), noninteraction between V1 responses to different feature values or feature dimensions can be viewed as a crude approximation). We will discuss in the final section how our experimental findings relate to different models of saliency maps; in particular, we will show that, if the previous models of saliency maps should be adopted, then our psychophysical observations will constrain the combination rules of the separate feature maps into a master saliency map.

In the next section, we will simulate the saliency map using a physiologically and anatomically based, and computationally designed, V1 model. This simulation is a necessary substitution of physiological observations since current experimental techniques can not yet provide sufficient information on a real V1 saliency map, which requires sufficiently dense or high spatial resolution recordings of V1 responses covering whole scenes of visual search or segmentation stimulus patterns. Next, we apply the model saliency map to the stimulus with both colour and orientation features, accounting for existing data on colour–orientation interference and providing testable predictions. Later, we describe the psychophysical experiment testing the prediction and the confirming results. We end with summary and discussions.

IMPLEMENTING THE SALIENCY MAP BY A V1 MODEL

A V1 model (Li, 1999b, 2000), based on physiological and anatomical data (Fitzpatrick, 1996; Gilbert & Wiesel, 1983; Hirsch & Gilbert, 1991; Kapadia et al., 1995; Knierim & van Essen, 1992; Nothdurft, Gallant, & van Essen, 2000; Rockland & Lund, 1983; Sillito et al., 1995), has been used to validate the saliency map theory. For clarity, we start by describing a model (Li, 1999b, 2000) that includes only cells tuned to orientation. The model (Figure 1A) focuses on layer 2–3 of V1 where there are prevalent intracortical connections that are responsible for the contextual influences to determine the saliency map. Each model pyramidal cell receives direct visual inputs within its CRF. CRFs are distributed in space. Each spatial location has 12 model pyramidal cells with overlapping CRFs, roughly modelling a hypercolumn. Each pyramidal cell is tuned to one of the 12 different orientations spanning 180°, with a half tuning width of roughly 15°. Local inhibitory interneurons form reciprocal interactions with the local excitatory pyramidal cells. Longer range interactions between pyramidal cells are mediated by the horizontal collaterals from the pyramidal cells (Gilbert & Wiesel, 1983; Rockland & Lund, 1983), reaching a distance of about a few CRF sizes in the model (or a few millimetres in the real cortex).

A: V1 model, its input, and outputs

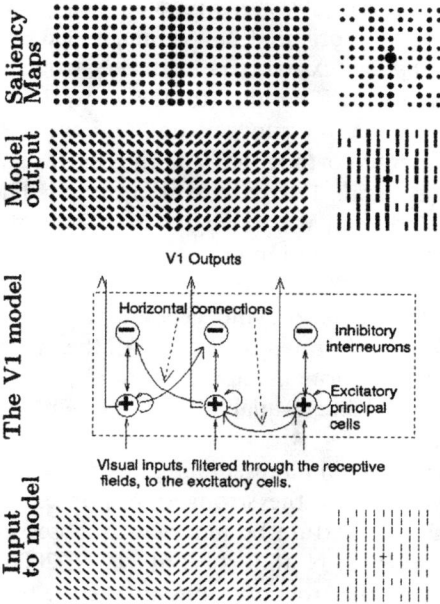

B: The histogram of V1 responses to the image of cross in bars in A

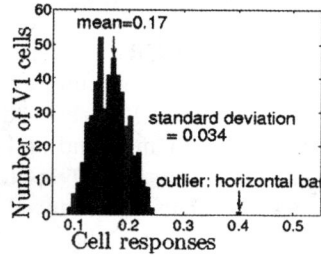

C: Lateral connection schematics. Thick solid bar: (oriented) CRF of the pre-synaptic pyramidal. Thin solid (dashed) bars: post-synaptic pyramidal CRFs via mono-synaptic excitation (di-synaptic inhibition)

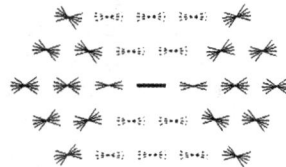

Figure 1. The V1 model. (A) A principal pyramidal cell receives direct visual contrast input from a bar within its CRF, comparable in size with the bars in the two input images. Pyramidal cells interact reciprocally with the local interneurons, and interact monosynaptic-excitatorily and disynaptic-inhibitorily with other pyramidal cells tuned to similar orientations within a distance of a few CRFs (see C). Each input/output/saliency map image plotted is only a small part of a large extended input/output/saliency map image. The thickness of the bars are plotted as proportional to the input/output strengths of bars for visualization (as in other figures). For example, all input bars in the two input images have the same input contrast, but evoke different V1 response levels (from the pyramidal cells) due to input context via intracortical interactions in the model. In the saliency maps, the radius of a disk is plotted proportionally to the firing rate of the most active cell responding to that visual location. (B) The histogram of all nonzero model responses (regardless of the preferred orientation of the cells) to the right input image (cross in bars) in A. The model responses are always within range [0,1]. (C) The schematics of the lateral connection pattern between pyramidal cells.

These connections enable a pyramidal model cell to excite another monosynaptically, or inhibit another disynaptically via inhibitory interneurons. They link cells tuned to similar (not necessarily identical, see Figure 1C) orientations (Fitzpatrick, 1996), and tend to be monosynaptic excitatory when the two CRFs are colinear or align to potentially form parts of a smooth curve, and disynaptic inhibitory otherwise (Figure 1C). Orientation unspecific local surround suppression is also implemented phenomenologically as local activity normalization (Heeger, 1992; Nothdurft, Gallant, & van Essen, 1999). The response to each bar depends on both the input contrast and the contextual stimuli via the lateral connections. The model produces the usual contextual influences observed physiologically. In particular, a cell's response to an optimally oriented bar within its CRF is suppressed if the CRF is surrounded by contextual bars, with the strongest suppression from surrounding bars oriented parallel to the central bar within the cell's CRF (termed iso-orientation suppression) and weakest suppression from surrounding bars oriented orthogonally to the central bar (Knierim & van Essen, 1992; Nothdurft et al., 1999; Sillito et al., 1995). The cell's response can be enhanced when contextual bars align with the central bar to form a smooth contour—colinear facilitation (Kapadia et al., 1995). The model parameters are designed (Li, 2001) to be consistent with the known physiology and anatomical data, and to avoid generating spontaneous or hallucinating model outputs not generated by inputs. All the model details and parameters (including activity normalization procedures, lateral connection strengths, etc.) of this model are available in Li (1999b) for interested readers to reproduce the results.

When the model is presented with visual stimuli resembling those in visual search and texture segmentation experiments, the strongest responses are located at or near the pop-out targets or texture boundaries, as observed physiologically (Knierim & van Essen, 1992; Nothdurft et al., 1999, 2000). In the example in Figure 1A on the right, the cross pops out among the bars since its horizontal bar, the only one that does not experience any iso-orientation suppression from other (vertical) bars in the image, evokes the highest response in the image. Hence, iso-feature suppression is the neural basis for the ease of feature search, when the target has a feature (horizontal orientation) not present in the distractors (Treisman & Gelade, 1980). Being the maximum response at its location, the response to the horizontal bar signals the saliency of the location of the cross. If we pick the dominant response to each visual location regardless of the cell's preferred feature, a histogram of the nonzero dominant responses will show the response outlier to the horizontal bar away from the population responses to the background (Figure 1B). The degree to which this response as an outlier could be quantitatively measured by a z-score (Li, 1999a) and phenomenologically linked to the perceptual saliency. Meanwhile, a sufficient orientation contrast at the border between two textures of uniformly oriented bars (Figure 1A, left) can pop out because a border bar, having half as many iso-oriented contextual neighbours as those of bars away from the border, experiences reduced iso-orientation suppression and evokes relatively higher responses. This V1 model has been applied to many other visual stimulus patterns similar to those used in visual search and segmentation tasks, giving results consistent with human visual behaviour (Li, 1999a, 1999b, 2000), such as the quantitative dependence of the strength of orientation pop-out on the quantitative orientation contrast in the stimulus. It elucidates how the just-noticeable-difference for orientation pop-out relates to the structure of the lateral connections. Although all kinds of contextual influences, including iso-feature suppression, colinear facilitation, and general feature unspecific surround suppression, contribute to the final V1 outputs and the saliency map (Li, 1999a, 1999b, 2000), iso-feature suppression is usually the dominant one, and is the most responsible and relevant for the stimulus examples in this paper. Hence, for simplicity of presentation in this paper, we sometimes estimate a cell's response by the number of iso-feature contextual neighbours for the optimal feature value and dimension of the cell. However, no such approximation is used in the actual model simulation or the figures, where a cell's response is quantitatively influenced by specific spatial configurations and quantitative feature values of stimulus at and around the CRF and by the level of the local neural activities.

EXTENDING THE MODEL TO THE COLOUR–ORIENTATION FEATURE SPACES

To account for the colour–orientation interference, the original V1 model was augmented by adding the colour feature dimension without changing any parameters in the original model. At each hypercolumn location, three model cell units, one each tuned to red, green, and blue colours respectively, are added to the set of orientation tuned model units. They have the same pyramidal–interneuron interactions as the orientation tuned units, thus the same input response properties. In this simplified model, a cell is either tuned to colour or to orientation but not to both. The mutual suppressive interactions between neighbouring units tuned to the same colour, i.e., iso-colour suppression, as observed physiologically (Wachtler et al., 2003), is implemented analogously to the iso-orientation suppression between the orientation tuned cells, except that, since colour tuned cells are untuned to orientation, iso-colour suppression depends only on the magnitude but not the direction of the displacement between the pre- and postsynaptic cells. Like the orientation tuned cells, each colour unit is subject to the same local activity normalization (see Li, 1999b, for details), thus the feature unspecific local suppression from neighbouring (colour or orientation tuned) cells. Besides the activity normalization which introduces interactions between cells tuned to different colours or different feature dimensions, we make the simplest assumption that no additional interactions exist between cells tuned to different colours or different dimensions. For the ease of analysis and discussion in this paper, without loss of generality, each colour unit is modelled as tuned to a primary colour feature of either red, or green, or blue, rather than to the opponent colour features (such as red–green opponency) or other hues in real V1 (Gegenfurtner, 2003). (Broad tuning to the wavelength of light enables the model cells to respond to nonprimary colour as well.)

A coloured bar evokes response O from an orientation tuned cell and response C from a colour tuned cell, in the same hypercolumn, giving a saliency signal $\text{Max}(O,C)$, the maximum of the responses. Let a neuron's response to a bar of preferred orientation be O_{single} when the bar is an orientation singleton, and O_{ground} when the bar is one of the elements in an iso-orientation texture. Let C_{single} and C_{ground} be the analogous responses from colour tuned cells to a colour singleton and a colour element in a uniform colour texture. Iso-feature suppression means $O_{single} > O_{ground}$ and $C_{single} > C_{ground}$. In typical stimulus situations with coloured bars, colour singleton and orientation singleton pop out, implying that both O_{single} and C_{single} are significantly larger than both O_{ground} and C_{ground}. For illustration and in our simulations in Figures 2 and 3, we use examples in which $O_{single} \approx C_{single}$ and $O_{ground} \approx C_{ground}$, meaning that the colour and orientation dimensions have comparable input stimulus strength (for all bars in the figures) and comparable intracortical interaction strengths. With uniform colour stimuli as in Figure 2A and B, all bars evoke suppressed responses C_{ground} from colour tuned cells, while only the background bars evoke suppressed responses O_{ground} from orientation tuned cells. The orientation singleton and texture border bars, with no or fewer iso-orientation neighbours, evoke higher responses O_{single} and O_{border} respectively, with

Figure 2. (A–G) Colour interference in orientation feature based visual search or texture segmentaion tasks as demonstrated in the stimuli in the left column, and simulated by the V1 model in the other columns. Each stimulus/response pattern is a small portion of a spatially extended pattern. Second column: The model responses from colour tuned cells and from orientation tuned cells. The responses from the colour tuned cells are plotted as proportional to the sizes of the coloured disks of the corresponding colours. The same ratios, bar thickness:response and disk radius:response, are used in all plots in this column, and they are such that the response levels of the orientation tuned and colour tuned cells to the background bars are similar in A. In the saliency maps (third column), the colour of a dot is the preferred colour of the cell signalling the saliency. If it is black, an orientation tuned cell signals the saliency. The radius:response ratio is the same as that used in the second column. Fourth and fifth columns: The model outputs and saliency maps (using the same size:response ratios as in previous columns) when the model includes cells tuned to both colour and orientation, i.e., the conjunction cells. The half-length of the minor axis of the coloured ellipses is proportional to the responses from the conjunction cells tuned to the corresponding colour and orientation, and the ratio (half) minor axis:response is the same as the radius:response for colour tuned cells. Note that colour disks, which indicate the responses from colour tuned cells, are invisible when the superposing ellipses are larger, indicating stronger responses from the conjunction cells. In the saliency maps (fifth column), when a bar's saliency is signalled by a conjunction cell, the colour of the disk is dark-red, dark-blue, or dark-green to correspond to the colour tunings of the conjunction cells and distinguish from the saliency disks (lighter coloured) signalled by the colour tuned cells. Note that colour randomization increases mainly the responses in colour but not the orientation tuned cells. Note that the target or border saliency is the highest in A, B, C, and E but not in D, F, and G, indicating significant colour interference in D, F, and G. Note that this conclusion holds with or without the conjunction cells in the model.

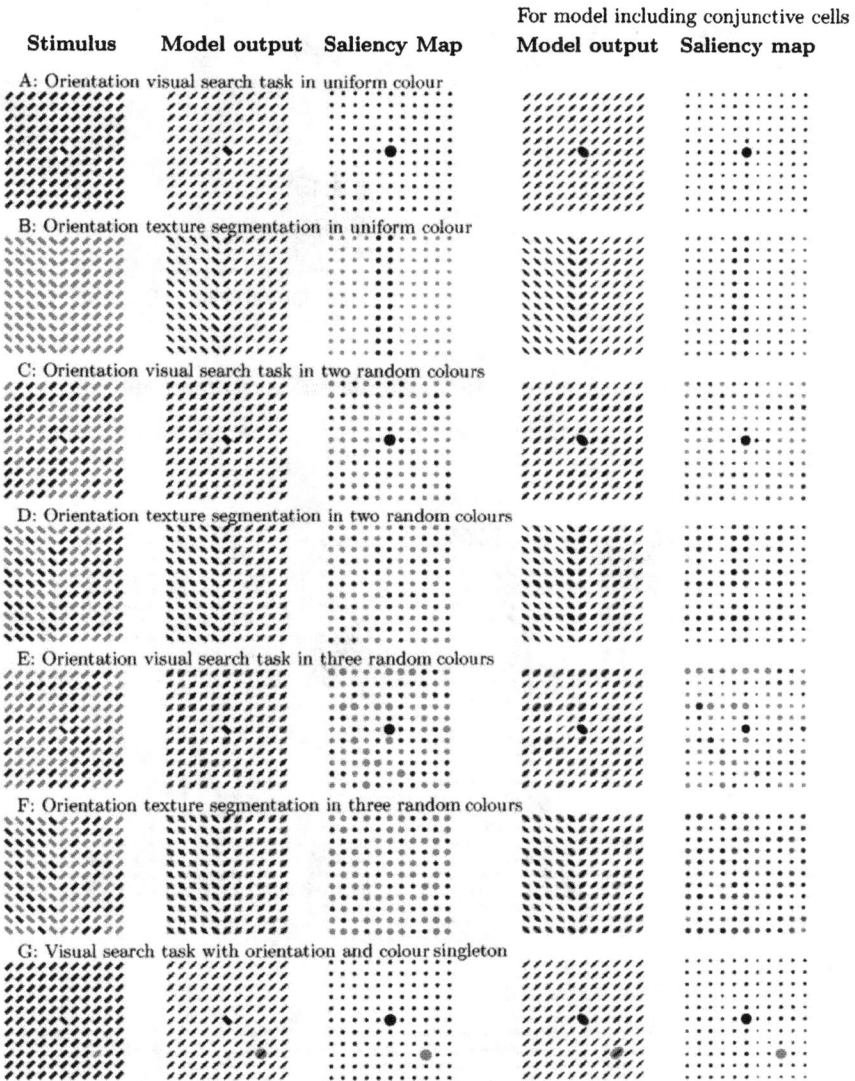

Figure 2. (See opposite for caption)

$O_{single} > O_{border}(> O_{ground})$ since the singleton is the only one with no iso-orientation neighbours. They pop out when their saliencies, Max(O_{single}, C_{ground}) and Max(O_{border}, O_{ground}) respectively, are significantly higher than the background saliency, Max(O_{ground}, C_{ground}). This is the case when $C_{ground} \sim O_{ground}$ or when C_{ground} is significantly weaker than O_{single} and

A: Experimental data

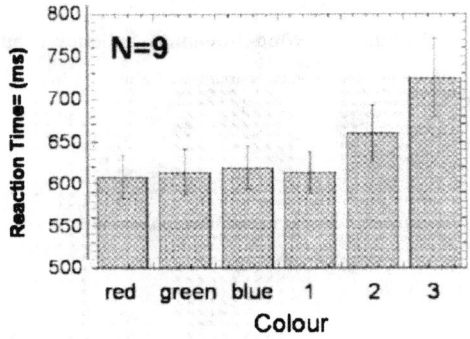

B: Model behavior on the test stimulus patterns

Stimulus   Model output   Saliency Map

Uniform color input

Two random color inputs

Three random color inputs

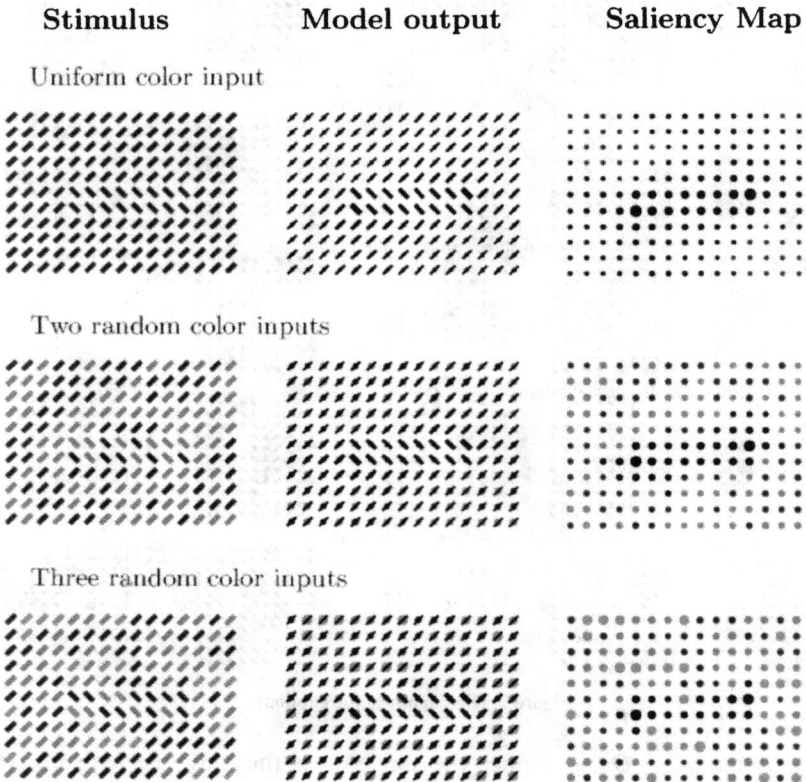

Figure 3. (See opposite for caption)

O_{border}. Note that the singleton is always more salient than the texture border as long as $C_{ground} < O_{single}$. When each bar randomly takes one of the two colours as in Figure 2C and D, the number of iso-colour neighbours of any bar is halved on average. Thus the colour tuned cell gives a less suppressed response $C_{random} > C_{ground}$. If $C_{random} > O_{ground}$ (which happens in stimulus of sufficient colour strengths and contrasts), the background saliency signal will increase from $\text{Max}(O_{ground}, C_{ground})$ to $\text{Max}(O_{ground}, C_{random}) = C_{random}$.

The texture border, less salient than the singleton, is more likely submerged by the background saliency to weaken its pop-out strength, explaining the observations by Snowden (1998). In particular, $C_{random} \sim O_{border}$ when $O_{single} \approx C_{single}$ and $O_{ground} \approx C_{ground}$, since on average a border bar has as many iso-orientation neighbours as a coloured bar has iso-colour neighbours. Thus the responses O_{border} to the border from the orientation tuned cells are submerged by the background responses C_{random} from the colour tuned cells.

Meanwhile, the orientation singleton pop-out is not impaired since its evoked response O_{single}, remains the most vigorous against the less-suppressed background responses C_{random}, and the excited cell is the only one tuned to either feature dimension to escape iso-feature suppressions. See Figure 2C. Therefore, assuming that object saliency rather than subject scrutiny (for feature values) plays a dominant role in such tasks (often performed under brief visual presentations and under time pressure), the essential reason for the colour interference is the following: Saliency is regardless of the feature dimension(s) of cells signalling it—hence the activity of a colour tuned cell signalling saliency of one bar is compared with the activity of an orientation tuned cell signalling saliency of another to see which bar is more salient for visual selection. Increased colour responses from the background make the orientation responses to border no longer response outliers (i.e., the z-score is lower). In other words, being regardless of features, saliency allows colour feature to interfere in an orientation feature-based task.

Figure 3 (opposite). (A) Data from experimental test of the model predictions: More random colour features should introduce more colour interference on orientation feature based segmentation tasks. Nine subjects performed the tasks of identifying the orientation (vertical or horizontal) of a 2×8 textured foreground area. Shown are averaged reaction times (and their error bars, 900 trials for each subject), as measurements of the difficulties of the tasks. Shortest reactions were for cases when all bars are of uniform colour (red, green, or blue, averaged in "one colour", the third column from right), longer reactions are for colours of bars randomly drawn from red and green (second column from right), longest reactions were for bars randomly drawn from the three colours (the right most column). (B) Model simulation of the tasks. Note that the averages and variations of the responses of the colour tuned cells to the background increase as more varieties of colour features are introduced randomly to the bars, submerging responses to the foreground.

From the analysis above, one can arrive at another observation. Suppose that only one distractor bar in an orientation singleton search stimulus has a different colour from other bars (Figure 2G), then, this colour (distractor) singleton also pops out when its evoked colour response C_{single} is significantly higher than the background responses O_{ground} and C_{ground}. When $C_{single} \sim O_{single}$, the orientation singleton target and the colour singleton distractor have comparable saliencies, $\text{Max}(O_{single}, C_{ground}) = O_{single}$ and $\text{Max}(O_{ground}, C_{single}) = C_{single}$ for visual selection. This impairs the visual search task for the orientation singleton, as has indeed been observed (Pashler, 1988; Theeuwes & Burger, 1998).

We can also predict phenomena that have not been previously observed. Suppose that the number of colour categories available to randomly assign to each stimulus bar increases from two to three, the texture segmentation task should become even more difficult. This is because each bar now has on average only one-third of its neighbours of the same colour, further reducing the iso-colour suppression on the colour tuned cells. This gives further elevated response C_{random} and background saliency, see Figure 2E and F. The next section describes a psychophysics experiment to test this prediction.

Our simple assumption so far of no conjunction cells (i.e., cells tuned conjunctively to colour and orientation) agrees more with some physiological data (Conway, 2001; Livingstone & Hubel, 1984; Ts'o & Gilbert, 1988) and less with other data (Friedman. Zhou, & Heydt, 2003; Gegenfurtner, Kiper, & Fenstemaker, 1996; >Hegde & Felleman, 2003; Johnson, Hawken, & Shapley, 2001; Leventhal, Thompson. Liu, Zhou, & Ault, 1995). Although there is a tendency for colour tuned cells to be less tuned to orientation and vice versa, as seen from data (see Fig. 5 in the review by Gegenfutner, 2003) and argued from efficient coding considerations (Li & Atick, 1994), we show here that including the conjunction cells in the model will not change our conclusions qualitatively. In each model hypercolumn, six conjunction units are added, each tuned to one of the six colour–orientation conjunctions (red, green, blue) $\times (45°, -45°)$ relevant in our stimulus, and each has the same input response properties as that of other model units. The pattern of the intracortical connections between conjunction cells tuned to similar conjunction features is modelled as a weighted average of that between colour tuned cells and that between the orientation tuned cells. Such an interaction pattern and strength are consistent with the limited physiological data (Hegde & Felleman, 2003) so far about the contextual influences using both feature dimensions. The conjunction cells are also modelled to suppress and be suppressed by the single feature tuned cells preferring similar orientation or colour, but with a 90% reduction in suppression strength compared to the iso-feature suppression within a single cell class. This interaction between the single feature tuned cells and conjunctive feature tuned cells is included so that, as in behavioural data (e.g., Treisman &

Gelade, 1980), the colour–orientation conjunction search tasks may not be as easy as the feature search tasks. The conjunction cells also participate in the feature unspecific surround suppression. The response from a conjunction cell to a coloured bar can be estimated approximately by the number of the bar's neighbours of the same conjunction feature, due to the iso-conjunction feature suppression. Analogous to notations for other cell types, CO_{single}, CO_{ground}, CO_{ground}, CO_{random}, and CO_{border}, respectively, are the responses from a conjunction cell to a preferred conjunction bar presented as a conjunction singleton, surrounded by iso(conjunction) feature neighbours, in a colour randomized iso-orientation field, and at an orientation texture border, respectively. Then, to an iso-orientation background texture stimulus with or without colour randomization, conjunction cells and the colour tuned cells respond with comparable strengths $C_{ground} \sim CO_{ground}$ and $C_{random} \sim CO_{random}$, since the orientation feature is uniform. To an orientation singleton, the conjunction cell and the orientation cell respond comparably $O_{single} \sim CO_{single}$, since both cells experience no iso-feature suppression. Hence, introducing the conjunction cells does not qualitatively change the saliency of the orientation singleton, whose pop-out remains insensitive to colour interference. To an orientation texture border, the responses from the conjunction cells should be comparable to or higher than those from the orientation tuned cells, $CO_{border} \gtrsim O_{border}$, when the stimulus have uniform or random colours, since a border bar has the same or fewer iso-conjunction feature neighbours as iso-orientation neighbours. Hence, conjunction cells make the border saliency higher or roughly unchanged when the stimulus colour is or is not randomized. However, these enhanced border responses from the conjunction cells are not sufficient to offset the increased mean and variances of the responses to the background also due to colour randomization. This means, orientation texture segmentation should remain susceptible to colour interference when the conjunction cells are included. This is confirmed in model simulation shown in the two right columns in Figure 2. Increasing colour randomization makes the texture border increasingly submerged by responses to the background, whereas the orientation singleton continues to evoke the highest response against the background.

TESTING THE MODEL PREDICTION OF INCREASED COLOUR–ORIENTATION INTERFERENCE

Methods

Stimuli. Texture patterns consisted of a grid of 12×12 elements that occupied a square of side 6.6 cm (6.6 deg); thus the average separation between elements was 0.60 deg. The actual position of each individual element within this grid was randomly jittered in both the horizontal and vertical axis by up to 0.135 cm (deg) using a flat probability profile. Most of the elements were assigned to be background; an area of 2×8 elements was designated to be foreground (or target, like that in Figure 3). The position of this target area was random, except that it was not allowed to intrude into the outermost elements so that it was always surrounded by background elements. The orientation of the target area (vertical or horizontal) was randomly chosen from trial to trial, and this was the judgement that the observer was required to make. To define this target area the orientation of the target elements was 90 deg different to that of the background elements. On each trial the orientation of all the target elements was randomly chosen to be either $+45$ deg or -45 deg with respect to the vertical, and thus the background elements were either -45 or $+45$ deg, respectively.

On each trial the colour of any element could be red, green, or blue, simply defined here as the output of each of the three colour guns in isolation. The salience of the elements was adjusted to be equal in pilot experiments so that it matches the apparent brightness of the elements in three observers. (We do *not* mean to imply by this that the differently coloured elements were equiluminant.) The average brightness matches of the observers were then used throughout all the experiments. Each colour was approximately 8 cd/m^2; the background was a dark grey at 0.1 cd/m^2. For reasons not expounded further here, the elements could have a length of either 3 or 6 mm, and a width of 0.6 or 1.2 mm (on any single trial all elements had the same length and width, chosen randomly for each trial). The data from these manipulations are not analysed further in this paper and data were simply collapsed across these conditions.

In all, five conditions were run (red, green, blue, two-colours—red and green, and three-colours—red, green, and blue). Each single colour condition was run in order to check that there were no overall differences due to the different colours used. Each observer received 100 trials in each of these conditions. In the next condition each element (both target and background) was randomly assigned to be either red or green; we term this the two-colour condition. The two-colour condition does not include other colour pairs in order to shorten the total duration of an experimental block. In the final condition each element (both target and background) was randomly assigned to be either red, green, or blue; we term this the three-colour condition. Observers received 300 of each of these last two conditions. Thus in total each observer saw 900 trials, which were presented within a single block of trials in a random order.

Procedure.   Each subject was given instructions as to the nature of the task and had a small practice session (approximately 30 trials) before any data were gathered. The observers were told to perform as quickly as possible while trying not to commit errors. Each trial consisted of a blank interval (375 ± 125 ms), followed by a fixation cross (375 ± 125 ms) placed at the centre of where the stimulus array would be presented (i.e., the centre of the screen). Following the extinguishing of the fixation cross the stimulus array appeared. The observer then made a speeded two-option forced choice (vertical or horizontal) as to the orientation of the target area. Stimuli were presented until the observer responded and then the screen was blanked. Reaction times and correctness of response were recorded by the computer and feedback was given via an auditory signal for incorrect responses. Observers were given breaks (approximately 5–10 min) every 300 trials; they could also stop at any time if they so wished (but none did).

Observers.   Nine observers were used (seven female) with an age range of 19–38. Eight of them were naive to the aims of the experiment; one was one of the authors (RS). All were screened for colour deficiencies using the Ishihara test.

Data analysis.   Reaction times were first screened for extreme outliers (>3000 ms or less than 100 ms) and these were removed (<1% for any observer). As RT scores do not form a normal distribution the median RT was then calculated for each observer in each of the five colour conditions using only trials on which the observer was correct. The percentage of trials on which the observer was incorrect was also noted. Differences in RTs and errors were examined via a series of a priori planned comparisons using *t*-tests.

Results

Figure 3A displays the means and standard error of measurement for the five conditions. Comparison of the data from each of the three single colour conditions revealed that performance was not statistically different for each of the colours (two-way *t*-tests; RvG $t(8) = -0.08$, *ns*; RvB $t(8) = -1.22$, *ns*; GvB $t(8) = -0.59$, *ns*) and thus data from these conditions were collapsed so as to form a single variable termed "one colour". As predicted, the two-colour condition gave reaction times that were significantly longer than the one colour condition (one-way *t*-test: $t(8) = 2.89$, $p = .010$), and the three-colour condition was slower than the two-colour condition (one-way *t*-test: $t(8) = 2.61$, $p = .015$). Not surprisingly the three-colour condition was significantly slower than the one-colour condition (one-way *t*-test: $t(8) = 2.89$, $p = .005$). Error rates were always quite low (0.2 –8.1%) for all subjects tested. Statistical analysis (ANOVA) did not reveal any significant effects ($ps > .05$).

Figure 3B shows the model simulations that agree qualitatively with the experimental outcome. For simplicity, only the simulations in a model without conjunction cells were shown, since those including conjunction cells are qualitatively the same. Note that although the stimuli are mainly of a texture segmentation type, they have an element of orientation search stimuli in them, since the foreground region has only 2×8 elements. (When the foreground has only one element the stimulus pattern is the same as that in the singleton search task.) This is manifested in the most vigorous responses to the two of the corners of the foreground since they have the fewest iso-orientation neighbours, and they have a particular spatial configuration of the bars around them to enable favourable contextual influences. Hence, the rate of deterioration of the foreground saliency with increasing colour randomization is somewhat between those for the texture segmentation stimulus and the orientation singleton stimulus in Figure 2. In realistic stimuli, this is common since a texture region has to be spatially bounded with the extreme corners, unlike in the model simulation where the space boundary is wrapped around to simulate an infinitely large spatial texture. Note that, although colour randomization may shift the most salient image location from foreground to background, such as in Figure 2D and F and Figure 3B, this does not mean that the foreground becomes invisible. Visibility and saliency pop-out are two different things. Less salient targets simply require longer reaction times, to allow visual attention to visit more salient locations first before being registered in the awareness (i.e., become visible).

SUMMARY AND DISCUSSION

We applied the theory of a saliency map in V1 to the colour–orientation interference phenomena using a model of V1. This theory is unique in proposing that saliency of a visual location or an object (e.g., a short coloured bar) is signalled by the activity level of the most active V1 cell responding to it, and is regardless of the feature tuning properties of the V1 cells signalling it. Hence, the activity of a colour tuned cell signalling saliency of a coloured bar can be compared with the activity of an orientation tuned cell signalling saliency of another bar to see which bar is more salient. Meanwhile, whether a colour tuned or an orientation tuned cell signals the saliency of a coloured bar depends on (1) the input strength in colour and orientation and (2) the colour and orientation contextual input of the bar concerned. This contextual dependence is computed by the intracortical interactions in V1 linking neighbouring cells, and demonstrated in this paper by a V1 model.

This model explained the existing data (Pashler, 1988; Snowden, 1998) on the interference of the colour features in orientation feature based tasks, in particular, the orientation singleton search and orientation texture segmentation. The ease of these tasks, especially when performed under time pressure, depends largely on the saliencies of visual objects. Specifically, our framework explains why randomizing the colours of the bars impairs performance in some segmentation tasks but not others. In addition, we predict from our model that the colour interference should increase with increasing colour categories used in the colours of the oriented bars in the stimulus. A psychophysics experiment was carried out to test the prediction, and reaction times in a texture segmentation task were shown to increase with increasing colour categories, confirming the model prediction.

Nothdurft (1997) has observed that non-iso-luminant stimuli could contribute to interference in orientation feature-based segmentation. Since our experiments used different luminance values for bars of different colours, it could happen that luminance variations in the background texture contributed to the observed interference. However, we believe that such a luminance factor is minimal or nonsignificant in our experiment since the reaction times of the orientation segmentation under uniform colour are similar (Figure 3A) for all three colours, implying that the saliencies of differently coloured bars are comparable in uniform textures without colour randomization. This implies that any changes of saliency values in colour randomized stimuli are caused by changes in colour feature values rather than the luminance values.

One could ask if the previous models of bottom-up saliency map (Itti & Koch, 2000; Koch & Ullman, 1985) could also explain our experimental data. These models assume that separate feature maps, such as colour feature maps and orientation feature maps, are constructed to obtain the saliency highlights in separate feature dimensions, and these separate feature maps are then subsequently combined into a master, feature unspecific, saliency map. Without diving into details of how separate feature maps are constructed, these separate maps obtain as highlights feature discontinuities such as singletons or borders in each feature dimension (Itti & Koch, 2000; Koch & Ullman, 1985). These mechanisms correspond to contextual interactions between cells tuned to the same dimension in our V1 model. These models then assume some mechanism that combines the results from different feature maps. The combination rule used has been to sum (or feature weighted sum) the outcomes from the feature maps into a scalar master map (Itti & Koch, 2000; Müller et al., 1995). Given that the orientation feature map gives a highlight at the texture border whereas the colour feature map has its high lights spatially distributed in the whole image, the summation of the two maps would produce saliency highlights along the texture border. This means, the orientation segmentation task should not be sensitive to colour interference. Arguably, it is possible that some degree of feature interference could still be predicted by this summation rule, considering that the colour feature map gives very unhomogeneous highlights due to the random assignments of colours to the bars. This creates a noisy background in the master map and this noisy background makes the border highlight not as conspicuous as it is under uniform colour (Duncan & Humphrey, 1989; Rubenstein & Sagi, 1990). Alternatively, if the feature map combination rule into a master map is the maximum rather than summation rule, i.e., the master map takes the maximum among the feature maps at each spatial location, the outcome would be qualitatively equivalent to our model without the conjunction cells. Hence, the colour–orientation interference phenomena argue that if the previous models of the saliency map were to be adopted, the combination rule from separate feature maps to the master map is more likely a maximum or winner-take-all rule, in which case, separation of feature maps is no longer relevant. Meanwhile, it has been observed that double feature search or searching for a dimensionally redundant target, such as searching for a vertical red bar among horizontal green bars, is faster than either of the single feature searches in either dimension alone, e.g., a vertical bar among horizontal bars, or a red among green (Krummenacher et al., 2001; Nothdurft, 2000). This observation can not be explained by a maximum rule of the feature maps since it would argue that a double feature search should not be easier than the easiest of the single feature searches. In particular, the maximum rule means that the reaction time to the double feature target should be the shorter one of the two single feature search reaction times. This is called the race model inequality, i.e., taking the reaction time of one of the two single feature dimensions that reaches the task decision first in a race between the two feature dimensions (see Krummenacher et al., 2001). However, in our theory, where there are neither separate feature maps nor any combination of them, the faster double feature search can be explained by introducing the conjunction cells (Li, 2002). This introduces a third racing element in the reaction time race which is now between three competitors: The colour tuned cell, the orientation tuned cell, and the conjunction tuned cell. While each of the former two competitors determines the reaction time for the single feature search, the double feature search can be faster when the conjunction cell's signal becomes the race winner in some of the trials.

We also note that top-down mechanisms (Cave, 1999; Müller et al., 1995; Wolfe et al., 1989), whether or not constructing the saliency map, could not explain the interference phenomena in this paper. This is simply because top-down control would argue instead that colour, being the irrelevant feature for the tasks, should not interfere.

To summarize, we applied the theory and model of the saliency map in V1 to the phenomena of colour interference in orientation feature-based tasks. Our framework explains the existing data, and provided a prediction that is tested and confirmed psychophysically. While our results here favour the V1 saliency map theory over others, they do not conclusively rule out any particular theory. However, our findings and our analysis of the scenarios here can motivate future investigations to better distinguish the alternative theories. One of these new investigations (Zhaoping and May, 2004) has already generated additional findings that strengthen our conclusions here and will be reported in a future paper.

REFERENCES

Cave, K. R. (1999). The FeatureGate model of visual selection. *Psychological Research*, *62*, 182–194.

Conway, B. J. (2001). Spatial structure of cone inputs to color cells in alert macaque primary visual cortex (V-1). *Journal of Neuroscience*, *21*, 2768–2783.

Duncan, J., & Humphreys, G. (1989). Visual search and stimulus similarity. *Psychological Review*, *96*, 1–26.

Fitzpatrick, D. (1996). The functional organization of local circuits in visual cortex: Insights from the study of tree shrew striate cortex. *Cerebral Cortex*, *6*, 329–341.

Friedman, H. S., Zhou, H., & Heydt, R. R. (2003). The coding of uniform color figures in monkey visual cortex. *Journal of Physiology*, *548*(Pt, 2), 593–613.

Gegenfurtner, K. R. (2003). Cortical mechanisms of colour vision. *Nature Reviews Neuroscience*, *4*(7), 563–572.

Gegenfurtner, K. R., Kiper, D. C., & Fenstemaker, S. B. (1996). Processing of color, form, and motion in macaque area V2. *Visual Neuroscience*, *13*(1), 161–172.

Gilbert, C. D., & Wiesel, T. N. (1983). Clustered intrinsic connections in cat visual cortex. *Journal of Neuroscience*, *3*, 1116–1133.

Gottlieb, J. P., Kusunoki, M., & Goldberg, M. E. (1998). The representation of visual salience in monkey parietal cortex. *Nature*, *391*(6666), 481–484.

Heeger, D. J. (1992). Normalization of cell responses in cat striate cortex. *Visual Neuroscience*, *9*, 181–197.

Hegde, J., & Felleman, D. J. (2003). How selective are V1 cells for pop-out stimuli? *Journal of Neuroscience*, *23*(31), 9968–9980.

Hirsch, J. A., & Gilbert, C. D. (1991). Synaptic physiology of horizontal connections in the cat's. *Journal of Neuroscience*, *11*, 1800–1809.

Itti, L., & Koch, C. (2000). A saliency-based search mechanism for overt and covert shifts of visual attention. *Vision Research*, *40*(10–12), 1489–1506.

Itti, L., & Koch, C. (2001). Computational modelling of visual attention. *Nature Reviews Neuroscience*, *2*(3), 194–203.

Johnson, E. N., Hawken, M. J., & Shapley, R. (2001). The spatial transformation of color in the primary visual cortex of the macaque monkey. *Nature Neuroscience*, *4*(4), 409–416.

Kapadia, M. K., Ito, M., Gilbert, C. D., & Westheime, G. (1995). Improvement in visual sensitivity by changes in local context: Parallel studies in human observers and in V1 of alert monkeys. *Neuron*, *15*(4), 843–856.

Knierim, J. J., & van Essen, D. C. (1992). Neuronal responses to static texture patterns ion area V1 of the alert macaque monkeys. *Journal of Neurophysiology*, *67*, 961–980.

Koch, C., & Ullman, S. (1985). Shifts in selective visual attention: Towards the underlying neural circuitry. *Human Neurobiology*, *4*, 219–227.

Krummenacher, J., Müller, H. J., & Heller, D. (2001). Visual search for dimensionally redundant pop-out target: Evidence for parallel-coactive processing of dimensions. *Perception and Psychophysics*, *63*(5), 901–917.

Leventhal, A. G., Thompson, K. G., Liu, D., Zhou, Y., & Ault, S. J. (1995). Concomitant sensitivity to orientation, direction, and color of cells in layers 2, 3, and 4 of monkey striate cortex. *Journal of Neuroscience*, *15*(3, Pt. 1), 1808–1818.

Li, C. Y., & Li, W. (1994). Extensive integration field beyond the classical receptive field of cat's striate cortical neurons: Classification and tuning properties. *Vision Research*, *34*(18), 2337–2355.

Li, Z. (1999a). Contextual influences in V1 as a basis for pop out and asymmetry in visual search. *Proceedings of the National Academy of Sciences, USA*, *96*, 10530–10535.

Li, Z. (1999b). Visual segmentation by contextual influences via intracortical interactions in primary visual cortex. *Network: Computation in Neural Systems*, *10*, 187–212.

Li, Z. (2000). Pre-attentive segmentation in the primary visual cortex. *Spatial Vision*, *13*(1), 25–50.

Li, Z. (2001). Computational design and nonlinear dynamics of a recurrent network model of the primary visual cortex. *Neural Computation*, *13*(8), 1749–1780.

Li, Z. (2002). A saliency map in primary visual cortex. *Trends in Cognitive Science*, *6*(1), 9–16.

Li, Z., & Atick, J. (1994). Towards a theory of striate cortex. *Neural Computation*, *6*, 127–146.

Livingstone, M. S., & Hubel, D. H. (1984). Anatomy and physiology of a color system in the primate visual cortex. *Journal of Neuroscience*, *4*(1), 309–356.

Müller, H. J., Heller, D., & Ziegler, J. (1995). Visual search for singleton feature targets within and across feature dimensions. *Perception and Psychophysics*, *57*, 1–17.

Nothdurft, H. C. (1997). Different approaches to the coding of visual segmentation. In L. Harris & M. Jenkins (Eds.), *Computational and psychophysical mechanisms of visual coding* (pp. 20–43). New York: Cambridge University Press.

Nothdurft, H. C. (2000). Salience from feature contrast: Additivity across dimensions. *Vision Research*, *40*, 1183–1202.

Nothdurft, H. C., Gallant, J. L., & van Essen, D. C. (1999). Response modulation by texture surround in primate area V1: Correlates of 'pop-out' under anesthesia. *Visual Neuroscience*, *16*(1), 15–34.

Nothdurft, H. C., Gallant, J. L., & van Essen, D. C. (2000). Response profiles to texture border patterns in area V1. *Visual Neuroscience*, *17*(3), 421–436.

Pashler, H. (1988). Cross-dimensional interaction and texture segregation. *Perception and Psychophysics*, *43*, 307–318.

Rockland, K. S., & Lund, J. S. (1983). Intrinsic laminar lattice connections in primate visual cortex. *Journal of Comparative Neurology*, *216*, 303–318.

Rubenstein, B., & Sagi, D. (1990). Spatial variability as a limiting factor in texture discrimination tasks: Implications for performance asymmetries. *Journal of the Optical Society of America, Part A*, *9*, 1632–1643.

Shipp, S. (2004). The brain circuitry of attention. *Trends in Cognitive Sciences*, *8*(5), 223–230.

Sillito, A. M., Grieve, K. L., Jones, H. E., Cudeiro, J., & Davis, J. (1995). Visual cortical mechanisms detecting focal orientation discontinuities. *Nature*, *378*(6556), 492–496.

Snowden, R. J. (1998). Texture segregation and visual search: A comparison of the effects of random variations along irrelevant dimensions. *Journal of Experimental Psychology: Human Perception and Performance, 24*, 1354–1367.

Tehovnik, E. J., Slocum, W. M., & Carvey, C. E. (2003). Behavioural state affects saccadic eye movements evoked by micro-stimulation of striate cortex. *European Journal of Neuroscience, 18*(4), 969–979.

Theeuwes, J., & Burger, R. (1998). Attentional control during visual search: The effect of irrelevant singletons. *Journal of Experimental Psychology: Human Perception and Performance, 24*(5), 1342–1353.

Treisman, A., & Gelade, G. (1980). A feature integration theory of attention. *Cognitive Psychology, 12*, 97–136.

Ts'o, D., & Gilbert, C. (1988). The organization of chromatic and spatial interactions in the primate striate cortex. *Journal of Neuroscience, 8*, 1712–1727.

Wachtler, T., Sejnowski, T. J., & Albright, T. D. (2003). Representation of color stimuli in awake macaque primary visual cortex. *Neuron, 37*(4), 681–691.

Wolfe, J. M., Cave, K. R., & Franzel, S. L. (1989). Guided search: An alternative to the feature integration model for visual search. *Journal of Experimental Psychology, 15*, 419–433.

Zhaoping, L., & May, K. (2004). Irrelevance of feature maps for bottom up visual saliency in segmentation and search tasks. Program No. 20.1. 2004 Abstract Viewer/Itinerary Planner [Online] Washington, DC: Society for Neuroscience.

VISUAL COGNITION, 2006, 14 (4/5/6/7/8), 934–957

Ψ Psychology Press
Taylor & Francis Group

On the roles of the human frontal eye fields and parietal cortex in visual search

Jacinta O'Shea, Neil G. Muggleton, and Alan Cowey

Department of Experimental Psychology, University of Oxford, UK

Vincent Walsh

Institute of Cognitive Neuroscience and Department of Psychology, University College London, UK

Successful search for a target in a visual scene requires many cognitive operations, including orienting, detecting the target, and rejecting distractors. Performance in search is affected by a number of factors, including the number of targets and distractors, their similarity, motion in the display, location, and viewing history of the stimuli, etc. A task with so many stimulus variables and behavioural or neural responses may require different brain areas to interact in ways that depend on specific task demands. Until recently the right posterior parietal cortex has been ascribed a pre-eminent role in visual search. Based on recent physiological and brain imaging evidence, and on a programme of magnetic stimulation studies designed to compare directly the contributions of the parietal cortex and the human frontal eye fields in search, we have generated an account of similarities and differences between these two brain regions. The comparison suggests that the frontal eye fields are important for some aspects of search previously attributed to the parietal cortex, and that accounts of the cortical contributions to search need to be reassessed in the light of these findings.

Visual search for a target in a cluttered display is now a common, almost standard task in studies of higher visual functions. Several brain regions have been identified as important to normal visual search, but if one particular area can be said to have a pivotal role it is the right posterior parietal cortex. There are good reasons for this view, which we first outline and then question in this paper. Three main lines of evidence support a central role for the parietal cortex in search and related functions.

Please address all correspondence to Vincent Walsh, Institute of Cognitive Neuroscience & Dept. of Psychology, University College London, UK. E-mail v.walsh@ucl.ac.uk

This work was funded by the Wellcome Trust, the Medical Research Council, and the Royal Society.

http://www.psypress.com/viscog

DOI: 10.1080/13506280500197363

Neurological patients with damage to the parietal cortex, particularly the right parietal cortex, show a variety of deficits in search behaviour (see Robertson & Brooks, 2006 this issue) including an increase in "illusory conjunctions" (i.e., false positive responses) (Friedman-Hill, Robertson, & Treisman, 1995). Global deficits in spatial functions that follow extensive parietal cortex damage (e.g., spatial neglect) also support the view that the parietal cortex is particularly important in conjunction searches. This is because theories of visual search argue that detecting conjunction targets requires spatial localization and orienting and that the binding of the features that contribute to the conjunction target also require spatial localization (see the contributions of Robertson & Brooks, 2006 this issue, and Treisman, 2006 this issue). This neuropsychological and psychological evidence is perhaps the most convincing and direct case for a key role for the parietal cortex in visual search.

The second line of evidence for the role of parietal cortex in visual search stems from brain imaging studies, which frequently find right parietal cortex activations associated with visual search tasks and in tasks such as orienting, which are thought to be components of search. Search is a highly complex task, however, and the cognitive operations actually giving rise to BOLD activation patterns are rarely clear. Proposed explanations for parietal activations during imaging studies of search include: Visual filtering, visual binding, eye movement preparation, spatial localization, orienting, and target selection (Corbetta, Shulman, Miezin, & Petersen, 1995; Gitelman, Nobre, Parrish, LaBar, Kim, Meyer, & Mesulam, 1999; Leonards, Sunaert, van Hecke, & Orban, 2001; Nobre, Coull, Walsh, & Frith, 2003; Pollmann, Weidner, Müller, & von Cramon, 2000; Wilkinson, Halligan, Henson, & Dolan, 2002). An exception here is the work of Donner et al. (2000, 2002), whose stimuli, task designs, and interpretations have partialled out difficulty from other elements of the task and allow an assessment comparable with the single unit experiments. This evidence from Donner's human brain imaging work provides a strong impetus to reinvestigate the role of the FEF vis-à-vis the PPC. Other work also leads us to emphasize the role of visuomotor transformations in the parietal cortex at the expense on motorically independent visual functions (Caminiti, Ferraina, & Johnson, 1996; Johnson, Ferraina, Bianchi, & Caminiti, 1996).

The final line of evidence often presented in support of the role of the parietal cortex in visual search is recordings from neurons in the lateral intraparietal sulcus. These cells are selective for saccade-related spatial localization (Bisley & Goldberg, 2003) and for task-relevant stimulus-association parameters (Andersen & Buneo, 2002). Such studies, rather than providing direct evidence of involvement in search, indicate that parietal regions are involved in some of the component processes of search. Lesion studies of parietal cortex in nonhuman primates provide more direct search-related evidence. For example, inactivation of the intra-parietal sulcus by reversible muscimol lesions produces impairments in saccade latency and accuracy when more than one stimulus is present and impairs conjunction search times significantly (Wardak, Olivier, & Duhamel, 2002).

WHY QUESTION THE ROLE OF THE PARIETAL CORTEX?

On examining the neuropsychological evidence, the cornerstones supporting the putative pre-eminent role of the parietal cortex in search are the data outlining a parietal role in spatial orienting, spatial localization and binding of individual visual features. Two recent pieces of evidence challenge the need to invoke the parietal cortex as critical to binding in conjunctions *per se*. Wokciulik and Kanwisher (1998), for example, showed that implicit binding can occur in a patient with Balint's syndrome, suggesting that the issue may instead be one of the results of binding reaching awareness. More compellingly, Jackson, Swainson, Mort, Husain, & Jackson (2004a) and Jackson, Newport, Mort, Husain, Jackson, Swainson, et al. (2004b) have shown that a patient with Balint's syndrome can report conjunctions of features correctly in a guided selection paradigm and, under some conditions, report on more than one object in a visual array. A recent transcranial magnetic stimulation (TMS) study also showed that if subjects know the location of an upcoming conjunction target they can report on conjunctions accurately even when TMS is delivered over the right posterior parietal cortex. In other words, feature binding *per se* can be achieved without a normal contribution from an intact right posterior parietal cortex (Ellison, Rushworth, & Walsh, 2003).

With regard to the view that binding is required in target absent displays, because "distractors must be bound correctly to be discarded as potential targets", we do not subscribe to this view as we believe it is not parsimonious. The concept of binding on target present trials requires that the subject (and underlying neural mechanisms) carry out search for a particular colour and shape that cooccur at a particular spatial location. In the sensory visual areas that code for these features (colour, shape), retinotopic information will be preserved. For efficient search then, this means that only those stimuli that coactivate both feature maps at the same spatial location need undergo binding. In Ashbridge, Walsh, and Cowey (1997) we show that the times at which TMS is effective are relatively singular, arguing against an iterative process of binding and rejection. In that study we showed that interference with the right parietal cortex impaired subjects' ability to decide whether a target was present or absent in conjunction search tasks. The impairment on target absent trials is important because on these trials there is no target whose two features have to be bound. Further, the time course of these TMS effects is inconsistent with any interpretation based on binding, filtering, orienting, or localizing. A subsequent study (Walsh, Ashbridge, & Cowey, 1998) showed that the right parietal cortex was only important for visual conjunction search when the targets were novel (see also Ellison et al., 2003; Walsh, Ellison, Ashbridge, & Cowey, 1999), suggesting that the conditions used to evaluate search (typically naïve subjects and novel stimuli) may not be good predictors of how real search is carried out when one looks for a familiar target (spouse, wallet, keys, pen) against backgrounds in which one has practised the task many times (shopping centre, handbag, kitchen table, desk).

So there is evidence from the studies of parietal cortex that questions the prevailing view that the PPC plays a fundamental role in the visual binding of the features that form an object.

WHY STUDY THE HUMAN FRONTAL EYE FIELDS IN VISUAL SEARCH?

In addition to a reexamination of the role of the parietal cortex in search, we have paid particular attention to the role of the frontal eye fields (FEF) in vision and search. There are several reasons for this.

Recent physiological studies, predominantly from Schall and colleagues (e.g., Bichot & Schall, 1999, 2002; Murthy, Thompson, & Schall, 2001; Schall & Bichot, 1998; Schall & Hanes, 1993; Schall & Thompson, 1999; Thompson, Bichot, & Schall, 1997; Thompson, Hanes, Bichot, & Schall, 1996; Thompson & Schall, 1999), suggest that the frontal eye fields of the macaque are involved in visual target selection. Prior to this work, the frontal eye fields were almost exclusively studied with a view to further understanding their role in eye movement programming. However, these single unit studies have shown that FEF neurons may have a perceptual role in vision that is independent of their role in eye movements. Microstimulation studies, in which the frontal eye fields are stimulated a few milliseconds prior to presentation of a visual stimulus, have revealed that preactivation of the FEF reduces the threshold of neuronal responses in V4 (Moore & Armstrong, 2001). When human FEF is stimulated by TMS prior to onset of a visual stimulus, subjects' sensitivity to the stimulus is similarly increased (Grosbras & Paus, 2003). Intracranial recordings from human subjects further suggest a role for the FEF in perceptual analysis of the contralateral visual field (Blanke et al., 1999). Thus, there are indications that the FEF may have some top-down role in visual detection. This is the kind of interpretation frequently offered to describe the role of the parietal cortex in higher level vision. It is also a hypothesis that has been proposed to account for search deficits in monkeys with unilateral FEF lesions (Collin, Cowey, Latto, & Marzi, 1982; see also Lawler & Cowey, 1987). The proposal that FEF makes a *perceptual* contribution to vision is also consistent with the early temporal onset profile of FEF neurons. In a review of single unit response latencies throughout the visual system, Bullier (2001) showed that FEF neurons form part of what he calls the "fast brain"—those regions which show the earliest responses to visual stimuli (Figure 1). If temporal response profiles provide a marker of the order of activation of visual areas, then the early responses of FEF neurons place them on par with other visual sensory areas such as V1, V2, V4, MT, and MST (Nowak & Bullier, 1997; Schmolesky et al., 1998).

New anatomical data also prompt a reassessment of the role of the FEF. In early models of the visual hierarchy (e.g., Maunsell & van Essen, 1987), the FEF were placed at a level above the parietal cortex. In a more extensive review of the laminar organization of corticocortical connections (Felleman & van Essen, 1991), the FEF were demoted to occupy the same level of the visual hierarchy as the parietal cortex, above the level occupied by the extrastriate visual areas. More recently, the FEF have been shown to have patterns of connectivity with extrastriate areas which may place them at the

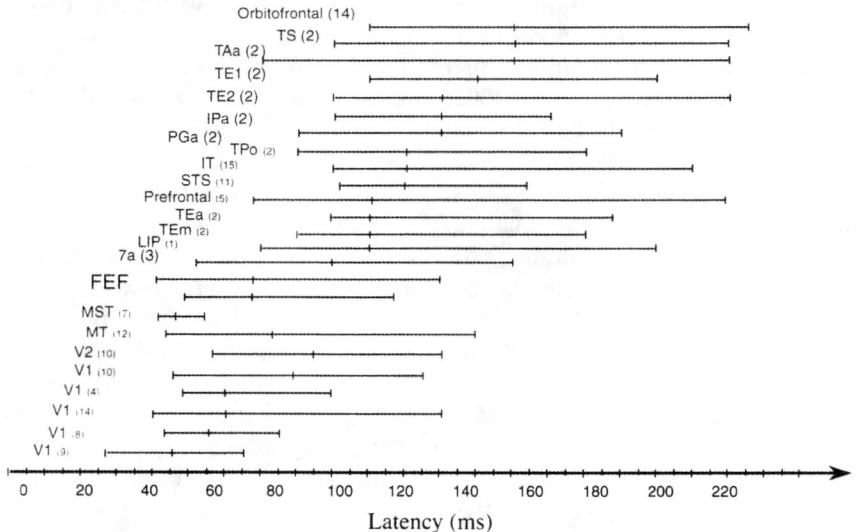

Figure 1. Review of studies measuring single unit response latencies in the visual system. For each study, the central bar represents the median and the extremities of the line the 10 and 90 percentiles. Numbers refer to individual studies detailed in Bullier (2001). Note that the FEF latencies are similar to those in V1 despite the large distance between these two areas in the anatomical hierarchy. (Reproduced from Bullier, 2001, with permission.)

same level in the visual hierarchy as the visual extrastriate areas (Barone, Batardiere, Knoblauch, & Kennedy, 2000).

In functional neuroimaging studies, the FEF are commonly activated along with the parietal cortex in search tasks or other tasks involving orienting, selection, localization, and other components of complex visual search and detection tasks. Because of the known role of the parietal cortex in spatial localization, binding, etc., and the known role of the FEF in saccade programming, these activations are, somewhat recursively, attributed to the role of the parietal cortex in binding, selection, and orienting, followed by saccade programming in the case of the FEF (see, for example, Gitelman et al., 1999).

The predominance of a view of visual cognition that places the parietal cortex at the hub of any function that can be related to spatial analysis and search, and reduces the role of the FEF to programming eye movements, is perhaps one reason why early evidence for the role of the FEF in search and contralateral orienting was not always considered in analyses of the "frontoparietal network". It has been known for more than a century that unilateral prefrontal lesions produce a visual neglect (Bianchi, 1895). Later work (reviewed by Latto & Cowey, 1971) established that it was the destruction of the frontal eye fields that produced this neglect. Discrete lesions of the FEF in the macaque produce deficits that would be considered typical of parietal damage in patients. Latto and Cowey (1971), for example, found that FEF lesions produced a contralateral neglect that is even greater than that seen following lesions of the PPC. A follow- up experiment showed that this neglect persisted even after the monkeys had recovered normal oculomotor functions and fixations.

Motivated by the new physiological and anatomical data, and by the emerging evidence which, in our view, weakens the assumption that the parietal cortex has a special role in feature binding *because* it is important for spatial localization, we have begun a programme of research that aims to identify the similarities and differences between the parietal cortex and the FEF in search. There are so many functional similarities between the two areas that the question "Why do we need both of them?" is a legitimate one. FEF and PPC are heavily interconnected; both occupy an interface between sensory input and motor output; both are important for eye movements; both are activated in search studies; both have been put forward as important in establishing stimulus salience; both have been associated with some form of attention and both give spatially driven responses (see Caminiti et al., 1996; Johnson et al., 1996).

Table 1 summarizes the findings from our previous TMS studies regarding the role of the parietal cortex in visual search. In what follows we summarize our findings so far in trying to match the studies on FEF and parietal cortex.

TABLE 1
Conclusions from TMS studies of the posterior parietal cortex in visual search

- Lateralization: Right hemisphere more important than left (Ashbridge et al., 1997)
- PPC required for target present *and absent* responses (Ashbridge et al., 1997; Walsh et al., 1998)
- PPC important for conjunction but not feature search (Ellison et al., 2003)
- Right PPC important for target detection in both visual hemifields (Walsh et al., 1999)
- The involvement of PPC does not change as a function of set size (Ellison et al., 2003)
- As subjects learn a search task the PPC becomes unnecessary for search (Walsh et al., 1998, 1999)
- The timing of TMS effects on PPC in search is yoked to RT (Ashbridge et al., 1997)
- The PPC is not required in visual priming (Campana, Cowey, & Walsh, 2002)

GENERIC DETAILS OF EXPERIMENTS

Cortical site localization

In the studies reviewed here the FEF was localized for TMS using the Brainsight frameless stereotaxy system (Rogue Research, Montreal, Canada). The stimulation site was identified on each subject's T_1-weighted MRI scan and was then coregistered with scalp coordinates over which TMS was applied (see Figure 2). The probabilistic location of each subject's FEF was determined according to anatomical landmarks. Stimulation was applied over the posterior middle frontal gyrus, just rostral to the junction of the precentral sulcus and the superior frontal sulcus (Blanke et al., 2000). The site of stimulation was also referenced to each subject's motor hand area (e.g., Ro, Cheifet, Ingle, Shoup, & Rafal, 1999). Using this method, on average, TMS was applied 5 cm lateral of the saggital midline and 3–4 cm rostral of each subject's motor hand area. This site corresponds well with scalp coordinates used in other TMS studies of FEF (Leff, Scott, Rothwell, & Wise, 2001; Muri, Hess, & Meienberg, 1991; Tobler & Muri, 2002; Wipfli et al., 2001). After registration of the MRI images to the Montreal Neurological Institute series average (Evans, Collins, & Holmes, 1996), mean Talairach coordinates for the stimulated site were 32, −2, 61 (standard error: 1.34, 6.09, 1.55) (Talairach & Tournoux, 1988). These coordinates correspond well with mean Talairach coordinates for FEF derived from a review of PET imaging studies (Paus, 1996). The vertex was chosen as the principal control site for the nonspecific effects of TMS, such as somatosensory and acoustic artefacts. Area V5 was chosen as an additional and easily accessed control site to demonstrate that any effects of frontal eye field TMS on visual search are specific and not a general consequence of interference with the visual system. Vertex stimulation was applied at electrode site "Cz" according to the 10–20 International

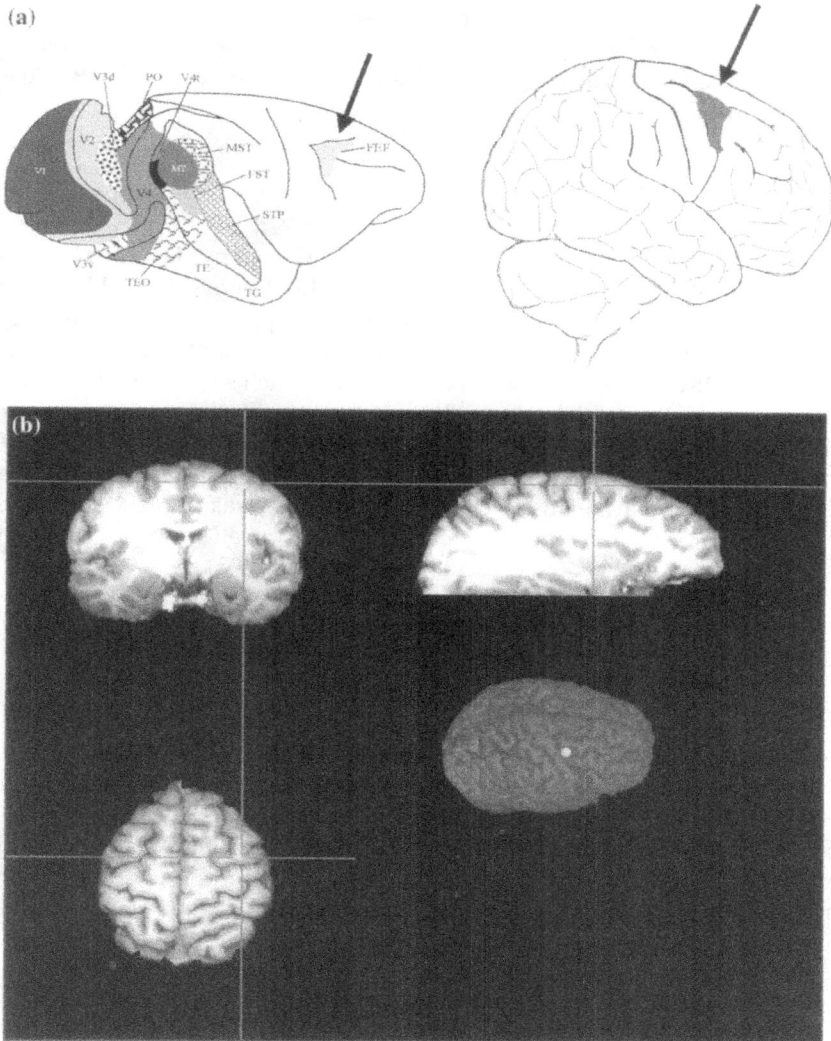

Figure 2. (a) The location of FEF in the macaque brain, in the rostral arch of the arcuate sulcus (Brodmann's area 8). The putative human homologue of FEF (based on neuroimaging studies) is located at the junction of the superior frontal sulcus and precentral sulcus (Brodmann's areas 6/8). (b) The anatomical landmarks used in combination with frameless stereotaxy to localize FEF on each individual subject's anatomical MRI. The mean point of FEF stimulation is marked by the filled white circle. (Top left) Transverse section showing FEF location at the caudal end of the middle frontal gyrus, at the junction of the precentral sulcus and superior frontal sulcus. (Top right) Saggital section showing FEF location at the level of the insula. (Bottom left) Coronal section. Arrow indicates superior frontal sulcus. (Bottom right) 3-D rendered image showing FEF location.

941

Electrode System. V5 was localized functionally using the established method of moving phosphene elicitation (Battelli, Black, & Wray, 2002; Stewart, Battelli, Walsh, & Cowey. 1999).

Transcranial magnetic stimulation

A Magstim Super Rapid machine (Magstim Company, Dyfed, UK) was used to deliver repetitive- and double-pulse TMS. A series of small diameter (50 mm) figure-of-eight TMS coils were used to apply stimulation over the cortical sites of interest. Coils were cooled before use to prevent overheating during a block and were replaced at the end of each block. Over FEF and vertex, each coil was oriented parallel to the floor with the handle running in an anterior–posterior direction and was clamped in position using a mechanical arm. Over V5, each coil was oriented at a right angle with the floor. In rTMS paradigms, 10 Hz TMS (500 ms) was applied at 65% of stimulator output over each site. Subjects wore earplugs to attenuate the sound of the coil discharge (Pascual-Leone et al., 1993).

Eye movement recording

To monitor fixation and any blinks during search trials, horizontal eye movements were recorded using infrared light transducers in the Skalar IRIS 6500 system attached to the forehead rest. Signals were sampled at a rate of 1000 Hz by an analogue to digital converter card (Type PCM-DAS 16d/12; Computerboards, Pittsburgh, PA) and recorded using DASYlab 5 software on an IBM compatible PC. Eye traces were recorded for the duration of the visual stimulus on every trial and the equipment was recalibrated between blocks.

Visual stimuli and task

All experiments were conducted using standard visual search tasks of three kinds: Conjunction search (colour/form or colour/orientation), feature search (colour singleton target remained constant from trial-to-trial), and odd-man-out search (colour singleton target that switched with distractor colour unpredictably from trial-to-trial). Each search task was one of two array sizes: The large search arrays subtended $20° \times 20°$ and contained sixteen $2° \times 2°$ array elements; the small search arrays subtended $2° \times 2°$ and contained twelve $1.6° \times 1.6°$ array elements. In all experiments, the subjects' task was to give a manual key-press response to indicate whether a particular target was present or absent. Target present probability was always 50%. Accuracy and speed of response were emphasized to subjects.

ARE THERE HEMISPHERIC DIFFERENCES BETWEEN THE LEFT AND RIGHT FEF IN VISUAL SEARCH?

There is clear evidence that the right hemisphere parietal cortex is more important for search than the left, so our first question was whether this is also the case in the FEF. Muggleton, Juan, Cowey, and Walsh (2003) presented the large visual conjunction search paradigm and analysed response time as the dependent measure. As in most experiments with TMS and search, a single set size was used. Repetitive TMS was applied over either the left or right FEF at 10 Hz for 500 ms at 65% of stimulator output beginning with the onset of the visual stimuli. Eye movements were monitored as described above. As Figure 3 shows, stimulation over the right, but not the left, FEF resulted in a significant increase in response times on target present trials. This result suggests that, like the parietal

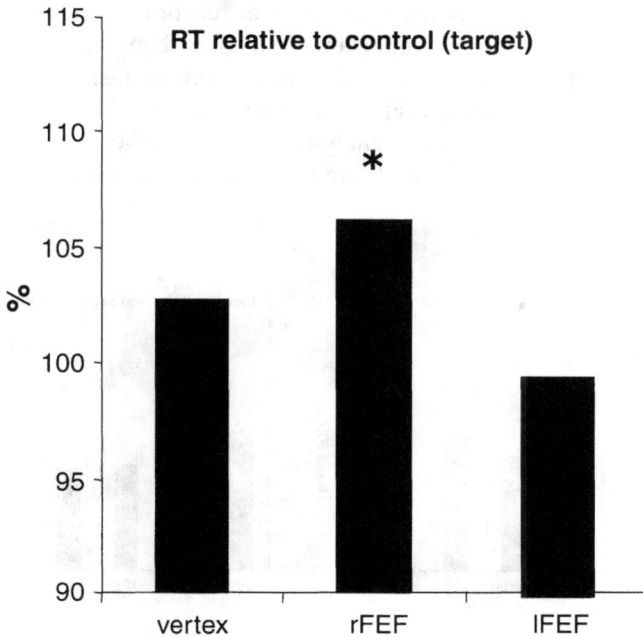

Figure 3. The lateralization of the frontal eye fields in visual search. TMS over the right, but not left, FEF significantly increases reaction times on target present trials, $F(3, 15) = 4.955$, $MSE = 2076.7$, $p = .014$, left FEF vs. right FEF, mean difference $= 40.49$, $p = .022$.

cortex, right hemisphere human frontal eye fields are necessary for normal visual conjunction search performance.

ARE THE FEF INVOLVED IN TARGET ABSENT TRIALS AS WELL AS TARGET PRESENT TRIALS?

Magnetic stimulation of the right posterior parietal cortex slows down performance on both target present and absent trials, and the timing of these effects correlates with subjects' reaction times. Given that a target is not present, the interference on absent trials cannot be a function of disrupting the binding of target features. In a recent paper we have argued, on the basis of a visuomotor learning experiment, that the role of the posterior parietal cortex may not be related to visual target analysis at all, but rather to forming visuomotor associations in novel tasks (Ellison et al., 2003). Muggleton et al. (2003) analysed the effects of rTMS on reaction times in target present and absent trials using the same stimuli and parameters as described above. As Figure 4 shows, compared with rTMS of the vertex or left FEF, or control trials in which TMS was not delivered, stimulation of the right FEF significantly increased manual reaction times only on target present trials. This is an important difference between the effects of stimulating FEF and parietal cortex under similar task conditions. We interpret this as indicating that the role of the FEF is related to target detection or some kind of visual analysis leading to target detection: If there is no target in the array, the FEF are not required to make a target absent

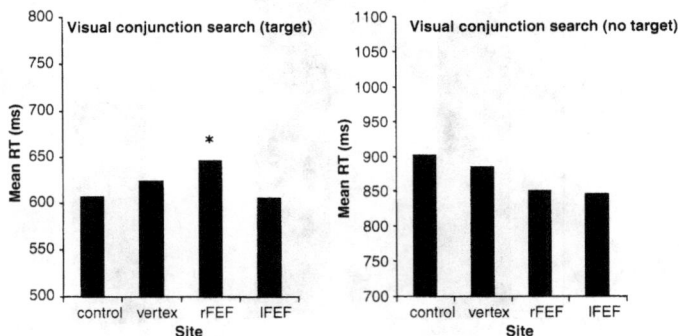

Figure 4. The frontal eye fields are involved in detecting targets but are not required for target absent trials. TMS over right FEF, but not over left FEF or vertex delays reaction times on target present trials but has no effect on target absent trials. Target absent, $F(3, 15) = 0.771$, $MSE = 4092.2$, $p = .0528$.

decision. This is in contrast to the target absent effect observed with TMS of the parietal cortex.

IS THE RIGHT FEF REQUIRED FOR TARGET DETECTION IN BOTH VISUAL HEMIFIELDS?

Stimulation of the right parietal cortex delays target detection in either visual hemifield, whereas TMS of the left parietal cortex has an effect only on targets in the right visual field. Intracranial recordings from human FEF (Blanke et al., 1999) and the effects of TMS over FEF during saccade tasks suggest that each FEF is entirely concerned with contralateral hemispace. TMS of either the right or left FEF, for example, tends to delay contralateral but not ipsilateral saccades (Ro et al., 1999). Muggleton et al. (2003) investigated whether this lateralization extended to visual analysis by using large conjunction search displays in which targets could be presented at up to 10° eccentricity. The result (Figure 5) yields the conclusion that, like the parietal cortex (Walsh et al., 1999), TMS over the right FEF delayed reaction times on target present trials irrespective of the location of the target in the visual field.

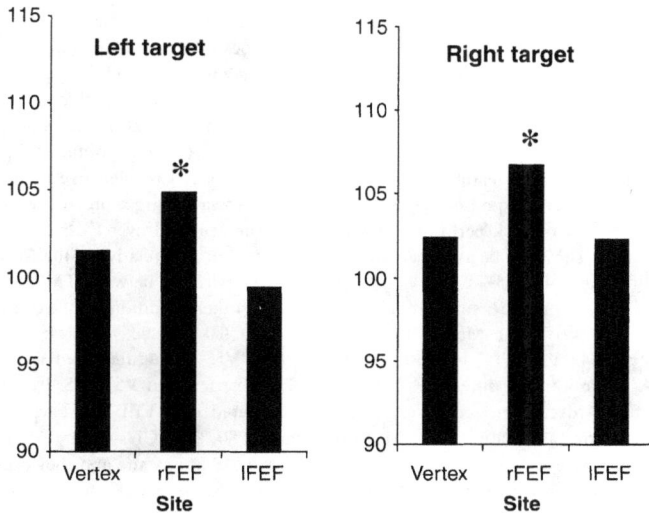

Figure 5. The right FEF is important for target detection in both hemifields. TMS over right FEF slows reaction times for target detection irrespective of whether the target is in the right or left visual hemifield. Repeated measures ANOVA with TMS site and target location as factors: Site, $F(3, 15) = 5.179$, $MSE = 3822.5$, $p = .012$; no significant main effect of hemifield, $F(1, 15) = 0.0$, $MSE = 0.376$, $p = .994$; nor an interaction, $F(3, 15) = 0.153$, $MSE = 202.3$, $p = .922$. Left vs. right FEF, mean difference $= 39.2$, $p = .018$.

DO CONJUNCTIONS HAVE SPECIAL STATUS IN THE FEF?

Much of the case for the role of the parietal cortex in feature binding is built upon the finding that patients with damage to the parietal cortex show a variety of feature binding deficits (Robertson & Brooks, 2006 this issue; Treisman, 1996; but see above and Wokciulik & Kanwisher, 1998; Jackson, Swainson, et al., in press; Jackson, Newport, et al., in press), the cardinal symptom being a failure to report conjunctions accurately. In seeking to find the similarities and differences between the parietal cortex and FEF, it is important to know whether the feature/conjunction distinction holds for FEF. To investigate this, Muggleton et al. (2003) used three tasks (Figure 6a): A simple feature search in which the target was constant, a feature oddball task in which the target and distractors could change identity between trials, and a classical colour/orientation conjunction search. Only one set size was used. In this experiment, subjects' search performance was matched across all three tasks by using a staircase procedure that varied array duration until subjects performed at a 75% accuracy level. The search

---

Figure 6 (opposite).   Behavioural task and performance data. **(a)** Time course of a trial and the three stimulus displays used. (i) In the constant feature search task the target was always a blue circle (CIE $x = 0.163$, $y = 0.140$, luminance 20 cd.m^{-2}; 0.2 ×0.2) amongst an array of 11 red circles (CIE $x = 0.615$, $y = 0.346$, luminance 20 cd.m^{-2}; 0.2 ×0.2). (ii) In the interleaved search condition, the target was either a red circle amongst blue circle distractors or vice versa. The order of red target or blue target trials was randomized with the constraint that each block of 60 trials contained 15 of each trial type in 30 target present trials. (iii) In the conjunction task the target was a blue diagonal amongst an array of six red diagonals (0.2 ×0.2) in the same orientation and five blue diagonals in the orthogonal orientation. **(b)** d' data ($\pm SEM$) obtained in (i) constant feature search, (ii) interleaved feature search, (iii) conjunction search task. **(c)** Log (bias) values ($\pm SEM$) obtained in (i) constant feature search, (ii) interleaved feature search, (iii) conjunction search task. Positive values indicated a bias towards target absent responses, negative values a bias towards target present responses. There was a significant effect on task performance when TMS was delivered over FEF. $F(2) = 5.011$, $p = .026$. This effect was shown to be a d' decrease in the conjunction task relative to the constant feature task: Mean difference 1.02, 95% CI 0.17, 1.87, $p = .02$. Comparisons between TMS sites showed a significant d' decrease with FEF stimulation compared to all other conditions in the conjunction task (TMS over FEF vs. no TMS): Mean difference 0.47, 95% CI 0.02, 0.92, $p = .044$; FEF vs. vertex: Mean difference 0.649, 95% CI 0.44, 0.86, $p = .001$; FEF vs. V5: Mean difference 0.44, 95% CI 0.10, 0.79, $p = .024$. There were no differences between no TMS, vertex, and V5 TMS. In the interleaved feature task, the d' decrement seen when TMS was delivered over FEF approached significance compared to the constant feature task: Mean difference 0.80, 95% CI −0.05, 1.65, $p = .056$. No difference in blinks or eye movements was associated with TMS at any site and they occurred rarely during trials. Log values showed that in the conjunction task subjects were biased towards making target absent responses in no TMS trials (value: 1.35) as well as in TMS conditions (vertex 1.77, FEF 0.91, V5 1.59). However, comparison of the three TMS conditions indicated a significant reduction in bias with FEF stimulation: Two-tailed paired Student's t-test: FEF vs. V5, $t(4) = 8.43$, $p = .001$; FEF vs. vertex, $t(4) = 3.26$, $p = .031$. Bias values for both the simple feature task were higher (values: No TMS 0.16, vertex 0.69, FEF 0.80, V5 0.86) and the interleaved task (values: No TMS 0.11, vertex 0.46, FEF −0.15, V5 0.59) but no significant differences between the effects of the stimulation sites were seen.

TMS (10 Hz, 500 ms)

(i) Fixation
500 ms

(ii) Search array
40–180 ms

(iii) Mask
Until response

(b)

(c)

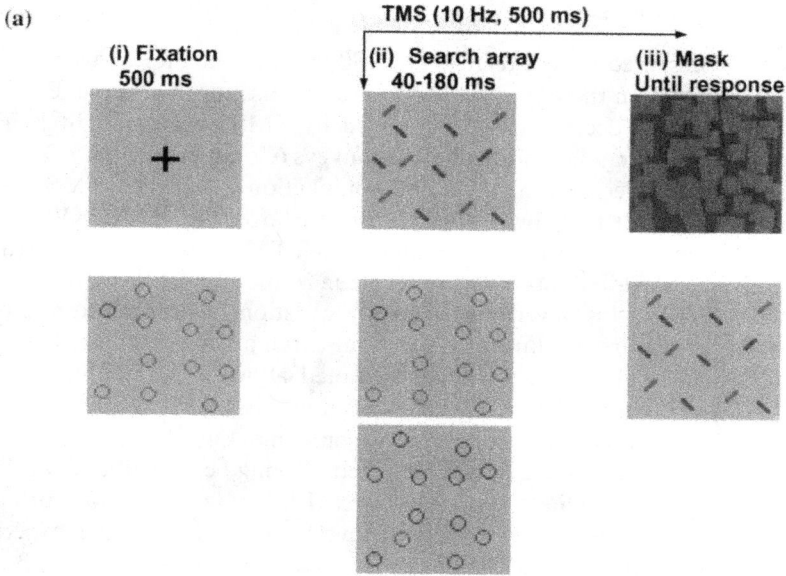

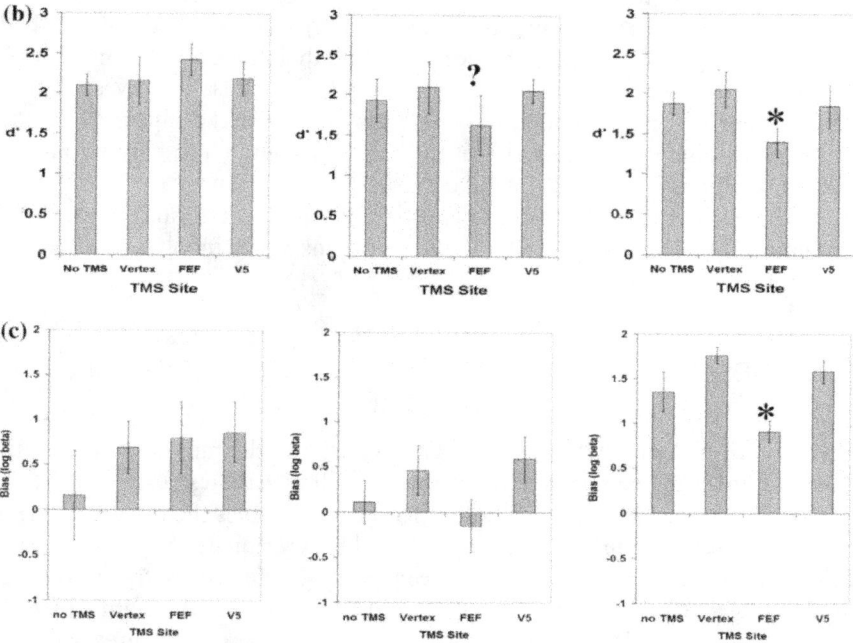

Figure 6. (See opposite for caption)

arrays were presented for between 40 and 180 ms according to each subject's ability. The results in the upper histograms show that, for the simple feature task, there was no decrease in d' produced by TMS over the right FEF, vertex, or V5, echoing the findings from monkeys (Collin et al., 1982). There was a significant decrease in d' in the conjunction task when TMS was delivered to the right FEF, but not when delivered over the vertex or V5. An intriguing intermediate result was obtained when TMS was applied over the right FEF in the oddball task. The decrease in d' did not reach significance here ($p = .056$) but this nevertheless raises a question regarding the role of FEF when targets are not known before the search array is presented. This may indicate that the FEF, which as we noted above is part of the "fast brain" (Bullier, 2001), is important in generating a first pass analysis of the stimuli in the visual array, akin to what is sometimes called a saliency map (although saliency seems to a portable concept, having been attributed to the superior colliculus, pulvinar, parietal cortex, FEF, inferotemporal cortex, extrastriate, and striate cortex). We will investigate this in further experiments. The lower panel of histograms in Figure 6 show changes in log β, a measure of bias. The only change in bias in any of the three tasks and with any of the three stimulation sites is in the conjunction condition in which TMS over right FEF causes subjects to shift their criterion to make more target present responses in the absence of a target (false positives). This is reminiscent of the tendency of parietal patients to make illusory conjunctions and to incorrectly report the presence of target. Thus, here we have at least preliminary evidence a similarity between FEF and parietal cortex— both increase the tendency to see conjunction targets; and a potential difference—FEF, under some conditions may be involved in feature detection.

DOES THE ROLE OF FEF CHANGE WITH INCREASING SET SIZE?

In a search task distractors need to be rejected and the more distractors, the longer it takes to examine and reject them. In all the studies described so far a single set size was used because adding a set size doubles the number of trials and therefore the number of TMS trials in an experiment. Any cortical area involved in the visual analysis of a scene will be affected by the amount of clutter. Recently Ellison et al. (2003) applied TMS over the right posterior parietal cortex while subjects carried out a search task with three set sizes. The increase in reaction time caused by TMS over parietal cortex was replicated, but there was no effect of the number of elements in the array. Together with our evidence that the parietal cortex is only involved in novel search (Walsh et al., 1998, 1999), that the parietal effects are time-locked to motor responses (Ashbridge et al., 1997), and that the parietal cortex is required for target absent trials (let's call them *nonbinding trials*), the lack of an effect of set size makes it difficult to attribute a visuovisual role to the parietal cortex in search. To assess the role of the FEF with respect to set size, we gave subjects five set sizes of the small array conjunction search task (methods described as above and in Muggleton et al., 2003) with sets of 4, 6, 8, 10, and 12 stimuli. There was no effect at any set size of TMS over the vertex or left FEF. However, on target present trials there was a prominent and significant increase in slope from approximately 6 to 12 ms per item when TMS was applied over right FEF (Figure 7). As with the studies reported above, there was no significant effect of TMS over FEF on absent trials. Here then we have a disruptive effect of TMS over right FEF as a function of the amount of visual clutter in the array, an effect not seen with stimulation of the parietal cortex. At the Munich Symposium, this effect was described by the speaker as "statistically significant but not necessarily biologically meaningful". This caution was expressed because although a conjunction search task was used, the baseline slope was somewhat shallow and we need to see this replicated under conditions with steeper slopes. The array size ($2° \times 2°$) may also lead to an underestimation of set size effects and we shall attempt to replicate this with larger visual arrays. Nevertheless, the basic pattern of FEF effects replicates that described in Muggleton et al.'s baseline experiment (i.e., an effect on present but not absent trials) and the effect is specific to right FEF (no effect of vertex or left FEF), so our prediction is that this finding will be replicated with more difficult conjunctions.

WHEN IS THE FEF INVOLVED IN SEARCH?

Bullier's (2001) contention that the FEF is part of the "fast brain" and the evidence that the FEF may be involved in early visual processes or, as argued on the basis of the lesion data from nonhuman primates, in top-down processes (Collin et al., 1982), suggests that the timing of the FEF

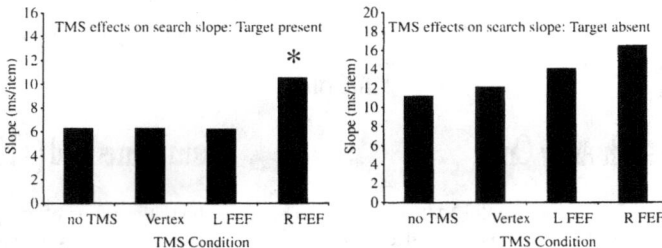

Figure 7. TMS over the right FEF causes a significant increase in visual search slopes on target present but not on target absent trials.

contribution to search may be different from that of the parietal cortex. In our first TMS study of search we identified two critical time windows around 100 and 160 ms after stimulus onset, during which TMS over the right parietal cortex interfered with target detection or search termination, respectively. To explore the timing of FEF involvement in search we employed a temporal hierarchy of TMS experiments (O'Shea, Muggleton, Cowey, & Walsh, 2004). An experiment using 500 ms of TMS was carried out to replicate the effects reported in Muggleton et al. (2003). To select the time window in which the FEF may make a critical contribution to search, TMS was applied for 500 ms, initiated either: (a) At visual array onset, (b) at 100 ms, or (c) at 200 ms later, in order to leave the first 100 or 200 ms of stimulus processing free of TMS interference. Only condition (a) produced a deficit in sensitivity (d'), so the timing experiment was aimed at the first 100 ms of visual stimulus processing. Figure 8 shows the timing of double

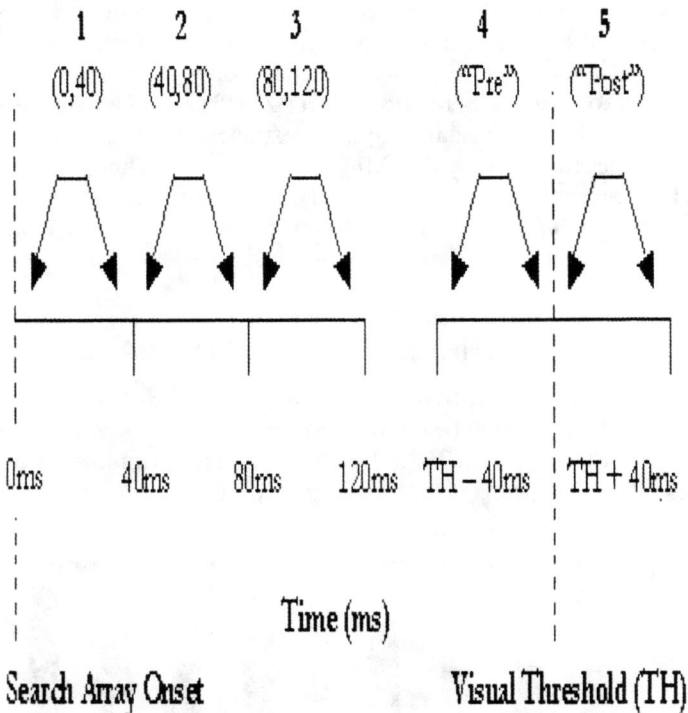

Figure 8. Timing of double pulse TMS application. The figure shows the timing of first and second TMS pulses applied in five experimental conditions. The timing of the first three conditions was determined relative to the onset of the search array, and these were identical for each subject. The last two conditions were determined relative to each individual's visual threshold and differed across subjects.

pulse TMS applied in this experiment. Subjects received two pulses per TMS trial and the pulses were either at 0 and 40 ms after array onset, 40 and 80 ms after array onset, or 80 and 120 ms after array onset. Because the duration of the visual stimulus was determined by each subject's ability to detect the target with 75% accuracy, we also applied pulses at two further times: Within the last 40 ms period below the subjects' visual threshold ("Pre" TH − 40 in Figure 8) and within the first 40 ms above the subjects' visual threshold ("Post" TH + 40 in Figure 8). These TH ± 40 conditions were included to have some measure of timing interference relative to individual differences in visual array exposure time. The spacing of pulses by 40 ms was chosen purely on the grounds of experience. We have noted that two pulses spaced by 30 or 40 ms are likely to yield more interference than a single pulse and thus give a reasonable temporal resolution without incurring the cost of the large numbers of trials demanded by single pulse timing experiments (see Walsh & Pascual-Leone, 2003).

Of these five timing sequences only one time window showed an effect of TMS over the right FEF. Sensitivity was significantly reduced when the two pulses were applied at 40 and 80 ms after stimulus onset (Figure 9). There was no effect of vertex stimulation. This time window is considerably earlier than that obtained in the experiments on the parietal cortex and therefore suggests that the FEF have a role in visual search that precedes that of the parietal cortex, and is too early to be explained on the basis of saccade preparation.

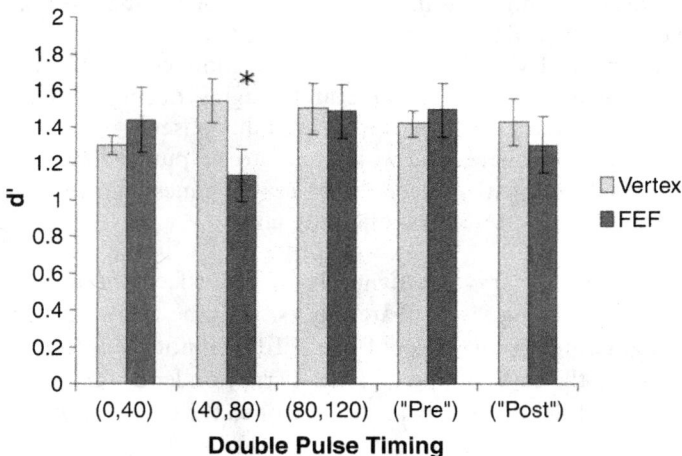

Figure 9. Effect of double pulse TMS over FEF on search performance. Double pulse TMS applied over FEF at 40/80 ms significantly reduced d' (* refers to MANOVA with "TMS time" and "TMS site" (vertex, FEF) as factors, $p < .044$) ($n = 9$).

CONCLUSIONS AND PROPOSALS FOR
FUTURE EXPERIMENTS

The aim of the research programme of which these experiments form a part is to reassess and compare, under conditions as similar as possible, the roles of the human posterior parietal cortex and the FEF in visual search. Repetitive transcranial magnetic stimulation over the human frontal eye fields has revealed that:

1. Like the parietal cortex, the right FEF plays an important role in search.
2. The FEF is important in search even when eye movements are not required.
3. The increased reaction times caused by TMS over right FEF only occurs for target present trials, unlike the parietal cortex, which is important for both target present and absent trials in the case of reaction times.
4. The FEF is clearly involved in conjunction search, but under some conditions may also be important in feature detection, for example when the subject lacks foreknowledge of target features.
5. The decrease in sensitivity caused by TMS over right FEF is accompanied by a criterion shift which leads subjects to make more false alarm reports.
6. The right FEF is important irrespective of the hemifield in which the target is located.
7. TMS over the right FEF increases the slope of a search task. This is not the case with stimulation over the parietal cortex.
   Double pulse TMS experiments add two more conclusions:
8. The involvement of FEF in search begins during a time window between 40 and 80 ms after visual stimulus onset.
9. Data not shown here, and which need to be pursued further, suggest that in subjects with longer visual search times, the timing of FEF involvement may be correspondingly later.

From our preliminary investigations of the effects of using TMS to disrupt the FEF during visual search tasks, it seems that a full description and understanding of the role of the FEF cannot be confined to eye movements and the early timing of TMS disruption lends further support to a visual analytic role for FEF, while leaving open the question of the bottom-up versus top-down nature of its contributions to perception.

Comparing these effects with a summary of the effects of TMS over the parietal cortex leads to the conclusion that the visual processing role of the parietal cortex in search has been overemphasized and perhaps bolstered by an absence of appreciation of the visual functions of the FEF. Indeed, the view that parietal cortex activity is indicative of visuospatial processing and that FEF activity is indicative of saccade programming has led to a sometimes recursive analysis of the functions of these components of the frontoparietal network. We propose instead that some of the visual functions often attributed to the parietal cortex may in fact be functions carried out by the frontal eye fields, and that the role of the parietal cortex in search is better explained as a visuomotor role, especially in novel search tasks (see Ellison et al., 2003, for a full exposition).

Inevitably there are many further experiments to be done and comparisons to be made between the parietal cortex and FEF, but two of the speakers at the Munich Symposium made particularly pertinent presentations that highlight important shortcomings of these experiments, indeed of the vast majority of visual search experiments.

Treisman (2006) this issue) presented data from experiments in which the subjects were shown to take note of the statistical properties of the stimulus displays, something that is almost always ignored in standard visual search experiments. Now consider *real* visual search. Real search is carried out in environments about which we have a great deal of statistical knowledge—objects we look for are of a certain size and at a certain distance: One searches for keys and diaries on a desk within reaching range and for spouses and cars on a street at greater distances. We may have a few sets of keys and possibly more than one diary, but as busy people on academic salaries we are probably looking for one spouse at a time and have only one car. In other words, we bring a great deal of knowledge to real visual search and this knowledge may provide a way of further parsing functions of the different areas involved in search. For example, the role of the parietal cortex in visual search may be limited to near space and not extend to far space. This has already been seen in line bisection (Bjoertomt, Cowey, & Walsh, 2002). So when, as we so often do, we begin a research paper by writing "Imagine looking for your yellow Ferrari against a background of other faculty members' yellow Lamborghinis and red Ferraris ...", we may be guilty of more than economic wishful thinking—we may be fondly imagining that our laboratory visual search tasks address real visual search problems. Clearly we have to test this by adopting more realistic search arrays or, at the very least, by taking into account the statistical properties of the arrays we present.

Now let's consider laboratory visual search again. The data we present here have been published elsewhere following peer review, and our care in monitoring eye movements was viewed as methodological strengths. However, as Gilchrist noted in his presentation, "we don't do much vision without eye movements" (Gilchrist & Harvey, 2006 this issue), and we can extend this to other actions: You identify your keys in order to fixate and reach and you identify your spouse in order to point/wave/move towards him or her. In addition to isolating visual search from the statistics of the environment in our paradigms, we may be imposing an additional constraint on our understanding of real search by divorcing visual search from action. We hope to pursue these factors in forthcoming studies.

REFERENCES

Andersen, R. A., & Buneo, C. A. (2002). Intentional maps in posterior parietal cortex. *Annual Review of Neuroscience*, 25(1), 189–220.

Ashbridge, E., Walsh, V., & Cowey, A. (1997). Temporal aspects of visual search studied by transcranial magnetic stimulation. *Neuropsychologia*, 35(8), 1121–1131.

Barone, P., Batardiere, A., Knoblauch, K., & Kennedy, H. (2000). Laminar distribution of neurons in extrastriate areas projecting to visual areas V1 and V4 correlates with the hierarchical rank and indicates the operation of a distance rule. *Journal of Neuroscience*, 20(9), 3263–3281.

Battelli, L., Black, K. R., & Wray, S. H. (2002). Transcranial magnetic stimulation of visual area V5 in migraine. *Neurology*, 58(7), 1066–1069.

Bianchi, L. (1895). The functions of the frontal lobes. *Brain*, 18, 497–522.

Bichot, N. P., & Schall, J. D. (1999). Effects of similarity and history on neural mechanisms of visual selection. *Nature Neuroscience*, 2(6), 549–554.

Bichot, N. P., & Schall, J. D. (2002). Priming in macaque frontal cortex during popout visual search: Feature-based facilitation and location-based inhibition of return. *Journal of Neuroscience*, 22(11), 4675–4685.

Bisley, J. W., & Goldberg, M. E. (2003). Neuronal activity in the lateral intraparietal area and spatial attention. *Science*, 299(5603), 81–86.

Bjoertomt, O., Cowey, A., & Walsh, V. (2002). Spatial neglect in near and far space investigated by repetitive transcranial magnetic stimulation. *Brain*, 125(Pt. 9), 2012–2022.

Blanke, O., Morand, S., Thut, G., Michel, C. M., Spinelli, L., Landis, T., & Seeck, M. (1999). Visual activity in the human frontal eye field. *Neuroreport*, 10(5), 925–930.

Blanke, O., Spinelli, L., Thut, G., Michel, C. M., Perrig, S., Landis, T., & Seeck, M. (2000). Location of the human frontal eye field as defined by electrical cortical stimulation: Anatomical, functional and electrophysiological characteristics. *Neuroreport*, 11(9), 1907–1913.

Bullier, J. (2001). Integrated model of visual processing. *Brain Research Reviews*, 36(2–3), 96–107.

Caminiti, R., Ferraina, S., & Johnson, P. B. (1996). The sources of visual information to the primate frontal lobe: A novel role for the superior parietal lobule. *Cerebral Cortex*, 6, 319–328.

Campana, G., Cowey, A., & Walsh, V. (2002). Priming of motion direction and area V5/MT: A test of perceptual memory. *Cerebral Cortex*, 12(6), 663–669.

Collin, N. G., Cowey, A., Latto, R., & Marzi, C. (1982). The role of frontal eye-fields and superior colliculi in visual search and non-visual search in rhesus monkeys. *Behavioral Brain Research*, 4(2), 177–193.

Corbetta, M., Shulman, G. L., Miezin, F. M., & Petersen, S. E. (1995). Superior parietal cortex activation during spatial attention shifts and visual feature conjunction. *Science*, 270, 802–805.

Donner. T.. Kettermann, A., Diesch, E., Ostendorf, F., Villringer. A.. & Brandt. S. A. (2000). Involvement of the human frontal eye field and multiple parietal areas in covert visual selection during conjunction search. *European Journal of Neuroscience*. *12*(9). 3407–3414.

Donner, T. H., Kettermann, A., Diesch, E., Ostendorf, F., Villringer, A., & Brandt. S. A. (2002). Visual feature and conjunction searches of equal difficulty engage only partially overlapping frontoparietal networks. *NeuroImage*, *15*(1), 16–25.

Ellison, A., Rushworth, M., & Walsh, V. (2003). The parietal cortex in visual search: A visuomotor hypothesis. *Supplements to Clinical Neurophysiology*, *56*, 321–330.

Evans, A. C., Collins, D. L., & Holmes, C. J. (1996). Computational approaches to quantifying human neuronatomical variability. In J. C. Mazziotta (Ed.), *Brain mapping: The methods* (pp. 343–361). San Diego, CA: Academic Press.

Felleman, D. J., & van Essen, D. C. (1991). Distributed hierarchical processing in the primate cerebral cortex. *Cerebral Cortex*, *1*(1), 1–47.

Friedman-Hill, S. R., Robertson, L. C., & Treisman, A. (1995). Parietal contributions to visual feature binding: evidence from a patient with bilateral lesions. *Science*, *269*, 853–855.

Gilchrist, I. D., & Harvey, M. (2006). Evidence for a systematic component within scan paths in visual search. *Visual Cognition*, *14*, 704–715.

Gitelman, D. R., Nobre, A. C., Parrish, T. B., LaBar, K. S., Kim, Y. H., Meyer, J. R., & Mesulam, M. (1999). A large-scale distributed network for covert spatial attention: Further anatomical delineation based on stringent behavioural and cognitive controls. *Brain*, *122*(Pt. 6), 1093–1106.

Grosbras, M. H., & Paus, T. (2003). Transcranial magnetic stimulation of the human frontal eye field facilitates visual awareness. *European Journal of Neuroscience*, *18*(11), 3121–3126.

Jackson, G. M., Swainson, R., Mort, D., Husain, M., & Jackson, S. R. (2004a). Implicit processing of global information in Balint's syndrome. *Cortex*, *40*, 179–180.

Jackson, S. R., Newport, R., Mort, D., Husain, M., Jackson, G. M., Swainson, R., et al. (2004b). Action binding and the parietal lobes: Some new perspectives on optic ataxia. In G. W. Humphreys & M. J. Riddoch (Eds.), *Attention in action*. Hove, UK: Psychology Press.

Johnson, P. N., Ferraina, S., Bianchi, L., & Caminiti, R. (1996). Cortical networks for visual reaching: Physiological and anatomical organization of frontal and parietal lobe arm regions. *Cerebral Cortex*, *6*, 102–119.

Latto, R., & Cowey, A. (1971). Visual field defects after frontal eye-field lesions in monkeys. *Brain Research*, *30*(1), 1–24.

Lawler, K. A., & Cowey, A. (1987). On the role of posterior parietal and prefrontal cortex in visuo-spatial perception and attention. *Experimental Brain Research*, *65*(3), 695–698.

Leff, A. P., Scott, S. K., Rothwell, J. C., & Wise, R. J. (2001). The planning and guiding of reading saccades: A repetitive transcranial magnetic stimulation study. *Cerebral Cortex*, *11*(10), 918–923.

Leonards, U., Sunaert, S., van Hecke, P., & Orban, G. A. (2001). Attention mechanisms in visual search: An fMRI study. *Journal of Cognitive Neuroscience*, *12*(Suppl. 2), 61–75.

Maunsell, J. H., & van Essen, D. C. (1987). Topographic organization of the middle temporal visual area in the macaque monkey: Representational biases and the relationship to callosal connections and myeloarchitectonic boundaries. *Journal of Comparative Neurology*, *266*(4), 535–555.

Moore, T., & Armstrong, K. M. (2003). Selective gating of visual signals by microstimulation of frontal cortex. *Nature*, *421*(6921), 370–373.

Muggleton, N. G., Juan, C.-H., Cowey, A., & Walsh, V. (2003). Human frontal eye fields and visual search. *Journal of Neurophysiology*, *89*(6), 3340–3343.

Muri, R. M., Hess, C. W., & Meienberg, O. (1991). Transcranial stimulation of the human frontal eye field by magnetic pulses. *Experimental Brain Research*, *86*(1), 219–223.

Murthy, A., Thompson, K. G., & Schall, J. D. (2001). Dynamic dissociation of visual selection from saccade programming in frontal eye field. *Journal of Neurophysiology*, *86*(5), 2634–2637.

Nobre, A. C., Coull, J. T., Walsh, V., & Frith, C. D. (2003). Brain activations during visual search: Contributions of search efficiency versus feature binding. *NeuroImage*, *18*(1), 91–103.

Nowak, L. G., & Bullier, J. (1997). The timing of information transfer in the visual system. In E. A. Rockland (Ed.), *Cerebral cortex* (Vol. 12, pp. 205–241). New York: Plenum Press.

O'Shea, J., Muggleton, N. G., Cowey, A., & Walsh, V. (2004). Timing of target discrimination in human frontal eye fields. *Journal of Cognitive Neuroscience*, *16*, 1060–1067.

Pascual-Leone, A., Houser, C. M., Reese, K., Shotland, L. I., Grafman, J., Sato, S., et al. (1993). Safety of rapid-rate transcranial magnetic stimulation in normal volunteers. *Electroencephalography and Clinical Neurophysiology*, *89*(2), 120–130.

Paus, T. (1996). Location and function of the human frontal eye-field: A selective review. *Neuropsychologia*, *34*(6), 475–483.

Pollmann, S., Weidner, R., Müller, H. J., & von Cramon, D. Y. (2000). A fronto-posterior network involved in visual dimension changes. *Journal of Cognitive Neuroscience*, *12*(3), 480–494.

Ro, T., Cheifet, S., Ingle, H., Shoup, R., & Rafal, R. (1999). Localization of the human frontal eye fields and motor hand area with transcranial magnetic stimulation and magnetic resonance imaging. *Neuropsychologia*, *37*(2), 225–231.

Robertson, L. C., & Brooks, J. L. (2006). Visual search and spatial deficits. *Visual Cognition*, *14*, 851–862.

Schall, J. D., & Bichot, N. P. (1998). Neural correlates of visual and motor decision processes. *Current Opinion in Neurobiology*, *8*(2), 211–217.

Schall, J. D., & Hanes, D. P. (1993). Neural basis of saccade target selection in frontal eye field during visual search. *Nature*, *366*, 467–469.

Schall, J. D., & Thompson, K. G. (1999). Neural selection and control of visually guided eye movements. *Annual Review of Neuroscience*, *22*, 241–259.

Schmolesky, M. T., Wang, Y., Hanes, D. P., Thompson, K. G., Leutgeb, S., Schall, J. D., & Leventhal, A. G. (1998). Signal timing across the macaque visual system. *Journal of Neurophysiology*, *79*(6), 3272–3278.

Stewart, L., Battelli, L., Walsh, V., & Cowey, A. (1999). Motion perception and perceptual learning studied by magnetic stimulation. *Electroencephalography and Clinical Neurophysiology*, *51*(Suppl.), 334–350.

Talairach, J., & Tournoux, P. (1988). *Co-planar stereotaxic atlas of the human brain*. Stuttgart, Germany: Thieme.

Thompson, K. G., Bichot, N. P., & Schall, J. D. (1997). Dissociation of visual discrimination from saccade programming in macaque frontal eye field. *Journal of Neurophysiology*, *77*(2), 1046–1050.

Thompson, K. G., Hanes, D. P., Bichot, N. P., & Schall, J. D. (1996). Perceptual and motor processing stages identified in the activity of macaque frontal eye field neurons during visual search. *Journal of Neurophysiology*, *76*(6), 4040–4055.

Thompson, K. G., & Schall, J. D. (1999). The detection of visual signals by macaque frontal eye field during masking. *Nature Neuroscience*, *2*(3), 283–288.

Tobler, P. N., & Muri, R. M. (2002). Role of human frontal and supplementary eye fields in double step saccades. *Neuroreport*, *13*(2), 253–255.

Treisman, A. (1996). The binding problem. *Current Opinions in Neurobiology*, *6*(2), 171–178.

Treisman, A. (2006). How the deployment of attention determines what we see. *Visual Cognition*, *14*, 411–443.

Walsh, V., Ashbridge, E., & Cowey, A. (1998). Cortical plasticity in perceptual learning demonstrated by transcranial magnetic stimulation. *Neuropsychologia, 36*, 45–49.

Walsh, V., Ellison, A., Ashbridge, E., & Cowey, A. (1999). The role of the parietal cortex in visual attention—hemispheric asymmetries and the effects of learning: A magnetic stimulation study. *Neuropsychologia, 37*(2), 245–251.

Walsh, V., & Pascual-Leone, A. (2003). *Transcranial magnetic stimulation: A neurochronometrics of mind*. Cambridge, MA: MIT Press.

Wardak, C., Olivier, E., & Duhamel, J. R. (2002). Saccadic target selection deficits after lateral intraparietal area inactivation in monkeys. *Journal of Neuroscience, 22*(22), 9877–9884.

Wilkinson, D. T., Halligan, P. W., Henson, R. N., & Dolan, R. J. (2002). The effects of interdistracter similarity on search processes in superior parietal cortex. *NeuroImage, 15*(3), 611–619.

Wipfli, M., Felblinger, J., Mosimann, U. P., Hess, C. W., Schlaepfer, T. E., & Muri, R. M. (2001). Double-pulse transcranial magnetic stimulation over the frontal eye field facilitates triggering of memory-guided saccades. *European Journal of Neuroscience, 14*(3), 571–575.

Wojcuilik, E., & Kanwisher, N. (1998). Implicit but not explicit feature binding in a Balint's patient. *Visual Cognition, 5*, 157–181.

Section IV.

Neuro-computational modelling of visual search

VISUAL COGNITION, 2006, 14 (4/5/6/7/8), 959–984

Ψ **Psychology Press**
Taylor & Francis Group

Quantitative modelling of perceptual salience at human eye position

Laurent Itti

Departments of Computer Science, Psychology and Neuroscience Graduate Program, University of Southern California, Los Angeles, CA, USA

We investigate the extent to which a simple model of bottom-up attention and salience may be embedded within a broader computational framework, and compared with human eye movement data. We focus on quantifying whether increased simulation realism significantly affects quantitative measures of how well the model may predict where in video clips humans direct their gaze. We hence compare three variants of the model, tested with 15 video clips of natural scenes shown to three observers. We measure model-predicted salience at the locations gazed to by the observers, compared to random locations. The first variant simply processes the raw video clips. The second adds a gaze-contingent foveation filter. The third further attempts to realistically simulate dynamic human vision by embedding the video frames within a larger background, and shifting them to eye position. Our main finding is that increasing simulation realism significantly improves the predictive ability of the model. Better emulating the details of how a visual stimulus is captured by a constantly rotating retina during active vision has a significant positive impact onto quantitative comparisons between model and human behaviour.

Over the past decades, visual psychophysics in humans and other primates have become a particularly productive technique to probe the mechanisms of visual processing, attentional selection, and visual search (Verghese, 2001; Wolfe, 1998). In typical visual psychophysics experiments, visual stimulus patterns are briefly presented to observers, for example on a computer monitor. Observers are instructed to describe their perception of the stimuli, for example by pressing one of several possible answer keys corresponding to alternate responses to a question asked by the experimenter (e.g., whether the stimulus was horizontal or slightly tilted off horizontal). Over the course

Please address all correspondence to Laurent Itti, Departments of Computer Science, Psychology and Neuroscience Graduate Program, University of Southern California, Los Angeles, CA 90089-2520, USA. E-mail: itti@usc.edu

Supported by NSF, NEI, NIMA, the Zumberge Fund, and the Charles Lee Powell Foundation.

http://www.psypress.com/viscog   DOI: 10.1080/13506280500195672

of many experimental trials, quantitative measures are collected and subjected to statistical analysis, to establish a relationship between the ability of observers to perceive some aspect of the presented stimuli and the hypothesis tested by the experimenter.

As visual psychophysics experiments become more sophisticated and stimuli more complex, the need for quantitative computational tools that can relate experimental outcomes to putative brain mechanisms is becoming more pressing than ever before. Indeed, in the presence of complex stimuli such as natural scenes, formulating hypotheses on how stimulus attributes may influence perception is hampered both by a difficulty in providing a quantitative formal description of the stimuli, and by the understanding that complex nonlinear interactions among the perceptual representations of diverse components of the stimuli at many processing levels will affect overall perception (Kofka, 1935; Sigman, Cecchi, Gilbert, & Magnasco, 2001).

A particularly successful experimental technique to evaluate perception of complex visual stimuli has been to track eye position of human subjects while they inspect visual displays. Using this technique, several studies have recently demonstrated how local image properties at the locations fixated by humans significantly differ from image properties at other locations in static images. These include studies by Zetzsche and colleagues (Barth, Zetzsche, & Rentschler, 1998; Zetzsche et al., 1998), who inferred from human eye tracking that the eyes preferentially fixate regions in greyscale images with multiple superimposed orientations, including corners. Similarly, Reinagel and Zador (1999) found that local spatial contrast of greyscale static images was significantly higher at the point of gaze than, on average, at random locations, whereas pairwise pixel correlations (image uniformity) were significantly lower. Privitera and Stark (2000) further computed the linear combination of a collection of image processing operators (e.g., local cross detector, Laplacian of Gaussian, local entropy measure, etc.) that maximized overlap between regions of high algorithmic responses and regions fixated by human observers, thus deriving bottom-up feature detectors that captured some of the local image properties which attracted eye movements. Extending on these purely local analyses, and considering colour scenes, Parkhurst, Law, & Niebur (2002) compared human scan paths to bottom-up saliency maps computed from static images (Itti, Koch, & Niebur, 1998). Thus, this study not only accounted for local image properties but also for long-range interactions among the cortical representations of distant image regions, which mediate visual salience and pop-out (Itti et al., 1998; Treisman & Gelade, 1980). This study revealed significantly elevated model-predicted salience at human fixations compared to random fixations, and more strongly so for the first few fixations on an image than for subsequent fixations.

Previous studies thus have abstracted most of the dynamics of human active vision, and have focused on intrinsic properties of local distributions of pixel intensities in an image. This contrasts with attempting a more realistic simulation of how the recent history of dynamic patterns of retinal stimulation, as the eye jumps from one image location to the next, may predict candidate target locations for a subsequent eye movement. As a first step in this direction, Parkhurst et al. (2002) noted a human bias for shorter saccades, and applied a spatial modulation filter to the static saliency map computed for each image, whereby the salience of locations increasingly further from current fixation was increasingly suppressed before salience distributions for the following fixation were analysed. Although this increased the model-predicted salience at human eye fixations compared to random fixations, the authors correctly noted that applying such foveation filter to the saliency map rather than the retinal inputs only is a coarse approximation of how active foveation may modulate salience.

Building on these previous studies, here we jointly use human eye tracking and a computational model of low-level visual perception to quantitatively evaluate dynamic attentional allocation onto visual stimuli. We develop a more realistic simulation framework, to transition from evaluating local *image properties* at human eye fixations to evaluating a measure of *perceptual saliency* at human eye fixations. For the purpose of this study, we thus operationally define perceptual saliency as depending not only on local image properties, but also on how these are captured by a foveated retina, and how their cortical representations interact over visual space and time. Thus, we attempt to more realistically account for a larger fraction of the details of how information present in an image may first be processed by the visual system of the observer, such as to eventually yield neural signals that may direct the observer's attention and eye movements. The main question addressed here is whether using such a realistic framework would significantly affect the outcomes of quantitative comparisons between model-predicted saliency maps and locations fixated by human observers. If it did, this would indicate that the details of active vision do play a non-negligible role in the selection of eye movements, and hence should be taken into account in future psychophysics studies.

Our approach relies upon and extends our previously proposed computational model of visual salience and bottom-up attentional allocation (Itti & Koch, 2000; Itti & Koch, 2001a; Itti et al., 1998). Previously, we have used this model in a "generative" mode, yielding predictions of the visual attractiveness of every location in a display (in the form of a graded topographic saliency map; Koch & Ullman, 1985) and predictions of attentional scan paths and eye movements (Itti, Dhavale, & Pighin, 2003). In contrast, here we use it in a "human-driven" or "servoed" mode: Using actual eye movement scan paths recorded from human subjects, we simulate the retinal input received by the observers, process it through the low-level visual stages of the model, and continuously recompute the saliency map over the course of the human scan path. To effectively exercise and challenge the framework, we employ dynamic (video clip) natural stimuli rather than static imagery. We explore three variants of the model, with increasing realism. The first variant simply computes saliency maps from the raw video frames shown to human observers, similar to previous studies. The human eye movement recordings are then used to compare the model-predicted salience at human eye positions compared to random locations within the video frames. The second variant adds a foveation filter, by which each input frame is increasingly blurred with distance from current human eye position before it is processed by the model. Finally, the third and most realistic variant embeds the raw video frames into a background photograph of the experimental room and computer monitor, shifts the resulting image to centre it at human eye position, crops the shifted image to simulate a retinal field of view, and applies a foveation filter to the field of view before processing by our model.

The present study focuses on whether increasing the realism of model simulations significantly affects the measures of model-predicted salience at the image locations visited by the human eye compared to random locations. We here use our available model of bottom-up attention as an approximation to early visual processing in humans. However, it is important to keep in mind that the computations operated by this model represent only a very coarse approximation to a small subset of the many factors that influence attentional deployment onto a visual scene (Henderson & Hollingworth, 1999; Itti & Koch, 2001a; Rensink, 2000). Hence, we do not expect perfect agreement between model-predicted salience and human eye position. In particular, our bottom-up model as used here does not yet account, among others, for how the rapid identification of the gist (semantic category) of a scene may provide contextual priors to more efficiently guide attention towards target objects of interest (Biederman, Teitelbaum, & Mezzanotte, 1983; Friedman, 1979; Hollingworth & Henderson, 1998; Oliva & Schyns, 1997; Potter & Levy, 1969; Torralba, 2003); how search for a specific target might be guided top-down, for example by boosting visual neurons tuned to the attributes of the target (Ito & Gilbert, 1999; Moran & Desimone, 1985; Motter, 1994; Müller, Reimann, & Krummenacher, 2003; Reynolds, Pasternak, & Desimone, 2000; Treue & Maunsell, 1996; Treue & Trujillo, 1999; Wolfe, 1994, 1998; Wolfe, Cave, & Franzel, 1989; Yeshurun & Carrasco, 1998); or how task, expertise, and internal scene models may influence eye movements (Henderson & Hollingworth, 2003; Moreno, Reina, Luis, & Sabido, 2002; Nodine & Krupinski, 1998; Noton & Stark, 1971; Peebles & Cheng, 2003; Savelsbergh, Williams, van der Kamp, & Ward, 2002; Tanenhaus, Spivey-Knowlton, Eberhard, & Sedivy, 1995;

Yarbus, 1967). Nevertheless, our hypothesis for this study is that a more realistic simulation framework might yield better agreement between human and model than a less realistic one. The present study quantifies the extent to which this hypothesis may be verified or rejected. The finding of significant differences between the three versions of our simulation framework would indicate that the details of foveation, eye movements, and background should not be ignored in the analysis of future psychophysics experiments.

METHODS

The proposed quantitative analysis framework allows us to derive an absolute measure of salience compounded over a human scan path, and to compare it to the same measure compounded over a random scan path. Although the absolute value of this measure is difficult to interpret, given all the factors influencing eye movements but not accounted for by the model, it allows us to rank the three variants of the model, and to suggest that the model variant with highest ranking may be the one that best approximates human bottom-up visual processing.

Human eye movement experiments

Eye movement recordings were collected from eight human observers watching a heterogeneous collection of 15 video clips, including outdoors scenes, video games, television newscasts, commercials, sports, and other content. Each clip comprised between 309 and 2083 frames (10.4–69.1 s), for a total of 13,770 distinct frames (totalling 7 min 37.0 s). The experimental protocol used to collect the data evaluated here has been previously described in detail (Itti, 2004; Itti, 2005). In short, stimuli were presented to four normal volunteer subjects on a 22-inch computer monitor (LaCie Corp; 640×480, 60.27 Hz double-scan, mean screen luminance 30 cd/m^2, room 4 cd/m^2) at a viewing distance of 80 cm ($28° \times 21°$ usable field-of-view). Subjects were instructed to attempt to "follow the main actors and actions" in the video clips, and thus were biased towards the scene elements that were the most important according to their current cognitive understanding of the scenes. The extent to which the selection of these cognitively important locations would be more or less predictable by variants of a simple bottom-up computational analysis of image pixels is a side issue addressed by the present study, with again our main focus being the influence of model realism onto agreement between model and humans. Eye position was tracked using a 240 Hz infrared video-based eyetracker (ISCAN, Inc model RK-464). Raw eye movement traces were remapped to screen coordinates using a nine-point calibration procedure (Stampe, 1993). Each calibration point consisted of fixating first a central cross, then a blinking dot at a random point on a 3×3 matrix. After a nine-point calibration had been completed, five video clips were played. For every clip, subjects fixated a central cross, pressed a key to start, at which point the eyetracker was triggered, the cross blinked for 1206 ms, and the clip started. Stimuli were presented on a Linux computer, under SCHED_FIFO scheduling to ensure accurate timing (Finney, 2001). Frame displays were hardware-locked to the vertical retrace of the monitor. Microsecond-accurate timestamps were stored in memory as each frame was presented, and later saved to disk to check for dropped frames. No frame drop occurred and all timestamps were spaced by $33.185 \pm 2 \, \mu s$. During offline remapping of raw eye position to screen coordinates, data was discarded until the next calibration if residual errors greater than 20 pixels (0.90°) on any calibration point or 10 pixels (0.45°) overall remained.

The dataset used here is a subset of the entire dataset collected (which was for 50 clips and eight subjects each watching a subset of the 50 clips, so that four to six valid eye movement traces were available for each clip; Itti, 2004). The fifteen clips used here were randomly chosen so that we would use two clips from any category (e.g., outdoors, video games, TV news, etc.) that had at least two clips in the original dataset, except for the last one (the original dataset had 12 categories, of which 8 had two or more clips). In addition to the 14 clips thus obtained, we included one very simple synthetic clip of a coloured disk jumping to various locations on a static textured background, which is a useful control stimulus. Once the subset of 15 clips had been decided upon, the four observers who had watched the most clips were selected and alphabetically ordered, and the first three eye movement traces for each clip were selected. Hence, we used calibrated eye movement data for three subjects on each of the 15 clips, yielding a total of 45 calibrated eye movement traces. The reason of using a subset of the available data here was solely computational cost (a run of the three variants of the model for comparison to the 45 eye movement traces takes approximately two CPU-months, or 4 days on a 16-CPU Beowulf cluster of interconnected Linux PC computers).

Comparing model predictions to human eye movements

The computational model variants were used in the following manner. Each of the 45 human eye movement recordings was considered in turn. For a given recording, the corresponding video clip was presented to a model variant, at the same resolution (640×480) and frame rate (33.185 ms/frame) as it had been presented to human subjects. In the more sophisticated model variants, recorded human eye position was then used to drive the foveated eye of the model and to generate a coarse simulation of the pattern of inputs actually received by the observer's retinas. For every human eye position recorded (240 Hz), several measurements of the internal state of the model were taken: Instantaneous model-predicted salience at current human eye position, maximum and average salience over the current video frame, and salience at a randomly chosen location in the image. Our analysis focuses on comparing how salience differed at human eye position compared to random locations, and on quantifying this effect so that the different variants of the model may be ranked according to their agreement with human eye movements.

Baseline model

To relate our findings to previous analyzes of local image properties at locations fixated by human observers, we begin with a simple model that analyses the raw video clips shown to observers, without including any realistic simulation of how human eye movements affect visual inputs that actually enter the eyes. Thus, the first model variant is mainly concerned with local *image* properties but disregards most of the byproducts of dynamic human *vision* (e.g., decrease of contrast sensitivity with eccentricity, motion transients due to eye movements, etc.).

At the core of the framework is our previously described model of bottom-up visual attention, which computes a topographic saliency map from the input images (Itti & Koch, 2000; Itti & Koch, 2001a; Itti et al., 1998; Koch & Ullman, 1985). Video input is processed in parallel by a number of multiscale low-level feature maps (Figure 1), which detect local spatial discontinuities in various visual feature channels using simulated centre-surround neurons (Hubel & Wiesel, 1962; Kuffler, 1953). Twelve neuronal features are implemented, sensitive to colour contrast (red/green and blue/yellow double-opponency, separately), temporal flicker (onset and offset of light intensity, combined), intensity contrast (light-on-dark and dark-on-light, combined), four orientations ($0°$, $45°$, $90°$, $135°$), and four oriented motion energies (up, down, left, right). The detailed implementation of these feature channels, thought indeed to guide human attention (Wolfe & Horowitz, 2004), has been described previously (Itti et al., 1998, 2003; Itti & Koch, 2001a). In the presentation of our results, these 12 features are combined into five categories: Colour, flicker, intensity, orientation, and motion. Centre and surround scales are obtained using dyadic pyramids with nine levels (from level 0, the original image, to level 8, reduced by a factor 256 horizontally and vertically). Centre-surround differences are then computed as pointwise differences across pyramid levels, for combinations of three centre scales ($c = \{2, 3, 4\}$) and two centre-surround scale differences

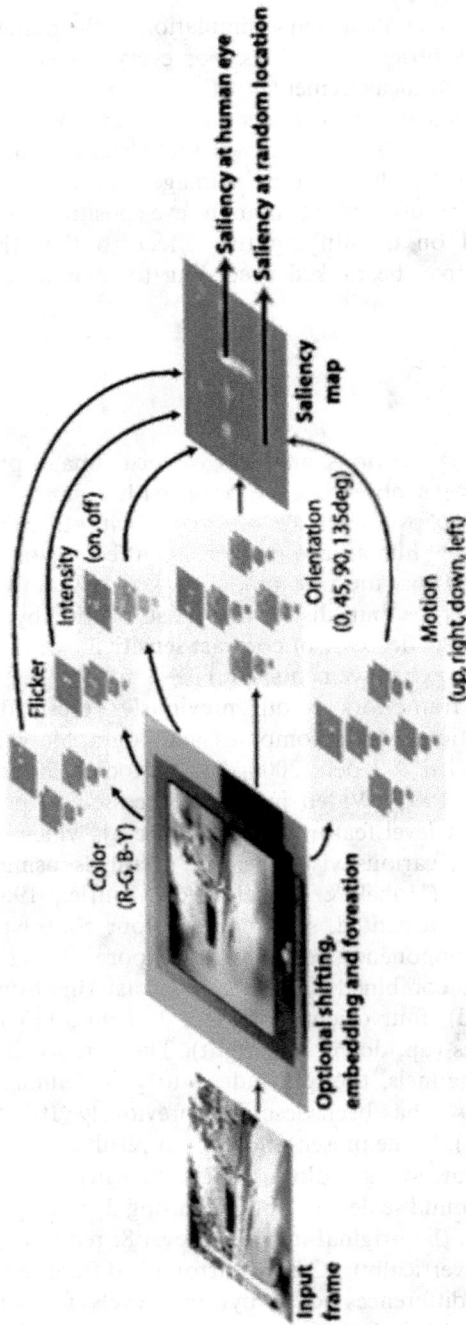

Figure 1. Overview of the computational framework. Depending on the model variant used, incoming video input may be used as it is, foveated around human eye position, or embedded within a background image, shifted so as to become centred at current human eye position, and foveated at the centre. Low-level visual features are then computed in a set of multiscale feature maps tuned to five classes of low-level visual properties (colour, intensity, orientation, flicker, motion). After nonlinear within-feature and across-feature competition for salience, all feature maps provide input to the saliency map. At each human eye position sample, measures are taken for the salience at eye position, the salience at a random location, and the maximum and average salience over the display area.

($\delta = \{3, 4\}$); thus, six feature maps are computed for each of the visual feature channels. Each feature map is endowed with internal dynamics that operate a strong spatial within-feature and within-scale competition for activity, followed by within-feature, across-scale competition (Itti & Koch, 2001b; Itti et al., 1998). As a result, initially possibly very noisy feature maps are reduced to sparse representations of only those locations which strongly stand out from their surroundings. All feature maps are then summed (Itti & Koch, 2001b) into the unique scalar input to the saliency map.

The saliency map is modelled as a two-dimensional layer of leaky integrator neurons at scale 4 (40×30 pixels given 640×480 video inputs) and with a time constant of 500 ms (Itti & Koch, 2000). Its main function is to provide temporal smoothing of the saliency values computed from each video frame. Consequently, in our study we directly evaluate the saliency values at current human eye position, even though some reaction delay exists between appearance of a stimulus element and the possible decision to orient the eyes towards that location. Thus, we here do not investigate in details the effects of stimulus–response latency, but instead temporally low-pass filter the saliency map. The integrators are simulated using difference equations at a temporal resolution of 0.1 ms of simulated time, that is, 10,000 frames/s (Itti & Koch, 2000).

The spatial within-feature competition operated within each feature map is a crucial component of the model, mainly responsible for the model's ability to reproduce psychophysical "pop-out" effects observed behaviourally in visual search psychophysics (Treisman & Gelade, 1980; Wolfe, 1998). In a first approximation, the computational effect of the model's long-range, within-feature competitive interactions is similar to applying a soft winner-take-all to each feature map before it is combined into the saliency map (Itti & Koch, 2001b). That is, the competitive interactions tend to enhance locations that are spatial outliers over the extent of the visual input. Hence, the salience of a patch of pixels at a given location in the visual field not only depends upon the local distribution of pixel values within that patch, but also on how that distribution compares to surrounding distributions. If the patch under consideration is similar to its neighbours (distant by up to approximately one-quarter of the width of the input image, with Gaussian decay; Itti & Koch, 2000), it will be strongly inhibited by its neighbours and will strongly inhibit them as well. This behaviour was included in the model to coarsely replicate nonclassical surround inhibition as observed in striate cortex and other early visual processing areas of mammals (Cannon & Fullenkamp, 1991; Levitt & Lund, 1997; Sillito, Grieve, Jones, Cudeiro, & Davis, 1995). Hence, while a vertical line segment would always excite a local vertical feature detector, irrespectively of the image contents far away from that stimulus, its salience will depend upon the possible presence of other vertical line segments throughout the entire visual field. If many other vertical elements are present, the salience of the one under consideration will be low; but it will be much higher if no other vertical line element is present in the display (Itti & Koch, 2000). We have proposed several implementations for the long-range interactions, with varying degrees of biological plausibility and computational cost (Itti & Koch, 2000; Itti & Koch, 2001b; Itti et al., 1998). Here we use one iteration of the method introduced in Itti and Koch (2001b), which yields fairly sparse saliency maps as exemplified in Figure 4 (see later).

Foveation

To progress from local measures of image properties to measures of predicted perceptual salience at the point of gaze, a first improvement upon the simulation framework described above was to coarsely replicate the decrease of contrast sensitivity with eccentricity from the centre of fixation, as observed in humans (Spillmann & Werner, 1990; Wandell, 1995). To this end, we designed a simple foveation filter, which would blur the input video frames, increasingly so with distance from the current human eye position. Our results compare agreement between humans and model with and without this additional filter.

Recorded human eye position determined the location of the model's foveation centre. The foveation filter was achieved through interpolation across four levels of a colour Gaussian pyramid C_σ (Burt & Adelson, 1983) computed from each input frame, where the natural number σ represents spatial scale. Scale zero is the input colour image, and each subsequent scale is obtained by first blurring the image at the current scale by a 9×9 two-dimensional Gaussian kernel, and further decimating that low-pass-filtered image by a factor two horizontally and vertically:

$$\forall \sigma \geq 0. \quad C_{\sigma+1} = \downarrow^{x:2,y:2} (C_\sigma \otimes G_{9\times 9}) \tag{1}$$

where $\downarrow^{x:2,y:2}$ is the decimation (downsampling) operator, $\otimes$ is the convolution operator and $G_{9\times 9}$ is a (separable) 9×9 approximation to a Gaussian kernel. To determine which scale to use at any image location, we computed a 3/4-chamfer distance map $D(x,y)$ (Borgefors, 1991), encoding at every pixel with coordinates (x, y) for an approximation to the Euclidean distance between that pixel's location and a disc of $2°$ diameter (the model's fovea and perifovea), centred at the current eye position of the human observer:

$$\forall x, y. \quad \sigma(x, y) = K \times D(x, y) \tag{2}$$

where K is a scaling constant converting from distance into a fractional scale $\sigma(x,y)$. The fractional scale $\sigma(x,y)$ thus computed at every location in the image was used to determine the relative weights assigned to the immediately lower and higher integer scales represented in the pyramid C_σ, in a linear interpolation scheme. Consequently, pixels close to the fovea were interpolated from high-resolution scales in the pyramid, while more eccentric pixels were interpolated from coarser-resolution scales. The process is illustrated in Figure 2. In a first step, we did not attempt to measure visual acuity of our subjects and to more accurately model the rate at which contrast sensitivity decreased with eccentricity for particular observers, although this could be included in a future implementation (Geisler & Perry, 2002). Although approximate, this model enhancement unveiled one additional contribution to perceptual saliency: Highly contrasted but small image regions far away from the observer's centre of gaze were unlikely to contribute much to the saliency map, since they were less or not detected by the low-level feature channels of the model once the foveation filter had been applied.

Input shifting and embedding

The realism of the simulation framework was further increased by dynamically shifting the input frames, so as to more faithfully simulate the changing patterns of retinal stimulation as the centre of gaze moved from one image location to another. That is, instead of considering that the model received inputs in the world-centred frame of reference attached to the stimulus frames, as implicitly assumed previously, we here transitioned to an eye-centred representation.

Hence, an explicit dissociation was made between retinotopic and world-centred (or head-centred since the head was fixed in our experiments) coordinate systems. The rationale for this enhancement was that the low-level visual processing of the model should operate not on the raw video frames, but on an approximation to the current retinal input received by the human observers. Thus, the first image processing step in the computational framework was to shift incoming raw video frames, such as to recentre them around the current human eye position. Hence, in the resulting images given as inputs to the model, human eye position was always at the centre of the field of view, and the raw video frames were shifted and pasted around that location. A background image consisting of a photograph of our experimental room and monitor (Figure 3) was used at retinal locations where there was no video clip input (e.g., at the top and left of the visual field when subjects fixated towards the top-left corner of the monitor). Finally, the image was cropped by a field of view larger than the raw video frames, centred at current eye position (Figure 3).

This transformation from stimulus to retinal coordinates unveiled two possible new contributions to perceptual salience that the simplified model did not account for: First, high contrast was often present at the boundary

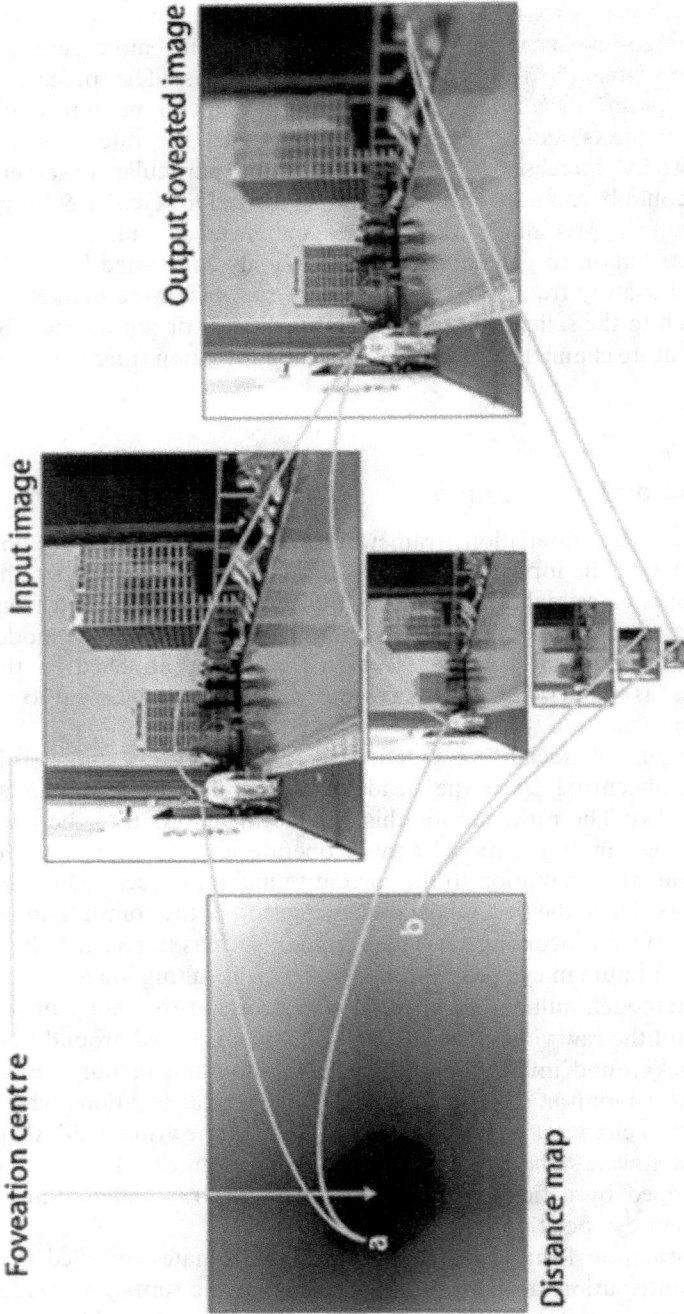

Figure 2. Foveation using a Gaussian image pyramid. Given a location for the foveation centre, the value at every location (x, y) in the distance map approximates the distance from the foveation centre to (x, y); brighter shades in the distance map correspond to larger distances. The appearance of (x, y) in the output foveated image is then read out from levels in the input image pyramid, which are increasingly coarse (and blurred) depending on the distance map value at (x, y). For example, the appearance of location a, close to the foveation centre, is interpolated from the two finest scales in the input pyramid, and hence is only lightly blurred. Conversely, the appearance of location b, more distant from the foveation centre, is interpolated from the two coarsest scales in the pyramid, and hence is highly blurred.

Frame 3   Frame 14   Frame 23   Frame 38

Figure 3. Embedding the video clips within a background. A 2048×1400 photograph of our eyetracker setup (top) was taken with a digital camera (here shown with slightly higher luminosity than actually used, for reproduction purposes). Incoming raw 640×480 frames from the video clips (middle; with current human eye position shown by the crosshairs) were pasted into this image, such as to appear within the monitor's screen area. Finally, the resulting image was cropped by a 1024×768 field of view centred at current human eye position (bottom, and also shown as a yellow rectangle in the top image), to simulate a human retinal field of view slightly larger than the monitor area. The resulting frames used as inputs to the shifted and foveated model thus had a fixed size of 1024×768 pixels, and depicted the room and monitor with the raw movie clip frames, shifting rapidly so that human eye position (crosshairs) would always remain at the centre of the field of view.

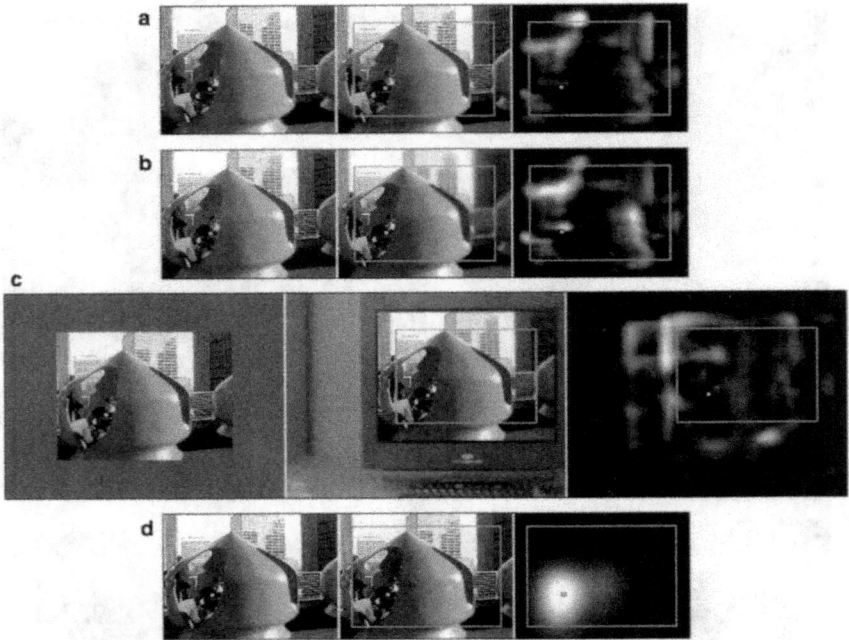

Figure 4. Example frame from a video clip. for the three model variants and the human-derived control model. The small cyan squares indicate current human eye position. (a) The simple model simply processes the raw video frames. (b) The second model variant applies a foveation filter centred at current human eye position before processing each frame. (c) The third model variant embeds the frame within a background, centres it to human eye position. crops it by a fixed field of view. and processes the contents of the field of view through the model. The green rectangles show the area over which maximum. average. and random salience were computed. (d) The human-derived control model uses a "saliency map" that contains three blobs. each corresponding to the instantaneous eye position of a human observer (with some temporal blurring provided by the internal dynamics of the saliency map). In the example frame shown. all three control observers are gazing at the same location as the fourth subject being tested (cyan square). This model provides a baseline for comparison with the bottom-up computational models.

between the shifted video frames and the background image, often strongly affecting model-predicted salience values within the video display area because of the long-range competitive interactions implemented in the model. Second. eye motion during human smooth pursuit and saccades significantly excited the model's low-level feature detectors sensitive to flicker and motion. thus adding an intrinsic motion component (due to the moving eye) in addition to extrinsic motion components (moving objects within the video clips).

Sample frames and saliency maps for the three model variants are shown in Figure 4.

RESULTS

At each human eye movement sample, several measurements were made on the model's current internal state, to quantify the extent to which salience at current eye position may compare to salience at other image locations.

The first of these measures was to read out salience and also low-level feature values (e.g., colour, orientation, etc.) at human eye position. To calibrate these measures, we also computed the maximum and average salience and feature values over the extent of the video display area, as well as salience and feature values at one random location (with uniform probability) within the display area. The goal of the random samples was to evaluate a baseline level of salience obtained by fixating a location by chance, for comparison to salience measured at human gaze location. Because we sampled a single point in the saliency and feature maps (which are at spatial scale 4, that is, downsized by a factor 16 horizontally and vertically compared to the original image), we expected that, on average over all frames, salience at random locations should be equal to the average salience over the entire frame. This was verified (see below), indicating that the random sampling worked properly.

There is one difficulty with defining what the random sampling area should consist of for the third variant of the model, which embeds the raw video frames within a larger background. With this model, the field of view over which feature and saliency maps are computed is larger than the actual video display (Figures 3 and 4). However, our human eye movement recordings contained no instance where the observers had looked either outside or right at the edges of the monitor's video display area. This was not a limitation of our eyetracking apparatus, which is capable of tracking over wider fields of view than the $28° \times 21°$ of our display monitor. We hence assumed that observers used top-down knowledge of the extent of the visible screen area to restrict their eye movements within that area. Under these conditions, it would seem an unfair comparison to allow random saccades to be distributed anywhere within the larger field of view. On the one hand, the background around the monitor often contained no or very few highly salient objects; including this area within the random sampling area hence would tend to artificially lower the average salience at random locations. On the other hand, the edges of the visible screen area often were salient, due to high contrast between the contents of the video frames and the dark grey plastic enclosure of the monitor, which would tend to artificially increase the average salience at random locations. Consequently, we here decided to only consider for random sampling (and for the computation of maximum and average salience) an area corresponding to the visible video display area, minus a border of three pixels at the scale of the saliency map (48 pixels at the scale of the original video frames; green rectangles in Figure 4).

Given this, the comparison between human and random samples concerns the following question: Given that observers knew to restrict their gaze to within the video display area, would the addition, in the simulations, of a surrounding background that observers never looked at influence the distribution of salience within the video display in a significant manner? If the model (and, presumably, the low-level visual processing stages of our observers) operated purely local processing, no influence would be expected. However, since model-predicted salience of a location within the video display area may be modulated by the presence of objects outside that area (due to the nonlinear spatial competition for salience at the core of our model), some significant effect was possible. It is important to remember that our goal in this study is not to make a point about the particular bottom-up visual attention used here, but rather to use this model to evaluate whether details like an ignored background scenery may significantly influence quantitative comparisons between model and human data.

The results of our measures are shown in Table 1. To allow comparison across model variants, the results are expressed in terms of a metric defined by the ratios:

$$F(x.y.t) = \frac{F_{max}(t) - F(x.y.t)}{F_{max}(t) - F_{avg}(t)} \tag{3}$$

where $F(x, y)$ is the feature (or salience) value at location (x, y) and time t, $F_{max}(t)$ is the maximum such value over the sampling area and at instant t, and $F_{avg}(t)$ is the average such value over the sampling area and same instant t. The motivation for using this metric is that it is more robust to varying dynamic range and varying baselines than other, simpler metrics like $F(x,y,t)/F_{avg}(t)$ or $F(x,y,t)/F_{max}(t)$.

The values shown in Table 1 are the values of the above metric, averaged over all video clips and observers (45 eye movement traces and a total of 324,036 valid eye position samples), for both human and random samples. A compound measure of 0% would indicate perfect agreement between humans and model, whereby humans would always gaze exactly at the single most salient pixel within the entire sampling area. In contrast, a compound measure of 100% would indicate that humans did not gaze at salient locations more than expected by chance, and measures above 100% would indicate that humans preferentially gazed at locations predicted to be of salience lower than average.

Clearly, a score of 0% is not possible as different observers often gazed to different locations while watching the same video clip. This intersubject variability makes it impossible for a model to highlight a single most salient pixel in the display that always corresponds to instantaneous human eye position. However, scores closer to 0% indicate models that more often

TABLE 1

Measures of agreement between model and humans (second column) and between model and random (third column), for saliency as well as individual visual features implemented in the model. A value of 0% would indicate that salience (or feature value) at the human (or random) sampling point was always the maximum over the entire display, while a value of 100% would indicate that it was average. In practice, 0% is unattainable because interobserver variability makes it impossible for a model to always exactly pinpoint a single best location for gaze. The score of 52.21% obtained when three humans predict one represents a more practical lower bound. The comparisons between human and random distributions of salience or feature values relied on a nonparametric sign test (fourth column). Finally, the fifth and sixth columns compare the values obtained for humans across two variants of the model, also using a sign test.

Visual feature	Average human $\dfrac{F_{max}(t) - F(x,y,t)}{F_{max}(t) - F_{arg}(t)}$	Average random $\dfrac{F_{max}(t) - F(x,y,t)}{F_{max}(t) - F_{arg}(t)}$	Compare human to random	Compare human to human NS.NF	Compare human to human NS.F
Three humans predict one:					
Humans	**52.21%**	**100.02%**	$p < 10^{-10}$		
No shifting/embedding, no foveation (NS.NF):					
Salience	**87.51%**	**99.97%**	$p < 10^{-10}$		
Colour	93.38%	100.00%	$p < 10^{-10}$		
Flicker	93.71%	99.98%	$p < 10^{-10}$		
Intensity	97.54%	99.98%	$p < 10^{-10}$		
Orientation	93.80%	100.02%	$p < 10^{-10}$		
Motion	93.73%	100.01%	$p < 10^{-10}$		
No shifting/embedding, foveation (NS.F):					
Salience	**81.85%**	**100.05%**	$p < 10^{-10}$	$p < 10^{-10}$	
Colour	93.44%	100.03%	$p < 10^{-10}$	$p < 10^{-10}$	
Flicker	87.13%	99.98%	$p < 10^{-10}$	$p < 10^{-10}$	
Intensity	97.18%	99.97%	$p < 10^{-10}$	$p \geq 0.1$	
Orientation	87.02%	99.97%	$p < 10^{-10}$	$p < 10^{-10}$	
Motion	92.01%	99.98%	$p < 10^{-10}$	$p < 10^{-10}$	
Shifting/embedding, foveation (S.F):					
Salience	**77.24%**	**99.94%**	$p < 10^{-10}$	$p < 10^{-10}$	$p < 10^{-10}$
Colour	95.85%	99.96%	$p < 10^{-10}$	$p < 10^{-10}$	$p < 10^{-10}$
Flicker	84.41%	100.03%	$p < 10^{-10}$	$p < 10^{-10}$	$p < 10^{-10}$
Intensity	97.34%	99.96%	$p < 10^{-10}$	$p < 10^{-10}$	$p < 10^{-10}$
Orientation	89.82%	99.99%	$p < 10^{-10}$	$p < 10^{-10}$	$p < 10^{-10}$
Motion	90.11%	99.98%	$p < 10^{-10}$	$p < 10^{-10}$	$p < 10^{-10}$

correlate with human behaviour. To provide a practical lower bound for scores that may be attainable by a computational model, we applied our scoring scheme to an alternate model, whose saliency map was derived from eye movement traces of three humans and tested against a fourth one. In this human-derived model, the "saliency map" contained three continuously moving Gaussian blobs (standard deviation $\sigma = 0.7°$), which followed in real-time the current eye positions of three human subjects who had watched the video clip of interest. By sampling this human-derived saliency map along the gaze locations of a fourth observer, we obtained a score of 52.21% for how well that fourth observer could have been predicted by the other three (Table 1). The human-derived model encompasses both bottom-up and top-down factors, some of which are well beyond the capabilities of our computational bottom-up saliency models (e.g., building a cognitive understanding of the story depicted in a video clip). Our computational models are hence expected to score somewhere between 100% (chance level) and approximately 50% (a remarkably good model that could predict human eye movements as well as other humans could).

Results for the first bottom-up saliency model variant (no shifting/embedding of the video frames, no foveation filter) confirm with dynamic video stimuli previous results indicating that human observers preferentially gaze at locations with model-predicted salience higher than average (Parkhurst et al., 2002), with a compound metric value of 87.51%. In contrast, the compounded metric for random samples was very close to 100%, as expected above. A nonparametric sign test of whether human and random measures for all 324,036 valid eye position samples could have been drawn from distributions with same median suggested highly significant differences between human and random distributions ($p < 10^{-10}$). It is interesting to note that the average metric was better for salience than for any of the individual visual features contributing to salience. This suggests that some of the locations visited by our observers were salient according to the model not only for a single feature (e.g., high colour contrast) but for combined features (e.g., high colour contrast and high motion energy). The figure of 87.51% for salience suggests that our simple, purely bottom-up model does predict locally higher salience at image regions likely to be visited by human observers, in a highly significant manner. But, obviously, there is more to human vision than bottom-up salience: 87.51% is rather far from the score near 50% achieved by our human-derived model. This point is further explored in our discussion: here we accept this figure as a baseline corresponding to a low-realism version of the simulation framework, and compare it to the other two model variants with increased realism.

Results for the second model variant (adding a foveation filter around current human eye position) overall improved the metric for humans (down to 81.85%), whereas random figures remained close to 100%. Comparing human metric values for the various features between the first and second model variants suggested a mixed pattern of changes, though all were highly significant except for the intensity feature. Colour, intensity, and motion energy metrics were little affected by the addition of a foveation filter, whereas flicker and orientation improved more substantially. Hence, the model benefited from foveation predominantly in that it reduced the competitive influence of previously salient fine oriented textures and flicker far from fixation (often present due to the fairly low quality of our video clips, digitized from analogue, interlaced NTSC video sources), which would tend to lower salience at fixation due to the long-range interactions. Irrespective of the details of the different feature responses, and keeping in mind that the model used here is only a very coarse approximation to low-level human vision and that its internals should not be overinterpreted, comparing first and second model variants showed that adding a foveation filter had a highly significant outcome onto the quantitative measure of agreement between model and humans.

Results with the third variant of the model (including embedding the video frames within a larger background, shifting to eye position, cropping around that position by a field of view larger than the video display area, and foveating the resulting image) fairly surprisingly suggested even better agreement between model and humans (metric down to 77.24% for the salience values). We believe this result was surprising because shifting the input, in a coarse attempt to simulate the dynamic motions of a retina, makes the task of computing perceptual salience with a computational model much more difficult, as large motion transients and smearing of the saliency map during saccades may occur (see Discussion). Interestingly, the better agreement for the salience measure was obtained despite the fact that slightly worse agreement was obtained, for this third variant than for the second, for the colour, intensity, and orientation features. Remarkably, the two features we had originally thought would suffer from rapidly shifting the input (and the associated high transients), flicker and motion, actually improved in their agreement with humans between the second and third variants of the model. This suggests that the simulation operated with the third variant may actually more closely approximate the patterns of motion and flicker signals received by a moving human retina. Again, one should be careful, however, not to overinterpret these detailed results and to keep in mind that the model only simulates a very approximate and small fraction of human visual processing. As for the second variant, however, the high-level conclusion for the third variant of the model was that the increased realism of the simulation highly significantly affected the outcome of the comparison between model and humans.

To summarize, Table 2 shows the results of a one-way ANOVA test for whether model variant was a factor that significantly influenced our metric, for both humans and random. The test suggested that the metric for salience as well as for all features was highly significantly affected for humans, but not nearly as much for random. Note, however, that the random salience metric was slightly affected by model variant, $F(2, 972,105) = 3.82$ (three groups for three model variants, and $3 \times 324,036 = 972,108$ data samples where valid measurements could be sampled), which would be considered a significant result in typical statistical analysis (with the conclusion that

TABLE 2

Analysis of variance (ANOVA) to test whether model variant was a factor in our measures of agreement between models and humans (ANOVA, human) and between models and random (ANOVA, random), for saliency as well as the individual visual features implemented in the models. All F-values reported here are for three groups (corresponding to the three model variants) and $3 \times 324,036 = 972,108$ data points where valid measurements could be sampled, hence should be read as $F(2, 972105)$.

Feature	ANOVA, Human		ANOVA, Random	
salience	$F = 9,803.86$	$p < 10^{-10}$	$F = 3.82$	$p \geq .02$
color	$F = 1,015.15$	$p < 10^{-10}$	$F = 2.04$	$p \geq .13$
flicker	$F = 11,275.84$	$p < 10^{-10}$	$F = 2.11$	$p \geq .12$
intensity	$F = 32.17$	$p < 10^{-10}$	$F = 0.04$	$p \geq .96$
orientation	$F = 5,761.22$	$p < 10^{-10}$	$F = 0.66$	$p \geq .52$
motion	$F = 2,194.56$	$p < 10^{-10}$	$F = 0.61$	$p \geq .54$

model variant was a factor, with significance $p < .02$, rather than the conclusion that it was not a factor, with $p \geq .02$, as reported in Table 2). Indeed, one difference which affected random sampling in the third variant of the model was that rarely only a portion of the video display area fell within the field of view of the model (e.g., frames 23 and 38 in Figure 3 are slightly cut off on the right side as the human eye position is close to the left side), resulting in a slightly truncated sampling window over which maximum, average, and random salience were computed. Nevertheless, the random metric was clearly affected to an extent that simply does not compare with the extremely high F-values found for the human metric. Of all features, the metric for intensity was the least affected by model variants, with colour a far second. The high-level conclusion here again is that the level of detail used for the simulations very highly significantly affected the agreement between humans and model, but very little affected that between random sampling and the model.

Finally, a breakdown histogrammed by metric values for the salience measures is shown in Figure 5. This shows how, for all three model variants, the basic difference between humans and random was that the distributions of metric values for humans had heavier tails towards 0% (salience at point of gaze higher than on average over the video display area), whereas the distributions for random were more concentrated around 100% (salience at sampled location close to the average over the video display area). This difference is increasingly emphasized from the first to second and to third model variants, hence showing in a graphical manner why the metric values reported in Table 1 also became better with increased simulation realism.

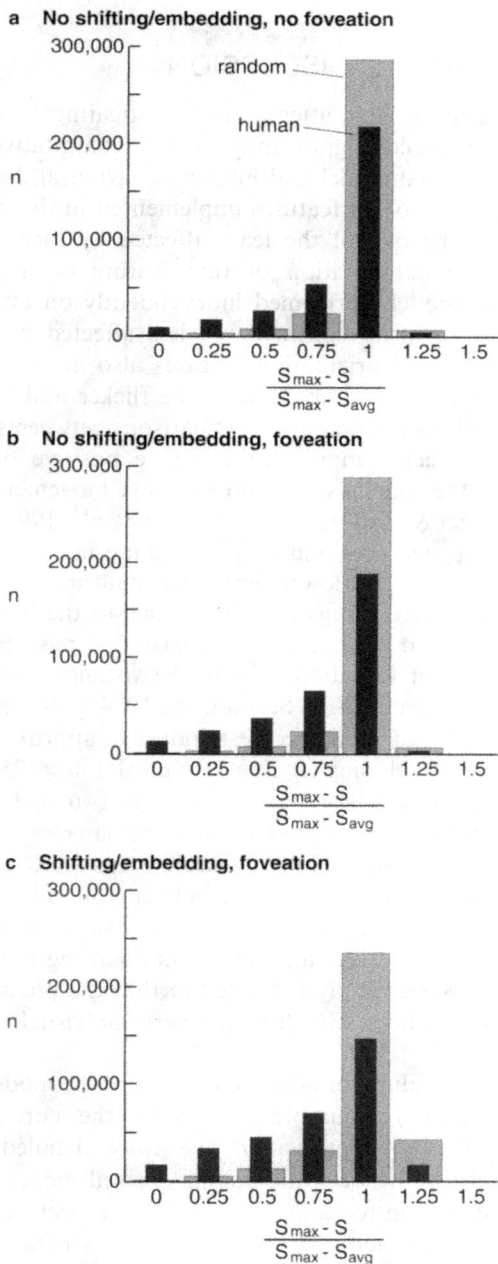

a No shifting/embedding, no foveation

b No shifting/embedding, foveation

c Shifting/embedding, foveation

Figure 5. Histograms of the distributions of our metric values for humans (thin dark grey bars) and random (wide light grey bars), for the three model variants.

979

DISCUSSION

This study represents a first attempt at investigating whether increased simulation realism could significantly affect quantitative comparisons between a computational model and human behavioural data.

It is interesting that, of all features implemented in the model, intensity contrast seemed to be overall the least affected by increased simulation realism. Indeed, the computation of that feature is instantaneous and memoryless in the model, performed independently on every frame. This could explain why intensity was less affected by input shifting. However, the colour and orientation features also are instantaneous and memoryless in our model (as opposed to the flicker and motion features, which are computed from differential comparisons between successive video frames) but were affected more strongly. One positive outcome of this observation is that the conclusions of previous eye movement studies (Barth et al., 1998; Reinagel & Zador, 1999: Zetzsche et al., 1998), which largely focused on contrast measures and greyscale static images, might not have been affected too strongly by lower simulation realism.

There are many shortcomings and limitations to the implementation of our model, which should be considered a coarse first pass. First, we did not attempt to calibrate our foveation filter to the visual acuity profiles of our observers (Geisler & Perry, 2002). Second, the 1024×768 field of view used in the third variant of our model, corresponding to approximately $45^\circ \times 33^\circ$ of visual angle, was much smaller than a typical $160 \times 175^\circ$ subtended by each human retina (Wandell, 1995). There were two main reasons which restricted our model's field of view: One was computer memory available to run the simulations (remember that 72 feature maps are computed from the input image); the other was that obtaining a background image of this width would require special apparatus, and a more sophisticated method to simulate the rotation of the eye than the planar shifting used here in a first approximation. Thus, our study is limited in that the possible influence of objects or otherwise salient stimuli in the very far visual periphery is not accounted for.

Overall, the metric values for all three variants of the model, ranging from 77.24% to 87.51%, were honourable compared to the score near 52% of the human-derived model—in particular, the fully detailed model scores approximately half-way between the human-derived model and chance. As briefly reviewed in our introduction, we did not expect perfect agreement given all the additional factors (biasing by the gist of a scene, top-down guidance of search, etc.) that contribute to eye movements and are not simulated by the model (Itti, 2003). It is interesting to note that the additional machinery implemented in our model compared to, for example, a simple local contrast detector, significantly improved the correlation between humans and model (the metric values for salience were always better than for intensity contrast alone). Although it is not our main aim here to advocate that the specific bottom-up saliency model tested in this study can account for a significant fraction of human gaze allocation, the fact that the models perform significantly below 100% is interesting as it suggests that bottom-up salience plays a sustained role in attracting attention in dynamic video scenes. Another study explores this question in further detail (Itti, in press).

We found it surprising that the third variant of the model performed best. Indeed, as the input image rapidly shifts during saccades in this model variant, possibly large motion transients may be elicited, which could easily over-whelm the saliency map. Remarkably, however, these were seldom observed in our dynamic saliency maps, suggesting that the long-range competition for salience implemented in our model was very efficient at suppressing full-field motion transients. Indeed, shifting the entire input at a given velocity and in a given direction would excite a single motion feature map (tuned to that velocity and direction) throughout the entire visual field. Strong local motion responses would thus be elicited in that feature map, but at many locations in the visual field, so that the entire feature map would become inhibited by the long-range competition mechanism because not containing any single location that significantly differs from most other locations. A consequence of this for human vision is that, at least in our model, an explicit mechanism for top-down saccadic suppression may be unnecessary (Thiele, Henning, Kubischik, & Hoffmann, 2002), although this remains to be tested (i.e., maybe even better agreement between model and humans could be obtained after addition of explicit saccadic suppression to the model). Additional difficulties which would tend to make the simulation with the third model variant more difficult include smearing of the low-pass filtered saliency map as the input shifted (which we often observed when inspecting the dynamic saliency maps predicted for various video clips), competition between possibly salient objects outside the video screen area and objects within that area, and lack of sufficient persistence to allow for salience to build up over time (remember that the saliency map is modelled as leaky integrator neurons, which respond better when inputs are somewhat stable). By computer vision standards, these may be regarded as artifacts, limitations of the feature detectors, or fundamental problems that inevitably deteriorate the output of the model. However, our results suggest that they actually might be a feature rather than a shortcoming of the model, in that biological early vision is subjected to similar situations as the eye moves, in a manner that eventually will affect biological computation of salience and eye movements.

It is important to again stress that one should not overinterpret the absolute quantitative measures of agreement between model variants and human scan paths. Indeed, these absolute numbers are highly dependent upon software implementation details of our model, various model parameters that we have here not attempted to tune, such as the strength of the long-range interactions, and even architectural choices, such as which preattentive visual features may guide attention (Wolfe & DiMase, 2003). Thus, the important conclusion of our work is not in the absolute performance value of each model variant, but in the comparison between the three variants. The fact that increased realism affected the comparison outcomes in such a significant manner stresses how attempting simulations that are as realistic as possible is important when using computational models to interpret empirical data. Translating these findings to human vision, in particular for psychophysical studies like visual search, our results strongly caution against an often fairly intuitive interpretation of the data in terms of the intrinsic local features of the target and distractor items. Instead, the outcome of a search may much more strongly be influenced than one may think at first by the spatiotemporal dynamics of eye movements operated over the course of the search.

REFERENCES

Barth, E., Zetzsche, C., & Rentschler, I. (1998). Intrinsic two-dimensional features as textons. *Journal of the Optical Society of America. Part A, Optics, and Image Science and Vision*, *15*(7), 1723–1732.

Biederman, I., Teitelbaum, R. C., & Mezzanotte, R. J. (1983). Scene perception: A failure to find a benefit from prior expectancy or familiarity. *Journal of Experimental Psychology: Learning, Memory, and Cognition*, *9*(3), 411–429.

Borgefors, G. (1991). Distance transformations in digital images. *CVGIP: Image Understanding*, *54*, 301.

Burt, P. J., & Adelson, E. H. (1983). The Laplacian pyramid as a compact image code. *IEEE Transactions on Communications*, *31*, 532–540.

Cannon, M. W., & Fullenkamp, S. C. (1991). Spatial interactions in apparent contrast: Inhibitory effects among grating patterns of different spatial frequencies, spatial positions and orientations. *Vision Research*, *31*(11), 1985–1998.

Finney, S. A. (2001). Real-time data collection in Linux: A case study. *Behavior Research Methods, Instruments, and Computers*, *33*, 167–173.

Friedman, A. (1979). Framing pictures: The role of knowledge in automatized encoding and memory for gist. *Journal of Experimental Psychology: General*, *108*(3), 316–355.

Geisler, W. S., & Perry, J. S. (2002). *Real-time simulation of arbitrary visual fields*. Paper presented at the ACM symposium on Eye Tracking Research and Applications.

Henderson, J. M., & Hollingworth, A. (1999). High-level scene perception. *Annual Review of Psychology*, *50*, 243–271.

Henderson, J. M., & Hollingworth, A. (2003). Global transsaccadic change blindness during scene perception. *Psychological Sciences*, *14*(5), 493–497.

Hollingworth, A., & Henderson, J. M. (1998). Does consistent scene context facilitate object perception? *Journal of Experimental Psychology: General*, *127*(4), 398–415.

Hubel, D. H., & Wiesel, T. N. (1962). Receptive fields, binocular interaction and functional architecture in the cat's visual cortex. *Journal of Physiology (London)*, *160*, 106–154.

Ito, M., & Gilbert, C. D. (1999). Attention modulates contextual influences in the primary visual cortex of alert monkeys. *Neuron*, *22*(3), 593–604.

Itti, L. (2003). Modeling primate visual attention. In J. Feng (Ed.), *Computational neuro-science: A comprehensive approach* (pp. 635–655). Boca Raton, FL: CRC Press.

Itti, L. (2004). Automatic foveation for video compression using a neurobiological model of visual attention. *IEEE Transactions on Image Processing*, *13*(10), 1304–1318.

Itti, L. (2005). Quantifying the contribution of low-level saliency to human eye movements in dynamic scenes. *Visual Cognition*, *12*, 1093–1123.

Itti, L., Dhavale, N., & Pighin, F. (2003, August). Realistic avatar eye and head animation using a neurobiological model of visual attention. In B. Bosacchi, D. B. Fogel, & J. C. Bezdek (Eds.), *Proceedings of the SPIE 48th Annual International Symposium on Optical Science and Technology* (Vol. 5200, pp. 68–78). Bellingham, WA: SPIE Press..

Itti, L., & Koch, C. (2000). A saliency-based search mechanism for overt and covert shifts of visual attention. *Vision Research*, *40*(10–12), 1489–1506.

Itti, L., & Koch, C. (2001a). Computational modeling of visual attention. *Nature Reviews Neuroscience*, *2*(3), 194–203.

Itti, L., & Koch, C. (2001b). Feature combination strategies for saliency-based visual attention systems. *Journal of Electronic Imaging*, *10*(1), 161–169.

Itti, L., Koch, C., & Niebur, E. (1998). A model of saliency-based visual attention for rapid scene analysis. *IEEE Transactions on Pattern Analysis and Machine Intelligence*, *20*(11), 1254–1259.

Koch, C., & Ullman, S. (1985). Shifts in selective visual attention: Towards the underlying neural circuitry. *Human Neurobiology*, *4*(4), 219–227.

Kofka, K. (1935). *Principles of Gestalt psychology*. New York: Harcourt & Brace.

Kuffler, S. W. (1953). Discharge patterns and functional organization of mammalian retina. *Journal of Neurophysiology*, *16*, 37–68.

Levitt, J. B., & Lund, J. S. (1997). Contrast dependence of contextual effects in primate visual cortex. *Nature*, *387*(6628), 73–76.

Moran, J., & Desimone, R. (1985). Selective attention gates visual processing in the extrastriate cortex. *Science*, *229*(4715), 782–784.

Moreno, F. J., Reina, R., Luis, V., & Sabido, R. (2002). Visual search strategies in experienced and inexperienced gymnastic coaches. *Perceptual Motor Skills*, *95*(3, Pt.1), 901–902.

Motter, B. C. (1994). Neural correlates of attentive selection for color or luminance in extrastriate area V4. *Journal of Neuroscience*, *14*(4), 2178–2189.

Müller, H. J., Reimann, B., & Krummenacher, J. (2003). Visual search for singleton feature targets across dimensions: Stimulus- and expectancy-driven effects in dimensional weighting. *Journal of Experimental Psychology: Human Perception and Performance*, *29*(5), 1021–1035.

Nodine, C. F., & Krupinski, E. A. (1998). Perceptual skill, radiology expertise, and visual test performance with NINA and WALDO. *Academic Radiology*, *5*(9), 603–612.

Noton, D., & Stark, L. (1971). Scanpaths in eye movements during pattern perception. *Science*, *171*(968), 308–311.

Oliva, A., & Schyns, P. G. (1997). Coarse blobs or fine edges? Evidence that information diagnosticity changes the perception of complex visual stimuli. *Cognitive Psychology*, *34*(1), 72–107.

Parkhurst, D., Law, K., & Niebur, E. (2002). Modeling the role of salience in the allocation of overt visual attention. *Vision Research*, *42*(1), 107–123.

Peebles, D., & Cheng, P. C. (2003). Modeling the effect of task and graphical representation on response latency in a graph reading task. *Human Factors*, *45*(1), 28–46.

Potter, M. C., & Levy, E. I. (1969). Recognition memory for a rapid sequence of pictures. *Journal of Experimental Psychology*, *81*(1), 10–15.

Privitera, C. M., & Stark, L. W. (2000). Algorithms for defining visual regions-of-interest: Comparison with eye fixations. *IEEE Transactions on Pattern Analysis and Machine Intelligence*, *22*(9), 970–982.

Reinagel, P., & Zador, A. M. (1999). Natural scene statistics at the centre of gaze. *Network: Computation, and Neural Systems*, *10*, 341–350.

Rensink, R. A. (2000). The dynamic representation of scenes. *Visual Cognition*, *7*, 17–42.

Reynolds, J. H., Pasternak, T., & Desimone, R. (2000). Attention increases sensitivity of V4 neurons. *Neuron*, *26*(3), 703–714.

Savelsbergh, G. J., Williams. A. M., van der Kamp, J., & Ward, P. (2002). Visual search, anticipation and expertise in soccer goalkeepers. *Journal of Sports Sciences*, *20*(3), 279–287.

Sigman, M., Cecchi, G. A., Gilbert, C. D., & Magnasco, M. O. (2001). On a common circle: Natural scenes and Gestalt rules. *Proceedings of the National Academy of Sciences, USA*, *98*(4), 1935–1940.

Sillito. A. M., Grieve, K. L., Jones, H. E., Cudeiro, J., & Davis, J. (1995). Visual cortical mechanisms detecting focal orientation discontinuities. *Nature*, *378*(6556), 492–496.

Spillmann, L., & Werner, J. S. (1990). *Visual perception: The neurophysiological foundations*. San Diego, CA: Academic Press.

Stampe, D. M. (1993). Heuristic filtering and reliable calibration methods for video based pupil tracking systems. *Behavior Research Methods, Instruments, and Computers*, *25*(2), 137–142.

Tanenhaus, M. K., Spivey-Knowlton, M. J., Eberhard, K. M., & Sedivy, J. C. (1995). Integration of visual and linguistic information in spoken language comprehension. *Science*, *268*(5217), 1632–1634.

Thiele, A., Henning, P., Kubischik, M., & Hoffmann, K. P. (2002). Neural mechanisms of saccadic suppression. *Science*, *295*(5564), 2460–2462.

Torralba, A. (2003). Modeling global scene factors in attention. *Journal of the Optical Society of America. Part A, Optics, and Image Science and Vision*, *20*(7), 1407–1418.

Treisman, A. M., & Gelade, G. (1980). A feature-integration theory of attention. *Cognitive Psychology*, *12*(1), 97–136.

Treue, S., & Maunsell, J. H. (1996). Attentional modulation of visual motion processing in cortical areas MT and MST. *Nature*, *382*(6591), 539–541.

Treue, S., & Trujillo, J. C. M. (1999). Feature-based attention influences motion processing gain in macaque visual cortex. *Nature*, *399*(6736), 575–579.

Verghese, P. (2001). Visual search and attention: A signal detection theory approach. *Neuron*, *31*(4), 523–535.

Wandell, B. (1995). *Foundations of vision*. Sunderland, MA: Sinauer Associates.

Wolfe, J. (1998). Visual Search. In H. Pashler (Ed.), *Attention*. London: University College London Press.

Wolfe, J. M. (1994). Guided Search 2.0: A revised model of visual search. *Psychonomic Bulletin and Review*, *1*, 202–238.

Wolfe, J. M., Cave, K. R., & Franzel, S. L. (1989). Guided Search: An alternative to the feature integration model for visual search. *Journal of Experimental Psychology: Human Perception and Performance*, *15*(3), 419–433.

Wolfe, J. M., & DiMase, J. S. (2003). Do intersections serve as basic features in visual search? *Perception*, *32*(6), 645–656.

Wolfe, J. M., & Horowitz, T. S. (2004). What attributes guide the deployment of visual attention and how do they do it? *Nature Reviews Neuroscience*, *5*(6), 495–501.

Yarbus, A. (1967). *Eye movements and vision*. New York: Plenum Press.

Yeshurun, Y., & Carrasco, M. (1998). Attention improves or impairs visual performance by enhancing spatial resolution. *Nature*, *396*(6706), 72–75.

Zetzsche, C., Schill, K., Deubel, H., Krieger, G., Umkehrer, E., & Beinlich, S. (1998). Investigation of a sensorimotor system for saccadic scene analysis: An integrated approach. In *From animals to animals: Proceedings of the fifth international conference on Simulation of Adaptive Behavior* (Vol. 5, pp. 120–126). Cambridge, MA: MIT Press.

VISUAL COGNITION, 2006, 14 (4/5/6/7/8), 985–1005

Ψ Psychology Press
Taylor & Francis Group

Top-down guidance of visual search: A computational account

Dietmar Heinke, Glyn W. Humphreys, and Claire L. Tweed

Behavioural Brain Sciences Centre, University of Birmingham, Birmingham, UK

We present a revised version of the Selective Attention for Identification Model (SAIM), using an initial feature detection process to code edge orientations. We show that the revised SAIM can simulate both efficient and inefficient human search, that it shows search asymmetries, and that top-down expectancies for targets play a major role in the model's selection. Predictions of the model for top-down effects are tested with human participants, and important similarities and dissimilarities are discussed.

Recently, we have presented a connectionist model of human visual attention, termed SAIM (Selective Attention for Identification Model; Heinke & Humphreys, 2003). SAIM uses an interactive approach to object recognition and visual selection in which units within and between processing modules compete to gain control of behaviour. SAIM produced a qualitative fit to a broad range of phenomena concerned with human visual selection. This included results on: Two-object costs (e.g., Duncan, 1980), object familiarity (Kumada & Humphreys, 2001), global precedence (Navon, 1977), spatial cueing both within and between objects (Egly, Driver, & Rafal, 1994; Posner, Snyder, & Davidson, 1980), and inhibition of return. When simulated lesions were conducted, SAIM also demonstrated both unilateral neglect and spatial extinction, depending on the type and extent of the lesion. Different lesions also produced view-centred and object-centred neglect, and both forms of neglect could even be simulated within a single patient (see Humphreys & Riddoch, 1994, 1995, for evidence). In essence, SAIM suggested that attentional effects in human behaviour could result

Please address all correspondence to Dietmar Heinke, Behavioural Brain Sciences Centre, University of Birmingham, Birmingham B15 2TT, UK. E-mail: d.g.heinke@bham.ac.uk

This work was supported by grants from the European Union, the BBSRC, and the EPSRC (UK) to DH and GWH, and by grants from the MRC (UK) to GWH, and from the EPSRC to CLT.

http://www.psypress.com/viscog   DOI: 10.1080/13506280500195482

from competitive interactions in visual selection for object recognition, whereas neurological disorders of selection can be due to imbalanced spatial competition following damage to areas of the brain modulating access to stored knowledge.

In this paper we present an extended version of SAIM in which a feature extraction process was added, while maintaining the basic principles of SAIM (e.g., competitive interactions leading to selection). Our aim here is twofold. First, to demonstrate that this new version still successfully performs translation-invariant object identification—a basic tenet of the original SAIM. Second, to assess the viability of "extended SAIM" as a psychological model, particularly when applied to data from visual search tasks and to data on the influence of the top-down guidance of human visual search.

Over the past 20 years the visual search paradigm has generated a vast amount of experimental evidence on visual selection (see Wolfe, 1998, for a recent review). Here we will focus on the most important outcomes. One common result is that, when a target shares features with the distractors, the search function shows a linear increase of reaction time with the number of items in the display. The slope and the intercept of the search function can vary with the properties of the target and distractor, though a search slope of less than 10 ms/item is typically considered to indicate efficient search, whereas search slopes of 20 ms/items and above are considered as examples of inefficient search (Wolfe, 1998). For target-absent trials the overall reaction time is typically longer than for present trials and slopes are usually higher. In some cases the efficiency of the search can change dramatically when targets and distractors are interchanged. So the search for target "X" amongst distractor "Y" can be very efficient, whereas the search for "Y" with "X" as distractor can be very inefficient. This phenomenon was termed a "search asymmetries" by Treisman (1988) and has been demonstrated with a variety of search displays (see Wolfe, 2001, for a more recent review). Here we will demonstrate that SAIM is capable of generating both efficient and inefficient (apparently spatially serial) search from its parallel processing architecture, and that it can capture basic search asymmetries such as the more efficient detection of oblique relative to vertical targets (e.g., Foster & Ward, 1991).

Like old SAIM, new SAIM is responsive to top-down processing as well as bottom-up factors in guided search. For example, preactivating a template (to expect a particular target) can lead to early biases on selection to favour the expected target over other (unexpected) items in the field. Here we will report simulation results examining the role of top-down guidance in visual search. Recently, a few experimental papers have looked at the issue of top-down influences in visual search (e.g., Hodsoll & Humphreys, 2001; Kristjansson, Wang, & Nakayama, 2002; Müller,

Reimann, & Krummenacher, 2003; Wolfe, Butcher, Lee, & Hyle, 2003). However, as we will discuss in the section dealing with the simulations, none of these papers can be seen as a test of SAIM's performance. An experimental test of a novel prediction derived from SAIM is then reported.

SAIM

Overview

Figure 1 gives an overview of SAIM's architecture highlighting its modular structure. In a first stage of processing in the model, two features, horizontal and vertical lines, are extracted from the input image. The contents network then maps a subset of the features into a smaller focus of attention (FOA), a process modulated by spatial attention. This mapping of the contents network into the FOA is translation invariant and is gated by activity from all retinal positions competing through the selection network to gain control of units in the FOA. This enables SAIM to perform translation-invariant object recognition. The selection network controls the contents network by competitive interactions between its processing units, so that input from only one (set of) locations is dominant and mapped into the FOA. At the top end of the model, the knowledge network identifies the contents of the FOA using template matching. The knowledge network also modulates the

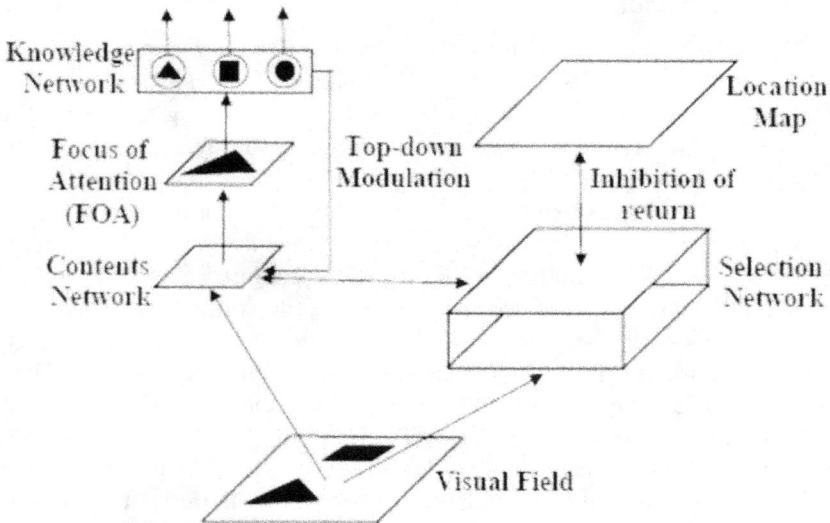

Figure 1. Architecture of SAIM.

behaviour of the selection network with top-down activation, with known objects preferred over unknown objects. In addition to these modules, there is also a location map that enables SAIM to make multiple selections. Essentially units in the location map store the object position each time an object is recognized and then inhibits the selection network from reselecting these locations (inhibition of return). This biases selection to move from one object to the next.

The design of SAIM's network follows the idea of soft constraint satisfaction in neural networks that use "energy minimization" techniques (Hopfield & Tank, 1985). In SAIM the "energy minimization" approach is applied in the following way: Each module in SAIM carries out a predefined task (e.g., the knowledge network has to identify the object in the FOA). In turn each task describes allowed states of activation in the network. These states then define the minima in an energy function. To ensure that the model as a whole satisfies each constraint, set by each network, the energy functions of each module are added together to form a global energy function for the whole system. The minima in the energy function are found via gradient descent, as proposed by Hopfield and Tank (1985). In the Appendix the energy functions for each module in SAIM are stated.

Simulation results and discussion

Basic behaviour

Figure 2 demonstrates the basic behaviour of the new version of SAIM, when presented with two objects (a "2" and a "+"). It shows that both objects are selected in a serial manner, here the "2" being followed by the "+". Similarly to SAIM version 1 (Heinke & Humphreys, 2003) there was a bottom-up preference towards certain objects, in this case the "2". This bottom-up preference results from the fact that the "2" is assembled through an inhomogeneous arrangement of vertical and horizontal lines. Such a heterogeneous representation facilitates the selection processes as independent object parts are assigned more easily to the contents network by the selection network (see Equation 1). We do not claim psychological plausibility for the two being preferred in selection over the cross, but it does illustrate asymmetries in bottom-up bias in the model. Figure 3 shows that the bottom-up bias can be overcome by giving the cross-template a higher initial value. This higher activation filters through the selection network via the top-down modulation process (see Figure 1). The top-down bias was used in simulations of visual search tasks where SAIM was required "to look for a particular target".

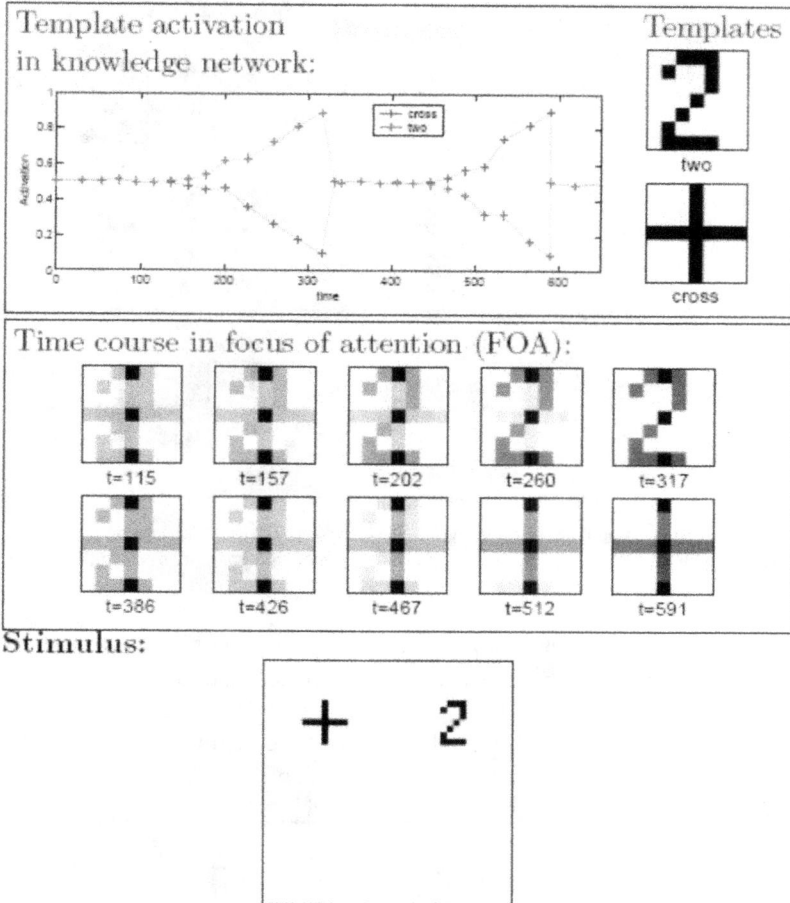

Figure 2. Basic behaviour of new SAIM. At the bottom of the figure we show the activation of units in FOA at a series of time steps, based on network iterations (the *t*-values). The top of the figure we show the variations in activation over time for the "2" and "+" units in the knowledge network.

Simulation of visual search

Rechecking strategy and initial values.   Due to noise in the system, SAIM has a certain probability of missing a target. This probability depends on the display size. To reduce the likelihood for missing a target, SAIM can be "re-run", to effect a rechecking process. A similar rechecking operation was used in simulations of search by the SEarch by Recursive Rejection (SERR) model (Humphreys & Müller, 1993). To equate the likelihood of detecting a target across the display sizes, the probability of rechecking was proportional to the display size. For the model, the display size is derived from overall

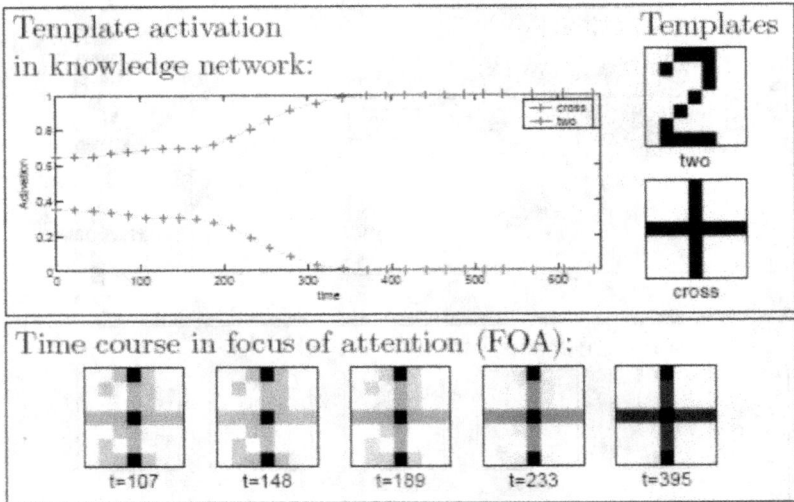

Figure 3. The simulation is set to select the " + " in preference to the "2", based on preactivation of the " + " unit in the knowledge network. The preactivation is apparent in the difference in the activation of the knowledge network at $t = 0$.

activity in the selection network, which rises to different levels dependent on the display size (see Figure 4). In the present simulations in SAIM, rechecking stops entirely when either the target is found or a predefined percentage of items have been selected. This percentage is determined by

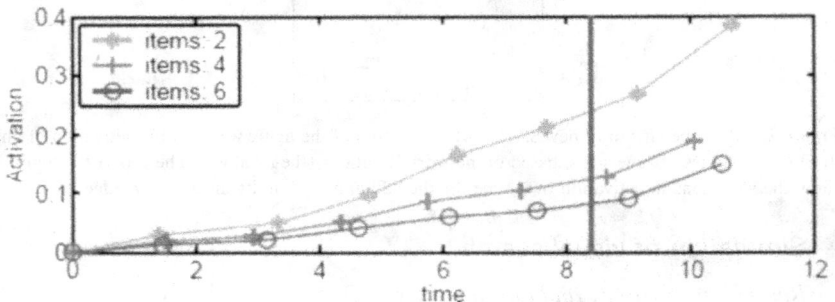

Figure 4. The plots show the time course of the activation of one unit in the selection network for different display sizes (2, 4, and 6). The units represent the location of the item that was finally selected. The time course illustrates the increased competition in SAIM as the number of distractors increase. At the point in time marked by the vertical line SAIM makes a probabilistic decision, as to whether to perform a "re-rechecking" operation. The rechecking operation is set into effect, in order to reduce missed targets to a psychologically plausible level. This decision is modulated by the height of the activation whereby the higher the activation, the less likely SAIM will recheck. Hence, as the plot illustrates, rechecking is less likely the smaller the display size.

process within the location network. The total number of locations inhibited by IOR is divided by the total number of locations occupied by the initial stimulus.

As explained earlier, the setting of a higher initial value for the template unit of the target can be seen as related to the instruction "Search for item X". The exact choice of initial values has to balance several factors. If the initial value is too high, SAIM is more likely to produce a false positive response, because the knowledge network would converge into a target response irrespective of the bottom-up information from the selection and contents networks. Also an absent decision could take longer, since the more the knowledge network is biased towards the target, the greater the time taken for the knowledge network to switch from "present" to "absent". However, there is also a lower bound for the initial activation. If the top-down bias is not high enough to override a bottom-up bias towards the distractor, rechecking would occur frequently and search would be very slow. In each of simulations here the initial values were set to balance the two constraints so that targets were found with a psychologically plausible error rate.

Linear search function and search asymmetries.   Figure 5 illustrates that the new version of SAIM is capable of simulating a result frequently interpreted as indicating a spatially serial search process—where there is a linear increase in search and absent responses are slower and show a greater slope than present responses. This arose when the target was a vertical line and the distractors oblique lines, and in this case the absent:present slope ratio was 2.1:1, consistent with a serial, self-terminating search (cf. Treisman & Gelade, 1980). In contrast to this, a "flat" search function arose when the target was the oblique line and the distractors were vertical. This search asymmetry matches the pattern found in human subjects (Foster & Ward, 1991). In SAIM, the asymmetry arises because of a bottom-up bias in the model, favouring the oblique target. This bias occurs because the oblique is coded as a mixture of horizontal and vertical edges, so that it has a heterogeneous representation at the feature level. This heterogeneous representation in turn allows the selection network to assign parts to locations in the contents network more easily than when the lines are coded in a homogeneous feature space. In humans, this bias in coding could come about because horizontal and vertical feature detectors are more prevalent in early vision (see Appelle, 1972, for an interpretation of the "oblique effect" in human vision along these lines; cf. Wang, Ding, & Yunokuchik, 2003). When searching for the vertical line, the linear increase of SAIM's reaction time originates from two factors: First the time to select an item increases with the number of items, reflecting greater competition for selection (see Figure 4). Second, the number of rechecks increases with the number of

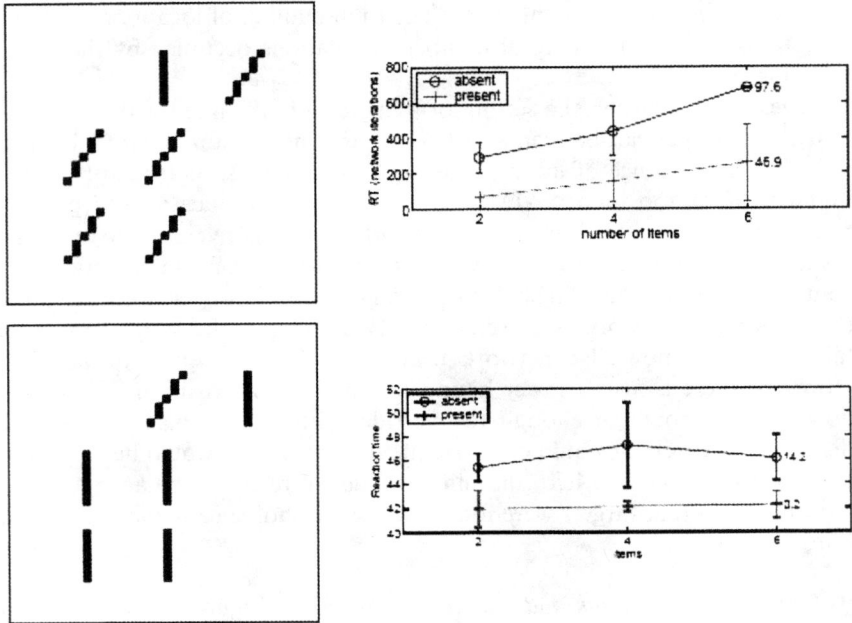

Figure 5. Simulation of a search asymmetry. Search for an oblique line among vertical lines is "parallel" (0.2 ms/item), whereas search for a vertical line target amongst oblique lines produces a "serial" search (49.9 ms/item).

items, reflecting the greater probability of missing a target at larger display sizes. Third, the bottom-up bias in the model favours selection of an oblique over a vertical stimulus (see above). When the target is vertical, this bias can only be overcome by top-down activation from the knowledge network. This top-down activation takes time to be effective, since activation has to propagate through the contents network to the selection network.

Prediction. In a series of simulations we tested the influence of the top-down bias introduced by varying the initial activation values of template units in the knowledge network. Figure 6 shows that the search slope decreased with increasing initial activation values for a moderately difficult search ("T" vs. "L"s) and for a more difficult search for the model (vertical line vs. oblique lines). The size of the benefit in terms of the search slope was roughly equal in the two cases. This pattern results from the fact that larger top-down biases lead to a decrease in selection time and an increase in the hit rate, so that rechecking is in turn reduced.

Extrapolating from these data to human data, we can ask whether top-down knowledge of the target can modulate competition from distractors, so

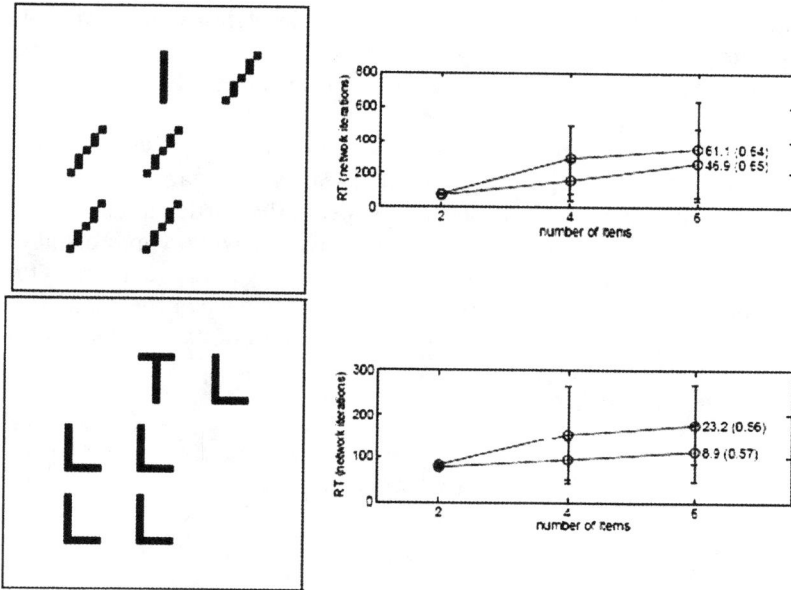

Figure 6. This figure illustrates the simulation results with different initial activations of templates units. The initial values are noted in brackets behind the slopes. The effect of varying the initial values was tested for a moderately difficult search ("T" vs. "L"s) and a difficult search task (vertical line vs. oblique lines). In both cases the search slope decreases with increasing template values ("T" vs. "L"s: 23.2–8.9; horizontal vs. oblique: 61.2–46.9).

that there is a reduced effect of display size on search for an expected target. This can come about without any increase in false positive responses, provided that template activation is not set too high. There have been several attempts to examine what have been termed top-down influences on human visual search. For example, some studies have evaluated effects of foreknowledge of the target being in a particular dimension (without knowing the target's feature value along that dimension) or knowing the target's features but not in which dimension the target may be defined (e.g., Found & Müller, 1996; Müller et al., 2003; Wolfe et al., 2003). Others have evaluated priming effects from one trial to another (Hillstrom, 2000; Kristjansson et al., 2002; Maljkovic & Nakayama, 1994, 1996; Zelinsky, 2001). In a third set of studies by Bravo and Nakayama (1992) and Hodsoll and Humphreys (2001), visual search for the odd-one out (unknown target condition) was compared with the situation when participants knew the target. In general, the data from these studies show that search benefits from top-down foreknowledge, with search operating more efficiently when such knowledge can be applied. However, the type of top-down influence these experiments explore is different from the way of top-down influence is manipulated in SAIM's simulations. In the simulations the target always known to SAIM, as indicated by higher initial values for the target template relative to any other template. The variation of initial values only indicates the degree to which SAIM looks for the target. Hence, we assume that the initial value is proportional to the expectation of the presence of a given target. Manipulating expectation in visual search tasks can be done by using a cue preceding the search display and instruct the participants that the cue gives a hint of what could be the target in the following search display. For such a priming experiment SAIM predicts that participants are better in terms of search slope and the overall reaction time when the prime is valid compared to when there is no prime is given. Additionally, when the prime was wrong, as in the simulated absent trials, the slope and the overall reaction time would be higher.

EXPERIMENT

Method

Participants.   Participants in this experiment were 24 undergraduates (2 male and 22 female) from the University of Birmingham. The average age was 21.5 years. All participants had normal or to corrected-to-normal vision and were naive to the purpose of the experiment.

Apparatus and stimuli.   The experiment was conducted by a Gateway 2000 computer using E-prime software package. Stimuli could appear at eight possible locations evenly distributed around the perimeter of an imaginary circle of diameter 2.96°. Items were white with a visual angle of 0.7° by 0.7° from an approximate viewing distance of 60 cm. They appeared on a black background. The search array contained either four or six items. The target was either an upright "L" or "V", and the distractors were "L"s rotated 90° clockwise or counterclockwise from the target orientation (see Duncan & Humphreys, 1989, for a similar display).

Procedure and design.   All participants completed all trials in one session. The trial sequence is illustrated in Figure 7. A fixation point appeared in the centre of the screen for 1 s. This was then replaced by a star (neutral prime), a "V" or an "L" for 1200 ms (the prime). Then, after an ISI of 100 ms, the search display appeared. Observers were asked to respond as quickly as possible while maintaining a high degree of accuracy. Responses were made by pressing the "z" key for target present ("V" or "L") or the "m" key for both absent. The left hand was used to indicate target presence and the right to indicate absence. The final display remained visible until a response was

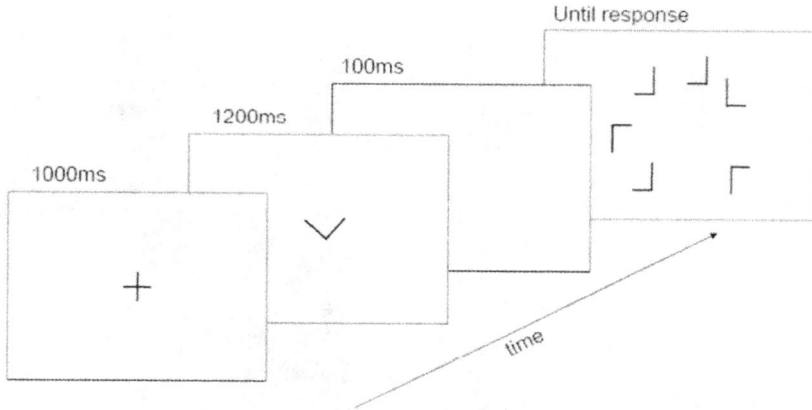

Figure 7. Schematic illustration of the experimental paradigm. Here the prime is invalid.

made. A repeated measures design was adopted with a total of 16 conditions. These conditions involved all possible permutations of the three factors: Validity (33% valid, 33% neutral, 33% invalid), target (36.1% "L", 36.1% "V", 27.8% absent or catch trials), and number of items (50% 4, 50% 6). The 18 practice trials were followed by a total of 576 trials (four blocks of 144). Participants were asked to take at least a 1 min break after each block.

Results

Overall accuracy was 96%. One participant was removed due to an error rate of 50%. Figure 8 plots the mean RTs versus the set size for the quick ("V") and slow ("L") targets as a function of validity. For present trials a three-way within-subjects ANOVA was conducted with the following factors: Validity (valid, neutral, invalid), target ("L", "V") and number of items (4, 6). All three main effects were significant: Validity, $F(2, 44) = 20.23$, $p < .001$, target, $F(1, 22) = 67.37$, $p < .001$, and items, $F(1, 22) = 83.14$, $p < .001$. No significant interaction was found between validity and number of items, $F(2, 44) = 0.474$, $p = .626$, but all other two-way interactions were significant: Validity × Target, $F(2, 44) = 13.62$, $p < .001$, and Target × Items, $F(1, 22) = 16.95$, $p < .001$. The three-way interaction between validity, target, and items was not significant, $F(2, 44) = 3.01$, $p = .059$.

For the slow target ("L") there were significant main effects of validity, $F(2, 44) = 7.83$, $p < .001$, and number of items, $F(1, 22) = 71.36$, $p < .001$. The interaction between validity and items was not significant, $F(2, 44) = 0.54$, $p = .589$.

For the quick target ("V") there were significant main effects of validity, $F(2, 44) = 26.95$, $p < .001$, and number of items, $F(1, 17) = 25.84$, $p < .001$.

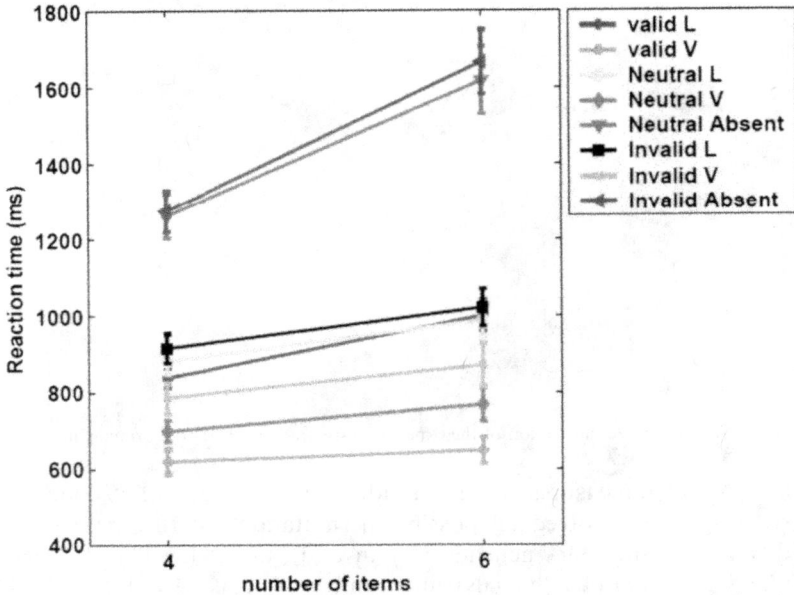

Figure 8.   Human search times to respond to the presence or absence of targets predicted by a prime.

Their interaction was also significant, $F(2, 34) = 4.11$, $p = .023$. The slopes were 17.7 ms/item for the valid prime, 31.2 ms/item for the neutral prime, and 40.7 ms/item for the invalid insert prime (see Figure 9).

Discussion

The results showed three qualitatively different outcomes. For both types of target RTs for the valid priming condition were overall faster than for the neutral condition, and the neutral condition showed an overall faster reaction time compared to the invalid condition. However, performance differed for the slow ("L") and quick targets ("V"). For the quick target, the slope increased in the invalid condition compared to the neural condition; the slope was reduced further when the prime was valid. That is, the effect of the prime increased with the number of items. In contrast to this, the search slope for the slow target was unaffected by target foreknowledge, though there was an overall RT decrease in the valid priming condition.

For the moderately difficult target these results fit with the predictions of SAIM, where effects of top-down knowledge emerge on the slopes of the search functions. However, for the very difficult target human performance does not show an effect of prime validity on search efficiency, as predicted by

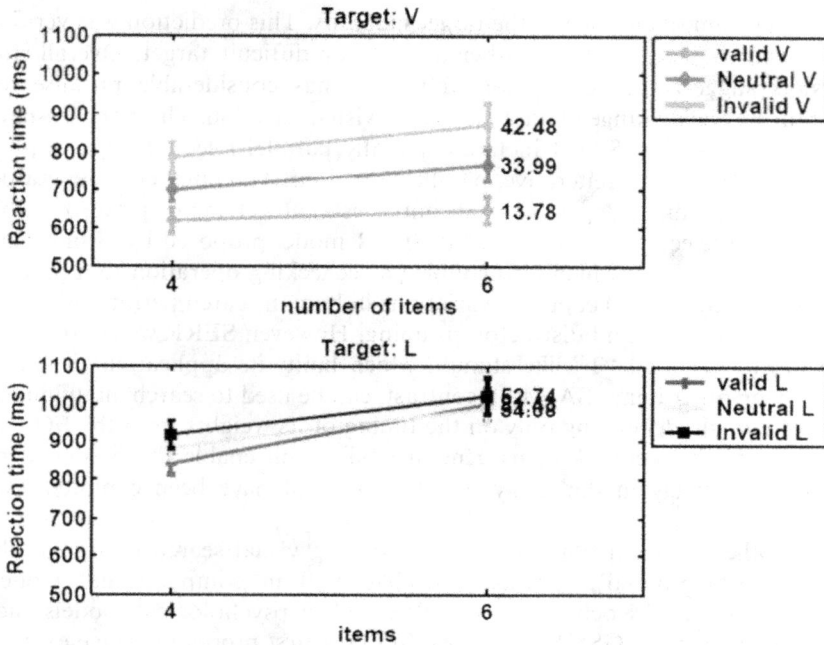

Figure 9.   Mean reaction times for present responses to slow and quick targets in relation to set size and prime validity.

SAIM. The prime influenced only the overall RT. In the framework of SAIM this discrepancy can be explained by the fact that difficult targets might warrant more rechecks than easier targets and that, in contrast to the simulations presented here, the initial template values are lowered with each recheck, leading to smaller search benefits for difficult targets. This decline of the benefit increases with display size, since the number of rechecks increases with display size as well. This may counter any benefit from top-down activation at the larger display sizes. Such a modification in SAIM would allow the model to simulate the experimental findings. Moreover, it would predict that for fast reaction times (with fewer rechecks) human responses to the difficult target would show a similar interaction between search efficiency and prime validity as for the quick target.

GENERAL DISCUSSION

We have demonstrated that SAIM can be successfully extended to include a feature extraction process, and to simulate search for a target amongst multiple distractors. We also predicted a particular pattern of top-down priming from knowledge of the target's identify. This prediction was verified in a search task involving either an easy or difficult target. Overall, the results suggest that this modified version has considerable promise for capturing a wide range of data on human visual selection. The mechanism of search involved in SAIM includes spatially parallel selection of a display, followed by further reiterative, parallel selections. The number of reiterative selections required depends on an initial estimate of the display size. This reiterative selection is similar to the SERR model proposed by Humphreys and Müller (1993), which also coupled a rechecking operation to a parallel selection process and captured variations in human search performance as a function of target and distractor grouping. However, SERR was hard-wired to detect "T" and "T"-like stimuli, which limits its application to search involving other items. SAIM, in contrast, can be used to search an unlimited set of stimuli, depending only on the tuning of its weights from the FOA to the knowledge network. This generalizability will enable the model to be tested effectively in the many search tasks that have been explored with human participants.

Another alternative approach to modelling visual search represents the "saliency-map-based" approach, implemented in computational models such as those of Koch and Itti (2001), and in psychological models such as Guided Search (GS; Wolfe, 1998). In GS, a first processing stage extracts features from the input display, which are represented in independent, retinotopically defined feature maps (see also Treisman & Gelade, 1980). Activation in these maps is determined both by the strength of the input and by the contrast between each part of the image and its neighbouring regions (in each feature space). A feature that contrasts with its local neighbourhood gains enhanced activation through lateral inhibition. A saliency map (or master map) combines additively the activation from the feature maps, and weights each location of the input according to its saliency. Based on this saliency map the scene is scanned serially, starting with the most salient location, and at each location a form of object recognition takes place, testing if the location contains the target. In addition to this bottom-up computation of the saliency map, top-down process can influence search by increasing activation at locations in the features maps that contain the features of the target. For instance, if the target is a red, left-tilted line, the feature maps for red and left orientation show an increased activation at positions where these features are present in the scene. The increased activation leads to an enhanced saliency of the target making selection more efficient. Hence, like SAIM, GS would predict that foreknowledge of the target should facilitate selection, though it is unclear whether the gains should be most for a high or a low salient target without operationalizing the parameters of the model. However, top-down modulation operates differently in SAIM and GS. For example in GS, top-down guidance involves activating feature maps for expected target features. In SAIM, the guidance is for a specific object. SAIM is, thus, consistent with experimental data on object-based top-down effects (Soto, Heinke, Humphreys, & Blanco, 2005). Moreover, it is interesting that, in data on human search, there is evidence for search to be influenced by associates of expected targets (Moores, Laiti, & Chelazzi, 2003), suggesting that templates for specific objects are set up and that there is even a spread of activation across templates, so that search is guided towards associates and not just the features of the expected target. In addition, in SAIM the activation throughout the system declines gradually when there is a blank screen. Thus, if a blank appeared between the offset of a prime and a search display, the action of the preactivated template should decline, and the top-down influence should decrease. This decrease in priming should be monotonically related to the interval between the prime and the search display. This prediction is currently being tested in our lab. Of course, such a mechanism could be also implemented in GS, but this is not an emergent property of the model, as it is in SAIM.

Relative to GS, SAIM may also provide a more adequate way of modelling grouping and of linking grouping processes in search to object recognition (e.g., with grouped parts being matched to a template). As we have noted, GS uses lateral inhibition to enhance the saliency of stimuli but it does not group elements together to form structured representations. SAIM does do this, with parts being coded in relation to the centre of gravity of the stimulus. We suggest that this again adds to the generality of the approach, since SAIM provides both a model of attention and object recognition. Also, unlike SAIM, GS has not been explored in relation to neuropsychological data, so we do not know whether the model will degrade in a manner consistent with human data. SAIM, on the other hand, can capture neuropsychological disorders, such as visual extinction and neglect.

MORSEL (Mozer, 1991; Mozer & Sitton, 1998) is another model of selection which has been used to simulate some aspects of visual search. MORSEL has two main components: An object-recognition system and a spatial attention system. The object recognition system operates in an hierarchical manner, pooling visual information across increasingly large receptive fields. The spatial attention network gates activation entering into the object recognition system, which is then biased in favour of attended objects. In visual search mode, MORSEL operates very similar to GS with its serial scan controlled by top-down modulated feature maps. MORSEL's object recognition model can respond to perceptual groups formed from activation pooled together in units at the higher end of the recognition hierarchy, and so, like SAIM, it may be able to capture effects of perceptual grouping on search. However, since top-down processes in the model operate in a feature-based manner, as in GS, it seems difficult to explain human data demonstrating object-based top-down effects in search (Moores et al., 2003;

Soto et al., 2005). By having item-specific feedback from templates, SAIM can address data on early top-down guidance.

In sum, though there are other explicit models of visual search that capture aspects of human data, we suggest that SAIM may provide the widest-ranging account, that can generalize across stimuli, that models grouping effects, and that accounts for the interaction between bottom-up and top-down effects in search.

REFERENCES

Appelle, S. (1972). Perception and discrimination as a function of stimulus orientation: The "oblique effect" in man and animals. *Psychological Bulletin*, *78*, 266–278.

Bravo, M. J., & Nakayama, K. (1992). The role of attention in different visual-search tasks. *Perception and Psychophysics*, *51*(5), 465–472.

Duncan, J. (1980). The locus of interference in the perception of simultaneous stimuli. *Psychological Review*, *87*, 272–300.

Duncan, J., & Humphreys, G. W. (1989). Visual search and stimulus similarity. *Psychological Review*, *96*(3), 433–458.

Egly, R., Driver, J., & Rafal, R. D. (1994). Shifting visual attention between objects and locations: Evidence from normal and parietal subjects. *Journal of Experimental Psychology: Human Perception and Performance*, *123*, 161–177.

Foster, D. H., & Ward, P. A. (1991). Asymmetries in oriented-line detection indicate two orthogonal filters in early vision. *Proceedings of the Royal Society of London: Series B*, *243*, 75–81.

Found, A., & Müller, H. J. (1996). Searching for unknown feature targets on more than one dimension: Investigating a "dimensional-weighting" account. *Perception and Psychophysics*, *58*, 88–101.

Heinke, D., & Humphreys, G. W. (2003). Attention, spatial representation and visual neglect: Simulating emergent attention and spatial memory in the Selective Attention for Identification Model (SAIM). *Psychological Review*, *110*(1), 29–87.

Hillstrom, A. P. (2000). Repetition effects in visual search. *Perception and Psychophysics*, *62*, 800–817.

Hodsoll, J., & Humphreys, G. W. (2001). Driving attention with the top down: The relative contribution of target templates to the linear separability effect in the size dimension. *Perception and Psychophysics*, *63*(5), 918–926.

Hopfield, J. J., & Tank, D. (1985). "Neural" computation of decisions in optimization problems. *Biological Cybernetics*, *52*, 141–152.

Humphreys, G. W., & Müller, H. J. (1993). SEarch via Recursive Rejection (SERR): A connectionist model of visual search. *Cognitive Psychology*, *25*, 43–110.

Humphreys, G. W., & Riddoch, M. J. (1994). Attention to within-object and between-object spatial representations: Multiple side for visual selection. *Cognitive Neuropsychology*, *11*(2), 207–241.

Humphreys, G. W., & Riddoch, M. J. (1995). Separate coding of space within and between perceptual objects: Evidence from unilateral visual neglect. *Cognitive Neuropsychology*, *12*(3), 283–311.

Koch, C., & Itti, L. (2001). Computational modelling of visual attention. *Nature Reviews: Neuroscience*, *2*, 194–203.

Kristjansson, A., Wang, D., & Nakayama, K. (2002). The role of priming in conjunctive visual search. *Cognition*, *85*, 37–52.

Kumada, T., & Humphreys, G. W. (2001). Lexical recovery on extinction: Interactions between visual form and stored knowledge modulate visual selection. *Cognitive Neuropsychology*, *18*(5), 465–478.

Maljkovic, V., & Nakayama, K. (1994). Priming of pop-out: I. Role of features. *Memory and Cognition*, *22*(6), 657–672.

Maljkovic, V., & Nakayama, K. (1996). Priming of pop-out: II. The role of position. *Memory and Cognition*, *58*(7), 977–991.

Mjolsness, E., & Garrett, C. (1990). Algebraic transformations of objective functions. *Neural Networks*, *3*, 651–669.

Moores, E., Laiti, L., & Chelazzi, L. (2003). Associative knowledge controls deployment of visual selective attention. *Nature Neuroscience*, *2*(6), 182–189.

Mozer, M. (1991). *The perception of multiple objects: A connectionist approach*. Cambridge, MA: MIT Press.

Mozer, M. C., & Sitton, M. (1998). Computational modeling of spatial attention. In H. Pashler (Ed.), *Attention* (pp. 341–393). Hove, UK: Psychology Press.

Müller, H. J., Reimann, B., & Krummenacher, J. (2003). Visual search for singleton feature targets across dimensions: Stimulus- and expectancy-driven effects in dimensional weighting. *Journal of Experimental Psychology: Human Perception and Performance*, *29*(5), 1021–1035.

Navon, D. (1977). Forest before trees: The precedence of global features in visual perception. *Cognitive Psychology*, *9*, 353–383.

Posner, M. I., Snyder, C. R. R., & Davidson, B. J. (1980). Attention and the detection of signals. *Journal of Experimental Psychology: General*, *109*(2), 160–174.

Schuster, H. G. (1989). *Deterministic chaos*. Cambridge, UK: VCH Publishers.

Soto, D., Heinke, D., Humphreys, G. W., & Blanco, M. J. (2005). Early, involuntary top-down guidance of attention from working memory. *Journal of Experimental Psychology: Human Perception and Performance*, *31*, 248–261.

Treisman, A. (1988). Features and Objects: The Fourteenth Bartlett Memorial Lecture. *Quarterly Journal of Experiment Psychology*, *40A*(2), 201–237.

Treisman, A. M., & Gelade, G. (1980). A feature integration theory of attention. *Cognitive Psychology*, *12*, 97–136.

Wang, G., Ding, S., & Yunokuchik, K. (2003). Difference in the representation of cardinal and oblique contours in cat visual cortex. *Neuroscience Letters*, *338*, 77–81.

Wolfe, J. M. (1998). Visual search. In H. Pashler (Ed.), *Attention* (pp. 13–74). Hove, UK: Psychology Press.

Wolfe, J. M. (2001). Asymmetries in visual search: An introduction. *Perception and Psychophysics*, *63*(3), 381–389.

Wolfe, J. M., Butcher, S. J., Lee, C., & Hyle, M. (2003). Changing your mind: On the contributions of top-down and bottom-up guidance in visual search for feature singletons. *Journal of Experimental Psychology: Human Perception and Performance*, *29*(2), 483–502.

Zelinsky, G. (2001). Visual priming contributes to set size effects. *Investigative Ophthalmology and Visual Science*, *42*, S927.

APPENDIX: MATHEMATICAL DESCRIPTION OF SAIM

Feature extraction

The feature extraction results in a three-dimensional feature vector: Horizontal and vertical lines and the image itself. The lines are detected by filtering the image with 3×3 filters:

$\begin{array}{ccc} -2 & +1 & -2 \\ -2 & +1 & -2 \\ -2 & +1 & -2 \end{array}$ for vertical lines and its transposed version for horizontal lines.

The feature vector is noted as f_{ij}^n hereafter, with indices i and j referring to retinal locations and n to the feature dimension. This feature extraction process provides an approximation of simple cell responses in V1. As becomes obvious in the following sections, the use of just this simple feature extraction is not of theoretical value and arises only from practical consideration (e.g., the duration of any simulations). In principle, a more biologically realistic feature extraction process can be substituted (e.g., Gabor filter).

Contents network

The energy function for the contents network is:

$$E^{CN}(y^{SN}, y^{CN}) = \sum_{ijlm} (y_{lmn}^{CN} - f_{ij}^n)^2 \cdot y_{lmij}^{SN} \tag{1}$$

y_{lmij}^{SN} is the activation of units in the selection network and y_{lmn}^{CN} is the activation of units in the contents network. Here and in all the following equations the indices i and j refer to retinal locations and the indices l and m refer to locations in the FOA. The term $(y_{lmn}^{CN} - f_{ij}^n)^2$ ensures that the units in the contents network match the feature values in the input image. The term y_{lmij}^{SN} ensures that the contents of the FOA only reflect the region selected by the selection network ($y_{lmij}^{SN} = 1$). Additionally, since setting an arbitrary choice of y_{lmij}^{SN} s to 1 allows any location to be routed from the feature level to the FOA level, the contents network enables a translation-invariant mapping.

Selection network

The mapping from the retina to the FOA is mediated by the selection network. In order to achieve successful object identification, the selection network has to fulfil certain constraints when it modulates the mapping process. These constraints are that: (1) Units in the FOA should receive the activity from only one retinal unit; (2) activity of retinal units should be mapped only once into the FOA; (3) neighbourhood relations in the retinal input should be preserved in mapping through to the FOA. Now, to incorporate the first constraint, that units in the FOA should receive the activity of only one retinal unit, the WTA-equation suggested by Mjolsness and Garrett (1990) turns into:

$$E_{WTA}^{SN1}(y^{SN}) = \sum_{lm} \left(\sum_{ij} y_{lmij}^{SN} - 1 \right)^2 \tag{2}$$

The second term implements the second constraint:

$$E_{WTA}^{SN2}(y^{SN}) = \sum_{lm} \left(\sum_{ij} y_{lmij}^{SN} - 1 \right)^2 \tag{3}$$

In both terms the expression $(\Sigma y_{ikjl}^{SN} - 1)^2$ ensures that the activity of one location is mapped only once into the FOA.

The energy following energy function implements the neighbourhood constraint:

$$E_{neighbor}^{SN1}(y^{SN}) = -\sum_{i,j,l,m} \sum_{\substack{s=-L \\ s \neq 0}}^{L} \sum_{\substack{r=-L \\ r \neq 0}}^{L} g_{sr} \cdot y_{lmij}^{SN} \cdot y_{i+r, k+s. j+r. l+s}^{SN} \tag{4}$$

with g_{sr} being defined by a Gaussian function:

$$g_{sr} = \frac{1}{A} \cdot e^{-\frac{s^2 + r^2}{\sigma^2}} \tag{5}$$

where A was set, so that the sum over all g_{sr} is 1. When units linked via g_{sr} are activated to $y_{lmij}^{SN} = 1$, the energy is smaller than when these units have different values, e.g., zero and one. Since g_{sr} connects units that relate to adjacent locations in both the FOA and the input image, this implements the neighbourhood constraint.

To implement inhibition of return, the location map prevents the reselection of an inhibited location through the following energy function:

$$E^{SN3}(y^{SN}) = -\sum_{lmij} \left(1 - \sum_{lm} y_{ij}^{LM} \right) y_{lmij}^{SN} \tag{6}$$

The term $(1 - y_{ij}^{LM})$ suppresses already-selected locations and supports the selection of new locations.

Knowledge network

The energy function of the knowledge network is defined as

$$E^{KN}(y^{KN}, y^{CN}) = a^{KN}\left(\sum_k y_k^{KN} - 1\right)^2 - b^{KN}\sum_{lmn}(y_{lmn}^{CN} - w_{lmn}^k)^2 y_k^{KN} \qquad (7)$$

The index k refers to template units whose templates are stored in their weights (w_{lmn}^k). The term $(\Sigma_k y^{KN} - 1)^2$ restricts the knowledge network to activate only one template unit. The $\Sigma_{lmn}(y_{lmn}^{CN} - w_{lmn}^k)^2 \cdot y_k^{KN}$ ensures that the best-matching template unit is activated, a^{KN} and b^{KN} weight these constraints against each other.

Rechecking

In order to implement rechecking, a "location map" is computed based on activity in the selection network:

$$y_{ij}^{LM} = y_{ij}^{LM}(old) + a^{IR}\sum_{l=1}^{M}\sum_{m=1}^{M} y_{lmij}^{SN} \qquad (8)$$

When a template unit in the knowledge network passes a threshold 0, the location map is used to reduce the activity in the visual field. a^{IR} controls the amount of inhibition. All units in the selection network and the knowledge network are set to the initial state they had at the beginning of the simulation.

Noise

The noise in SAIM was inserted into the input stimulus and was based on the following equation:

$$\ddot{\Theta} + \gamma\dot{\Theta} + \sin\Theta = A \cdot \cos\omega t \qquad (9)$$

This equation was inspired by the motion equation of a periodically driven pendulum where γ is the damping constant and the right side describes a driving torque with amplitude A and frequency ω (e.g., Schuster, 1989). This equation was chosen on merely technical grounds. It exhibits chaotic behaviour, hence a quasistochastic temporal behaviour. It does not produce big leaps in amplitude and therefore does not distort the process of the gradient descent.

To ensure that each pixel of the input stimulus receives a different signal, each pixel has its own pendulum equation initialized with a different value:

$$\ddot{\Theta}_{ij} + \gamma\dot{\Theta}_{ij} + \sin\Theta_{ij} = A \cdot \cos\omega t \qquad (10)$$

For each pixel (ij) a different initial value is chosen randomly. To limit the amplitude of the noise, Θ was fed into the following equation:

$$\epsilon_{ij}(t) = .5 \cdot \sin \Theta_{ij}(t) \cdot (\text{max} - \text{min}) + (\text{max} - \text{min}) \tag{11}$$

ϵ_{ij} was added to the input stimulus I_{ij}

VISUAL COGNITION, 2006, 14 (4/5/6/7/8), 1006–1024

Ψ Psychology Press
Taylor & Francis Group

The neurodynamics of visual search

Gustavo Deco

Institucio Catalana de Recerca i Estudis Avancats, Universitat Pompeu Fabra, Barcelona, Spain

Josef Zihl

Ludwig-Maximilian University, and Max Planck Institute of Psychiatry, Munich, Germany

We review different functions in visual perception associated with attention and memory that have been integrated by a model based on the biased competition hypothesis. The model integrates, in a unifying form, the explanation of several existing types of experimental data obtained at different levels of investigation. At the microscopic level, single cell recordings are simulated. At the mesoscopic level of cortical areas, results of functional magnetic resonance imaging (fMRI) studies are reproduced. Finally, at the macroscopic level, the outcome of psychophysical experiments like visual search tasks are also described by the model. In particular, the model directly addresses how bottom-up and top-down processes interact in visual cognition, and shows how some apparently serial processes reflect the operation of interacting parallel distributed systems. Attentional top-down bias guides the dynamics to focus attention at a given spatial location or on given features.

To understand how the brain in general, and the visual brain in particular, works, it is necessary to combine different approaches, including neural computation. Neurophysiology at the single neuron level is needed because this is the level at which information is exchanged between the computing elements of the brain. Evidence from neuropsychology is needed to help understand what different parts of the system do and what each part is necessary for. Neuroimaging is useful to indicate where in the human brain different processes take place, and to show which functions can be dissociated from each other. Knowledge of the biophysical and synaptic

Please address all correspondence to Gustavo Deco, Computational Neuroscience, Dept. of Technology, Institucio Catalana de Recerca i Estudis Avancats (ICREA), Universitat Pompeu Fabra, Passeig de Circumval.lacio, 8, 08003 Barcelona, Spain. E-mail: Gustavo.Deco@upf.edu
Gustavo Deco was supported by ICREA.

http://www.psypress.com/viscog
DOI: 10.1080/13506280500195425

properties of neurons is essential to understand how the computing elements of the brain work, and therefore what the building blocks of biologically realistic computational models should be. Knowledge of the anatomical and functional architecture of the cortex is needed to show what types of neuronal network actually perform the computation. And finally the approach of neural computation is needed, as this is required to link together all the empirical evidence to produce an understanding of how the system actually works. This review utilizes evidence from some of these disciplines to develop an understanding of how vision is implemented by processing in the brain, focusing on visual attentional mechanisms.

VISUAL ATTENTIONAL MECHANISMS

As it is well known, because of the limited processing capacity of the visual system, attentional mechanisms are required in order to process information from a given scene. The dominant neurobiological hypothesis to account for attentional selection is that attention serves to enhance the responses of neurons representing stimuli at a single relevant location in the visual field. This enhancement model is related to the metaphor for focal attention in terms of a spotlight (Treisman, 1982, 1988). This metaphor postulates a spotlight of attention that illuminates a portion of the field of view where stimuli are processed in higher detail whereas the information outside the spotlight is filtered out. According to this classical view, a relevant object in a cluttered scene is found by rapidly shifting the spotlight from one object in the scene to the next one, until the target is found. Therefore, according to this assumption the concept of attention is based on explicit serial mechanisms. The Feature Integration Theory of visual selective attention (Treisman & Gelade, 1980) explains the outcome of numerous psychophysical experiments on visual search and offers an interpretation of the binding problem. In the Feature Integration Theory, the first preattentive process runs in parallel across the complete visual field extracting single primitive features without integrating them. The second attentive stage corresponds to the serial specialized integration of information from a limited part of the field at any one time. The main evidence for these two stages of attentional visual processing comes from psychophysical experiments using visual search tasks where subjects examine a display containing randomly positioned items in order to detect an a priori defined target.

There exists an alternative mechanism for selective attention, the *biased competition* model (Desimone & Duncan, 1995; Duncan, 1996; Duncan & Humphreys, 1989). According to this model, the enhancement of attention on neuronal responses is understood in the context of competition among all of the stimuli in the visual field. The biased competition hypothesis states that the multiple stimuli in the visual field activate populations of neurons that engage in competitive mechanisms. Attending to a stimulus at a particular location or with a particular feature biases this competition in favour of neurons that respond to the location or the features of the attended stimulus. This attentional effect is produced by generating signals within areas outside the visual cortex, which are then fed back to extrastriate areas, where they bias the competition such that when multiple stimuli appear in the visual field, the cells representing the attended stimulus *win*, thereby suppressing cells representing distracting stimuli (Desimone & Duncan, 1995; Duncan, 1996; Duncan & Humphreys, 1989). According to this line of work, attention appears as an emergent property of competitive interactions that work in parallel across the visual field (for alternative approaches see Heinke & Humphreys, 2003).

Several neurophysiological experiments have been performed suggesting biased competition neural mechanisms that are consistent with such a hypothesis (Chelazzi, 1998; Chelazzi, Miller, Duncan, & Desimone, 1993; Luck, Chelazzi, Hillyard, & Desimone, 1997; Moran & Desimone, 1985; Reynolds, Chelazzi, & Desimone, 1999; Spitzer, Desimone, & Moran, 1988).

Further evidence comes from functional magnetic resonance imaging (fMRI) in humans (Kastner, de Weerd, Desimone, & Ungerleider, 1998; Kastner, Pinsk, de Weerd, Desimone, and Ungerleider, 1999). According to the biased competition hypothesis, these results show that when multiple stimuli are present simultaneously in the visual field, their cortical representations within the object recognition pathway interact in a competitive, suppressive fashion, which is not the case when the stimuli are presented sequentially. It was also observed that directing attention to one of the stimuli counteracts the suppressive influence of nearby stimuli.

THE NEURODYNAMICAL MODEL

The overall systemic representation of the model is shown in Figure 1. The system is essentially composed of six modules (V1, V2–V4, IT, PP, v46, d46), structured such that they resemble the two known main visual paths of the mammalian visual cortex: The *what* and *where* paths (Deco & Zihl, 1999, 2001; Hamker, 1999; Rolls & Deco, 2002). These six modules represent the minimum number of components to be taken into account within this complex system in order to describe the desired visual attention mechanism.

Information from the retinogeniculostriate pathway enters the visual cortex through areas V1–V2 in the occipital lobe and proceeds into two processing streams. The occipital-temporal stream *(what* pathway) leads ventrally through V4 and IT (inferotemporal cortex) and is mainly concerned with object recognition, independently of position and scaling.

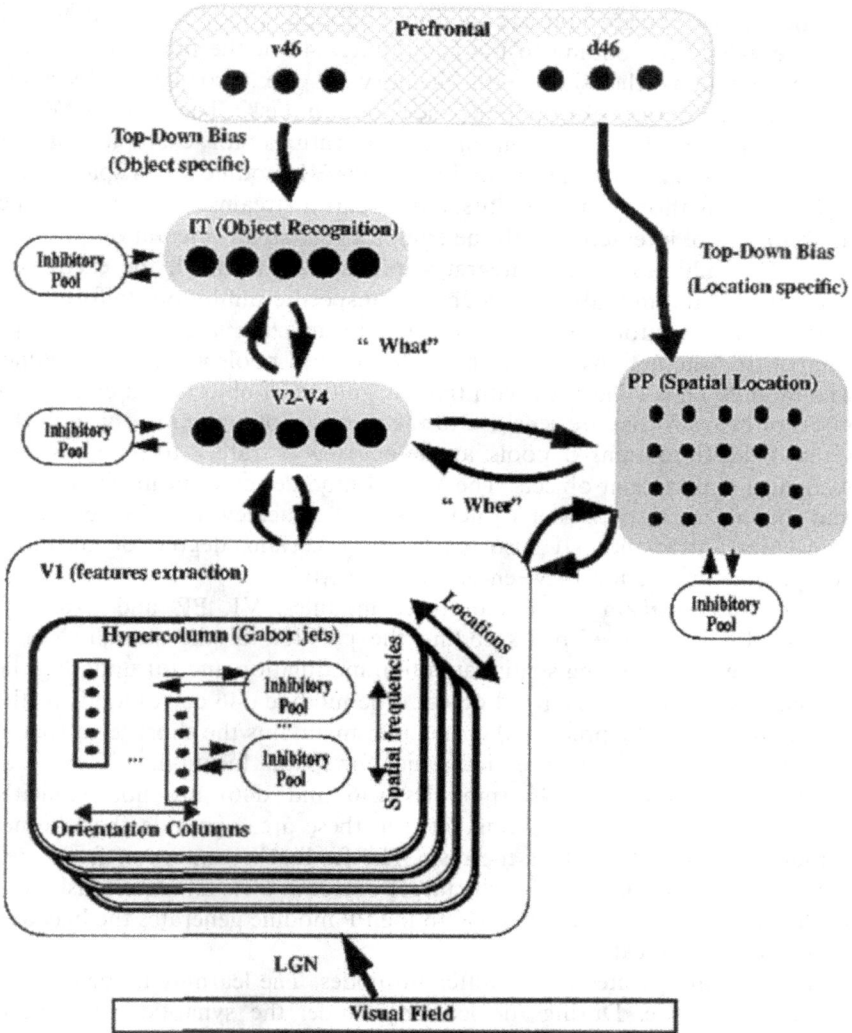

Figure 1. Architecture of the neurodynamical approach. The system is essentially composed of six modules structured such that they resemble the two known main visual paths of the visual cortex.

The occipitoparietal stream (*where* pathway) leads dorsally into PP (posterior parietal cortex) and is concerned with the location of objects and the spatial relationships between objects. The model considers that feature attention biases intermodular competition between V4 and IT, whereas spatial attention biases intermodular competition between Vl, V4, and PP.

The ventral stream consists of four modules: V1, V2–V4, IT, and a module v46 corresponding to the ventral area 46 of the prefrontal cortex, which maintains the short-term memory of the recognized object or generates the target object in a visual search task. The module V1 is concerned with the extraction of simple features, for example bars at different locations, orientation. and size. This V1 module sends spatial and feature information up to the dorsal and ventral streams. There is also one inhibitory pool interacting with the complex cells of all orientations at each scale. This inhibitory pool integrates information from all the excitatory pools within the module and feedbacks unspecific inhibition uniformly to each of the excitatory pools. It mediates normalizing lateral inhibition or competitive interactions among the excitatory cell pools within the module. The module IT is concerned with the recognition of objects and consists of pools of neurons that are sensitive to the presence of a specific object in the visual field. It contains C pools, as the network is trained to search for, or recognize C particular objects. The V2–V4 module serves primarily to pool and channel the responses of V1 neurons to IT to achieve a limited degree of translation invariance. It also mediates a certain degree of localized competitive interaction between different targets.

The dorsal stream consists of three modules: V1, PP, and d46. The module PP consists of pools coding the position of the stimuli, and is responsible for mediating spatial attention modulation and for updating the spatial position of the attended object. The module d46 corresponds to the dorsal area 46 of the prefrontal cortex that maintains the short-term spatial memory or generates the attentional bias for spatial location.

The prefrontal areas 46 (modules v46 and d46) are not explicitly modelled. Feedback connections between these areas provide the external top-down bias that specifies the task. The feedback connection from area v46 to the IT module specifies the target object in a visual search task. The feedback connection from area d46 to the PP module generates the bias to a targeted spatial location.

The system operates in two different modes: The learning mode and the recognition mode. During the learning mode, the synaptic connections between V4 and IT are trained by means of Hebbian learning during several presentations of a specific object. During the recognition mode there are two possibilities of running the system. First, an object can be localised in a scene (visual search) by biasing the system with an external top-down component at the IT module which drives the competition in favour of the pool associated with the specific object to be searched. Then, the intermodular attentional modulation V1–V4-IT will enhance the activity of the pools in V4 and V1 associated with the features of the specific object to be searched for. Finally, the intermodular attentional modulation V4-PP and V1-PP will drive the competition in favour of the pool localising the specific object. Second, an object can be identified (object recognition) at a specific spatial location by biasing the system with an external top-down component at the PP module. This drives the competition in favour of the pool associated with the specific location such that the intermodular attentional modulation V4-PP and Vl-PP will favour the pools in V1 and V4 associated with the features of the object at that location. Intermodular attentional modulation V1–V4-IT will favour the pool that recognized the object at that location.

The neurons in the pools in V1 have receptive fields performing a Gabor wavelet transform. Let us denote by I_{kpql}^{V1} the sensory input activity to a pool A_{kpql}^{V1} in V1 which is sensitive to a spatial frequency at octave k, to a preferred orientation defined by the rotation index l, and to stimuli at the centre location specified by the indices pq. The sensory input activity to a pool in V1 I_{kpql}^{V1} is therefore defined by the modulus of the corresponding Gabor wavelet transform of the image. Since in our numerical simulations the system needs only to learn a small number of objects (usually two to four), we temporarily did not include the V4 module for simplicity in some of the simulations. In fact, the large receptive fields of V2 and V4 can be approximately taken into account by including them in V1 pools with receptive fields corresponding to several octaves of the 2-D Gabor transform wavelets (i.e., not only the typical narrow receptive fields of V1 but also larger receptive fields are included in the modelled V1). The reduced system connects all cell assemblies in V1 with all cell assemblies in IT.

The connections with the pools in the PP module are specified such that the modulation is Gaussian. Let us define in the PP module a pool A_{ij}^{PP} for each location ij in the visual field. The mutual (i.e., forward and back) connections between a pool A_{kpql}^{V1} in V1 and a pool A_{ij}^{PP} in PP are therefore defined by

$$w_{pqij} = A\exp\left\{-\frac{(i-p)^2 + (j-q)^2}{2S^2}\right\} - B \tag{1}$$

These connections mean that the V1 pool A_{kpql}^{V1} will have maximal amplitude when spatial attention is located at $i=p$ and $j=q$ in the visual field, i.e., when the pool A_{ij}^{PP} in PP is maximally activated and provides an inhibitory contribution—B at the locations not being attended to. The V1-PP attentional modulation, in combination with the Hebbian learning that we will define later in this section, generates translation-invariant recognition pools in the module IT.

Let us now define the neurodynamical equations that regulate the temporal evolution of the whole system.

The activity level of the input current in the V1 module is given by

$$\tau \frac{\partial A^{V1}_{kpql}(t)}{\partial t} = -A^{V1}_{kpql} + \alpha F(A^{V1}_{kpql}(t)) - \beta F(A^{I,V1}_k(t)) + I^{V1}_{kpql}(t) \tag{2}$$

$$+I^{V1-PP}_{pq}(t) + I^{V1-IT}_{kpql}(t) + I_0 + v$$

where the attentional biasing coupling I^{V1-PP}_{pq} due to the intermodular "where" connections with the pools in the parietal mode PP is given by

$$I^{V1-PP}_{pq} = \sum_{i,j} W_{pqij} F(A^{PP}_{ij}(t)) \tag{3}$$

and the attentional biasing term I^{V1-IT}_{kpql} due to the intermodular "what" connections with the pools in the temporal module IT is defined by

$$I^{V1-IT}_{kpql} = \sum_{c=1}^{C} w_{ckpql} F(A^{IT}_c(t)) \tag{4}$$

w_{ckpql} being the connection strength between the V1 pool A^{V1}_{kpql} and the IT pool A^{IT}_c corresponding to the coding of a specific object category c. We assume that the IT module has C pools corresponding to different object categories. For each spatial frequency level, a common inhibitory pool (designated with a superscript I) is defined. The current activity of these inhibitory pools obeys the following equations:

$$\tau_P \frac{\partial A^{I,V1}_c(t)}{\partial t} = A^{I,V1}_k(t) + \gamma \sum_{p,q,l} F(A^{V1}_{kpql}(t)) - \delta F(A^{I,V1}_k(t)) \tag{5}$$

Similarly, the current activity of the excitatory pools in the posterior parietal module PP is given by

$$\tau \frac{\partial A^{PP}_{ij}(t)}{\partial t} = -A^{PP}_{ij} + \alpha F(A^{PP}_{ij}(t)) - \beta F(A^{I,PP}(t)) + I^{PP-V1}_{ij}(t)$$

$$+I^{PP,A}_{ij} + I_0 + v \tag{6}$$

where $I^{PP,A}_{ij}$ denotes an external attentional spatially-specific top-down bias, and the intermodular attentional biasing I^{PP-V1}_{ij} through the connections with the pools in the module V1 is

$$I^{PP-V1}_{ij} = \sum_{k,p,q,l} W_{pqij} F(A^{V1}_{kpql}(t)) \tag{7}$$

and the activity current of the common PP inhibitory pool evolves according to

$$\tau \frac{\partial A^{I,PP}(t)}{\partial t} = -A^{I,PP}(t) + \gamma \sum_{ij} F(A^{PP}_{ij}(t)) - \delta F(A^{I,PP}(t)). \tag{8}$$

The dynamics of the inferotemporal module IT is given by

$$\tau \frac{\partial A_c^{IT}(t)}{\partial t} = -A_c^{IT} + \alpha F(A_c^{IT}(t)) - \beta F(A^{I,IT}(t)) + I_c^{IT-V1}(t)$$ (9)

$$+I_c^{IT,A} + I_0 + v$$

where $I_c^{IT,A}$ denotes an external attentional object-specific top-down bias, and the intermodular attentional biasing I_c^{IT-V1} between IT and V1 pools is

$$I_c^{IT-V1} = \sum_{k,p,q,l} w_{ckpql} F(A_{kpql}^{V1}(t))$$ (10)

and the activity current of the common PP inhibitory pool evolves according to

$$\tau_P \frac{\partial A^{I,IT}}{\partial t} = -A^{I,IT}(t) + \gamma \sum_c F(A_c^{IT}(t)) - \delta F(A^{I,IT}(t)).$$ (11)

A more detailed explanation of the model can be found in (Deco, Pollatos, & Zihl, 2002; Rolls & Deco, 2002).

SIMULATIONS OF BASIC EXPERIMENTAL FINDINGS

Single cell experiments

Reynolds et al. (1999) first examined the presence of competitive interactions in the absence of attentional effects, making the monkey attend to a location far outside the receptive field of the neuron they were recorded from. They compared the firing activity response of the neuron when a single reference stimulus was located within the receptive field with the response when a probe stimulus was added to the visual field. When the probe was added to the field, the activity of the neuron was shifted towards the activity level that would have been evoked had the probe appeared alone. When the reference is an effective stimulus (high response) and the probe is an ineffective stimulus (low response) the firing activity is suppressed after adding the probe. In contrast, the response of the cell increased when an effective probe stimulus was added to an ineffective reference stimulus. Working within the neurodynamical model presented in the previous section, Corchs and Deco (2002) and Deco and Lee (2002) carried out numerical calculations to simulate these single cell experiments. Compared with the experimental results, the same qualitative behaviour was observed for all experimental conditions analysed. The competitive interactions in the absence of attention are due to the intramodular competitive dynamics at the level of V1, i.e., the suppressive and excitatory effects of the probe. The modulatory biasing corrections in the attended condition are caused by the intermodular interactions between V1 and PP pools, and PP pools and prefrontal top-down modulation.

fMRI experiments

The experimental studies of Kastner et al. (1998, 1999) show that when multiple stimuli are present simultaneously in the visual field, their cortical representations within the object recognition pathway interact in a competitive, suppressive fashion. The authors also observed that directing attention to one of the stimuli counteracts the suppressive influence of nearby stimuli. These experimental results were obtained by applying the functional magnetic resonance imaging (fMRI) technique in humans. In the first experimental condition the authors tested the presence of suppressive interactions among stimuli presented simultaneously within the visual field in the absence of directed attention, in the second experimental condition they investigated the influence of spatially directed attention on the suppressive interactions, and in the third condition they analysed the neural activity during directed attention but in the absence of visual stimulation. The authors observed that, because of the mutual suppression induced by competitively interacting stimuli, the fMRI signals were smaller during the simultaneous presentations than during the sequential presentations. In the second part of the experiment there were two main factors: Presentation condition (sequential vs. simultaneous) and directed attention condition (unattended vs. attended). The average fMRI signals with attention increased more strongly for simultaneously presented stimuli than the corresponding signals for sequentially presented stimuli. Thus, the suppressive interactions were partially cancelled out by attention.

The dynamical evolution of activity at the cortical area level, as found in the behaviour of fMRI signals in experiments with humans, can be simulated in the framework of the neurodynamical model of the previous section by integrating the pool activity in a given area over space and time. The integration over space yields an average activity of the considered brain area at a given time. With respect to the integration over time, it is performed in order to simulate the temporal resolution of fMRI experiments. Corchs and Deco (2002) simulated fMRI signals from V4 under the experimental conditions defined by Kastner et al. (1998, 1999). As in the experiments, their simulations showed that the fMRI signals were smaller in magnitude during the simultaneous than during the sequential presentations in the unattended conditions because of the mutual suppression induced by competitively interacting stimuli. On the other hand, the average fMRI signals with attention increased more strongly for simultaneously presented stimuli than the corresponding ones for sequentially presented stimuli. Thus, the suppressive interactions were partially cancelled out by attention.

Simulation of psychophysical experiments: Visual search

We now concentrate on the macroscopic level of psychophysics. Evidence for different temporal behaviours of attention in visual processing comes from psychophysical experiments using visual search tasks where subjects scan a display containing randomly positioned items in order to detect an a priori defined target. All other items in the display that are different from the target serve the role as distractors. The relevant variable typically measured is search time as a function of the number of items in the display. Much work has been devoted on two kinds of search paradigm: feature search and conjunction search. In a feature search task the target differs from the distractors in one single feature, e.g., only colour. In a conjunction search task the target is defined by a conjunction of features and each distractor shares at least one of those features with the target. Conjunction search experiments show that search time increases linearly with the number of items in the display, implying a serial process. On the other hand, search times in a feature search can be independent of the number of items in the display. Deco and Lee (2002) and Deco and Zihl (2001) showed that the attentional architecture described in the previous section performs search across the visual field in parallel but, due to the different latencies of its dynamics, can show the two experimentally observed modes of visual attention, namely serial focal attention and the parallel spread of attention over space. The model demonstrates that neither explicit serial focal search nor saliency maps need to be assumed. The focus of attention is not provided to the system but only emerges after convergence of the dynamic behaviour of the neural networks.

To further elucidate these assumptions, Deco and Lee (2002) simulated the search of a letter located between other distractor letters. They defined the task of searching for a letter "E". Figure 2 illustrates the basic observations concerning parallel and serial search.

The stimulus in Figure 2a contains shapes "E" and "X". Because the elementary features in "E" and "X" are distinct, i.e., their component lines have different orientations, "E" pops out from "X", and its location can be rapidly localized independently of the number of distracting "X" shapes in the display. On the other hand, the stimulus in Figure 2b contains the letters "E" (target) and "F" (distractors). Since both letters are composed of vertical and horizontal lines, there is no difference in elementary features to produce a preattentive pop-out, so they can be distinguished from each other

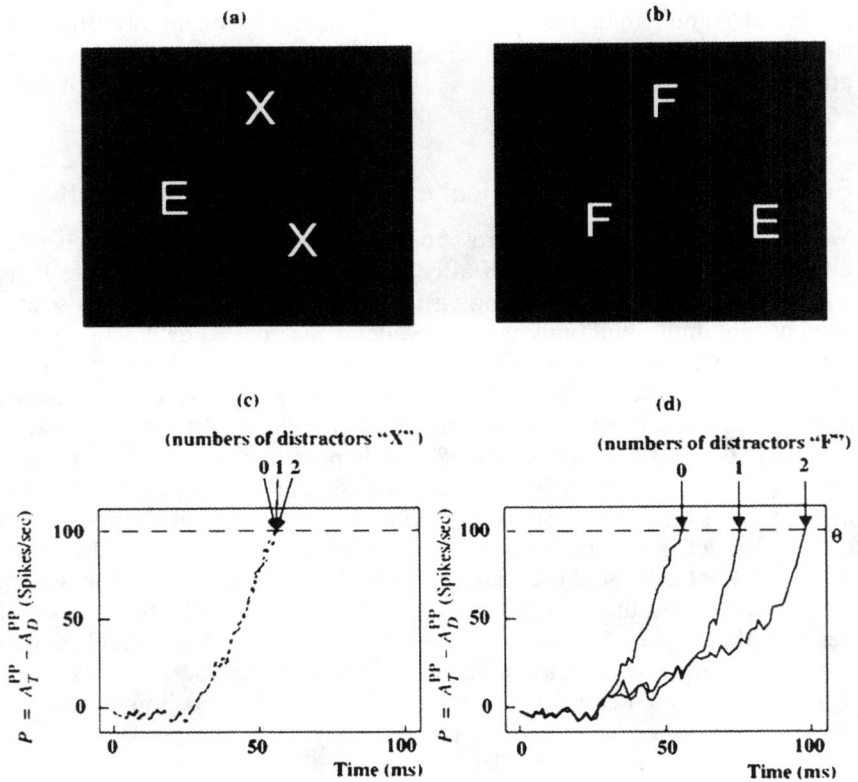

Figure 2. (a) Parallel search example: an image that contains a target "E" in a field of "X" distractors. Target "E" pops out from "X". (b) Serial search example: an image that contains a target "E" in a field of "F" distractors. The "E" and "F" can be distinguished from each other only after their features are bound by attention. (c–d) Simulation result of the network described in the previous section performing visual search on images (a) and (b), respectively. The difference (polarization) between the maximum activity in the neuronal pool corresponding to the target locations and the maximum activity of all other neuronal pools in the dorsal PP module is plotted as a function of time.

only after their features are glued together by attention. It has been thought that because attention is serial, the time required to localize the target in such images increases linearly with the number of distractors of the display. The serial movement of the attentional spotlight has been thought to be governed by a *saliency map* or *priority map* for registering the potentially interesting areas in the retinal input and directing a *gating* mechanism for selecting information for further processing. Does the linear increase in search time observed in visual search tests necessarily imply a serial search process, a saliency map or a gating mechanism? Could both the serial and parallel search phenomena be explained by a single parallel neurodynamical process without an additional serial control mechanism?

To investigate this issue, Deco and Lee (2002) presented the stimuli shown in Figure 2a and Figure 2b to the system described in the previous section, which has been trained to recognize "X", "E", and "F" in a translation invariant manner. The system received a top-down bias for the "E" pool in the ventral IT module, and was then presented with stimuli containing "E" in a variable number of "X" shapes, or "E" in a variable number of "F" shapes. Polarization (the difference between the maximal activity of the pools indicating the "E" location and that indicating the "F" location, i.e., $P = A_T^{PP} - A_D^{PP}$), is used as a measure to determine whether detection and localization of the target had been achieved or not. The authors found that for the "E" in "X" case, the time required for the polarization to reach a certain threshold in the dorsal PP module was almost identical whether the number of "X" shapes was equal to 0, 1, or 2, as shown in Figure 2c. On the other hand, when "E" and "F" were presented, the time required for polarization to reach threshold increased linearly with the number of distracting items. Although the system was running with the same parallel dynamics, it took an additional 25 ms for each additional distractor added to the stimulus as shown in Figure 2d. Therefore, the system works across the visual field in parallel, but, due to the different dynamic latencies, resembles the two apparent different modes of visual attention: serial focal search and parallel search. The typical linear increase in search time with the display size is clearly obtained as the result of a slower convergency (latency) of the dynamics. In this case, the strong competition present in V1 and propagated to PP delays the convergence of the dynamics. The strong competition in the feature extraction module V1 is finally resolved by the feedback received from PP. In other words, stimulus similarity in the feature space is decided by competition mechanisms at the intramodular level of V1 and the intermodular level of V1-PP. The simulation results show that parallel search and serial search might not represent two essentially different independent stages as previously thought (Treisman & Gelade, 1980). In the computational model described in the previous section, the two stages of processing (preattentive and attentive) involve the same mechanism, and feature integration is accomplished dynamically by the interaction between the ventral IT module and the early V1 module. Feature integration is an emergent phenomenon due to interactive activation among the cortical areas, rather than a separate stage of visual processing, or involving a separate visual area.

Recently, we extended the neurodynamical model to account for the different slopes observed experimentally in complex conjunction visual search tasks (Deco et al., 2002; Deco & Zihl, 2001; Rolls & Deco, 2002). The authors assume that selective attention results from independent competition mechanisms operating within each feature dimension.

Quinlan and Humphreys (1987) analysed feature search and three different kinds of conjunction search, namely standard conjunction search and two kinds of triple conjunction, with the target differing from all distractors in one or two features. Let us define the different kinds of search tasks by using a pair of numbers m and n, where m is the number of distinguishing feature dimensions between target and distractors, and n is the number of features by which each distractor group differs from the target. Using this terminology, feature search corresponds to a 1,1-search; a standard conjunction search corresponds to a 2,1-search; a triple conjunction search can be a 3,1- or a 3,2-search depending of whether the target differs from all distractor groups by one or two features. Quinlan and Humphreys showed that in feature search (1,1) the target is detected in parallel across the visual field. They also show that the reaction time in both standard conjunction search and triple conjunction search conditions is a linear function of the display size. The slope of the function for the triple conjunction search task can be steeper or relatively flat, depending upon whether the target differs from the distractors in one (3,1) or two features (3,2), respectively.

In Figure 3, the computational results obtained by Deco and Zihl (2001) (see also Deco et al., 2002) for 1,1-, 2,1-, 3,1-, and 3,2-searches are presented. The items are defined by three feature dimensions ($M = 3$, e.g., size, orientation, and colour), each having two values ($N(m) = 2$ for $m = 1, 2, 3$, e.g., size: Big/small; orientation: Horizontal/vertical; colour: White/black). Figure 3 shows examples for each kind of search. For each display size, the experiment is repeated 100 times, each time with different randomly generated targets at random positions and randomly generated distractors. The mean value T of the 100 simulated search times is plotted as a function of the display size S. The slopes for all simulations are consistent with existing experimental results (Quinlan & Humphreys, 1987).

WORKING MEMORY AND ATTENTION

In previous sections we have not explicitly modelled working memory, and we have used a mean-field based neurodynamical approach in a set of networks with an externally applied attentional bias which affects the networks in a biased competition scenario. In this section we summarize a model containing some of the working memory functions of the prefrontal cortex which provide the source of the biased competition for the posterior perceptual areas in the parietal and temporal cortex. Moreover, we utilize a different approach to the dynamics in which each neuron in the network is

Reaction Time (ms)

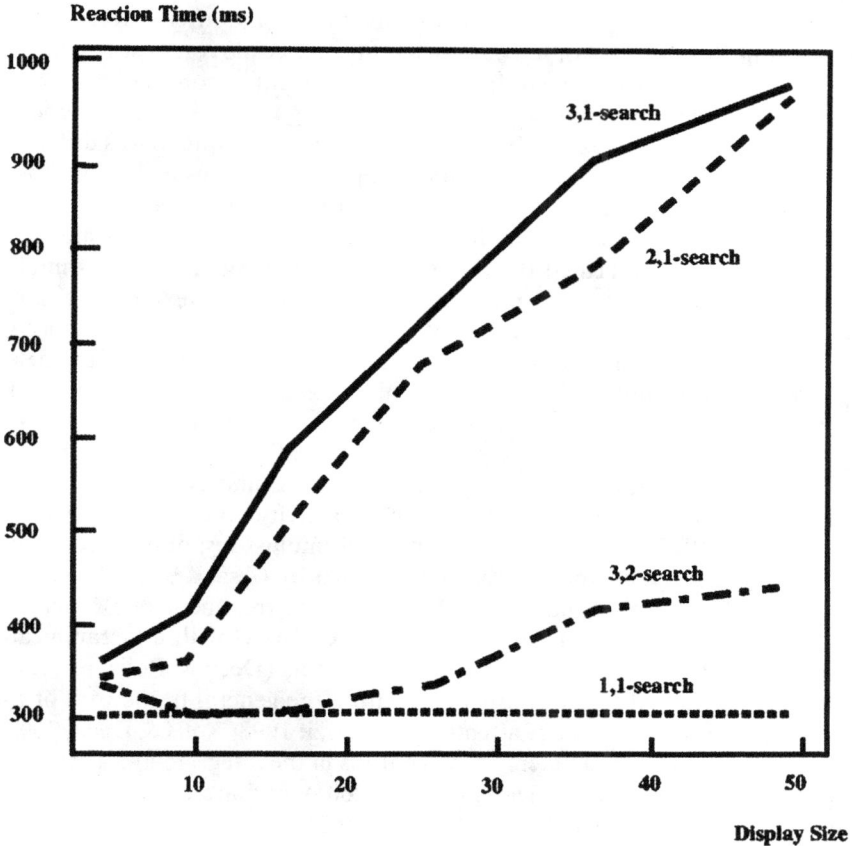

Figure 3.   Search times for feature and conjunction searches obtained utilizing the extended computational cortical model.

modelled at the integrate-and-fire level, so that we can produce spiking from the neurons in the network which can be directly compared with recordings from single neurons.

Working memory refers to an active system for maintaining and manipulating information in mind, held during a short period, usually of seconds (see Fuster, 2000, for a more comprehensive definition). The prefrontal cortex is involved in at least in some types of working memory, and neuronal activity in it continues during short-term memory periods (Fuster, 2000). Asaad, Rainer, and Miller (2000) investigated the functions of the prefrontal cortex in working memory by analysing neuronal activity when a monkey performs two different working memory tasks using the same stimuli and responses. In a *conditional object-response (associative) task* with a delay, the monkey was shown one of two stimuli, and after a delay had to make either a rightward or leftward oculomotor saccade response depending on which stimulus was shown. In another experiment, recordings were made both during the object-response task and during a *delayed spatial response task*, in which the same stimuli were used, but the rule required was different, namely to respond towards the location where the stimulus had been shown (Asaad et al., 2000). The main motivation for such studies was the fact that for real-world behaviour, mapping between a stimulus and a response is typically more complicated than a one-to-one mapping. The same stimulus can lead to different behaviour depending on the context or the same behaviour may be elicited by different cueing stimuli. In the performance of these tasks prefrontal cortex neurons were found that respond in the delay period to the stimulus object, the stimulus position ("sensory pools"), to combinations of response and stimulus object or position ("intermediate pools"), and to the response required (left or right) ("premotor pools").

The model is designed to help understand the underlying mechanisms that implement the working memory-related activity observed in neurons in the primate PFC in the context-dependent stimulus–response (associative) and delayed spatial response tasks investigated by (Asaad et al., 2000). We build on the integrate-and-fire attractor network treatment of Brunei and Wang (2001) and introduce a prefrontal cortex model with a hierarchically organized set of different attractor network pools (Deco & Rolls, in press). The hierarchical structure is organized within the general framework of the biased competition model of attention (Chelazzi, 1998; Rolls & Deco, 2002). The operation and parameters of the neurons in the integrate-and-fire model are similar to those of Brunei and Wang (2001), and are provided by Deco and Rolls (in press) and Rolls and Deco (2002).

Figure 4 shows schematically the synaptic structure assumed in the prefrontal cortical network. There are four excitatory populations or pools of neurons, namely sensory, task or rule-specific, premotor, and nonselective. The sensory pools encode information about objects, or spatial location. The premotor pools encode the motor response (in our case the leftward or rightward oculomotor saccade). The intermediate pools are task-specific and perform the mapping between the sensory stimuli and the required motor response. The intermediate pools respond to combinations of the sensory stimuli and the response required, e.g., to object 1 requiring a left oculomotor saccade. The intermediate pools receive an external biasing input that reflects the current rule (e.g., on this trial when object 1 is shown make the left response after the delay period). The remaining excitatory neurons do not have specific sensory, response, or biasing inputs, and are in a nonselective pool. All the inhibitory neurons are clustered into a common inhibitory pool, so that there is global competition throughout the network.

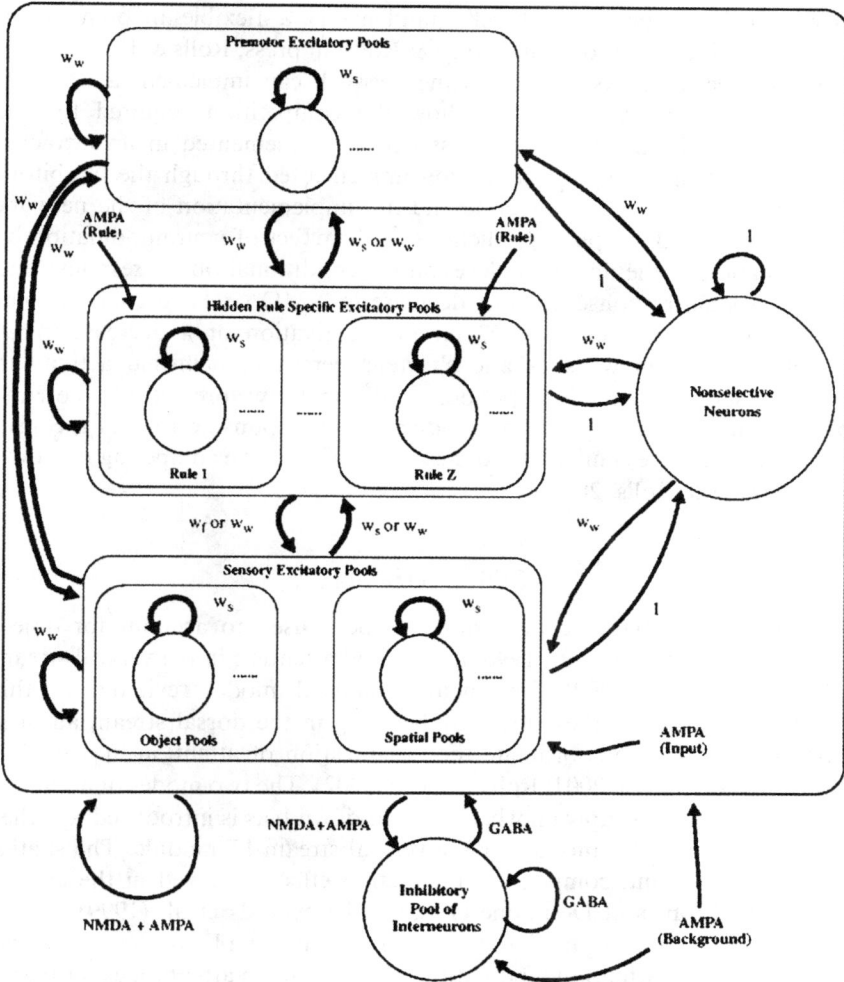

Figure 4. Prefrontal cortical module.

Overall, the network has the architecture of a single attractor network with multiple activated populations or pools of neurons. These different pools engage in competitive interactions, are organized with some hierarchy imposed by the asymmetrically strong forward and backward connections, and receive biasing inputs to influence the relative activity of the different pools, thus implementing attention-based or rule-based mapping from sensory inputs to motor outputs. This model thus shows how a rule or context input can influence decision making by biasing competition in a hierarchical network that thereby implements a flexible mapping from input stimuli to motor outputs (Deco & Rolls, in press; Rolls & Deco, 2002). The model also shows how the same network can implement a transient short-term memory, and indeed how the competition required for the biased competition selection process can be implemented in an attractor network that itself requires inhibition implemented through the inhibitory neurons. Even more, the integrate-and-fire implementation of the network enables us to make explicit predictions of the effect of neuromodulation by manipulation of the dopamine level on the conditional object response and delayed spatial response tasks. A decrease in NMDA-related conductances produced by an increase in D2 receptor activation or a decrease in Dl receptor activation weakens and shortens persistent neuronal activity in transient short-term memory periods. Additionally, we predict that the same pharmacological manipulations produce more response errors as a consequence of the more similar level of neuronal firing in the competing neuronal pools (Deco & Rolls, 2003).

CONCLUSIONS

The concept of biased competition has been used to account for object attention (Usher & Niebur, 1996) and spatial attention in the ventral stream (Reynolds et al., 1999). The neurodynamical model reviewed in this manuscript advances these ideas by bringing in the dorsal stream and the early visual areas to coordinate the organization of attention in a unified system (Deco & Zihl, 2001; Rolls & Deco, 2002). The two modes of attention emerge depending simply on whether a top-down bias is introduced to either the dorsal stream PP module or the ventral stream IT module. The spatial attention effect and competition interaction effect observed in the experiments of Moran and Desimone (1985) and Reynolds et al. (1999) can be accounted for by this model. It also shows and explains the dynamical competition and attention modulation effects found in attention experiments at the level of gross brain area activation as measured with fMRI (Corchs & Deco, 2002; Kastner et al., 1999). In the context of visual search, the model shows that Treisman's feature integration (Treisman & Gelade, 1980) can be implemented as an emergent phenomenon arising from the interaction between early visual cortical areas and the various extrastriate areas in the ventral and dorsal visual streams (Deco & Zihl, 2001). The system works across the visual field in parallel, but, due to the different dynamic latencies, resembles the two apparent different modes of visual attention: serial focal search and parallel search.

In summary, computational neuroscience provides a useful mathematical framework for studying the mechanisms involved in brain function, like visual attentional mechanisms, that we have reviewed in the present work. The neurodynamical model here analysed is based on evidence from functional, neurophysiological, and psychological findings. The simulations obtained with this theoretical model can successfully reproduce the experimental results of neurophysiological and fMRI experiments on spatial attention, as well as studies on serial and parallel search.

REFERENCES

Asaad, W. F., Rainer, G., & Miller, E. K. (2000). Task-specific neural activity in the primate pre-frontal cortex. *Journal of Neurophysiology*, *84*, 451–459.

Brunei, N., & Wang, X. (2001). Effects of neuromodulation in a cortical networks model of object working memory dominated by recurrent inhibition. *Journal of Computational Neuroscience*, *11*, 63–85.

Chelazzi, L. (1998). Serial attention mechanisms in visual search: A critical look at the evidence. *Psychological Research*, *62*, 195–219.

Chelazzi, L., Miller, E., Duncan, J., & Desimone, R. (1993). A neural basis for visual search in inferior temporal cortex. *Nature (London)*, *363*, 345–347.

Corchs, S., & Deco, G. (2002). Large-scale neural model for visual attention: Integration of experimental single cell and fMRI data. *Cerebral Cortex*, *12*, 339–348.

Deco, G., & Lee, T. S. (2002). A unified model of spatial and object attention based on inter-cortical biased competition. *Neurocomputing*, *44–46*, 775–781.

Deco, G., Pollatos, O., & Zihl, J. (2002). The time course of selective visual attention: Theory and experiments. *Vision Research*, *42*, 2925–2945.

Deco, G., & Rolls, E. T. (2003). Attention and working memory: A dynamical model of neuronal activity in the prefrontal cortex. *European Journal of Neuroscience*, *18*, 2374–2390.

Deco, G., & Zihl, J. (1999). A neural model of binding and selective attention for visual search. In D. Heinke, G. Humphreys, & A. Olson (Eds.), *Connectionist models in cognitive neuroscience: The 5th Neural Computation and Psychology workshop* (pp. 262–271). Berlin: Springer.

Deco, G., & Zihl, J. (2001). Top-down selective visual attention: A neurodynamical approach. *Visual Cognition*, *8*(1), 119–140.

Desimone, R., & Duncan, J. (1995). Neural mechanisms of selective visual attention. *Annual Review of Neuroscience*, *18*, 193–222.

Duncan, J. (1996). Cooperating brain systems in selective perception and action. In T. Inui & J. L. McClelland (Eds.), *Attention and performance XVI: Information integration in perception and communication* (pp. 549–578). Cambridge, MA: MIT Press.

Duncan, J., & Humphreys, G. (1989). Visual search and stimulus similarity. *Psychological Review*, *96*, 433–458.

Fuster, J. (2000). Executive frontal functions. *Experimental Brain Research*, *133*, 66–70.

Hamker, F. (1999). The role of feedback connections in task-driven visual search. In D. Heinke, G. Humphreys, & A. Olson (Eds.), *Connectionist models in cognitive neuroscience: The 5th Neural Computation and Psychology workshop* (pp. 252–261). Berlin: Springer.

Heinke, D., & Humphreys, G. (2003). Attention, spatial representation and visual neglect: Simulating emergent attention and spatial memory in the Selective Attention for Identification Model (SAIM). *Psychological Review*, *110*, 29–87.

Kastner, S., de Weerd, P., Desimone, R., & Ungerleider, L. (1998). Mechanisms of directed attention in the human extrastriate cortex as revealed by functional MRI. *Science*, *282*, 108–111.

Kastner, S., Pinsk, M., de Weerd, P., Desimone, R., & Ungerleider, L. (1999). Increased activity in human visual cortex during directed attention in the absence of visual stimulation. *Neuron*, *22*, 751–761.

Luck, S., Chelazzi, L., Hillyard, S., & Desimone, R. (1997). Neural mechanisms of spatial selective attention in areas V1, V2, and V4 of macaque visual cortex. *Journal of Neurophysiology*, *77*, 24–42.

Moran, J., & Desimone, R. (1985). Selective attention gates visual processing in the extrastriate cortex. *Science*, *229*, 782–784.

Quinlan, P. T., & Humphreys, G. W. (1987). Visual search for targets defined by combination of color, shape, and size: An examination of the task constraints on feature and conjunction searches. *Perception and Psychophysics*, *41*, 455–472.

Reynolds, J., Chelazzi, L., & Desimone, R. (1999). Competitive mechanisms subserve attention in macaque areas V2 and V4. *Journal of Neuroscience*, *19*, 1736–1753.

Rolls, E. T., & Deco, G. (2002). *Computational neuroscience of vision*. Oxford, UK: Oxford University Press.

Spitzer, H., Desimone, R., & Moran, J. (1988). Increased attention enhances both behavioral and neuronal performance. *Science*, *240*, 338–340.

Treisman, A. (1982). Perceptual grouping and attention in visual search for features and for objects. *Journal of Experimental Psychology: Human Perception and Performance*, *8*, 194–214.

Treisman, A. (1988). Features and objects: The fourteenth Bartlett memorial lecture. *Quarterly Journal of Experimental Psychology*, *40A*, 201–237.

Treisman, A., & Gelade, G. (1980). A feature-integration theory of attention. *Cognitive Psychology*, *12*, 97–136.

Usher, M., & Niebur, E. (1996). Modelling the temporal dynamics of IT neurons in visual search: A mechanism for top-down selective attention. *Journal of Cognitive Neuroscience*, *8*, 311–327.

Author Index

Subject Index